THE TENNESSEE SAMPLER

Peter Jenkins and Friends

Thomas Nelson Publishers
Nashville • New York • Camden

Published in Nashville, Tennessee, by Thomas Nelson, Inc. and distributed in Canada by Lawson Falle, Ltd., Cambridge, Ontario.

Printed in the United States of America.

Library of Congress Cataloging-in-Publication Data

Jenkins, Peter, 1951–
  The Tennessee sampler.

  1. Tennessee—Description and travel—
1981–   Guide-books. I. Title.
F434.3.J46   1985   917.68'0453   85-21673
ISBN 0-8407-5964-9

Dedication

We, Peter Jenkins, Wallace Hebert, Terri Baker and Judy Roberson, dedicate this book:

To the great state of Tennessee and its even greater people. May this book help share the many special qualities that make our state so terrific. Also, thanks to UFO, for all his hard work while living on our farm the last few years.

Peter Jenkins

To Brenda, Andrea, and Julia, with much love. And to Millard and Mary Mitchum, who taught me to love Tennessee.

Wallace Hebert

To my grandmothers, Estalee Graves and Mavis Loveless, who helped give me a love for Tennessee, my family, and God.

Terri Loveless Baker

To my husband, Joe, and my daughters Amy and Abby, who survived the difficulties of living with a wife and mother turned writer.

Judy Roberson

Acknowledgments

The *Sampler* thanks those special friends who helped make it all happen:

Governor Lamar Alexander and his wife, Honey; Commissioner William Long, Jim Fuller, Phil Armour, Roy and Ruth Cunningham, Debby Patterson Koch, friends at the Departments of Tourist Development, Conservation, Transportation; the State Library and Archives, state photographers, and the *Tennessee Traveler* for taking us to some wonderful places; the folks at Opryland and at Graceland; Joe and Junebug Clark; and Kathy Gangwisch.

Thanks to Dennas Davis, our talented deisgner, for a beautiful cover and artwork.

Our thanks to *Memphis Magazine* and *Nashville Magazine* for permission to quote from various articles, to marvelous media people all over the state who helped us spread the word about the *Sampler*, to friends from the *Tennessee Cooperator, Tennessee Magazine*, and the Tennessee Farm Bureau.

At Thomas Nelson, Inc., our terrific Tennessee publisher, thanks to: Sam Moore, Bob Wolgemuth, Mike Hyatt, Etta Wilson, Mikemail, Lori Quinn, Joan Boyle, Walt Quinn, Sondra Estes, and Bruce Nygren.

And special thanks to Jerry Evans, Kim Hutto, and Mary Margaret Reed at Sweet Springs Press.

HELLO

My name is Peter Jenkins, and I'm one proud Tennessean! I live here not because I was born here, or transferred here with a company, or wanted to make it in country music. My wife Barbara and I decided on Tennessee after we had walked all across this great nation and had written two books about our adventure. I call Tennessee home because it's *the* place in this world I want to be.

Many of you love Tennessee even though you live elsewhere. Why, last year alone almost nine million of you visited the Smokies, over half a million of you came to Graceland, Elvis's home in Memphis, and two million enjoyed the Grand Ole Opry and Opryland!

Now some of my friends and I have the honor to present to all of you who love Tennessee and want to know more about it, wherever you live, this very special book, the *Tennessee Sampler.*

Actually, the *Sampler* started happening almost from the time we became Tennesseans. I was traveling around America asking people to tell me the good things about where they lived, and a woman named Ruby Winchester wrote a beautiful letter about the seasons around her Tennessee farm. She said winter was when they "put the porches to sleep" by moving all the plants inside for the cold weather. What a wonderful image! Ruby's letter and many more made me realize that Tennesseans can express their great love for their state and their families, their jobs, and their beliefs as powerfully as any professional writer can.

Then Tennessee Governor Lamar Alexander invited me to attend his inauguration, and I heard him announce a statewide celebration of Tennessee called "Homecoming '86." So I committed Sweet Springs Press, my company, to produce a beautiful calendar for Homecoming which would be written and photographed by the people of Tennessee. We had a statewide contest, received thousands of entries, and awarded $15,000.00 in prizes which were donated by some of Tennessee's great corporations.

Our *Homecoming '86* calendar turned out to be a heartfelt tribute to Tennessee, but there were many more wonderful entries that could have been used in the calendar. They taught us so much about Tennessee that we started thinking of a book that would let these voices be heard. Research revealed that Tennessee needed a truly comprehensive guidebook, and the idea for *The Tennessee Sampler* was born.

We would let Tennesseans themselves tell about their crafts, their restaurants, music places, and scenic trails, rivers, and parks. We would call upon special friends across the state who were experts on food, antiques, caves, hiking trails, quilts, or whatever, to tell us about their specialties. As "The Sampler," we would go all over Tennessee listening to music and attending festivals and checking out information. *And* we would put this all together in time for our great celebration of Homecoming '86!

Fortunately, I had a publisher right here in Tennessee, Thomas Nelson, Inc., who believed in me. And Sweet Springs Press had a staff (I call them my "SWAT Team"!) who could make it all happen. They are all gifted teachers with four master's degrees and most of a Ph.D. between them.

Judy, Terri and Wally

I'd like you to meet them. Wallace Hebert is a historian, musician, and good friend who has been managing editor of the *Sampler* project. He's also served as Music, Outdoors, and Wit and Wisdom Editor. Wally's a transplanted Louisiana Cajun (His name's pronounced "A-bear"). He and his wife, Brenda, a nurse at Vanderbilt Hospital, and their two daughters, Andrea and Julia, live in the hills outside Columbia.

Terri Loveless Baker is our Tours and Trails and Eatin' and Sleepin' Good Editor. She's a native Tennessean and a super organizer who has put together some Tennessee Tours we know you'll enjoy. Terri lives in Columbia with her husband Jim and their two children, Mark and Lajuana. Jim operates a John Deere dealership.

Judy Roberson is another home-grown Tennessean who compiled the extensive Insider's Shopping Guide and also edited the Fun Times section. Judy and her schoolteacher-photographer husband, Joe, and their two children, Amy and Abby, live on a farm outside Columbia.

Wally, Terri, and Judy share with me a tremendous love for Tennessee and its people which is reflected in the pages of *The Tennessee Sampler.*

We hope you have as much fun reading the *Tennessee Sampler* as we had writing it for you. It is packed with entertaining information. But as much as this book has to offer, Tennessee has much more. We have just scratched the surface in this first *Sampler.* Come and discover Tennessee with us!

Peter Jenkins

Contents

Music

Tours and Trails

Eatin' and Sleepin' Good

Insider's Shopping Guide

The Greatest Outdoors

Map of Tennessee follows page 283

MUSIC

MUSIC HIGHLIGHTS

The Most Complete Guide to the Opry & Opryland

Tickets, tapings, music, rides, special shows, and Nashville's newest riverboat

That Nashville Music

12 feature articles and listings of Nashville's great listening places including Fan Fair, the Volunteer Jam, the Ralph Emery Show, Contemporary Christian Music, the Station Inn, and the Bluebird Cafe

That Memphis Music

An Elvis tour, Beale Street, and a dozen great blues, country, jazz, and rock places in Memphis

Music Festivals and Contests

6 Feature articles plus listings of festivals, symphonies, and operas statewide including Memphis in May, the Old Time Fiddler's Jamboree, and the Sewanee Music Center

Gospel and Grass-roots Music

The Sampler's unique guide to finding community singings, pickings, and dances all across the state. *Plus* an entertaining section on Tennessee's buckdancers and where to find them

13 Best Kept Secrets

One-of-a-kind picking places across Tennessee, such as Down Home, the Pastime Cafe, and Clyde Blalock's

Music Is in Tennessee

Music is in Tennessee. Has been for thousands of years. Before man came to this area, it was already making music. Water music. Bird music. Great kettle-drum thunders, brushed cymbal rainstorms, and high-land rim-shot rock slides filled the ears of the first inhabitants with an endless earth symphony. Even Tennessee's name—"Tanasie," given to it by those who first listened to its wonderful sounds—is musical. Nowadays, our engines drown out the natural music just as our lights at night obscure the incredible sky our great-grandparents knew. But there are still places to find the old music, the kind made by Tennessee and the kind made by Tennesseans. We at *The Tennessee Sampler* aim to tell you about some of them.

Another kind of music is made in Tennessee too. This music happened because an Italian named Marconi invented the wireless radio and an American named Edison invented the phonograph. Both marvels made it possible for music to be performed in one place and heard in another. They produced a supernova of information and music and profound changes in the way people lived and entertained themselves. Music entered the electronic consumer era.

Memphis blues and Tennessee traditional music were both part of radio and recorded music from the very beginning. Beale Street and Smoky Mountain trails reached to Broadway in New York City, and from there all over our nation, but they returned very soon to radio stations in Memphis and East Tennessee and, above all, to Nashville and WSM's Grand Ole Opry. These two main streams branched all over the state, producing such blends as rockabilly and bluegrass and rhythm and blues but, most important of all, *country.*

The Grand Ole Opry and Opryland

The Opry

"The Grand Ole Opry is as simple as sunshine. It has a universal appeal because it is built upon good will, and with folk music expresses the heartbeat of a large percentage of Americans who labor for a living."—George D. Hay, founder of the Grand Ole Opry.

It is no exaggeration to say that without the Opry, Nashville wouldn't have become Music City. But when the WSM barn dance started on November 28, 1925, no one could have foreseen its glorious future. George Hay was the announcer, and a fiddler, Uncle Jimmy Thompson, played traditional hoe-down music for an hour. The show kept increasing in popularity, outgrowing auditorium after auditorium. Sometime in the late thirties the instrumental music emphasis began to shift to vocals,

largely due to the influence of Roy Acuff and his Smoky Mountain Boys. But even today, you'll hear groups that bring back the early string band sound of the Opry.

Whether you listen to the Opry on radio any Friday or Saturday night, watch it on TNN, or order your tickets and come to Nashville to see it in person, you'll find a unique experience waiting for you. It is nothing less than a still lively and still enormously successful living history of country music.

On any given night, perhaps 30 bands or individual performers will play their songs, which are all pure country gold. Some of them have been sung on the Opry for almost 50 years. Some were hits in the sixties. Some are today's hits. But you'll hear them all sung by country music's legends.

Sadly, the Opry changes from time to time as one of its stars passes from the scene. Ernest Tubb, Marty Robbins, and Kirk McGee have died in the past few years. But at any performance, you can still see performers who have been extolling the virtues of Martha White's self-rising flour (with hot rise) for decades.

The Opry wisely doesn't try to be what it's not. This isn't a place where established stars try to sing the newest country hits. At the Opry, you'll laugh at Cousin Minnie's classic attempts to latch onto a man, clap to Roy Acuff's "Wabash Cannonball," or hear Dottie West's "Here Comes My Baby" plus her latest hit. You'll see Porter Wagoner flash his famous rhinestone "hello" and listen to Hank Snow's "I'm Movin' On." But then again, you might see Ricky Skaggs pick everything in sight on his new hot single, "Country Boy," because he's a member of the Opry too.

Even at the new Opry House, with all its electronic sophistication, the Opry remains as down-to-earth as you can get. The performers keep it that way, reading out birthdays and anniversaries and greeting the folks who have come to the show, sometimes from across the nation and occasionally from across the world.

It's better than a museum. It's alive. It's real. "Sophisticated it ain't, but it don't have to be 'cause it's country. It's the Grand Ole Opry!"

How to Get Opry Tickets

Grand Ole Opry tickets, though reputed to be impossible to come by, are not always that hard to obtain. Every week roughly one-third of the seats for each performance of the upcoming weekend are held open, and there are seven Opry performances each weekend at the height of the summer tourist season.

The trick to obtaining tickets is knowing the sales system, because schedules and procedures for purchasing tickets never vary. Understanding them is the key to finding tickets for the date you want to visit Nashville.

At least three performances of the Opry take place every weekend—two on Saturday night and one on Friday night—and they are broadcast over WSM, a clear-channel radio station at 650 on the AM dial. A Saturday matinee is scheduled when the Opryland theme park is open (late March through October), Sunday matinees are offered from late May through September, Friday matinees are offered from early June through mid-August, and a second Friday night show is performed from early May through October.

For evening and matinee performances alike, tickets are sold on a reserved and a general admission basis. All tickets are for specific seats. Reserved seat tickets are available only through the mail and must be ordered well in advance, especially for summer performances. About two-thirds of the Opry House's 4,400 seats are sold in this fashion.

The remaining one-third of the house is covered by general admission tickets. These tickets go on sale every Tuesday for that weekend's show and are sold on a first-come, first-serve basis at the Grand Ole Opry ticket office at the main Opryland USA parking lot. Depending largely on the number of tourists, general admission tickets sometimes are available until showtime. Another, less certain, method is to obtain unclaimed or cancelled tickets a half-hour before showtime at the Grand Ole Opry ticket office.

The most readily available Opry tickets are those for the matinees in spring, summer, and autumn. Although matinees are not broadcast, they are as informal and spontaneous as their evening counterparts.

Address inquiries about Grand Ole Opry tickets to Grand Ole Opry Ticket Information, 2802 Opryland Drive, Nashville, TN 37214. (615) 889-3060.

A SAMPLER

SPECIAL

Big Don Goes to Nashville

An Indiana wanderer heads south to Music City
for the ultimate Tennessee vacation.

Tom Adkinson is a good friend of The Sampler *and one of the most knowledgeable people around when it comes to Opryland USA, where he's Manager of Public Relations. Tom's also a fine writer whose articles have appeared in* Southern Living Magazine, Travel & Leisure, *the* Los Angeles Times, *and the* Chicago Tribune.

We posed a question to Tom—"What if a country music fan could take a dream trip to Nashville and to the Opry? What would he see and do while he was here?" Tom thought about our question and wrote "Big Don Goes to Nashville" for us.

"That tears it!" Big Don muttered as he slammed the telephone receiver back in the cradle.

"The only way I'm going to get to talk to Ralph Emery is to go to Nashville myself. After months of trying, I finally got a call in to 'Nashville Now,' and I *knew* the answer to his silly trivia question.

"But do I get to tell him that Sylvia's from right here in Kokomo? Noooo! It was some caller from Connecticut of all places! I know Sylvia's cousin personally. I even liked him before Sylvia got that fancy Nashville recording contract."

Martha watched in amused silence. She'd seen Don work himself into a tizzy before. Still, she felt a bit sorry for him. Before Ralph Emery opened the toll-free phone lines on "Nashville Now" (their favorite television show), he'd said that the first caller who could tell him the name and home town of the country music star whose first job in Nashville had been as a Music Row secretary and who now records using only one name would win a fancy pair of Laredo boots. Big Don didn't particularly want the boots, but he did want to brag on Sylvia Kirby, the cousin of one of his coworkers at Delco Electronics.

When Big Don declared he was heading to Nashville, he and Martha were ready to become tourism statistics. Something like seven million people visit Nashville each year, and a whole lot of them want to do what Big Don wanted to do. Not necessarily to talk to Ralph Emery, host of a television show on The Nashville Network, but to see why Nashville claims to be Music City, USA.

More than two million of them go to Opryland, the theme park that calls itself "the home of American music." Almost another million ride a pew at the Grand Ole Opry, the longest-running radio show in the history of broadcasting.

Thousands of them walk reverently through the Ryman Auditorium, the home of the Opry for more than 30 years and the place where such stars as Roy Acuff, Ernest Tubb, Hank Snow, Hank Williams, Patsy Cline, and Loretta Lynn began to burn their brightest.

Hank Williams and Country's most famous call letters

Others visit the Country Music Hall of Fame and Museum and browse through the souvenir shops near Music Row that bear the names of performers such as Mel Tillis, Hank Williams, Jr., and Boxcar Willie.

Quite a few hop on tour buses to see the stars' homes, especially the collection of homes on and near Franklin Road. (See "Tours and Trails.") Every one of them gets a laugh when the tour guide tells them that one of the rewards for being governor of Tennessee is living next door to Minnie Pearl.

Martha realized Big Don was serious about going to Nashville when he continued to talk about it the next morning. There usually isn't too much morning conversation between Big Don and Martha as they head for their jobs at Delco. But Big Don wouldn't shut up about going to Nashville.

"I thought we were going back up to the cabin for vacation again this year," Martha protested, although weakly. She was talking about their vacation cabin on Shafer Lake north of Kokomo.

"Hang the cabin," he declared. "We're going to Nashville. I've wanted to go for a long time, and this is the year.

"We're going to do it right. We're not going to take the pickup truck with the camper-top. Ray, back in the shipping department, has promised to loan me his Winnebago anytime I want it, and I'm asking for it today, and you're writing for Opry tickets tonight. Maybe Dottie West will be there."

Actually, Martha had been watching The Nashville Network and reading travel stories in *The Kokomo Tribune* long enough to know how to plan a trip to Nashville. She wasn't quite as impulsive as Big Don, so she was ready to get things organized.

First off, she called Opryland USA to find out when Opry tickets were available. The woman on the telephone told her how to order her tickets by mail and even offered to send Martha some current information about several other activities in the city.

Although Martha thought she knew a lot about what was at Opryland USA, the woman told her about a couple of new things. The newest, she learned, was a $12 million paddlewheel showboat called the *General Jackson*. As Big Don observed dryly, "That sounds bigger than anything on Shafer Lake."

Second, she called The Nashville Network to get a seating reservation for "Nashville Now." Since The Nashville Network is part of Opryland USA, she couldn't understand why it didn't have the same phone number as the Opry, but she wasn't going to leave Kokomo without knowing she and Big Don could see "Nashville Now."

Finally, she found a KOA campground directory on the bedroom bookshelf (next to her last high-school annual and the phone directory from church) and looked up the KOA nearest Opryland. "Full hookups," it said, "and transportation to Opryland." That was enough for Martha, and she dialed the telephone number listed.

Big Don and Martha left Kokomo one afternoon after work. By the time they fumed their way through the rush hour traffic in Indianapolis, Big Don had

figured out what most of the knobs and switches in the borrowed Winnebago were. As night fell, they picked up WSM on the radio, and their anticipation grew.

The DJ played something by Alabama, then a new song by Barbara Mandrell, and an old, old one by Rex Allen. Big Don nearly ran a little Toyota off the interstate near Mammoth Cave as he listened to Kenny Rogers and Dottie West sing "Everytime Two Fools Collide." Martha grasped the irony of the moment, but she held her tongue.

They found the campground in the middle of the night and settled in. Despite the quiet surroundings, they didn't sleep much.

Big Don and Martha's day began as they set out to discover Nashville, knowing that "Nashville Now" was on the schedule for that night, the Opry for the following night, and Opryland was available for the next three days.

"Let's start at the beginning," Big Don said, as he pointed the big Winnebago into downtown traffic in search of the Ryman Auditorium.

The Ryman was easier to find than was a parking place, but even that was worth the effort. Inside the imposing Gothic structure, Big Don and Martha tagged along with a tour group and heard the guide explain that the Opry had begun in 1925 in the studios of WSM and had been in several locations around Nashville until it settled into the Ryman Auditorium in 1943.

It stayed there for the next 31 years—through cold winter nights, hot and humid summer days. Those oak church pews accommodated many faithful fans who came to see Acuff, Tubb, Kitty Wells, Cowboy Copas, and the rest. A chunk of the stage, the guide explained, was taken from the Ryman and was built into the stage of the Grand Ole Opry House at Opryland USA. That way some of the tradition of the Opry was carried to the Opry's new home when it was finished in 1974.

Big Don felt as if he'd died and gone to heaven, standing on the stage of the Ryman.

After the Ryman, Big Don and Martha checked out the Country Music Hall of Fame. They saw Elvis Presley's solid gold Cadillac; Martha liked the exhibit on the many categories of country music, even though Big Don claimed that the only categories were "cheatin' songs, cryin'-in-your-beer songs, and train songs"; and Big Don felt like a champ when he punched the right button in the songwriters' exhibit to prove Bill Anderson wrote "City Lights."

That night, Big Don and Martha got their first taste of Nashville entertainment. The KOA shuttle bus took them to Opryland USA in plenty of time to find the Gaslight Studio and to watch the camera crews get ready for "Nashville Now." They listened intently as the guy doing the audience warm-up explained that "Nashville Now" is an honest-to-goodness live show.

For 90 minutes, the satellite beams of The Nashville Network would carry the show to homes across the United States and Canada. "It's possible," the warm-up announcer said, "for the show to be seen in more than 21 million homes."

Big Don just hoped that some of the guys from work were watching this night. He'd brought a sign that read, "Hello Delco," to hold up when the camera scanned the audience.

When the show went on the air, Big Don and Martha clapped louder than anyone. Jack Greene was on, and he sang "Statue of a Fool." John Hartford danced, played the banjo, and sang about Uncle Dave Macon, the "Dixie Dewdrop."

Richard Sterban from the Oak Ridge Boys popped in unexpectedly (Martha was quite pleased) to plug a celebrity softball game he was playing in. And Ralph Emery came out into the audience to talk to some folks. He gave the guy sitting next to Big Don a sweatshirt, and Don was so excited that he forgot to hold up his sign.

After "Nashville Now," Martha insisted they stop at the Opryland Hotel to look around. She wanted to see the Conservatory, an indoor tropical garden filled with waterfalls, walkways, and 10,000 plants and crowned with an acre of glass to form one of the largest skylights in the world.

As they stood on the elevated walkway, Big Don looked out over the Conservatory and said, "I think this means we don't have to go to Hawaii now."

Back at the KOA, Big Don and Martha slept better than the night before. Their Nashville dream was coming true.

The next morning, Big Don woke up early and slipped back over to the Opryland Hotel. He'd seen a sign about a radio show called "The Waking Crew," and he wanted to see what that was all about.

What he found was a bit of Nashville madness and a lot of Nashville tradition. "The Waking Crew," he discovered, is on WSM, just like the Grand Ole Opry. In fact, the only radio show that's older than "The Waking Crew" is the Opry itself.

Big Don eased into the Stagedoor Lounge to watch "The Waking Crew" and was astounded at the sight. At 7:45 A.M., a six-piece band was backing up two singers. Big Don has trouble talking before he's had his third cup of coffee, and he couldn't imagine anyone being able to sing at that hour.

At 9:00, the show ended, and Big Don went back to the KOA. HIs absence hadn't bothered Martha, but she was perturbed when he told her that one of the singers on "The Waking Crew" that morning was an Indiana boy from Lafayette.

"We'll never get a show like that at home on WWKI," Martha said.

For the rest of the day, Big Don and Martha roamed around Opryland. They'd read in a guidebook about how the theme park was the first part of Opryland USA.

In the late 1960s, the folks who owned the Opry knew that the Opry had to leave the deteriorating Ryman Auditorium, so they decided to do more than just build a new auditorium. They built a family park dedicated to many styles of American music, and they've made a habit of attracting more than two million guests every year to enjoy the entertainment offered.

Opryland opened in 1972; the 4,400-seat Grand Ole Opry House was finished in 1974, and the Opry took up residence that same year; the Opryland Hotel opened in 1977; and in 1983 The Nashville Network made Nashville the only city in the world with a television network named after it.

Big Don and Martha found more entertainment than they expected at Opryland. Every time they turned a corner, it seemed they found another stage show.

Martha fell in love with the tenor singer in a gospel group that performed a show called "Sing the Glory Down," and Big Don said he'd never seen or heard anything like the 16 performers in "Country Music USA."

"Johnny Cash had better watch out for that boy who sang 'I Walk the Line.' He's a better Johnny Cash than Johnny Cash," Big Don said to Martha, but she observed that June Carter probably could tell a difference.

In all, they saw six shows, ate a fried chicken lunch, won a Cincinnati Reds batting helmet playing a game that measured how fast Big Don could throw a baseball, and rode two rides—a cable car that gave them a bird's-eye view of the park and a train that looped around the park. Big Don wanted to ride some more, but Martha wouldn't go for it.

"I'll do a lot of things," Martha told him, "but ride on a roller coaster that turns you upside down two times isn't one of them."

Big Don didn't even bother asking her to ride on something called the Grizzly River Rampage. Big Don said the people getting off the Grizzly River Rampage were all smiling and laughing; Martha noted that they were soaking wet too.

A Saturday night performance of the Grand Ole Opry was to be the crowning touch to Big Don and Martha's visit to Nashville.

They arrived an hour hearly, just to watch the crowd assemble and to savor the anticipation of being in the congregation of "the mother church of country music." Their seats were on the main level about halfway back on the left side. Big Don had a clear path to the concession stand and to the area right in front of the stage where guests could walk right up and take pictures of the performers.

As they entered, Big Don bought a *Grand Ole Opry Picture-History Book* and a six-pack of Goo-Goos. "Something for the mind and something for the stomach," he laughed.

They had decided not to get a program. They wanted to be surprised as each member of the Opry came out to perform. "It's going to be just like listening at home," Big Don said. "We won't know who's appearing until the host tells us."

It was a marvelous night. Jeannie Pruett sang "Satin Sheets." Del Wood got her ragtime piano cranked up into fourth gear for "Down Yonder." Bill Monroe sang "Blue Moon of Kentucky." Hank Snow did "Traveling On." Porter Wagoner did "Green, Green Grass of Home."

From 9:30 until 11:30 P.M., there were 21 performers. Big Don had counted. And there still was a half-hour to go. It appeared nothing could improve on an apparently already perfect night until Whisperin' Bill Anderson came on to host the last segment.

He sang "Southern Fried," joked about Po-Folks Restaurants, and then put the star on Big Don's Christmas tree when he said: "I want you to give a special welcome to an unexpected guest of mine tonight. Ladies and gentlemen, here's that 'Country Sunshine' girl herself...Dottie West!"

For information about any aspect of Opryland USA, write Opryland Customer Service, 2802 Opryland Drive, Nashville, TN 37215. (615) 889-6611.

The *Sampler* Guide to Opryland

The Tennessee Sampler wants to make sure you have some information at your fingertips when you make your own visit to America's greatest musical theme park. We'll let you know in advance the places to target for certain age groups and give you a behind-the-scenes glimpse of the park's wonderful music productions.

Park. Opryland is 120 acres of great entertainment set in a great American crossroads city, Nashville, Tennessee. Music City. Where over half the 45s released in America are recorded. Opryland has helped Nashville become entertainment's "third coast," along with Hollywood and New York. A place where not just country but any type of music can be recorded, where videos can be produced, and where sophisticated television series, awards shows, and comedies can be filmed. What is remarkable about Opryland is that this talent and this state-of-the-art electronic sophistication are all showcased for you at unbeatable prices.

The park schedule is keyed to the calendar each year, but it is usually open weekends in spring and autumn and seven days a week in summer. Gates usually open at 10:00 A.M. and close at 6:00 or 10:00 P.M., depending

on the season. Right now admission to the park is $13.50 ($11.85 for groups of 25 or more), which includes three consecutive days. That gives you up to 36 hours to enjoy the rides, see the shows, try your hand at games of skill and luck, and sample the best of America's foods. All rides and shows inside the park are included in the price of admission, and there's no limit except time on what you can see and do.

Over a three-day period, you are apt to get a little hungry. Food at Opryland ranges from popcorn, nachos, and ice-cream-cone munchies to the specialties of eight full-service restaurants. The Cafe Mardi Gras has food with a French flavor; other restaurants offer pizza, seafood, chicken, or barbecue; and the Gaslight Beef Room is a top quality steakhouse. You can spend anything from $1 to $10 or more on your meal depending on your tastes. So be sure to budget for snacks and food. Some picnic tables have been placed outside the park by the Cumberland River, and you can eat there and return to the park just by getting your hand stamped. Food may *not* be taken inside the park itself, though.

Rides and activities. Sections of the park are geared just for the little ones, say up to 7 years old. There's a petting zoo that's always a great favorite in the State Fair Area near Eagle Lake. An area sponsored by General Mills is called "Big G's Kid Stuff" which sometimes has such characters as Frankenberry walking around. It includes a miniature space needle, a boat ride, and several playground activities such as the Trix Crawl, where the little ones roll around in a big enclosure full of plastic balls. When the *Sampler* checked this section out again this year, one 9-year-old's day was almost ruined when she discovered she was too tall to get into these activities. Children's rides are in the area next to Eagle Lake—Red Baron airplanes, dune buggies, a mini-Rockin' Roller Coaster, and a mini-Ferris wheel. A children's theater in the Riverside Area has The Laughing Place, a fast-paced magical show. It's always a favorite with everyone.

Grizzly River waterfall

Next come the 7 to 12 year olds, and parents know how difficult it is to keep this bunch entertained. Well, rest assured, because it'll be a snap at Opryland. You might even find some kid still left in you as you try to keep up with the preteens in the park. They will enjoy the skyride over the park, the trains that run around Opryland, and the Rockin' Roller Coaster. DoWahDiddy City's fifties area is geared to this age group, and that's where they can ride the Little Deuce Coupes. The Tennessee Waltz in the State Fair Area is a swing ride that goes really high and fast. The Fair Area also has a lot of carnival-type games.

The two favorite rides for this age group are unquestionably the Flume Zoom in the Hill Country Area and the Grizzly River Rampage over in Grizzly Country. The Flume Zoom is a 4-person floating tub that winds around a water-filled flume to a steep descent into a pool of water. Everyone loves it. Now, the Rampage is another story. To use a Woody Allen line, "It's the most fun we ever had without laughing." Actually, we did laugh at everyone else getting wet as we drifted in a 12-person round craft down a real white-water river, including a cave complete-with-grizzly. However, we stopped laughing when *we* got soaked, and all the ink in our *Sampler* notebook ran! So, if you're taking a preteen to the park, make sure he or she dresses in clothes that will dry fast. If the night promises to be cool, you might need to bring a change of clothing for the ride home.

The teenager at Opryland prefers to run in packs. Among younger teens these packs tend to be of the same sex, loud, and competitive. "This is our tenth time on the Rampage today!" "What, only ten?" Whole busloads of junior high and high schoolers pull up into the parking lot from Poplar Bluff, Missouri; Indianapolis, Indiana; and anywhere else you can name. Opryland is wonderful to them. Teens will really enjoy two of the shows at the park. "At the Hop" is in DoWahDiddy City at the bandstand. (Be sure to get a look at the drums mounted on an old Chevy body.) The show features fifties music and is simply irresistible. Another show for this age group is performed by the Tennessee River Boys at the Flip Side Theater. They sing today's country hits, the chart-toppers, and do them incredibly well.

Favorite rides for teenagers are the Rampage (of course), the Barnstormer—some very high-flying airplanes—and two rides that are among the most sophisticated at any amusement park. The Wabash Cannonball is a modernistic roller coaster that turns its intrepid riders upside down twice in big loops. It was almost more than the *Sampler* could take, but we didn't want the teen-agers to ride it alone! The other ride is the Screamin' Delta Demon, six-person tobogganlike cars on rollers that twist at high speed through curved steel chutes. The engineering that went into it is marvelous. It's exciting, but not quite as intense as the cannonball. The lush area where the line forms for the Demon has Cajun fishing cabins, skiffs, and crab traps and old nets hanging all around, and Cajun music plays through loudspeakers. For older dating teens, Opryland is a great place to get to know one another, and trying to win a teddy bear for a date still seems to be a favorite activity.

There are also plenty of things for families to do together at Opryland. The entire American West area has a family appeal. The Tin Lizzies offer a chance for mom and dad to see how much fun driving lessons will be in a few years. And the beautiful antique carousel is enchanting.

Now, one other group runs Opryland in packs. They have just as much fun as the young people, because they are truly young at heart. Perhaps they don't cover the park as rapidly as the younger set, but they get around, and the *Sampler* has seen them on every ride at Opryland. Of course, we're talking about some of Opryland's greatest fans, the senior citizens. The three-day tickets enable them to catch all the shows and rides they want to enjoy, and the skyride and trains are a great help in cutting down on the walking necessary to enjoy the park.

Some of Opryland's guests are confined to wheelchairs or cannot walk for extended periods. For their convenience the park is entirely barrier-free, and wheelchairs are available at the park entrance for any who might need them.

Now is as good a time as any to talk about the Opryland staff. They are excellent and getting better all the time. Trained and courteous personnel are ready to help with any sort of problem.

Shows. We've really saved the best for last! Opryland has the capability to stage a dozen shows simultaneously, complete with stages, sound and lights, costumes, singers and dancers, production people, and live instrumentalists and pit orchestras. No other park in the world has strictly live orchestras and bands for every show. No "sweetened" vocal tape-recorded tracks are used. Hand-held microphones or sophisticated wireless body mikes enable these shows to be of studio-quality sound. In other words, what they sing and play on stage is what you hear.

The shows cover the whole spectrum of American music. This is something the *Sampler* really wants to emphasize. There's great country music at Opryland. The "Bluegrass Show" is sponsored by Martin guitars. At "Country Music USA," a score of young singers and dancers perform the all-time great country hits, past and present, including some very good vocal imitations of Ronnie Milsap, Loretta Lynn, the Gatlins, and others. The Tennessee River Boys offer their renditions of today's chart-toppers. "Sing the Glory Down" is a great gospel show. But, and this is very important to realize, you can hear a lot of other music at Opryland.

Two shows in particular will help you trace the history of American pop music from the Civil War almost to the present. They are "For Me and My Gal" and "I Hear America Singing Its Song." "For Me and My Gal," in the American Music Theater, takes American love songs and patriotic songs and brings them from 1880 or so all the way to 1917, when we entered the First World War. "I Hear America Singing Its Song," in the Tennessee Music Theater, picks up where that show leaves off, including music from the 1920s to the present. This year's "I Hear America Singing Its Song" has been totally rewritten, but it still features the extravagant costuming and production that have made it a favorite among the more than seven million people who have seen it. It is the longest-running major theme park production in the world.

Now, something you need to know about "For Me and My Gal" is that admission is free, but you'll need a ticket to get in. So, whatever day you're going to see this show, as soon as you get to the park, head on over to the American Music Theater, and get a ticket to the performance you prefer. If you wait even an hour past park opening time on the busiest days, the tickets are liable to be gone. Also, you'll notice a long line forming as much as a half-hour before the performance. Unless you just enjoy standing in lines, the *Sampler* recommends that you wait until the doors are open and the line starts moving. The seats inside are good, better, and best. They all provide a fine view of the show, but if you want to be down front in the middle, by all means get there a half-hour before show time and line up.

Once you're inside, you'll see a wonderful 40-minute performance hosted by George M. Cohan himself. It features the comedy of rowdy Bowery Boys' characters and Keystone Cops, romantic ballads, and a patriotic finale. The timing is great, and special effects are effective. We'll not give away the show's surprises, because we want you to see them for yourself, but you won't believe the bird in a gilded cage, or Ragtime Cowboy Joe, or the old-time-movie sequence. The *Sampler* took two kids in under protest. They didn't want to see a stuffy show with grandma's music in it. But they loved the show and were totally captivated by the energetic choreography and good humor.

Backing the singers and dancers is an orchestra with a string quartet (something you'll find only at Opryland), a rhythm section, woodwinds, and a brass section. Bobbie Jean Frost directs the show from the piano without a note of music in front of her! Bobbie Jean is a music teacher at Hillsboro High School in Nashville. She gave the *Sampler* a behind-the-scenes glimpse of one of Opryland's great shows. "There were two understudies in today's show," she said, "but I'll bet you couldn't tell." (We couldn't.) "We start rehearsing weekends in February. From scratch. The singers don't know a line of their part, and all the choreography has to be worked out. By opening day, we're really tight." The performers average around 21 years old, and the musicians tend to be symphony players and teachers. "We're always ready for anything to happen, and being totally live, we can usually deal with a skipped beat so that the audience doesn't even know about it. That wouldn't be possible with sound track music."

New at Opryland this year. Now, what if you've spent three days at Opryland and still have one more day in town? Or maybe you're in town just for a day on business and you don't have time for the park. Well, you need to know about two great new attractions at Opryland. The first is the *General Jackson*, a multimillion-dollar riverboat that started running up and down the Cumberland in midsummer of 1985. It will run year-round and boarding is at the rear of the Opryland parking area. It features two-hour cruises during the day at $8.95 per person (kids three and under are free). Food is available but not included in the price. Entertainment

Opryland's newest show "Music! Music! Music!"

includes strolling pickers and such. In the evening there's a dinner cruise. It's $28.00 per person, and kids four to eleven get in for $22.50. This price includes dinner and a full show.

The second great attraction is a brand-new Broadway-caliber show in the Roy Acuff Theater called "Music, Music, Music." Admission is $4.95. This is accessible without going into the park, just like the Opry House. This show has 22 singers and dancers, a 16-piece orchestra, and over 130 costume changes. It salutes the three coasts of entertainment—Hollywood, Broadway, and Nashville—in a 75-minute show featuring dazzling special effects, excellent musicianship, and some truly incredible young performers. Some of them are literally show-stoppers, like sultry Shawn Johnson from Connecticut. There are two shows daily, except on Tuesdays. This top-quality Opryland show is a must-see for everyone.

How to Attend Free Tapings at Opryland

Want to see Barbara Mandrell or Conway Twitty while visiting Nashville? How about Lily Tomlin, Della Reese, Robert Duvall, or Cybill Shepherd?

These performers—and scores of others—from all

parts of the entertainment world have appeared on "Nashville Now," a television show produced at Opryland and available to Opryland guests. "Nashville Now" is on The Nashville Network (TNN), which, like the Opryland theme park, is part of the Opryland USA entertainment complex.

"Nashville Now" and several other TNN shows are produced before live studio audiences, adding a regular attraction to Opryland that no other theme park can claim. Park guests can be in the audiences for concerts, game shows, dance shows, and other types of programs. Some can become game show contestants or be used in other roles on camera. Tapings are held year-round at the Opryland complex.

Admission to tapings almost always is free, and when shows are taped inside Opryland, the shows are part of the entertainment that park guests can enjoy. When ticketing is required, tickets usually are distributed free at Opryland's Passport and Guest Relations Centers. Both of these are in the Plaza Area.

"Nashville Now" is one show certain to be in production every week. Produced every weeknight in the TNN Gaslight Studio, it combines music, interviews, and occasionally some audience participation. Country music personality Ralph Emery is the host, and his guests run the gamut of country music stars and other performers whose travels bring them through Nashville.

The best way to find out about taping schedules is to call the Opryland Information Center at (615) 889-6611 or TNN Information Services at (615) 883-7000 to see whether any shows will be in production during your visit to Nashville.

TNN, a cable television service with a country music emphasis, went on the air in 1983. In less than a year, it reached 12 million households nationwide and is cable television's fastest growing service. At Opryland, it can produce shows in the 4,400-seat main auditorium of the Grand Ole Opry House, a 300-seat studio in the same building, the 800-seat TNN Gaslight Studio, and other theaters and locations. Shows also are produced at the nearby Opryland Hotel.

Besides its own shows, TNN provides its staff and state-of-the-art technical facilities for other television projects. Examples are the tapings in June and October of "Hee Haw," the long-running country music and comedy syndicated series.

Duane Allen of the Oaks

land, unless he rented the whole place for himself. Well, even Elvis couldn't have rented this whole place for himself. But when the *Sampler* asked Duane Allen, of The Oak Ridge Boys, what was his favorite thing to do when home, he said he loved to take himself, his wife, and Jamie and Dee, his two children to Opryland. Notice we say he likes to take himself, as well as the kids.

Duane enjoys the rides as much as his kids, maybe more. In fact, Duane told us that, "Opryland is not the kind of place that you go to once as a tourist and never again. No, you go back again and again." Fact is, one of the most important things to any Tennessean is his family. Family ties around these parts are mighty thick, and that's what makes Opryland so special for Duane and his family. They can all laugh together, have a blast together and then go watch Mama sing. Mama sing? I thought that Duane was the one doing all that singing. Mrs. Duane Allen is not just the wife of an Oak Ridge Boy but is one of the back-up singers at the Grand Ole Opry.

We're sure Duane can afford to take his family anywhere he wants, and we know he's seen just about all that the world has to offer. But when he has the chance to spend precious time with his family, he just drives down the road a piece to Opryland.

A SAMPLER
*****Exclusive*****
An Oak Ridge Boy Goes to Opryland

Y ou wouldn't really picture one of the most famous singers of one of the most successful singing groups ever to come out of the USA heading to Opry-

That Nashville Music

If you're going to be in Music City a few days, one sure source to check for the most up-to-date information on pickers, clubs, concerts, and who's playing where is the Sunday edition of the Nashville morning newspaper, the *Tennessean*. It has a supplement called "The *Tennessean* Sunday Showcase," which is put together just for entertainment seekers. It showcases not only Nashville but also surrounding areas. It has every place that's any place for any type of music. So if you are inspired by the *Sampler's* articles to want to hear jazz at J. C.'s, bluegrass at the Station Inn, or rock at Cantrell's, then the "Showcase" is a must for your week in town.

Music City Country

Country Music Fan Fair

There's no music like country music, no musicians like country musicians, and most of all no fans like country fans. Country fans are the most loyal in the music industry. They love to travel, to meet their favorite entertainers, and to organize. Put the music, the stars, and the fans together in a gigantic celebration, and you get International Country Music Fan Fair. No other form of music has anything quite like it.

By 1986, Fan Fair will be in its fifteenth year. For those of you who have never been, Fan Fair is a weeklong interaction between country stars and country fans. Over 300 booths are set up with exhibits about the musicians. Autograph and picture-taking sessions are held with country's most popular entertainers. Over 30 hours of concerts are sponsored by the various record labels. A bluegrass concert, an international show, a Cajun show, and the Grand Masters Fiddling Championship are also part of the festivities. The registration fee of $60 per person includes all this, plus tickets to the Country Music Hall of Fame, Opryland USA, and Ryman Auditorium, historic site of the Grand Ole Opry. Oh, there's also the All American Country Games, where the likes of Barbara Mandrell compete in athletic events for the benefit of Tennessee's Special Olympics.

As impressive as these events are, the real story of Fan Fair takes place in and around the official events and exhibits. For one thing, many of the stars put on wingding events just for their fan clubs during Fan Fair. Ricky Skaggs gave his fans their own private concert on the Marriott Hotel grounds last year. Barbara Mandrell puts on a big breakfast spread for her fans so she can meet and talk with them. Conway has a big bash for his fans out at Twitty City.

Then, too, the fan clubs are a show unto themselves. They spend months preparing for Fan Fair, getting in touch with all their people, constructing the booths for the week-long extravaganza, and then stocking them with souvenirs and club members who are great at pot-lickin' and recruitin' new members. A happy, intense, and harmless rivalry among the clubs spices up the week. Loretta Lynn's fan club was showing a letter last year from a fan who wrote: "I'm sorry I'm strapped right now, but I promise to renew as soon as I get my next unemployment check."

But beyond all this, Fan Fair is great because of all the people who are country fans and the spontaneous, poignant, or hilarious events that just happen all week long. Last year there was a wedding at one of the booths. Fans B. W. Sipes and Edith Newsome tied the knot in singer Billy Blanton's booth. A red bandanna, gift of Boxcar Willie, served as the bride's garter. Some other couples got engaged after they met through the fan clubs.

Fan Fair inevitably spills some of its craziness into the streets of Nashville. Night spots rock and jump just a little harder and higher. A lot of out-of-town media are in evidence, and they seem to create events just for the cameras.

If you want to hear country's greatest songs sung by the stars themselves, meet the songwriters, visit for awhile, get everyone's autograph, blitz Music City's greatest attractions, and hear world-class instrumentalists, then Fan Fair's for you. June is a great time of year, too, as Tennessee sports its summer best. Y'all come!

Information Address: Fan Fair, 2804 Opryland Drive, Nashville, TN 37214.

The Music Country Radio Network

So you want country? Well, you can hear it any night all over the USA on the Music Country Radio Network. From 10:00 P.M. until 5:00 A.M. the country flows on a live variety radio show broadcast by satellite to affiliated stations coast to coast. There's one near you. Write to the network in care of WSM radio and find out the call letters and frequency of your local station. WSM is the flagship station of this network, and whoever's in town recording is just liable to show up for an interview. Stars like Willie Nelson, Alabama, and Ronnie Milsap have been guests on the show. Whether you're in Washington, D.C., or Washington State, tune in to country on the Music Country Radio Network.

The Midnight Jamboree

Those of you who have your radios on after the regular Saturday evening Grand Ole Opry broadcast on WSM have already heard the Midnight Jamboree. Broadcast live from the Ernest Tubb Record Shop on Music Valley Drive off McGavock Pike, near Briley Parkway, this live music session welcomes visitors and admission is free! The Midnight Jamboree has been going on for 37 years now and has seen performances by Hank Williams, Elvis, Loretta Lynn, Willie Nelson, George Jones, Ricky Skaggs, and Barbara Mandrell. Justin Tubb hosts the show, which is a pleasing mix of country entertainment and a great place to meet some country music stars in a fun, informal setting.

The Ernest Tubb Record Shops remain Music City's best places to find rare or recent country music records. They'll look up records for you and will be happy to mail you a catalog. Just write them at P. O. Box 500, Nashville, TN 37202.

The Ralph Emery Show

What is the highest rated locally produced morning television show in the United States? Why, it's "The Ralph Emery Show," of course. Ralph and his collection of characters have been waking up Nashville and environs since 1963. The show features a live, tried-and-true unique format of country music backed up by a studio band, do-it-yourself commercials, weather, traffic reports, schoolbus reports, and viewers' birthdays. Most Middle Tennessee households get their start every morning by tuning in Ralph and his crazies to see what will happen next. And something always does.

Emery presides over the antics with a calm akin to Tennessee limestone—that is, it can dissolve under the right conditions! He has been known to remove hype from commercials on the spot and has even asked singers to redo song endings that weren't just exactly right. One morning, most of the band was late, and the only music Ralph had for about 45 minutes was Us Two and Him, a group from Chapel Hill specializing in songs about outhouses. The show does highlight some great new country talent, and how they can sing so well at 5:30 A.M. is one of Music City's mysteries.

The group of commercial sponsors includes such local characters as Steamatic Man and his singing duo the Dirtbusters, and Jerry from Burke Building Salvage, who can put a model of anything on a hard hat. Another star is Albert McCall, head of a Middle Tennessee furniture empire, who has no shame when it comes to participating in skits.

But the most famous of Emery's cohorts are Maude and Dorothy Paul, two sisters who just started dropping in for the show 20 years ago. Their off-key singing, idiosyncratic sense of rhythm, and general lack of musical ability and inhibitions border on genius. They are so bad they are wonderful, and Middle Tennessee has taken them to its heart.

If you're visiting in Nashville, ask for a wake-up call and tune in the Emery show. It's an experience you'll never forget!

WSMV Channel 4: The Ralph Emery Show, Monday through Friday, 5:30 A.M.

The Country Music Foundation

If you just can't seem to remember the name of Gid Tanner's band, the way the original title went to "Will the Circle Be Unbroken," the color of Ernest Tubb's eyes, or Roy Acuff's birthplace, then you need to know about the Country Music Foundation's Library and Media Center. Ronnie Pugh and his coworkers can answer any question that's really bothering you about country music or musicians.

Fan Fair: Close encounters with ALABAMA

Hold on, now, before you rush to the phone over a Trivial Pursuit question! There are charges for research time, so make sure it's something you really need to know. Also, if you're in Nashville, you can stop in and look it up yourself, and there will be no charge unless the staff has to spend an exceptional amount of time stepping and fetching for you. They welcome anyone with a serious interest. By all means, include a stamped self-addressed envelope with your question. If you're coming by the library, you'll need an appointment, so contact them in advance.

The foundation itself is dedicated to preserving, interpreting, and spreading information about country music, and they love people who love their country. Let them help you learn more about your favorite singers and pickers. Oh, by the way, Gid Tanner's band was the Skillet Lickers. The original title to the Carter family song was "Can the Circle Be Unbroken." Ernest Tubb's eyes and Roy Acuff's birthplace—well, we'll just have to call Ronnie and his researchers and find out!

The Country Music Foundation, 4 Music Square East, Nashville, TN 37203. (615) 256-1639.

The Station Inn

"Redneck Reggae!" someone in the audience shouted. There we were, 200 or so people packed into the Station Inn, all of us screaming our lungs out, and swaying on our feet, clapping as hard as we could, and the band was only three songs into its second set! But none of us could believe what we'd just heard. It had to be the best music being played in the whole world at that moment!

We were listening to Crucial Country, the performance bluegrass band centered on tall, handsome Peter Rowan, guitarist and singer. Other members in the superpickers that night included acoustic bass player Roy Huskey, Jr.; Sam Bush, one of newgrass's founders, on mandolin; simultaneous world fiddle and guitar champion Mark O'Connor on fiddle; and jazz-bluegrass synthesist Bela Fleck on five-string banjo.

They had just done some reggae songs by Jamaican Bob Marley. Rowan's incredible voice had soared over imaginative instrumentals by these best-of-bluegrass practitioners. Fleck played with machinelike precision, virtually immobile. Huskey tossed off balletlike bass runs with deadpan efficiency. Bush was restless as a caged tiger, his whole body pulsing, keeping the rhythm for the entire group as he played reggae mandolin.

Mark O'Connor was phenomenal. Around hypnotic repetitions of the chorus, he first wove an amazing fabric of melody and variations all over the fingerboard of his fiddle. Then his flowing fingers left the wood and began to just lightly touch the strings in subtle harmonics, producing achingly beautiful sounds, the like of which had probably never come before come out of any fiddle anywhere. They originated in an instantaneous coordination between O'Connor and his fingertips, floated by us for a majestic moment, and were gone.

Everyone in the audience was totally blown away, and that's saying something, because night after night, the Station Inn has some of bluegrass music's most discriminating listeners. That night, Gove Scrivenor, half The Nitty Gritty Dirt Band (in town for a recording session), Jessie McReynolds, and other famous names in bluegrass and country dotted the audience.

As soon as the *Sampler* got a chance, we took J. T. Gray off to the side to ask about his establishment. "There's no question about it," he said, "the music's the main thing here. We are a family of people who love their bluegrass."

Almost as important as the word *bluegrass* is the word *family*. A few years ago, when J. T. had a bout with serious illness, everyone in bluegrass from founding father Bill Monroe on down pitched in with benefit concerts to help him with expenses and keep the Station Inn open.

Why do the musicians keep coming to the Inn to play and listen? We asked mandolinist Roland White, leader of the New Kentucky Colonels. "Well, many of us play and record here in Nashville. This is where we come to hang out and hear the latest. And on tour, Nashville is a great in-between stop to and from just about anywhere. It's like an oasis. You know there'll be people at the Station Inn who have come to listen to you. J. T. often gets up to play acoustic bass and sing high tenor with us. There's just no other place quite like it."

J. T. never throws away any poster anyone sends him of bluegrass performers or festivals. He just keeps putting them up on the walls, and they remain the Inn's only decoration except for the digital Michelob clock. The floors are a bit uneven, hardwood alternating with well-worn sheet plywood, but people who jump up to buck dance seem to have no trouble with them.

Tuesdays through Sundays the Station Inn is one of America's premier listening rooms for bluegrass music, featuring nationally known groups such as the Country Gentlemen and the Bluegrass Cardinals as well as local bands. Individual headliners like Dan Crary or Norman and Nancy Blake also appear regularly.

When we say bluegrass, we mean any kind of bluegrass! One of the favorite groups that occasionally plays at the Inn is Hot Rize, which alternates sets of true-blue bluegrass with sets of light-hearted spoofing performed by their alter egos, Red Knuckles and the Trailblazers. The Trailblazer set includes the best rockabilly music you'd ever want to hear, Motown-like choreography, and understated comedy. One of the Trailblazers, the sinister Slade, even has a guitar strap with three skulls complete with blinking red lights for eyes. Hot Rize is always a real treat.

Music starts nightly at 9:00 P.M. and continues until at least 1:00 A.M. Sets usually last just longer than an hour. Cover charges range from $4 to $6. Sunday night is a jam session of whoever's in Nashville, and it's always a lot of fun; there is no cover charge. Beer, soft drinks, and munchies are served. Don't forget, though, people just rent beer, they don't buy it! So if you can sit on the left side of the room, you'll miss the never-ending stream of patrons making their way to the rest rooms.

The *Sampler* recommends showing up at least by 8:30 if you want to be sure of a seat on the nights favorites are in town. Call J. T. and ask if you're not sure

who's playing. A schedule is available by mail for hardcore fans of the Inn.

The Station Inn, 402 Twelfth Avenue South, Nashville, TN 37203. (615) 255-3307.

Music City Playhouse/Reel Country

This is a one-of-a-kind restaurant and country music showcase. It wouldn't be possible anywhere else but in Music City. They have live country music seven nights a week and there is no cover charge. Mostly studio bands of high quality perform. Monday and Tuesday it's the Jean Shepard Band, and Wednesday through Sunday, the Real Country Band. These groups play mainstream country, says Jeff the manager. A full bar, a steakhouse-type restaurant, and a dance floor that will accommodate at least 300 add to the place's appeal. What makes Reel Country different? Well, when the bands take a break, vintage country videos are shown—clips from old television appearances dating back to the fifties and some old movie clips as well. A few times, country stars just visiting Reel Country have been surprised to see themselves on the screen looking 30 years younger!

Music City Playhouse/Reel Country, 1520 Hampton, just off I-65 at Trinity Lane, across from Drury Inn.

Country Music Clubs:

Nashville Palace, 2400 Music Valley Drive. (615) 885-1540. Live country seven nights a week.

Stagecoach Restaurant and Lounge, 870 Murfreesboro Road. (615) 361-9806. Live music seven nights a week.

The Country Playhouse, 3940 Dickerson Road. (615) 865-9237. Live country music Thursdays through Saturdays at 9.00 P.M.

The Four Guys Harmony House. Live country music, often by the Four Guys, evenings Tuesday through Sunday.

The Bluegrass Inn, 1914 Broadway. (615) 329-1112. Bluegrass music most nights by bands that are booked in for several nights at a time.

Music City Jazz, Rock, Etc.

The Volunteer Jam

"Ain't it great to be alive and in Tennessee!" Charlie Daniels has shouted those words just after the first few bars of the "Tennessee Waltz" and over the full-throated roar of 9,900 rock-and-roll fans to introduce Volunteer Jam concerts. "The Jam" is the Charlie Daniels Band's annual homecoming performance in the Volunteer State of Tennessee and much more. It is a special spark of remembrance and love that fans and

Ted Nugent, Rock's wild man, with Charlie at the Jam
Photo by Larry Dixon

over to attend, and in 1985 not even a major winter storm could keep them or the performers away.

The Jam now is broadcast live worldwide over the Voice of America and over cable networks. This year's Jam included those rare moments which have become typical at this music celebration. The tender tones of Amy Grant's "Amazing Grace" were still floating over the audience when Ted Nugent, rock's wild man, strode to the microphone and started his ear-blistering guitar riffs. Legendary Little Richard threw most of his wardrobe to the crowd while belting out gospel tunes. Kris Kristofferson showed he is still the complete song crafter with some new material. Nicolette Larson, EmmyLou Harris, Dickey Betts, Alabama, Dobie Gray, Tommy Shaw (formerly of Styx), and a host of others just blew the audience away.

A traditional secrecy shrouds the list of performers. Neither Daniels nor people who are coming to play will divulge the information before the Jam. There are always very big surprises, and rumors about who has been seen at the airport flow around the audience like water around creek stones.

What can we say about the Jam? Volunteer Jam is one of Tennessee music's main courses, always satisfies, and gives you a year to get hungry all over again!

For Volunteer Jam ticket information, write the Sound Seventy Corporation, 210 Twenty-fifth Avenue North, The Sound Seventy Suite N-101, Nashville, TN 37203, or call (615) 327-1711.

---

performers alike carry with them from one year to the next. If you've ever experienced the Jam, you feel like family—it's as simple as that. The concert has grown from a showcase for southern rock to include country, rhythm-and-blues, pop, jazz, Christian contemporary, and classical musicians.

What does Charlie Daniels say about the Jam? "First off, let me just say that the Volunteer Jam is the busiest, the friendliest, the greatest, the most efficiently run, the happiest and the downright damndest outpouring of love to take place at any musical event I've ever been a part of.

"It is the Grand Ole Opry, a Saturday night jam session, the circus, and the Super Bowl all rolled up into one great big multicolored ball. It is a honky-tonk juke box and redneck beer joint. It's a hillbilly, rock-and-roll, jazz-picking, blues-shouting, low-riding, high-stepping, hymn-singing, 24-carat phenomenon."

But, Charlie, what *is* the Jam? On October 14, 1974, at Nashville's War Memorial Auditorium, the Charlie Daniels Band decided to celebrate their first-ever sold-out concert in their home town by inviting some friends over to do some jamming. Members of the Marshall Tucker Band and the Allman Brothers Band dropped by, and the Jam was born. By 1977 the Jam found a home in Municipal Auditorium in Nashville where it has been held ever since, usually in January or early February. The show begins at 5:30 or 6:00 P.M. and typically features 9 hours of music and more than 80 songs performed by various artists. Loyal Jam fans come from all

J.C.'s

Maybe you're a musical omnivore and one evening you feel like hearing some jazz. Or perhaps you're a strictly jazz person. Either way, the *Sampler* says go to J. C.'s. Once there, you'll be hooked on the music and the great food. Jazz is J. C.'s only music format—contemporary, bebop, original, and fusion. For those who think Tennessee's only fusion happens around Oak Ridge, what we are talking about here is a high-energy style of jazz built around a rock rhythm section and a jazz horn section.

The jazz is live six nights a week, with Sundays off. There is no cover charge on Monday nights, which offer a free-flowing jam session. Other cover charges are usually $2 weeknights and $3 or $4 on weekends. The groups that play J. C.'s are mostly Nashville-based studio musicians, but out-of-towners occasionally play, and a different group plays every night.

Some crowd favorites are Jeff Kirk, alto sax player, and his quartet, who do very structured and disciplined sets; and Mickey Basil (keyboards) and his quintet, which features Stan Lassiter on guitar. Stan may be the only person you'll ever hear play jazz fretless guitar. He's even written a solo piece for it entitled—what else?—"Don't Fret!" He's only one of several players at J. C.'s known worldwide in jazz circles.

The musicians at J. C.'s make their licks look easy, but believe us, this music is very demanding. Many of the groups do their own arranging. Sometimes they use head arrangements, but often you'll see them playing with their charts in front of them, riding riffs faster than hummingbird wings and twice as delicate with their eyes closed, peeking every now and then at their music.

All this jazz is in J. C.'s restaurant, owned by John and Sylvia Cicatelli. Out front is a full bar. Oh, and the restaurant has live piano music from noon to 2:00 P.M. Tuesday through Friday. All the food is freshly prepared by Sylvia and is definitely and delightfully Italian. It's an intimate room, with seating capacity for about 125. A sound system and lights are available, but not every group uses them.

More than any other Nashville listening room, J. C.'s really shows the versatility of Music City musicians. These players might be backing up Dottie West in the morning, playing with a Nashville Symphony ensemble in the afternoon, and laying down hot or cool jazz at J. C.'s in the evening. Music starts at about 9:00 P.M. Don't miss J. C.'s!

J. C.'s, 2227 Bandywood Drive (just off Hillsboro Rd). (615) 383-8160.

Bendin' those notes at J.C.'s

The Bluebird Cafe

If you're wondering why the Bluebird Cafe isn't the Redbird or the Mockingbird, you should visit on a Monday night. Monday is strictly blues night, with the house band, Blue Monday, furnishing the framework for some of the best jamming on God's blue earth. Plenty of hot musicians are in Nashville, and many times people will come out of the audience to play with the band to produce some genuine Nashville funk. No cover charge for this evening makes this one of Nashville's great entertainment values.

The Bluebird has an impressive variety of live music seven nights a week. Tuesday through Saturday different bands or performers play rock, jazz, or crossover country. These top national entertainers are stopping in at one of their favorite places to play, and the shows are always something extra special. These nights there will usually be a modest cover charge.

But many Bluebird regulars will say that we've saved the best for last. That's because Sunday night is writer's night. Again no cover. On these nights the Bluebird features new material by songwriters and performers in the Nashville area and also a special guest slot for the industry's best-known songwriters. Sunday night last, for example, John Prine showed up and played for an hour and a half! Friend, believe us, the Bluebird is a unique listening room not to be missed!

The Bluebird is also a fine cafe with a full bar. They serve lunch from 11:00 A.M. to 2:30 P.M. and feature several specials for dinner from 5:30 to 8:30 every night. Owner Amy Kurland and a staff of three chefs make sure that every palate is satisfied. Everything is fresh, and the menu includes sandwiches, salads, vegetarian dishes, and casseroles, all moderately priced. So come for the music and enjoy the good food. Seating capacity is about 100.

The Bluebird Cafe, 4104 Hillsboro Road (US 431). (615) 383-1461. From Nashville, go southwest on Hillsboro Road. The Bluebird is on the left in a row of storefronts just past Green Hills Mall. Additional parking at Payne Furniture, two doors south.

Cantrell's

Cantrell's isn't much to look at, but it's a heck of a lot to listen to! Within Cantrell's walls reverberate, consistently, Nashville's most electrifying music and its rawest, raunchiest rock. Cantrell's features live music Wednesday through Sunday, although there is sometimes variation in the schedule. It's Nashville's place to hear "alternative music." In fact, the night of the Volunteer Jam, Cantrell's had the Alternative Jam and rocked out until the wee hours.

Cantrell's features most types of rock music and even some country. Reggae, punk, heavy metal, and new wave rock styles are all heard at Cantrell's. And we do mean heard! We might as well say that "decibellacious" Cantrell's has the best light and sound of any of Nashville's listening rooms. It definitely has a concert atmosphere and provides just the right setting for groups like the Stray Cats or Asleep at the Wheel. The *Sampler* asked Cantrell how they pull such well-known groups into Nashville. He replied: "Nashville is one of the most important music markets in the nation. Any band with new material has to play this town."

Cantrell's opens at 8:00 P.M. and showtime is always 9:30, with closing about 3:00 A.M. There is a full bar, and snacks are available. Each night they're open, 300 or so patrons fill the seats and crowd the dance floor. The music is hot and the folks are friendly, so go on down to 1901 Broadway and hear whoever's at Cantrell's. (615) 327-2356.

The Boardwalk Cafe

"White collar casual," that's how the people at the Boardwalk describe their atmosphere.

Ginny Underwood, one of the owners, said, "Our clientele changes from night to night. When Delbert Mc-Clinton is playing, people just rock off the walls. The place goes berserk. When John Hartford plays, things quieten down a little. The music has a lot to do with the audience."

The Boardwalk Cafe is a restaurant providing a varied menu, most of which is homemade and cooked to order, at good value; a music room of above-standard size but still personal enough to make it a favorite to people in the industry; a neighborhood bar and gathering place where everybody knows your name; and an intimate environment for private parties.

Some of the best musicians and entertainers in the country have appeared at the Boardwalk, including Jimmy Hall, Pat McGlaughlin, Doc and Merle Watson, John Hartford, Delbert McClinton, Gary Lewis and the Playboys, the Neville Brothers, Dianne Davidson, The Nerve, and Ray Sawyer. Upcoming are Rare Earth, Leon Redbone, David Bromberg, Sonny Throckmorton, Jessie Winchester, John Sebastian, and the Butterfield Blues Band. The Boardwalk leans toward most rock forms and middle-of-the-road to crossover types of country music.

Most shows range from $3 to $7, depending on the artist, and they always have entertainment on Friday, Saturday, and Sunday evenings, with no cover on Sundays. On special occasions there are shows during the week, usually on Thursdays. Also depending on the date and artist, shows start anywhere from 8:00 to 11:00 P.M. Sunday, the Boardwalk tries to give new bands a chance.

The Boardwalk opens for meals at 11:00 A.M. Monday through Friday, noon on Saturday, and currently 4:30 on Sunday, closing at 1:00 A.M. weekdays and 2:00 A.M. on weekends.

Dress is casual, and most major credit cards are accepted. Tickets to some shows are sold in advance, with seating capacity of 200.

Boardwalk Cafe, 424 Nolensville Road, Nashville, TN (615) 832-5104.

Cafe Unique and Other Uniques

Cafe Unique, 2406 Batavia Street. (615) 320-5126.

Cafe Unique features some of the best jazz in the city, Friday through Sunday, 9:30 P.M. A lot of big names on the jazz national scene also come through the Unique's portals tooting their horns. Call for directions if you can't find Batavia.

Brass A, Hickory Hollow Mall, (615) 833-6436; and Rivergate Plaza, (615) 859-4549. Rock-and-roll, seven nights a week, at 9:30 P.M.

The World's End Restaurant, 1713 Church Street. Sunday classical music brunch—Music City tradition. Live classical music performed by musicians dressed in formal wear. Delightful.

Ziggy's, 2054 Gallatin Road. (615) 859-0108. Rock Thursday through Saturday to some great bands.

Bogey's, Lion's Head Village, 80 White Bridge Road. (615) 352-2447. Live rock-and-roll, Monday through Saturday.

Music City Contemporary Christian

Brian Mason's 6:00-9:00 A.M. Sunday radio show on WLAC FM is the best place to hear the songs, catch the vision, and meet contemporary Christian artists in lively interviews. We've asked Brian to tell you how Nashville came to be the home of this exciting new music.

Many people do not realize that Nashville, with its reputation as Music City USA, is also the capital of contemporary Christian music. Besides being the major recording center, Nashville is also responsible for much of contemporary Christian music's direction and ever-changing form.

It hasn't been too many years ago that the mention of Christian music meant a southern, a black, or even a traditional style of gospel music. However, early in the 1970s it became apparent that a new, original style of "gospel" music was happening.

I remember the first time I visited the Belmont Church on Music Row. It was the fall of 1971. Walking in the door, I was stunned! Long hairs were sitting next to businessmen, and old ladies were sharing hymnals with people I would have guessed would never have known how to find a church. This same thing was happening all over the country and even all over the world, but the gift of love that God had given those people was something different.

In the Bible, there's a word that describes this love and the fellowship that the Belmont people shared. The word is *Koinonia.* Right across the street from the church building, the people decided to open a Christian bookstore, and guess what they named it—Koinonia! As if a Christian bookstore smack dab in the middle of Music Row wasn't enough by itself, the Koinonia people decided to open up a coffeehouse too.

A couple of fellows from West Virginia always had the place so packed that people would sit on each other's laps. Steve Chapman made weekly pilgrimages to Koinonia to sing the songs the Lord had given him. Songs that told stories. Songs that the listeners could take and chew on, and then chew on some more. It wasn't long before Steve called back home to his old friend and fellow musician Ron Elder.

Ron began performing regularly with Steve at Koinonia. Their style was a raw and natural folk-country-pop balance. They used acoustic guitars, and both of them sang. They were known for a long time simply as "Steve and Ron" but eventually named themselves Dogwood. Soon they added a third member, Bobby Dennis, a fellow who had a fairly impressive history in rock-and-roll music, had been in and out of the drug routine, and finally had given everything in himself completely over to Jesus.

They traveled extensively around the Southeast, but it was during one of their appearances at Koinonia that a young man by the name of Chris Christian heard Dogwood. Chris was fresh out of college in Texas, and he was quite an accomplished musician himself. In recent years, he has played guitar for Wayne Newton in Las Vegas; he was then working at Opryland at one of the country music shows. Chris wanted to produce Dogwood, but he had never really produced anything in his life. Also, the group wasn't sure that they wanted to do a record.

Well, the record *was* produced, and if it was Chris's first attempt, you certainly couldn't tell it! Dogwood's first record, *After the Flood, Before the Fire,* was released by Pat Boone's Christian record label, Lamb and Lion, in 1975. Chris was proven to be a gifted producer. He was called on to produce the first gospel album for B. J. Thomas when he became a believer. In addition, Chris produced the Imperials, a group that had been together since 1964. He produced Debby Boone and her sisters, Pat Boone, David Meece, Fireworks, and Dan Peek (former leader of the group America), among others.

Someone else was there with Chris at those Dogwood sessions, another Texan named Brown Bannister. And if Chris was green as a producer, Brown was even greener as the album's engineer. However, wouldn't you know it, a few years later one of the albums Brown engineered (*Home Where I Belong* by B. J. Thomas) won a Grammy. And since that time, Brown has become one of the most respected producers in contemporary Christian music, with credits like Amy Grant, Debby Boone, Kathy Troccli, the Imperials, and many others. Brown himself is also considered a strong writer and artist. When his schedule allows, he performs with his group The Vocal Band.

All these people I've mentioned so far have had at least one thing in common—the Belmont Church on Music Row in Nashville. The preacher of that church is Don Finto. Don is probably as responsible for the strong spiritual content of contemporary Christian music as anyone could be. He was once warned on the credits of Gary Chapman's first album, "If you were a songwriter, I'd be out of a job." (Gary is married to Amy Grant and has written, among other giant hits, T. G. Sheppard's "Finally" and Amy's "Father's Eyes," which actually introduced him to Amy.)

Koinonia's still there too! And the Spirit that led them in the beginning is still in charge. Almost every Saturday night you can attend a Koinonia concert. Most of them are held across the street in the old Belmont church building, but some are just intimate sessions held in the coffeehouse with the same type songs and people who have been drawn to that place for all these years.

The names of artists who have performed at that place would read like a who's who of contemporary Christian music. Dogwood went on to release a total of four albums. The last concert the group ever did was at Koinonia (of course) in December of 1980. Steve Chap-

Amy Grant, contemporary Christian pioneer

man continues to record with his wife, Annie. In fact, the two of them have released three LPs since Dogwood.

When she was just 15, Amy Grant wanted to share some songs that the Lord had given her, so Koinonia gave her the opportunity. The folks loved her, and it seems as if that's still happening. She shares her heart, sings her songs, tells her stories, and her ever-growing army of listeners continues to grow and love not only her but also the One who sends her.

Amy started out in Nashville. Many did not, but knew that Nashville was where they'd have to start. The group Fireworks, Michael W. Smith, Kathy Troccoli, Billy Sprague, Alan Robertson, Lanier Ferguson, Tricia Walker, Jim Weber, and many others simply followed their hearts to Tennessee.

Before I give you the impression that you would have had to pass through Koinonia's portals to be blessed and/or be a blessing, let me tell you about some other folks.

The number one Christian rock band in the world today is Petra. They've been together, goin' strong, since 1973. A few years back, the members of the group moved themselves, their families, and their business to use Nashville as their home and base of operations.

In 1980, Cheryl Prewitt was crowned Miss America. She grew up in Akerman, Mississippi. After she handed down her scepter, because of the Lord's call on her life and an incredible incident early in her life, she began Miracle Ministries. She too has moved to Nashville.

Scott Wesley Brown is truly a pioneer in contemporary Christian music. He grew up in the Washington, D.C. area. He tours all over the country and, in fact, the world. He is a special kind of singer/songwriter. As a result of missionary journeys behind the iron curtain, he has begun a nonprofit organization called I Care. A few years back, Scott too moved all he had to Nashville.

Scott Douglas is the lead singer for the Christian group Whiteheart. Before Scott ever heard of Whiteheart, he and his wife and kids left family and friends behind in Michigan because he knew that God had something for him here in Nashville.

Or how about Dan Keen? Dan is from Denver, Colorado, and has always wanted to be a singer and dancer. He wanted to move to Nashville to get into the business. His story is a little different because Dan was an atheist when he arrived in Tennessee. He went to work at Opryland, where he met his wife Bonnie, and she introduced him to many of her friends. The one who made the biggest impact on Dan was her friend Jesus. Now, Dan, Bonnie, and two other friends, Wayne and Nan Gurley, have teamed up to form the Christian comedy group Ariel.

Don Potter, originally from New York, is another fine example. His extraordinary work as a guitarist is most impressive. Among other credits, Don is one of the few people to do vocals on Chuck Mangione albums. When Don met the Lord a few years ago, he and his wife Christine moved to Nashville where he gave up music and took up carpentry. Although we all have idols in our lives, Don just wanted to make sure that the Lord was his idol, not music. Well, Don waited and God finally said yes. Now Don plays better than ever; now Don plays His music.

Also in Nashville are John and Patti Thompson. John and Michael Card, another Middle Tennessean, wrote the music to "El Shaddai," and John and Patti have released a new album, *Hope of the Heart*. John has been producing records here for years.

Of course, not only musicians make up this ever-growing musical forum. It takes record companies, publishing companies and, obviously, recording studios. Some of the best are in Nashville. Probably the biggest studio I know of is at the Benson Company. Benson is the home of Benson Publishing, as well as the head of several Christian record labels.

Most Christian labels have moved or at least set up branch offices in Nashville. Both Word and Star Song records have publishing companies here. Milk & Honey, Reunion, and many other labels are actually based in Nashville.

One of the largest, if not *the* largest, publishing companies on Music Row is Tree International. Tree for

years now has recognized the valuable impact of contemporary Christian music and even formed a special division for Christian music, Meadowgreen Music.

Every year, usually in March, the Gospel Music Association holds its annual National Gospel Radio Seminar in Nashville. This major event draws professionals from the radio industry all over the country. There they can meet and exchange ideas with one another as well as meet face to face artists and folks from the record labels they deal with on the phone or on the turntable everyday.

The big question is, Why Nashville? What's the attraction? Even the people who grew up here can't think of anywhere else they'd rather be. Nashville is so much more than just Music City. It's the place where God has drawn us. Musicians, singers, arrangers, producers, engineers, writers, even radio announcers, and *especially* the music supporters. This is home.

Koinonia

Koinonia is a book-and-record store and much more. It is a coffeehouse which has for years featured Christian contemporary music's key writers and singers. It is also a meeting place and nerve center for Nashville's Christian community. Koinonia's music room will pack about 400, and most Saturday nights it's filled with eager listeners. Concerts begin at 7:30. Dress is informal, and the regulars go out of their way to make you feel at home. There is almost always no admission charge, but a pass-the-hat love offering is taken for the singers. Not only Nashville-based singers, but musicians from all over come to Koinonia.

Koinonia, 1000 Sixteenth Avenue South. (615) 254-6414. On Music Row, four blocks up Seventeenth from the Country Music Hall of Fame and four blocks over from the Upper Room.

That Memphis Music—
Something Old, Something New, Something Borrowed, Something Blue

Bridal necessities in a former time, today these phrases aptly describe Memphis's ageless romance with her music. Old music, new music, borrowed music, and blue music are still being played by Memphis's world-class musicians. Just like the Mississippi flows by this Delta city, American music flows through Memphis in all its forms. Which is old, which is new, which is borrowed, we'll let you figure out. There's no doubt about which is blue. Few other cities have produced such an incredible line-up of performers as W. C. Handy, Furry Lewis, B. B. King, and Elvis Presley. They made, and were all made by, the blues.

Memphis gave birth to the blues, as they say. It was the music of field hands and levee workers, brought to

Outrageous Country Song Titles

"If I Said You Had a Beautiful Body, Would You Hold It Against Me."

"You're Wife's Been Cheatin' on Us Again."

"Get Your Biscuits in the Oven and Your Buns In the Bed."

"Fat Girls Jog at Night."

"He's Got a Way with Women and He Got Away with Mine."

town by traveling minstrels and entertainers. Then a genius named W. C. Handy scored the melodies, the patterns, and above all the rhythms, and the blues became a distinct form. He arranged, improvised, and composed blues classics like "St. Louis Blues," "Beale Street Blues," and "Memphis Blues," among others. Handy took the blues out of cottonfields and back-alley bars and into the best music halls in America.

A musical generation later, Memphis became headquarters for rhythm and blues (R and B), another enduring black musical style. B. B. King, Bobby "Blue" Bland, Herman "Junior" Parker, and others developed the style by fusing big band arrangements and jazzy lead guitar with country blues and gospel. It has continued strong with such Memphis performers as Booker T. (Jones) and the M.G.s, and the Bar-Kays leading the way.

Then in the 1950s, at Sam Phillips's Sun Recording Studio in Memphis, another wave of music began to be recorded. It was a fusion of black R and B and white honky-tonk country. It was most definitely rock-and-roll, though some called it rockabilly. Carl Perkins, Jerry Lee Lewis, Johnny Cash, B. B. King, Charlie Rich, Roy Orbison, and Conway Twitty all circulated through Memphis and Sam Phillips's Sun Recording Studio in the rockabilly days. But the man who made it all happen, Elvis Aaron Presley, the "King of rock-and-roll," made Memphis the place where the heart of rock-and-roll is still beating. After 30 years he's still a moving force in rock, one of its sources, the "Big Train from Memphis," as rock great John Fogerty calls him today.

ELVIS—A *Sampler* Tour

"Nothing really affected me until I heard Elvis. If there hadn't been an Elvis, there wouldn't have been the Beatles."—John Lennon

"You may not have liked Elvis or listened to his music, but he changed your life."—David Brinkley, NBC News.

"If love could find a stairway
And memories build a lane,
I'd find a way to heaven
And bring you back again."
— Graffito from Graceland's famous wall

Elvis loved Memphis. If Graceland became a velvet prison to him, Memphis remained a place where he could roam alone or with friends, driving shiny new cars up and down the strip. Perhaps he thought of all the water that had flowed down the Mississippi past the city where it all happened for him scarcely a year after he graduated from L. C. Humes High School. For the curiosity-seeker or the dedicated fan, more of Elvis's career mileposts are in Memphis than anywhere else. Beyond that, it was home. Here is the shrine where the faithful keep the faith and the mourners mourn what was and what might have been.

Graceland

Unquestionably, the place to begin is Graceland. From Memphis International Airport, turn west on Winchester and go on to US 51 South (Elvis Presley Boulevard). Turn left on US 51 South into the Graceland parking area on the right. Don't expect to see any Elvis Presley Boulevard street signs, however. Souvenir-seeking fans have removed them as fast as the city put them up, so Memphis has given up on replacing them!

Graceland was opened to the public in 1983. It is operated by Elvis Presley's estate, held in trust for Lisa Marie Presley, his daughter. Since it opened, almost a million fans have visited the King's palace.

Tickets are now $6.50 for adults and $4.50 for children 3 to 12. If it's summer or close to Elvis's birthday, there may be a wait before your group of 14 leaves for the mansion in one of the vans with its guide and taped Elvis music.

Elvis and his most famous Cadillac

Inside the grounds, magnolias surround the colonial mansion that Dr. and Mrs. Thomas Moore built in 1939. From the front porch, the tour moves through the living room which permits a glimpse into the music room with its grand piano covered with gold leaf, down into the basement where the TV room and pool room await. From there the tour goes up to the King's den, sometimes called the "Jungle Room," the teak-furnished exotic room where several of Elvis's albums were cut, including his last one, *Moody Blue*. After seeing the racquetball room where a video presentation is shown, guests are taken to Meditation Gardens, the final resting place of Elvis, his parents, and his grandmother.

During the course of the tour, you will be able to visit the "Hall of Gold," the largest privately owned collection of gold records in the world. Several of Elvis's costumes are on display, including the incredible eagle cape which weighs a shoulder-sagging 60 pounds! Equally stunning are the jewelry exhibits, including the famous 17-carat diamond-studded ring. If you're not blown away by all this yet, just wait till you see some of Elvis's vehicles: motorcycles, supercycles, snowmobiles, dune buggies, a Stutz-Blackhawk and of course, Cadillacs. One local Caddy dealer remembers selling Elvis more than 100 luxury cars.

But wait, there's still more to see. Graceland has added a "Relive the Magic" museum which is a masterpiece of sight and sound, including live concert footage. If that's not enough, you can board Elvis's private jetliner, the *Lisa Marie*, or his customized touring coach. The jet tour is $3.50 for adults and $2.75 for children, the museum is $2.00 for adults and $1.00 for children, and the coach is $1.00 for everyone. Food and officially licensed souvenirs can be purchased too.

Graceland is usually open seven days a week. Closed Tuesdays from November 1 through February 28. Closed Thanksgiving, Christmas, and New Year's Day. Hours: June through August—8:00 A.M. to 6:00 P.M.; September through April—9:00 A.M. to 5:00 P.M. May—8:00 A.M. to 5:00 P.M. Ninety per cent of the tour is protected from the weather.

The *Sampler* recommends ticket purchases in advance for Graceland. Long waits in the summer months can be avoided by this precaution. Tickets may be reserved by calling (901) 332-3322 inside Tennessee or (800) 238-2000 from the continental United States. The friendly staff at Graceland will help with room reservations in Memphis, which should also be arranged before your visit.

Lansky's, The Old Chisca Hotel, and Overton Park

Downtown Memphis has some significant Presley sites as well. Down on Beale Street, you'll see the statue of Elvis by Eric Parks, dedicated in 1980. Don't miss visiting Lansky Brothers, on the corner of Beale and Second, where Bernard Lansky outfitted Elvis with some of his more flamboyant costumes early in his career.

At the corner of Maine and Linden streets, and now headquarters for the Church of God in Christ is the old Chisca Hotel building, the site of Elvis's first radio interview. Dewey Phillips, the WHBQ DJ who played "That's All Right Mama" and "Blue Moon of Kentucky" for Sam Phillips, had to send someone to find the unknown singer after his telephone lines lit up with calls for the tunes. The story goes that he got the interview by convincing Elvis the microphone was turned off!

Another good place to soak up some Elvis vibes is Overton Park Shell, where Elvis first performed before a big crowd and began his patented gyrations while doing a song called "Good Rockin' Tonight." The crowd's reaction was so intense, some say, that one of the headliners for the evening declined to follow Elvis onstage.

While you're in the neighborhood, just over from Overton Park on Broad Street is the Broadway Pizza House, where you can eat pizza and view Elvis memorabilia including a lock of the King's hair, and two tickets to the concert Elvis never performed, the one at the Coliseum on August 27, 1977.

Sun Recording Studio and American Sound Studio

Some fans might want to drive down Union Avenue to pass Baptist Memorial Hospital, where Elvis was pronounced dead on August 16, 1977. If you're not the morbid type, just cruise on by, and a few blocks west of the hospital you'll find the Sun Recording Studio at 706 Union Avenue (at Marshall Street). Sun Studio has been restored to its 1954 appearance for the benefit of Elvis's fans.

Here Elvis made a recording for a birthday present for his mother Gladys (three months after her birthday) for $4.00 using a $12.75 guitar she had given him for his birthday in 1946. Here too Sam Phillips burst out of the control booth in July of 1954 when he heard something special as Elvis and two other musicians laid into "That's All Right Mama." Here also, on December 4, 1956, the Million Dollar Jam Session took place with Elvis, Johnny Cash, Carl Perkins, and Jerry Lee Lewis swapping piano and guitar licks.

Another sound studio of importance to Elvis fans is to be found at the corner of Chelsea and Thomas. There at American Sound Studios, in 1969, Elvis recorded "Suspicious Minds," "In the Ghetto," and 34 other songs in a 12-day period.

Can You Believe?—Elvis Souvenirs and Trivia

Can you believe Elvis recorded songs like "Ito Eats," "Song of the Shrimp," "Do the Clam," "Queenie Wahine's Papaya," "Yoga Is as Yoga Does," and "Fort Lauderdale Chamber of Commerce"?

Can you believe that the RCA country and western boxed set of nine extended play discs intended for juke boxes which has one Elvis disc with four songs on it is worth almost $3000 (with juke-box labels)?

Can you believe the 33 RPM single, "Good Luck Charm," could fetch $2,000 if it has the color picture sleeve?

Can you believe that white vinyl copies of Elvis's final studio album, *Moody Blue,* could earn you over $1,000 each?

Can you believe the wall around Graceland, with its

overwhelming variety of graffiti? Examples include: "It's all your fault I'm here with my woman—Joe"; "Elvis rules"; "I like the Doors better—Boyd"; and "I, Frank A. Cook, came to see your home—11/7/83."

Can you believe the 1957 Elvis doll with plaid shirt and blue pants could be worth $1,500, if he still lives in his original box and if no one has stepped on his blue suede shoes?

Beale Street or Gettin' the Blues in Memphis

From the turn of the century until the l940s, Beale Street was the jumpingest scene between Bourbon Street and Times Square. Outlandish zoot suits, top hats and tails, *and* bib overalls and straw hats meandered up and down the street, which always pulsed with a beat that was Memphis's own. Now Beale Street is jumping again, *and* music is the lure that will make it all work. Now frequented by tourists and home folks alike, Beale Street includes some of the old landmarks restored and some brand-new spots as well.

Today, Beale Street has come to life, thanks to Memphis's dedicated citizenry and the work of the Beale Street Development Corporation. Blues artists are performing again in free, impromptu summer concerts in Handy Park at the corner of Third and Beale, under the magisterial eye of a statue of W. C. Handy himself, standing with cornet in hand, looking toward his beloved Club Handy.

Blues Alley

Some of the old-time blues artists still perform regularly at Memphis nightspots. One of the favorites of blues audiences is an old cotton warehouse on Front Street which has been converted into the showplace Blues Alley. Some of its featured performers recall the great days when Beale Street was smoking and jumping with the blues beat. Blues enthusiasts from around the world come to hear the likes of Little Laura Dukes, a 76-year-old who can really belt 'em out. Other artists include Ma Rainey, and Big Sam and Evelyn "The Whip" Young, who once led her own recording orchestra on Beale Street. *Memphis Magazine* calls Blues Alley the "Temple of the True Sound, where you'll find the survivors of the old-time blues scene."

Blues Alley, 60 South Front Street, (901) 523-7144

The Old Daisy Theatre

The Old Daisy has been restored and is now being managed by the Center for Southern Folklore. Daily exhibits of interest include an extensive depiction of Beale Street life in its heyday which includes many rare photographs. An impressive permanent multimedia show is, "If Beale Street Could Talk," a 25-minute show using 18 projectors and four screens, hundreds of unique photographs, rare film footage, and sound recordings. This show alone is worth a trip to Memphis. From W. C. Handy's understated and lyrical blues style to the raw soulful blue notes of B. B. King's everlasting romance with Lucille (his guitar), the music really brings old Beale Street to throbbing life.

Friday and Saturday nights, recline in the old theatre seats and listen to a wide range of performers: traditional ones like James "Son" Thomas, or Booker T. "Slopjar" Laury; jazz people like Prince Gabe and the

Hulbert's Lo-Down Hours

Millionaires, or Fred Ford and Honeymoon Garner (whose musical collaboration spans decades and beggars description); rockabilly players like Mud Boy and the Neutrons; bluegrass folks like Doug Cole and the Dixie Bluegrass Boys; or gospel like the Spirit of Memphis. Admission to the live concerts is $4, making this one of the best bargains in Memphis.

The Old Daisy Theatre, 329 Beale Street. (901) 527-8200. Open from 11:00 A.M. to 6:00 P.M. Tuesday through Saturday, and 2:00 P.M. to 7:00 P.M. on Sunday as a museum and interpretive center for Delta life and music. Friday and Saturday, live music shows at 8:00 P.M. and 10:00 P.M.

Club Handy and W. C.'s Cafe

The showbar upstairs features live music nightly, with blues and pop predominating in a crowd-pleasing mixed bag, but Sunday afternoon features the blues. Recently Herman Green has been playing at the Club Handy. Herman's career began on Beale in the 1940s when he was a 15-year-old high-school sophomore. Back in those days, Club Handy, featuring Bill Harvey's band, served as the acid test for up-and-coming musicians as they jammed with the pros. Since then, Herman Green has played jazz in San Francisco, New York City, and most points in between, with such legends as Lionel Hampton and John Coltrane. But now he's back in his home town and back at the club where he learned a lot of his craft in the early days. He makes a detour to Memphis well worth the trip.

Club Handy and W. C.'s Cafe, 340 Beale Street. (901) 521-0213.

Marmalade

A real find. Just south of Beale, in the post office area, the food is home-style, and the R and B music some of the best in town. 153 Calhoun Avenue East. (901) 522-8800.

Some Old, New, and Borrowed Music Places:

The Antenna Club, 1588 Madison Avenue. (901) 725-9812. The cutting edge of rock-and-roll styles, that's where the Antenna Club is. Punk, new wave, heavy metal, and experiments that may never achieve the benediction of a name, these can all be found among the Antenna's players and participants. You've got to see it to believe it. This place really rocks! Memphis Magazine says, "It's loud, and raunchy, just like you walked up to your television and jumped right into the latest MTV video."

Fantasia, 1718 Madison Avenue. (901) 725-6748. We have to include this relaxed bar. Tuesdays through Saturdays it is a strictly classical music place. A variety of classical small ensembles regularly performs including string quartets, guitarists, flutists, and violinists. In between sets, taped classical music plays. For the quiet aficionado. Sunday and Monday, it's jazz time at Fantasia.

Foren's Vapors, 1743 Brooks. (901) 345-1761. An old Presbyterian church building is the location for the Vapors, a fine supper club. Most of its female clientele are probably old enough to remember getting "the vapors" or hearing mother talk about them. This club is primarily a place to dance in the more intimate styles of a bygone era. *Memphis Magazine* calls it "one of the few places in town a fox trot won't be laughed at." A large dance floor, seating for over 700, and a house band that plays plenty of slow dance music make this a place with a dedicated crowd of regulars. The 3:30 to 7:30 tea dance is the only one of its kind in the city. So grab the missus, take a break from the tube or the blues, and waltz an evening gently away at the Vapors.

Jefferson Square, 79 Jefferson Avenue. Behind the small bar, dark and just right for a good neighborhood tavern, is a good alternative listening room for jazz, folk, and blues, a typical Memphis mix. Outstanding local musicians with occasional cover charges.

Morocco Town Club, 616 Washington Street. The Morocco has a bright disco sound without the glitzy decor. Live music on the weekends features some of the best rhythm-and-blues performers in Memphis.

Memphis Was Country Since Before There Was Cool!

Music historians have long noted that bluegrass and country pickers home-grown in Memphis played in a unique style. Although it hasn't had the pivotal importance in country and western that it has had in rhythm and blues, Delta country has always has its own definite flavor. In fact, in the twenties and thirties, Memphis, not Nashville, was Tennessee's recording center for country music.

The main reason was the Delta string bands that captured the attention of talent scouts from the recording companies. The Delta string band usually had a tenor banjo which was strummed, rather than a five-string banjo played claw-hammer-style as predominated in the Appalachian string bands. This produced a driving rhythmic sound which allowed Memphis string bands to play blues, pop songs, and polkas as well as country. Country music in Memphis has always kept this eclectic characteristic of drawing on any style for material or inspiration. So if "cash-box country" settled in Nashville and drew from all directions, Memphians just stayed put and grew to love their country music. Several places in Memphis provide country music that is strictly state-of-the-art.

Hernando's and Other Hideaways

Hernando's Hideaway, 3210 Hernando Road. (901) 398-7496. An occasional Jerry Lee Lewis hangout, the Hideaway features great country and western anytime—mostly truck-stop country. There is lively dancing too. The walls are covered with the obligatory publicity photos of music stars.

Leon's Club, 5099 Old Summer Road. (901) 767-9847. Leon's is another dance club, but with good ole' boys and girls as its high steppers. Located in the Summer/White Station area, it's a gathering place for "honky-tonk angels" and their hard-dancing admirers. Leon's has a house band which intersperses just enough of the King's music with country and western to keep its folks happy. Prime steaks are the main food attraction.

Western Steakhouse, 1298 Madison. (901) 725-9896. Great steaks and beer-guzzling country. Live music on weekends is excellent. According to *Memphis Magazine,* firearms and dice have to be checked at the bar!

Bad Bob's, 3126 Sandbrook. (901) 332-9559. Tennessee's Gilleys, Bad Bob's is always replete with cowpersons. First-class live music is the main attraction, and country performers on the way up are almost always showcased at Bad Bob's. The parking lot is set up for 18-wheelers, and *Memphis Magazine* calls it "a hell-raisin' " joint, a vast warehouse where the truck drivers come to drink away their troubles, dance, and listen to a country-western band. In years past, performers included Razzy Bailey, Mickey Gilley, and Barbara Mandrell.

Miller's Cave, 2615 Overton Crossing. (901) 353-9301. Wonderful country music in a smoky honky-tonk setting. Live music Wednesday through Sunday. You're apt to hear some good dance rock-and-roll at Miller's also.

For who's playing where during your Memphis visit, grab a copy of *Memphis Magazine* and consult their city section. Also, buy Friday's *Memphis Commercial Appeal's* "Playbook" tabloid which has complete details on musicians and music places.

Larry Gatlin Says:

"I've been a lot of places in the last 30 years, but there's an old 150-year-old log house sitting on 84 acres of Tennessee farmland that's very special to me. In fact, it's the most special place on earth to me. The big-city bright lights sometimes entice us, but they're gonna have to drag me off that place feet first. No matter where I go, Brentvale Farm, my home, is the most special place to me."

Tennessee's Music Contests and Festivals

A SAMPLER FEATURE

Clyde Hartman, Tennessee State Champion Fiddler

■ "This tune's called 'Whistling Rufus.' It's one of my favorites," said Clyde Hartman as he settled his chin down on a beautiful old fiddle. We were sitting in Bruce and Elaine Peden's music room outside of Columbia, Tennessee, a dozen or so pickers playing the jazzy style of bluegrass that dominates these gatherings. Pediatrician Bob Thompson laid down an intricate and bassy rhythm guitar foundation, and Clyde's fingers just took flight! It was wonderful. In fact, the most amazing fiddling we'd ever heard! He played both parts of the tune three or four times and kept building variations and subtle harmonies until when he returned to the basic melody the last time it was like an old friend. Several other tunes followed, from Texas swing-style to "Fisher's Hornpipe," and Clyde just kept getting better.

When everyone's left-hand fingertips were almost bleeding and right forearms were ready to fall off, it was break time. "Clyde, the fiddle must be your life, to be able to play like that," someone said.

"No," he said, "I used to think it was, when I started playing in competitions a few years back. Then I had a serious illness, and I learned that music is just part of what I am. Family and friends, they mean so much. The good Lord helped me see that. I think that experience helped my fiddle playing."

It sure must have. Clyde is fiddling better than he has in his whole life, and that's really saying something. In recent years the soft-spoken district engineer for Ma Bell has won the coveted Tennessee Valley Fiddle King title down in Athens, Alabama, and the Tennessee Fiddle Championship at Clarksville, Tennessee.

It turns out champion fiddle players are both born and made. Clyde's parents and his six brothers and two sisters all played music in their Sequatchie Valley home, but none of them fiddled. "People would come for miles around. We'd pull all the furniture out of a couple of rooms and really pack them in dancing. The sheriff of Sequatchie County was the dance caller, and they'd fetch a cattle rustler out of jail to play the fiddle."

The *Sampler* wanted to know how Clyde got into the fiddle.

"In 1932, when I was eight years old, two men drove

Clyde Hartman

up in a brand-new Chevrolet. They were looking for a musician, and my daddy invited them to stay with us. Two weeks later we went into Chattanooga to a picture show. When we came out, we were surrounded by G-men with drawn guns. Turned out one of the men had robbed a bank in Texas using a gun stuffed with cotton in the cylinders. He got $22,000, bought the Chevrolet, and had picked up the other fellow, Joe DeWees, who was totally innocent, along the way. Anyway, my father sort of adopted Joe. He lived with us for years, and he taught me jazz fiddle.

"I guess Hugh Farr of the Sons of the Pioneers had the most to do with my fiddle style. I'd be listening to them on the radio and hear a tune I liked. Then I'd have to remember it clear till I got home and could figure out how to play it. We didn't have tape recorders to remember the tunes for us!"

The seven Hartman boys formed a western band and played for years on radio and TV. "We still get together and play for special occasions, but since we all lost our hair, we play as the Bald Eagles instead of the Hartman Brothers!" Clyde grinned as he said this.

"But, now, fiddling in a contest is a lot different than fiddling in a band. Contests have junior and senior fiddlers. Senior fiddlers are 60 or over. Each person plays usually three pieces—one free-style to sort of get the butterflies out, one fast reel or jig, and one waltz tune. Then after all the other winners have been named in banjo, guitar, mandolin, no-holds-barred buck dancing,

or spoons, the junior and senior fiddlers will be selected and play off for the trophy. It's very unusual for the senior fiddler to defeat the junior in the play-off, but I did that last year in Clarksville.

"You're apt to hear some tunes in several different versions. It takes younger players years to accumulate the number of tunes in their heads that some of us carry around. But they get incredibly good on the ones they do know. And don't get me wrong; some of them know an amazing number of tunes. I've had the privilege of playing off against Mark O'Connor for a trophy. You might as well relax and enjoy the music, because he's going to beat you. He's the equal of anyone in the world on fiddle and guitar and even other instruments, from what I hear.

"I guess the greatest thing about contests and festivals is seeing old friends and making new ones, and seeing the great young fiddlers growing up. People come to hear the music and make the music, and it just happens all over the contest site. There's just nothing else quite like it."

The Old Time Fiddler's Jamboree

One of Tennessee's biggest contests takes place every year on the Fourth of July weekend at the Old Time Fiddler's Jamboree and Crafts Festival in Smithville, Tennessee. As many as 50,000 people from all over the world have attended the Jamboree. Prize money will total over $3,000 this year.

The competition takes place on an outdoor stage in front of the county courthouse at Smithville. Contests are held in 21 different categories: fiddle, banjo, dulcimer, harmonica, gospel singing, folk singing, string bands, bluegrass bands, and buck dancing, among others. There's even a contest for novelty instruments like spoons, saws, or collard greens. First-prize money ranges from $35 to $100, with lesser cash prizes going to second- and third-place finishers.

As exciting as the competition can be, for many spectators the greatest music just happens all around the courthouse in impromptu jam sessions. A guitar player will carefully aim his tobacco juice away from his old Martin and ask a fiddler, "You know 'June Apple' or 'Indian on a Stump'?" When they swing into the tune, up will come a banjo picker, do a hasty tuning job, and before you can break a G-string, he'll run off with the melody. A foot-patting crowd will gather and out will come the cameras and tape recorders, but the players will be lost in the tune, savoring that June apple, looking each other directly in the eyes while they trade it back and forth.

Sometime late Saturday evening comes the climax of the Jamboree—the Junior and Senior Fiddlers' Showdown, a head-to-head competition between the best of the fiddlers at Smithville for a $100 prize and the Berry C. Williams Memorial Trophy. Friends, it don't get any better than this!

For information, write or call: Smithville Jamboree, P. O. Box 64, Smithville, TN 37166. (615) 597-4163.

Directions: From Nashville on I-40 East turn off at Lebanon-Watertown-Smithville (exit 239) and come 30 miles east on US 70. From Knoxville on I-40 West turn off at Smithville (exit 273) and come 10 miles south on State 56.

The Sewanee Music Center

What's the difference between a fiddle and a violin? Well, one you hear at Smithville in the summertime, and the other you hear at Sewanee. Nestled high atop the Cumberland Plateau just off Interstate 24, Sewanee is 90 minutes south of Nashville and 45 minutes north of Chattanooga. It is the site of a 10,000-acre Episcopalian institution which is modeled after Oxford University in England. The government of the university and the town are linked in a 700-year-old English pattern. Among the many distinctive Gothic-style buildings is the stunning All Saints Chapel with some of the most beautiful stained-glass windows in North America.

The campus is the location each year of the Sewanee Music Center, an intensive, high-caliber, five-week music camp now in its twenty-eighth year under the capable direction of Martha McCrory. Held in June and July, the festival boasts an international faculty and gifted students from America and abroad. Nearly 200 classical works are typically performed in a series of 30 concerts, ensembles, and recitals, all open to the public. Selections include everything from string quartets to trombone solos.

Most performances during this renowned program take place Saturday afternoons and evenings and Sunday afternoons. Some are held indoors at Guerry Hall, while others take place outside under shady trees at the Garth, a popular area on the lawn.

The Music Center's culmination occurs during nine concerts staged for a special four-day festival. For brilliance in execution and incredible musicianship, this festival is the equal of any in the classical music world. It highlights a wide variety of music including brass ensembles, original compositions, concertos, symphonies, and overtures.

Although the music brings people to the Sewanee Music Center, many students, faculty, and visitors keep coming back year after year because of the friendly campus atmosphere, the wonderful scenery, and the interesting countryside and people around Sewanee. Nearby is Wonder Cave, where visitors are handed lanterns to light their way through dark passages. Hundred Oaks, a mansion fashioned after a medieval castle, is in Winchester, Tennessee. Other favorites include the Jack Daniels Distillery in Lynchburg and Tims Ford State Rustic Park, which offers recreational activities for the entire family.

Tennessee's Got the Classics

We've got oboe music as well as hobo music. Across the state, there are 51 college departments of music; 35 dance companies; 59 drama theaters, clubs, and players' groups; 5 opera companies; and 10 symphony orchestras.

Here are the addresses of the operas and orchestras:

Opera Memphis, Inc., Memphis State University, Memphis, TN 38152.

Knoxville Civic Opera Company, P.O. Box 16, Knoxville, TN 37919.

Chattanooga Opera Association, 801 Oak Street, Chattanooga, TN 37402.

Appalachian Opera Company, University of Tennessee, Music Department, Knoxville, TN 37916.

Southern Opera Theatre, Memphis State University, Memphis, TN 38152.

Johnson City Symphony Orchestra, P.O. Box 533, Johnson City, TN 37601. (615) 926-8742. Guy R. Mauldin, General Manager.

Kingsport Symphony Orchestra Association, Fine Arts Center, 509 Watauga Street, Kingsport, TN 37663. John Gordon Ross, Music Director.

Knoxville Symphony Society, Arcade Building, 618 Gay Street, Knoxville, TN 37902. (615) 523-1178. Constance Harrison, General Manager.

Oak Ridge Civic Music Association, P.O. Box 271, Oak Ridge, TN 37830. (615) 482-4809. Jane Palmer, Development Director.

Chattanooga Symphony Orchestra, 8 Patten Parkway, Chattanooga, TN 37402. (615) 267-8583. Dean Corey, General Manager.

Tennessee Tech Community Symphony, P.O. Box 5045, Tech Campus, Cookeville, TN 38501.

Nashville Symphony Association, 208 Twenty-third Avenue North, Nashville, TN 37203. (615) 329-3033. Matt Maddin, Executive Director.

Jackson Symphony Association, Box 3098, Murray Station, Jackson, TN 38301. James Petty, Music Director.

Memphis Orchestral Society, 3100 Walnut Grove Road, Suite 402, Memphis, TN 38111. (901) 324-3627. Florence Young, General Manager.

Germantown Symphony Orchestra, P.O. Box 38038, Germantown, TN 38138.

For more information, write the Tennessee Arts Commission, Suite 1700, 505 Deaderick Street, Nashville, TN 37219. (615) 741-1701.

Tennessee Grassroots Days

For nine years now the Southern Folk Cultural Revival Project has been presenting Tennessee Grassroots Days in September in Centennial Park in Nashville. The project is a nonprofit organization operating under grants and contributions from individuals. Led by Anne Romaine, Judith Lovin Stiles, and Alice Merritt, the project has operated for almost 20 years, bringing traditional music and crafts of all types together on concert tours and in recordings and program series for PBS and other stations.

Grassroots Days is a statewide cultural event bringing together the music, folklife, and old-time survival ways of Tennessee's working people, Indian, black and white. All sorts of traditional crafts are demonstrated from quilting and coopering to broom- and banjo-making. If you ever used a plunker or a knuckle-buster, you'll want to see the Roley Hole marble-playing contingent from Clay County demonstrate how to make and shoot flint marbles. If you think your eye's still sharp, try to beat these guys! Other demonstrations include show posters by Hatch Show Print, of Fourth Avenue in Nashville; they have been making show posters in Nashville since 1879!

One of the festival's crossover performers is Bud Garrett, of Freehill, Tennessee, up on the Cumberland Plateau. His community is on land deeded to freed slaves in 1865, and their descendants still own the land. Bud makes flint marbles which sell for as much as $30, and he demonstrates marble-making techniques. He also sings traditional and original blues at the festival.

Groups such as Afrikan Dreamland, a three-piece reggae group from Nashville, and the Roan Mountain Hilltoppers with their generations-old mountain tunes illustrate the musical variety of Grassroots Days. String bands such as the Long Hollow Ramblers from Sumner County furnish the hoe-down tunes, and Robert Spicer

Chet Atkins with Carter girls, ca, 1948
Courtesy of Les Leverett

and Jacky Christian are there to demonstrate buck dancing in all its forms. In recent years the solo performers who have appeared include Anne Romaine, Peter Rowan, Sparky Rucker, a wonderful young blues player from Knoxville, and Frazier Moss, Tennessee's premier old-time fiddler.

Grassroots Days remains the best occasion in Middle Tennessee to hear all kinds of gospel music, especially black gospel. The Clouds of Heaven, the Faithful Few, and The Exciting Jones Brothers are just some of the gospel groups which have performed. The two-day festival features music at two stages simultaneously from noon to 7:00 P.M. or so.

The best news of all—although foods and crafts are offered for sale, the festival is absolutely free to the public!

For information write: Southern Folk Cultural Revival Project, 339 Valeria Street, Nashville, TN 37210. (615) 331-0602.

Memphis In May

On weekends in the month of May, don't expect to zip through Memphis on the interstate. Why? Nearly a million people flock to Memphis in May, the largest festival of its kind in North America. Each year this celebration has grown bigger, and the May calendar in Memphis is packed with entertaining activities for the whole family.

The celebration centers on festivals held the five weekends of May, but other activities include sporting events, daily concerts, educational programs, art exhibits, and more. Each year the festival salutes a country. Since l977 when the festival began, Japan, Canada, Germany, Venezuela, Egypt, the Netherlands, Israel, Mexico, and Australia have been honored. Foreign trade is promoted, and international flavor and culture is brought to Memphis.

But Memphis does have a culture of its own, and barbecue, Beale Street, and the Memphis Symphony are wonderful living reminders. In May, the excitement and imagination of Memphians are whetted. Businesses contribute over half the $1 million budget for the event, and over 700 citizens volunteer their time.

Annual highlights include these events:

The International Barbecue Cooking Contest held at Tom Lee Park. Some 200,000 spectators brave the crowds and eye-stinging smoke to see 200 amateur teams from across the nation test their barbecue-cooking skills in Memphis, "the pork barbecue capital of the world." The teams compete for awards in ribs, shoulders, and whole hogs, as well as an award for showmanship. The outlandish costumes and team names of Sooey Side Squad and Swine Lake Ballet make this a wild but delightful culinary treat.

Beale Street Music Festival. Each year Beale Street, the Old Daisy Theatre, and the adjacent W. C. Handy Park throb day and night with rhythm-and-blues sounds, rock, jazz, and gospel concerts by national and local artists.

The **Sunset Symphony** in Tom Lee Park is the concluding event of the festival, with some 200,000 people watching the sun set over the Mississippi River. The Memphis Symphony plays popular hits as well as classical masterpieces, and a concluding fireworks display makes this a one-of-a-kind experience.

For a complete schedule of events, write to Memphis in May, Dept. KO, 245 Wagner Place, Suite 220, Memphis, TN 38103, or call (90l) 525-4611. For information about other things to see in Memphis, as well as a listing of accommodations and restaurants, write to the Convention and Visitors Bureau of Memphis, 203 Beale Street, Suite 305, Memphis, TN 38103, or call (901) 526-1919.

The Cosby Dulcimer and Harp Convention

Jean and Lee Schilling's Folk Life Center of the Smokies is the site of two important East Tennessee music festivals, the annual Dulcimer and Harp Convention in June and the Folk Festival of the Smokies every autumn. At the Dulcimer and Harp Convention, continuous workshops, jam sessions, and concerts feature these ageless instruments. The sounds of hammered dulcimers, autoharps, bowed psalteries, and fretted dulcimers fill the valley for two days and nights.

Every autumn the Folk Festival covers a broader range of traditional entertainment. Workshops and concerts for guitar, fiddle, recorder, dulcimer, and saw are held. Other events include storytelling, a liars' contest, and even a teaching session on how to play the bones. A potluck supper Saturday night is followed by a concert spotlighting well-known folk musicians.

Jean told the *Sampler* that Paul Simon, formerly of Simon and Garfunkel, showed up incognito at one Folk Festival of the Smokies. He purchased a dulcimer while he was there.

"He was recognized by one of our young friends, and we told him he had a fan who would certainly like to meet him. He didn't want to be announced and didn't wish to perform; he was just out camping and having a good time. However, he did agree to meet a few friends. Soon a guitar was produced, and he was in the back room with some of the performers and staff of the festival, giving them a few pointers and a private concert."

For more details, contact Jean and Lee Schilling, P.O. Box 8, Highway 32, Cosby, TN 37722. (615) 487-5543.

The Old-time Country Radio Reunion

This music festival recreates the days when live country music broadcasts were conducted at barn dances, high-school auditoriums, and fiddling conventions. It also commemorates the 'discovery' here of country music in the l920s. In 1927 Ralph Peer, a Victor talent agent, came to Bristol to audition new musical talent.

When word got out, musicians came any way they could to Bristol. Among the acts that Peer's search uncovered were the Carter Family and Jimmie Rodgers. In 1929, radio station WOPI went on the air in the Tri-Cities area. Thousands of faithful listeners enjoyed its long-running Saturday Night Jamboree.

The Old-time Country Radio Reunion at Jonesborough is the reenactment of the traditional old-time barn dance where many live country broadcasts took place. It features many of the musicians who were actually on the air through the years. In addition to the live stage shows, the musicians will jam under the large shade trees at Christopher Taylor Park, headquarters for the reunion. Tape and slide shows, collections of songbooks and advertisements of the 1920s and 1930s, and lots of reminiscing make this a memorable event for country music fans.

The Radio Reunion is usually held in May, and information can be obtained by writing the Jonesborough Office of Cultural Affairs, Town Hall, Jonesborough, TN 37659.

Other Tennessee Music Festivals

JANUARY
Annual Bluegrass Music Awards, National Convention, Opryland USA Hotel, Nashville, TN. Sponsor: SPBGMA. Contact: SPBGMA, c/o Chuck Stearman, Box 271, Kirksville, MO 63501.

MARCH
Annual Bell Witch Opry, Mini-Fan Fair, Springfield Civic Center, Adams, TN. Contact: Bell Witch Opry, Ken or Nina Seeley, Adams, TN 37010.

MAY
Blues in the Park, Handy Park, Beale Street, Memphis, TN. Sponsor: The Blues Foundation. Contact: Joe Savaring, The Blues Foundation, P.O. Box 161272, Memphis, TN 38186-6459. All blues performers. Daily from May through September. 100 artists. No admission.

Appalachian Music Days, Steele Creek Park, Bristol, TN. Contact: Bristol Chamber of Commerce, Box 1039, Bristol, VA 24201. A bluegrass and old-time band competition.

JUNE
Summer Lights Festival, Legislative Plaza, Nashville, TN. Sponsor: Metro Arts Commission. Contact: Metro Arts Commission, Nashville, TN.

Cedar Grove Campground Bluegrass Festival, Cedar Grove Campground, New Tazewell, TN. Sponsor: Cedar Grove Campground. Contact: Chester H. Wolfe, Box 249, Middlesboro, KY 40965. Festivals throughout the year.

Festival Favorites Red Knuckles and the Trailblazers

Blue Grass Festival, Slagles Pasture, Elizabethton, TN. Sponsor: Clayton Slagle. Contact: Clayton Slagle, Route 3, Elizabethton, TN 37643.

One For the Sun, Hermitage Landing, Nashville, TN. Sponsor: 103 WKDF. Contact: Carl P. Mayfield, 506 Second Avenue South, Nashville, TN 37210. Rock music.

Old-Time Fiddlers' Convention and Music Festival, Eastgate Center, Chattanooga, TN. Two-day festival.

Country Music Days, Elizabethton, TN. Five-day festival of country, gospel, and bluegrass.

Smith County Bluegrass Festival, Carthage, TN. Three-day bluegrass festival.

Arts and Crafts Festival and Fiddlers' Championship, TVA's Land Between the Lakes.

National Mountain Music Festival, Silver Dollar City, Pigeon Forge, TN. June–July, three weeks.

JULY
Tennessee River Bluegrass Festival, Savannah City Park, Savannah, TN. Contact: Randy Wheeler, 1020 Main Street, Savannah, TN 38372.

Annual Fentress County Bluegrass & Craft Festival, Fentress County Fairgrounds, Jamestown, TN. Contact: Roy T. Smith, P.O. Box 947, Jamestown, TN 38556.

East Tennessee Old Time & Bluegrass Championships, Kinser Park, Greeneville, TN. Contact: Sheryl Donovan, 103 1/2 College Street, Greeneville, TN 37743.

AUGUST
Annual Bell Witch Bluegrass Festival, Adams School, Adams, TN. Contact: BWBF—Ken Seeley, Adams, TN 37010.

Wartrace Pickin' and Fiddlers' Convention, Wartrace, TN. Sponsor: Wartrace Pickin' & Fiddlers' Association, Contact: Gallagher Guitar Co., Box 128, Wartrace, TN 37183.

OCTOBER
Annual Fall Color Cruise & Folk Festival, Shellmound Recreational Area, Chattanooga, TN. Contact: Chattanooga Area Convention and Visitors Bureau, John Payne, 1001 Market Street, Chattanooga, TN 37402.

Oktoberfest, Civic Center Plaza, Memphis, TN. Contact: Wanda Carruthers, Center City Commission, 147 Jefferson, Memphis, TN 38103.

Gospel and Grassroots Music

Tennessee Gospel Music

"I've anchored my soul in the Haven of Rest.
I'll sail the wide seas no more.
The tempest may sweep o'er the wild stormy
    deep;
In Jesus I'm safe evermore."

It was a fifth-Sunday night singing at a Baptist church in Middle Tennessee. Soft piano chords framed the chorus of this gospel song. Her right hand held high, palm open, her eyes tightly closed, the tall, tanned, willowy lead singer had tears streaming down her cheeks. Then, other members of the quintet were overcome with emotion. The deep, rich alto of the lead singer's sister began to waver as the tears flowed. Out on the third row of pews where she always sat, their mother began to shout. The tenor stopped even pretending to sing and just prayed.

Their song had clearly become something more than just a song. Now it was a prayer, a testimony, a key to open the sweet release of weeping. As remembered griefs, joys, and shared prayers for lost and backslidden loved ones swept over the congregation like Holy Spirit-Wind, people said, "Amen," clapped their hands, and lifted them up to the Lord. There would be no sermon tonight, but the words to these beloved songs would summarize for these people a lifetime of listening to preachers and serving the Lord.

Across town, a different kind of singing was taking place at another church. Electric guitars, basses, and drums strained to keep up with the organist who played the music as he felt it, eyes shut and sweat pouring off his face. Singers and choir swayed, and the music poured out like a flood, with improvised verses, answering choruses, and a natural ebb and flow of intensity. Here too were shouting, clapping, and deep-throated "Amens."

In both churches, hours and even decades of rehearsal had gone into the offering up of this music before the Lord in a worship service. Some of these songs were learned from parents and grandparents. They were the ones that brought the bittersweet memories and tears. Some of the music was brand-new, but all of the songs were intensely personal, testimonies of the writers that the singers had made their own.

Across Tennessee there are more types of gospel music being heard on just about any Friday, Saturday, or Sunday than you can shake a shaped note at! In fact, some of the most beautiful gospel singing in all Tennessee has no instrumental accompaniment whatever. It is found in churches which do not believe in instrumental music, such as Primitive Baptist or Church of Christ, or among groups determined to keep the old shaped-note unaccompanied tradition of "Harp" singing alive. This singing is named after the "Harp of Columbia" hymnal of the mid-1800s, published in Knoxville, which dominated church music in East Tennessee. Singers learned to read a different shape for each pitch of the scale—do, re, mi—and could sing their part just by looking at the shape of the note. Such singing is a rarity now.

Not all of Tennessee's gospel music is in church, either. If you'll consult local newspapers in the religious news sections, you'll usually find some sort of regularly scheduled or benefit gospel singing near you. Many bluegrass groups play almost exclusively gospel tunes, and you're liable to hear them picking at some community center. Often, when someone in the community has been injured on the job or loses belongings in a fire, a benefit singing will be held and collections taken to help.

At most singings out in the community, several groups will sing and testify, and people in the audience will come and go for as long as the singing lasts. Refreshments are usually available. Just go and enjoy the music, and you'll find the friendliest folks in the world.

Sometimes the singings will be held in churches on Saturday or Sunday. You might even be fortunate enough to experience an all-day singing and dinner on

Old-time banjo plunkin'

the ground. Again, you'll be welcome, but remember you're a visitor in the place that these people consider very dear to their hearts. You'll find politeness and friendliness reciprocated.

The Nashville Gospel Show

Teresa Hannah and Tommy Lewis host this wonderful musical program of black and white gospel music on Channel 4. All forms of gospel—old-time to contemporary, country and bluegrass to blues shouting—are featured on this excellent program. At publication time, "Nashville Gospel" airs at 6:30 A.M. on Sunday, and 1:00 A.M. Monday. Tapings of the show are open to the public every Tuesday evening at WSMV studios at 5700 Knob Road. There is no charge. To attend, just call Nashville Gospel Productions at (615) 876-9566, and let them know how many will be coming. Video and audio cassettes of programs are available, and Lewis and Hannah have cut a 45 with some gospel favorites.

Tennessee Grassroots Music

They dot Tennessee's landscape every few miles, weathered wood-frame remembrances of separate-but-equal education. One-room schoolhouses they are, many built in the first few decades of this century. These were the first to fall victim to the vinelike creepers of school-bus routes in rural counties. Some still contain the wood-burning stoves where teachers cooked pots of beans for students during Depression days. In these schools were forged some of Tennessee's greatest leaders and thinkers, people who have left their mark on us all. But most Tennesseans who went to these schools took the character they developed in that concentrated setting, helping the younger children, or adding up columns of numbers for the chance to walk through the woods to gather kindling, and put their lives back into their land and families. They stayed at home, and helped define it.

Years later, when their empty old school started to fall down, they got busy and fixed it up again. Today, many of these schools are community centers and provide polling, eating, and singing places for folks thereabouts. They're back in their rightful place at the heart of the community. Chances are that just about any Tennessee Friday or Saturday night one of these old schools close to you will be ringing with the sound of folks making music. Local papers or radio stations usually know about these events, and many of them operate on a regular schedule, such as the third Saturday of every month. If you persevere and find one of these treasures, you'll probably be able to talk to people who went to that school a generation or two ago.

The *Sampler* attended one of these every-third-Saturday-night gatherings at Bethel Community Center in Maury County. It is located on Leipers Creek Road, 3 miles north of Fly, Tennessee.

At least 250 people in their best Duck Head overalls or most comfortable jeans were in the old Bethel School, a sizable rectangular building with 15-feet-high ceilings, a potbellied wood stove, and solid wood walls with cracking yellow paint. Naked bulbs hung from the ceiling on long wires. Handlettered signs forbade smoking, alcoholic beverages, or fighting.

An area about 16 by 25 feet was left open in front of the stage for dancers. A 4 by 8 piece of sheet iron was situated so that any of them with taps on their shoes could really go to town.

Homemade desserts and on-the-spot hamburgers went down just right with the bluegrass music. A donated quilt was raffled off, and several cakes and pies were auctioned to help with utilities and repairs to the building. Local groups such as the Pickin' Crew from Theta, the Backyard Stompers, the Shade Tree Bluegrass, and a special invited group, the Pinewood Ramblers, each played for an hour or so. Some came to play, some to dance, some to visit and maybe catch up on the latest local information. Some just came to chew and spit. The young folks had obviously come to court and spark.

Some caught up on old friendships: "How you been doin', Bobby Joe?" "Best you ever seen!" was the response. One newcomer asked an old-timer, "Been living in Tennessee all your life?" "Not yet" came back the answer.

We talked to Clifton Anderson who informed us that music had always been important at Bethel School. "They had Uncle Dave Macon here one time. Drove right up in that horse-drawn wagon with Sam McGee. And another time they had a fellow who drove up to the school, got out, played the guitar, sang, and drove back off, all with just his feet; he had no hands!"

Speaking of feet, the dancers were a show in themselves. Two-stepping couples, buck dancers, or just plain stompers hit the dance floor as soon as the songs grabbed them. Just before the bands quit playing, judges deliberated carefully to award a coconut cake to the best buck dancer, Emily Tomlin, who came out of the band to win and claim her prize.

It was a typical grassroots, get-down-home, everyone-welcome Tennessee Saturday night, one being echoed all across the state! You haven't sampled rural Tennessee until you've been to one.

Buck Dancing in Tennessee

The Sampler *wants you to meet two Tennesseans you'll always catch flat-footed. They are Robert Spicer and Jacky Christian, Tennessee's best-known buck dancers. Mr. Spicer taught Jacky just like he's been teaching people to buck dance for decades. Jacky'll tell you right away that she's still learning from Robert and other old-time dancers.*

Jacky has danced on the Grand Ole Opry and for Bill

Monroe's band, and she has many other professional credits as well. She teaches buck dance and is now involved in documenting (with videotape equipment) Tennessee's traditional dancers and their steps.

Jacky's going to tell you what buck dancing is and where to watch and learn it in Tennessee. She will feature major festivals which offer great dancing as well as places you can find the buck dancers every week. So grab your Tennessee Sampler, *slip on your dancing shoes, and get ready to get down-home with Jacky and Mr. Spicer.*

What Is Buck Dancing?

Buck dancing is to Tennessee as honey is to a bee. Most often you'll find some of the best buck dancers in out-of-the-way places, but when you find them, you're sure to meet some colorful characters and have a wonderful old-time good time.

Buck dancing is an American folk dance. It should not be confused with clogging. Clogging evolved from the European country dance traditions such as Irish jigs, reels, step dances and clog dances. The European style concentrated on very intricate footwork and the production of sound while the upper body was kept erect and almost motionless. Clogging became the major rural dance form in the southern Appalachian Mountains.

Buck dance evolved in America from the African tribal dance traditions which emphasized using the entire body but in a flat-footed style. Improvising to the complex and pulsating rhythms of African music also characterized these dances. After the Slave Act of 1740 which prohibited slaves from "beating drums, blowing horns or the like," slaves substituted handclaps and footbeats to create their own rhythm and sound.

Today, buck dancing is constant percussive rhythm produced by the feet. The feet must not only keep the basic beat but also add sounds between the beats of the music. This is most often referred to as "rhythm buck dance." "Flat-footing" uses this same emphasis on the production of rhythm but the feet are kept low (about 3 inches or less) to the floor. "Buck-and-wing" is another type of buck dance that uses the entire body and allows for the addition of more exaggerated leg and body movements while still adhering to the same rhythms and a general flat-footed style.

Buck dance was popularized when white dancers appeared in black face in minstrel shows during the mid-to-late 1800s. Traveling medicine and tent shows also included buck dancers. Uncle Dave Macon, the Grand Ole Opry's first big star, took a buck dancer with him when he entertained. Especially during the vaudeville era, the Afro-American buck dance and the Euro-American clogging folk dance traditions blended and evolved into what we know as tap dance today. The famous "time step" of tap dance is credited as having evolved from buck dance along with dances such as the Virginia essence, sand dancing, and the soft shoe.

But the authentic free-style buck dance has survived and is enjoying a tremendous revival. Robert Spicer can be credited with keeping the purest style of flat-foot, rhythm buck dance alive in Tennessee. He has been buck dancing for over 50 years, teaches buck dance, and has trained buck dance teams for over 40 years. Robert Spicer is *"Mr. Buck Dance"* and quite a character.

We doubt that Mr. Spicer has ever met a stranger. No matter where you are, you'll find him chatting with somebody. And if he's not talking, you can bet he'll be clapping rhythm for the dancers. "Putting the rhythm in a person is what makes them dance," he says. Mr. Spicer trains all the dancers by clapping a constant, pounding, pulsating rhythm with his hands on the upbeat and patting his foot on the downbeat. A buck dancer should be "hitting a lick"—making a step and sound—for every beat that Mr. Spicer is clapping and patting.

Mr. Spicer, as everyone calls him, learned to buck dance from his mother and from a former slave in Dickson. He was a very small boy when Fiddling Arthur Smith would stand him in a chair to call square dances. He just naturally loves the old-time music and dancing and people. He has combined that love and shares it by teaching folks how to relax and enjoy themselves by dancing. He'll often tell you that "what most people need is to get out and dance and they wouldn't need to take medicines and such."

Some Regular Buck Dances

Dances are held all over Tennessee. Just ask around (bluegrass musicians are a good source), and you'll find a place you can dance. Here are some of the dances that Mr. Spicer and I frequent.

Cedars of Lebanon State Park. A square dance is held every Saturday night in the Assembly Hall of the park. The dance is held year-round, and the park facilities are open during the summer season. The Assembly Hall is a nice air-conditioned building with a large dance floor, a stage at one end, and seating at the other. There's a fireplace for the winter months. They do old-time (slow dancing), square (Appalachian-style), buck and clog dancing to live bluegrass and country-western music. There's always a large crowd of regulars, and visitors come from all over the country. You'll see mamas and daddies out dancing with their little ones. Lots of folks wear taps on their shoes. Everyone is welcome on the floor even if you don't happen to know exactly how to do the dancing.

Lloyd McCormick runs the dances, and Charles Taylor, Jr., is the square dance caller. Mr. McCormick said that visitors should ask for him and he would see that they are taken care of. The park has camping, cabins, hookups, horseback riding, bicycles, a swimming pool, and miles of trails. There is a small admission charge to the square dance. You can contact the office of Cedars of Lebanon State Park (just off I-40 east of Nashville) at (615) 444-9394 from 8:00 A.M. to 4:30 P.M.

Pickin' and Grinnin'. In Dickson County a local dance is held every Saturday night (except the last of each month) at the old Carr's Market location about 5 miles north of State 100 on Spencer Mill Road. The local community regularly attends, but there is always a dash of visitors. The dance room is actually the other side of the country store. You'll know you're close when you see cars and trucks lining both sides of the road. A small stage is at the back, and several local bands alternate sets for the dancers. They do some square dances, a few line dances, and a lot of buck dancing. You'll be welcome and will get a real glimpse of a very informal Saturday night get-together. You can contact William Spicer, Jr., at (615) 670-3758.

Foxhunter's Club. This club in Hickman County holds a dance and community dinner the last Saturday night of every month. You pay for the supper and then stay for the music and dancing. This is the real thing. It really is a club for foxhunters, and the dinners are usually some type of game such as rabbit, dove, squirrel, or other country vittles. You'll most often find Robert Spicer clapping away and making sure that everyone is welcome and gets out on the dance floor. They do a lot of line dances, the old-time (Appalachian-style) square dancing which always ends with everyone doing an individual brand of buck dance, and a lot of old-time round dancing. Visitors are welcome, and you will be included in the dancing by the regulars.

The Foxhunter's is located (north) off State 100 West,

Jacky Christian, Photo by Hope Powell

down a little gravel road, and it sits in the middle of a field. Better pay attention because there is only a small sign nailed to a tree where you turn off the highway onto the gravel road. The Foxhunter's also holds a community barbecue and festival on Labor Day with the same good music and dancing. You can contact William (W. D.) Tidwell, Jr., at (615) 446-6018 for more details.

Longhollow Jamboree. A small square dance is held every Friday night, with great live music. The dance floor is small and pretty crowded. You will see some fine buck dancers, though. To get there from Nashville, take the Long Hollow Pike Exit off I-65 North and go east until you get there. You can't miss it, it's on the left. Contact Long Hollow Jamboree at (615) 824-4445.

Hendersonville VFW Post 9851. This group holds a square dance every Saturday night which is open to the public. This dance is usually well attended and a real friendly place to go. The live band plays good dance music for square dances, round dances, and buck dancing and will even throw in a polka if requested. One of the fun traditions is that they will have a "grand march" sometime during the night that circles out the side door and back in the front door. The big dance floor is surrounded by seating around the room. Located on New Shackle Island Road in Hendersonville. From Nashville go out Gallatin Road North and turn west on New Shackle Island Road, go about one block, and turn left at the VFW sign.

You can call (615) 824-9836 for additional information.

Tennessee Buck Dancing Festivals

You will find some fine buck dancers competing in the many festivals and old-time fiddlers' conventions held all across Tennessee. This is just a sample of some of the really enjoyable events.

State of Tennessee Old-time Fiddlers' Championships. These are held annually in Clarksville, Tennessee, at Austin Peay State University, Winfield Dunn Center, on the first weekend in April. The forerunner of this competition began in 1927, and it has existed in its present form for the past 12 years. The official state fiddle championships are held during the weekend along with competitions for old-time singing, dulcimer, old-time banjo, old-time string band, harmonica, guitar, Dobro, junior fiddle, bluegrass banjo, mandolin, band, senior fiddle and, of course, two categories of flat-foot dancing—age 13 and under, and 14 and over. Rules for the flat-foot dancing are no holds barred which means that contestants can do absolutely anything they want. You'll see just about anything, too, from clogging to real flat-foot and somewhere in between. This is one of the bigger events, and there is always a lot going on in addition to what's on stage. A congregation of musicians and dancers is always in the lobby with the dancers going for as long as the band will hold out. The dancers and spectators just naturally gather 'round in a tight little ring, and first one and then another dancer will pop out in the center of the circle to "take a break" until the next dancer moves out to take over. There is a small ad-

mission charge. For information, contact: Clarksville Chamber of Commerce, P.O. Box 883, Clarksville, TN 37041. (615) 647-2336.

Old-timers' Day. Held annually in Dickson, Tennessee on the first weekend of May, this wonderful family-oriented happening is "home" to Robert Spicer. He has been involved in starting and perpetuating this event for the past 27 years. There's a parade with steam engines, plenty of horses, buggies, and wagons, and a flatbed truck with Robert Spicer and his Dickson County Square Dancers just a dancin' and wavin' as they pass by. You'll want to attend the square dance on Friday night, and the old-timers beauty contest is delightful. To be eligible for the beauty contest, you must be over 65 and dressed in old-fashioned attire.

There is plenty of good food available, and the music and entertainment go on all day. There is always a platform next to the stage for buck dancing. A lot of folks bring their lawn chairs and blankets and sit on the side of the hill facing the stage. The music is infectious, and all of a sudden folks will just pop down to the dance floor and let go with a free-style buck dance.

You'll see some of the real authentic dancing at this celebration. On one occasion an older gentleman was supporting himself with crutches under both arms and his feet were just dancing away. Now, *that's* the spirit of buck dance! An arts and crafts fair and a flea market are underway at the same time. So, just be prepared to wander about and stop to enjoy and join in some of the impromptu music and dancing. And be sure to look up Mr. Spicer. He'll enjoy meeting you and chatting with you for a while. I'll be there too. This one's free. Contact Robert Spicer, Rt. 1 Box 113, Dickson, TN. (615) 446-6351.

Grinder's Switch Fiddlers' Convention. The Fiddlers' Convention in Centerville, Tennessee, is an annual event and is held on the last weekend in June. There is a no-holds-barred junior buck dance competition for 15 and under and a senior buck dance competition for 16 and over. There are probably more buck dancers in this area than anywhere else in Tennessee, and Robert Spicer has likely had a hand in teaching most of them. Mr. Spicer has also helped with the organization and establishment of this event, so you can bet he's going to turn out the dancers! A jam session and square dance are held on Friday night, and competition begins on Saturday. Camping space is available with hookups. A flea market is also set up. So, bring your lawn chairs and enjoy a weekend of music and fun and dancing. There is a small admission. For information, contact: Grinder's Switch, Centerville, TN. (615) 729-5558.

Smithville Jamboree and Crafts Festival. Held on the square in Smithville every Fourth of July weekend, this event began in 1972 and just keeps growing. An estimated 35,000 to 50,000 people attend during the two days. This is one of the only events where clogging and buck dancing are separated into distinct competition categories. There are categories for junior and senior clogging, junior and senior buck dancing, as well as square dancing. There is certainly a lot to see and do at this jamboree. Arts and crafts booths surround the court house, and bands and musicians play under every tree. Robert Spicer's special place is the outside entrance to the basement on the right side of the building, and you'll spot large groups of people hanging over the railings looking down at his dancers. Free camping for self-contained campers is available, and campers needing hookups can contact Edgar Evins State Park, Lancaster, TN 38569. (615) 548-8135. Admission is free. For information contact: Smithville Jamboree, P.O. Box 64, Smithville, TN 37166. (615) 597-4163.

Uncle Dave Macon Days. This annual event at the Rutherford County Square in Murfreesboro, Tennessee is a tribute to Uncle Dave Macon, "the Dixie Dewdrop." It also celebrates old-time music and crafts, and it's just plain fun. This extremely well-organized event has attractions and activities for the entire family. There is everything from an ice-cream-eating contest and a tobacco spittin' contest to the State of Tennessee Banjo Championships.

The buck dancing competition is divided between junior (under 30) and senior (30 and over) categories, and the rules state that "no particular form or style is necessary." The dancer's information sheet points out that "dancers may freely move their arms, legs, and whole bodies as they swish, in time with the music." Since both types (cloggers and flat-footers) are entered under one category (buck dancing), "each dancer will be judged individually, on their own merit, for the type of dance being performed." You'll find the dancers trading licks under the trees surrounding the courthouse, and there are special clogging and buck dancing workshops and exhibitions. You'll also enjoy the Uncle Dave Macon Days Motorless Parade and the "Dixie Dewdrop Classic" Bicycle Race. Admission is free. For more information, contact: Uncle Dave Macon Days Committee, P.O. Box 864, Murfreesboro, TN 37130.

Bell Witch Bluegrass Festival. This event has been held annually on the second weekend in August since 1979. In addition to the junior flat-foot dance competition on Friday night and the senior flat-foot dance competition on Saturday, there is also a variety of music competition. An arts and crafts show is set up on the grounds, and special concerts on both days featuring bluegrass and country bands.

The dance competitions are fierce, and there's more than a lot of parking-lot pickin' going on—and where there's music, you'll find the buck dancers. You should bring your lawn chairs. Rough camping is welcome, and there are several hookups. Admission is charged. For information, contact: Bell Witch Bluegrass Festival, P.O. Box 127, Adams, Tennessee 37010. (615) 969-9919 or 696-2589.

Wartrace Pickin' and Fiddlers' Convention. Held annually in Wartrace, Tennessee, on the third weekend of August, this festival was started in 1979. It is the home of the State of Tennessee Guitar Championships competition. Buck dance competitions are divided into

two categories: junior buck dancers (39 and under) and senior buck dancers (40 and older).

The festival is held on the football field, so bring your lawn chairs. Camping in the rough (without hookups) is available. An arts and crafts fair is also held on the premises. Registration and jam sessions are on Friday night, and the competition begins on Saturday. Look for the parking lot pickin' and dancin'. Admission is charged. For information, contact: Wartrace Pickin' and Fiddlers' Association, Inc., c/o Gallagher Guitar Company, P.O. Box 128, Wartrace, TN 37183. (615) 389-6455.

Tennessee Fall Homecoming. This annual event is scheduled for the second weekend in October at the Museum of Appalachia in Norris, Tennessee. The spacious Museum of Appalachia mountain farm and homestead complex is the most authentic and complete replica of pioneer Appalachian life in the world. There are over 120 mountain activities and craft demonstrations: spinning wool, cotton, and flax; riving fence palings; Kentucky rifle firing; coopering; molasses making; cream separating and butter churning; hominy making; and a seemingly endless list of other things. You'll hear hundreds of old-time mountain, folk, hymn, traditional, and bluegrass musicians and see buck dancers and mountain cloggers. You'll even hear the rare mountain mouth bow played. Continuous entertainment takes place on a stage plus the parking lot and shade tree picking livens the place up. The Homecoming is a must for everyone. The resident buck dancer, Hoot King, literally dances all day long. Country food is cooked on open pits and wood stoves right on the compound. Norris, Tennessee, is 16 miles north of Knoxville, 1 mile off I-75. A small admission is charged. For information, contact: John Rice Irwin, Museum of Appalachia, P.O. Box 359, Norris, TN 37828. (615) 494-7680.

If you can't manage to get to any of these events, Jacky will bring the dancing to you. The Tennessee Arts Commission Touring Program brings professional performers to communities across the state by providing financial assistance to qualified sponsors. Any Tennessee nonprofit organization or community is an eligible sponsor.

Jacky and old-time fiddler Frazier Moss and his band are available through the Touring Program. They would love to hold a community square dance for you. If you're interested, contact Tennessee Arts Commission, Touring Program, 505 Deaderick Street, Suite 1700, Nashville, TN 37219. (615) 741-1701.

The Tennessee Sampler hopes everyone will get out there and get involved in the dancing. Buck dancing is just plain good for your soul as well as your body. Hope to see *you* getting caught flat-footed.

For more information call or write Jacky at the Old-time American Dance Center, P.O. Box 381, Madison, TN 37116. (615) 876-8765.

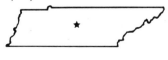

A Special Picker's Section

Gruhn's Guitar Store

For 15 years, guitar and banjo pickers have felt like they've died and gone to heaven when they walk into Gruhn's. On walls, behind counters, and in cases are usually over 1,000 fine vintage stringed instruments for sale. Printed brochures have long lists of old Martin and Gibson guitars and mandolins, all types of banjos, fiddles, and Dobros. The list is updated every three weeks, and its descriptions and prices can really help you determine what a vintage instrument is likely to be worth. George Gruhn is a recognized authority on these instruments and a featured writer in *Frets* magazine and in *Guitar Player* magazine. Appraisals are offered for $10, and Gruhn's does have a consignment sales service. Gruhn's also has a "want" file for people who are looking for certain instruments. Many of Nashville's finest session people are in and out daily. The store has five full-time craftsmen who repair electric, acoustic, fretted, and fretless instruments.

Gruhn's is also a place to get one of the real collector's items on the guitar market today. Selling for $100 each, these experimental plastic guitars were made in the United States under the direction of Mario Maccafferi himself. They are real guitars, not toys, and they feature removable and adjustable necks. Each one is in its original case and has been warehoused since 1953.

Gruhn Guitars, Inc., 410 Broadway, Nashville, TN 37203. (615) 256-2033. Hours: 9:30–5:30, Monday through Saturday.

The Apprentice Shop

Does your guitar sound like a brick or your chord like a clothesline? Have you ever wanted to build your own guitar or learn to do your own instrument repair work? Sounds like you need to talk to the boys at The Apprentice Shop in Spring Hill. Bruce Scotten and Mike Lennon operate one of Tennessee's most unique music shops.

First of all, they offer extensive courses in acoustic guitar construction, electric guitar construction, and fretted instrument repair. Students come from all over the world to this small, picturesque Middle Tennessee town to take their courses. Sixty per cent of their students are now making a living by building or repairing musical instruments. Others just sign up because they want to build their own dream instrument, but with some professional guidance.

Bruce and Mike are both gifted luthiers (guitar builders) and can repair or build any type of guitar or dulcimer. Mike handles most repairs, and the *Sampler* can vouch for the quality and reasonable prices of his work. He has repaired old Martins that became too involved in marital disputes, and old Gibsons with bullet holes and blood stains. He's even pulled items such as oak floorboards out of vintage guitars, placed there by amateur repairmen with a lot of imagination and no other way to anchor down a bridge!

Bruce does most all of the custom building of guitars and dulcimers. He can build with any wood, any type action, fingerboard width, or body style. He also does painstaking wood and abalone inlay work. When they say custom building, they mean just that. Their shop and showroom are open for serious inquiries. Please call for an appointment.

The Apprentice Shop, on US 31 north of Spring Hill, P.O. Box 267, Spring Hill, TN 37174. (615) 486-2615.

Gallagher Guitars

The beautiful town of Wartrace is home to the famous Walking Horse Hotel, final resting place of Strolling Jim. It is also home to what many musicians consider the finest guitars made in recent decades. The Gallagher guitars made by old J. W. Gallagher and now by his son Don are prized among bluegrass and old-time pickers. Doc Watson plays one that rings just like a bell. The guitars are as reasonably priced as they are beautifully crafted. Don does mostly custom building now, so get in touch with him if you're ready to buy an instrument for a lifetime. Or even longer, if you can figure out how to take it with you!

Gallagher Guitars, P.O. Box 128, Wartrace, TN 37183.

Tennessee's Best-kept Secrets— Some Out-of-the-way Listening Rooms

Yarbrough's Pickin' Post

This unique and internationally known music store and sound shop has a full line of music products and services. But on Tuesday nights from 6:00 to 9:00 it reverberates with bluegrass, country, folk, and old-time music in a jam session which is one of the best musical experiences Memphis has to offer. Friendly folks and good music combine to make this a great evening for patting your feet, making new friends, or just enjoying the music.

Yarbrough's hosted the World's Longest Jam Session a few years back, all strictly according to the official guidelines of the *Guinness Book of World Records*. The session lasted 11 days. So a Tuesday evening full of good music is rather easy for these folks to accomplish. Free coffee and homemade pastries help fuel the nimble fingers of musicians and the tapped-out toes of the audience.

Acoustic and amplified instruments coexist in this no-holds-barred music session. No telling who'll show up to play, and many times old-timers can be seen sharing their musical know-how with the younger set.

If you're interested in making music yourself, the Pickin' Post has everything from the smallest guitar pick to sound systems for huge auditoriums, plus a full staff of teachers for all instruments.

But the jam sessions on Tuesday nights at Yarbrough's are still a favorite place to meet old friends and make new ones. Just drop off the ramp at I-240 and I-40, and they'll be there waiting for you.

Yarbrough's Pickin' Post, 741 White Street Road North, Memphis, TN. (901) 761-0414.

The Country Harvest Bluegrass Show, Memphis.

The Country Harvest Bluegrass Show (formerly the Lucy Opry) is located at the International Harvester Union Hall Building, which seats about 500. Admission is free but hats are passed to pay the bands. Joe Taylor and Ken Bingham run the Country Harvest Show, which remains one of the great places in Tennessee to hear live bluegrass music.

Doug Cole helped run the Lucy Opry for 17 years, and he says its daughter, the Country Harvest Bluegrass Show, is still the place to be in Memphis on Friday night. The CHBS is a free-wheeling, unstructured, bluegrass concert that begins at 8:00 P.M. Right off the bat, the stage will be crowded with fiddlers, guitarists, banjo pickers, mandolin and Dobro players, and a family of string basses. This is the traditional beginning, which features everybody at once who has come to play. This giant opening jam session can last up to 45 minutes.

After this rather amazing experience, two shows follow, equally good and equally inexpensive. One is the series of bands that play in the auditorium for whatever the crowd chooses to put into the hat. Part of the allure of this show is that no one can predict exactly who will show up to play, and some of the biggest names in bluegrass have been known to stop by.

The second show has its own dedicated audience and participants. It happens out in the parking lot as bands tune up and rehearse before moving inside, and other musicians who strictly come for parking lot jamming either play with them or in their own little groups. The Country Harvest Bluegrass Show has some dedicated fans who hardly ever make it into the auditorium; they're too busy prowling the parking lot with their tape recorders.

Saturday nights, the host band, the Country Volunteers, and a guest band present the Country Harvest Country Show featuring everything from tunes of the old Carter Family, Jimmie Rodgers, and Hank Williams to recent country hits. Again, there's no admission charge, just a pass-the-hat contribution to help pay expenses.

Directions: Get off I-240 at the Millington Exit. Veer to the right and continue until you hit US 51. Turn right on 51 North and go to the second traffic light. Turn left there (Whitney Street), and go about 1/4 mile. When you see the International Harvester plant, turn right on Harvester Lane, and the Union Building will be directly across the street from the plant. The actual address is 2984 Harvester Lane, Memphis, TN.

A SAMPLER FEATURE

Cayce Russell

"Learning comes from books, travel, and people; but Wisdom comes from above."—Cayce Russell

■ It's worth a trip to Lafayette, Tennessee, just to meet Cayce Russell and his wife Doney. Cayce is almost 80 years old and has been a fighter all his life. He still remembers hearing the doctor say, "Well, he'll never live. And if he does live, he'll never have brain one. His fever's cooked his brain." Polio left Cayce totally paralyzed for two years.

Then his daddy started carrying him to school until Cayce could walk on crutches. He persisted in spite of the odds and finished eighth grade by the time he was 24 years old. Cayce finished high school and even enrolled at Western Kentucky University in Bowling Green until the Depression finally cut his schooling short. Then Cayce campaigned all over Macon County in a buggy drawn by an old blind mule and was elected Register of Deeds for the county, an office he held for 16 years.

No question about it, Cayce is an original, and *The Tennessee Sampler* wishes him all the best. He and his wife Doney have performed for years around Macon County, and his music store is the recommended place in Lafayette to hear some great stories and a wealth of old-time songs and to pick up what you need in the way of musical supplies.

Here's what Cayce has to say about his music and his shop:

Cayce Russell

"People come to play music with me, and listen to old songs from the past. I collect and play old songs from the bygone days. People want to hear old Civil War stories and old haunted tales of the past. They want stories of how people lived and communicated back then. They come from other states to hear me play old-time banjo. Most every Saturday people gather here and spend most of the day.

"I sell medium-priced guitars, mandolins, and banjos.

"I never see any strangers. To me we are just people put here alike and each one has their own role to fill. I have never seen a person that I couldn't love.

"If a person ever comes here once, he will come back again. They love the old southern hospitality they receive. I guess there are as many people who come here to ask questions about old-time music and get a history of the customs and ways of the people in early days and just for entertainment than any other place around. Young people come for stories and just to see me because they love me."

Cayce Russell Music Store, 206 Times Avenue, Lafayette, TN 37083. (615) 666-4366.

The Full Moon Bluegrass Party, Nashville

Back in 1975, Ted Walker started having parties out at his farm on Old Hillsboro Road for his friends. People started bringing their instruments and playing bluegrass music, and the Full Moon Bluegrass Party was born. Now it is something of an institution around Nashville. Every full moon from May to September, Ted's farm is open from dusk till dawn for people to listen to, dance to, and play bluegrass music.

A large, picturesque barn is the setting for many of the pickup groups, but hundreds usually mill around outside, buck dancing or walking from one group to another to listen to an incredible variety of bluegrass practitioners. Some groups appear heavily weighted toward endless repetitions of "Rocky Top" or "Fox on the Run," the two most overplayed tunes in bluegrass. Other knots of musicians feature old-timers and young young pickers who can apparently play all night and never repeat a tune. Almost 1,000 people were at the May 1985 Full Moon Bluegrass Party, with scores of talented musicians. In particular, James McKinney, a banjo picker who works at Opryland, was absolutely amazing.

When the weather is just right, and the full moon falls so that rest is possible the next day, there is nothing like the Full Moon Party *if you are really into the music.* A saying often repeated goes, "Bluegrass is like a lot of things, it's more fun to do than to watch!" Anyway, only the truly hardy souls are able to make it till the last fiddle is laid to rest in its case come the sunrise after the world's one-and-only Full Moon Bluegrass Party.

Directions: From I-65 South, take the Brentwood/Old Hickory Boulevard Exit. Turn west on Old Hickory Boulevard, traveling about 4 miles to Hillsboro Road. Turn left on Hillsboro Road, and travel about 3 miles. Turn right on Old Hillsboro Road, and the driveway to the party is on the right about 6/10 of a mile from the turn.

Admission is $5. Party goers bring their own ice chests and refreshments.

The Full Moon Bluegrass Party, 2108 Parkway Towers, Nashville, TN 37219.

The Pastime Cafe, Fayetteville

Clay Sawyer's Pastime Cafe is a pleasant country eating spot with its clientele of regulars and visitors to Lincoln County. For most of the week, that is. Then Thursday mornings roll around, and the place fills up with instruments and musicians of every description. Clay's uncle, fiddler Ernest Norman, opened the cafe in 1947. Some years back, all of them started playing on Thursday mornings, a date they chose because of everyone's work schedules. Now they're apt to be joined by pickers from all over Tennessee and some from Alabama.

The Thursday morning sessions have even given birth to a song, "An Even Deal," which writer Tom Leach says came from a conversation he overheard at the Pastime. Charles Higgins, a local funeral director, was talking to Bill Trigg, another regular picker, about the possibility of trading a funeral for Trigg's vintage Martin guitar!

There is some singing and buck dancing at these sessions, but most of the music is instrumental, with players trading tunes and techniques in a friendly old-time jam session.

Directions: From Nashville take I-65 South to the US 64 Exit. Head east on 64, just over 20 miles to Fayetteville.

The Pastime Cafe, Main Street, Fayetteville, TN 37334.

The Tennessee Valley Jamboree, Lawrenceburg

The Tennessee Valley Jamboree is the place to be every second and fourth Saturday nights for lively country, bluegrass, and gospel music. The sprightly show is staged live at the City Administration Building in Lawrenceburg from 7:00 to 11:00 P.M. The Jamboree is composed of 108 groups of talented musicians governed by a board of directors, president, and vice-president. Eight groups perform each Jamboree night. Over 40,000 people attend the 24 regular shows and 22 special shows including 18 benefits. The Jamboree performs Memorial Day, July 4, and Labor Day at the amphitheater in David Crockett State Park, Lawrenceburg. Every Friday evening during the summer, the Jamboree picks and sings at Campsite 2 in the state park to the delight of many tourists. The musicians comprising the Tennessee Valley Jamboree offer their time and talents as a public service, absolutely free of charge.

Admission is free to all shows. When you find yourself at the crossroads of US Highway 43 and 64 stop by. You'll enjoy a hearty welcome and four hours of toe-tappin', foot-stompin' music.

The Tennessee Valley Jamboree, Town Square, Lawrenceburg, TN 38464.

The Picking Post, Lafayette

Owner J. V. Deering says, "We have live country and bluegrass music every Saturday night, giving people hereabouts some fine entertainment they'd otherwise have to travel quite a ways to see. We use a lot of local talent, and have a house band that plays every week."

The Picking Post is in a large building with plenty of room for dancing, and it has a snack bar and soft drinks available. Admission charges are adults $2, children and senior citizens, $1. Music is from 6:00 P.M. to midnight.

Directions: From Lafayette, take State 10 north, the highway to Scottsville, Kentucky. Turn on the Apersville, Kentucky road. Go about 4 miles and follow the signs.

The Picking Post, Fiddlers Lane, Lafayette, TN 37083. (615) 666-3712.

A SAMPLER

SPECIAL

Some Secrets Are Best Kept

Located right at an intersection of two highways in Middle Tennessee is a truly unusual bar called Joe's. When you drive by, you know this is a special place. Joe's is a haven for artists and craftsmen down on their luck. Most of the time there's an interesting array of chain-saw carvings and other objets d'art in front, some of them quite impressive.

Once inside, you can see that Joe's is a typical country bar. Dark interior, juke box with country hits and southern rockers like the Marshall Tucker Band. Downstairs, on Saturday nights, they play music in a freewheeling, redneck jam session. The *Sampler* went with our friend Billy Bob Thudpucker, a regular. "Just keep your mouth shut and pick," he advised. We were just walking up to the front door when it opened and out flew a patron who had just come out on the losing end of a fist fight.

"Sorry," Joe said as he met us at the door. "He didn't know the rules."

As we bellied up to the bar for a sarsaparilla, the fight had momentarily crowded President Reagan, the economy, and The Judds aside as the main topic of conversation. "Well, it's as plain as day, he just didn't know the rules," said a man wearing a farmer's Co-op hat and a Charlie Daniels T-shirt.

We were just about to ask what the rules were when Billy Bob shot us a glance that definitely said shut up, so we kept quiet.

We heard the sounds of someone downstairs trying to short out a guitar amp, so we picked up our guitar cases and headed down the stairway. After an hour or so, a crowd of pickers and listeners had gathered, and the music was as thick as the smoke.

Practically everyone had two drink bottles close at hand. One was to drink out of, and the other was for the tobacco juice. We hoped no one close to us would get their bottles mixed up.

Meanwhile, at least two other fights had occurred, both followed by the exchange of knowing glances among the regulars, and general agreement that the troublemakers "didn't know the rules." We still didn't know the rules, but we were beginning to surmise some of them from observing the disputes. Some of the rules obviously involved wives and girlfriends, and one or more dealt with spitting on other people's boots, intentional or otherwise.

By the time we'd played every kind of song in the world, including every hit George Jones ever had, it was time to quit. Only then did we realize they'd been taping through the P.A. the whole session. One of the players took the tape, wrote something on it, and tossed it onto a table piled with other tapes. We went over to look at the cassettes, and every one of them had "Last Night" written on it. No date. Just "Last Night."

We began to think we were in the Twilight Zone. When we got back outside with Billy Bob, we could hardly wait to find out the rules.

"We don't talk about the rules," he said. "That's the first rule!"

That's why the *Sampler* really can't tell you how to get to Joe's or its real name. You might not know the rules.

Down Home, Johnson City

Music is the centerpiece of an evening at Down Home. If you want to really listen to some of the greatest names in acoustic music, in a family setting, then Down Home is just the place for you. Recent players have included Doc and Merle Watson, Dan Crary, Tony Trischka, Jesse Winchester, and Taj Mahal. The Down Home Grabbag is almost always acoustic, but includes jazz and newgrass as well as bluegrass, blues, all folk styles, and storytelling.

Down Home also hosts a series of 13 one-hour programs entitled "Down Home Music" which is offered by ultramodern satellite uplink on National Public Radio. The first year over 90 stations picked up the series, which features such people as Doc and Merle Watson, Southern Manor, and Ralph Stanley and the Clinch Mountain Boys.

A great favorite with the crowds at Down Home is the Roan Mountain Hilltoppers, a family which plays traditional mountain music going back four and five generations. Such groups keep alive the music which became the basis for country a half-century ago and still furnishes much of the subjects and melodies of bluegrass.

Phil Leonard, one of the owners of this music collective, says "Our purpose is to provide a place for musicians to share their music with patrons who have come to listen." Seating capacity is about 150, with rustic barnwood decor. The menu emphasizes delicious natural foods. Beer, natural drinks, and colas are served.

Opens at 5:00 P.M. Wednesday through Saturday and at 3:00 P.M. Thursday and Friday. Admission charges usually vary from $4 to $6. Some shows are sold in advance. Wednesday evenings feature "Open Hoots" with no admission charge and some incredibly talented local musicians, with many surprises.

Down Home, 300 West Main Street (Main at Watauga), Johnson City, TN 37601. (615) 929-9282.

The Mountain Opry, Chattanooga

Just outside Chattanooga, atop Signal Mountain every Friday night, folks enjoy the Mountain Opry. The Opry originated in 1979 as a way of preserving the music of Appalachia. The musicians who play at the Opry are not paid; they do it on an informal, volunteer basis just to enjoy the music. There are no electrical instruments; it's strictly bluegrass and mountain music. Players include a number of national champions in banjo, guitar, and mandolin. They include Dr. Ray Fox, dean of admissions at the University of Tennessee at Chattanooga; Curtis Hicks, who does small engine repair and old-time banjo; Morris "Bull" Robinson, a long-distance truck driver, and his boys; and others from all walks of life with one common bond: their music. There is no admission charge, and soft drinks are available. No alcoholic beverages are allowed. A pass-the-hat collection pays the utility expenses for the building. Come and join the folks at the Mountain Opry for good family entertainment every Friday night from 8:00 to 11:00 P.M.

Directions: Take US 127 to the top of Signal Mountain, and continue past the shopping center on the right 2 miles to Fairmount Orchard and the "Mountain Opry" sign. Then turn right on Fairmount Road and go 3/10 of a mile to Walden Ridge Civic Center on the left.

Telephone number for information: (615) 886-3252 or 886-1525 and ask for Ken.

The Clyde Blalock Music Co., Hixson

A visit to Clyde Blalock in Hixson is an unforgettable experience, especially if you can make it on a Saturday night. Clyde's easygoing country manner and his passion for bluegrass music are so captivating that the visitor may not realize he is shopping at one of the premier sales outlets for high-quality acoustic instruments in the eastern United States. Clyde is on hand at the shop daily from 8:30 A.M. to 9:30 P.M., teaching bluegrass musical styles and catering to his customers' needs.

But on Saturday nights, Clyde and his family (including his 10-year-old son who "picks like a house afire") and pickers from all around gather on the huge porch at his store and play bluegrass from 7:30 or so to midnight. Such players as Curly Fox, a retired Grand Ole Opry fiddler, come to help them out. The audience fills up the parking lot, many bringing lawn chairs and sitting around the pickers. "Them as gets hungry or thirsty can slip into the restaurant next door for refreshments," says Clyde. There is no admission charge for this East Tennessee bluegrass happening, which has been going strong for over six years now.

Just head north over the Market Street Bridge out of Chattanooga on Hixson Pike, and you'll see Blalock's when you get into Hixson. Very close by is Chester Frost County Park. The fishing and camping are great, with a lot of Indian history thereabouts. So plan a weekend trip to the park, and you'll have Saturday night entertainment to equal any in Tennessee. Clyde loves to wheel and deal. Who knows? You might walk away the proud owner of one of his Martin guitars or Stelling banjos.

The Clyde Blalock Music Co., Hixson, TN 37343. (615) 842-4000.

Roy Acuff with tourist

The Jubilee Arts Center, Knoxville

The Jubilee Arts Center is in an old church building which provides a fine setting for its traditional, bluegrass, blues, and old-time music. The building is at Sixteenth and Laurel in the university area. Bill Daniel is the director of this nonprofit corporation. Jubilee has been alive for 16 years now and has always been a place where old-time music, poetry, and local performers could be showcased to appreciative crowds. Groups like the New Grass Revival, the Louisiana Aces, Skyline, John McCutcheon, and Knoxville's own Sparky Rucker have played at the Jubilee. Bill says there is a $6 admission on music nights, but they never turn anyone away who is a little short on cash and wants to hear the pickers. Music is usually on Friday, or Friday and Saturday. Most Wednesday nights poetry readings feature local writers.

The Jubilee Arts Center, 1538 Highland Avenue, Knoxville, TN. (615) 522-5851.

TOURS & TRAILS

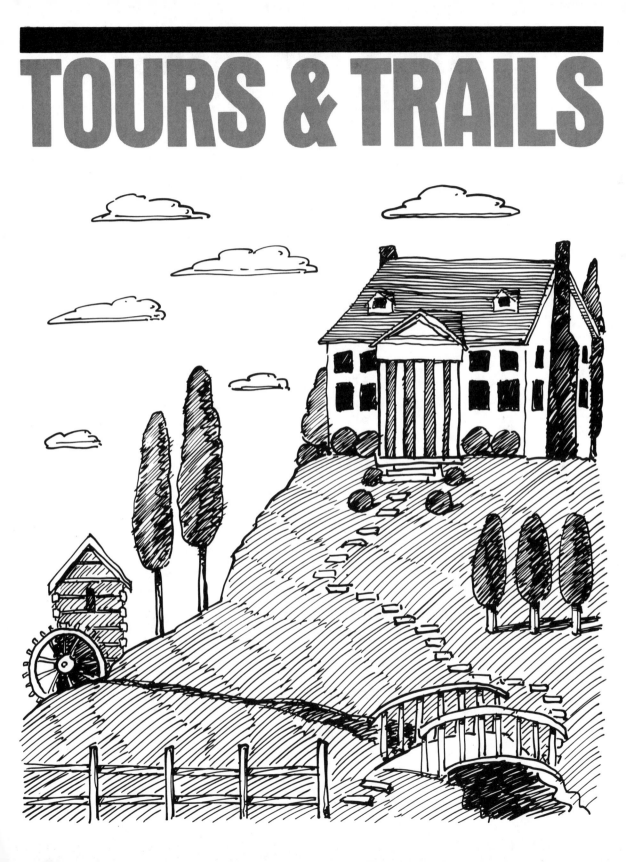

TOURS AND TRAILS HIGHLIGHTS

Six Comprehensive Tours

Upper East Tennessee

Sites in Greeneville, Historic Jonesborough, and Kingsport including the Doe River Covered Bridge, National Fish Hatchery, and Rocky Mount

Knoxville Area

Places in Gatlinburg, Pigeon Forge, and Cherokee National Forest such as The Lost Sea, Silver Dollar City, and Historic Rugby
A *Sampler* Exclusive: T. G. Sheppard

Chattanooga Area

Sites in Sequatchie Valley and Cleveland, such as Rock City, Ketner's Mill, and the Chattanooga Choo-Choo

Nashville Area

Visit Jamestown, Murfreesboro, and Franklin;
Opryland, the Parthenon, and Loretta Lynn's Dude Ranch
The studios, museums, and homes of the stars
Tennessee's most significant Civil War sites
A *Sampler* Exclusive: John Seigenthaler
A *Sampler* Special: The First Jet Tour for Country Music's Super Rich, Super Fans
Oak Ridge Boy William Lee Golden's guide to Tennessee's prettiest roads

South Central Tennessee Area

Bell Buckle, Sewanee, the Jack Daniel Distillery, Tennessee Walking Horse Country, and Falls Mill

Memphis Area

Skullbone, Mud Island, Memphis Riverboats, Beale Street, Trenton Teapots
A *Sampler* Special: An Original Monument to the King

Explore Tennessee!

To help you explore the best Tennessee has to offer—our theme parks, historic houses, battlefields, museums, zoos, and other unique sites—the *Sampler* has divided Tennessee into six travel regions. We start in mountainous and historic Upper East Tennessee, home of Jonesborough and beautiful Roan Mountain. Our next stop is the Great Smoky Mountains area of Gatlinburg, Pigeon Forge, and Knoxville. Moving south to picturesque Chattanooga, we see Rock City and Civil War sites; there we can take advantage of opportunities to travel by railway or by riverboat as well as by car.

Middle Tennessee is divided into two sections. Country music flourishes and Tennessee history comes to life in Nashville and the counties surrounding it. South Central Tennessee boasts of walking horse farms, antebellum plantations, and rugged natural beauty.

West Tennessee's activities center in the Volunteer State's largest city, Memphis. However, towns in other western counties have a lot to offer, so don't overlook them.

You'll find a directory listing phone numbers and many addresses at the end of the six "tour" sections. Also listed are numerous chambers of commerce, which are happy to send information to you about their areas. (These lists appear as they are mentioned, not in alphabetical order.)

There's more to do in Tennessee than you ever thought possible. Yet, the *Sampler's* "Tours and Scenic Trails" is only a sample of the good things in our state. Get out and explore and have a great time doing it!

Follow the Mockingbird

Tennessee's Scenic Parkway runs the length of the Volunteer State—from Tiptonville and Reelfoot Lake to Ducktown and the Ocoee River; from Mountain City, as far east as you can go in Tennessee, to Beale Street in Memphis, about as far west as you can travel before you cross the Mississippi River. The Parkway takes you to scenic sights such as Gatlinburg, the Chattanooga Choo-Choo, Jack Daniel Distillery, the Grand Ole Opry, and Graceland, Elvis's home.

Tennessee's state bird, the mockingbird, is the symbol for the state's Parkway system and is the first thing you see on the signs marking the scenic routes. The *Sampler* suggests you escape the bustle and boredom of interstate travel, and let the mockingbird guide you to the Heartland for a close-up look at Tennessee and Tennesseans.

To order the brochure which maps out the Scenic Parkway System, contact: Department of Tourist Development, 601 Broadway, P. O. Box 23170, Nashville, TN 37202. (615) 741-2158.

To order an official Tennessee highway map, contact: Department of Transportation, Map Sales Office, Suite 1000, James K. Polk Building, 505 Deaderick Street, Nashville, TN 37219-5538.

Tennessee county maps may be ordered for 50 cents each. If you order 10 maps or more, there is a small handling fee. To order county maps, contact the Department of Transportation at the above address.

Upper East Tennessee

Historic Jonesborough, a covered bridge in Elizabethton, and mountains and mountains of rhododendron—what a beautiful weekend getaway! This part of the state was known as the "Gateway to the West" in the 1770s and 1780s. Davy Crockett's stomping grounds as a child were here. We're talking about Upper East Tennessee, the place we'll start our travels across Tennessee.

This beautiful little eight-county section of Tennessee is sometimes called "First Tennessee." Although many travelers drive through on I-81, few have explored this area to discover the beauty and history it offers. Upper East Tennessee can be a quiet retreat, a place to escape to, not escape from.

We'll make a loop as we tour this area, by starting in Greeneville and ending up in Rogersville. From Greeneville we'll travel US 11E to Jonesborough and Johnson City, over to Elizabethton, and south on US 19E to Roan Mountain State Park. From there we'll travel west to the Nolichucky River and white-water rafting, then go to Erwin. From Erwin, we go north to Bristol, then Blountville, Kingsport, and finally Rogersville.

Greeneville

In Greeneville is the **Andrew Johnson National Historic Site**. Since Johnson lacked formal education, as a young man he hired a reader to keep him abreast of current events by reading aloud newspapers, government reports, political speeches, and books while he worked at his tailor's bench. At this location are Johnson's tailor shop, the home in which he lived during and after his term as our seventeenth president, and the National Cemetery where he was buried.

Visitors may take a walking tour, which takes in almost 40 other historic sites in Greeneville. The restored capitol of the state of Franklin is located here, and the **Samuel W. Doak House** is on the Tusculum College campus. Samuel Doak, often referred to as the "apostle of learning and religion in the West," built the two-story brick home in 1818. He founded the first school west of the Allegheny Mountains.

In nearby Limestone, on the banks of Limestone Creek is a replica of the log cabin in which **Davy Crockett** was born. The five-acre historic park is enclosed by a rail fence.

The Chester Inn in historic Jonesborough

Jonesborough

Jonesborough is sometimes called the "Mother of Tennessee." It boasts of being the oldest town west of the Allegheny Mountains during the time Tennessee was serving as the "back door of the early colonies." Andrew Jackson was admitted to the bar here, and Daniel Boone is said to have "killed a bar" nearby. Through ongoing restoration efforts, many buildings over a century old may be seen in Jonesborough. This historic town served as the capital of the "Lost State of Franklin" for a couple of years in the 1780s before Tennessee officially became the sixteenth of the United States in 1796. For overnight lodging, reservations can be made with Jonesborough Bed and Breakfast. (See "Eatin' and Sleepin' Good.")

A good way to begin sightseeing in Jonesborough is by stopping at the Visitors Center. **The Jonesborough History Museum** is located here, and you can obtain many brochures listing local sites. A helpful pamphlet, *Historic Jonesborough,* gives the names of all the interesting shops along this five-block stretch of Main Street which is bordered by bricked sidewalks. Many contrasting styles of architecture, including Federal, Greek revival, Gothic revival, and Victorian, are in evidence. If you decide not to walk, you can take an antique bus tour.

Built in the 1790s, the **Chester Inn** is considered the oldest frame structure in Jonesborough. Its long covered porch has welcomed the three Tennessee Presidents of the United States, Andrew Jackson, Andrew Johnson, and James K. Polk, along with many other dignitaries. **Sister's Row**, built in the 1820s, is the oldest surviving brick building in town.

For dining, there are the Parson's Table located in a century-old church building (see "Eatin' and Sleepin' Good"), Widow Brown's, The Dinner Bell, and The Blue Iris Tea Room. Numerous places to stop and sample goodies along Main Street include the Main Street Cafe, Beverly Farms Old Sweet Shop, with homemade ice cream, The Jonesborough Confectionery, and Another Roadside Attraction.

Each fall the famous **National Storytelling Festival** (see "Fun Times"), is held in Jonesborough, and the four days ending the Fourth of July celebrate the festival

known as Jonesborough Days. Christmas in Old Jonesborough is delightful with its buggy rides, old-fashioned caroling, and shopping by candlelight. During the Christmas season many historic private homes are open for tours.

Johnson City

Johnson City, also in Washington County, is a historian's delight. **The Tipton-Haynes Living Historical Farm** spans four eras of American history—the colonial, Revolutionary War, War of 1812, and the Civil War periods. The **B. Carroll Reece Museum** on the campus of East Tennessee State University displays items and implements from the earliest colonial days of the region.

Also in Johnson City is **Rocky Mount**, a large log house built atop a limestone hill and overlooking the Watauga River. Rocky Mount is one of the few territorial capitols still existing. William Blount, in 1790, used Rocky Mount as his base of operations to serve as the governor of the newly organized "Territory South of the River Ohio," a post to which President George Washington had appointed him.

Elizabethton

Between Johnson City and Elizabethton is **Sinking Creek Baptist Church**, the oldest church in Tennessee. The **Doe River Covered Bridge** in Elizabethton is believed to be the oldest such bridge in the state still in use. Known as the "kissing bridge," it spans the river 154 feet, and it originally cost $3,000 to build back in 1882.

Sycamore Shoals State Historic Area in Elizabethton is the site of the first permanent American settlement established outside the original 13 colonies. In 1772, the Watauga Association, the first majority-rule system of American democratic government, was formed at this location. One of the largest real estate transactions in our country's history took place here in 1775 when Richard Henderson's Transylvania Company purchased 20 million acres of land from the Cherokees for 10,000 pounds of goods. In 1780 the "Overmountain Men" mustered at Sycamore Shoals prior to victory over the British at the battle of Kings Mountain, South Carolina. A replica of **Fort Watauga** has been reconstructed at Sycamore Shoals. During July the Watauga Historical Association produces an outdoor drama depicting the events during the 1770s and 1780s at Fort Watauga.

The **John and Landon Carter Mansion** near Sycamore Shoals is one of the oldest houses remaining in Tennessee. The Carters were father and son, prominent in governmental and military affairs during the 1770s. In 1772 John Carter was elected chairman of the Watauga Association.

A little south of Elizabethton is one of the quiet, restful reasons many people travel to this area of Tennessee, **Roan Mountain State Park.** Cabins nestled in the valley at the foot of the mountain are available. Often even on June nights in these Tennessee mountains, it's cool enough to build a fire in the fireplaces. Roan Mountain in June is a spectacular sight. A 600-acre rhododendron garden at the summit of the 6,285-feet-tall mountain makes up the largest natural stand of rhododendron in the world. The mountains are vivid with many shades of pink, rose, coral, white, and red. The panoramic view looking toward North Carolina is breathtaking. The Rhododendron Festival (see "Fun Times") is held in late June, and the mountains are alive with dancing color that seems to gently reach down out of the mountain tops and soothe weary nerves. In the winter, Roan Mountain serves as the South's only cross-country ski resort state park. (See "Outdoors.")

Once a resort hotel, Cloudland Hotel, crowned this mountaintop. Although the steps are all that are visible now, you can imagine the joy of waking on a bright beautiful June day, looking out the hotel window, and feeling like you're wrapped in the largest "flower garden" quilt ever crafted! *The Miller Homestead* is also nearby with its frame house, log barn, and outbuildings. It took tough mountain people to settle this rugged area in the days before Tennessee became a state.

Erwin

For those interested in white-water rafting, one of the best places to shoot the rapids in the state is nearby, outside of Erwin. The *Nolichucky Canyon* provides a spectacular setting for what's been called the "South's premier white-water experience." (See "Outdoors.")

Also in Erwin is the *National Fish Hatchery* which welcomes visitors. It began operation in 1897 and produces 18 million disease-free rainbow trout eggs annually, shipping them to other hatcheries around the country.

The old frame Victorian house that formerly was home to the superintendent of the fish hatchery is now the *Unicoi County Heritage Museum*. A few years ago this lovely old house was scheduled for demolition, but community leaders and the citizenry of Erwin saved the house and renovated it. Now it's a fine museum. A display of antique clothing, the Blue Ridge Pottery Room, and "Main Street" exhibit are three interesting features.

Near Bluff City, on US 19E, you'll see *The Ridgewood*, which has been dubbed "America's best barbecue restaurant." (See "Eatin' and Sleepin' Good.")

Iron Mountain Stoneware, in Laurel Bloomery, is the only high-fired stoneware plant in the nation. (See "Shopping.")

Bristol

In the twin city of Bristol, you can spend the afternoon seeing the sights in this town that's half in Tennessee and half in Virginia. The geographic border runs down the middle of State Street. The fabulous *Bristol Caverns* are the largest series of caves in the Smoky Mountain region and are located just outside of town. Paved, well-lighted walkways in this subterranean world wind through the chambers past an underground river, stalagmites, and stalactites.

Also located in Bristol are the Historic Bristol Train Station, The Bristol International Raceway, and the Grand Guitar, the world's only guitar-shaped music museum. Beautiful South Holston Lake is nearby.

Blountville

The *Sampler* recommends that you take the time to walk around the town of Blountville. The *Old Deery Inn* and *Anderson Townhouse* are but two of the many eighteenth- and nineteenth-century log and frame buildings along State 126.

Kingsport

Coming toward Kingsport you'll pass by *Warriors' Path State Recreational Area*, which was named for the park's proximity to the ancient "warriors' path" used by the Cherokees when they went raiding or hunting in Virginia. Golfing, swimming, fishing, and hiking are available.

Also in Kingsport is *Exchange Place*, a restored nineteenth-century farm complex which once served travelers along the Old Stage Road. It served as a place for exchanging Virginia currency for Tennessee currency and for exchanging horses. The sassafras leaf is the symbol for Exchange Place, based on the discovery of a leaf-shaped cookie cutter among the original family's effects. The saying, "Drink sassafras in March, and you won't need a doctor all year," was an admonition exported to England along with the plant itself.

Allendale Mansion was the home of Harvey C. Brooks, a prominent Kingsport businessman. The plantation-style residence houses a fine collection of antiques and artwork.

Netherland Inn and Boat Yard Historical District is in Kingsport. Purchased in 1818 by Richard Netherland, it became a celebrated stop on the Great Stage Road, often playing host to Presidents Jackson, Johnson, and Polk. Netherland Inn is located on the banks of the Holston River and near *Long Island*, the sacred treaty ground of the Cherokees and the starting point of Daniel Boone's Wilderness Road. The boat yard was where pioneer families made their boats for the trip West.

The wonderful city park called *Bays Mountain Park* is a 3000-acre natural reserve with a 44-acre lake of which the city of Kingsport is amply proud. Twenty-five miles of hiking trails, a Puppet Ecology Theater, and an excellent planetarium are prominent features. Not too far from Bays Mountain is a well-known restaurant many people enjoy for the atmosphere as well as the good food. It's called Skoby's. (See "Eatin' and Sleepin' Good.")

Rogersville

The *Hale Springs Inn*, on the square in Rogersville, is a historic place to spend the night. (See "Eatin' and Sleepin' Good.") This is the oldest inn in the state in continuous operation since opening in 1824, except for a period during the Civil War when it served as Union Army headquarters. Other sites in historic Rogersville are the *Amis House*, Clay Kennedy House, Rosemont, Masonic Temple, Walker House, and the Hawkins

County Courthouse, one of the few original courthouses still in official use.

Fascinating Tennessee history, adventures by waterway or mountain trail, and some of the prettiest natural scenery to be found anywhere are all waiting for you in Upper East Tennessee. Get off the interstate and discover what this northeastern section of Tennessee has to offer. You'll be pleasantly surprised.

DIRECTORY:

For information on all of Upper East Tennessee, contact: Upper East Tennessee Tourism Council, P.O. Box 375-P, Jonesborough, TN 37659; (615) 753-5961.

Greeneville: Greeneville Chamber of Commerce, 207 North Main Street, 37743; (615) 638-4111. Andrew Johnson Site, corner of Depot and College streets, 37743; (615) 638-3503. Samuel Doak House, (615) 639-4681.

Jonesborough: Jonesborough Visitors Bureau, P.O. Box 375, 37659; (615) 753-5961.

Johnson City: Johnson City Conventions and Visitors Bureau, P.O. Box 1674B, 3760l; (615) 926-2141. Tipton-Haynes Farm, (615) 926-3631. Carroll Reece Museum, (615) 929-4392. Rocky Mount, US 11E, Route 2, Box 70, Piney Flats, TN 37686; (615) 538-7396.

Elizabethton: Carter County Chamber of Commerce, P.O. Box 190, Elizabethton, TN 37643; (615) 543-2122. Sycamore Shoals, P.O. Box 1198, Elizabethton, TN 37643; (615) 543-5808. Roan Mountain State Park, Route L, Box 50, Roan Mountain, TN 37687; (615) 772-3303.

Erwin: Unicoi Chamber of Commerce, P.O. Box 713, Erwin, TN 37650; (615) 743-3000. National Fish Hatchery, P.O. Box 548, 37650; (615) 743-4712. Unicoi County Heritage Museum, (615) 743-9449.

Bristol: Bristol Chamber of Commerce, P.O. Box 519, Bristol, VA 24203; (615) 669-2141. Bristol Caverns, (615) 878-2011.

Kingsport: Kingsport Visitors Council, 408 Clay Street, 37662; (615) 246-2010. Warriors' Path State Recreational Area, P.O. Box 5026, 37663; (615) 239-8531. Exchange Place, 4812 Orebank Road, 37664; (615) 288-6613. Netherland Inn, P.O. Box 293, 37662; (615) 247-3211.

Rogersville: Rogersville-Hawkins County Chamber, 403 East Main Street, 37857; (615) 272-2186.

Also, for more information about many places mentioned in the article, contact Tennessee Department of Tourist Development, P.O. Box 23170, Nashville, TN 37202; (615) 741-2158.

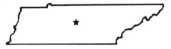

Knoxville Area

Take your pick of seasons—when snowfall's blanketing the mountaintop villages or when the trees are splashed with vivid fall colors. When summer wildflowers carpet broad valleys and meadows, or when spring is bursting on the hillsides with pastel shades from redbuds, dogwoods, and mountain laurel. In the Great Smoky Mountain area of Tennessee, you can't go wrong in choosing any time of the year as the right time to visit.

Pigeon Forge

Pigeon Forge was at one time a sleepy little village that you just passed through on your way to Gatlinburg. In recent years it's exploded as a family entertainment center, offering water slides, wave pools, and theme parks featuring magic and dinosaurs, among other appealing activities. Pigeon Forge takes its name from the pigeons that roosted on the river beside a pioneer forge.

The Old Mill, on the bank of the Little Pigeon River, has been in continuous operation since 1830 and is one of the most visited sites in this small community.

Silver Dollar City has a full day's worth of shows, craft demonstrations, rides, and entertainment. "Craftsmen's Valley" provides visitors with a look-over-the-shoulder of authentic mountain craftsmen at work. Take a trip back in time and enjoy the beauty and charm of 100 years ago at Silver Dollar City. (See "Outdoors.")

Mill Creek is a family park with friendly animals that love to be petted, tire tubes for floating down the stream, fishing poles, and a grassy playground. **Ogle's Water Park** is a giant water playground with water slides, a wave pool, and a manmade beach.

Magic World has realistic dinosaurs on display built by the owner, James Sidwell. There's everything from Tyrannosaurus Rex to Stegosaurus, the original walking tank with armor shields up and down his spine, spikes on his tail for defense, and two brains (one in his head and one in his hip). Magic and fantasy are the themes, and there's even an old-time European organ grinder complete with his monkey!

The Great Smoky Mountain Water Circus is one of the largest outdoor show extravaganzas in the nation. Comprised of a water ski show and circus thrills in the sky, the ultramodern covered amphitheater can comfortably seat over 4,000 guests. Country music stars often appear at concerts here.

Other tourist attractions in Pigeon Forge are Flyaway, indoor sky diving (see "Outdoors"); Smoky Mountain Car Museum; Carbo's Police Museum; and Pigeon Forge Pottery. There are two nightly country music shows and a "Salute to Elvis" show.

Gatlinburg

Gatlinburg is located at the main entrance to the Great Smoky Mountains National Park, and its 3,500 residents play host to over eight million visitors a year to the park. More than 300 specialty shops carry everything from University of Tennessee sweatshirts to antique grandfather clocks. Stop at the Chamber of Commerce and get any of the hundreds of brochures as well as a directory listing accommodations, shops, restaurants, and information on the Smoky Mountains. A Twelve Days of Christmas Festival in December and a month-long Crafts Fair in October are only two special events in the area.

The Gatlinburg Municipal Bear Habitat is located atop Mount Harrison at **Ober Gatlinburg**. The habitat helps educate the public about black bears. Although the bears aren't pets and never come in contact with humans, they live in a natural-looking environment where people can watch them play. Most of the bears were orphaned at a young age, and the goal is to return them to nature someday.

Also at Ober Gatlinburg are ice skating, an alpine slide, Old Heidelberg Castle, a shopping mall, and skiing year-round.

Other attractions in Gatlinburg are the World of Illusions, World of Unexplained Museum, Elvis Hall of Fame, American Historical Wax Museum, Guinness World Records Museum, Ripley's Believe It or Not Museum, Christus Gardens, and Cinema 180.

Pioneer Cemetery at Cades Cove Church

Great Smoky Mountains National Park

The Indians gave the name of "The Land of the Thousand Smokes" to the **Great Smoky Mountains**. The climbs to Clingman's Dome and The Chimney Tops are two favorites with hikers. (See "Outdoors.") LeConte Lodge is located above Gatlinburg and can be reached only by horse or hiking trail. (See "Eatin' and Sleepin' Good.")

Cades Cove, in the Great Smoky Mountains, takes you back to the life of America's pioneers. An 11-mile Loop Road circles the western perimeter of the cove and leads past open fields, log cabin pioneer homesteads, split-rail fences, and tiny white frame churches. The two most popular attractions are the John Oliver cabin and John P. Cable homestead with grain grist mill.

Sunrise and sunset are the most likely times for seeing deer, usually in a clearing near a wood. Hundreds of black bears are in these mountains, as well as wild turkey and the usual mountain critters. There's a mule-powered sorghum mill that operates in the fall when the sorghum cane is ripe. Hikers enjoy the miles of nature walks that lead to places such as Abrams Falls. Bikes, camping spaces, and horses are available for rent.

Cherokee National Forest

Cherokee National Forest borders the park on both north and south. Its 600,000 acres extend along the entire Tennessee/North Carolina border. There are over 500 miles of hiking trails, mountain streams, cascades, and waterfalls. (See "Outdoors.")

A unique photography/guide service is available for those who want to explore the Cherokee Forest and capture the sights on film. The service is *Mountaineer Photo Adventures*. Guides will lead you to the best spots for photographing loads of beautiful scenery and provide instruction, transportation, and equipment rental. "Color Camps" are available in October as the fall colors peak. Wildflower tours are held in the spring. There's even a service "For MADMEN ONLY!" (See listing at end of article.)

Maryville

The **Sam Houston Log Schoolhouse** in Maryville is where Sam Houston became the schoolmaster in 1812. At the high tuition rate of $8 per term, he earned $2 more than previous schoolmasters. He was paid one-third in cash, one-third in corn, and one-third in bright-colored calico that he liked for his shirts. He had a short teaching career (one term) due to his enlistment in the army. Houston served under General Andrew Jackson in the army, and later he was a lawyer and the governor of Tennessee. He went on to become president (of the Republic of Texas!).

Also in Maryville is the **Thompson-Brown House**, a two-story log house which now serves as the Smoky Mountains Visitors Center.

Knoxville

Knoxville is Tennessee's third largest city and the home of the University of Tennessee. Knoxville was the site of the 1982 World's Fair, and the Sunsphere, focus of the fair, is still visible. The Tennessee Valley Authority, the nation's largest public utility, is headquartered in Knoxville. Six of TVA's Great Lakes of the South are within an hour's drive of Knoxville. (See "Outdoors.")

The **Knoxville Zoological Park** is one of the most outstanding zoos in the country, and it is known for its collection of large cats, including African and Asian lions, Siberian and Bengal tigers, and jaguars. Most of the animals are threatened and endangered species. More than 1,200 animals inhabit the 120 acres. Favorites at the petting zoo are llamas, pygmy goats, and donkeys.

Knoxville is proud of its many historic sites. Three broad areas of the city are labeled historic districts: Jackson Avenue, Fort Sanders, and Mechanicsville. The **Ramsey House**, built of native pink marble with blue limestone trim, was the first stone house built in Knox County. James White Fort, Speedwell Manor, and the Armstrong-Lockett House are other significant historic sites.

Marble Springs is so named because of the numerous springs and marble deposits nearby. It was the farm home of Tennessee's first elected governor, John Sevier. He had also served as the governor of the Lost State of Franklin. **Blount Mansion** is called "the birthplace of Tennessee history," since the Tennessee constitution was written here. Built in 1792, it served as the home of William Blount who was appointed governor of the Southwest Territory under George Washington.

Knoxville has 17 museums. Dulin Art Gallery, McClung Museum, and the Knoxville Academy of Medicine Museum house fascinating exhibits and artifacts. (See phone number at end of article for museum information.)

The Dogwood Festival in April features 50 miles of auto trails that take you to some of the South's most beautiful lawns, gardens, and blooming trees. (See "Fun Times.")

Sweetwater and Fort Loudon

The **Lost Sea**, located deep inside a mountain near Sweetwater, is the world's largest underground lake and is part of the Craighead Caverns. Glass-bottom boats powered by electric motors carry visitors out onto the lake stocked with some of the largest rainbow trout in North America. The lake itself is 4½ acres, and there are more rooms completely filled with water. On guided tours you can see rare crystalline structures called anthodites. They are fragile, spiky clusters known as "cave flowers," found only in a few of the world's caves.

Near Sweetwater is "The Gold District of the Volunteer State." **Coker Creek Gold Mine** is a great place for the amateur or serious prospector to spend a weekend or a vacation. The Autumn Gold Festival takes place there annually. (See "Fun Times.")

Fort Loudon in Vonore is a state historic area. It was built in 1756–57 and is an imitation of European forts, nothing like our American forts. This fort played a role in determining that America would be an English-speaking nation. It also helped Great Britain secure the trans-Appalachian region from France during the French and Indian War. It was the first British fort in the East Tennessee area to fall to the Cherokee Indians. The **Tellico Blockhouse** is also at this site.

The **Tennessee Valley Winery** is located on a hill in Loudon County with a fantastic view of the Smoky Mountains. Tours of the winery are offered.

Oak Ridge

Known as the "Atomic City" and the "Energy Capital of the World," Oak Ridge, west of Knoxville, was a site of great secrecy in the early 1940s. The secrecy protected the huge Manhattan Project, the code name for the development of the atom bomb. The self-guided **Energy/Environment Loop** is a 38-mile motor tour that takes about one day to complete. Nine sites including the **American Museum of Science and Energy,** packed with models, movies, and computer games, tell the story of energy. The **Children's Museum** is a hands-on learning center. The graphite reactor is the oldest nuclear reactor in existence and its control room and operating areas are open to the public also.

Crossville

It's worth getting off the interstate to drive through Crab Orchard and Crossville to see the churches, schools, and businesses built from the unique crab orchard stone. With an earthtone and mauve cast it's quarried *only* in this section of the United States. The stone is shipped to New York, New Jersey, Texas, and many other states to be used in construction.

South of Crossville is the unique planned community of **Homestead**, developed in the 1940s. The entire community is on the National Register of Historic Places. The many buildings, built of all-native products, feature The Homestead School and Homestead Tower Museum, constructed of field stone found in this area. They're located just across the road from the delightful Cumberland General Store. (See "Shopping.")

Also in Crossville are the Cumberland Mountain State Rustic Park and Cumberland County Playhouse.

Be sure to stop outside of Crossville at **The Talavera De La Reina,** which means "The Tavern of the Queen." The restaurant, run by Amy Brissler, is far more than a place to stop and eat. Amy began her Hollywood career in 1935, and for more than 40 years she was a costume designer for motion pictures and television. The "tavern" is filled with Amy's mementos of Tinseltown—a pair of Betty Grable's shoes, one of Mae West's gowns, a coat worn by Marilyn Monroe. Each room contains a large montage of autographed pictures of stars from several eras, as well as some of Amy's own costume creations and sketches of costumes she designed. It is open to any visitor who telephones ahead for reservations—and *do* ask for a map or instructions. Just for the record, you may reach the Talavera De La Reina by taking US 70 North approximately 12 miles from Crossville and turning right on Jim Garrett Road.

Rugby

North of Crossville is a community that's a must for everyone's tour of Tennessee—**Historic Rugby.** Calling Rugby a "lovely corner of God's earth," Thomas Hughes in 1880 formed his "New Jerusalem" in a corner of the Cumberland Plateau in Tennessee, far from his native England. Hughes, an eminent Victorian novelist and social reformer, began this new community as a place where Britishers and anyone else who wished to come could build a strong agricultural community through cooperative enterprise. Private ownership of land and freedom of religion and expression would prevail.

The idea for such a colony grew out of Hughes's concern for the younger sons of the British gentry, victims of the primogeniture system in which inherited estates usually went to the eldest son. The tradition left the younger sons with few choices. Any type of manual labor was unacceptable, and the "honorable" professions—law, medicine, and the clergy—were already overcrowded at that time. In America, Hughes hoped, these young men's energies and abilities could be directed to manual trades and agricultural endeavors.

Hughes's ideal community didn't turn out as he'd hoped, however. The first winter was the worst one in 25 years, and the summer brought a devastating drought along with an outbreak of typhoid. The citizens of Rugby often were more eager to quit work at 4:00 P.M. and dress for tea than hoe in their gardens, build new roads, or tame the wilderness around them. Although it didn't flourish, it did survive and is now a twentieth-century village building a future on its past.

The buildings open for tours are Christ Church, the 7,000-volume Thomas Hughes Library, the Hughes Home, Percy Cottage Bookshop, and the Rugby Commissary. In May a Music and Crafts Festival is held. (See "Fun Times.")

The new Harrow Road Cafe specializes in Cumberland Plateau cooking. Lodging is offered at the historic Pioneer Cottage and Newbury House Inn. Near Rugby is Beggar's Castle at Jamestown; German food is the focal point. (See "Eatin' and Sleepin' Good.")

Harrogate

The Lincoln Memorial University and **Lincoln Library and Museum** are located in Harrogate in Claiborne County. Founded in 1896 by Union General O. O. Howard as a living memorial to his former Commander in Chief, Abraham Lincoln, it houses the third largest collection of Lincoln memorabilia and Civil War items in the world.

The **Cumberland Gap** is a prominent V-shaped indentation in the mountains which marks the common borders of Tennessee, Kentucky, and Virginia. It served as a natural passage through the Appalachian Mountain chain. Although the Cumberland Gap was used earlier, Daniel Boone was the one who opened the floodgates for the western migration that followed. Boone and 30 axmen blazed a trail known as the "Wilderness Road." Today a four-lane highway winds through the gap. There are many trails, short, self-guided ones, and longer overnight ones.

Morristown, Jefferson City, Dandridge, and Newport

Located in Morristown's first public school building is the **Rose Center.** It's a cultural center for arts and features a gallery and a children's "touch museum." **Davy Crockett Tavern and Museum,** also in Morristown, is a reproduction of the Crockett tavern Davy's father operated in the 1790s. The **Glenmore Mansion,** in Jefferson City, is a 27-room, five-story Victorian mansion built in 1869 by John Roper Branner, president of East Tennessee-Virginia Railroad.

In Dandridge is the **Jefferson County Museum** which includes a marriage bond signed by "D. Crock-ett" in 1806. A self-guided walking tour in Dandridge takes you past 30 structures on the National Historic Register. There's a Revolutionary War "burying ground," and in this second oldest town of Tennessee is the Shepherd's Inn where it's said James K. Polk, Andy Jackson, and Andrew Johnson all stayed.

In Newport is the **Cocke County Museum** which displays Indian artifacts and pioneer implements.

Whether you're looking for the peaceful solitude offered on a hiking trail in the Smokies, or nonstop family fun at the theme parks of Pigeon Forge, or stepping back in time at Rugby and the Lincoln Museum, the area from the Smokies to the Cumberland Plateau can provide the vacation spot you're seeking. Hope you'll do some exploring in this part of Tennessee.

DIRECTORY:

Pigeon Forge: Pigeon Forge Department of Tourism, P. O. Box 209PJ, 37863; (615) 453-8574; toll free out of Tennessee (800) 251-9100. The Old Mill, (615) 453-3883. Silver Dollar City, (615) 453-4616. Magic World, (615) 453-8044. The Great Smoky Mountain Water Circus, (615) 453-9473.

Gatlinburg: Gatlinburg Chamber of Commerce, P. O. Box 527, 520 Parkway, 37738; (615) 436-4178 or (800) 251-9868. Great Smoky Mountains National Park, (615) 436-5615.

Mountaineer Photo Adventures, Route 2, Box 217, Vonore, TN 37885; (615) 295-2181.

Knoxville: Knoxville Convention and Visitor's Bureau, P. O. Box 15012, 500 Henley Street, 37901; (615) 523-2316. Knoxville Chamber of Commerce, P. O. Box 2688, 37902; (615) 637-4550. Knoxville Zoological Park, (615) 637-5331. Ramsey House, (615) 546-0745. Marble Springs, (615) 573-5508. Blount Mansion, (615) 525-2375. For information on Knoxville's museums, call (615) 974-2144.

Sweetwater:
Coker Creek Gold Mine: Attn: Harold Witt, Route 2, Box 186, Tellico Plains, TN 37385. Lost Sea, (615) 337-6616.

Loudon: Tennessee Valley Winery, Route 3, Box 307-A, Hotchkiss Valley Road, 37774; (615) 986-5147.

Oak Ridge: Oak Ridge Visitor Center, P. O. Box 160, 37830; (615) 482-7821.

Crossville: Cumberland County Chamber of Commerce, P. O. Box 453, 38555; (615) 484-8444. Talavera De La Reina, (615) 277-3749.

Rugby: Historic Rugby Inc., P. O. Box 8, 37733; (615) 628-2441.

Harrogate: Lincoln Museum, campus of Lincoln Memorial University, 37752; (615) 869-3614.

Morristown: Morristown Area Chamber of Commerce, P. O. Box 9, 37814; (615) 586-6382.

Jefferson City: Jefferson City Chamber of Commerce, Broadway Boulevard, 37760; (615) 475-3819.

Newport: Newport Chamber of Commerce, 803 Prospect Avenue, 37821; (615) 623-720l.

Publications: A newspaper called "the leading magazine about the Smokies" is *Mountain Trails.* It's published monthly and can be ordered by contacting P. O. Box 120, Pigeon Forge, TN 37863.

Also for many places mentioned in the article, contact Tennessee Department of Tourist Development, P. O. Box 23170, Nashville, TN 37202; (615) 741-7994.

A SAMPLER
·····*Exclusive*·····
A Place T. G. Loves

The man T. G. has had bunches of country music hit songs. T. G. is loved by fans from the upper corners of Washington State to the white beaches of the Gulf of Mexico and everywhere else in the world humans like country music. When the pressures of this world get to Mr. T. G. Sheppard, he goes back to a place he's loved since he was five years old. That place is Gatlinburg, Tennessee.

That's right. T. G. goes to a place in the state where he and his family live. Certainly, there are more exotic sounding spots. But T. G. goes to Gatlinburg for himself.

T. G. Sheppard

When T. G. gets to feeling troubled and frazzled from being on the road too long, he heads for his home away from home on top of Mt. Harrison. Every morning is special, because he can usually step out on his deck and look down on the clouds and mists covering the valley where most of Gatlinburg lies. When the sun's morning rays color the tops of the clouds a woolly gold, he says, "I feel like I'm walking out into heaven."

"There is something special about the air there. It smells cleaner, makes breathing more wonderful. It's hard to explain," T. G. told the *Sampler.* "But I can never get enough of that mountain air."

It's obvious the way he talks about this place that he'd like to go there as soon as we quit talking.

"The food tastes better there. And my morning coffee never smelled so good. Everything seems more special, and I can spend a short time on top of our mountain and get my days and nights straightened out and just be right with life again." T. G. paused a moment and said, "You know I was born and raised in this state, and there are many things I love about it, but I guess Gatlinburg is one of my very favorites, and a place I'd send my best friend."

Thanks, T. G.

Driving the Roads of Tennessee with Bobby and Hugh Lee

"Every year I drive 15,000 miles in Tennessee, and I reckon I've seen about everything," said Bobby Dias as he and Hugh Lee Quarles settled into the *Sampler* office and began talking about something they know a lot about—Tennessee highways. Bobby and Hugh Lee, Tennessee Department of Transportation employees, drive each state highway every year, checking the surface of roads. If anyone would know about scenic routes, rarely advertised sights, or just great places to take a Sunday afternoon drive, these good ol' boys are the folks to ask.

"Have you ever heard about the white squirrels in Kenton?" asked Bobby. "They's a lot of 'em. You can see 'em any time of the year," he reassured us.

"We thought that was a joke when we heard about it," we told Bobby.

"No, you can see 'em sitting up in those tree limbs. They're just snow white. You don't see 'em anywhere but down there. And they don't let any other squirrels live with 'em.

"Yeah, and what about the world's largest pecan tree at Natchez Trace State Park. It's bolted to hold it together. Boy, it's a big thing!"

He went on to tell us about Skullbone, Tennessee, also in the western part of our state, where a sign post has arrows indicating mileage to such faraway places as Brazil and Israel. "It's got signs pointing all over the world, and we see it ever' year. Sure glad we ain't got to drive the roads of Brazil," Bobby said. "And near

Skullbone, over at Dresden there's a place that has Martin birdhouses....Posts just as thick as they can stand, and on one post there may be five to six birdhouses. There ain't no telling how many, I bet there's a thousand."

"They're all different shapes, some of 'em real fancy like colonial houses," added Hugh Lee. "He can't even mow back there."

"We know they's some chickens in the state of Tennessee with hair on 'em, but we can't figure out where they're at."

"Chickens with hair?" we asked in astonishment.

"Yeah, with knobs on their heads; it just hangs off like human hair and it's on their legs and feet too."

"It looks like they got leggin's on," Hugh Lee pointed out. "They're just kinda woolly all over. They're really funny looking things."

As Bobby continued to look at the road map we had spread across the front of the desk, other places with strange sights come to mind. "Down out of Winchester, there used to be an ostrich farm. This man had a big ol' field, and these ostriches would be out in the pasture just like cattle. He raised 'em to sell their eggs. That fellow took us to his house one time, and he had an ostrich as tall as this ceiling."

Hugh Lee added, "You don't get behind an ostrich, because if it kicks you it could knock you 50 feet."

We asked how the man got the ostrich to the house.

"He told us he blindfolded it one night, and then the next morning led it to the house."

We wondered about the dangerous parts of their job. Over 16 years, surely there had been run-ins with unfriendly people, wrecks, and other such mishaps.

Bobby told us he was run over one time and stayed off the job "for almost three year. Another time I had a little run-in with a bear at Gatlinburg. He got between me and the car. I ran at him, and he took off. Then I got to the car, and the boy inside had the door locked on the car and wouldn't let me in! He was afraid to open the door! Then there were several times we've had road or bridge problems," Bobby remembered.

"Have you ever gotten over a bridge and had it wash away?" we asked.

"I've had one break through. We'd go off a road and couldn't go back up. The bridge would be out. We have dug our way out, taken rocks, and built a bridge. I've tried to jump 'em."

"Like on the 'Dukes of Hazzard'?"

"Yeah, like that. I made a small ramp, but I hit right in the middle of the little branch. Had to call someone to come get us out. All but the back wheels cleared. A state car is hard to jump a small creek with."

Bobby talked about many other things they'd experienced from one end of the state to the other. Covered bridges, springs with wonderful mountain water and, of course, good places to eat. "Hey, I wanted to tell you about this one place we ate at." Bobby laughed as he recalled it. "You go in there, it's got old wooden tables and long benches. This man comes out and says in a gruff voice, 'What do you want?' I say, 'What have you got? Just bring me some meat, beans, and taters.' Here

he comes, draggin' bowls out, pullin' his corn bread out of the oven in an old black skillet. 'Eat all you want, boys.' I said, 'Bring me some milk,' and he brings out milk in a quart jug. When I got ready to pay off, it was $1.40 or $1.80. I couldn't believe it the first time I ate in there."

Hugh Lee chimed in, "It's just an old log building painted green, and it's got cement between the logs that's painted white."

We asked, "Do you know the man's name?"

"No, he probably wouldn't tell you. You just have to let him do his thing. He didn't act like he did it for the money. It's rough. People sort of spit on the floor and carve on the seats."

Although this wasn't the type place Bobby and Hugh Lee would recommend we stop to eat, they did tell us of such wonderful eating places as Bozo's, Blue Bank, Rendezvous, and the Old Country Store. (We've written about all these in "Eatin' and Sleepin' Good.")

Bobby and Hugh Lee stayed with us a couple of hours, telling us of some sights we'd never heard of and other better-known stops listed in "Tours and Trails." So thanks, Hugh Lee and Bobby, for taking us on a Tennessee tour.

Hugh Lee and Bobby's Favorites

Prettiest scenes in the state: State 32 (US 25E) going across the mountain from Morristown to Tazewell has one of the best views. "You can see lakes, bridges that cross the river, and the valley...even over to Morristown. On top of the mountain they've got a viewer sitting right up there. You can see a bunch."

Hugh Lee and Bobby's favorite drive in the state is from Cleveland to Ducktown to Copperhill on State 40 (US 64). This is where the water flume is seen. It goes across Ocoee Wildlife Management Area.

State 28 going from Jamestown to Pall Mall. Pickett State Park in this area has a swinging bridge and many natural wonders.

Old State 68 going through Sweetwater.

State 8 from McMinnville to Dunlap going past Savage Gulf.

State 111, Cookeville to Spencer, has a lot of mountains and woods. You go by Calfkiller River, and it's a brand new road. "I understand the way that got its name, it would wash some cows away ever' time there came a flash flood."

State 1 (US 70) at Bon Air takes you to the top of the mountain where you can see for miles.

State 85 is a crooked road from Gainesboro to Livingston. Out of Livingston on top of the mountain, you can see Dale Hollow Lake miles away.

State 76 (US 79) around Dover goes across Kentucky Lake to Paris Landing State Park.

Hugh Lee, Bobby, and state car

The Great River Road is built on the levee beside the Mississippi River in West Tennessee.

State 9, outside of Newport where you cross the French Broad River.

Prettiest part of West Tennessee—Reelfoot Lake.

Prettiest part of East Tennessee—Johnson City and around Greeneville.

Prettiest part of Middle Tennessee—Cookeville, Sparta, and Celina, or anywhere around Center Hill and Dale Hollow lakes. "I love Dale Hollow, all those roads are good. Anytime you get to where you can see the lake, it's pretty."

Prettiest rivers—Buffalo in Perry County and the Ocoee in Polk County.

Favorite state park—Pickett State Park.

Chattanooga Area

Almost everyone in America has seen the barns or at least heard of them. You know, the ones with "See Rock City" painted on them. In the 1950s there were more than 800 barn signs in 18 states, from Canada to as far west as Texas. Chattanooga is the home of Rock City, but as the *Sampler* carries you through this city and the surrounding countryside, you will soon learn it's home to many other fascinating places as well.

It's easy to see why Chattanooga is called "The Scenic Center of the South" and "The City Next Door to Outdoors." Chickamauga Lake and Nickajack Lake offer fishing, boating, and other outdoor recreation. Hang gliding, white-water rafting, nature trails, and the state parks in this part of Tennessee provide abundant variety for both the avid and the not-so-avid outdoor lover.

The Ocoee Flume and The Tennessee Badlands outside of Ducktown are unique to this part of the state.

Lookout Mountain

In Chattanooga, several sites are located on **Lookout Mountain**. **Rock City Gardens** has 10 acres of trails that lead through landscaped gardens and deep crevices like Fat Man's Squeeze, under boulders like the 1,000-ton Balanced Rock, and over unusual formations such as Tortoise Shell Rock. **Lover's Leap** offers a panoramic view of seven states below. Always favorites with little ones are Fairyland Caverns and Mother Goose Village.

The Cravens House is halfway up Lookout Mountain. It served as headquarters for both the Union and Confederate armies during the Civil War. From there you can walk up to **Point Park** to enjoy the sweeping views of Chattanooga and the Tennessee River below. The name *Chattanooga* comes from an Indian word meaning "rock coming to a point." In the park Civil War cannons, winding trails, and the **Ochs Museum** offer something of interest for everyone.

Lookout Mountain is where the Battle Above the Clouds was fought in 1863. This area is now part of the huge **Chickamauga-Chattanooga National Military Park** which embraces 8,000 acres. Road tours, bicycle tours, and trails for horseback riding and hiking take you to the many historic spots dotting the fields. Park personnel provide scheduled talks and demonstrate actual firing of weapons from muzzleloaders of pioneer days—all at the Visitor Reception Center.

Any way you go up the mountain will be scenic, but be sure at some point to ride the **Incline Railway,** "America's most amazing mile." It's the world's steepest and safest incline.

Near the beginning of the Incline Railway is the **Confederama** which re-creates the movements of the mighty armies that battled at Chattanooga and Chickamauga. With tiny guns flashing in battle and miniature cannons puffing real smoke, there is a shot-by-shot explanation of this historic conflict. More than 5,000 toy soldiers show where the armies were located. This is the world's largest electronic miniature battlefield display of its kind.

When you come down the mountain, stop at **Ruby Falls.** This spectacular natural waterfall (145 feet) was named after the wife of the discoverer. At this stop you will see the highest underground waterfall open to the public, and the deepest commercial caverns in the United States. You descend via elevator to view the waterfall located 1,120 feet below the surface of Point Park.

In April each year there's a wildflower pilgrimage at **Reflection Riding,** a 300-acre botanical park and wildlife refuge at the base of Lookout Mountain. A 3-mile loop can be driven, or several trails have been opened for hikers. More than 1,000 trees, flowers, and shrubs have been identified and labeled.

At the entrance to Reflection Riding is the **Chattanooga Nature Center** which has displays relating to various types of animal life in Chattanooga. A hands-on learning experience involves close-up looks at snakes, insects, raccoons, and other animals. It's a favorite with the Chattanooga school children.

Lover's Leap at Lookout Mountain

An interesting legend is told about the Indian profile on Lookout Mountain which stands out in bold relief against the sky 1,200 feet above Reflection Riding. Here's how it goes: in the old days a great Indian chief lay dying in Lookout Valley. He was the last member of a once-powerful tribe. The old chief regretted that there was no one to mourn for him after his death, that no one would ever know he had lived. He prayed to his gods for a token, a sign that he and his tribe should not perish utterly but in some way be remembered in days to come.

As he prayed, a great storm swept up the valley, shaking the mountain and throwing down huge rocks. The next day the dying chief looked up and saw on the side of the mountain his own likeness carved from rock. He died content, knowing that he would not be forgotten as long as his image looked out over the valley.

When the Cherokees came to this section of the country in later times, it was said that they often took food to the base of the stone profile and eventually called it *do-da nun-yu,* or "Father Rock," even though the old chief had not been a Cherokee.

Also in Chattanooga

Any machairologist will enjoy visiting the *National Knife Museum,* which is the headquarters for the 16,000-member National Knife Collectors Association. Some of the knives on display include an oyster shucker's knife with an attachment that looks like brass knuckles; novelty knives decorated with slogans such as "Pepsi Cola 5 ¢ "; and knives with handles of bone, stag, wood, metal, plastic, ivory, or mother of pearl. (By the way, a machairologist is a knife collector.)

Hunter Museum of Art is perched on a 90-feet-high bluff that overlooks the Tennessee River. The museum contains eighteenth- and nineteenth-century American art. The *Houston Museum* has one of the largest collections of glassware in the United States. Given to the city by Anna Safley Houston, the pitchers hanging from the ceiling are of every conceivable design, texture, and color.

The Tennessee Valley Railroad and Museum is located on 40 acres and includes several miles of track, four railroad bridges, and a historic pre-Civil War tunnel. The tunnel goes through Missionary Ridge which played a prominent role in the Civil War battle for Chattanooga. It's a fun place where passenger trains still run, steam locomotives still hiss and spout soot and smoke, and conductors in black coats still summon passengers with cries of "All aboard." A 6-mile round trip is part of the museum operation.

In the fall, the *Autumn Leaf Special* between Chattanooga and Crossville, Tennessee, leaves from here. You can dine southern-style on the train and enjoy seeing the countryside the way passengers did in the early 1900s when the railroad was *the* way to travel. It's a trip to remember. Trips in the spring are to destinations such as Huntsville, Atlanta, Nashville, and Oak Ridge.

Visit the namesake that put Chattanooga on the map—*The Chattanooga Choo-Choo.* There are five unique restaurants: The Palm Terrace, Grand Dome, The Trolley Cafe, Le Grand Diner, and The Station House. The Grand Dome dining room is thought to be the world's highest free-standing dome.

The 30-acre Choo-Choo Complex offers a variety of things to see. Some turn-of-the-century shops include the Depot Gift Shop, the Southern Bell Shop, and many more. Gardens are perfectly landscaped, and in the evening a lamplighter lights each of the 40 gas torches that ring the gardens.

Of course a real "Chattanooga Choo-Choo," the world's largest H. O. Gauge Model Railroad Exhibit, and two authentic antique trolley cars that shuttle passengers throughout the Choo-Choo complex are all there. Passenger train cars with 48 rooms are now restored as unique sleepers. The 325-room Hilton Hotel designed to carry out the train motif is also part of the complex. (See "Eatin' and Sleepin' Good.")

Other places of interest in Chattanooga are the National Cemetery, Confederate Cemetery, and Harris Swift Museum of Religious Art.

Recommended as a Sunday afternoon outing is a drive along Tennessee's first official "scenic highway" (State 4l) as it parallels the Grand Canyon of the Tennessee River. Considered one of the five most beautiful canyons in the nation, it begins a few miles west of Chattanooga. The annual Fall Color Cruise through the canyon attracts boaters and auto travelers by the thousands. It takes place during the last two weekends in October. All types of boats, from small speedboats to cabin cruisers to houseboats, sail along the river enjoying the brilliant fall colors. (Write Visitors Bureau for information.)

For another river-cruising experience, board the new 500-passenger riverboat, the *Southern Belle.* It's docked at Ross's Landing in downtown Chattanooga.

Raccoon Mountain

In January, TVA's Pumped Storage Reservoir on Raccoon Mountain is a wonderful location for sighting eagles. At the *Raccoon Mountain Pumped Storage Project,* an elevator takes visitors over 1,100 feet down inside the mountain to view the giant generators and turbines. The 230-feet-high dam at Raccoon Mountain is the largest rock-filled dam ever constructed by TVA.

Also on Raccoon Mountain are the *Alpine Slide,* which offers a view of Lookout Mountain; *Sky Ride,* the nation's only hang-gliding simulator; three-quarter-scale *Grand Prix Race Cars,* where you can race to beat the clock; and *Raccoon Mountain Caverns,* filled with interesting formations.

A "castle" atop Lookout Mountain always arouses everyone's curiosity. It's Covenant College, and visitors are welcome at this private college. A nationally known hang-gliding site is at *McCarthy's Bluff.* (See "Outdoors.")

Sequatchie Valley

West of Chattanooga is the Sequatchie Valley, which is sixty miles long and about 5 miles wide. With the valley's craggy mountains and forests on both sides, State 27 goes up to *Ketner's Mill.* For four generations, the Ketners have operated the picturesque waterpowered grist mill on the banks of the Big Sequatchie River in Marion County.

Ketner's is the only remaining continuously operating waterpowered grist mill in the area. The millstone, over 100 years old, must be sharpened often. Unlike modern roller mills which crush the grain, the millstone slices the grain, producing a unique texture and flavor. Clyde Ketner is there, every day, adjusting the speed of the turbines or checking the texture of the corn in the hopper.

Clyde also operates an extremely rare wool carding machine in the back of the mill. It was built before 1850 and is of solid cherry with brass bearings. A carding machine combs and stretches raw wool to ready it for spinning.

The Ketner's Mill Fair is held each October, and craftsmen of this region display their wares then. (See "Fun Times.")

Several roads enter the Sequatchie Valley from neighboring small towns, and all offer panoramic views of the valley below. State 30 from Pikeville to Mount Crest leads to one of Tennessee's favorite state parks, *Fall Creek Falls State Park.* It's the state's second largest and boasts of having the highest waterfall east of the Rocky Mountains. (See "Outdoors.")

Dayton

Rhea County Courthouse in Dayton, north of Chattanooga, was the site of the famous Scopes Monkey Trial in 1925. It all began when a Dayton high-school teacher named Scopes was accused of teaching the Darwinian theory of evolution. This was in violation of a Tennessee statute which made it unlawful to teach any theory that denied the story of divine creation of man as taught in the Bible. The two legal giants William Jennings Bryan and Clarence Darrow met in battle in the three-story, red brick Rhea County Courthouse.

This trial was one of the nation's first major "media" events; it was broadcast live on a Chicago radio station, and reporters from newspapers everywhere crowded the courtroom of this tiny Tennessee community. Loudspeakers were set up on the courthouse lawn for those who could not jam into the courtroom. The second floor of the courthouse where the trial was held has been restored and opened to visitors. A museum containing artifacts and photographs of the trial as well as actual newsreel footage is in the basement of the building.

Two toll ferries cross the Tennessee River from Dayton. Blythe's Ferry is located where State 60 disappears into the river and takes you to Cleveland. The Washington Ferry, where State 30 meets the Tennessee, goes over to Decatur.

Athens

In Athens, the *McMinn County Living History Museum* is housed on the campus of Tennessee Wesleyan College in the Old College Building. The museum's diverse collection reflects life in this region from the time of the Cherokee Nation to the Great Depression.

Blockhouse at Fort Marr on the Trail of Tears

Cleveland

The *Red Clay State Historic Area,* south of Cleveland, was the final council ground of the eastern Cherokee Nation. You can see a historical replica of the council house and an Indian farm as well as a museum featuring a film. The spring-fed pool which originally attracted the Indians to this area is still flowing as pure and abundant as it was hundreds of years ago.

The *Trail of Tears Historic Route* begins at Red Clay. In 1838 the United States government uprooted 13,000 Cherokees from their native land and forcibly exiled them to Oklahoma Territory. This cross-country march, much of it during midwinter, was an exodus of sorrow and despair—a "trail of tears." This trail continues from Red Clay 260 miles across Middle Tennessee and ends in Guthrie, Kentucky.

Also near Cleveland, off US 64E, is a *Primitive Settlement.* This collection of nineteenth-century log cabins has been restored and furnished with household and farming items used by early Americans. These cabins were gathered from their original locations, moved to this site, and restored. The oldest is 150 years old.

Ducktown Area

Driving from Cleveland to Ducktown to Copperhill (State 40; US 64) you can view the *Ocoee Flume.* The wooden flume was originally built in 1912 by the East Tennessee Power Company. It's the largest such structure known to exist in the country and certainly one of the oldest. This European invention is also known as a siphon spillway.

The 5-mile-long, 11- by 14-feet flume was shut down in 1976 by the Tennessee Valley Authority (TVA) so it could be completely rebuilt, but it is now open again. The Ocoee can function as a recreational waterway, because TVA's flume management controls the amount of water that flows into it at certain times of the day. At some stretches along the highway (east of the powerhouse about 1 1/2 miles), an optical illusion makes it look like the water in the flume is running uphill.

The Ocoee has been called the most popular white-water river in the South. Slingshot, Tablesaw, Hell's Hole, and Osterizer are the names of a few of the rapids you can encounter if you're a white-water enthusiast.

The *Tennessee Badlands* are a most unusual area of Tennessee. Along US 64E is a valley reminiscent of the deserts of the western states or the badlands of South Dakota. The desertlike landscape of Tennessee's Copper Basin was not created by nature but by man when extensive copper mining took place there in the l840s. It's said that from space the basin's 56 square miles of barren hills make it one of the few identifiable landmarks inland from the coast. The *Ducktown Museum* has historic photos of the men and the work they did in this area.

Scenic vistas, Civil War remembrances, and the excitement offered by the Incline, riverboats, or railroad travels make the Chattanooga area a vacation destination for the entire family to enjoy.

DIRECTORY:

Chattanooga: Chattanooga Area Convention and Visitors Bureau, Civic Forum, 1001 Market Street, 37402; toll-free (in Tennessee) (800) 338-3999, (out of state) (800) 322-3344. Information on most of the places discussed here can be obtained from this address. Be sure to ask for the brochure telling about the Nickajack Lake-Chattanooga Scenic Loop. This drive will take you past many of the stops mentioned here. Rock City Gardens, (404) 820-2531. Cravens House, (615) 821-6161. Incline Railway, (615) 629-1473. Confederama, 3742 Tennessee Avenue; (615) 821-2812. Ruby Falls, Route 148; (615) 821-2544. Reflection Riding, The Chattanooga Nature Center, Route 4, Garden Road, 37409; (615) 821-1160. National Knife Museum, 7201 Shallowford Road; (615) 892-5007. Hunter Museum of Art, 10 Bluff View; (615) 267-0968. Houston Museum, 201 High Street; (615) 267-7176. Tennessee Valley Railroad and Museum, 4119 Cromwell Road, 37421; (615) 894-8028. Chattanooga Choo-Choo, 1400 Market, 37402; (615) 266-5000. Raccoon Mountain Pumped Storage Project, 4328 Cummings Highway, (615) 821-9403. Chickamauga and Chattanooga National Military Park, Ft. Oglethorpe, GA 30741; (404) 866-9241.

Dayton: Dayton Chamber of Commerce, 305 East Main Avenue 3732l, (615) 775-0361.

Athens: Athens Area Chamber of Commerce, 13 North Jackson Street, 37303; (615) 745-0334. McMinn County Living Heritage Museum, P.O. Box 889, 37303; (615) 745-0329.

Cleveland: Cleveland-Bradley County Chamber of Commerce, P.O. Box 2275, 37311; (615) 472-6587. Red Clay State Historic Area, Route 6, Box 734, Cleveland, TN 37311; (615) 472-2627. Trail of Tears, for map contact Division of Planning and Development, TN Conservation Dept., 2611 West End Avenue, Nashville, TN 37203. Primitive Settlement, Route 7, Box 236, Cleveland, TN 37311; (615) 476-5096.

Also, for many places mentioned in the article, contact Tennessee Department of Tourist Development, P.O. Box 23170, Nashville, TN 37202; (615) 741-2158.

Marking Tennessee's Past

Anyone who drives the highways of Tennessee sees the gray metal markers on the roadside. These historical markers can teach you a lot about Tennessee history. More than 1,200 of them have been erected by the Tennessee Historical Commission.

The stories they tell are often about the famous people or happenings of Tennessee but sometimes about the not-so-famous, the notorious, and the hilarious. They cover stories of Indian raids, Civil War skirmishes, and early settlements.

A *Guide to Historical Markers* is published by the Tennessee Historical Commission. Write them at 701

Broadway, Nashville, TN 37203; (615) 742-6716. The $2.50 guide has a good index for easy reference and lists both locations and contents of the markers.

For a free color brochure from the state, highlighting historic sites in Tennessee, contact: Tennessee Tourism Development, P.O. Box 23170, Nashville, TN 37202; (615) 741-2158. Information on location, fees, dates open, and historical significance is included.

For information on Tennessee's 13 historic homes maintained by the Association for the Preservation of Tennessee Antiquities (APTA), write: APTA, 110 Leake Avenue, Nashville, TN 37205. These homes are beautifully restored and opened regularly to the public.

Nashville Area

Country music is certain to come to mind when you think of Nashville. It's true that this "Home of the Grand Ole Opry" is synonymous with country music. Yet the capital city of Tennessee proudly boasts of being the "Athens of the South" as well as the home of country music. The massive Parthenon in Centennial Park and many colleges and universities throughout the city have earned Nashville this appropriate title.

Historic sites such as the Hermitage, Andy Jackson's home; the sophisticated Performing Arts Center where operas and Broadway plays are presented; and excellent museums such as the Tennessee State Museum offer evidence that there *is* life beyond country music in Nashville, although it proudly waves the banner "Music City USA."

You've already read about everything you ever wanted to know about Opryland in the "Music" section of the *Sampler.* The Music Row tour and ways to see the stars' homes are featured below. Then the *Sampler* invites you to come on along as we take you to the other places in and around Nashville that make it a fun place to visit.

A Music Row Tour

Probably the most excitement in Nashville is generated by the activities on the world-famous Music Row, less than 1 mile from downtown. Located between Sixteenth and Seventeenth Avenues, the area gets its name by being the home of a majority of the nation's recording houses; RCA, MCA, CBS, Monument, Polygram, Tree International, Capitol, and United Artist all have offices here. It is also the home of ASCAP, BMI, and the Country Music Foundation.

A must on everybody's list is The Country Music Hall of Fame, recently declared America's "Favorite Music Museum." The Hall of Fame includes not only great memorabilia but also a special exhibit on country music in the movies. Before leaving, be sure to take the tour of RCA Studio B, where you can see an actual recording studio in action.

Right across the street from the Hall of Fame is Barbara Mandrell's new museum, Barbara Mandrell Country. This museum is impressive for several reasons, but one of them is that Barbara played a large part in its development. Here you can see films of her musical career and one of her Rolls Royces, and you can even sign her autograph book.

You've always wanted to record a country music song? Go downstairs at Barbara Mandrell's and visit Ted and Barbara McCraken at Recording America. The McCrackens will help you do what many people dream of doing, recording their own country music hit single. They'll show you how simple it is, and you get to keep the copy of your private masterpiece all for well under $10.

Right next door to Barbara Mandrell's is Music Row's newest addition, the Minnie Pearl Museum which features highly personalized touches from both Minnie and

Minnie Pearl's Museum

her husband, Henry. In fact, one of the great things about this museum is that Minnie makes a special effort to be there whenever possible to greet her fans. Across the street from Minnie's and Barbara's is a bevy of shops and museums including the Guinness World Records Museum, the Country Music Wax Museum, George Jones's Car Collectors Museum, and Waylon Jenning's Museum. Once you get to Music Row you can park and easily walk from shop to shop.

Just about 10 miles north of Music City in Hendersonville, several country music stars have made their homes. The House of Cash, a colonial-style building, includes the Johnny Cash Museum. The highlight of any visitor's trip north of Nashville, though, will be a stop at the Music Village Complex. This complex features top-name country concerts with the likes of Conway Twitty, Loretta Lynn, and Ronnie Milsap on a regular basis from April till October. Also here are the Marty Robbins and Ferlin Husky Museums.

Be sure and see Twitty City. There is truly nothing else like this in the country. The entire Twitty City portion of Music Village includes Conway's museum, his gift shop, and his house. Conway's Christmas activities include turning his city into a winter wonderland full of Christmas lights, snow, reindeer, and other seasonal decorations. He always wishes everyone a "Merry Twismas."

Other fine attractions include the Jim Reeves Museum at 5007 Gallatin Road, Bill Monroe's Bluegrass Hall of Fame and Museum, Boots Randolph's Nightclub in the famous Printer's Alley, and The Ryman Auditorium in downtown Nashville.

Andrew Smith encourages your group to take an *Enjoy Nashville* package tour (526 Hickory View Dr., 37211; [615] 333-1344). You can hear about some of the area's great folklore from courteous tour directors while driving by some of Nashville's most famous residences. These include Dolly Parton, Waylon Jennings, Eddy Arnold, Porter Wagoner, Ronnie Milsap, Kitty Wells, Roy Acuff, Johnny Cash, and Hank Snow.

Other tour agencies:

Country & Western Roundup Tours, 2416 Music Valley Drive, Nashville, TN 37214; (615) 883-5555.

Grand Ole Opry Tours, 2100 Opryland Drive, Nashville, TN 37214; (615) 889-9490.

Gray Line of Nashville, 501 Broadway, Nashville, TN 37203; (615) 244-7330.

Johnny Walker Tours, 97 Wallace Road, Nashville, TN 37211; (615) 834-8585.

Smile-A-While Tours (groups only), P. O. Box 15957, Nashville, TN 37215; (615) 228-6239.

Stardust Tours, P. O. Box 120396, 1504 Demonbreun, Nashville, TN 37203; (615) 244-2335.

Our thanks go to Andrew Smith of Enjoy Nashville Tours for letting us know about what to see and do on Music Row and at the other country music sights in and around Nashville.

A SAMPLER

$SPECIAL$

The First Jet Tour for Country Music's Super-rich, Super Fans

Presented by Black and Gold Tours,
Nashville, Tennessee

Have you listened to country music and loved it since you were a child? Are you one of those fans who started out driving a 1959 Chevy pickup but now drive a Silver Shadow Rolls Royce? Have you made it big, and yet still love country music? Well, now, Black and Gold Tours, Inc., has put together a tour for *you.*

Does it include seats on the stage of the Grand Ole Opry? NO! Will you be driven by the stars' homes in a 1982 custom Ford van? NO! Are you going to stop at the Country Music Hall of Fame? NO! "Certainly not," says Winston Morton, Jr. (Vanderbilt, B.A.,'71; Princeton Law School, '76), owner and originator of Black and Gold Tours.

You will be picked up at the Nashville airport in a fully restored 1967 Cadillac, first owned by Elvis Presley. Your chauffeur will be one of Elvis's original drivers, having driven for the King from 1968 to 1970. Thomas, although Elvis called him by his given name, Tommy Lee, will tell you informative and often exciting stories of his life with the King.

You will be dropped off at your room in the home of a country music star. You may find yourself bunking in with Jerry Reed's family or at Ronnie Milsap's place by the governor's mansion. You may see our present governor, Lamar Alexander and his exceptionally delightful wife, Honey, jogging near Ronnie's home. You may stay with Webb Pierce; there you can take a moonlight dip in his guitar-shaped pool. You'll enjoy a quiet evening with "your" star. Black and Gold promises that the country music star you'll be staying with will not be on the road playing concerts. But you better rest up because the car will be back the next day at 5:30 A.M. to take you to where the jet is parked.

Jet? Yes! Black and Gold Tours took the *Sampler* on a two-hour tour of their 727 customized tour jet. Black and Gold spared no expense on the interior of the tastefully outfitted plane. They used one of Tennessee's most famous interior decorators, Rodney Treveckian. The interior is done in specially imported birchwood from Holland, with calf leather and cream-colored suede. Cool smells of leather mingle with the scents of your favorite colognes, especially collected for your pleasure by your touring hostess, Terri Roberson. For three summers Terri had a lead part in one of the most popular Opryland musicals ever, "I Hear America Singing."

Black and Gold's extremely sophisticated stereo sound system was installed by John and Patti Thompson, who recently came to Middle Tennessee from England where they've installed stereo systems for The Beatles, Boy George, and Sting of Police. For an extra $12,000, shared by the whole tour group, B and G can provide a live band, just a hair away from being real stars, which will play a total of 40 sets of original music during the length of your 10-day tour. Four private, sound-proofed phone booths are at your disposal if a business emergency should arise during this time.

Since all the clients are usually heavily insured (one had a whole life policy for $50 million on him and $12 million on one of his Arabian stallions), they usually enjoy meeting the pilot, B. T. Hyatt. He's one of aviation's most experienced pilots and a character from the best-selling book, *The Right Stuff*. B. T.'s flown well over one million miles, and he gave up his job with a commercial airline because he gets to do more than just fly as a part of his duties with B and G. He also sings the Top 50 greatest country music hits while in flight for the guests' listening pleasure. B. T. never sings while landing, however. Also on board will be 10 flight attendants, 2 copilots, your host, Winston Morton, Jr., and your special chef. Trained at The Tower in Paris, Michael will be cooking highly guarded recipes collected by B and G that consist of the stars' favorite foods. One exciting meal is greens and quiche, and an especially thrilling breakfast consists of corn bread, fertilized eggs, peanut-butter toast, and a chilled diet Pepsi.

Where is the tour going to go? After all, how many 10-day tours cost $17,500 (not including tips, spending money for the flying casino, and cash for souvenir buying)? Costs may be higher based on full occupancy of the jet, which holds 20 paying tourists.

Leaving Nashville you'll head for Hank Williams's home town deep in the heart of Dixie, in "sweet home" Alabama. Once on the ground you'll be whisked away to the modest home where Hank was born. Then on to Lone Pine Elementary School where he first learned how to count past 20. From there it's a leisurely drive to the red-dirt road just past the Singing Creek Community where Hank went to church and performed his first songs.

You think this seems too good to be true? Well, what will you say when you land in the Delta of Mississpppi, just 6 miles from the home of country music's beloved Charley Pride? As you flew over Alabama and Mississippi you were treated to specially recorded tapes of his 20 greatest hits. You'll be picked up in 10 Pontiacs and driven by 10 of Charley's childhood buddies and cousins to the part of town where he was raised. You'll visit the little country store at the edge of this predominantly black commu-

nity, owned by Bill Luther, city champion bowler, where Charley heard his first country music playing on Bill's radio.

Then you'll head over to VFW Lodge #1287, where Charley played before his first white audience. Many of them were amazed that a black man could sing such good country. On the cinderblock walls of the lodge are a prized collection of pictures and framed newspaper clippings of this Mississippi Delta town's most famous native, Charley Pride.

You'll eat a special soul-country meal prepared by Charley's aunt, Ophelia, before leaving for a stop at Conway's and Tammy's in northern Mississippi. Conway has been kind enough to allow B and G to print limited edition sweatshirts with "Twitty City" printed in a specially prepared silver ink, highlighted with real gold thread stiching.

After the Mississippi experience, you'll fly to Texas for three stops, then touch down for a few moments in Colorado to visit John Denver and his newly opened Whale Museum. Then it's on to California, with brief stops on the way home in Oklahoma and Arkansas.

The folks at Black and Gold would love to tell you more, but they wouldn't want to spoil the surprises they have in store for you. So if you're a Super Fan of that original American form of music, country, beloved around the world, call them for a lavishly illustrated brochure at 1-800-The *Sampler*'s Just Kidding.

P.S. Stay tuned for the soon-to-be-available tours especially for the fans of punk, bluegrass, jazz fusion, church choir conventions, and The Bee Gees.

Nashville Historic Residences

In Nashville (Davidson County) there are several famous historic homes. The **Hermitage,** with its massive white columns, was the home of President Andrew Jackson and his beloved wife Rachel. It houses countless personal belongings of the Jacksons from jewels and swords to rifles and carriages. The tomb of Rachel and Andy Jackson rests in the corner of the old-fashioned garden.

Travellers' Rest was the home of Judge John Overton, who made many contributions to the early development of Tennessee. Andy Jackson and Sam Houston were frequent guests in the judge's parlor, and as its name suggests, its doors were always open to weary travelers.

The Belle Meade section of Nashville is one of the most beautiful and affluent neighborhoods in America. The drive along Belle Meade Boulevard and adjoining streets such as Tyne Drive and Harding Place features homes that are outstanding in architecture and landscaped to perfection.

When you're in this part of Davidson County, visit the **Belle Meade Mansion,** once the mansion house of the 5,300-acre plantation for which this section of Nashville is named. World famous as a Thoroughbred breeding farm, its most famous horse was Iroquois. The carriage

Carriage House at Belle Meade Mansion

house and stable, which cover almost an acre, house some of the finest carriages in the South. In May the Iroquois Memorial Steeplechase draws choice Thoroughbred horses from around the world.

Cheekwood, Tennessee's Botanical Gardens and Fine Arts Center, is nearby. This 60-room Georgian mansion houses an outstanding art collection, and the Botanic Hall features horticultural exhibits. In December the famous Trees of Christmas display draws people from across the state to view exquisitely decorated Christmas trees.

Near Cheekwood you'll enjoy driving through **Percy Warner** and **Edwin Warner parks.** Get out of your car and walk around or simply sit and enjoy the beautiful vista from the top of the park. Since you'll be just down the road from the Loveless Cafe, stop in and eat some of the best country ham and biscuits anywhere. (See "Eatin' and Sleepin' Good.")

The **Executive Residence,** where the governor and his family reside, is open to the public Tuesday and Thursday mornings from 9:00 A.M. to 11:00 A.M. You don't have to make reservations unless there is a large group.

Downtown Nashville

Downtown Nashville has become an interesting place to walk around and view the results of the restoration of many historic buildings. On Second Avenue, formerly a rundown warehouse district, restaurants, shops, private residences, galleries, apartments, and offices are now at home in the renovated buildings which are detailed with outstanding Victorian architecture. The Market Street Festival (held here the first weekend in October) gives festival goers a chance to tour many offices and apartments which are not usually open to the public. Several have received architectural awards for excellence.

More activities are being held along the Cumberland River thanks to the revitalization of the downtown district. **Riverfront Park** on the banks of the river offers an ideal place for picnicking and lazily watching the river traffic pass by. During summer months free band concerts feature jazz, Top 40 hits, and big band music. The Fourth of July Celebration has become a popular event at Riverfront Park.

The **Belle Carol Company** has two riverboats for taking scenic tours along the Cumberland River. The *Music City Queen* and the *Captain Ann* can be boarded at First Avenue at Broadway and at the end of McGavock Pike West near Opryland. Prime rib or a southern-style buffet are dinner selections, and live entertainment nightly features country music and Top 40 hits. Opryland's *General Jackson* is the newest spectacular addition to Nashville's river traffic. (See "Music.")

A helpful brochure called *Downtown Nashville Art and Architecture* lists three walking tours of downtown Nashville (see ordering information at end of article). It tells the history of **Fort Nashborough,** a replica of the fort where Nashville began in 1780. The multistoried *Life and Casualty Tower* has an observation deck from which you can get a bird's-eye view of Nashville.

The two-tiered shopping arcade connecting Fourth and Fifth Avenues was inspired by one in Milan, Italy. This turn-of-the-century structure houses 52 businesses, from a button shop to an umbrella repair shop, and it is one of only a handful left in America. The *Ryman Auditorium* was from 1943 to 1974 the home of the Grand Ole Opry and during those years was called the Grand Ole Opry House. First Presbyterian Church is in Egyptian revival style and features an elaborate interior.

Another part of downtown filled with much of Nashville's history is the Capitol Hill area. The *Tennessee State Capitol* offers free tours on the hour. It's one of the most highly regarded Greek-revival-style buildings in the nation and is the second oldest working capitol in the United States, completed in 1859. The designer, William Strickland, chose to be buried in one of the walls. In late May the Summer Lights Festival, which benefits the Nashville Symphony, is held on the Legislative Plaza of the Capitol. (See "Fun Times.")

The *Tennessee State Museum* is housed in the James K. Polk Building, one of Nashville's newest and most modern. The museum displays more than 5,000 historic objects. (See "Civil War.") The *Tennessee Performing Arts Center* (TPAC), also in this building, offers Broadway plays, operas, concerts, and other excellent presentations throughout the year.

The elegant *Hermitage Hotel* is in this part of the city and is worth stopping to see. (See "Eatin' and Sleepin' Good.") The stained-glass skylight in the lobby area is breathtaking. The Hermitage Dining Room is one of Nashville's premier restaurants.

You may want to just drive by some of the old buildings on Broadway between Tenth and Seventh avenues. Union Station is one of Nashville's most visible landmarks. It served as an L & N railroad station and is a fine example of the Romanesque style of building. Christ Episcopal Church, the U.S.Customs House, and Hume Fogg High School also feature Victorian Gothic detail and make Nashvillians proud that historic preservation is alive and well in our city.

In downtown Nashville, *Printer's Alley* was the home of nineteenth-century saloons which were gathering places for the workers in the printing industry centered there. The printers later moved, but the name of their trade remained. Ten clubs and restaurants are now located there.

Tennesseans Are Dirt Rich

Tennessee agriculture ranges from the farming practices of 100 years ago still in use by the Mennonites and Amish to high-tech operations such as Spring Creek Ranch, which uses embryo transfer in producing high-grade Brangus cattle in Collierville, Tennessee.

A SAMPLER
·····*Exclusive*·····
John Seigenthaler

J ohn Seigenthaler is one of thousands of Tennesseans having a great impact on our world. In years past, John was an administrative aide to Robert Kennedy when Kennedy was United States Attorney General.

John now maintains two residences, one in Nashville where he is publisher and editor of the *Tennessean* newspaper and one in Washington, D.C., where he serves as editorial director of *USA Today.*

We asked John to tell us what makes Tennessee, and particularly Nashville, special to him. We wanted to know where he likes to take his friends and business acquaintances for dinner.

For "northern Italian cuisine as good as anywhere in the U.S.A." John likes to dine at Mario's on West End Avenue. "The food is authentic, and the service is outstanding," he says. His good friend Mario Ferrari is a well-known Nashville restauranteur and a real character.

John feels the Hermitage Hotel Dining Room reflects the character of the city. "Its desserts are particularly traditional Nashville." The Loveless Cafe (see food section) is great for "country" cooking. Opryland Hotel's fabulous conservatory is another of John's favorite spots to relax.

What are John's favorite books about Tennessee? One is Robert V. Remini's three-volume work on Andrew Jackson. "This book absolutely flows; it's better than all the other books on Jackson. Remini explains why Tennessee was so important to this country in its formative years.

"Absolutely indispensable is *I'll Take My Stand,* a retrospect by Vanderbilt's 'fugitive' writers who were in Nashville in the twenties. These included John Crowe Ransom, Robert Penn Warren, Donald Davidson, and Andrew Nelson Lytle."

Will D. Campbell's *Brother to a Dragonfly* is a great book about the Civil Rights Movement. John also recommends *The Nashville Storyteller* and *The Laughing Man of Woodmont Cave* by Tom T. Hall, a unique country music storyteller.

Half of John's week is spent in Washington and the other half in Nashville. "Washington may be the most beautiful city in the country, but there's an element of unreality because so much revolves around the government. It's difficult not to discuss the government at breakfast, lunch, and dinner. You're talking about 'what's the President going to do?' You're much less likely to talk about family and home.

"But in Nashville, there's a more comfortable—more 'real' feeling. It's home. You can still get anywhere around town and back home without feeling like you've been through an all-day ordeal.

"Tennessee is more than the place I was born," John said, with emotion. "It's the place I choose to live."

Museums and Galleries

Several excellent museums in Nashville should not be missed. The **Cumberland Museum and Science Center** has an excellent planetarium and laservision program in addition to animal exhibits and displays of Indian artifacts, fossils, and more.

The **Museum of Tobacco Art and History** houses such unusual pieces as a meerschaum "skull" pipe and pipes of clay, deer horn, glass, and porcelain. Cigars, cigarette containers, Chinese snuff bottles, peace pipes, and even a 6-feet-tall cigar store Indian chief can be found at this museum honoring one of Tennessee's biggest cash crops—tobacco.

The **Upper Room Chapel and Museum** features a woodcarved copy of Leonardo Da Vinci's *Last Supper,* and a stained glass window depicts events of Pentecost. In this same area of town is the **Vanderbilt University Art Gallery.**

The **Parthenon** and **Centennial Park** are wonderful places to visit. The Parthenon is the only full-scale exact replica of the original Greek temple. It was built originally of frame and stucco in 1897 for the Tennessee State Centennial Exposition but later burned. The present concrete structure was completed in 1931, and now it houses an art gallery. Ice Centennial is an indoor ice skating rink that is open year-round except in August.

The **Conservatory** at the Opryland Hotel is a 2-acre garden under glass. Its stone walkways, flowing streams, waterfalls, San Francisco-style street lights, and 8,000 plants, are all covered by a one-acre ceiling of glass that is 150 feet high. Rhett's is a southern-themed restaurant located in the Conservatory, and the adjacent lounge, Jack Daniel's Saloon, is decorated with many pieces of memorabilia from the historic Lynchburg distillery for which it is named. (See "Eatin' and Sleepin' Good.")

The **Tennessee Agricultural Museum** at Ellington Agricultural Center has exhibits showing the history of farming in Tennessee and displaying tools, implements, and other farming-related equipment.

For lots of information and good feature articles about the city, its people, and attractions, pick up a copy of *Nashville Magazine* at any local newsstand.

Sumner County

Sumner County, north of Nashville, has several outstanding historic houses. Three-story gray-stoned **Cragfont,** near Gallatin, was built by General James Winchester in the late 1700s. Winchester brought stonemasons and ship carpenters 700 miles from his native Maryland to build this house. **Wynnewood** served as a stagecoach inn in the early 1800s, and it is probably the

largest log structure ever erected in Tennessee. **Trousdale Place,** built around 1813, is a two-story brick house near Gallatin's public square, and it was the home of Governor William Trousdale.

In Hendersonville is **Rock Castle** which took 12 years to build because the Indians kept killing the workmen. A secret room behind a panel in the attic was used to hide from the Indians.

Jamestown to McMinnville

Seven miles from Jamestown (Fentress County) is the **Alvin C. York Grist Mill and Park.** Sergeant Alvin York of this area was described as "the greatest soldier of the war" (WWI). He operated the grist mill located here in his later years. Nearby are scenic **Pickett State Park** (see "Outdoors") and a wonderful restaurant, Beggar's Castle (see "Eatin' and Sleepin' Good"). Byrdstown, the birthplace of Cordell Hull who was the secretary of state under Franklin D. Roosevelt, is in Pickett County. In nearby Overton County are Standing Stone State Park and beautiful Dale Hollow Lake.

Dale Hollow Lake and Center Hill Lake, in Dekalb County, are often considered to be the two most beautiful lakes in Tennessee. Fishing, boating, skiing, camping, or just enjoying scenic vistas are all favorite activities here. (See "Outdoors.") In nearby McMinnville (Warren County) are the **Cumberland Caverns,** 200 feet beneath the Tennessee mountains.

Murfreesboro

The best-known residence in Murfreesboro is the **Oaklands Mansion.** The original two-story cabin faced the grove of tall oaks for which the plantation was named. It was alternately occupied by Southern and Northern forces during the Civil War. (See "Civil War.") **Cannonsburgh** is a reconstructed pioneer village which has replicas of houses, churches, stores, and other buildings from yesteryear. Cannonsburgh was the original name of the present city of Murfreesboro. Other remembrances of southern life are a cotton gin, a chapel, a blacksmith shop, a waterpowered grist mill, and a one-room schoolhouse.

The **Stones River National Battlefield and Cemetery** in Murfreesboro is a must for anyone interested in the Civil War. (See "Civil War.") For the more adventurous who want to see the county by bicycle, an excellent bicycle touring map and brochure direct you to picturesque Readyville Mill, Stones River, the site of the geographic center of Tennessee, show barns, and the Sam Davis Home (see information at end of section for address).

In nearby Smyrna the **Sam Davis Home** is the home of the "boy hero of the Confederacy." Young Davis was hanged as a spy by the Union Army when he refused to reveal the source of the accurate information on Federal troop movement discovered under his saddle and in his boots. (See "Civil War.")

Franklin

Williamson County, south of Nashville, boasts of *Franklin,* a quaint little town proud of its heritage. This community has gone to great lengths to preserve and restore many private homes, the downtown Main Street, and numerous historic buildings. The entire downtown section of Franklin is on the National Register of Historic Places.

The **Carter House,** which still has bullet holes in its walls, was in the center of fighting in the Battle of Franklin. **Carnton Mansion** saw the five bodies of the Confederate generals who were killed in the Battle of Franklin lying side by side on the front porch. (See "Civil War.") The Visitor's Information Center in Franklin is located in a small renovated former doctor's office. A brochure with a self-guided walking and driving tour map of this area is available. You can find excellent restaurants (see "Eatin' and Sleepin' Good") and shopping here.

Franklin is a great little community to drive around and discover the old homes that have been restored. Franklin hosts at least two home tours during the year—The Town and Country Tour in April and the Christmas Candlelight Tour in December. The back roads of Williamson County offer hours of driving pleasure for those who like to explore pretty countryside.

To the West of Nashville

The **Loretta Lynn Dude Ranch** is in Humpreys County. Loretta and Moony live here at Hurricane Mills. A restaurant, a western store, arts and crafts shop, campgrounds, and cabins are all part of the ranch. Loretta's personal museum is located in the old mill and includes everything from costumes to mementos donated by her country music contemporaries. Horseback riding, canoeing, buggy and stagecoach rides, hayrides, rodeos, and cookouts are only some of the things to do here.

Montgomery Bell State Park is west of Nashville in Dickson County (see "Outdoors"), as are Ruskin Cave and Jewel Cave.

In Cheatham County, northwest of Nashville, is the **Narrows of the Harpeth,** where two channels of the Harpeth River are separated only by a peninsula of limestone bluffs. Montgomery Bell in the early nineteenth century blasted a tunnel through the base of the narrow ridge and built huge water wheels, thereby creating a usable source of power. A pool at the tunnel outlet is now a popular swimming hole. From the top of the 200-feet-high bluff is a panoramic view of the river and adjoining countryside.

Also northwest of Nashville is Montgomery County, location of **Fort Campbell Military Reservation.** The reservation is the home of the famed 101st Airborne Division. A museum is open to the public. The **Montgomery County Historical Museum** provides a walking tour map to point out historic sites and beautiful old buildings in the downtown area. Clarksville is home to some of the best eating anywhere at Phila Hach's Hachland Hill Inn. (See "Eatin' and Sleepin' Good.")

If you've been following a map through this tour, you know we started in Nashville, then went clockwise around Nashville pointing out sites in many of the surrounding counties. All of these are within easy driving distance of Nashville. There's a lot available—ice skating to boating; Broadway theater to Civil War battlefields. The choices are exciting. Hope you enjoy them!

DIRECTORY:

Nashville: Nashville Tourist Information Center, 300 Main Street, (615) 242-5606. Nashville Area Chamber of Commerce, 161 Fourth Avenue North, 37219; (615) 259-3900. Metropolitan Historical Commission, 701 Broadway, 37203; (615) 259-5027 (walking tour of Nashville). Hermitage, (615) 889-2941. Travellers' Rest, (615) 832-2962. Belle Meade Mansion, ll0 Leake Avenue, (615) 352-7350. Cheekwood, (615) 352-5310. Executive Residence, 822 Curtiswood Lane; (615) 383-5401. Riverfront Park, (615) 259-6314. Belle Carol Riverboat Co., 6043 Charlotte Avenue, 37209; (615) 356-4120. Fort Nashborough, First Avenue North; (615) 255-8192. Tennessee State Capitol, (615) 741-3211. Tennessee State Museum, James K. Polk Cultural Center, 505 Deaderick; (615) 741-2692. Cumberland Museum, 800 Ridley Boulevard; (615) 242-1858. Museum of Tobacco Art and History, Eighth Avenue North and Harrison; (615) 242-9218. Upper Room Chapel, 1908 Grand Avenue; (615) 327-2700. Parthenon, (615) 327-3413. *Nashville Magazine,* The Advantage Building, 1719 West End Avenue, 37203.

Gallatin: Gallatin Chamber of Commerce, P.O. Box 26, 37066; (615) 452-4000. Cragfont, Route 1, Box 73, Castalian Springs, TN 37031; (615) 452-7070. Wynnewood, Castalian Springs, TN; (615) 452-5463. Rock Castle, 139 Rock Castle Lane, Hendersonville, TN 37075; (615) 824-0502.

Fentress County Chamber of Commerce, P.O. Box 496, Jamestown, TN 38556; (615) 879-9948.

Overton County Chamber of Commerce, P.O. Box 354, Livingston, TN 38570; (615) 823-6421.

Smithville-Dekalb County Chamber of Commerce, P.O. Box 64, Smithville, TN 37166; (615) 597-4163.

McMinnville-Warren County Chamber of Commerce, P.O. Box 574, McMinnville, TN 37110; (615) 473-2468.

Murfreesboro: Rutherford County Chamber of Commerce, P.O. Box 64, 37130; (615) 893-6565. Oaklands Mansion, 900 North Maney Avenue; (615) 893-0022. Cannonsburgh, South Front Street; (615) 893-6565. Stones River Battlefield, (615) 893-9501. To receive bicycle tour write Rutherford County Planning Commission, 100 North Maple, Room 200, Murfreesboro, TN 37130; (615) 896-5590.

Sam Davis Home, Smyrna, TN; (615) 459-2341.

Franklin: Williamson County Chamber of Commerce, P.O. Box 156, 37064; (615) 794-1225. Historic Franklin, P.O. Box 723, 37064. Carter House, 1140 Columbia Avenue; (615) 794-1733. Carnton Mansion, Route 2, Lewisburg Pike; (615) 794-0903.

Humphreys County Chamber of Commerce, P.O. Box 733, Waverly, TN 37185; (615) 296-4865.

Loretta Lynn Dude Ranch, Highway 13; (615) 296-7700.

Dickson County Chamber of Commerce, P.O. Box 612, Dickson, TN 37055; (615) 446-2349.

Ashland City Chamber of Commerce, United Citizens Bank, 37015; (615) 792-5672. Narrows of the Harpeth, ranger's office; (615) 797-2099.

Clarksville: Clarksville Chamber, P.O. Box 883, 37040; (615) 647-2331.

Montgomery County Historical Museum, Commerce and Second streets, Clarksville, TN; (615) 645-2507. Fort Campbell, Highway 41A; (502) 798-3215.

For more information on many places mentioned in this article contact Tennessee Department of Tourist Development, P.O. Box 23170, Nashville, TN 37202; (615) 741-2158.

A SAMPLER
★★★★★ *Exclusive* ★★★★★

An Oak Ridge Boy
Hits The Road

We think that William Lee Golden is fantastic. He's the Oak who looks like he just got back from a two-year trapping expedition in the Colorado Rockies. His hair is way down his back, his beard is one of the longest we've ever seen, and his eyes reflect the wild

William Lee Golden

adventurer that he is. We love "Wild" William's clothes, his custom-made buckskins and moccasins and Indian beads. In a world of look-alikes and act-alikes, he's not afraid to be himself.

William Lee Golden lives in a magnificently restored pre-Civil War home north of Nashville. "I'm proud of the fact they fought a Civil War battle right in the front yard," William said. In fact, during the painstaking restoration of William's home they found bullet holes from that battle inside the house. William Lee wanted them to remain so that they would be a reminder of times long since past, but still deeply meaningful to every true southerner.

When this Oak gets to feeling like he's got to hit the road and feel free, there's no place he'd rather drive than down the winding, enchanted backroads of Middle Tennessee. William Lee made sure that the *Sampler* understood that when he said he loved driving the roads of Middle Tennessee he meant the *back* roads. A back road ain't a back road if it has an unending line of shopping malls and red lights. A back road in Tennessee usually has farmers living along it, weathered shacks, and an occasional country store.

Here are the *Sampler's* tips to tell you whether you are on one of our back roads. On a Tennessee back road you must be able to see wood smoke coming out of almost every house you pass in winter and a tractor in about every other field, plowing up the moist, rich dirt, in the spring. In the summer you should be able to see someone working a pair of mules in the tobacco patch and pass at least one pickup filled with teen-age boys, their shirts off, headed for the local swimming hole. In the fall you should pass a few yards where some good ol' boy or girl is skinning out a buck or cutting fire wood.

A lot of people who have been to New England say that Tennessee is just as quaint with its small towns with white clapboard houses, many church spires, stone walls, and vibrant fall colors. If you're visiting us or already live here, William Lee would love for you to hit the back roads. The driving is fantastic, as you hug the corners and whip by the piles of maple leaves in fall. You'll see the old-timey Tennessee, and no matter what season you're driving around there will be inspiring eye-filling visions for you and yours to appreciate in the privacy of your car, truck, motorcycle, bike, or motorhome.

If you see some guy in a convertible pass you and he looks like a trapper from the 1800s, his hair flying way back in the wind, then wave. It may be William Lee Golden. But don't hit the back roads of Tennessee looking for him. Nope. Hit our back roads for your own peace of mind. Be inspired. Get shed of the frantic pace that gets to all of us. That's this Oak Ridge Boy's prescription and ours. Now, hit a back road!

The Civil War in Tennessee

Although the Civil War was fought over 100 years ago, thousands of people still want to visit the sites where it *really* took place. Civil War battlefields are spread all across Tennessee—from Bloody Pond and the Sunken Road near Shiloh to the slopes of Lookout Mountain where the Battle Above the Clouds was fought.

The Tennessee State Museum in Nashville has opened a new wing to deal specifically with the Civil War in Tennessee. The huge exhibit sprawls over 15,000 square feet and two levels of the museum in the James K. Polk Building. Tennessee personalities who played leading roles in the drama of the Civil War are featured here: Sam Davis, Nathan Bedford Forrest, John Hunt Morgan, Andrew Johnson, and many others. Tennessee's major Civil War engagements are graphically illustrated in photographs, drawings, and battlefield artifacts.

We asked our friend, Bob Womack, a recognized Civil War authority and professor at Middle Tennessee State University, to list 15 of the most significant Civil War sites in Tennessee. He suggested the following locations.

15 of Tennessee's Most Significant Civil War Sites

1. *Fort Donelson National Military Park, Dover, Tennessee.* The site of Tennessee's first major battle. Located on the Cumberland River just north of Dover. Here General Ulysses S. Grant pinned the Confederate army against the river and forced it to surrender. Attractions: Park headquarters and museum, National Cemetery, entrenchments, rare display of naval guns, and the Surrender House and Museum.

2. *Stones River National Military Park, Murfreesboro, Tennessee.* This park commemorates the battle which took place December 31, 1862, through January 2, 1863. Following the battle General William S. Rosecrans's Federal army held possession of the field. The Confederates under General Braxton Bragg retreated south. Attractions: Park headquarters and museum, National Cemetery, Hazen Brigade Monument (the oldest Civil War monument in America), and the railway monument marking the place where 58 Federal cannon repulsed the Confederates during the last day's fighting.

3. *Chickamauga-Chattanooga National Military Park, Chattanooga, Tennessee.* Although this park is not in Tennessee, it should definitely be a major attraction to Civil War enthusiasts visiting Chattanooga. It was the

Confederate Veterans' Reunion, Murfreesboro

scene of a bloody battle fought on September 19–20, 1863. Attractions: Park headquarters and museum, a unique gun collection, an unusually well-marked battlefield, and buildings contemporary with battle.

4. *Missionary Ridge, Chattanooga, Tennessee.* The storming of this ridge by Federal forces on November 25, 1863, assured the Confederacy's loss of Tennessee. Located east of the business area of Chattanooga. Well marked.

5. *Shiloh National Military Park, Savannah, Tennessee.* The place where Grant's Federal army was surprised by the Confederates under General Albert Sidney Johnston. After two days of intense fighting the Confederates were forced to retreat. Attractions: Park headquarters and museum, Bloody Pond, Sunken Road, National Cemetery, and Indian mounds not directly associated with the battle.

6. *Orchard Knob, Chattanooga, Tennessee.* A focal point in the fighting around Chattanooga. Located between the Chattanooga business district and Missionary Ridge. First served as a Confederate outpost, then as Grant's command post. Now the site of a National Cemetery.

7. *Franklin, Tennessee.* Located just south of Nashville. Franklin, in terms of men and time involved, was one of the war's most savage battles. While no park commemorates the battle, there is much to see. Attractions: Carter House, museum and bookstore; Carnton House where the bodies of five Confederate generals were laid out; a rare Confederate cemetery on the McGavock property. The town possesses many pre-Civil War homes.

8. *Lookout Mountain, Chattanooga, Tennessee.* An imposing height on the western edge of Chattanooga. On its slopes was fought the so-called Battle Above the Clouds. The Cravens House which figured prominently into this battle still stands. The summit of the mountain furnishes a spectacular view of the surrounding area.

9. *Greeneville, Tennessee.* The East Tennessee site of Confederate General John Hunt Morgan's death. Although the original house is gone, the site is marked. Greeneville is one of the few places in the United States whose courthouse yards contain monuments to both Confederate and Union soldiers.

10. *Oaklands, Murfreesboro, Tennessee.* A pre-Civil War home which formerly served as a plantation mansion. General Nathan Bedford Forrest attacked a Federal regiment in its yard during his raid on Murfreesboro on July 13, 1862. Jefferson Davis used the home when he visited Murfreesboro on December 10, 1862. The home has been fully restored with appropriate furnishings.

11. *Sam Davis Home, Smyrna Tennessee.* Sam Davis was a Confederate scout who was captured near Pulaski, Tennessee, in November of 1863. He was hanged in Pulaski on November 27, 1863. Offered a pardon if he disclosed the sources of information found in his shoes, Davis replied, "If I had a thousand lives I would lose them all before I would betray my friends or the confidence of my informer." Attractions: the Davis home, Sam Davis's grave, museum items, and restored grounds.

12. *Nashville, Tennessee.* Site of the last major battle in Tennessee (1864). Attractions: Shy's Hill where the Confederates made one of their last stands, earthworks still visible; rocks fences used as shields by both armies; Belle Meade Mansion which served as headquarters for Confederate cavalry; Travellers' Rest, which served as headquarters for Confederate generals during the battle; the Tennessee State Museum which houses a fine collection of Civil War-related material; and many other marked locations pertaining to the Battle of Nashville.

13. *The Highway between Columbia and Mount Pleasant (US 43).* Perhaps no comparable stretch of road in Tennessee gives a better impression of the Old South than this. Located on the drive are Rattle and Snap and Clifton Place, beautiful pre-Civil War mansions. They are not open to the public. Many other historic homes are located in Maury County and are open in the fall on the Majestic Middle Tennessee Home Tour.

14. *Pulaski, Tennessee.* A museum now occupies the place where Sam Davis was hanged. The office in which the original Ku Klux Klan was organized is still standing.

15. *New Johnsonville, Tennessee.* A central point in General Forrest's action against the Federal navy in the fall of 1863. Attractions: A state museum and park headquarters; beautiful scenery.

South Central Tennessee

Harold Twitty Introduces Us to Walking Horse Country

Harold Twitty is one of the most enthusiastic Tennessee Walking Horse promoters around. He lives in Lewisburg, writes for the walking horse publication Blue Ribbon, *and takes care of advertising and public relations for the Celebration. Of course, one of his favorite pastimes is riding Tennessee Walking Horses. The Sampler knew that Harold would be the person to tell us about the background of the much-celebrated Walking Horse and pass along information about interesting places around "Walking Horse Country." Here are his comments.*

Principal activities around here are the breeding, training, and showing of beautiful, easy-riding Tennes-

Walking Horse Celebration, Shelbyville

Lewisburg is the home of the Tennessee Walking Horse Breeders' and Exhibitors' Association, organized in 1935 for the breed's registry and promotion. More than 200,000 Tennessee Walking Horses have been registered by the TWHBEA since its beginning. Visitors are welcome at the association's handsome building on Ellington Parkway in Lewisburg; it has a "Wall of Fame" showing paintings and color photographs of World Champion Tennessee Walking Horses. The many Walking Horse training stables throughout the area also welcome visitors to see horses worked and trained.

Harold also pointed out some other places of interest in Middle Tennessee's Celebration Country; and we'll briefly describe them for you.

Famed for its role in Walking Horse history, the three-story Walking Horse Hotel offers quaintly furnished rooms and "country gourmet" meals. Located in Wartrace on State 64, 12 miles from Shelbyville. (See "Eatin' and Sleepin' Good.")

see Walking Horses. Many of the farms around Wartrace, Manchester, Beech Grove, Fayetteville, Lewisburg, and Shelbyville—throughout this central basin of Middle Tennessee—raise Tennessee Walking Horses.

This is the center of the unique breed's origin and development. The Tennessee Walking Horse is a breed born of necessity and pride, developed during more than a century of selective breeding to implant the stamina, style, and spirit of the magnificent show and pleasure horse celebrated today as one of Tennessee's most important assets.

The ancestry of the Tennessee Walking Horse includes most of America's popular light breeds: Morgan, Saddlebred, Standardbred, Thoroughbred, Canadian and Narragansett Pacers, and, more distantly, Arabian.

In the late 1800s and early 1900s, Middle Tennessee became the center of the breeding of these easy-riding, "walking" horses. Three basic gaits evolved: the flat-foot walk, the running walk, and the canter. The Walking Horses, with their four-beat walking gaits, differ from their ancestry in their avoidance of the jolt of the trot and the sway of the pace; their canter is a collected gallop, an easy "rocking chair" action.

Tennessee Walking Horse National Celebration

The horse's national showcase—the Super Bowl, the Kentucky Derby, the World Series of the breed—is the *Tennessee Walking Horse National Celebration* in Shelbyville. It began here in 1939 and has been held each year since, stretching now to 10 days and nights with an annual attendance of 120,000. More than 3,000 entries in 93 classes compete for more than $100,000 in prize money and World Championship honors.

This "World's Greatest Horse Show" is scheduled so that the final Saturday night performance occurs on the weekend preceding Labor Day each year, ending in late August or early September. Ticket and room information is available at the Celebration office, (615) 684-5915.

Bell Buckle and Webb School

Bell Buckle is a unique town. Founded as a railroad shipping point, it now is an artist's mecca, producing sculpture, ceramics, handmade quilts, and other craft products. (See "Shopping," "Crafts.") Its Railroad Square has the look of a Western movie set. It is also home of the famed *Webb School.*

This private secondary school, founded more than a century ago, has produced more Rhodes scholars than any other preparatory school in the South. Open to visitors seven days week, it is on State 82 in Bell Buckle.

George Dickel Distillery

In 1869, George Dickel started a distillery near Tullahoma after finding a pure spring flowing through a place called Cascade Hollow. Tennessee sour mash whiskey is still made here by the original recipe. There's a turn-of-the-century general merchandise store called appropriately enough, "Geo. A. Dickel Gen. Merchandise," but it's really more of a museum than a store. Both the distillery and the store are open weekdays for touring.

The distillery has its own post office and will mail as many free Dickel postcards as you want to write, and they'll furnish the stamps, compliments of the house. The postmark reads "Dickel Station, TN." You can meet your tour guide here at the general store.

University of Tennessee Space Institute

Aerospace programs in picturesque buildings are located on Woods Reservoir on AEDC (Arnold Engineering Development Center) reservation, between Tullahoma and I-24 at Manchester. This facility is devoted to graduate education and research in engineering and science.

Roger Brashears tells Us about Lynchburg and Jack Daniel Country

Roger Brashears is Lynchburg's promotions manager for Jack Daniel Distillery and has been with the distillery about 20 years. Roger told the Sampler, *"I'm head flunky here, and proud of it. It took me 22 years to reach that position." When we asked Roger how many people work at the distillery, he quipped, "Oh, about half of us!" Of his educational background, Roger said, "I went to Tennessee Technological University, majored in five card stud and minored in accounting. I crammed four years of education into seven-and-a-half years."*

Actually Roger runs the distillery's tour program and accompanies photographers Joe Clark or his son June-bug Clark on photographic assignments for Jack Daniel advertisements. Roger told us a little about his stomping grounds, Lynchburg, Tennessee, and the area around those parts. Here's what he had to say.

Every year some 300,000 folks come from all over everywhere to visit Lynchburg. They all seem to enjoy themselves, though I expect there's some of them a little surprised at what they find here.

Lynchburg is not a Williamsburg. It is not a Disneyland. It's not somebody's designed reconstruction or authentic restoration of what used to be, with townsfolk in costume, acting like 60 or 100 years ago. Lynchburg is real; a working county-seat town that somehow has never outgrown itself. That it has never really changed much isn't due to lack of interest. Just lack of necessity.

Everything in Lynchburg works well enough to satisfy the everyday needs of the town and its 567 inhabitants. The old brick courthouse, for instance, and the jail. Modernization for its own sake seems a whole lot of work and bother that doesn't accomplish much when it's done. Built in the early 1880s, both of them. They do their intended jobs just as well as if they had been built a century later. In fact, the jail could have been built in 1780 for all the use it gets any more.

Around Town

The Bobo Hotel—just a half-block off the square on the old highway—was built right after the Civil War. It has been in business continuously ever since. Miss Lynne Tolley—a great-grandniece of Jack Daniel—is the proprietor and hostess. She carries on the tradition started by Mrs. Mary Bobo herself in 1908, of serving the finest southern family-style midday dinner to be found most anywhere. This unforgettable experience can be yours on a reservation-only basis, six days a week at 1:00 P.M. (See "Eatin' and Sleepin' Good.")

There have been a few changes in the **Lynchburg Hardware and General Store** since Herbie Fanning started his mail-order department some years back. But the basic store is pretty much the way it was when Mr.

Lem Motlow started it in 1912. It is well worth a visit, especially if you are a fan of Jack Daniel.

The old White Rabbit is a lunchroom now, but it was a saloon in the old days. (See "Eatin' and Sleepin' Good.") Lynchburg had several saloons in the old days, but none since 1909. That's when Moore County voted itself dry.

At the Ladies' Handiwork Shop, you'll meet the makers of the handmade quilts and afghans and needlework specialties that are for sale. The Lynchburg ladies take turns clerking in their store and will even give you a quilting lesson if you have the patience.

The Distillery

I guess of the 300,000 visitors to Lynchburg each year, 299,990 of them come to see the old **Jack Daniel Distillery.** (The other 10 are my wife's relatives, and they've seen it already.)

Jack Daniel's is the oldest registered distillery in the country and is designated as a National Historic Site. So it is old and historic and mighty picturesque. But it is not a museum either. It is real. A working, functioning, old-time distillery turning out what many believe—and that includes me—the finest whiskey there is.

It's nestled up in the Jack Daniel Hollow on the edge of Lynchburg, right next to the limestone cave where its famous pure cold water comes from. It's all there—just like the pictures: the fat sassy ducks, the unique rick yard with its hard maple bonfires, the charcoal mellowing tanks, Mr. Jack's old office, everything. A guided walking tour of the Hollow takes about an hour and is available year-round seven days a week, except Thanksgiving, Christmas, and New Year's Day. Admission is free. It's easy to feel at home at Jack Daniel's and in Lynchburg. The pace is slow, the people are friendly. (For walking tour information or other brochures on Lynchburg, see address at end of article.)

When you leave Lynchburg, no matter which side of town you decide to take off from you will find beautiful country and several things of interest to stop by and see.

Tims Ford Dam

Going out State 50 to Winchester, you will pass Tims Ford Dam, one of the larger earthen-filled dams in this part of the country. If you take the Lexie Road, off State 50, and over to State 64, you will go by **Falls Mill,** which is a restored mill built in 1873 as a textile mill. It's located on Factory Creek and stands as the sole survivor of a once-thriving cotton- and wool-processing industry in Franklin County. In the 1960s it was converted into a grist and flour mill. It has one of the largest operating water wheels in the Southeast and grinds corn, wheat, and other grains on grinding stones powered by the water.

Winchester

Turning left on 64, continue on to the city limits of Winchester. On your left you will find **Hundred Oaks Castle** with its battlements and tower (75 feet high) and hundreds of battlements. It was built in 1891 by Arthur Handly Marks, son of Albert S. Marks, twenty-first governor of Tennessee. The library is an exact replica of the one in Sir Walter Scott's home in Abbotsford, Scotland. Lunch is served Tuesday through Friday and Sunday, and tours of the castle are available on the same days.

Roger went on to tell us about more things to see in and around the Lynchburg area. These are included in the following section, as well as other points of interest the Sampler *wanted to share with you.*

The **Old Jail Museum,** *built in 1897, is also in Winchester. Indian artifacts, Civil War memorabilia, and other items of historical interest are housed there.*

Cowan

At the foot of Monteagle Mountain on US 64 is Cowan, where the **Cowan Railroad Museum** is located. The old train station has been renovated, and an antique locomotive and caboose are parked there. A tunnel, cut through the Cumberland Mountain, is near the depot, which was the home of the unusual Cowan Pusher District that assisted trains up the steep mountain grade.

Sewanee

On US 64, you'll come to the mountaintop town of Sewanee and the stately old **University of the South.** Built in the 1860s as a replica of the Oxford, England, campus, the university is proud of its unique architecture. The **All Saints Chapel** contains Shapard Tower with its 56 bell carillon, one of the largest in the world. Sunday afternoon performances are held each week during July. All Saints Chapel has the history of the university in its stained glass. This 10,000-acre mountaintop campus has produced 20 Rhodes scholars so far.

Be sure to see the **Sewanee Memorial Cross** built in 1923. The 55-feet-tall white marble monument was erected to "The Sons of Sewanee Who Answered Their Country's Call to Service in the World War 1917–1918." The sweeping panorama from the base overlooks Hawkins Cove, Cowan, and Winchester, and at night the many lights of the country homes create a tranquil view.

Monteagle

Also on Monteagle Mountain is the **Monteagle Sunday School Assembly.** Founded in 1882 as the "southern Chautauqua," it features an octagonal bandstand, six footbridges dating from the 1890s, and 163 cottages, many of Victorian architecture. Founded as a permanent, though seasonal community, it was—and is—a place to escape from the rat race of urban living. Meander along the nature trails, or enjoy the picnic area at Warren's Point located on the edge of the mountaintop, which overlooks Pelham Valley. During two-and-one-half months of the summer when guests are in residence, permission to go on the grounds must be obtained at the gate.

Wonder Cave, near Monteagle is the South's oldest, most fascinating underground experience and one of the largest caves in Tennessee. The domed chamber is 120 feet high and has interesting stalagmites and stalactites with names such as Madonna and Child, Onyx Billygoat, Totem Pole, and Lot's Wife. Three Vanderbilt students discovered the cave in 1897.

Falls Mill at Belvidere

Grundy County

Not far from Monteagle near Tracy City, is the **Grundy Forest Natural Area.** Sycamore Falls, Chimney Rocks, and Fiery Gizzard Gorge are located in this 211-acre recreational area. (See "Outdoors.")

Near Palmer, still in Grundy County, is one of the state's most spectacular natural areas—**Savage Gulf.** Some of the most impressive virgin timber east of the Mississippi is located in this 10,000-acre wilderness. Twenty-five miles of hiking trails and spectacular Savage Falls are also here. (See "Outdoors.")

Also in Grundy County is the community of **Beersheba Springs**. Built in 1850, the hotel was once a bustling resort and health spa. In the old days the stagecoaches would sound their horns at the bottom of the mountain, once for each passenger. By the time they reached the top, the French band would be playing, and a hot meal and clean linens would be ready for the number of guests indicated. The hotel is now owned by the United Methodist Church, and an arts and crafts fair is held during the last weekend of August each year.

One of the state's finest bakeries is located in Tracy City. **Dutch Maid Bakery** has been operated by the Baggenstoss family for almost a century. The original Mr. Baggenstoss (his name was John) and Jack Daniel were good friends and drinking buddies. The Baggenstoss famous fruit cakes take at least 30 days to be ready to eat after baking. They must first be "cured" by a fine liquor. Reckon that tradition started back when John and Jack were trading fruit cakes and whiskey with each other?

Old Stone Fort Archaeological Area

In Coffee County is a unique site, the Old Stone Fort Archaeological Area, a 94-acre state park near Manchester. It's a system of walls built by the Indians in the woodlands period, which extended over hundreds of years (B.C. 30–430 A.D.). The rock and earthen walls are 3 to 6 feet high and enclose an area of 54 acres. The purpose of the structure is still a mystery. It's along the bluffs of the Duck River and overlooks waterfalls on the Little Duck. Union Civil War troops were stationed here.

Columbia

The *James K. Polk Home* is on picturesque West Seventh Street in downtown Columbia. Many furnishings used by Polk in the White House are on display, including the inaugural Bible he used when he was sworn in as the eleventh President of the United States and the interesting fan the president had made for Mrs. Polk for the inauguration. On the front of the fan are portraits of the first eleven presidents, and on the reverse side is a picture of the signing of the Declaration of Independence.

One of Mrs. Polk's ball gowns, made in Paris, is on display at the home. An exact replica of one of her inaugural gowns has been created by Gloria Rasbury, a Maury County resident, and presented to the Polk Home.

Down the street from the Polk Home is the *Athenaeum,* the last remaining building of the Columbia Athenaeum, a private school for girls. It's one of the 13 historical buildings across our state maintained by the APTA (Association for the Preservation of Tennessee Antiquities).

The *Majestic Middle Tennessee Fall Tour of Homes,* held the second and third weekends of October, gives you a chance to go inside many of the historic old homes in Maury County. For anyone interested in viewing antebellum homes which are private residences and not open to the public, drive down US 43 South and see Rattle and Snap and Clifton Place, along with the historic churches, St. John's Episcopal and Zion Presbyterian.

US 31 North is a Tennessee Scenic Parkway and features such plantation homes as Haynes Haven Farms and Rippavilla. *Grace Episcopal Church* in Spring Hill, between Columbia and Nashville, is open any time for people to view. The unique altar rail of walnut featuring leaves and grapes was handcarved by a teacher at a private boys' school in Spring Hill back in the 1800s.

Centerville

Outside of Centerville, in Hickman County, is legendary *Grinder's Switch* featuring a small museum and camp store open during summer months only. Labeled as "a country adventure," this old railroad switch was made world famous by Grand Ole Opry star Minnie Pearl. Activities include a fishing pond and wildflower trails and on holidays and special weekends old-time skill demonstrations, country music, square dancing, and clogging are held.

Lewis County

In Lewis County is the *Meriwether Lewis Monument* which marks the grave of the famous American explorer Meriwether Lewis of the Lewis and Clark expedition. A Country Fair and Arts Festival is held here each October. (See "Fun Times.")

This is one of the sites at which the *Natchez Trace Parkway* is accessible. This scenic parkway follows the path of the old Natchez Trace, an important highway in the late 1700s. When completed, the 450-mile parkway will roughly follow the route of the original Natchez Trace through the states of Mississippi, Alabama, and Tennessee, connecting the cities of Natchez, Jackson, Tupelo, and Nashville.

Many archaeological sites, historical landmarks, nature trails, and recreational areas are off the parkway. You can walk or ride over typical sections of the old trace and see what it looked like. Here and there you will find obscure remains—a house, an abandoned mine, or an old stream crossing—all associated with the people who lived on or traveled over this thoroughfare.

Waynesboro

Near Waynesboro, you can see the only double-span *Natural Bridge* in the world. It spans a length of 70 feet and is 44 feet high. The natural shelter served as the site for the Wayne County Courthouse in bygone days, and Davy Crockett launched his political career on "Pulpit Rock" located there. The Indians used it as council chambers and sealed treasures there before going on the Trail of Tears. It was a hideout for outlaws who preyed on travelers along the Natchez Trace.

The excitement of this South Central Tennessee area lies in its diversity. The ruggedness of scenic attractions such as Savage Gulf and Fiery Gizzard Gorge; the splendor of majestic antebellum homes; the quaintness and novelty of the little hamlet of Lynchburg, yet the sophistication of its world-famous distillery; the beauty and charm of the unique Tennessee Walking Horse; and the nostalgic appeal of Monteagle and Beersheba Springs. There's a lot this part of Tennessee has to share with you. Hope you'll come be a part of it.

DIRECTORY:

Walking Horse Information: Walking Horse Breeders and Exhibitors Association, 250 North Ellington Parkway, Lewisburg, TN 37091; (615) 359-1574. The Celebration, P.O. Box 1010, Shelbyville, TN 37160; (615) 684-5915. Shelbyville-Bedford County Chamber of Commerce, 100 North Cannon Boulevard, Shelbyville, TN 37160; (615) 684-3482.

Tullahoma: Tullahoma Chamber of Commerce, P.O. Box 339, 37388; (615) 455-5497. George Dickel Distillery, Cascade Road, 37388; (615) 857-3124. UT Space Institute, (615) 455-0631.

Lynchburg: Jack Daniel Distillery, 37352; (615) 759-4221.

Franklin County: Franklin County Chamber of Commerce, P.O. Box 280, Winchester, TN 37398; (615) 967-6788. Hundred Oaks Castle, Highway 64W, Winchester, TN 37398; (615) 967-0100. Old Jail Museum, 400 First Avenue NE, Winchester, TN 37398; (615) 967-0524. Cowan Railroad, P. O. Box 53, Cowan, TN 37318; (615) 967-7233. University of the South, Sewanee, TN 37375; (615) 598-5931.

Grundy County: Grundy County Chamber of Commerce, Tracy City, TN 37387; (615) 592-8795.

Coffee County: Manchester Chamber of Commerce, 305 Murfreesboro Highway, Manchester, TN 37355; (615) 728-7635. Old Stone Fort, Manchester, TN 37355; (615) 728-0751.

Maury County: Maury County Chamber of Commerce, P.O. Box 1076, Columbia, TN 38401; (615) 388-2155. James K. Polk Home, 301 West Seventh Street, Columbia, TN 3840l; (615) 388-2354.

Grinder's Switch, P.O. Box B, Centerville, TN 37033; (615) 729-5558.

Natchez Trace, Tupelo Visitor Center, RR1, NT-143, Tupelo, MS 38801; (601) 842-1572.

Natural Bridge, (615) 722-9218.

Other informative publications:
Brochure: *Nature's Beauty at its Best,* South Cumberland Visitor Center, Route 1, Box 144-H, Tracy City, TN 37387; (615) 924-2980.

For the brochure *Country Roads of Tennessee's Mountains and Hollows* write: James David Oliver, P.O. Box 579LT, Monteagle, TN 37356; (615) 924-2268.

The Funlander (an excellent newspaper for midstate attractions), Lakeway Publications, P.O. Box 400, Tullahoma, TN 37388; (615) 455-4545

Also for more information on many places mentioned in this article, contact: Tennessee Department of Tourist Development, Box 23170, Nashville 37202. (615) 741-2158.

West Tennessee Area

Memphis

Extending from shore to shore (the shores of the Tennessee River to the Mississippi River, that is), West Tennessee contains as great a variety of things to see and do as anywhere in the state. Some of the most stately old homes in Tennessee are located in Memphis and in nearby LaGrange. The Bluff City of Memphis, sitting atop the Chickasaw Bluffs, is proud of its colorful heritage, and The Peabody Hotel and Beale Street, recently renovated and ready for company, are significant parts of the city's rich traditions.

Quaint sights become the ordinary rather than the unusual in West Tennessee, from white squirrels to doodle soup and from Skullbone to Mud Island. State parks and natural areas abound, and cotton is "king" in this agricultural stronghold of Tennessee's fertile bottomlands.

Since Memphis contains the most sites to visit in West Tennessee, we'll start our tour there. Settle back, get out your map, and enjoy West Tennessee.

Victorian Village

Victorian Village located on Adams Avenue has two houses open to the public, Fontaine House and Mallory-Neely House. One of the houses is rumored to be haunted. In the Fontaine House people have reported someone or something unseen walking up or down the stairs behind them. The curator of the house says that there are times when it suddenly gets very cold in the upstairs rose bedroom, just as shivery as it can be. The bed in that room always seems to be mussed as if someone had been lying or sitting on it.

The cluster of nineteenth-century mansions in Victorian Village range in style from neoclassical through late Gothic revival. The Mallory-Neely House, a three-story Italianate Victorian mansion, has a tower and arcaded porches. The Massey Schaeffer House, Molly Fontaine Taylor House, and Pillow McEntire House are other homes here.

Lee House was the home of Captain James Lee, Jr., who loved to watch steamboats on the river from the mansion's tower. Also nearby is the Magevney House, an 1830s cottage believed to be the oldest known private residence in the city. Just driving around the historic areas of Memphis offers glimpses of street upon street of magnificent old homes.

Memphis in May

Memphis is beautiful in the spring. The azaleas and dogwoods blooming all over the city are simply breathtaking. The event the whole city looks forward to and makes preparations for practically year-round is Memphis in May. This month-long festival is the largest event of its kind in North America, and each year honors a different foreign country.

Area museums and schools offer exhibitions and units of study centered on the chosen country. Japan, Canada, Germany, Venezuela, and Egypt are just a few countries that have been honored so far. There are "fun runs "; a children's festival, with dozens of events on Mud Island; canoe and kayak racing; the Beale Street Music Festival; and a Memphis Symphony Orchestra outdoor concert. Most of the festivities are spread along downtown streets, in parks, and along the river. (See "Music.")

One of the most popular events during Memphis in May is the International Barbecue Cooking; some 200 championship cooking teams from across the United States participate in a two-day competition. Culinary experts begin cooking Friday morning and continue non-stop until the winners are announced late Saturday afternoon. Usually it turns into an all night-party with bands playing and plenty of well-wishers and sample snitchers participating along with the competitors. Attendance of nearly one million people is evidence of the popularity it has gained nationwide.

The Great River Carnival, formerly known as the Memphis Cotton Carnival, is held each year in conjunction with Memphis in May. (See "Fun Times.")

The Memphis Queen on the Mississippi

Memphis Zoological Garden, Brooks Museum, and Overton Square

Memphis is really proud of its zoo, officially known as the Memphis Zoological Garden and Aquarium. Located on 36 acres in Overton Park, the zoo is home to more than 2,000 animals. The bears, just as you enter on the right, have always been the favorites of Memphians. The Memphis Brooks Museum of Art is also in the park. Overton Square, just a few blocks from Overton Park, has sidewalk cafes, music, and a variety of specialty shops.

Mud Island and the Mississippi River Museum

Mud Island is one of Memphis's newest attractions. You can get to Mud Island via overhead walkway, or you can ride the monorail or ferry. The 50-acre development tells the history of the much-sung-about and written-about Mississippi River. A five-block-long scale model called "River Walk" depicts 1,000 miles of the Mississippi River, from Cairo, Illinois, to the Gulf of Mexico.

The Mississippi River Museum at Mud Island tells the heritage of the waterway by featuring full-size replicas of part of an 1870s steamboat and a Union gunboat, in which you can go below the deck. The earthquakes of 1811–1812 that formed Reelfoot Lake are depicted in an audiovisual presentation.

Also at Mud Island you can enjoy riverboat excursion rides, marina retail shops, playground areas, strolling musicians, places for picnicking and quiet spots to just sit and watch the river roll by. The River Terrace Restaurant specializes in foods expressing the traditions of the South.

The Pink Palace Museum

The Memphis *Pink Palace Museum* on Central Avenue has always been a favorite with the citizens of Memphis—young and old alike. Although once housed in the famous pink marble building from which it took the name Pink Palace, it's now located in a new $5.5 million facility adjacent to the original museum.

The museum contains an exact replica of the world's first Piggly Wiggly self-service supermarket from 1917. A turn-of-the-century drugstore complete with soda fountain and hundreds of patent medicines is also re-created here. Part of the museum contains one of the country's newest and most modern planetariums where weekly celestial and laser shows are held.

Another of the museum's favorite attractions is the miniature, animated three-ring circus scaled 1 inch to 1 foot, which comes to life with jugglers juggling and acrobats flying on the high trapeze. The 2,000 pieces in the circus were hand carved over a 30-year period by one man.

The newest and most exciting addition to the Pink Palace is the life-size dinosaur which stomps toward you and snorts—all for the price of a quarter! Children absolutely love it! The insect zoo, reconstructed log cabin, and Civil War exhibits are other attractions.

Graceland

Graceland, the home of Elvis Presley, is visited by millions of fans from around the world. (See "Music.")

National Ornamental Metal Museum

Of interest to anyone who enjoys hand-crafted items is the *National Ornamental Metal Museum,* the only one of its kind in the world. Everything from gold jewelry to handmade nails to exquisitely crafted wrought iron gates are on exhibit. The exhibits change often so that the type of work on view today will be entirely different from what will be on display another time. A working blacksmith shop is located on the premises.

Repair Days are held two days each year during October, and about 30 craftsmen repair broken, bent, or otherwise mutilated metalwork, except jewelry. Shoeshine boxes, horse trailers, sterling pieces of flatware, and metal sculptures for front yards are just some of the items people bring in for this event.

Downtown Memphis

If you want to take a walking tour of downtown Memphis, the **Peabody Hotel** makes an ideal place to start. At II:00 A.M. the event that always warms people's hearts to Memphis takes place. The famous ducks of the Peabody take the elevator from their penthouse shelter down to the lobby. A red carpet runway is rolled from the elevator to the fountain, and to the accompaniment of a drum roll and lively march tune, the four mallard ducks waddle proudly down the carpet to the fountain. Everyone cheers and applauds when they appear! (See "Eatin' and Sleepin' Good.")

Cotton Row is nearby where Robert Farrish owns and operates **Shelby Cotton Company** at 48 South Front Street. He delights in sharing his love and knowledge of cotton growing and marketing with visitors. Farrish has tale after tale about this part of town and the famous "white gold" that put Memphis on the map in the late 1800s.

Carter Seed Store has been located on Cotton Row for 65 years and is a wonderful place to shop. You'll find seeds, antiques, baskets, and all sorts of goodies displayed on its storefront and inside the crowded, fun-to-visit store.

The Orpheum Theater, now restored to its full splendor at 89 Beale Street, reopened its doors to the delight of Memphians in 1984. The elegant Czechoslovakian crystal chandeliers and meticulous giltwork of the theater make the Orpheum glitter and glow. Operas, ballets, Broadway shows, and special film series are offered to the public.

Beale Street, the "Birthplace of the Blues," has experienced a rebirth in the past few years. W. C.'s Cafe, Club Handy, Kublai Khan's, and other nightspots offer good music, eats, and drinks. The statue of W. C. Handy, the "Father of the Blues," looks down approvingly at the revitalization that has taken place on Memphis's most famous address. (See "Music.")

Riverboat cruises are offered by the **Memphis Queen Line** and last about an hour and a half. You'll see sights such as Memphis's famous Riverside Drive, the historic cobblestone levee, and a lot of interesting river traffic as the captain shares the history of the river with you. The river is one mile wide here, and because there's nothing built on the western side of the river, Memphis has some of the most spectacular sunsets of any city. The riverboat departs from the foot of Monroe Avenue and Riverside Drive.

Also in Memphis

In Memphis you can also find Libertyland, a patriotic theme park; the Stroh Brewery; the Lorraine Motel, site of the assassination of Dr. Martin Luther King which now contains a shrine to Dr. King's memory; Memphis Botanic Garden; Dixon Gallery and Gardens; the Center for Southern Folklore; and the Lichterman Nature Center which includes nature trails, a 12-acre lake, and an outdoor amphitheater.

A major dog racing track, **Southland Greyhound Park,** is about 10 miles away in West Memphis, Arkansas. Many tourists and Memphians enjoy going over for a night at the dog races.

Chucalissa Indian Village and Museum, at T. O. Fuller State Park, was a village founded around the year 1,000 and was occupied by several different groups till 1500 when it was abandoned. Although the Choctaws did not live there, they gave it the name *Chucalissa* which means "abandoned village." In the 1940s it was fully excavated, and a re-created village is now on display including the medicine man's hut and the chief's house.

Federal Express, the Memphis-based firm which originated the overnight package delivery concept, is another impressive sight. The daily one-and-a-half hour tour begins at 11:30 P.M. as 2,800 employees sort an average of 400,000 packages and documents each night. In the main sorting room 23 miles of high-speed conveyor belts rush material to the destination loading areas. Now that's a sight to see!

Memphis Magazine can be very helpful to anyone wanting to know more about Memphis, whether you're a tourist or a resident who doesn't want to miss out on happenings in the Bluff City. The magazine lets you know everything going on in this area with really great feature articles like their annual survey of the restaurants with the "best" barbecue in Memphis. The competition is stiff since West Tennessee is known as the "Pork Barbecue Capital of the World."

History Lives at TVA's Homeplace

Other West Tennessee Sites

In the fall, when the weather gets cool, is a good time to go on an all-day drive to see some of the historic homes in West Tennessee. A good way to start is by eating breakfast at the Silver Moon Cafeteria in Somerville. (See Eatin' and Sleepin' Good.")

La Grange

Over in La Grange is **La Belle Village,** once a center of culture, gracious living, and agriculture. When La Grange incorporated in 1836, it was known as the wealthiest and most cultured town in the South. The gracious old homes in this small community give a hint of what small-town life was once like.

In La Grange you'll see **Woodlawn Mansion,** once a headquarters for Union General Sherman and once a military hospital. Hillcrest features Swiss chalet architecture, and Reverie and Tiara are both outstanding in design. The cupola on Tiara was blown away in 1900 by a tornado. It landed 10 miles away but was brought back and put atop the house. Every other year, in October, these homes are open to the public through home tours.

In February each year the **National Field Trials** are held at nearby **Ames Plantation.** This is known as the "World Series" of bird dog competition and is open to the public. (See "Outdoors.")

Bolivar

In Bolivar are several interesting historical sites. **The Pillars,** which served as a Civil War headquarters, is the oldest brick home in Bolivar, and historical figures such as Sam Houston and President James K. Polk gathered there. The two-story **Little Courthouse Museum** is the oldest remaining courthouse building in West Tennessee. These buildings and many homes are open to tour at certain times during the year. Just on the outskirts of town is the **Polk Cemetery.** Among those buried there is Ezekiel Polk, President Polk's grandfather whose epitaph makes a trip to the cemetery worthwhile.

Jackson

The **Casey Jones Home** and **Railroad Museum** are located in Jackson, northeast of Memphis. At this same location, known as **Casey Jones Village,** is the **Carl Perkins Music Museum** and Brooks Shaw's Old Country Store and Restaurant. (See "Eatin' and Sleepin' Good.") Casey Jones is America's most famous engineer who became a legend when he met his death in Mississippi, the only casualty of a collision he tried valiantly to prevent. A replica of his steam engine, old 382, is on display at the museum.

South of Jackson is the **Pinson Mounds State Archaeological Park,** the second-largest Indian ceremonial and burial mounds in the eastern United States. In nearby Adamsville is the **Buford Pusser Museum,** containing personal effects belonging to the famous *Walking Tall* lawman.

Gibson County

The **Trenton Teapots** comprise the world's largest collection of teapots. In the small West Tennessee town of Trenton (pop. 4,600), this rare collection of art is housed in city hall. When city hall is closed, a sign on the door directs visitors to the fire station where they can pick up a key from the fireman on duty! The teapots are porcelain "veilleuse-theieres"—night-light teapots—and were given to the city by Dr. Frederick Freed in 1955. Some of the shapes include cathedrals, castles, Romeo and Juliet, woodchoppers, ice skaters, and musketeers.

Near Trenton, also in Gibson County, is the little community of **Skullbone,** Tennessee, or the kingdom of Skullbonia. "Skullbone" fighting was bare-knuckle fighting, swapping punches to the head until only one man would remain standing. The winner would receive the coveted prize of a stalk of bananas.

This form of fighting took place in the late 1800s and early 1900s and was known throughout the country, because one of the residents of Skullbone constructed

signs everywhere he went telling the direction and distance to Skullbone, Tennessee. In Skullbone, he also erected signs giving the distance and direction to all the major cities of the world.

Now, you'll find a general store with a map of Skullbone painted on one side and lots of mementos inside promoting the area.

Nearby (about 3 miles) is Bradford, the "Doodle Soup Capital of the World." Doodle soup is a hot, spicy, savory dish which is served during the **Doodle Soup Festival** held here during the fourth week in July each year. (See "Fun Times" and "Eatin' Good.")

You might want to travel to *Kenton,* a little north of Trenton on US 45W, either early morning or late afternoon because that's the best time to see Kenton's natural wonders. This little West Tennessee town is one of four places in the United States that is home to a community of **white squirrels.** No one really knows how they got there, but since the 1870s the rare breed has laid claim to this small town, driving off any gray, brown, or red squirrels that try to join their ranks. They're protected by a city ordinance which prohibits trapping and killing them, and they love to put on a show, probably because the townsfolk have spoiled them so much over the years.

Union City and Puryear

In Union City, the **Dixie Gun Works** features firearms from many periods of our nation's history, gun parts, bullet molds, powder horns, and other gun-related items. (See "Shopping.") The **Old Car Museum,** at the same location, contains 31 antique automobiles.

Near the Kentucky border, in Henry County, Dora Anderson lives in the little community of Puryear. She has on display in her home over 80 *Character Dolls* that she has authentically dressed, after carefully studying the history behind each character. The 11 1/2 inch replicas are of first ladies, Henry VIII, Sir Walter Raleigh, Jeff Davis, Lady Diana, and scores of others. Mrs. Anderson tells the *Sampler,* "They are authentic, to the last detail, including undergarments!" She invites people to call her ([901] 247-3788), and come by and see her collection.

Other West Tennessee sites include Shiloh National Military Park near Savannah (see "Civil War"), famous Reelfoot Lake near Tiptonville, Pickwick Landing State Park, Chickasaw State Park, and Natchez Trace State Park. (See "Outdoors.") At The Homeplace-1850, a living history farm located at TVA's Land Between the Lakes, people "live" there and do all the farming and housekeeping with nineteenth-century tools. Land Between the Lakes is located between Lake Barkley and Kentucky Lake. Fort Pillow State Historic Area is a Civil War fort overlooking the Mississippi River 50 miles north of Memphis.

West Tennessee offers history dating back to the ancient Chucalissa Village; music of every description including blues and rock-and-roll; education from museums and galleries; and loads of fun in the theme parks, zoos, and riverboat rides. Come on over to West Tennessee. It's got a lot to offer.

DIRECTORY:

Memphis: Convention and Visitors Bureau of Memphis, P. O. Box 3543, 38103; (901) 526-1919. Memphis Area Chamber of Commerce, P. O. Box 224, 555 Beale Street, 38101; (901) 523-2322. Fontaine House, (901) 526-1469. Mallory-Neely House, (901) 527-7965. APTA, 680-690 Adams Avenue, 38105; (901) 526-1469. Memphis Zoological Garden and Aquarium, (901) 725-4768. Memphis Brooks Museum of Art, (901) 726-5266. Mud Island, (901) 528-3595. Memphis Pink Palace Museum, 3050 Central Avenue; (901) 454-5600. National Ornamental Metal Museum, 374 West California Avenue; (901) 774-6380. Peabody Hotel, 149 Union Avenue, 38103; (901) 529-4000 or toll-free (800) 258-7273. Orpheum, 89 Beale Street; (901) 525-2121. Memphis Queen Line departs at foot of Monroe Avenue and Riverside Drive, (901) 527-5694. Federal Express, (901) 369-3613. Chucalissa Museum, (901) 785-3160. *Memphis Magazine,* P.O. Box 370, 38101; (901) 521-9000.

Somerville (La Grange): Fayette County Chamber of Commerce, P.O. Box 411, Somerville, TN 38068; (901) 465-8690.

Bolivar: Hardeman County Chamber of Commerce, P.O. Box 313, 500 West Market Street, Bolivar, TN 38008; (901) 658-6554.

Jackson: Jackson Area Chamber of Commerce, P.O. Box 1904, 38301; (901) 423-2200. Casey Jones Village, (901) 668-1222. Pinson Mounds, (901) 988-5614. Pusser Museum, (901) 632-1401.

Trenton: Gibson County Chamber of Commerce, P.O. Box 464, 38382; (901) 855-0973.

Union City: Obion County Chamber of Commerce, P.O. Box 70, 38261; (901) 885-0211. Dixie Gun Works, (901) 885-0700.

Also for many places mentioned in this article, contact: Tennessee Department of Tourist Development, Box 23170, Nashville, TN 37202; (615) 741-2158.

A SAMPLER

SPECIAL

An Original Monument to the King

About an hour's drive north of Memphis you will find Gail Spinner's soybean farm. It's about 500 acres of good level land between Fort Willow and Blimp, Tennessee. Gail has been in love with Elvis since she was 15 and saw one of his first concerts. Fact is she has never married, although she's "a fine-looking woman," according to the man who runs the Farmers Co-op in Wipley. Anyway after the King's death, Gail felt compelled to do something for him. Should she put together a traveling slide show and spend her life traveling and speaking at high schools across America telling young Americans of Elvis's contributions to American music and culture? No, she had to run her farm. So one night after seeing the movie, *KING KONG,* Gail got an idea.

Gail placed ads in fan magazines, Elvis newsletters, even *The National Enquirer,* asking people to sell her anything having to do with Elvis. It didn't matter whether it was newspaper clippings, plastic cups with Elvis's face on them, just absolutely anything that had anything to do with the Man. Gail was swamped with Elvis memorabilia. In fact, after the first year she had two barns filled up, as well as her seven-room home and a bunch of rent-a-storage places. What did Gail have in mind? What idea did she get after watching the King Kong movie ?

Well, Gail would take all these things and find a sculptor to fashion them into a statue of Elvis 30 feet tall. She put an advertisement in a leading art magazine for a sculptor who loved Elvis. She heard from nine men and three women. Five of them were from Communist countries and couldn't leave. The one that she thought would be best was a man named Victor Marchioni, from Venice, Italy, now living in Australia. Vic moved to western Tennessee and began work. He planned to hold everything together with Crazy Glue. His work created a real stir around Fort Willow and Blimp and all over that part of Tennessee. Even the crew of "That's Incredible" came and filmed the giant Elvis the day Vic finished.

It's been about three years since Vic finished and moved back to Australia. Gail doesn't have to shine her monument because all that Crazy Glue gives a natural shine to it, but every day you can find her there collecting the $3 entry fee from the fans who come to see it. The glued-together Elvis can be seen from 6:00 A.M. till 3:30 P.M.. "The King in a Soybean Field Gift Shop" is open for your Elvis shopping pleasure. To get there follow State 877 till you get to Elmer's Barbecue, then pull off the road, and look at your map and find Blimp, Tennessee. If you miss this, you've missed a big piece of Tennessee.

EATIN' & SLEEPIN' GOOD

EATIN' AND SLEEPIN' HIGHLIGHTS

Eatin' Good in Tennessee

50 RESTAURANTS: The Crosseyed Cricket to a Music Row restaurant frequented by the stars
A Sampler Feature: Phila Hach, Tennessee's first Lady of food
A Sampler Exclusive: Where Gary Morris likes to eat
Our greatest recipes
Sampler Specials: The Chitlin' Hut and The Secret of Lonnie B's
Country ham, chitlins' and the best barbecue
Dinner on the ground, southern style
College kids—Where They Go

Sleepin' Good in Tennessee

4 GRAND HOTELS
TENNESSEE INNS—quaint and nostalgic
BED AND BREAKFAST…southern hospitality at its best!
A corporate retreat businesses will love!
Smoky Mountain chalets
A Sampler Feature: One Lodge "You Can't Hardly Get To"

EATIN' GOOD IN TENNESSEE

You'll find Tennessee's great food in restaurants of every description, from one with a country-ham-shaped swimming pool to one in a century-old church building; one overlooking the Great Smoky Mountains to one smack dab on Music Row in Nashville; one where you can eat the freshly cooked fish you just caught to one where you go back to the kitchen and dip your own food from pots on the stove!

There's most every type food represented: Italian, German, southern, country, deli, French, the all-American hamburger, Cajun, fish, steak, and on and on.

Some of the restaurants have a modern elegance, while others haven't changed their looks in 30 years. A few are right off the interstates, but others require a drive along a country road or down a hollow to enjoy their fine food. You might be offered a comfortable rocker to sit in while you wait or perhaps a game of checkers or dominoes. We'll give you fair warning right here, some of these fine eating places are pretty small, and when you go there to eat, you just may have to wait awhile. But you'll find in every case, the food will be worth waiting for!

Excellent food is served at many of the fine hotels and bed and breakfast facilities we've listed in "Sleepin' Good." We hope you'll give those restaurants a try as well.

We realize that *many* excellent restaurants are not listed in this section. But we've tried to give you, the reader, a sample of what's available for eatin' good in Tennessee. Our thanks to Phila Hach for helping the *Sampler* discover many of these fine restaurants.

One common denominator we found among these restaurants is that they are home owned and home operated. In some cases the owners or their families have been running the establishments for 30 years or more. They are there from early in the morning to late at night on many days. The *Sampler* thanks the restaurant owners for providing good eatin' places all across our state.

Eatin' Good in East Tennessee

Norris BP Grocery and Sub Shop, Mountain City
Grover and Beulah Norris, owners

Sandwiches are prepared while you wait, all "to go," although picnic tables are available. Features are submarine sandwiches, hot sandwiches, and side orders. Also ice cream, sundaes, and milk shakes.

Hours: Sub Shop open 11:00 A.M. to 9:00 P.M.

Directions: From Mountain City, take State 91 north 9 miles, located on corner of 91 and Sugar Creek Road in Laurel Bloomery. (615) 727-6471.

Skoby's, Kingsport
Fred "Pal" Barger, owner

The dining rooms at Skoby's have varying themes such as the Butcher Shop, the Bordello, the Diner, and an Oriental Room. The personality of each dining room is reflected in the tasteful decor. Antique Tiffany lamps, walls of yesterday's memorabilia, and a juke box playing hits of the forties and fifties provide atmosphere. The menu lists Chinese roast chicken, filet mignon, barbecue, shrimp, and lasagna. The 21-feet-long salad bar is another popular specialty of the house!

Hours: Monday–Thursday, 5:00 to 11:00 P.M. Friday–Saturday, 5:00 to 11:30 P.M. Closed Sunday. Reservations accepted.

Directions: 1001 Konnarock Road, next door to the Eastman Company. (615) 276-2761.

Parson's Table, Jonesborough
Jimmy Neil Smith, owner

Dining with the Parson in a century-old church building in the heart of Historic Jonesborough offers atmosphere and country dinners. Entrees include chicken and dumplings, pot roast of beef, southern-fried catfish, and country ham. Dinner is served with a mysterious "brew" plus peanuts, old-fashioned vegetable soup with flatbread, fresh relishes, green beans, sweet potato pudding, stewed apples, country slaw, freshly baked whole wheat bread, and hot apple fritters.

Hours: Dinner only, Monday–Thursday, 6:00 to 9:00 P.M. Friday and Saturday, 6:00 to 10:00 P.M. Sunday, 12:00 noon to 8:00 P.M.

Directions: From I-81 take State 81 south to Jonesborough. Parson's Table is on Woodrow Avenue in the historic district of Jonesborough. (615) 753-3982.

Ridgewood Restaurant, South of Bluff City on US 19E
Grace Proffitt, owner

"I got to go to New York and be on 'Good Morning America' to tell about my restaurant," says Mrs. Proffitt. Now in her sixties, she's run the Ridgewood from the same location for thirty-seven years.

The *Sampler* asked, "What was the response to your television appearance?"

"Why, hon, they were lined up plumb down the road to get in here. They're hunting us up off I-81 when they pass through Upper East Tennessee. People from all over the nation."

What's so special about the Ridgewood? *Barbecue* with a capital *B.* "We have two big pits and cook all week long over green hickory wood," says Mrs. Proffitt.

To go along with this world-famous barbecue are French fries, cole slaw, and barbecue beans. Of course, lots of other good eatin' is offered, but it's the barbecue that keeps 'em comin' back. The Ridgewood's been written up in *Goodfoods, Food and Wine,* and *People* magazine.

Hours: Tuesday–Thursday, 11:30 A.M. to 7:30 P.M. Friday, Saturday, and Sunday, 11:30 A.M. to 2:45 P.M. and 4:30 to 8:30 P.M.

Directions: US 19E, south of Bluff City. (615) 538-7543.

Little Dutch Restaurant, Morristown
George Angelos, owner

In 1939, Frank and Mattie Lorino established a Morristown tradition when they opened Little Dutch. Frank always had plenty of home-cooked food and a warm welcome for his customers. After Frank's death, George Angelos pledged to carry on the Lorino traditions.

Meals prepared in "Dutch" fashion include pork chops, baby beef liver, ham steak served with pineapple, and beef tips. Seafood, steak dinners, and Italian food also are house specialties with a children's menu offered. Dessert temptations are baklava—delicious Mediterranean pastry—cheesecake, and Greek custard pie prepared from scratch. Price range: $3.25 for a hamburger plate to $9.50 for New York Strip.

Hours: Monday–Saturday, 11:00 A.M. to 9:30 P.M. Closed Sunday.

Directions: Downtown Morristown, 1 block from US 11E. 5 miles from I-81, Exit 3 Morristown. 115 South Cumberland. (615) 581-1441.

Log Cabin Inn, Newport
Virginia and William Cureton, owners

The cane-bottomed rockers and old church pews on the front porch offer a place to sit and wait till the dinner bell rings at the Log Cabin. Even if you choose to take advantage of the top-of-the-world views of the Great Smoky Mountains, you'll hear the dinner bell and come a runnin' when you find out what's been cookin'.

The log restaurant, built originally as a summer cabin, is constructed of 100-year-old logs. "We hired a man from Cades Cove to come show us how to fit the logs together," said the Curetons. Furnishings inside are old-fashioned, with bright red carpeting and tablecloths. Chairs are ladder-back. The picturesque setting is often the site of club meetings, anniversary and bridal parties, and occasionally a wedding.

Food is served buffet-style. No menus. Offered are four to five meats, an incredible number of salads and vegetables, six to eight desserts, corn bread, sweet rolls, and muffins. From an Amish-made cart several hot, homemade soups and/or chili are served. Prices: For adults, $6.00 plus drink; for children, $3.20. A Log Cabin cookbook is available.

Other features: An antique shop is located within walking distance of the restaurant. The Ramp Festival is held annually at nearby Kineavista. (See "Fun Times.")

Hours: Thursday, Friday, Saturday, 5:00 to 9:00 P.M. Sunday, 11:00 A.M. to 2:00 P.M. Reservations recommended for large groups.

Directions: From I-40 take Newport Exit. Take a right at Holiday Inn onto State 32 and go 6 miles. A sign in the field will say "Log Cabin Inn." Take a left and stay to the left. Come up through the apple orchard. Follow signs to Log Cabin Inn. (615) 623-5959.

Green Valley Restaurant, Pigeon Forge
Ed Reagan, owner

When you're traveling to Gatlinburg on State 71, Pigeon Forge is a little community you pass through. A stop worth your time is the Green Valley Restaurant. For over 25 years they've been serving one of the biggest breakfasts around. Country ham, country fresh eggs, and locally made sausage with homemade biscuits and gravy start out your morning just right. The stone fireplace, bottomless coffee cup, and friendly service provide a homelike atmosphere.

The menu is extensive and prices are moderate. A variety of vegetables at lunch and dinner is available along with steaks, fresh rainbow trout, seafood, and lobster tails.

Hours: 7:00 A.M. to 10:00 P.M. daily.

Location: 804 Parkway South, Pigeon Forge; (615) 453-3500. Also one on Airport Road in Gatlinburg.

Burning Bush Restaurant, Gatlinburg
Jim Huff, owner

Known for their "bountiful breakfast," this Gatlinburg eatery offers a menu with a mountain view. "One foot away from our property line is the Great Smoky Mountains National Park boundary," says manager Don Smith. Breakfast begins with blueberry muffins and your choice of appetizers, typically strawberries, melon balls, and a bowl of strawberry jam. The meal to follow includes eggs with regular breakfast meats or your choice of trout, quail, or filet mignon.

Southern Living magazine said: "Many travelers fuel their energy for a day in the park with the Burning Bush Bountiful Breakfast. It's such an ample offering that if you're hungry again by noon, you certainly know you didn't eat all your breakfast."

The Burning Bush also serves lunch and dinner, with quail and country ham as favorites. Exquisite wines are available to accentuate your meal.

By the way, in the fall the shrubbery outside the restaurant bursts into fiery crimson red and becomes the Burning Bush.

Prices: Bountiful breakfast $7 to $l0; lunch $5 to $l0; dinner $10 to $19.

Hours: 7:00 A.M. to 2:00 P.M.; 5:00 to 10:00 P.M. (summer hours). Open daily 365 days a year. Reservations advised.

Directions: At the north entrance to Great Smoky Mountains National Park, 1151 Parkway. (615) 436-4669.

Gladys Breeden's Restaurant, Sevierville
Gladys Breeden, owner

Where did Jane Fonda eat when she was in the Smokies filming *The Dollmaker*? She ate at Gladys Breeden's Restaurant where you can dip your own plate from the pots on the stove and eat at the nine-stool counter, on one of three unmatched Formica-topped tables, or out on the porch if there's no room inside.

Gladys Hurst Breeden, a hard-working, delightful 74 year old, has combined the two things she enjoys most—cooking and people. Her country store restaurant, nestled in the foothills of the Smokies, has gained quite a reputation.

On a typical day Gladys prepares barbecued ribs,

country ham, pork chops, country steak, and fried chicken. Macaroni and cheese is daily fare, usually served with steamed cabbage, hominy, cole slaw, green beans, and mustard greens. The pies she bakes fresh each morning are coconut cream, chocolate, and cherry custard along with apple, peach, and cherry fried pies.

Is your mouth watering yet? Don't forget the hearty breakfast of sausage, bacon, ham, eggs, milk gravy, and homemade biscuits.

Gladys has never advertised. It seems she doesn't have to, seeing the number of people who take the time and effort to find her remote restaurant. The "decor"? Hundreds of business cards taped to the walls by "satisfied (and overstuffed) customers."

Price of the meal is $4 which includes two meats and an unlimited number of vegetables, homemade pie, and biscuits or rolls.

Leave your checkbooks and credit cards at home, and get ready for "good, plain food and generous portions of homespun, common-sense advice" as the *Knoxville Journal* put it.

Hours: 6:30 A.M. to 8:30 P.M. daily.

Directions: Gladys says, "You just come out Dolly Parton Parkway (US 411 in Sevierville) past Sevier County High School, then take the first road to the right. Go to a one-lane bridge. Bear to the left there and stay on that road till Howard's Grocery Store. Turn right at Jones Cove Road, and then turn left at the second blacktop. That's Wilhoite Road, and it's about 1 3/4 miles from there to the restaurant." If you get lost, her phone number is (615) 453-9908.

The Crosseyed Cricket, Lenoir City
Jim and Jean Lockwood, owners

"The next best thing to catching fish is eating them," say Jim and Jean Lockwood, of the delightful Crosseyed Cricket. Jim raises catfish and trout in two lakes he made himself. Then Jean fries the fish and serves them with other homemade specialties.

Located on Paw Paw Road, in a community the old-timers refer to as Whoopie Holler, is the log cabin restaurant. A 130-year-old grist mill next door is where the Lockwoods grind their own cornmeal. Lockwood and his wife virtually raised The Cricket out of the swamp as they built the lakes, restored the mill and cabin, built a fish-shaped swimming pool, and constructed a campsite.

Jim says, "Anglers can rent a boat or fish from the banks. Cane poles are provided, and The Cricket has a special license which covers all anglers who use the place. The campground staff cleans and dresses your catch, which you can have fried in the restaurant or take home packed in ice."

What about those real monsters swimming around in the trout lake? "They aren't trout," says Jim, "they're Chinese carp, a fish that savors weeds. I stock them to keep the lakes clean, and they do a fairly good job." The carp never take anglers' bait, though. "The only time they're caught is when they're snagged by mistake. We throw them back as quickly as possible. I always tell the people fishing, 'Don't catch the hired help.'"

Plan a leisurely visit to The Crosseyed Cricket. They have a limited seating capacity and don't accept reservations. It's not unusual to wait an hour for a seat, particularly on weekends. Even the wait can be an experience you'll enjoy with rambling paths, two lakes, and waterfalls. Wandering ducks delight young children.

A loudspeaker will announce when it's your turn to be seated. A friendly game of horseshoes can help pass the time, and the waiting room of the mill is complete with barrel seats and plenty of checker games.

The Lockwoods tell us, "Your dinner is prepared only after your order has been taken; no precooking or short-cut methods. Just fresh fish dipped in yellow cornmeal and fried to a golden brown, hushpuppies made from white cornmeal fresh from the grinding stone, specially prepared tangy homemade coleslaw, potatoes still hot and steamy, and homemade pies prepared fresh daily in our kitchen." Prices are $3.90 for a catch-your-own trout dinner to $6.85 for their charbroiled trout fillet dinner.

Hours: Fishing—9 A.M. till dark, Monday through Saturday. Fishing closed October through February. Restaurant—5:00 to 9:00 P.M., Tuesday through Saturday. (Open Mondays, too, April through September.)

Directions: Off I-40 take Exit 364 (Melton Hill Dam Exit). Turn toward Oak Ridge and go 1/8 mile. Turn left and follow signs 2 miles. Off I-75 take Exit 81. Turn toward Oak Ridge and go 5 miles. After going under I-40, take first road on the left and follow signs 2 miles. (615) 986-5435.

The Attic Restaurant, Talbott
Mildred Pokorny, owner

"The waitresses wear duster caps and long dresses with aprons, which adds to the 1800s theme," says restaurant manager Nancy Meinert. Selecting recipes, preparing food, and managing and operating the restaurant are a family effort. Even the solid oak tables are hand-crafted by family members.

The Attic Restaurant moved from the attic of a shoe store in Morristown to the 100-year-old farmhouse on County Line Farm. All the out buildings, such as the tractor shed, smokehouse, and caretaker's cottage, have been renovated and now house gift shops.

The food is homemade, from crepes to rolls to pie crusts. Lunch specialties include soup of the day; garden salads; ham and cheese, tuna, and chicken salad sandwiches—all priced $2.00 to $4.95. Dinner entrees include Cornish hen, crepes, and several steak selections priced from $7.95 to $15.95. Peanut butter pie is the dessert specialty.

Hours: Monday–Saturday, 11:00 A.M. to 2:30 P.M.; 5:00 to 9:00 P.M. Sunday, lunch only, 11:00 A.M. to 2:30 P.M.

Directions: From I-40 exit to State 92, Jefferson City. Located on US 11E, 3 miles east of Jefferson City. (615) 475-3508.

Annie's "Very Special Restaurant in the Old City," Knoxville
Annie McCarthy, owner

Annie McCarthy, English-born ballet dancer, opened her restaurant in the "old city" of Knoxville in 1983. The two dining rooms are small and intimate, featuring art deco interior in shades of light blue and melon. Fresh flowers, white linen tablecloths, and flickering candles set the mood for each table.

The menu changes daily, but it tends to feature northern Italian, French, and nouvelle cuisine. "It's a small, but perfectly wonderful menu," Annie boasts. Chicken, fish, and pasta are favorite entrees. A prix fixe menu of $15.95 includes one appetizer, a salad, entree, dessert, and coffee or tea.

Hours: Tuesday–Sunday, 6:00 to 11:00 P.M. Afternoon tea, Sunday, 3:00 to 5:00 P.M. Reservations are advisable on weekends.

Directions: From I-40 take business loop, first exit Summit Hill. Go right to first set of lights, turn right, and travel 2 blocks. Annie's is on the right with a pink neon sign and a tree with tiny lights. 106 Central North. (615) 637-4484.

Golden Dragon Chinese Restaurant, Knoxville
Robert Tsao, owner

Features Mandarin, Szechwan, Hunan, and Shanghai cuisine. Fresh seafood and lamb; steak and seafood dinner; carry-out and luncheon specials. Banquet room available. Lunch prices are from $2.95 to $4.00; dinner, $4.50 to $12.50.

Hours: Monday–Thursday, 11:00 A.M. to 10:30 P.M. Saturday and Sunday, 12:00 Noon to 11:00 P.M.

Directions: Cedar Bluff Shopping Center—I-40 Exit 378; after you exit, turn right at first light, shopping center is on the left. Golden Dragon is in the middle of the shopping center. 9117 South Executive Park Drive. (615) 690-2000.

Regas Restaurant and Gathering Place, Knoxville
William Regas, owner

In 1919 two young Greek immigrants, Frank and George Regas, opened a cafe near the railway station in downtown Knoxville. A lot has changed during Regas's 67 years as a leading restaurant in Knoxville, but the original credo still lives on, "Knowing that a satisfied customer is the best advertisement, we will do our utmost to please you."

Regas today is operated by Gus, Bill, and Frank, sons of the founders. The restaurant has been written up in the *Congressional Record* and received the Travel/Holiday Award as one of the best restaurants in the world. Regas Restaurant represented Tennessee during "A Taste of America" event at the last presidential inauguration.

Bill Regas tells the *Sampler*, "Homemade breads and pastries are made daily in our own bakeshop. Prime rib of beef and fresh steaks are cut a couple of hours before cooking. Fresh seafood is flown in daily from Boston. Our favorite dessert is the strawberry shortcake served with fresh whipped cream." Prices for lunch are $4.25 to $7.95 and for dinner, $6.50 to $23.95.

The Gathering Place Lounge features a piano bar and skylight with live trees and green plants throughout. The antique European cheese cart offers a variety of gourmet cheeses—compliments of Regas.

Hours: Lunch, Monday–Friday, 11:00 A.M. to 3:00 P.M.; dinner, Monday–Thursday, 5:00 to 10:30 P.M.; dinner, Friday–Saturday, 5:00 to 11:30 P.M.

Directions: Off I-40 take the business loop exit, turn right on Summit Hill Drive, right on Gay Street. Go 2 blocks and Regas is on the right. 318 North Gay Street. (615) 637-9805.

Apple Cake Tea Room, Farragut
Mary Henry, Jean Slagle, and Jenny Hines, owners

Family heirloom antiques, country-look wallpaper, and fresh flowers on the tables give a warm and homey appeal to this log cabin Tea Room. When asked the definition of a tea room, Jenny Hines said, "It usually designates being open for lunch only."

A menu featuring cream of broccoli or vegetable beef soup, spinach, crabmeat, or taco salad, a T-room club sandwich, chili, quiche, and "special" baked potatoes appeals to both men's and women's appetites.

The feature dessert is apple cake, but don't overlook the interesting ice-cream cornucopia which is a pizzelle (Italian cone-shaped sugar cookies) filled with ice cream and banana slices, topped with hot caramel or chocolate sauce.

Friendship, almond, and cinnamon rose teas complete the tea room menu. The price range is $2.00 to $5.25.

Other shopping: Also located in Appalachian Square are several antique and craft shops including The Oaken Mantle, Mulberry Bush, and Country Sunshine.

Hours: Monday–Saturday, 11:00 A.M. to 2:00 P.M.

Directions: From I-40/I-75 take Campbell Station Road—Farragut Exit. Turn right on Campbell Station. Log cabin is on the left (200 yards). 11312 Station West Drive. (615) 966-7848.

Atkins Restaurant, Sweetwater
Amos Patterson, owner

Tracy Patterson of Atkins Restaurant says, "We believe in trying to get to know each and every patron. Our specialty is my dad's bread. We feature hot homemade rolls with every vegetable plate and all entrees. My father has been rolling out these great rolls for 20 years."

Entrees served with potato and salad include

steak, fried chicken, fried chicken livers, and pork chops. All types of sandwiches are offered.

Ever-popular plate lunches feature country-style steak, chicken and dumplings, beef stew, or turkey and dressing. Vegetables are buttered corn, macaroni salad, pickled beets, and white beans. Desserts include cobblers, puddings, or pies.

Prices range from 15¢ for a homemade roll to $7 for a steak or seafood dinner. Tracy says, "If you would like something special that is not on the menu, ask our waitress and if there's any way possible, we'll give it a try!"

Hours: Monday–Saturday, 5:30 A.M. to 9:00 P.M. Sunday, 7:00 A.M. to 3:00 P.M.

Directions: From I-75 take exit for State 68 and go south for 2.5 miles until 68 and US 11 intersect. Take 11 north, Atkins is on the left on Main Street. (615) 337-9916.

Bean Pot Restaurant, Crossville
Merle and Charlet Courtad, owners

"Y'all is now in the Cumberland Mtn's of Tenasse whar mountain folks are aimin' to please you with good country cookin'. We hope you will relax and enjoy yourself cause we bin a-fixin' and awaitin' fer you ins."

Charlet Courtad says most visitors to their restaurant take one of the menus home to show friends. The "mountain talk" dictionary on the back explains that "aigs" are eggs and "vittles" means food. There's a dummy that's wired to move his arm and talk to the customers. If you happen to handle one of the country hams he's sitting next to, he'll probably tell you to "keep your hands off my ham!"

The red-and-white-checked shirts and bib overalls the waitresses wear are in keeping with the theme of the menu that offers country favorites of pinto beans, country ham, sawmill gravy, biscuits, turnip greens with corn bread and onion, grits, molasses, and a "cowjuice shake." Prices range 70¢ for sausage and biscuit to $5.50 for a country ham steak dinner.

As Mrs. Courtad says, "We also have a few of the local boys that call themselves the 'Bean Pot Pickers.' They make good music, and some of the children clog along with the music."

Hours: "Forever," said Mr. Courtad. In other words, they're open round the clock 365 days a year!

Directions: At I-40 and Peavine Exit (#322), Crossville. (615) 484-4633.

Mt. Vernon, Chattanooga
Mr. and Mrs. E. A. Evans, Mr. and Mrs. Jeffrey T. Messinger, owners

For 30 years this colonial-type building at the foot of Lookout Mountain has served good food to the folks of Chattanooga. Their southern-cooked lunches and dinners and fresh seafood are well known. Homemade breads and desserts such as amaretto cream pie, chocolate kahlua, blueberry cheese pie, and old-fashioned apple pie are mouthwatering specialties. Mt. Vernon has been recently remodeled and enlarged.

Hours: Monday–Friday 11:00 A.M. to 10:00 P.M. Saturday, 5:00 to 10:00 P.M. Closed Sunday.

Directions: At the foot of Lookout Mountain on US 41. 3509 Broad Street. (615) 266-6591.

Harvey's Pirate Drive Inn, South Pittsburg
Harvey Allison, owner

"We are well known for our Pirate or Harvey Burgers as well as our Dagwoods," says Wanda Crane of Harvey's. (The name Pirate comes from the local football team at South Pittsburg.) "People from Tennessee, Georgia, Alabama, and many other places come here to eat because they've heard about our hamburgers!" Harvey's also serves hot dogs, chiliburgers, French fries, and onion rings. Harvey has been in business 10 years and offers "eat in" facilities.

Hours: Monday–Saturday, 5:00 A.M. to 11:00 P.M. or midnight. Closed Sunday.

Directions: From I-24 take US 72 (South Pittsburg Exit). Go to second red light, turn on State 156 North. Harvey's is on the corner. Second Street. (615) 837-7763.

A SAMPLER FEATURE

Phila Hach, Tennessee's First Lady of Food

■ After enjoying a delicious meal of melt-in-your-mouth roast beef with gravy, luscious steamed green beans, crisp garden salad, flaky hot biscuits, and fudge pecan pie, the Sampler staff was ecstatic. Heading for the nearest easy chairs, we propped up our feet and proceeded to enjoy the wonderful company of the woman who probably knows Tennessee food best.

We were talking with Phila Hach (pronounced Ha) who prepared the out-of-this-world meal for the Sampler at Hachland Vineyard, a 200-year-old log house just outside of Nashville owned by Phila's son, Joe.

Phila has always been involved in one way or another with food preparation—from cooking on live TV broadcasts and catering all across our state to writing cookbooks and sharing recipes. Phila told the Sampler, "My love for culinary excellence comes from my mother, Sophia Shadow Rawlings, one of the state's first home demonstration agents."

When the United Nations Ambassadors visited Nashville in 1976, Phila prepared a Tennessee meal they would never forget! They ate fried chicken, Tennessee River catfish, baked country ham, boiled corn on the cob, fresh garden vegetables, slaw, tomatoes, cucumbers, and cheese. For this contribution to international friendship she received the Peace medal.

Phila helped pioneer live television in Nashville in the early 1950s with her show, "Kitchen Kollege." Phila says: 'You've never lived till you've prepared cake batter on live TV, and the spatula gets caught in the mixer and slings batter all over you!

"There were many embarrassing moments, but my friend and helper Martha Morman Gentry and I would just laugh and go on. Martha was the first black person on live TV in Nashville. When I told the producers I had to have a helper in the kitchen on my cooking show, they said, 'Fine, Phila, who do you want?' When I told them thay said, 'Oh, no. Blacks just aren't on TV.' I said, 'That's okay, if Martha isn't on the show, neither is Phila!' And they gave in. She was great, and I loved her dearly. She was a star herself because of her knowledge of food. I couldn't have done the show without her."

Each room of Joe's cedar log house is furnished in turn-of-the-century antiques, handmade quilts—many crafted by the Amish—woven rag rugs, and memorabilia of the Hach family. There are accommodations for lodging as many as twenty, and up to one hundred can be easily served for a private dinner or meeting.

"Just because you've seen Nashville, you haven't seen Tennessee," says Phila as she proudly explains the concept of the retreat. Family gatherings are often held at the Vineyard, but someone who just wants to spend the night in a "different atmosphere" is also welcome.

Phila Hach

Phila and her distinguished husband, Adolph, showed us around the sprawling residence. The Vineyard serves as a "country" corporate retreat (see lodging section). Walls of glass on the back of the structure look out onto fountains, rock gardens, hundreds of dogwood and redbud trees, and "creatures" of all sorts. The afternoon we were there, birds of every description were lighting in the trees and sunning on the window sills. They eat 300 pounds of seed each week in the winter and 100 pounds in the summer. Deer, opossum, racoons, and red fox also are frequent visitors.

Phila lives in Clarksville, Tennessee, about a forty-five-minute drive from Nashville at the handsome three-story mansion she and her husband Adolph built 30 years ago. It's called Hachland Hill Inn and is a restaurant with overnight lodging accommodations. It, too, can be reserved for private parties or dinners (see restaurant section). Phila oversees all cooking at the Vineyard as well as at Hachland Hill Inn.

During our afternoon with Phila, the *Sampler* was able to get some clear explanations of two terms that have become synonymous with good food in the south–country cooking and southern cooking.

Country Cooking

In the past, *country cooking* was "food cooked simply, fresh, at its best. Country cooking utilized produce grown right on the farm, for example, the apples raised in the orchard, the pumpkins from the field, the eggs and poultry from the chickens in the hen house. The hog provided the hams, sausage, and other pork products. However, the beef was usually sent to market, because that was a money-making commodity. The country cook used few herbs and spices except perhaps cinnamon or nutmeg. Maple sugar was available, but not plentiful, so honey and molasses were also used for sweetening. You would never see spinach in country cooking; turnip greens were the greens of choice. Most vegetables were seasoned with fat meat or bacon drippings.

"The dried beans cooked daily were beans from the garden they had dried the summer before. The milk and butter came from their cow. Around the turn of the century, and certainly before, families would go from fall to spring without buying a single food item. Everything they used would be fresh, home-canned or dried, or salted.

"The country cook used biscuit dough left from breakfast for her fried pies at noon. And the filling was fruit that had been sun-dried. She probably used a saucer or 6-inch plate to cut the rolled-out dough for the crust. She made sweets like custard pies or cobblers that had a lot of sustenance because the farm workers coming in for the noon meal had been working hard all morning.

Southern Cooking

"The same ingredients are used for fine *southern cooking* as were used for country cooking. Southern cooking is a refinement of country cooking. As the homemaker had more time she began to use her ingenuity to take the raw product and combine it with other ingredients for her special recipes. She used finer seasonings and butter, rather than fat meat.

"Southern cooking is more complex than country cooking, and uses more of the science of cooking. A variety of meats are used, and they are prepared in ways more sophisticated than in country cooking, even in combination with vegetables. Rather than just frying a chicken, cooks will combine it with soups, sauces, and rice for variety. Green beans might have cheese, onion rings, or other vegetables added for extra taste and texture. Just a meal of fried meat and plain vegetables is transformed to casseroles and dishes a little 'fancier' than country cooking. There are thousands of cookbooks on southern cooking because each community has its special tastes and special way to do things.

"With plantation cooking, there is more of an ethnic intermingling. Planters and their families traveled more than other Southerners and cost was no object. They brought in tutors for their children, entertained travelers, hired itinerant artists and craftsmen. Thus the people who lived at the mansion might not be typically southern.

Foods and recipes from exotic port cities like New Orleans might be used. Also, most of the food was cooked by slaves, and many details of preparations might have been influenced by the black heritage, as they employed their cooking habits from Africa.

"Thus we could say that plantation cooking was Southern cooking at its best, mingled with the ethnic background of the people of the mansion, and prepared by the wonderful hands of the black person.

"Southern cooking and country cooking are still practiced today, but plantation cooking, in its truest form, is probably gone forever."

Just as various types of southern cooking have developed through the years, so have the names for eating times. The *Sampler* has noticed that some people use the terms dinner and lunch to mean the same meal. Phila put us straight on these.

Dinner and Lunch

"*Dinner,* in the country, is the big meal of the day served at noon. The people get up at sunup, and while the men are in the field, the women are preparing dinner. Then for *supper,* there is a lighter meal, the leftovers from noon.

"But the white collar worker, who is in his office at noon, can't go home for dinner. So usually, the light meal he eats at noon is called a *lunch*. His dinner, the larger more elaborate meal, is eaten at night."

The *Sampler* left the Vineyard full of good food and good information. If you want the same, then come to the Vineyard or Hachland Hill Inn and sample Phila's cooking for yourself. If you can't manage a visit, then just grab one of Phila's wonderful cookbooks and stir up some great Tennessee food on your own.

Phila and Duncan Hines on Kitchen Kollege, 1950

Phila's cookbooks include *Kitchen Kollege,* recipes from her TV show; *From Phila With Love,* an inspirational and intimate collection of recipes from her famous inn; *Kountry Kooking,* a wonderful collection of down-on-the-farm favorites; *Plantation Recipes and Kountry Kooking,* the official cookbook of Opryland U.S.A.; *Phila Hach's United Nations Cookbook,* a great collection of international favorites from U.N. Ambassadors; *The Official 1982 World's Fair Cookbook,* and *Cracker Barrel Old Country Store Recipes.*

Phila has recently produced a *Tennessee Homecoming Cookbook: Famous Parties, People, and Places,* which features recipes served by famous Tennesseans to famous people who have visited our state. Also included are recipes she's used in catering large affairs such as parties at mansions across the state and for Don Williams, Barbara Mandrell, and Twitty City.

Phila's Favorites:

FLOUR AND CORN MEAL: White Lily produced in Knoxville. "Best I've ever cooked with."

BUTTER, ICE CREAM, MILK and DAIRY PRODUCTS: Mayfield Dairy, Athens, TN. "Made with real cream, natural." Favorite flavors of ice cream include black walnut, butter pecan, strawberry cheesecake, and tin roof, a mixture of chocolate, nuts, and marshmallow. Mr. Scottie Mayfield, owner P.O. Box 310, Athens, TN 37303. (615) 745-2151.

CANDY: Sally Lane's Candy Company, Paris, TN. 65-70 varieties of homemade candy. Their delicious pink and green mints are their trademark. Jerry and Jean Peterson, owners. Rt. 2, Box 41, Paris, TN 38242. (901) 642-5801.

BAKERY: Dutch Maid Bakery in Tracy City. "This bakery has been run by the Baggenstoss family for over 80 years. Their specialities are Christmas Sugar Plum Cakes and fruitcakes, also salt rising bread and sourdough." P.O. Box 487, Tracy City, TN 37387. (615) 592-3171.

EGGS: Hudson Brothers, one of the biggest suppliers in the state. Is an egg an egg? Phila says, "Any egg is not a good egg. The best eggs are eggs that have a rooster in the henhouse. The old timey folks always preferred fertile eggs for nutrition.

TEA: "I brew my own—McCormick is good. For a great cup of iced tea use 1 bag to 3 cups of water. Bring distilled water to a rolling boil, put tea bag in and set aside, covered in ceramic teapot. Let it steep for 45 minutes. The leaves must 'unfurl' to release full flavor. (If tea leaves are used, use 1 heaping teaspoon to 3 cups of water.) To serve it cold, add ice and an orange peel for special flavor. For hot tea, bring it back just below boiling point to serve it."

MEATS: "Buy choice beef or meats, 'prime' meat. The consumer must learn to choose meat, poultry and fish. I've got a man up the road who makes the best 'link' sausage. Jake's Sausage in Joelton. You have to buy it from him or at the farmer's market." And for country hams, Frank Rudy, Jr. has the 'old timey' country hams. He's located on Mint Springs Road in Adams, TN.

Is there a difference in cooking with one water compared to another?

"Absolutely...I use distilled water. There are so many additives to water now that coffee made with water from a purification plant tastes like chlorine. Spring water is 'wonderful,' but you can't use it in commercial places of business,"

A storehouse of knowledge on food in Tennessee ...that's what Phila was for the *Sampler.* We are indebted to her for sharing so freely and enthusiastically the information she's gleaned over a lifetime. This generous, lovely lady wins the heart of anyone who is around her for long. The *Sampler* hopes you've enjoyed meeting Phila Hach, Tennessee's First Lady of Food.

A sad note, however. Adolph, Phila's companion for over 30 years died shortly before *The Tennessee Sampler* went to press. Our sympathy to Phila, Joe, and the Hach family. "Eatin' Good in Tennessee" is lovingly dedicated to the memory of a fine Tennessean—Adolph Hach, 1918-1985.

Eatin' Good in Middle Tennessee

Beggar's Castle Restaurant, Jamestown
Roger Salomon, owner

Leaving the beaten track to wind your way down the mountains, you'll find Beggar's Castle. It's a rough-hewn, wood-and-natural-stone chalet with an inviting rustic bridge and sheltered garden terrace. Colorful awnings offer a protective screening for enjoying a refreshing European beverage while planning a stroll through one of the most varied landscapes in Tennessee. The 500 acres offer a range of landscape, from small coves to airy mountains and hiking trails.

The dining room has a huge central fireplace, and its picture windows overlook rugged cliffs. Fine German cuisine and mouth-watering steaks are menu selections. Don't be in a hurry—the Salomons cook to order. Some of their specialties include Lieber Augustine, a delicate chicken, veal, and pork sausage; Wiener Schnitzel, sauteed, milk-fed veal in lemon sauce; Bratwurst, prime, milk-fed veal and pork sausage; Sauerbraten, traditional German sweet-and-sour-marinated beef round; Hasenpfeffer, marinated rabbit with sauce; and other traditional German dishes. Vegetables served with meats include German potato salad, Bavarian red cabbage, and sauerkraut. Price range: $5.25 to $11.00; an average dinner costs $8.50.

A picnic lunch ordered ahead of time includes delicatessen hams, homemade bread, cheese, and smoked fish. Less than an hour's drive from Salomon's farm are Standing Stone, Pickett, and Cumberland Mountain state parks, and the historic nineteenth-century English town of Rugby. (See "Tours and Trails.")

Other features: Shop at The Hamlet, their small store featuring a variety of European specialties. Classical music concerts are offered at various times during the year. A true German Oktoberfest is celebrated the last week of September on into the first week of October, featuring day-long eating! At any time of the year German-cured hams, bacon, and sausage can be ordered. All meat is cured by Salomon at his farm. Inquire about mail-order service.

Hours: Open daily (except Mondays), 11:00 A.M. to 11:00 P.M.

Directions: From I-40, take the Jamestown-Crossville Exit, turning north on US 127. Drive 30 miles, and take the next left turn after the Farmers Co-op onto Glen Oby Road. (There may not be a road sign, but it is a paved road.) Travel 2½ miles on Glen Oby Road. A sign will direct you to turn left on a steep gravel road. (615) 879-8993.

Smoke House Restaurant, Monteagle
Jim Oliver, owner

Jim Oliver started a tiny eating place in 1960 called the "Bee Hive"—a popular drive-in curb-service-type business. Soon outgrowing this facility he and brother Melvin bought the Monteagle Diner where the specialties were country ham, hot biscuits, and plate lunches. In 1975, Jim established the operation he'd always dreamed of having—The Smoke House Restaurant and Trading Post.

Jim says, "There's something for everyone at the Smoke House." In addition to the restaurant are an Ole Tyme Soda Shop, 1920 player piano, country-ham-shaped swimming pool, convention facilities, campground, motel, lodge, and much more.

Almost all of the recipes used now originated from Jim's mother Irene. Known as Mama Rene, she personally oversees the cooking of 1 million biscuits annually for satisfied customers. Other specialties include barbecue dinners, catfish, shrimp, homemade spaghetti, hot sourdough bread, sandwiches of all kinds, vegetables such as white beans and turnip greens, a more than ample salad bar and, of course, country ham and homemade biscuits. Prices range $1.80 for a hamburger to $11.45 for prime rib roast. Average price for a dinner is $6.95. Breakfast served any time.

Other shopping: Catalog also available featuring meats, cheeses, barbecue sauce, jams, jellies, relishes, honey, and molasses. The Trading Post features seven specialty shops, all under one roof, with collections of antiques, brass, local handicrafts, unique gifts, and novelties. Their collection of Jack Daniel souvenirs is second to none.

Hours: Sunday–Thursday, 6:00 A.M. to 10:00 P.M. Friday and Saturday 6:00 A.M. to 11:00 P.M.

Directions: 300 yards from I-24, Exit 134. (615) 924-2268.

The Walton Hotel and Dining Room, Carthage
Fritz and Bettie Sircy, owners

The Walton Hotel looks much the same today as it did in 1908. Lots of things have changed in Carthage, but the Walton's long-standing tradition of good cooking still remains.

"Some people say we have the best fried chicken in Tennessee," says Bettie Sircy. "It's because I don't 'quick fry' anything. It's cooked slowly, the old-fashioned way."

The Walton serves breakfast and lunch seven days a week, featuring delicious country-style food—ham, roast, chicken, vegetables, and homemade desserts. Prices are moderate.

Hours: 6:30 A.M. to 2:00 P.M., seven days a week. Private catering in the evening.

Directions: From I-40 take the Carthage-Gordonsville exit, go 7 miles into Carthage. 309 Main Street. (615) 735-2529.

4 Seasons Restaurant, Sewanee
Daniel and Arlene Barry, owners

A restaurant built with their own hands atop Monteagle Mountain, this dream of the Barrys became reality when 4 Seasons opened with their specialty—pizza, made from scratch.

"We select all our meats and vegetables and make all our pizza stuff, from dough to toppings. We cook the hamburger, put the sausage on raw, grind our cheeses, and mix our spices," says Arlene.

Besides the pizza with eight toppings, the 4 Season Burger, colossal sandwiches, including "Homeboy Hero," and a meatball sandwich are some of their culinary creations. As the name 4 Seasons suggests, the menu varies with the seasons.

Fresh hand-pressed apple cider from the Barrys' orchard is a popular item at harvest time. Winter is time for chili and stew. There are fresh vegetables from their garden in the summer.

Hot fudge cake, chocolate chip pie, and cheesecake have become dessert specialties. Prices range from $1.65 for a half-sandwich to $12.95 for a 16-inch combo pizza. Average price on the menu is $4.00.

Hours: Friday–Saturday, 11:00 A.M. to 9:00 P.M. Sunday, 5:00 to 9:00 P.M.

Directions: From I-24, take Monteagle Exit, go toward Sewanee on US 41A. Turn left after railroad tracks onto Midway Road. Go 1/2 mile. 4 Seasons is on the left. (615) 598-5544.

Miss Christine's, Manchester
Charles and Shelba Miller, owners

"I've tried to maintain the house and entertain in the way Miss Christine would like," says Charles Miller, owner. "Miss Christine Vaughan had lived in the house since 1902. After she died, I heard rumors that the house was to be torn down, and I saw the restaurant as being a viable means of saving the home place."

Miss Christine was a teacher and was the first woman president of TEA (Tennessee Education Association). Her parents entertained lavishly and Miss Christine followed in their footsteps. She made many of the centerpieces and fashioned handmade favors for guests to take home from her parties.

Miller's favorite meal is Sunday buffet, served from a long table covered with a lace cloth and a huge bouquet of beautifully arranged fresh flowers in the center. Served are huge platters of homebaked ham, thinly sliced roast beef, dishes of creamed corn, lima beans, green beans, and a large relish dish. Dessert is usually cobbler, cake, or pie. Fluffy rolls smelling of yeast and corn bread fresh out of the oven are served by waitresses dressed in long dresses and crisp hand-sewn aprons.

"We're known for having good steaks. That's the dinner meal on Fridays and Saturdays." Other meals include barbecue, spaghetti, sandwiches, salads, and soups. Price range: $1.00 for a peanut butter and jelly sandwich for children to $8.99 for a bacon-wrapped filet.

Miller has tried to keep the appearance of the house exactly as Miss Christine had it. Her Christmas ornament tree is featured at Christmas time, and her hats festoon interior walls. A walnut corner cupboard, dining tables, and dining room chairs are original furnishings.

Hours: Monday–Friday 11:00 A.M. to 2:00 P.M.. Dinner, Friday and Saturday, 5:30 to 9:00 P.M. Sunday buffet, 11:00 A.M. to 2:00 P.M.

Directions: In Manchester, just off the town square across from the post office. 215 North Spring Street. (615) 728-5623.

Granny Fishes' House, between Shelbyville and Tullahoma
Richard and Gail Sells, owners

"We raise our trout right here on the farm, 65,000 to 70,000 a year," says Gail Sells, owner of Granny Fishes' House. "We have a catchout pond. You fish and just pay for what you catch."

Located at Nut Cave Trout Farm, the newly built log-type restaurant has a limited, but excellent menu. Rainbow trout and blue channel catfish are the specialties with a frog legs dinner on Thursday nights. Choice of potato, slaw, and hushpuppies come with the dinners. Average price is $5.45. For the nonfish lovers,

hamburger steaks are served. Granny's homemade pies include peach or apple fried pies and cherry or apple cobblers.

Gail tells the *Sampler*, "When the children were young and wanted to go visit their grandmother, they would say, 'Let's go to Granny Fishes' house.'" She and her husband Richard hope you, too, will want to come to Granny Fishes' House.

Hours: Trout farm 8:00 A.M. to 4:00 P.M. daily. Restaurant, 5:00 to 9:00 P.M., Thursday, Friday and Saturday.

Directions: From Tullahoma, go 5 miles on US 41A toward Shelbyville. Look for sign that says Nut Cave Trout Farm and Granny Fishes' House. Turn at Shippman's Creek Road and go 1/2 mile. (615) 857-3315.

Pope's Cafe, Shelbyville
Robert A. Pope and Raymond G. Sudberry, owners

"We serve home-cooked food and have earned the reputation of having the best chili, coffee, and homemade pies in town." Partners Pope and Sudberry have 47 years combined experience at the small city cafe. Counter service at the bar stools and lettering on the glass windows almost take you back to what it might have been like eating at Pope's in the l950s when it first opened.

Breakfast begins at 5:00 A.M. and features the normal breakfast fare for $1.55 to $2.25. The one-page cardboard menu includes steaks, flounder, chicken, oysters in season, ever-popular plate lunches, and all types of sandwiches. Prices range from 85¢ for a pimiento cheese sandwich to $7.65 for a large sirloin dinner.

Horse trainers and visitors to the world-famous Walking Horse Celebration have eaten at Pope's for years. Mrs. Paul Lovelace of Sarasota, Florida, was inspired to write of Pope's:

"Come, all ye horse lovers. Celebration time is here.

If Pope's Cafe is crowded, just move to the rear.

Everyone who knows good eatin' likes corn bread and navy beans

Apple sauce and barbecue, taters and turnip greens.

Rain or shine the show goes on, and you all gotta eat.

So, go on in at Pope's Cafe—it's worth waiting for a seat."

Hours: 5:00 A.M. to midnight daily except Sunday.

Directions: On the square in Shelbyville. 120 East Side Square. (615) 684-7933.

White Rabbit Saloon Restaurant, Lynchburg
Marie G. Clark, manager

In the 1800s and up until Prohibition, the White Rabbit was a true-to-life saloon. The Jack Daniel Distillery restored the building and opened the restaurant about 10 years ago. The early 1900s decor focuses on the back bar which is original to the saloon days. Mirrors, ornate carvings, and writing on the mirrors advertise Uncle Jack's light whiskey. You can imagine row upon row of whiskey lined along these shelves, although today the whiskey is surprisingly absent. Moore County, home of the famous distillery, is dry!

The two-story building on the square in Lynchburg serves roast beef, turkey, corned beef, and Tennessee barbecue. Also offered are an extensive salad bar, homemade soups, and chili served with corn bread. For breakfast, sausage or ham and biscuits are available. Homemade pies are baked daily. Prices: $2.75 to $4.25 for sandwich dinners.

Hours: Monday–Saturday, 7:30 A.M. to 4:00 P.M. (winter months). Seven days a week, 7:30 A.M. to 5:00 P.M. (summer months). Large groups with reservations can be served at night.

Directions: Lynchburg is on State 50 between Fayetteville and Tullahoma. White Rabbit is on the east side of the square, three blocks from Jack Daniel Distillery. (615) 759-7263.

Miss Mary Bobo's Boarding House, Lynchburg
Lynne Tolley, hostess

"An invitation to dinner at Miss Mary's was a valued prize," was the way one old-timer put it. Those who had the privilege of coming here for noon-time dinner always knew they'd been treated to southern hospitality at its finest and down-home cooking at its most delicious.

Mary Bobo was an institution in Lynchburg, Tennessee. She lived to be 101 and ran the boarding house where Jack Daniel himself ate his noon meals. Federal revenue agents assigned to the distillery were long-time boarders. When the boarding house closed after Miss Mary's death in 1983, its passing was mourned by everyone who ever visited the big two-story frame house with its distinctive white picket fence.

Miss Mary's has now reopened under the sponsorship of the distillery, and Lynne Tolley, great-grandniece of Jack Daniel, is the charming hostess. Invitations aren't so hard to come by—all it takes is a reservation by phone. Although Miss Mary's is no longer a boarding house, that portion of the operation may be reopened in the future.

The brass dinner bell lets everyone know it's time for dinner, not *lunch* mind you! "It's a tradition for everyone to introduce oneself before the meal begins," explains one of the hostesses who takes her seat at the head of the table.

At the three tables, it's get-all-you-want-and-then-pass-it-to-the-left-please. The hostess gladly shares with diners much of the local history of Lynchburg and the distillery.

All the food is prepared according to Miss Mary's original recipes. Favorites are fried chicken, fried okra, "riz" biscuits, sweet potato casserole, and cheese grits. "People just love our fried chicken because it's fried in old iron skillets. None of this deep-fat frying stuff—just the old-fashioned way," brags Lynne. "In the summer months three gardens maintained beside the house provide all the vegetables for the daily dinners."

Is Lynchburg's most famous drink served at Miss Mary's? (Of course, this question is always asked!) No, for two reasons. First, Moore County is dry. Second,

Miss Mary didn't allow the drink to be served in her house, except at Christmas when she allowed a little to be added to the boiled custard!

Cost of the meal is $7.50 for adults and $4.00 for children 12 years and younger.

P.S. Lynne passed along the secret of Miss Mary's style of frying chicken: 'You take freshly cut up chicken pieces and dip them in boiling water. Then you dredge the chicken in seasoned flour. Sticking it in the boiling water makes the flour stick better," she said.

Hours: Monday–Friday, 1:00 P.M. Phone for reservations.

Directions: One block off the square in Lynchburg. Lynchburg is on State 50 between Fayetteville and Tullahoma. (615) 759-7394.

The Magnolia House, Columbia
Merrill and Elizabeth Nabers, owners

Built around 1812, The Magnolia House is believed to be the oldest house in Columbia. It became known as the "Doctors' House" because of the many physicians who occupied it through the years.

The creative menu changes daily with offerings of cream of broccoli or cheddar cheese soup, salads, chicken salad on croissant, or ham on raisin-nut bread, asparagus-tomato, bacon-ham, or cheddar-ham quiches, homemade breads, and pastries. Prices: $1.50 to $4.50 for lunch.

Period antiques grace the dining rooms of this house listed on the National Register of Historic Places. Unique gifts are for sale in an upstairs gift shop. A special room is available for children's tea parties. Tableside modeling by local dress shops is often an added treat on Fridays.

Hours: Tuesday–Saturday 11:00 A.M. to 2:00 P.M. Catering available.

Directions: In Columbia, one block north of James K. Polk Home. 701 North High Street. (615) 388-0462. (See "Tours and Trails.")

Albert's Exceptional Dining, Columbia
Ric and Brenda Wilson, owners

Housed in the former Columbia Power Building, this restaurant underwent moderate renovation which gave it a warm, inviting atmosphere. Live plants, dark shades of green decor, and old movie posters along the walls provide a relaxed dining environment.

All breads, desserts, and salad dressings are homemade. Specialties are fresh beef and seafoods. Gourmet burger platters include the Eliot Ness, John Dillinger, and Legs Diamond. Kabobs and poultry are also favorites. Prices range from $4.95 for burger platters to $28.95 for Steak Diane for two.

Hours: Lunch, Tuesday–Friday, 11:00 A.M. to 2:00 P.M. Dinner, Tuesday–Saturday, 5:00 P.M. until—.

Directions: Located north side of courthouse in Columbia. 708 North Main Street. (615) 381-3463.

Henpeck Market, Franklin
Linda Henson, owner

This small deli features all kinds of sandwiches; homemade biscuits with country ham; barbecue plates with slaw, white beans, and corn muffins; chili; potato salad; and dressed eggs. Desserts include homemade fried pies, banana bread, lemon pound cake, brownies, and Italian cream cake.

According to 90-year-old Virginia Jefferson, who lives on Henpeck Lane, the infamous name came about this way, "Back around 1890 there was no water on the little dirt road, and the men were all out hauling water from a nearby well. Two city slickers turned up the road by mistake and asked these husbands where in the world were they and what was the name of the road. Mr. Jefferson set his pails down and said, 'I guess it should be called Henpeck Lane because all the property on the lane is owned by our wives who inherited the farms from their parents.'"

Hours: Monday–Thursday, 5:00 A.M. to 8:00 P.M. Friday and Saturday, 5:00 A.M. to 9:00 P.M. Sunday, 11:00 A.M. to 7:00 P.M.

Directions: Corner of Henpeck Lane and Lewisburg Pike. Exit off I-65 South at Peytonsville Road (Exit 61), Go west approximately 1 mile to a four-way stop. Turn right on Lewisburg Pike—1/2 mile on the left. (615) 794-7518.

Choices, Franklin
Calvin and Marilyn LeHew, owners

"Cooking 'close to nature'…only the freshest fruits and vegetables and superb entrees," says Rod Pewitt of Franklin's newly created Choices restaurant.

The restaurant is housed in the 100-year-old structure that was formerly the Bennett Hardware Building, and Calvin LeHew has provided it with relaxing atmosphere, charm, and character. Franklin's downtown Main Street has recently undergone a strong historic preservation movement.

The handwritten menu changes with the season and may offer Shepherd's Pie (beef round browned in burgundy gravy) or Vegetable Pasta Alfredo (broccoli, carrots, and snow peas with pasta in a white buttery Parmesan sauce). Seafood, chicken, and steak are dinner entrees. Freshly cooked vegetables of the day, delicious soups such as broccoli-cheese, and fresh salads

(chicken salad, congealed, or Boston bibb lettuce) delightfully complement the dinners. Spoon rolls and banana nut bread are baked daily. A child's special is available, and there are plate lunches too. The desserts are lemon souffle, chocolate cheesecake, and caramel pie. Lunches are $4 to $8, dinner, $6 to $15.

A lounge, Bennett's Corner, is located above Choices.

Hours: Monday–Saturday, 11:00 A.M. to 2:30 P.M. Sunday buffet, 11:00 A.M. to 2:30 P.M. Monday–Thursday, 5:00 to 9:00 P.M. Friday and Saturday, 5:00 to 10:00 P.M.

Directions: On the corner of Fourth and Main Streets in Franklin. (615) 791-0001.

Dotson's, Franklin

Clara Dotson, manager

When you see a line of people heading from the courthouse to Dotson's, it just might be the "locked up" jurors from a local trial going to enjoy Clara's home cooking. They've been doing this for 20 years, and Clara Dotson says, "We reserve them a table even when we're covered up."

Some of her customers you may recognize like Tom T. Hall. Clara says, "We have one entire wall covered with autographed pictures of country and western music stars who come all the time." The Back Table Gang are the men who meet from 5:00 till 10:00 A.M. each morning. Although through the morning hours the faces come and go, many of these are regulars who have been doing this for years.

Clara and her late husband, Chester, opened a snack shop on First Avenue back in 1947. Although the location is different now, the delicious food hasn't changed. It's kept Williamson Countians coming back for three generations.

Looking over her lunchtime crowd, Clara brags, "I served most of these people when they sat in a high chair. Now they have children of their own." Does she dream of the day she can retire? "I tried to retire once, but missed seeing and talking to my customers and friends so much that I got back as soon as possible!"

Besides the friendly atmosphere and inexpensive prices, her meals are what have kept the doctors, lawyers, farmers, factory workers, and people from all walks of life coming to Dotson's. "The fried chicken and meatloaf as well as all the home-cooked vegetables are what we've served for years. It just hasn't changed much and people love it."

Hours: Monday–Friday, 5:00 A.M. to 8:30 P.M. Saturday, 5:00 A.M. to 2:30 P.M. Sunday, 6:00 A.M. to 2:30 P.M.

Directions: 99 East Main Street in Franklin, 2 blocks from the square, at the Harpeth River Bridge. (615) 794-2805.

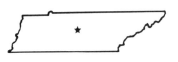

A SAMPLER
·····*Exclusive*·····
Where Gary Morris Likes to Eat

*From Forearm Smashes to "Between Two Fires";
From* La BOHEME *to Dotson's Cafe*

Today and tomorrow Gary Morris will be one of our favorite singers. When we tell our friends this, some of them don't know who he is till we mention the titles of his dozen Top 10 singles. We didn't know who he was until we heard a tremendously moving song called "The Love She Found in Me" on the radio. It was one of those tunes that touches you so deep you just have to find out who's singing it. So we'd listen real hard to the radio trying to hear the DJ say who the artist was. Finally we found out it was a guy named Gary Morris.

You would have to search long and hard to find songs sung anywhere—rock, pop, soul, or country—that are as deeply moving as Gary's. He cuts right to the bone with such hits as "Between Two Fires," "Second Hand Heart," "The Wind Beneath My Wings," and "The Love She Found in Me." In fact, in 1984, his recording of "The Wind Beneath My Wings" was honored as Song of the Year by both the CMA and the Academy of Country Music.

Gary grew up tough in Fort Worth, playing football so well that he won a scholarship to play in college. He liked to hit people, but he was destined for hit records, instead. It seemed a higher calling to touch people's souls than to try to hit them so hard they'd have a hard time getting up.

When the *Sampler* caught up with Gary, he told us that he loves living in Tennessee. He may hunt deer in south Texas and elk in Colorado, but when it comes time for singing, living, eating, enjoying friends and family, there ain't no place like Tennessee.

Gary Morris, the male lead of Joseph Papp's New York Shakespeare Festival production of the opera La Boheme, loves to entertain friends and family and visitors at Dotson's Cafe. Is Dotson's in Manhattan? No! Is it in Hollywood? No! Is it on Nantucket Island? No! Dotson's is in Franklin, *Tennessee*. Franklin, Tennessee, is the home of many of country music's hottest talent, including Gary and his son, Sam.

Gary tells the *Sampler* that one of his favorite things in the world is to take his friends to an early breakfast at Dotson's. His suggestion is get up real early and order sunny-side-up eggs, pan-fried chicken breast (he says it's the world's best), biscuits, juice, and coffee. When Gary's in there alone, he enjoys just eatin' and talkin' to the waitresses, Mrs. Dotson, and the other workin' people gettin' their day started off right.

So next time your radio's playing and you're moved by a song sung by a man who can squeeze as much

Gary Morris

emotion from a lyric as anyone, pay attention to who's singing. It could easily be Gary. Next time you're in Gary's part of Tennessee, munch a bunch of breakfast down at folksy and friendly Dotson's Cafe in Franklin, Tennessee!

Loveless Motel and Cafe, Nashville
Donna McCabe, owner

"We give the same hospitality to college kids as we did one night when Chet Atkins brought Paul McCartney and his wife," says Donna McCabe. It's just plain country hospitality specializing in excellent country ham and redeye gravy (made from ham drippings and doused in coffee). Breakfast is the house specialty and is offered all day. Many mornings 150 breakfasts are served. Besides country ham are fresh eggs, peach and blackberry preserves made daily, skillet-fried chicken, and piping hot homemade biscuits (their secret recipe).

The chief cook, Mrs. Mary Elizabeth Roberts, has been cooking there 6 days a week for 23 years. Her secret is never to use a recipe but a little of this and a little of that. It's her good country cooking that has earned this restaurant such a fine reputation that it attracts customers like Jimmy Buffet, Captain Kangaroo, Willie Nelson, B. J. Thomas, the Hee Haw gang, and many more.

This family-owned establishment began in 1951 when an unassuming little house in the country was turned into a restaurant and called the Harpeth Valley Tea Room. The Loveless couple bought it the next year, added the motel, and the name became simply Loveless Motel and Cafe. Donna McCabe, who's owned it now for close to 15 years, has chosen to keep the old-time neon sign and other originals to retain that homey atmosphere.

The busiest day of the week for the restaurant is Sunday, when the Loveless will satisfy between 500 to 800 appetites. Mrs. Roberts will sometimes make 3,500 biscuits for one Sunday, and by the end of the day they will be gone!

Breakfast prices are $2.45 to $5.60; lunch, $1.75 to $8.00; and dinner, $5.30 to $8.00.

Other features: Besides the restaurant, Donna offers the cafe's specialties by mail order. For a taste of the South at home, order the freshly made preserves, salty country ham, delicate honey, smoked or spicy sausage, slab bacon, or Benton County sorghum molasses. For a copy of the catalog, write Loveless Hams and Jams, Rt. 5 Hwy. 100, Nashville, TN 37221.

Hours: Tuesday–Saturday, 8:00 A.M. to 2:00 P.M.; 5:00 to 9:00 P.M.; Sunday, 8:00 A.M. to 9:00 P.M. If you plan to go to the Loveless at peak periods, especially Saturday and Sunday breakfast, be sure to make reservations.

Directions: From Nashville, go out West End Avenue. About 8 miles from downtown US 70 and State 100 fork, take State 100 about 7 1/2 miles. Restaurant on right. From I-40 West take Exit 192–go left, about 4 miles take another left and you can see the Loveless sign. (615) 646-9700.

Sylvan Park, Nashville
Louise and Lynn Chandler, owners

Sylvan Park is one of those places that doesn't worry about decorating in a trendy style, advertising extensively, or seeking a lot of tourist trade. What they do seem to dwell on is serving good, home-cooked food. It's kept diners coming back for 35 years. The waitresses are known for how quickly they get your food to you. Charles Etta Patterson, the cook, is one reason Sylvan Park is so well known in Nashville. She gets there about 4:00 A.M. each day to get all the pies made.

Phila Hach says Charles Etta's candied tomatoes are about the best she's ever eaten! Plate lunch specials feature fried chicken, roast beef, salmon, fried Tennessee country ham, and—lots of people's favorite—turkey and dressing. Potatoes, pole beans, stewed apples, cauliflower, potato salad, and turnip greens are some of the vegetables. Prices average about $3.

Hours: Monday–Saturday, 10:30 A.M. to 7:30 P.M. Closed Sunday.

Directions: From downtown Nashville, take West End Avenue to Murphy Road. Turn right, across from McCabe Park. 4502 Murphy road. (615) 292-9275.

Tavern on the Row, Nashville
Al Cartee, owner

A restaurant on Music Row that doesn't have country music playing in the background? That's right! Tavern on the Row was created as a restaurant catering to people in the music industry; therefore, owner Cartee feels the pop/jazz music played offers this crowd a diversion from their everyday surroundings. The comfortable interior is accented by exposed brick walls, brass fixtures, and original woodwork which is the result of the two years the owner spent in preparing the building, beginning with gutting the old two-story house.

A full course meal is served way into wee morning hours since hungry singers and pickers often wind up a recording session around midnight. Dinner entrees include seasoned prime rib, Shrimp Diane, veal with shrimp and artichokes, and the popular New Orleans dish—Blackened Redfish. The house salad includes a side dish of marinated vegetables and homemade dressings. A favorite appetizer is Buffalo Wings! The sandwiches are prime rib, sirloin strip, chicken salad, Tavern club, and a 7-ounce fresh ground beef burger. There is an impressive and varied wine list.

Hours: Monday–Saturday, 11:30 A.M. to 2:30 A.M.
Location: 26 Music Square East. (615) 255-3900.

Hachland Hill Inn, Clarksville

Phila Hach, owner

Hachland Hill Inn is a unique concept in lodging and dining in Tennessee. Located in Clarksville, about 45 minutes from Nashville, the inn is a wonderful setting for any occasion. The grand ballroom can hold a debutante ball or wedding reception, or it can seat 300 for a private dinner. Hachland Hill has an unlimited menu selection, down-on-the-farm country suppers of southern fried chicken or Tennessee country ham and biscuits or international cuisine.

Clarksville's three oldest log houses have been reconstructed in the garden area and are available for overnight lodging. Primitive antiques offer a "homey" atmosphere, yet central heat and air provide modern comfort.

A bird sanctuary and flower gardens offer peace and solitude to soothe your frazzled nerves, while square dances and old-fashioned barbecue suppers invite fun and good times, southern style.

Though Phila does all the menu planning and selection herself, she has a devoted staff of 35 who welcome and serve the guests and make their visit memorable. Phila explains, "All cooking is done from my cookbooks. If I walk through the kitchen and something isn't right, out it goes. I'm not a perfectionist, but it's got to be done the way I perceive it."

The Hachs have been offering fine dining and overnight lodging at Hachland Hill for 30 years. Phila invites you to Clarksville to enjoy the best in southern cuisine, served in the elegant manner of the Old South. Cookbooks containing Phila and Adolph's famous recipes are available at the Inn. (See more in this section.)

Rates for overnight lodging in the cabins are $45.00 for first person, $10 for each additional person, maximum of 10 per cabin. Breakfast and lunch are $7.75 per person. Dinner is $17.00 to $30.00 per person.

Hours: Lunch, 12 Noon to 2:00 P.M. Dinner, 6:00 to 8:00 P.M., by appointment only.
Location: 1601 Madison Street. (615) 647-4084.

Cross Plains Country Kitchen, Cross Plains

Anne and Herbert Mills, owners

"We have only one traffic light in Cross Plains," laughs Anne Mills as she gives the *Sampler* directions to the Country Kitchen, "and it's located in our front window! It's one I bought at a sale, and it works, too!

The restaurant began in the stock room of the Food Town grocery when Anne brought her stove and refrigerator from home and started making pies. As she says, "Then I decided I'd cook a small amount for our employees. Before long, one person, then another would come by and say they'd like a piece of pie and coffee, or 'could I possibly fix a plate for them?' Soon we had people sitting on crates in the stockroom trying to eat. One man even brought his own table so when folks came in from the fields at noon, they'd have a place to sit."

When the bank closed in 1984, Anne expanded her facilities to the bank building which can be reached through a door near the back of the grocery store. Now when the farm hands come in from the fields or the bank president comes by, they have a place to spread out and enjoy the abundant meal. The Carrs of Cross Plains run a burro and wild horse adoption center for the federal government. When the guys from Washington, D.C. come down on business, the Carrs take them to the Country Kitchen.

From the traffic light in the window to the hay rake and mole trap her friends have brought by for Anne to use, the decor is rustic, country, and thoroughly delightful. Old graduation pictures and Cross Plains's basketball team photos from the 1920s and 1930s line the walls, and people keep bringing in more. The guest book rests on a 6-feet-long butcher block covered with a quilt, and checkers are played everyday on the old checkerboard located on the dance floor.

Monday features fried chicken and pork chops. Minute steaks with gravy and salmon patties are Tuesday's specials. Meatloaf, baked country ham, and roast beef with gravy are the treats on Wednesday. Fresh-cooked vegetables, cobblers that simply melt in your mouth, beef stew, and barbecue are offered everyday. Twenty pork shoulders are barbecued every Friday night over an open pit. Price range: 89¢ for a sausage and biscuit to $3.95 for a dinner of meat and three vegetables.

Hours: Monday–Wednesday, 6:00 A.M. to 2:30 P.M. Thursday–5:00 P.M. dinner, 6:30 bingo. Friday and Saturday, 5:00 P.M. dinner. Live entertainment on the stage with colored lights. Country and western, bluegrass, and swing bands.

Directions: Located on State 25. From I-65, take Exit 112 which is State 25. Turn left, go 3 miles. Country Kitchen is just before the four-way stop. (Look for the traffic light in the window.) (615) 654-2588.

Swan View Restaurant and Motel, Hohenwald
Wilma Lindsey, owner

Combination country market, restaurant, and health food store, the Swan View can fill most of your needs with one stop. The picnic tables with benches and red-and-white-checked tablecloths are located right next to the toy trucks and down the aisle from the sun tan lotion and hairspray. Health food displays include vitamins, garbanzo beans, rolled oats, and buckwheat pancake mix.

Formica-topped tables and red plastic glasses await the weekend when the catfish crowd is overflowing and the dining room is opened. All-you-can-eat Tennessee River catfish dinners are served with your choice of potatoes, white beans, slaw, and hushpuppies. A full order is $5.49 and a half-order is $3.95. Also served are steak, chicken, freshly made hamburger steaks, and sandwiches of all kinds. Homemade pies are pecan, lemon, coconut, and chocolate.

Hours are long during turkey, rabbit, squirrel, and deer seasons when the Swan View opens at 4:00 A.M. to cater to hungry hunters. The Swan View is a check-in station for deer hunters, which allows game wardens to keep records of how many deer are killed in each county per year. Mrs. Lindsey says, "I get bicycle and motorcycle riders from the (Natchez) Trace. When they stay in my motel, I open when they'd like to have breakfast." Breakfast prices range from $2 for sausage or bacon, eggs, and biscuits, to $3 for country ham breakfast.

Although many deer can be seen, no hunting is allowed on Natchez Trace. There's plenty of superb hunting in Lewis County, however, making it one of the state's top deer hunting areas.

Hours: Monday–Thursday, 5:00 A.M. to 9:00 P.M. Saturday, 5:00 A.M. to 10:00 P.M. Sunday, 6:00 A.M. to 9:00 P.M. Special hours for hunting seasons!

Directions: Located right on State 99 between Columbia and Hohenwald (7 miles east of Hohenwald). One mile west of the Natchez Trace Parkway. (615) 796-8864.

Breece's Cafe, Centerville
Linda Breece Bates, owner

For three generations the Breece family has been serving home-cooked food and extending southern hospitality. In 1939 John Breece and his wife Bessie began operating a pie wagon. Today Linda Breece Bates, their granddaughter, carries on the family tradition.

Linda says, "We were honored to have six governors and Minnie Pearl eat with us in July 1984 for our Heritage Day celebration." The menu that day at Breece's was typical of each day's serving: fried chicken, fresh green beans, corn, baked squash, fried apples, sliced tomatoes, homemade rolls, and corn bread. The home-baked desserts are blackberry cobbler and pecan, apple, cherry, strawberry, coconut cream, and lemon ice box pies. Some say Breece's coconut cream and apple pies "can't be beat anywhere." Prices of plate lunches, $1.85.

Centerville is the home town of Minnie Pearl (Sarah Ophelia Colley Cannon) who grew up on the outskirts of town.

Hours: 5:00 A.M. to 8:00 P.M. daily

Directions: From Nashville go State 100 southwest about 50 miles to Centerville town square. 111 South Public Square. (615) 729-3481.

Turn of the Century Tea Room, Dickson
Harold and Jo Ann Sutton, owners

"I've been cooking since I was about seven years old," relates Jo Anne Sutton. Jo Ann uses the many recipes collected from friends over the years.

She enjoys changing the menus with the seasons, and a house specialty is the "Salad-a-Rama" on Thursdays. "We've been so pleased that the Tea Room has been accepted by the men of our community. About 60 per cent of our customers are men," beams the proud owner.

Wooden rockers and a porch swing grace the large front porch and balcony that wrap around the charming two-story frame house. The Suttons recently added a garden room which doubled the number they can serve.

Hours: Monday–Friday, luncheon 11:00 A.M. to 2:30 P.M.; dessert and beverages 2:30 to 4:30 P.M. Friday–Saturday, dinner 6:00–9:00 P.M. Sunday buffet, 11:00 A.M. to 2:00 P.M.

Directions: From I-40 take Exit 172 (State 46). Travel to Main Street and turn left. Across the railroad tracks, the house is on the left. 303 South Main Street. (615) 446-7300.

Other shopping: Upstairs is the Mulberry Garden Mini-mall featuring local residents' hand-crafted items. The hours are Monday–Friday, 10:00 A.M. to 5:00 P.M.; Sunday, 11:00 A.M. to 4:00 P.M.

Pizza Corner, Waynesboro
Glenda West, owner

"I started this restaurant when I was 19, right out of high school, and we've just celebrated our eighth anniversary in business," says Glenda West. "I guess our all-beef hamburgers might be the thing we get the most comments about. They've been a huge success. Our meat is bought fresh and patted out daily—nothing frozen."

Located right across from the courthouse, Pizza Corner gets travelers as well as the steady teen-age crowd. In square miles Wayne County is the second largest county in the state but has only 13,000 people, so out-of-town business must be depended upon. The Buffalo River, a popular, scenic canoeing site is nearby, and many of her customers are very hungry canoeists. Glenda enjoys meeting these interesting people and says they always have some *real* stories to tell. (Five canoe rental places are close to Waynesboro.)

Since the local teen-agers enjoy cruising around the square, they often stop for a burger or pizza. Thirteen toppings are offered for the pizzas. Prices are moderate.

Hours: Open seven days a week. Monday–Thursday, 11:00 A.M. to 9:00 P.M. Friday and Saturday, 11:00 A.M. to 10:00 P.M. Sunday, 12:00 Noon to 9:00 P.M.

Directions: State 13 and US 64 both lead to Waynesboro. Pizza Corner is on the square. Although there is not an interstate that runs close to Waynesboro, there are two easy access routes from the Natchez Trace Parkway (milepost 370 is US 64 and milepost 360 is State 13). (615) 722-5611.

Hog Wild in Tennessee

A controversy in Tennessee has been going on for years, and it looks like it'll continue for decades longer. It centers on that mouth-watering delicacy called "Tennessee country ham." Now, the controversy is not as to whether we Tennesseans like to eat it. That'd get a resounding yes pretty well statewide. The controversy is about the best way to cook it.

Some folks say the *only* way to cook country ham is to fry it. Others testify that boiling in a lard stand or roaster produces the most succulent meat, while others *always* bake their ham.

The *Sampler* isn't going to add any fuel to the fire and say one way is the *best*. But we will furnish you with cooking directions and let you decide for yourself! Our thanks to Louise Barker, food marketing, University of Tennessee, for providing us with these recipes.

A smokehouse hangs with Tennessee's finest

Frying country ham:

1. Skin should be removed only over the area from which the slices will be taken before attempting to slice the ham. Cut ham slices 1/4 to 3/8 inch thick.
2. Do not trim any excess fat from the slice until after frying.
3. Use heavy skillet that will distribute heat evenly.
4. Place slices in skillet with fat edges toward the center. Fat edges should be scored to prevent buckling.
5. Do not cover. Fry slowly. Turn slices frequently.
6. Do not overfry. Grease should not splatter. Cook until both sides of ham are very lightly brown.

Boiling country ham:

1. Cut off hock, clean whole ham thoroughly with a brush and rough cloth. Trim off any dark, dry, edges and discolored fat. Hams over 1 year old can be soaked 8–12 hours before cooking if you prefer. Be sure to change the water before boiling the ham.
2. Fill large roaster with rack about 1/2 full of water. Put ham in skin side up. Start ham at 450° F. and reduce heat to 300° F. when water boils. One tablespoon of brown sugar or molasses per quart of water may be added. (1/4 cup vinegar or red wine may be added to the water if desired.)
3. Simmer, do not boil. Cook approximately 30 minutes per pound or until meat thermometer registers 160° F.

4. Allow ham to cool in juice 4 or 5 hours.
5. Remove from broth, and skin ham. Use your favorite glaze.

Baking country ham:

1. Prepare the ham exactly as you would for boiling. Soak it about 12 hours if you prefer.
2. Place ham, skin side up, on a rack in an open pan.
3. Start ham covered or in aluminum foil in a hot oven (375° F.) 1 hour. Reduce heat to 200–225° F. and cook until the center of the ham registers 160° F. on a meat thermometer. This will take about 45 to 50 minutes per pound for whole hams. Hams continue to cook after removal from oven.
4. Remove skin and allow ham to cool slightly. You may either serve now or glaze.
5. After ham is cool, cover generously with your favorite glaze.
6. Place under broiler or in hot oven until glaze is melted.
7. Serve hot or cold. Baked hams are much easier to slice when chilled. Cut slices thin and perpendicular to the bone.
8. Cooked ham can also be prepared for serving by removing the bones, tying in a roll, then chilling before slicing.

To glaze baked or boiled country ham:

After ham is cooked, remove skin with sharp knife, score, cover with glaze, stick cloves about every inch and bake 350–400° F. for about 30 minutes or till lightly browned. Glaze may be made of combinations of brown sugar, fruit juice, and crushed pineapple, or you can baste ham with honey while baking.

Janice Stevenson of S & H Honey Farms, Columbia, Tennessee, (see "Shopping"), is happy to give her tried-and-true advice on fixing this Tennessee taste treat, country ham.

To cook slices of country ham:

1. Preheat oven to 300–325° F.
2. Trim off heavy rind but not fat, and place slices in a 13 x 9 x 2 baking dish or heavy iron skillet. Cover tightly with aluminum foil.
3. Bake 5 minutes. Turn slices, and bake other side 5 minutes. Test for tenderness and, if not tender, bake 3 or 4 more minutes.

To cook a whole country ham:

This is yummy for Christmas or Easter dinner, regardless of size. Here's what to do. Remember! *Don't* throw the ham away if mold is on the outside. That's okay.

1. Get a very large pan with lid, a lard stand if you have it.
2. Cut off the small end piece if too large to fit in the pan.
3. Scrub with warm water and a stiff brush.
4. Soak 8 hours.
5. Take out of that water, and scrub and wash again.
6. Put the ham back in rinsed-out container, and fill with hot tap water.
7. Place on stove and after coming to a boil, boil 30 minutes.
8. Put tight-fitting lid on the container, and place the container in a cardboard box, lined with several layers of newspaper.
9. Wrap container in an old quilt or sleeping bag.
10. Wrap with more newspaper and close cardboard box, if possible.
11. Let sit 24 hours.
12. Drain off all the hot water. The ham will still be very hot.
13. Before it completely cools, put on rubber gloves, and remove all loose fat and heavy outer skin. Work the bone out.
14. Press the good meat together while placing on a piece of cellophane wrap.
15. Refrigerate overnight. Ham will come out moist and tender. Slice and enjoy.

Country cured hams are produced in many areas, but Middle Tennessee is noted for this specialty. The traditional dry cured, smoked, and aged hams of this area are treasured for good eating. The country ham is a featured party food (often thinly sliced in tiny hot biscuits) and always a really appreciated gift remembrance even for those who may have everything or be hard to please.

A really neat little booklet is produced by the folks who cure Clifty Farm Real Tennessee Country Hams in Paris, Tennessee. Their name is well known across the state, and they've been performing this "country art" for years. The booklet tells the process used for curing country hams, at least as near as anyone will tell. Anyone who cures ham has "secret" ingredients that make hams special, but at least you'll find cut what's involved in getting the ham from the farmer to your dinner table.

This booklet also gives recipes from women across the state who use ham in casseroles, with greens, in soups, as sandwiches—in other words, more ways than

you thought were possible! Just write: Clifty Farms, P.O. Box 1146, Paris, TN 38242.

There's even a section on Slicin' and Storin'. "All Clifty Farm hams are fully cured and are easily stored by wrapping in a brown paper bag and hanging in a cool dry place. Do not wrap in plastic. Once the ham is cut you should slice the entire ham and wrap in individual or family size servings and freeze. Then your ham can be stored for long periods of time and can be thawed and prepared as needed. The hock and small pieces should be wrapped and frozen separately. They make excellent seasoning meat when you cook beans and vegetables."

The Chitlin Hut

The Chitlin Hut, Flypaper Circle, Fly, TN, (615) 555-4432.

Ray Jo Bullington, owner

"I guess you could say that we specialize in hog innards," said Ray Jo Bullington of Fly, Tennessee. "Everything we serve here at the Hut's got chitlins in it. We ain't like a lot of restaurants that just have special chitlin suppers on Thursday night, no sir."

In the background we could hear the water running and the hog entrails being slopped on the counter while being cleaned.

"Our breakfast menu's most popular item is our chitlin omelets. We got chitlins and cheese omelets, bacon and chitlin omelets (we call 'em, whole hog omelets), and my favorite, which we call 'high-bro omelet,' has a mixture of chitlins, greens, brains, jowls, and corn bread. People come all the way from Detroit for that one," said Ray Jo proudly.

"Our lunch specials here in Fly are barbecued innards with three veggies that are hog favorites, such as boiled ragweed, taters, and fried fescue grass. We also have chitlin burgers for them that feel they gotta have a burger. When you think about it, this is more of a *Ham*burger than the real thing," laughed Ray Jo.

"Now dinner, ain't nobody can outdo The Chitlin Hut for dinner. Not even one of them Five-Moon-Rated restaurants in San Francisco." We could hear music playing in the background. The owner said it was hog-eatin' music. "We only serve one thing for dinner here and that is real traditional Tennessee country chitlins. *Boiled,* of course.

"Ya'll come see us."

We couldn't wait. To get to Fly, take Highway 79 to Flypaper Circle, then go around the circle 10 times till you get dizzy. Ray Jo said that would help anyone who was afraid to eat chitlins. Then go down Rural Route 82 about 21 miles till you get to a crossroads. Take a right. If you go left, you'll end up in Mushroom Pasture, Tennessee. If you get lost, call 555-4432 and ask for Boss Hampshire.

Prices at The Hut are low to high, the most expensive item being their incredibly delicate chitlins and blueberry omelet. If you still think that this a real place, please don't head for The Hut. We're just kidding.

Preparing Chitlins

The *Sampler* has some friends, Dot and Frank Sowell, who host Chitlin Suppers, feeding hundreds of people at a time. We knew they'd be the ones to tell us how to prepare chitterlings. Below is their method:

25 pounds of frozen or fresh chitterlings, thaw if frozen. Remove all fat, clean and wash thoroughly. Scrubbing on an old-fashioned washboard is very helpful.

Place cleaned chitterlings in a black wash kettle. Cover with water. Add 1 cup vinegar, red pepper, bay leaf, 1 bunch celery, several white onions, salt. Boil outdoors over a wood fire until tender—about 2 to 3 hours.

If you prefer stewed chitlins, they are ready to eat when tender. If you prefer them fried, make a batter from the following ingredients.

5 pounds plain flour
1 dozen eggs
salt
pepper
milk to make a thick batter

Drop small amounts of chitterlings into batter until coated thoroughly and fry in deep fat, preferably Crisco, until golden brown. Drain and serve very hot with hot sauce, if desired.

Serve accompanied by cole slaw, French fries, and hushpuppies.

This amount will generously serve about 20 people.

Stewed chitlins may be placed in cold storage for 2 to 3 days, then reheated.

This recipe was used by J. B. Johnson, a well-known Maury County cook, for many years. He could prepare meals for 10 to 1,000 persons with ease.

Eatin' Good in West Tennessee

Broadway Farms, Decaturville
Thomas Broadway, owner

"We're just plain country and jest so proud" is the motto at Broadway Farms. Drinks are served in fruit jars, rocking chairs wait comfortably, and country cooking abounds. Served are Tennessee River catfish with hushpuppies, whole hog pit barbecue, chicken and dumplings, steak dinners, hoe cakes, corn fritters, and white beans. 'Nanner puddin', homemade chocolate, cherry, caramel, and coconut pies, and 'lasses sundaes are desserts. Children's dinners are also available. Price range: $1.50 for sandwiches to $4.70 for country ham dinners.

Thomas Broadway tells the *Sampler,* "This restaurant is operated by the greatest bunch of people, our family and close friends. We aim to please."

Hours: Friday and Saturday, 5:00 P.M. to 10:00 P.M. Will open anytime for special parties. Chuck wagon catering service. Will cater country or city style.

Directions: 3 miles east of Decaturville on Old Perryville Road. (901) 852-4559.

Silver Moon Cafeteria, Somerville
Eula Mae Richardson, owner

We're proud to feature in the *Sampler* an article written by one of the regulars of the Silver Moon Restaurant, Julia Blackwood. We feel this description is typical of happenings in many restaurants all across Tennessee—every day.

The Silver Moon Restaurant opens at 6:00 A.M. Unknowing persons who arrive at that predawn hour glance around the freshly painted, cozy cafe and select a table or booth far from the hub of local patrons. Shyly, they deposit their coats and purses, plop down, and hear a cheerful, "Good morning," from Eula Mae Richardson or from Cindy Fuller, her niece.

Soon, if they are observant, these visitors notice a peculiar happening. Locals begin to trickle in, and not shy at all about their love for Eula's steaming coffee and good food, they sashay up to The Round Table—located smack in the center of all the activity.

Attired in real work clothes (i.e., blue jeans and overalls), this early group passes along bits of local news, gossip, speculation, or downright lies to Eula Mae and Cindy. From the two ladies, they get any news left from the day before that is worthy of continued interest. These sunrise coffee drinkers complain about late sleepers, high taxes, the woes of farming, and marriage.

By now a few of the next group have arrived. The Round Table is never completely deserted unless the Silver Moon is closed. These new arrivals are more apt to be dressed in three-piece suits. Some carry important-looking folders or briefcases. They make a big production of reading the Memphis newspaper, especially financial and legal pages. Their conversations run to more heavy matters such as canoeing on the Wolf River or locating a duck blind.

Time ticks on, and the sun is up for the day. If it's Wednesday, several ladies have arrived to join the young professionals around The Table. Soon, the men are driven off because (they say) the talk has turned to new fashions, menus, and complaints about men.

By 9:00 A.M., the early crowd has thinned considerably. Those who work have gone reluctantly to tractors, typewriters, law books, and cash registers. But, around 10:00, the early risers are back to get midmorning coffee and to get a whiff of what will be served for lunch.

(Note: Rumor has it that many regular customers of "The Moon" have the restaurant on call forwarding.)

The early lunch crowd is usually women. They discuss (besides the news that Eula has gathered from the earlier groups) art, music, special events in theaters in Memphis and Jackson, and shopping excursions. One of this group is *always* going somewhere!

As others begin to arrive around 11:00, Eula and her staff are kept on the run trying to keep the pans and bowls full of hot meats and vegetables. The fresh homemade biscuits and corn bread are irresistible.

Through the luncheon hour, the membership of The Round Table changes several times. The morning events are mentioned, discussed, and reviewed for newcomers. It is said that all the best jokes and much of the true speculations come from the 11:00 to 1:00 gatherings.

Eula Mae and Cindy get to take a brief breather when 1:00 rolls around. They use this time to replenish the coffee pots and to set out fresh cups. By 1:30, the afternoon coffee break has begun, and by the time it is over, more than two hours will have elapsed.

The coffee break group is a mixed group. From the banks, the insurance agencies nearby, and the shops across the square, the afternoon coffee klatch gathers. They learn the latest on who is married, remarried, or calling it quits. They drain the coffee pots and leave Eula and Cindy to lock up, go home, get some sleep, and be back the next morning at the center of the universe as far as the folks of Somerville, Tennessee, are concerned.

The menu includes country ham, homemade biscuits, home-cooked vegetables, and cobblers.

Hours: Monday—Saturday, 6:00 A.M. to 4:00 P.M. Sunday, 7:00 A.M. to 2:00 P.M. Closed Thursday.

Directions: From I-40 take either State 59 or State 76 into Somerville. The Silver Moon is on the east side of the square. 117 East Fayette Street. (901) 465-2728.

The Old Country Store and Restaurant, Jackson
Brooks Shaw and T. Clark Shaw, owners

"When my daddy had a heart attack in 1960, the doc-tor told him to get a hobby. Twenty years and 15,000 antiques later, we've got The Old Country Store," says T. Clark Shaw. Although he'd never collected an antique in his life, when a friend gave Brooks Shaw three antiques, that whetted his appetite for more. Over the next five years he collected everything from Garrett snuff stored in a hog bladder to an extremely rare soda fountain.

The restaurant is part of the country store museum and started out simply as a bar counter with stools where cold cuts were served. Later white beans, Tennessee country ham, and cracklin' bread were added. "To serve more people, we added one table, then another. Now we've moved and developed our new Old Country Store and Casey Jones Village," says Clark.

"The gift shop, museum, and ice-cream parlor are favorites with all. Our good cooking like homemade cobblers and southern fried chicken seems to keep bringing people back too!"

Other features: Casey Jones Home and Railroad Museum and the Carl Perkins Music Museum are at this same location.

Hours: Sunday–Thursday, 6:00 A.M. to 9:00 P.M. Friday and Saturday, 6:00 A.M. to 10:00 P.M.

Directions: Located in Casey Jones Village on I-40 West. (901) 668-1222.

Rib Eye Barn, Jackson
Bert Holland, owner

"We have been in business 11 years and have not changed our format. We specialize in food and service," says Bert Holland.

As the name implies, aged rib-eye steaks are the specialty at this dinner restaurant. The meat is brought to your table for selection and is prepared exactly as you request.

The salad bar with 30 or more items offers smoked oysters, herring in wine sauce, sardines, and anchovies along with the regular salad fixings. "We have an orange honey butter that we make and serve with our bread and crackers," says Bert.

The decor is rustic western. The large open dining room has a cathedral ceiling and cedar walls. Old wagon wheels leaning against a split-rail fence out front complete the setting.

Hours: Monday–Saturday, 5:00 to 10:00 P.M.

Directions: From I-40 take Exit 80A onto 45 Bypass S. The restaurant is at the intersection of 45 Bypass and I-40. (901) 668-8777.

Mister B's Restaurant, Memphis
Richard Baker, owner

"We don't batter a single shrimp until we get an order for it," says Richard Baker, owner of Mister B's, one of the best-kept secrets in the city. Richard brags that his restaurant is "the only authentic Cajun seafood eatery in Memphis." Although Mister B's ancestors are English, he learned to cook Cajun from "my old girlfriend's mother."

A limited, but well-prepared menu features a well-seasoned and thick gumbo, batter-fried shrimp, "peel-um-

and-eat-um shrimp," shrimp creole, the popular red beans and rice, and red fish almondine. The oyster "po boy" is popular as are the fried frog legs. For those who have really big steak appetites, 2-pound steaks are available! Seafood $3.50 to $9.25; steaks $14.95 to $17.95.

Although the atmosphere is casual and the building humble, if you're a true Cajun food lover, it's a place you don't want to miss.

Hours: Monday–Thursday, 11:00 A.M. to 10:00 P.M. Friday, 11:00 A.M. to 11:00 P.M. Saturday, 5:00 to 11:00 P.M. Closed Sunday.

Location: 4632 Winchester Road at Perkins. (901) 362-1345.

Justine's, Memphis

Justine and Dayton Smith, owners

In a rented old warehouse in 1948 Justine Smith opened the original Justine's. This restaurant newcomer took only a very short time to be accepted as the "in" place for dining and entertainment in the Memphis area.

Deciding to move to surroundings more suitable for the classic French cuisine, the Smiths in the 1950s spent 14 months restoring stately Coward Place. They created a museum restaurant—from white marble steps to antique dining room chandeliers. The total atmosphere is graceful and elegant. The grounds are lush with boxwoods, magnolias, and a prize rose garden. An ancient octagonal gazebo and garden pavilions provide a perfect setting for the lovely old mansion. The Fourth Pavilion is a glassed-in piano bar—a popular Memphis gathering place.

The menu is extensive with offerings including Tournedos Beauharnaise (filet with artichoke hearts and bearnaise sauce); Flounder Louisianne (flounder stuffed with crab and mushroom); and Foie de Poulet de Champignons (fresh chicken livers and mushrooms sauteed in butter and served with rice). Salads vary from asparagus to watercress, and a wide variety of appetizers are available. Vichyssoise and creme de champignon are two typical soup choices, while desserts include Cerises Jubilees, Gateau Alaska (baked Alaska flamed with brandy), and Gateau de Fromage (fresh strawberry cheesecake). An average meal will be about $30 per person.

Hours: Monday–Saturday, 5:30 to 10:00 P.M.

Directions: 1 block south of Crump Boulevard, off East Street. East Street dead ends at Coward Place at the front door of the restaurant. 919 Coward Place. (901) 527-9973.

Grisanti's Restaurant, Memphis

John A. Grisanti, owner

A bottle of wine that cost $31,000? You've got to be kidding! A restauranteur in Memphis has made national headlines twice by paying never-before-paid prices for bottles of wine. The man's name is John A. Grisanti, and a special story explains his extravagance.

John Grisanti is a robust, bearded Italian who is not only a businessman and chef, but also a promoter. Be-

ing a lover of wine (he keeps 2,000 bottles in his private cellar), he came up with a scheme a few years ago to help contribute to three things he believes in—children, a hospital that fights cancer, and the city of Memphis.

In 1978 he attended Heublein's 10th Anniversary Premier National Auction of Rare Wines in Atlanta, Georgia. Collectors and wine enthusiasts attend these annual auctions, and up until 1978, the most that had ever been paid for a single bottle of wine was $14,200 for an 1806 Chateau Lafite. But Grisanti had a plan.

He made history by paying $18,000 for the last known bottle of 1864 Chateau Lafite. Yet, he didn't buy it as a collector's item or for resale as do most buyers at this auction. He shocked wine collectors by announcing his plan for "the grand old dame of all Bordeaux." "Wine is made to drink. I'll serve the wine at a special dinner to raise money for cancer research," he said. He proceeded to sell tickets to a lavish dinner to benefit St. Jude Hospital in Memphis. The dinner raised $34,800 for St. Jude's that year.

In 1980, Grisanti broke records once again by paying $31,000 for Lafite 1822, and in the fund-raising event that followed he raised $40,000 for St. Jude Hospital. He had lined up nine other Memphis residents to commit $6,000 apiece to buy the wine at the Heublein Auction, this time in San Francisco. Since the total bill was only $31,000, he came back home telling his friends, "You only owe me $3,100 each."

A love of cooking and eating led John Grisanti to write a cookbook. "Cooking should be fun and not a complicated process," according to him. *Wining and Dining with John Grisanti* features something for everyone, from the beginning cook to the expert. Learn how to make your own homemade pasta. In "Grisanti on Wine," the author suggests guidelines for choosing wines, for storing wines, and for selecting the proper glasses to use, among other helpful hints.

Grisanti is often seen at his Italian restaurant where everybody calls him by his first name.

The menu is extensive, and Grisanti himself recommends the following: Baked manicotti (tubular pasta with Italian spinach and Italian sausage stuffing served with spaghetti sauce and Mozzarella cheese), Pollo e Carciofi (chicken breast and artichoke hearts sauteed in wine, mushrooms, and spices), and Elfo Special (buttered spaghetti with mushrooms and shrimp). Price range for dinners is $5 to $15.

Hours: Monday–Thursday, 11:00 A.M. to 11:00 P.M. Friday, 11:00 A.M. to midnight. Saturday, 5:00 P.M. to midnight.

Directions: Corner of Airways and Lamar—2.3 miles north of I-240. Take exit 23A. 1489 Airways, (901) 458-2648.

Rendezvous, Memphis

Charlie Vergos, owner

"Now they're not barbecue ribs," emphasizes Nick Vergos. "They are *charcoal*-broiled pork ribs."

The *Sampler* was asking Nick what makes the Rendezvous such a well-known Memphis tradition. (The Rolling Stones bought $1,600 worth of world-famous ribs here one night.)

"The ribs are grilled over pure hardwood charcoal. We have four pits that are open, and you can watch us cook them. They are basted with a mixture of hot vinegar and water, sprinkled with some of our special seasoning, and they'll knock you out."

This unique taste has kept the Rendezvous the sought-out restaurant of college students, bank presidents, traveling business executives, and tourists for almost 40 years. To get to the Rendezvous, you go through a nameless alley and down into a basement. The decor is unique. The walls are lined with a gun collection, arrowheads, artwork, helmets, and Civil War artifacts. The museumlike atmosphere reflects Charlie Vergos's interests and the generosity of the many friends who have donated items to his collection over the past 30 years.

Other entrees are chicken, pork chops, beef ribs, and lamb ribs. Appetizer plates offer ham, sausage, and cheeses. Soft drinks and beer are served. No coffee, no desserts. Price range: $2.25 for appetizers to $7.00 for a full order of ribs.

Hours: Tuesday–Thursday, 4:30 P.M. to midnight. Friday and Saturday, 12:00 Noon to 1:00 A.M. Closed Sunday and Monday.

Directions: In downtown Memphis. The alley is between Union Avenue and Monroe right across the street from the Peabody Hotel. 52 South Second Street. (901) 523-2746.

A Cooking School in Memphis

La Maison Meridien,
The Memphis Culinary Academy

Are you interested in learning how to be a better cook in your own kitchen or, more specifically, how to be a chef and earn your living by cooking? Tennessee has an excellent facility in which to do this.

La Maison Meridien, The Memphis Culinary Academy, is the Mid-South's only school devoted exclusively to the culinary arts. The Academy is located at 1252 Peabody in Memphis (telephone 901-722-8892). It offers a basic professional course of study for the aspiring chef ($2900 for a 350-hour course) as well as periodic series of classes ($100 for five class meetings) in such specialties as "Wine and Food," "Creole and Cajun Seafood Cookery," "Northern Italian Cookery," and "Professional Pastries and Desserts," for professionals and laymen alike.

Operated by Joseph and Elaine Wallace-Carey, the first graduating class in 1984 received an A by the *Commercial Appeal* newspaper, "Not only was the food delicious, but it was all presented to appeal to the eye as well."

The prerequisites for taking the course are a personal love of food and an eagerness to learn how to prepare it. Mrs. Carey is a pastry specialist, and Joseph has been a professional chef and restaurant consultant in California for 13 years.

Carey said his class for professional cooks is limited to 10 students, and the course is broken down into five weeks of technical training and five weeks of "art." "We try to teach techniques rather than individual recipes or rote learning."

Advanced training is available in the Carey's restaurant, Cafe Meridien, located at Victorian Village.

Bozo's, Mason
Helen Williams, owner

"You've got to include Bozo's barbecue in your book," said the Federal Express man one day when he was making a delivery to our office. The name *Bozo's* kept coming up again and again when we would ask people about good barbecue in West Tennessee.

Run by the same family since 1923, Bozo's has earned a well-deserved reputation because quality is their goal. Miss Helen Williams told the *Sampler* her parents opened the restaurant, and she and her sister have owned it since 1972.

Although many articles have appeared in newspapers and magazines, when the *Sampler* asked for copies, Miss Williams said she didn't really know where they were. She said they've never advertised but have just depended on word of mouth and the good words of publications over the years. It seems Miss Williams doesn't have to brag about Bozo's. Plenty of other people have done that for her.

"We serve pork only, barbecued daily over charcoal." Served with the barbecue are potato salad, French fries, slaw, barbecue beans, or tossed salad. All types of sandwiches and salads are on the menu as well as fried chicken and steaks. Take-out orders include barbecue by the pound, beans, slaw, and chicken salad. Price range: 95¢ for beef stew to $5.95 for 8-ounce rib-eye steak.

Hours: Monday–Saturday, 10:30 A.M. to 9:00 P.M. Closed Sunday.

Directions: From Memphis, go US 70 approximately 38 miles from downtown. (901) 294-3400.

The Hut, Dyersburg
Mary Lou Parker, owner

Menus from all over the world stapled to the ceiling

make interesting reading at the Hut, Dyersburg's oldest restaurant.

In 1984 John Eagerton, *Washington Post* reporter, went on a "3 day barbecue safari" covering 300 miles from Memphis to Owensboro, Kentucky. The Hut was one of his stops. Mrs. Parker found out about the survey when Congressman Ed Jones (of Memphis) sent her the article placing the Hut among the very top establishments. Mrs. Parker says, "We have our own pits and smoke shoulders with hickory chips and charcoal daily."

Popular at noontime is the cold seafood bar with crabmeat salad, shrimp salad, fresh fruits, and other tempting treats. On Friday and Saturday nights, the fried seafood bar packs in the people as they enjoy shrimp, catfish, hushpuppies, white beans, and onions. The prices range from $1.90 for a barbecue sandwich to $6.25 for a steak.

Hours: Monday–Saturday, 11:00 A.M. to 10:00 P.M. Closed Sunday.

Directions: 1 mile from the intersection of US 51 bypass and Lake Road. 705 Lake Road. (901) 286-0821.

Blue Bank Dining Room and Motel, Tiptonville
Marvin Hayes Associates, owner

A family-owned restaurant for over 30 years, the Blue Bank overlooks picturesque Reelfoot Lake. The restaurant has facilities to serve over 200 with several private dining rooms. Banquet facilities are available too. Jill Hayes White tells the *Sampler*, "During summer months, vacationers are a large part of our crowd and often family reunions are held at the combination restaurant/motel."

All-you-can-eat dinners are served on large platters to the whole family. Included are country ham (home salt cured), fried chicken, and Reelfoot Lake catfish served with slaw, French fries, hushpuppies, onion rings, homemade rolls, and baked apples. Seafood specials brought from the Gulf weekly include fresh oysters, boiled or fried shrimp, crab legs, and fried oysters. Prices for dinners range from $7.00 to $10.95.

Lake County is the only county in the state where crappie can be caught and commercially sold. Blue Bank serves crappie along with other fish.

Jill shares two of the Blue Bank's most popular recipes:

Hushpuppies
2 c. self-rising flour
2 c. self-rising meal
2 c. chopped onions
6 eggs
2 1/2 c. milk
(If too thin, add more flour.)

Mix ingredients, drop by teaspoonfuls into hot 350° oil, cook 10–15 min., hushpuppies will float and then cook 2 min. longer.

Onion Rings
2 c. self-rising flour
2 1/2 tbsp. sugar
1 tsp. salt

Add cold water to make a thin consistency, add large onion ring to batter, drop into hot 350° oil, cook for about 10-15 min. until turns brown. They will float.

Hours: Summer, 6:00 A.M. to 9:30 P.M. daily. Winter, 10:00 A.M. to 9:00 P.M. daily (except Christmas Eve and Christmas Day).

Directions: Located on State 22. Restaurant is next to Blue Bank State Park and overlooks Reelfoot Lake. (901) 538-2166.

Boyette's Dining Room, Tiptonville
Jack and Mary Frances Richardson, owners

On the shores of Reelfoot Lake, Boyette's has been serving fine foods since 1922, specializing in family-style meals. When you order fish, fried chicken, or Tennessee country ham, the platter of meat—along with vegetables—is brought to your table and you help yourself, just like at home. Vegetables are green beans, white beans, casseroles, and slaw. Homemade rolls and pies are available. Also on the menu are quail and frog legs.

Jack Richardson says Boyette's seats about 300, so tour groups are always welcome. "We have lots of tourists in the summer, and now that eagle watching is getting popular, tourists are here during the winter as well."

Reelfoot has a large eagle population with sometimes as many as 25 eagles perched in the same tree. The time for eagle watching is November through March. Jack says many times people ask for information about Reelfoot—the names of guides, boat rental, good fishing spots. He says, "We're glad to help when we can."

Famous for their catering service, they'll go anywhere requested, but mostly cater in West Tennessee and Missouri. From hors d'oeuvres to full-course dinners, Boyette's is available. Prices of food range from $5.00 to $9.25.

Hours: 7:00 A.M. to 9:00 P.M. daily (except Thanksgiving and Christmas).

Directions: Located on State 22 (Lake Road), across the highway from Buford Ellington Convention Hall. (901) 253-7307.

College Kids—Where They Go

The *Sampler* wondered where the college kids like to eat in Tennessee. Usually there's a local hangout close to campus, with a price tag to fit the college students' funds (or lack of them!). We thought it would be fun to get a sampling across the state of eating establishments that cater to our college friends.

East. Rita Hubbard, University of Tennessee in Chattanooga, says David's Restaurant and Lounge is close to campus and has reasonable prices and good home cooking with a family atmosphere. Two doors down is The Vine Street Market. Lots of class meeetings and group get-togethers are held here where deli-type food is the fare.

Dan Batey, a University of Tennessee alumnus, tells us about the "Strip" up on the Hill in Knoxville. Anyone

who's ever been there on a football weekend will never forget it! Actually the strip is part of Cumberland Avenue, a street that runs through the campus. This eight-block section on the north side of the campus has been referred to as "Knoxville's Miracle Mile."

What's here? Dan says, "It ranges from your basic Krystal and deli where you can go and get a sandwich any time without spending too much money to the Copper Cellar, an 'up town' type place where you can use your American Express card." Dan told the *Sampler*, "Sometimes the businesses change before the paint's even dry on the sign." Things have ranged over the years from the strip's being a commercial district with car dealerships to nightclubs with live bands. Then in the seventies there was the tap room phase.

But some things don't change, and a few places, such as Sam and Andy's, have been on the strip as long as anyone can remember. You can't miss it, it's the one with the orange-and-white cow standing on the roof. It's kind of a combination restaurant, deli, and tap room— complete with a "Vol" burger (of course).

Then there's the Varsity Grill and the Torch. "The kids go there when they're sick of cafeteria food and want a plate lunch more like mom would fix," says Dan.

Dan knows a lot about his alma mater. As a matter of a fact he's written two publications that feature cartoons and essays on UT life. The first one, now out of print, is called *One More for the Hill*. *Return of the Alumni* can be ordered by sending $7.50 to Center Hill Communications, Box 1098, Columbia, TN 38402.

Middle. Harold Smith, director of student programming at Middle Tennessee State University in Murfreesboro, says for years the students have been going to the City Cafe on the square. It has a laid-back atmosphere, reasonable prices, home-cooked plate lunches, and rolls that people are crazy about!

Carol Hedden, in public affairs at Austin Peay State University in Clarksville, says The Brary serves pizza and sandwiches. "When people say they're going to the 'brary,' they don't mean the 'library' to study!" They mean the Brary to eat and have fun.

The Big Burger is just what it says, a great all-meat hamburger place that also offers fresh French fries. Poppy's Pizza delivers to the dorms and offers New-York-style pizza.

Libby Leverette-Crew, a medical illustrator for Vanderbilt University in Nashville, says an area of town called Elliston Place near the campus has TGI Friday's

and Obie's which offers homemade pizza with thick crusts. Order to go from Spat's on Twenty-first Avenue, a favorite for barbecue. Slice of Life is a health restaurant on Division Street.

West. Dr. Phillip Watkins, director of student affairs at the University of Tennessee at Martin, says, "The T-Room has been here for years. It's on Lovelace Avenue right across from the campus. The atmosphere is friendly, service good, home-cooked meals are like mom's cooking. For 30 years it's served the students of UTMB."

David Collins, Memphis State, says Captain Bilbo's on the banks of the Mississippi just south of Beale Street has live music, a dance floor, and Cajun food. It's an informal, friendly, unpretentious atmosphere.

The *Sampler* would like to know where the kids from *your* college like to go to get some really good food. Write us and let us know.

Dinners-on-the-ground, Homecomings, and Decoration Days

There are get-togethers of the southern variety, usually during summer months, that many Tennesseans look forward to like a child looks for Santa. They've been going on since 'way back. You may call it a Decoration Day at the country cemetery, a church homecoming, a family reunion, a dinner-on-the-ground for the gospel meeting, or a community club fund raising. They go by many different names, but what they mean to the folk who attend is that old friendships are renewed and good food is shared.

Sometimes the food is cooked en masse there at the location, but most often the ladies bring their dishes they're known for. Aunt Jean *always* brings corn lightbread, and Mama Graves fixes chicken and dressing like nobody else. Mama fixes corn, Ina Lou brings the coconut cake, and Dottie brings the barbecued venison. They've usually cooked the whole day before. Then everything is loaded up into the picnic basket and cardboard boxes, taken to the dinner, and spread along the long, long tables outside under massive old trees, along with everyone else's specialties.

This is the place to get your best recipes. Even if you don't know the people, they will usually share recipes with you. That is, if they have one! Even if it's not a "written down" recipe, you can get them to tell it to you, and you can put it in writing.

The other type of dinner is where everything is cooked beforehand, and you buy a ticket to eat. Phyllis Beasley of Springfield wrote the *Sampler* about one of the really popular events in Robertson County each year. It's the annual Martin's Chapel Barbecue Supper sponsored by her church the fourth Saturday night in June each year. It's been going on 30 years now and has grown to feeding 1,500 persons, country style, all-you-can-eat.

The barbecue pit has been enlarged twice, and the

men start work Friday morning cooking the pork shoulders slowly over an open pit fire of hickory chips. The women of the community boil tons of new potatoes, make gallons of cole slaw, and bake their mouth-watering corn bread and over 200 pies to serve at the dinner.

The politicians are there handing out cards, if it's an election year. Everybody brings flowers for the graves of grandparents and great-grandparents in the nearby cemetery. Sometimes there's a quilt auction, horseshoes, or a country store set up to sell homemade canned jams or craft items.

It may be a fish fry like the one down at the Methodist Church at Oak Grove, outside of Hohenwald, or it could be an ice-cream supper. Wherever it is, and whatever is served, you'll eat some of the best food anywhere. Although the people who have been going to these dinners for years enjoy the food, it's the friendships and fellowship that they come back for year after year.

A SAMPLER

SᴘEᴄᴵAᴸ

The Secret of Lonnie B's

For over 50 years the secret has been passed down from governor to governor here in Tennessee. Even the occasionally, lightly disguised hatred between the Republicans and Democrats didn't stop the secret of Lonnie B's from being passed from one chief executive to the next. The *Sampler* recently visited Lonnie B's and was served one of the most delectable meals ever imagined. In fact, the food and service were beyond imagination.

What is Lonnie B's? It's an extraordinary restaurant only two hours by limo from the capital or 30 minutes by plane from Nashville's airport. It's located on a bluff overlooking one of our state's most beautiful views. Lonnie B founded this extraordinary dining establishment in 1929. Lonnie was born and raised on a small hill farm in the tiny community of Snow Creek during some of the hardest years Tennesseans have ever had to exist through. Lonnie said to himself as a boy, *Lonnie B, there is no way you are going to spend the rest of your life on this here farm!*

So, as soon as he was 14 he hoboed to New York and caught a tanker to Europe, working as a boiler room attendant. He jumped ship in Wales and soon found himself working his way around the United Kingdom, learning the cooking secrets of this great WASP kingdom as he went. Lonnie crossed the English Channel and spent five years working his way up the ladders of some of Europe's most sophisticated eateries. Lonnie quickly learned the subtle art of roll making under the phenomenal Claude Monike, then went on to apprentice with Jean Paul Keal, the world's most honored dessert chef. From France, Lonnie, the slim, slow-drawlin' country boy, ambled on down to Italy where he learned the tricks of pasta, oil dressings, and wine making. Then he split for northern Africa and the cooking secrets of the desert nomads. He never imagined camel could taste so wonderful when prepared with palm leaves and oasis nuts, like the nomads did for the marriage feast. To put it mildly, when Lonnie came back to Tennessee, nine years later, he knew more about cooking than anyone in our state and probably anyone in the United States.

It wasn't two weeks after Lonnie opened his marvelous restaurant, On the Creek Bank, that some of the state's most powerful politicians began to frequent it, especially when they were attempting to impress out-of-town dignitaries. None of these influential and mostly wealthy Tennesseans had ever tasted such cooking prepared by such gifted hands. These men were so impressed they talked Lonnie B into calling the place just plain and simple Lonnie B's. They said they thought that On The Creek Bank sounded too country, and not chic enough. Lonnie didn't know how to spell *chic* and thought it was a French word for chicken. ''Them Frenchies had all kinds of strange names for things,'' Lonnie B said.

Only two years passed before some of the

Lonnie B's pap with his favorite ox, Lamar

world's wealthiest and best connected businessmen, politicians, and religious leaders were thinking of excuses to come to Tennessee just to eat at Lonnie B's. After three years Lonnie B had to limit the people he served to a top-secret list of movers and shakers.

Today, in 1986, the original Lonnie B is mostly retired, raising world champion coon dogs, and nearing his eightieth birthday. Lonnie's son, Scott B, is in charge. Not only did Lonnie B pass on all his own rare recipes, such as Rabitto El'Poplar, Le Green Beans and Hawg, and African Herbal Tea Cake l'Orange, but when Scott B turned 18, Lonnie B gave his son an airline ticket that would take him around the world for two years of cooking adventures.

Scott learned sauce secrets from the king of Sweden's chefs. He was taught amazing barbecuing techniques by New Guinea headhunters. Scott B was even invited to attend Szechwan University's incomparable cooking school in Chengtu, China; he was the first non-Communist ever accepted into their class for advanced whole-fish boiling.

At Lonnie B's, the *Sampler* experienced a 14-course meal we will never forget. The meal began with the Tibetan custom of sniffing the petals of a spring rose to prepare the palate. Then we had walnut broth soup with French onion muffins and a blackberry popsicle. The popsicle was properly aged at 29.5 degrees F. for 12 days to achieve that especially delightful flavor that recreates all the pleasant memories of a child's summer in Cape Cod.

Each course had a different server, all outfitted in costumes from different periods of Tennessee history. Next came our salads, a variation of three seafood combinations served on a bed of thistle leaves, freshly plucked from the side of Interstate 65 that morning. We were told that Japanese businessmen always stay an extra day here in Tennessee when they know that the salad will be shrimp, oysters, and jellyfish on thistle leaves. The dressing was the house specialty, consisting of aged mayonnaise, plump avocadoes, and Pepsi, blended at room temperature. Shredded pig nuts added a zesty texture to our wonderfully delightful salad experience.

We at the *Sampler* wish we could let you know what happened next but we can't. From this point, the eating experience that takes place at Lonnie B's is a secret. In fact, everyone that's ever eaten there must take a sworn oath never to reveal what happens after salad at Lonnie B's. We at the *Sampler* would give anything if we could tell you how to get to Lonnie B's, but we were driven there blindfolded, on a dark night when the winds were especially noisy so that we could hear nothing.

We've heard that a few of our governors have offered to give away the location of Lonnie B's, for the right price, which we heard was a cool

$35,000 cash. About the only thing the *Sampler* can suggest is to run for governor of Tennessee in 1986. If you win, our present governor, Lamar Alexander, will have to tell you where it is. The *Sampler* has heard that both Paul Prudhomme, America's favorite Cajun chef, and Willard Scott, of "The Today Show," are planning to set up residence here to run for governor. Winfield Dunn, Ned Ray McWherter, and Richard Fulton may have some real heavyweight competition!

Lonnie B's Egg Regius Gourmet Souffle

We did talk Lonnie B out of one of his prize recipes, named for King Faisal of Saudi Arabia. Faisal and an entourage of 100 rented the entire city of Snow Creek a few years back for a week. He brought in all the great country musicians to teach his bands how to play real country music. His dancing girls even learned to buckdance and belly dance at the same time during their stay. Faisal invited Lonnie B to cook a gourmet breakfast for everyone, and the result was the fabulous Egg Regius. We at the Sampler *are happy to offer it to our readers in an exclusive.*

Egg Regius Gourmet Souffle

3 fresh guinea eggs
2 wild turkey eggs
1 buzzard egg yolk
**4 rattlesnake egg whites, beaten
2 c. rattlesnake milk
1 tsp. marjoram
1/2 tsp. bloodroot
3 tbsp. chopped digitalis leaves (foxglove)
1/8 tsp. pepper
8 oz. grated goat cheese
4 oz. sliced Tennessee Monterey mushrooms
Possum sardine oil
Roasted 13-year cicadas

**These various egg components may be duplicated by using domestic hen eggs. However, the hens must be locked in the chicken house with a cock-fighting rooster for no less than six months and fed a steady diet of poke salad, sassafras root, and moonshine-soaked pellet corn.

Recipe directions:
Beat guinea eggs until frothy. *Slowly* fold in the wild turkey eggs. Be sure not to add too fast or the egg mixture will curdle. When the foaming and fizzing settle down, whip the buzzard egg into the beaten rattlesnake egg whites. Do this very quickly.

While you are savoring the aroma of this delicacy, add the marjoram, bloodroot, digitalis, and pepper. These spices will enhance the flavor tremendously. Whip the mixture while adding the rattlesnake milk till double in size.

Grease a souffle dish with Possum sardine oil. Fold into mixture the grated goat cheese and sliced Tennessee Monterey mushrooms. Pour immediately into heated dish. Garnish with ample amounts of the *Sampler*'s favorite roasted 13-year cicadas for a crunchy taste treat you won't soon forget. King Faisal told the *Sampler* that after a generous serving of Egg Regius Gourmet Souffle, his troupe of "Belly-buck dancers" were at their peak of performance.

Cookin' Good in Tennessee: Traditional Tennessee Recipes

The *Sampler* thanks Phila Hach for the recipes below reprinted with her permisson from *Official Cookbook of the 1982 World's Fair.*

East Tennessee Mountain Vittles

East Tennesseans, the first pioneers of our state, have long been serving these East Tennessee Mountain Vittles. Phila says, "When you really want to get back to cooking the way our ancestors did—country cooking—this is it!"

Fresh Backbone and Sauerkraut or Turnips Appalachian

Simmer backbone with water to cover, salt and pepper to taste, until tender—4 or 5 hours. Cook turnips or sauerkraut in the broth and serve hot.
'Tis worth moving to the country to taste this!

White Beans

Soak 1 lb. white beans overnight. Cook white beans in a large pan with 7 c. water, 1 ham bone, 1 pod red pepper and 1 big onion. Simmer for about 3 hours over low heat until done. Serve with sliced raw onions and corn pone.

Wild Greens and Nasturtium Salad

4 c. mixed wild tender greens
Dandelion
Lamb's quarters
Sorrel
Chickweed
Purslane
3 spring onions, chopped or ramps
8 nasturtium flowers
6 tbsp. oil
2 tbsp. vinegar
Salt and black pepper to taste
3 tbsp. hot bacon drippings
Juice of 1 lemon

Mix all together, adding hot bacon drippings and lemon juice last. Serve immediately.

Stack Cake or "Come Back Cake" Appalachian

It was called "Come Back Cake" because the children always came back for more.
Filling:
1 lb. dried tart apples
1 c. brown sugar
1/2 c. white sugar
2 tsp. cinnamon
1/2 tsp. cloves
1/2 tsp. allspice

Mash and cook apples until tender, mash thoroughly. Add sugar and spices and cool.

Cake
4 c. flour, unsifted
1 c. sugar
4 tsp. baking powder
1/2 tsp. soda
2 tsp. vanilla
1 tsp. salt
2 eggs
1/2 c. soft butter
1 c. buttermilk

Sift 3 3/4 cups flour into bowl. Add remaining ingredients in order given. Mix quickly and thoroughly into soft dough. Divide into 6 parts. Use remaining 1/4 cup flour to roll out dough. Bake in 9 inch cake pans at 450° until slightly brown. As you take the cake from the oven, spread each layer with the apple mixture. Do not put apples on the top layer. Place in a covered container for at least 12 hours before cutting.

Middle Tennessee Plantation Breakfast

When Phila wants to give some friends a special and historic meal, she serves them a Middle Tennessee Plantation Breakfast, much like Andy Jackson might have enjoyed at the Hermitage.

Chicken Hash
2 tbsp. butter
1/8 green pepper shredded
1 c. thinly sliced mushrooms
2 tbsp. flour
1/2 tsp. salt
2 c. cream
3 c. chicken, diced (cooked)
1/4 c. butter, creamed
3 egg yolks
1 tsp. onion juice
1 tbsp. lemon juice
1/2 tsp. paprika
2 tbsp. cooking sherry
Chopped pimiento

Saute green pepper and mushrooms in butter until done. Add flour, salt, cream, and stir until smooth. Add chicken. Cream butter with egg yolks, onion juice, lemon juice, and paprika. Add to hot chicken mixture. Simmer slowly until thick. Just before serving add sherry and chopped pimiento.

Serve in pastry shells.

Cheese Grits Casserole

4 c. boiling water
1 c. cheese, grated
(garlic cheese is great)
2 eggs
1 stick melted butter
1 tsp. salt
(garlic salt, if desired)
1 c. grits
½ c. milk

Bring water and salt to a boil. Stir in grits and cook slowly for 15–20 minutes, stirring frequently. Then add cheese, blending thoroughly. Beat eggs with milk and stir in butter. Add to grits and cheese. Place in casserole and bake 35 minutes at 350 degrees.

Curried Fruits

6 peach halves
6 pear halves
6 pineapple slices
6 sliced apples
1 tsp. curry powder
1 c. sugar
1 c. juice from fruit
1 stick butter

Place in casserole and bake after sprinkling with sugar and curry for 30 minutes at 350 degrees.

Basic Biscuit Dough

2 c. flour
2 tsp. baking powder
1 tsp. salt
1 tbsp. sugar
Shortening the size of an egg
Enough milk to moisten

Sift dry ingredients together. Blend in shortening and moisten with milk. Do not overmix. Turn out on floured board, cut out and bake in a 450° oven until brown, about 12 minutes.

And of course you'll want to serve blackberry jam like that alwaysfound on Andy Jackson's table.

West Tennessee Barbecue Supper

West Tennessee has long been known for its excellent barbecue. When Phila wanted to introduce the United Nations delegates to a wonderful southern meal, she chose this dinner-on-the-ground-type menu.

Open Pit Barbecue

Dig a pit the size that is required for the amount of

East Tennessee mountain farm

meat you have. A small hole is about 9 inches deep—say for a grill space up to 2 feet square. For large barbecues, I like a pit dug about 12 to 18 inches deep, 3 to 4 feet wide, and as long as you wish. Never get your pit so wide that you can't safely tend your fire and barbecue.

Never start to barbecue until your fire and coals have died down. Keep a fire of hickory wood going to continue feeding coals to the pit. This fire should be close to the pit. We call this the feeder fire.

We use heavy chicken wire frames to stretch across our pits. These should be a few inches above the embers. New brooms or mops are used to brush large portions of meat with the sop. Warm salted water is used to baste the meat until it gets hot enough to keep away insects and flies.

We then use the same sop or mopping sauce as for oven barbecue. Allow 12 to 18 hours to cook large pieces of meat over open pit. For whole hog or shoulders, allow 10 to 12 hours. For chicken, allow 2 to 3 hours. Cook *slowly.*

For a good mopping sauce recipe for larger amounts of meat (20 to 30 pounds) use:

1 qt. apple cider vinegar
1 stick butter
3 tbsp. crushed hot red pepper
Salt and pepper to taste
1 lemon, sliced thin
Bring to a boil and sop.

Quilter's Potato Salad

3 large potatoes, cooked	1 tsp. dry mustard
3 hard-cooked eggs	1 tsp. salt
4 tbsp. minced onion	3 tsp. sugar
Salt and pepper	

2 eggs, uncooked
3 tbsp. melted butter
1/2 c. hot vinegar
1 c. cream, whipped or sour cream

Mix first 6 ingredients. Put next 3 ingredients in a saucepan and cook until thick. Add to first mixture and add hot vinegar and whipped cream. Garnish with sweet pickle.

Slaw

1 medium head cabbage, shredded
1 medium onion, sliced thinly
7/8 c. sugar
1 c. vinegar
3/4 c. salad oil
2 tsp. sugar
2 tsp. salt
1 tsp. dry mustard
1 tsp. celery seed

Mix vinegar, salad oil, 2 teaspoons sugar, salt, mustard, and celery seed, and bring to a boil. Alternate layers of cabbage and onion rings in a large bowl. Top with 7/8 cup sugar. Pour hot mixture over cabbage and onion. Cover and let stand 4 to 6 hours. Mix well and serve. Will keep 2 to 3 weeks in refrigerator.

Apple Goody

3 c. of sliced apples
1 c. sugar
1 rounded tbsp. flour
1 pinch salt
1/4-1/2 tsp. cinnamon

Mix and put in baking pan. Top with the following ingredients.

Topping:

3/4 c. oatmeal, uncooked
3/4 c. flour
3/4 c. brown sugar
1/4 tsp. soda
1/4 tsp. baking powder
1/3 c. melted butter

Mix well and pat over apple mixture. Bake in a 350° oven for approximately 30 minutes. Serve with ice cream or whipped cream or plain.

Jim Oliver's Red-eye Gravy

After frying country ham, remove your slices of ham from the skillet. Pour 1 cup of fresh perked coffee into the ham drippings in the skillet. Let simmer for 1 minute, then pour into a bowl. Watch the dark liquid settle to the bottom…"Red Eye!" Great topping for fresh hot biscuits or your ham. Dip from the bottom of the bowl.

Corn Bread

1 c. white self-rising cornmeal
3 tbsp. self-rising flour
1 egg, beaten
2/3 c. buttermilk
1 tbsp. water
1 tbsp. melted shortening
Bacon drippings

Heat oven to 450° F. Grease thoroughly and heat in the oven a small black iron skillet or corn stick or muffin pans. Measure all ingredients in the order listed in a mixing bowl and stir to blend thoroughly. Pour batter into hot greased pan and bake 20 minutes for sticks; 25 to 30 minutes for skillet or muffins.

Cracklin' Corn Bread

Follow the same recipe for corn bread but add 1/4 pound country ham cracklings. To prepare cracklings:
Use the trimmings from country ham (meat scraps, fat, and skin). Chop the trimming into small pieces and fry in a skillet. Fry the trimming until most of the grease appears to be cooked out, good and crisp, but not burned. Now you've got "cracklin's." Place the cracklin's on several paper towels to soak up the extra grease. Store in the refrigerator until ready for use. The grease you cooked out of the trimmings may be kept also for future use as "country shortening" and for use in redeye gravy.

Pepper Relish

12 sweet green peppers
12 sweet red peppers
12 small onions
Boiling water
3 c. vinegar
1 1/2 c. sugar
4 tsp. salt
2 tsp. celery seed

Put peppers (seeds discarded) and peeled onions through food chopper. Add boiling water to cover, let stand 10 minutes; drain and discard liquid. Add remaining ingredients to vegetables. Boil slowly for 15 minutes. Ladle into hot, sterilized jars. Seal at once. Makes 6 pints. (Note: Peppers cut with knife look prettier.)

If you don't feel like cookin', you can enjoy Jim's gravy and corn bread at the Smoke House Restaurant on Monteagle Mountain.

Louise Barker's Chess Pie

Louise Barker tells us, "Chess pie is a favorite in the Nashville area. It has long been popular, and in some communities in past years it may have been known as 'Vinegar Pie' or 'Meal Pie'—descriptive of the ingredients. This recipe utilizes the ingredients that were produced and readily available. A small serving may be sufficient because it is a rich dessert but, oh, so delicious, especially nice served at a light meal."

1/2 c. butter, softened
1 1/4 c. sugar
1 tbsp. self-rising cornmeal
1 tsp. flour
1 tsp. cider vinegar
1/2 c. evaporated milk or cream
3 eggs, slightly beaten
2 tsp. vanilla
1 8-inch pastry shell, unbaked.

Add the cornmeal and flour to the sugar and blend well. Add softened butter and beat until fluffy. Slowly add milk and then the vinegar, blending as each is added. Add the eggs, mixing well into other ingredients. Blend in the vanilla. Pour into unbaked pastry shell.

Bake at 350° F. about 45 minutes. If tested with a knife in the center it comes out clean. It will be lightly browned on top and will shake lightly in the center but will set as it cools. Cool for about 2 hours before cutting.

Doodle Soup and Chicken

Cook hen in roaster with a lot of water (nearly covered), slow 350° for 2 to 3 hours (depending on size of chicken).

Measure and cook in deep skillet:

10 to 12 c. of broth

1 1/2 c. vinegar (to taste)

Add: red cayenne pepper or whole pods of red pepper (lots).

Bring to boil for 23 to 30 minutes, then simmer for at least an hour or longer.

Cut up livers, gizzards, and hard-boiled eggs to pour doodle soup over when ready to serve. Serve over crumbled crackers.

Always serve cream potatoes, English peas, and fruit salad with doodle soup and chicken.

Doodle soup recipe compliments of the Bradford Chamber of Commerce. (See "Tours and Trails—Memphis" and "Fun Times.")

Preparing Some Tennessee "Naturals"

Lorene Porter of Evensville tells the *Sampler*,, "We live on a farm in Rhea County near Watts Bar Dam on the Tennessee River. Some of our East Tennessee people enjoy the following foods in the springtime. As our beautiful, ethereal dogwoods and redbuds make their big show and our frogs start croaking, many of us head for the outdoors to search for poke salad or sassafras for tea. The following recipes are two early American foods which have been handed down and enjoyed through all the years."

Poke Salad or Greens

Collect the tender young shoots of poke. *DO NOT USE ROOTS.* Wash the poke greens well, place in deep kettle, add water. Bring to a boil, then parboil 3 or 4 minutes. Remove from kettle into a colander. Drain. Rinse again through colander. Fry some bacon in a skillet over medium heat until crisp. Set bacon aside and crumble.

Add the parboiled poke to the bacon drippings, salt and pepper to taste. Cover, cook over low heat about 25 minutes, stirring occasionally. When tender, beat about 3 eggs, pour over greens and stir until eggs are cooked. Or serve with sliced boiled eggs. Sprinkle top with the crumbled bacon. Pass the corn bread!

Sassafras Tea

Sassafras tea is an old-time favorite and is said to be a good spring tonic. After the ground thaws, find the young roots of a sassafras tree. Clean the roots, then drop into boiling water, and boil until your tea is as strong as you desire. The tea is a clear amber color, with a delicious taste and fragrance. Most people prefer the tea hot with sugar or honey added. Try a cup with your family on a cool spring Tennessee evening!

How To Order Information From one of Tennessee's Food Experts

Anyone who has ever listened to talk shows on the radio, watched them on TV, or read the newspaper in Tennessee has probably heard of Louise Barker, Extension Agent—food marketing, Agricultural Extension Service, University of Tennessee. We've always been fascinated by the wonderful information on food she's continually passing out.

When the *Sampler* contacted Miss Barker, we asked for general information people might be interested in knowing about foods, recipes, or food preparation that seem to be characteristic of Tennessee. We also asked for an address the public could use for finding the answers to questions about food preparation.

She replied, "Information on food production, marketing, preservation, and preparation is available from any County Agricultural Extension Office in Tennessee. Locations of specific food production sites are available from these offices."

To locate the extension office in a particular county, look in the phone book under the county name, such as:

MAURY COUNTY OF—Agricultural Extension Service...

The address and phone number is then given. Usually the extension service is the first listing under the county name. Miss Barker sent the *Sampler* some pamphlets characteristic of the ones that can be ordered. For example, the brochure on strawberries tells in which counties in Tennessee the crop is mainly harvested, at what time period the strawberries are ready to be picked, some of the history of the strawberry, the nutritional value of the berry, how to store berries, how to choose the best ones, and how to freeze them. Probably the best part of the information is the recipes for strawberry preserves, pastry for shortcake, and fresh strawberry pie. Other brochures are about blueberries, blackberries, peaches, green snap beans, cabbage, corn, sweet potatoes, and so on. Excellent information is only a phone call away.

October Means Sorghum Making in Tennessee

The sorghum cane, similar to sugar cane, matures during the month of October. That's when preparations for the laborious sorghum making begin. First the leaves are stripped from the plant, and the cane is brought in from the fields. The stalks are ground at an old horse-pulled mill, and the pungent juice is saved. The juice is boiled for hours while skilled hands skim the foam from the liquid. Finally, the thick, brown, bittersweet syrup is ready.

Sorghum making at Cades Cove

As ingredients for good home cooking, the sorghum and molasses are just waiting to be spread over hot, springy, buttered bread or pancakes made from fresh cornmeal.

At Cades Cove (see "Tours and Trails") you can turn back the pages of time to see how farm families lived and experience the rich tradition of pioneer self-sufficiency which continues today. The entire process of making sorghum which can be seen demonstrated here depicts traditions handed down from generation to generation.

However, because the sorghum is prepared so authentically by old-time methods, health standards prevent visitors from sampling or buying the sorghum at the park. Many stands dotting the nearby highways do sell homemade sorghum.

Perhaps you prefer a mountain-top chalet or remote country inn, with cows grazing outside your window. Maybe you want the glitter and glamour of the Hermitage Hotel in downtown Nashville, or the pageantry of the "March of the Ducks" at the Peabody. You may desire a campground or a rustic cabin in one of Tennessee's scenic state parks. But what you want is *something different*—not just the same old thing.

The *Sampler* looked far and wide to help you find your ideal "resting" place. We found some special ones—from an inn that serves brandy and pumpkin bread upon your arrival to grand hotels that offer you a full vacation experience without ever leaving the complex. Regardless of the establishment, we found a real love for people, and the guests and hosts often wind up as good friends.

SLEEPIN' GOOD IN TENNESSEE

Across Tennessee there are thousands of places to stay overnight, most of them well-established motels or hotels that are part of a nationwide chain. The Holiday Inns, Quality Inns, Ramada Inns, and many others offer a good place to sleep for the night. But what if you want to get off the beaten path? You don't want to stay in a room that looks the same from Maine to California. You want one that is nestled in the foothills of the Smoky Mountains or located right next to a bubbling brook.

The Grand Hotels

The Hermitage, *Nashville*

In 1910, this newly built $1 million hotel advertised its rooms as "fireproof, noiseproof and dustproof, $2.00 and up." Each of the 250 rooms provided hot- and cold-circulating water (distilled to avoid typhoid), private bath, telephone, electric fan, and a device to show the arrival of mail. It was magnificently furnished with velvet upholstered furniture, luxurious Persian carpets, and palm trees. Pretty special amenities for 1910, but the Hermitage still offers elegance and service found only in select hotels worthy of the Mobil Four Star rating.

This historic hotel was fully restored before it reopened in 1981. The marbled lobby features an exquisite skylight and glass panels crafted by an Italian artisan. Ornately hand-carved ceilings and richly paneled walls display craftsmanship reminiscent of another era.

Guest rooms were completely renovated into one- and two-bedroom suites decorated in traditional, contemporary, or Oriental style. Suites are divided into a separate living room and bedroom with a full bath and vanity.

Guests of The Hermitage are treated to courtesy airport transportation, complimentary shoeshine, continental breakfast served on The Veranda, morning newspaper delivered to the door of each room, and much more.

Add your name to the guest register which has included such notables as Howard Taft, Woodrow Wilson, Franklin D. Roosevelt, John F. Kennedy, Al Jolsen, Jack Dempsey, Al Capone, Billy Graham, Greta Garbo, and Gene Autry.

The Hermitage Dining Room has gained the reputation of being one of the finest dining establishments in Nashville. Continental cuisine is served by experienced waiters while you are entertained by Miss Myrna Rose at the piano. The dining room is open for breakfast and lunch. Room service is available 24 hours a day.

Directions: Downtown, just across from the Capitol. 321 Sixth Avenue North, Nashville, TN 37219. (615) 244-3121.

Edward Pembroke and the Peabody ducks

The Peabody, *Memphis*

For over a century, The Peabody has set the standards of excellence and served as the epitome of hospitality for an entire region. Even the ducks that grace the marble fountain in the lobby have become world famous as the Peabody's unique symbol.

Every day at 11:00 A.M. the Peabody ducks march to the fountain, having descended via elevator from their Royal Duck Palace. At 5:00 P.M. the festivities are reversed as the ducks leave for the night. This tradition, which began as a joke over 50 years ago, has expanded over the years to include the rolling out of a 50-foot carpet and the playing of John Philip Sousa's "King Cotton March." The elaborate Royal Duck Palace, in the penthouse suite, has been called a "fairyland bird cage with banners flying." The Palace has its own original mural of trees and waterfowl, a custom-designed ornate fountain, and a Royal Bed Chamber where the ducks sleep and roost. Edward D. Pembroke, the ducks' royal trainer and chaperone since May of 1940, said upon seeing the Royal Duck Palace the first time, "It's even more than it was 'quacked' up to be."

The Peabody underwent a $25 million renovation and reopened in 1981. The original guest rooms of The Peabody have been elegantly remodeled so that each of the 454 luxurious new rooms combines Old World elegance and modern conveniences.

Twenty-four-hour room service, an indoor pool, health club, gallery of exclusive shops, catering, and convention facilities are available at The Peabody. Dining at this hotel is done on just as grand a scale as everything else. Chez Philippe, their flagship restaurant, offers the finest French cuisine. Dux Restaurant is dedicated to American cuisine and the finest American wines. Emphasis is on unusual creations with all-American ingredients. (Duck is *not* on the menu!) Mallards, a "Neighborhood Bar," offers lunch and happy hour in sophisticated surroundings. Cafe Expresso is the combination of a New York deli and Viennese pastry shop.

For reservations and information, call toll-free: (800) 582-6204 (Tennessee) or (800) 238-7273 (outside Tennessee). 149 Union Avenue, Memphis, TN 38103.

Chattanooga Choo-Choo, *Chattanooga*

From all over America, "Track 29" leads to historic Terminal Station, beautifully restored home of the world's most famous train—the Chattanooga Choo-Choo. In the 1900s, wealthy families traveled across the nation by private railroad car, spending the nights in sleeper cars.

This atmosphere is still to be found in one of the 48 Victorian family suites at the Choo-Choo, each occupying half a tastefully restored passenger train car. A 325-room Hilton designed to carry out the train motif is nestled in among the train cars. Although the actual name is the Choo-Choo Hilton, from coast to coast people still call it the Chattanooga Choo-Choo.

The Victorian-style terminal was dedicated on a cold winter morning in 1909. For the next six decades, Chattanooga's Terminal Station became for the South the equivalent of Grand Central Station in New York City. With the decline of rail passenger service, however, the Terminal Station was closed in August of 1970 and later was scheduled to be demolished by Southern Railway. Because of the foresight of several Chattanooga businessmen, the terminal was spared and was elegantly restored. A new "grand opening" was held on May 30, 1973.

The Choo-Choo is a whole vacation experience. Five unique restaurants, formal gardens, an Olympic ice rink, a racquet club, convention and concert hall, model railroad, and shops of every description are all there. Two antique trolleys shuttle guests from the parking lot to various stops in the complex. A special treat for children is the year-round waterfall swimming pool. (For more information on the Choo-Choo and Chattanooga, see "Tours and Trails.")

Rates: $60 to $90, depending on number in room. Suites are from $200 up. (615) 266-5000.

Opryland Hotel, *Nashville*

The best term to describe the hotel complex located at Opryland, USA is *elegance*. When you approach the hotel, you get a feeling of traditional southern, from the massive white columns to the arches and cupolas of the sprawling structure. Inside, the elegance continues, with gleaming chandeliers, graceful winding stairways, murals depicting the heritage of Nashville, and fine Tennessee art displayed throughout the lobby.

The hotel's more than 1,000 guest rooms make it one of the largest convention sites in North America. The hotel can serve as a complete vacation destination in itself since it boasts of heated pools, a shopping arcade, lighted tennis courts, 18-hole golf privileges, and several excellent restaurants. One of the grandest of all theme parks, Opryland, USA, is located nearby. The world-famous Grand Ole Opry is just a stone's throw away too.

Rachel's Kitchen serves country-style meals, while the Old Hickory Restaurant offers superb continental cuisine in luxurious surroundings. Bucksnort's serves up fine barbecue and all the trimmings. Rhett's and Jack Daniel's Saloon are located in the one-of-a-kind Conservatory. (See "Tours and Trails.") The Staircase Lounge, The Veranda, The Stagedoor Lounge, and Pickin' Parlor are also located in the hotel. Even if you're not going to spend the night there, at least walk through Opryland Hotel and experience a grand hotel.

Rates: Average $100 for single or double occupancy, April–October. Suites are $200 up. (Lower rates rest of year.) Children under 12, free; sr. citizens rates available.

Directions: 5 miles northeast of I-40, just off Briley Parkway. 2800 Opryland Drive, Nashville, TN 37214. (615) 889-1000.

Quaint, Nostalgic Inns

Hale Springs Inn, Rogersville
Carl Netherland-Brown, owner

"I'd like the Andrew Jackson suite," says a woman as she makes reservations at Hale Springs Inn. Andrew Jackson, Andrew Johnson, and James K. Polk were guests in the 1800s, and rooms in the inn are named for these presidents as well as for persons important in area history. Located on the Great Stage Road, at that time the main road from the western frontier to Washington, Hale Springs is the oldest continuously operating inn in Tennessee.

The inn was built in 1824 by John A. McKinney, a prominent lawyer and judge with large landholdings in that area. Carl Netherland-Brown, a descendant of McKinney, bought the inn in 1982 and since then has undertaken massive restoration. Some of the restored woodwork was done by modern craftsmen using antique tools. Four-poster canopy beds, original fireplaces, and antique bathtubs on legs add a special touch. Many of the antiques were discovered in the hotel's attic during renovation.

The inn's hospitality is apparent in many ways. Bowls of fresh fruit and lots of ginger ale in the rooms when guests arrive. Tea is available in the afternoon. Dulcimer music in the inn's restaurant provides background for delightful luncheon and dinner meals.

Ten guest rooms are available, and rates range from $40 to $55 per room for two guests. Continental breakfast is included.

Directions: 110 West Main Street, Rogersville, TN 37857. (615) 272-5171.

Parish Patch Farm & Inn, Normandy,
Marty Parish Ligon, owner

Want to spend the night on a real Tennessee farm, a working farm complete with grazing cattle and crops in

Inside the Walking Horse Hotel, Wartrace

the fields? The *Sampler* has the perfect suggestion for you—Parish Patch Inn.

This home was built by the late Charles Parish, former head of the world's largest manufacturer of baseballs and bats. He wanted a place to entertain his friends and business acquaintances, somewhere rustic enough to get away from business yet close enough to his business to make it practical. The perfect solution was this 750 acres of rolling farmland bordered on two sides by the Duck River.

The warm cherry and walnut paneling in the living room, library, and dining room of the board-and-batten house can be called "elegant rustic." There are cottages for overnight lodging as well as bedrooms or a suite in the house itself.

A hearty breakfast consists of country ham, eggs, homemade biscuits, grits, fresh preserves, juice, and coffee. You'll be served in the dining room or, if the weather is favorable, on the dining porch. Country dinners or picnic basket lunches can be ordered ahead of time. Breakfast is included in the room rate; evening meals are served to house guests only with advance reservations.

Swimming, fishing, boating, canoeing, water skiing, and bird watching, are all activities to be enjoyed at or near the inn. Cortner's Mill, built in 1848, has been recently restored and is a favorite of the guests.

Parish Patch is the site of business retreats as well as retreats for ladies taking quilting lessons in quaint Bell Buckle, just down the road. (See "Shopping.") Tennessee Walking Horse country is nearby in Wartrace, Shelbyville, and Lewisburg. Jack Daniel and George Dickel distilleries are both located within easy driving distance, and they offer tours daily. (See "Tours and Trails.")

Rates: Bed and Breakfast, double $55; suite $75; cottage $100. Check-in time is between 2:00 and 4:00 P.M.

Advance reservations required. (615) 857-3441.

Tennessee *Walking Horse Hotel,* Wartrace
George Wright, owner

"There are no frills here—we are basing our service completely on charm and comfort," says George Wright, owner of what he refers to as "the ultimate southern hotel." As you enter the lobby of this three-story brick hotel in the tiny (pop. 600) Bedford County hamlet, you can picture what it would have been like in 1917 when the hotel was built. Little has changed since then.

George purchased the hotel in 1980 and has been refurbishing each of the 25 rooms. Two verandas offer ideal vantage points to sit and watch the trains go by in this little community which was once a booming railroad town. There are no telephones or televisions in the rooms and not all the rooms come with the luxury of a private bath. What you do find is the peace, quiet, and laid-back comfort of an old-fashioned hotel that is saturated with tradition.

The tradition of the Tennessee Walking Horse literally was born at this hotel. In 1939, a man with a dream took a magnificent plow horse, developed its natural gaits to perfection, named him "Strolling Jim," and strolled to a World Championship. Floyd Carothers, then owner of the hotel, was that man.

Carothers and Jim worked out daily behind the hotel, perfecting the distinctive Walking Horse gaits. In 1939 the team captured the first grand championship at the Walking Horse Show in Shelbyville. Today that show is known as the annual Tennessee Walking Horse National Celebration, and Wartrace is nicknamed, appropriately enough, "The Cradle of the Tennessee Walking Horse." (See "Tours and Trails.")

The stables which housed the first world's champion still stand behind the hotel near the marble headstone marking Strolling Jim's grave. One of George Wright's goals is to educate "anybody and everybody about Walking Horses." To do this he has opened the Walking Horse Center, featuring Walking Horse memorabilia, films about Walking Horses, and an actual demonstration of the breed's gaits.

George personally guides the tour which begins in the picture gallery of the hotel. The photos represent the world's largest collection of Tennessee Walking Horse pictures. Dating to the 1930s, they tell the history of this magnificent breed. Next, visitors are treated to a film which highlights some of the more famous Walking Horses and their trainers. Part of the film was shot in the 1940s and gives Walking Horse admirers a rare look at some of the early champions, including the celebrated Strolling Jim.

The trip "out back" allows visitors an up-close look at the famous breed. Training Walking Horses is an everyday activity, and guests can watch as the horses demonstrate the characteristic gliding gait that has made the Tennessee Walking Horse one of the world's most popular pleasure horses.

After the presentation, you are welcome to relax and soak up the atmosphere and hospitality of the historic hotel. In the dining room, George's mother, Pauline Wright, serves southern gourmet cooking, "the kind we put on our table at home." The menu features country ham, fried chicken, fresh vegetables, and home-baked breads and desserts. Lunches are served Monday through Saturday 11:30 A.M. to 2:00 P.M.. Dinner is 5:30 to 8:00 P.M., and reservations are required.

Room rates: Room with private bath $28. Room with semi-private bath $20. Suite $36.

Directions: From I-24, take exit 97 to State 64. Just a few minutes drive from the interstate. (615) 389-6407.

Blackberry Farm Inn, Walland

Gary and Bernadette Doyle, Innkeepers

Looking for seclusion, yet variety of activity? Country atmosphere, yet elegance and taste? Located on a 1,100-acre farm adjoining the Great Smoky Mountains National Park is Blackberry Farm Inn. The innkeeper, Gary Doyle, tells us, "The location, hospitality, and cuisine combine to make one's visit the ultimate in relaxation."

Your day starts about 8:15 with a soft knock at the door announcing that a tray of fresh-squeezed juice and coffee with a croissant or sweet roll has been left for you. A real country boy's breakfast follows at 9:00 and includes eggs, sausage, buttermilk biscuits with milk gravy and preserves, and hashbrown potatoes. Box lunches are available for the noon meal, but dinner that evening is a "dine by candlelight" affair (jackets recommended for gentlemen at this meal). Guests dine at a long antique oak table set with Spode china, Waterford crystal, and heavy silver. The cost of the meals and room is included in the basic charge per person per day.

A short drive takes you to various activities such as water skiiing, golf, and fishing. Cades Cove is only a few miles southeast, and excellent shopping is in nearby Gatlinburg. Visitors to Blackberry more often stay on the farm to enjoy the pool, tennis court, hiking trails, and trout fishing in Hesse Creek, which runs near the inn.

The inn has eight full bedrooms and baths, each with its own personality just as a home would have. The main lounge is arranged in conversational groupings with thick Oriental rugs underfoot. A fireplace takes the chill off the room on brisk evenings.

Porch sitting at the Wonderland Hotel

The farm is located in Miller's Cove, which abounds in rich history. The oldest church in this part of Tennessee is here—Miller's Cove Primitive Baptist Church. An old mill which produces water-ground cornmeal and a schoolhouse a century old are other attractions in this scenic valley.

Rates: Two types of rooms are available at $74.95 or $84.95 per person per day, based on double occupancy. This figure includes all meals. Children may stay in the same room with parents or guardian for $25.00 extra per day.

Directions: From Knoxville, take US 129 (Alcoa Highway). Follow the signs to the Great Smoky Mountains. The first right past the Foothills Parkway is Route 321. Turn here. There are signs at the turnoff to Blackberry Farm, which is about 3 1/2 miles from the turnoff. 3570 West Millers Cove Road. (615) 984-8166.

Wonderland Hotel, Gatlinburg
Darrell Huskey, innkeeper

Back in its early days, just getting to Wonderland Hotel was an adventure. In 1920 the only ways to reach it were on foot, on horseback, or on the logging train. A trip on foot or horseback started in Gatlinburg, a distance of 7 1/2 miles. The train ride involved taking the morning train on Southern Railway from Knoxville and then transferring to a logging train for the final 30-mile ride to the hotel. Today it's a short drive from Gatlinburg.

Built in 1912, Wonderland Hotel has survived to stand as the only hotel in the Great Smoky Mountains National Park. It was once the exclusive playground of the affluent and socially prominent from surrounding communities. Visitors or vacationers would stay at least a week and sometimes all summer long; these well-to-do families enjoyed this escape from the heat of the cities.

Set on a hillside, Wonderland Hotel overlooks its surroundings. The white, two-story clapboard building has an old-fashioned porch—complete with rockers and swings—that stretches all across the front. The rushing Little River in its gorge is visible and audible from here. The serenity of the hotel is enhanced because radios, televisions, and telephones are not in any of the 27 rooms.

The hotel's restaurant offers country-style meals. Breakfast and dinner are served on red-checked tablecloths in the dining hall. Meals are available to the public, and menus are posted at the desk in the hotel lobby. The hotel is open from the end of May (Memorial Day) through October. The average price for a room is $35 to $50.

Elkmont Campground, operated by the national park, is 1/2 mile from the hotel on Elkmont Road. Park personnel conduct programs and guided walks during the summer months.

Directions: From Gatlinburg, take US 441 South to Sugarlands Visitors Center, then State 73W 4 1/2 miles to Elkmont Campgrounds. Wonderland is about 1 mile from the campgrounds. (615) 436-5490.

Silver Leaf 1815 Inn, Lyles
Norma and Johnny Crowe, owners

Nestled by a small creek bank, the log cabin Silver Leaf Inn exudes the country's peacefulness. Dine by the fireside, swing on the porch, spend time at the nature retreat by the creek, or just relax and catch a glimpse of the deer and wildlife in the woods.

There are three guest rooms with private baths. Continental breakfast is served. The guest rooms have comfortable furnishings of antiques, handmade quilts, and fresh flowers.

In 1976 the Crowe family restored the house log by log to its present beauty. A country Christmas at Silver Leaf 1815 is the main attraction of the year with 15-feet-tall live trees and everything heart warming of an old-fashioned Christmas.

Norma Crowe does all the cooking with a devoted staff, and some of the southern favorites they prepare are Tennessee country ham, southern fried chicken, fresh vegetables, fruits, and homemade breads. She makes all her jams, jellies, and preserves from fruit produced on the farm. They are served along with buttermilk biscuits. A cookbook is available so that you can go home and fix some of her special treats too.

Moderate prices.

Hours: Tuesday–Saturday, lunch 11:00 A.M. to 2:00 P.M.; dinner 5:00 to 9:00 P.M. Sunday buffet, 11:00 A.M. to 2:00 P.M. Reservations recommended. Available for corporate meetings, seminars, and private parties.

Directions: From State 100 and US 70, go west 25 miles on State 100 to Gulf Station on right, turn left, go 1/4 mile. From downtown Nashville, go I-40 to Dickson-Centerville Exit 172, turn left. Go State 46 south to State 100. Turn right. Go 1 mile to Gulf Station on right, turn

---

A SAMPLER FEATURE

One Lodge "You Can't Hardly Get To"

LeConte Lodge, Inc., Gatlinburg
Tim Line, Manager
Jim Huff, President

■ "Well, you can't hardly get there from here," says one old-timer with a gleam in his eye. What he means is, you really can't *drive* to LeConte, you can only hike to it. Located in the Great Smoky Mountains National Park, the lodge is the highest overnight lodge in the eastern United States.

LeConte is primitive—no radio, no television, no hot baths, no electricity. It's for those special people who prefer solitude and an escape from the traffic, smoke, noise, and bright lights of our fast-paced society.

Five trails lead from Gatlinburg and US 441 to LeConte, the shortest a climb of over 5 miles, the longest 8 miles. Those who do choose to rough it are blessed with enjoying the freshness of the air and the hush all around. Catching a filtered sunset from Cliff Tops, drinking the icy-cold water from a 6300-feet-high spring, and eating delicious hot meals served promptly at the ringing of the breakfast and dinner bells are the luxuries of LeConte.

Seven small cabins and three group lodges are available for overnight guests, with a capacity of 40. Reservations must be made in advance. Solomon, Chestnut, and Chalkie, three-year-old llamas, carry fresh foodstuffs topside three times a week.

Daytime temperatures are about 20 degrees lower than at the base of the mountain. Since everything but personal articles are provided at the lodge, a light knapsack should hold all your necessities. Prices average $35 per adult, which includes dinner and breakfast. (615) 436-7878.

For reservations, contact Jim Huff, P.O. Box 350, Gatlinburg, 37738.

Bed and Breakfast

We want to share with you some of the homes that represent the wide diversity of Bed and Breakfast dwellings in Tennessee.

Sandra Pennington of *Nashville:*
"I have been a hostess to couples from all of the USA at my Bed and Breakfast. Our California stucco was built in the 1920s, largely Palladian in style with a touch of art deco. There is a tile floor central atrium which features a large, vaulted skylight. An elegant, oversized bath exhibits a Jacuzzi for four under yet another skylight. Tropical plants and flowers abound. Guests are treated to fresh orange juice, crisp Tennessee bacon with fresh eggs, and my own special buttermilk biscuits. I welcome my guests by telling them, 'This is your home and you can expect to be treated royally.' " 205 Jackson Boulevard, Nashville, TN 37205. (615) 352-4823.

Jackie Waddell of *Hendersonville:*
"My home is Monthaven and is on the National Register of Historic Places. It was used as a hospital during the Civil War." 1154 West Main, Hendersonville, TN 37075.

Mary Ellan Stevens of *Franklin*
"I'm a widow, a farmer and a jack-of-all-trades. I like people and welcome Bed-and-Breakfast guests. I have a 100-acre farm with various and sundry critters ranging from Angus cattle and Arabian horses down to fancy chickens, pheasants, peafowl, and a lop-eared rabbit. Visitors are welcome to come and watch or help with cutting, raking, baling hay, and especially with picking up the bales! I work with international women in Nashville, so would especially welcome visitors from other countries—just to show them a farm or as guests."

By the way, Mrs. Stevens has backpacked the Appalachian trail and has a second-degree brown belt in judo! She says of her accomplishments, "They're just enough off the beaten path to add a little spice!" Sweeney Hollow Road, Franklin, TN 37064. (615) 794-6162.

Memphis Bed and Breakfast
Offers a log cabin with a lake stocked with bass and brim. You're welcome to fish, and there's a pool for swimming. Contact *Helen Denton* for information (see Directory below).

Helen also told the *Sampler* about a unique bonus for businessmen relocating to the Memphis area. You know how it is. Daddy has to go ahead and start his new job in February. The house back in Iowa is for sale, and it looks like it'll take a few months to sell it. The children want to finish the school year before they move. So Daddy has to live in a motel room for four months. He doesn't want to buy a new house until the old one sells. When Mom and the kids come for the weekend, there's just not enough room to spread out.

Memphis Bed and Breakfast has solved this dilemma. Imagine a little cottage you can rent by the week or month, not for the cost of an arm and a leg as is the case with most rental houses. When the kids come, there's a pond where you can go fishing. There's a kitchen so that you can have some of the home-cooked meals you've been missing. All this is available. Just talk to Helen Denton, and she'll help make your relocation much more pleasant.

Listed below is a directory of Bed and Breakfast facilities in Tennessee including the contact person, address, and phone number. We've always been known for our southern hospitality, so give us a chance to share it with you. Stay in a Tennessee home. Be sure to let the *Sampler* know about your favorites. We also encourage those Tennesseans who have homes that would be ideal for Bed and Breakfast to consider opening your home. Contact the agency nearest you for more information. Happy sleepin'!

Bed and Breakfast Directory:
Nashville area: Nashville Bed and Breakfast, c/o Fran Degan, P.O. Box 150651, 37215. (615) 298-5674; 366-1115 (after 6:00 P.M.).

Memphis area: Bed and Breakfast in Memphis, c/o Helen Denton, P.O. Box 41621, 38174. (901) 726-5920.

Jonesborough: Lynn Lucas, 305 College Street, 37659. (615) 753-9223 or 753-2095.

Knoxville: Bed and Breakfast of Knoxville, 212 Greene Road, Knoxville, TN 37920. (615) 577-4111.

All Tennessee: Host Homes of Tennessee, Fredda Odom, P.O. Box 110227, Nashville, TN 37222-0227. (615) 754-1372 or 331-5244.

A Corporate Retreat

Hachland Vineyard, Nashville
Joe K. Hach, innkeeper

The Vineyard offers something totally unique to the Nashville business community. The retreat, which is log and stone in structure, combines the quiet and privacy demanded for a business meeting with the convenience of a very short drive out of the city. Rented to one organization at a time, privacy and freedom to enjoy the entire complex are assured. Walking paths are next to the creek, and the large meeting room has a working stone fireplace. The retreat can be rented for dinner only, overnight lodging, or several days at a time.

Each room is furnished in turn-of-the-century antiques, hand-made quilts (many crafted by the Amish), woven rag rugs, and memorabilia of the Hach family. There are accommodations for lodging for 20, and up to 100 can be served easily for a private dinner or meeting. Plans are underway to add a swimming pool, 50 bedrooms, and a dining room to seat 200.

Burgess Falls

All the food at Hachland Vineyard is catered by Hachland Hill, the Clarksville restaurant and catering firm Joe's parents, Phila and Adolph Hach established 30 years ago. (See "Eatin' Good.") Everything from a plantation breakfast for a small group of business personnel to a barbecue dinner on the patio for 200 can be served.

A place to enjoy abundant nature, outstanding food, and peaceful surroundings is offered at Joe Hach's Vineyard.

For information, contact JKH Marketing, P.O. Box 2567, Nashville, TN 37219. (615) 255-1727.

Chalets for Rent

Mountain Laurel Chalets, Gatlinburg
Ralph and Dot Egli, managers

"Had you rather stay in Camelot, Stone's Throw, Rockytop, Cloud Nine, or Smokies Paradise?" is the delightful question you might hear when you call Dot Egli about renting a mountain chalet. The Eglis offer for rent 59 privately owned chalets that provide a 'home away from home' just outside of Gatlinburg.

All chalets have fully equipped kitchens, linens furnished, wood-burning fireplaces, TV's, and air-conditioning, and they are just a few minutes away from the ski resort, Gatlinburg Golf Club, and the Great Smoky Mountains National Park. Amenities available in some chalets are microwaves, barbecue pits, whirlpools, hot tubs, pool tables, and waterbeds.

Chalets are located 1 to 4 miles from downtown, have from two to seven bedrooms, and have access to three private recreational areas which include free swimming pool and tennis courts.

Rates are from $65 to $90 for two adults; $12 for each additional adult. Children 10 to 16 are $3.50 each, and children under 10 stay free. One night's rent in advance is required to hold a reservation. Check-in time is 2:00 P.M. Make reservations by calling or writing the Eglis: Route 2, Box 648, Ski Mountain Road, Gatlinburg, TN 37738. (615) 436-5277.

Shagbark, Sevierville

Shagbark is a private 1,200-acre picturesque resort which has fine dining, entertainment, tennis, swimming, fishing streams, waterfalls, places to hike, and more for you to enjoy. The mountain chalets have fully equipped kitchens, spacious bedrooms, and a great room with stone fireplace.

Only a short distance from Gatlinburg, Shagbark overlooks the Great Smoky Mountains National Park. Rates are $90 per day for two people and $20 for each additional person. Weekly rates, which include seven full nights, are $500 for two people and $90 for each additional person. No charge for children under 12 years old.

Shagbark is located 3 miles off Highway 321, on Walden Creek Road. For reservations, contact Carrine Rich at Route 11, Sevierville, TN 37862. (615) 453-5522.

Other Unique Accommodations

Clardy's Guest House, Murfreesboro
Frank Clardy, owner

"A big white elephant?" Frank Clardy and his late wife Betsy bought this Victorian Romanesque house back in 1954. Frank says, "Ninety-eight per cent of the folks in town called it 'Clardy's big white elephant,' but I told them to wait and see." The house is certainly big, and Frank can be seen on many days of the year painting a patch here or there to keep it white—but it is not the "elephant" many had predicted.

He has catered to an active tourist trade for over 30 years, and his guests include tourists, permanent residents, a couple of college students, and others in town for an extended period of time. The house is furnished throughout with period antiques that Frank and his wife collected from auctions, sales, and antiques dealers. The beautiful stained-glass window on the stairway and the elaborate woodwork throughout are reminiscent of more opulent times.

Murfreesboro boasts of many turn-of-the century homes along Main Street. A driving tour of this part of the city will give tourists a look at several homes whose old South charm reflects the pride of the homeowners nearly a century later.

A light, continental breakfast is served, and Mr. Clardy says you can check in at any time of the day. Clardy's is listed in *Bed and Breakfast, USA.* Price to stay overnight is approximately $20 for one room. Because of limited accommodations, reservations are recommended, but not required. Directions: From I-24, take Murfreesboro Exit 78B. Clardy's is 4 blocks from the public square. 435 East Main Street, Murfreesboro, TN 37130. (615) 893-6030.

McMahan Place, Pigeon Forge
Ken and Polly Spencer, owners

Located on the Little Pigeon River, under the quiet shade of gigantic maple trees, is a vacation place in the middle of nature but only two blocks from the downtown parkway.

Since McMahan Place is small, accommodations are limited to a few guests per night. Individual kitchenette units are completely furnished, and Polly Spencer says she'll loan any of her cooking utensils to you if you need something else. Although there's no swimming pool, the old swimming and fishing hole is yours to enjoy.

Pigeon Forge is an ideal central location to stay while enjoying the Great Smoky Mountains. Historic stops as well as shopping outlets and theme parks are all within easy driving distance. (See "Tours and Trails," "Shopping," and "Outdoors.") Ken and Polly were both raised in this area, and they are proud to share their Tennessee heritage with guests.

Advance reservations are preferred. Check-in time 2:00 P.M. Open April 1 to December 3l. Varying rates depend on season; average summer rate for two adults is $40 per night. 648 McMahan Street, Pigeon Forge, TN 37863. (615) 428-1605.

Camping in Tennessee

Campgrounds of every description are spread across Tennessee. They're found in state parks, at KOA's (Kampgrounds of America), and at privately owned camping facilities such as The Crosseyed Cricket (see "Eatin' Good").

Travel camps have provisions for travel trailers, truck coaches, or campers, and tent campers and primitive camps are primarily for tent camping.

Camping in Tennessee is a booklet produced by the Department of Tourism. Included are 85 towns across the state, the names of campgrounds, directions to reach the camps, and facilities offered, from ice to firewood, pay phones to showers.

Some 330 campgrounds are listed, including KOA's and state park facilities. To receive the booklet contact: Tennessee Tourist Development, P.O. Box 23170, Nashville, TN 37202. (615) 741-2158.

State Parks Accommodations

State Parks in Tennessee is a booklet produced by the Department of Tourism. It lists the name, address, and phone number of each state park along with information such as which parks have swimming, fishing, stables, boat launching ramps, tennis, backpacking, group lodges, nature trails, playgrounds, golf courses, marina, restaurants, bike trails, and other activities. A brief description is given of each park.

Tennessee has 51 state parks that offer just about any activity, sport, scenery, or lodging that you could wish for. Seven parks boast of resort inns: Fall Creek Falls, Henry Horton, Montgomery Bell, Natchez Trace, Paris Landing, Pickwick Landing, and Reelfoot Lake.

Cabins are available at all the above-mentioned except Paris Landing. Other parks with cabins include Big Ridge, Cedars of Lebanon, Chickasaw, Cumberland Mountain, Edgar Evins, Norris Dam, Pickett, Roan Mountain, Standing Stone, and Tims Ford.

To make reservations at many of the state parks, call toll-free (800) 421-6683. If a reservation cannot be made for you directly, you will be given the phone number of the park in which you are interested.

Campsites are available at most of the 51 parks. For a free booklet listing all the parks, contact: Tennessee Tourist Development, P.O. Box 23170, Nashville, TN 37202. (615) 741-2158

(For more information on state parks in Tennessee, see "Outdoors.")

Brochures and booklets on a wide range of accommodations can be ordered free of charge from the Tennessee Tourist Department by contacting them at the above address. Listings include: *Camping In Tennessee, Accommodations in Tennessee* (comprehensive listing of motels across the state), and *Tennessee Travel Directory (comprehensive list of motels across the state, chambers of commerce, package tours, charter bus services, rental car companies, airlines, events, and attractions).*

AN INSIDER'S SHOPPING LIST

SHOPPING GUIDE HIGHLIGHTS

✳Antiques✳

Reupen Gulbenk–An Antique Authority
8 Antique Malls and 13 Antique Shops
Many more Reproduction Furniture, Crafts, and Restoration Experts

✳Country Stores✳

Special Sittin', Sippin', Spittin', Swappin', and Shoppin' Places

✳Outlet Stores✳

A Comprehensive Guide to more than 70 Outlet Stores
Save up to 75% on clothes, footwear, linens, and much more

✳Tennessee's Unique Shopping—East, Middle, West✳

The Sampler's Guide to All Kinds of Auctions and Flea Markets
A Sampler Exclusive: Go Shopping with an Oak Ridge Boy
Almost 100 places to buy everything from exquisite, handmade knives, to cheese, herb wreaths, and wild horses!
A Sampler Feature: Tennessee's Amish

✳Tennessee Crafts—East, Middle, West✳

100 incredible Tennessee Craftsmen including quilters, woodworkers, basket weavers, doll makers, crochet, tatting and weaving experts, and potters
A Sampler Exclusive: Janie Fricke and her Quilts

Antiques

A SAMPLER FEATURE

Reupen Gulbenk

■ Fifty-three years ago they forded the creek to get to the cabin. Chickens clucked lazily in the yard and sauntered across the front porch, but Reupen and his uncle walked straight to the door. They were 25 miles west of Columbia in the middle of a wooded never-never land, and another day of adventure was ahead.

Two boys, bare feet dangling, looked down from a sagging maple tree branch on the intruding visitors. The little girl in her flour-sack dress ran inside, announcing to Mama that "company had come." The pungent smell of fresh turnip greens mingled with wood smoke, but Reupen's mind was on something else.

"Ma'am, what would you take for that desk?"

"That ol' green thang? I reckon about $10."

The burly, sleepy-eyed husband spoke up and said, "And I'll take a 25-pound bag of sugar." Sugar was of more value to his moonshining operation than cash.

"But do you want that part upstairs?"

They went to take a look, but the stairs had been burned for firewood the winter before. All Reupen could see above him was the slanted lid of the desk. But that was enough to make him hope the offer was still good. Reupen wanted the desk like most 12-year-old boys want a new baseball glove.

The fire department and a hook-and-ladder truck were hired to get the upper part of the desk down. All that trouble for an old desk, in two pieces, with six coats of green paint! Yes, because that sensitive, inquisitive young boy saw more than many of us could see—fine lines, special details, and quality wood. Forty-five years later, that primitive Hepplewhite secretary of the Governor Winthrop type, beautifully adorned with bell-flower inlay, sold for $25,000. And Reupen Gulbenk still sees more than most of us can see as he deals in exquisite antiques.

In antique circles today, Reupen is what is known as a "picker," that is, a person who travels all over the country and "picks" exclusive seventeenth- or eighteenth-century antiques for a specific buyer—or for himself to resell later. Reupen's impressive list of clients includes Tennessee's Governor Lamar Alexander and his wife, Honey. Reupen is chairman of The Tennessee Executive Residence Foundation, and he was instrumental in furnishing the formal rooms of the Executive Residence with period and historical furniture. A few of the many other stately homes for which Reupen has picked furniture and/or decorated are featured in *Colonial Homes* magazine (six issues from 1980 to 1982), *House Beautiful* (June 1968), *Texas Homes* (March 1982), *Southern Accents* (September 1982), and *Antiques Magazine* (May 1985).

Reupen is known in the business as a knowledgeable, honest person, and he often gets calls from across the country to come and make an offer on an individual item. But sometimes Reupen has to wait for what he wants. He waited 20 years to get a matched set of mirrors that now hang in his dining room. Sometimes he is called in as an antique consultant to give his valued opinion on a piece of furniture or a roomful of furnishings. Once when viewing a person's several hundred thousand dollars worth of newly acquired antiques, Reupen observed a startling fact: all the pieces were fakes. "What did he say when you told him?" we asked. Reupen replied, "I didn't tell him. If he didn't want my opinion before he bought, why should I give it after?"

Reupen's own home, set on a hill overlooking a valley near Nashville, is a high-style New England saltbox, brimming with period antiques. His furnishings rival what is found in most museums, except no ropes keep you off the canopy beds and away from the downy cushions. If only the two griffins on the front porch could talk! Not only could they tell the unsuspecting visitor that they came from the gateposts of James Whitcomb Riley's home, but perhaps they could whisper something about what lies behind the double doors.

Hepplewhite secretary, bought for $10 and a bag of sugar, sold for $25,000

In the right front parlor is an exquisite tea table (ca. 1720). A perfect companion piece is the pole screen (ca. 1740) adorned with very fine needlework. Reupen explained that women often had pockmarks on their faces, little scars left as a reminder of the dreaded smallpox. So they covered their faces with wax in order to achieve smoother skin. Naturally they didn't want to get too close to the fire, so they shielded their faces with embellished pole screens, now very rare items. Much the same principle was applied with the use of high-backed wing chairs because the wide, side wings shielded them from drafts.

Reupen proudly showed us a 1723 copyrighted book he discovered in a secret pocket of a secretary. He bought the secretary from a family up East. The secretary had been in their family for years, and they never knew of the hidden book.

In the left front parlor a china hutch (ca. 1690) from the original Plymouth Colony sits beside a one-arm, wooden desk. The desk was initially owned by Elbridge Gerry, a member of the First Continental Congress who gave his name to gerrymandering politics.

Reupen's stories from his life of dealing in fine antiques are all captivating. One time he and his father's business partner, Clifton Greer, were riding out on Lebanon Pike from Nashville. They became intrigued by the majesty of one of the antebellum mansions and stopped to take a closer look. In walking to the big house, they passed a tenant house. Inside was a marvelous sugar chest. Mr. Greer bought it for $1.

We followed Reupen into the front parlor. This gentle, soft-spoken man sat down on the antique rug, and then lay down on his back beside a tea table valued in the tens of thousands of dollars. As he reverently rubbed his hand on its underside, he said with awe, "I want you to feel this smoothness. Remember this was done with an ax in the early eighteenth century."

As we examined the fine craftsmanship, we marveled that such quality was achieved using primitive tools. But we were more intrigued by this man who in a few short hours had given us an education in fine antiques.

Tips from Reupen:

1. If you like antiques, find places where you can see the best furniture. Visit high-quality shops or visit historic places where you can get an idea of what very fine furniture looks like. In Nashville visit the Tennessee State Museum, the Hermitage, or Travellers' Rest (Travellers' Rest has one of the finest antique collections anywhere). In Knoxville visit the Blount Mansion or Ramsey House.

2. Find a good cabinetmaker or furniture craftsman to make your antiques of tomorrow. Today most people who are unable to have $30,000 tables and $50,000 sofas might be able to spend $1,000 for a reproduction of a table and $3,500 for a reproduction of a sofa. Reupen says, "I'd rather have a good reproduction than a lousy antique." Above all, know your antiques or find someone you trust who does.

Reupen Recommends
Tennessee's Finest Antique Specialists

Alfred Sharp, Woodbury, Eighteenth-century English and American furniture reproductions

Alf Sharp has a proverb he applies to his work: "If you ain't got time to do it right, how come you've got time to do it over?" Alf feels his attention to design, construction detail, and skill using hand tools (many are antiques in their own right) all work together to set him above the usual furniture crafter. For those who want to re-create the appearance of earlier interiors and appreciate the quality that can result only from the individual attention of a master craftsman, serious reproductions are really quite a bargain. For example, Alf can expand a set of dining room chairs from 6 to 10 or 12, copying the originals so faithfully that the owners often can't tell the new from the old.

Given Alf's background, you would not expect to find him in a workshop, in dust-covered denims, using woodworking tools. He tells us: "I was raised in Nashville, received a B.A. degree from Vanderbilt University, and was preparing to enter law school when I came to the realization that I had no desire to be a lawyer. I had no idea, however, of what I did want to do. I floundered around for two or three years and once, lacking the money to pay my rent, offered to do some remodeling for my landlord. A fascinating realm was opened up!

"Seeing that fine hardwood furniture was the ultimate expression of this activity that I enjoyed so much, I set my sights on that goal. I sought out old craftsmen and haunted their shops, soaking up the tricks of the trade. I read everything available. Much of the knowledge, skills, tools, and techniques were literally in danger of being lost forever when I started out, although this is not so much the case today."

You must see Alf's work to believe it. Custom and limited production from $100 to $15,000 and up.

Directions: Doolittle Road turns north only off 70S in Woodbury. Home and shop are 3¼ miles from 70S, on the right-hand side of the road. Business hours, usually 8:00 A.M. to 5:00 P.M. weekdays, others by appointment. Calling ahead is suggested. Route 1, Box 34, Woodbury, TN 37190. (615) 563-2831.

Keath Poyner, Nashville, Restorer of art objects

Keath has a rare talent. He restores damaged, rare art objects of almost any material—ivory, glass, marble, or porcelain. It doesn't matter about size; he remakes parts too, if necessary.

Keath's talent had an interesting birth.

One day he inherited a piece of Dresden china. Having a background in antiques and art, he set about

Reproduction by Alfred Sharp

working up his own formula for repairing the lovely piece. In no time flat, working by trial and error, he had perfected his skill. He was so good at this newfound art, other people wanted him to fix their damaged art pieces. Soon he was spending so much time restoring, he didn't have time to run his antique business. One had to go...it was the antique business he'd been in 14 years. Now Keath receives and repairs things from all over the United States.

Approximate price range $25 per hour. Call for an appointment. 3622 Bellwood Drive, Nashville, TN 37205. (615) 292-4164.

Corlew and Perry, Inc., Nashville, Floor refinishing

How do you get a dirty, dull, scarred floor to glow with the beauty it once had? Who creates the old look from new materials? Search no further.

Steve Dizmon tells us that floors in most old homes are of oak, pine, or poplar, with a few walnut, pecan, hickory, or beech. Corlew and Perry refinishes these floors to the owner's specifications, offering suggestions based on their more than 30 years of experience.

When a new floor with the old look is installed, oak is generally used, although some homeowners prefer old heart pine. Boards can be as wide as 8 inches or as narrow as the standard 2¼-inch width. Edges can be beveled or square, with pegs at the end of each board, if desired.

Most customers want a stain applied as a final step. An oil-based stain is hand rubbed into the wood, followed by a coat of shellac and a paste wax with a high carnauba content. With this type of refinishing, the floor will take on a fine patina with age.

Call for a free estimate or a free brochure on your flooring needs. 3017 Nolensville Road, Nashville, TN 37211. (615) 832-0320.

Lillian Luna's Log Cabin's Antiques, Columbia
Antique furniture

Lillian and John Luna are brother and sister, and they were raised with a love for antiques. Their father, Rufe Luna, was one of the first antique "pickers" of Tennessee. The late Mr. Luna traveled the hills and dales of Tennessee 50 and 60 years ago picking authentic Tennessee antiques to buy and then resell in the larger populated areas of Middle Tennessee.

Today Lillian, John, and John's wife, Jane, carry on the tradition of dealing in quality antique furniture, specializing in southern walnut and cherry furniture. They do their own hand-refinishing work. Prices range from a few hundred to several thousand dollars.

Call for an appointment. Lillian's shop is on the Nashville Highway (US 31N), Columbia, TN 38401; (615) 388-2857. John and Jane's shop is on Route 9, Sante Fe Pike, Columbia, TN 38401. (615) 388-3859.

Eloise Jeffries, Nashville, Early American

Reupen tells us Miss Eloise is a fine lady of high integrity, so it stands to reason that her antiques will be of the same quality. She makes a point to handle only fine Early American pieces which she can guarantee in regard to age, condition, value, and source. In her shop you'll see mostly antiques dating before 1830, samplers, folk art, pewter, brass, and copper. There's a wide price range from small accessories to period furniture.

Business hours: 10:00 A.M. to 4:00 P.M., Friday, Saturday, and Sunday, and the rest of the week by chance or appointment.

Directions: The shop is in a tenant cottage at the back of her residence. 1101 Otter Creek Road, Nashville, Tn 37220. (615) 832-1611.

James L. Horne, Goodlettsville, American and English eighteenth-century furniture reproductions

Words do not capture the elegant beauty of this work. The epitome of a master craftsman, James restores and reproduces furniture of the Anglo-American community made between 1680 and 1825. All work is done by hand. Reproductions are priced by the piece—for example, a mahogany English candlestand, ca. 1760, is $425, and an ornately carved mahogany English side chair, ca. 1735, is $1,800.

Call for an appointment. 7773 Ridgewood Road, Goodlettsville, TN 37072. (615) 876-2969.

Sandor Bodo, Nashville, Artist and painting restorer

Sandor Bodo fled Hungary for political freedom. Here in a new homeland he carefully researched our history, making it come to life in his action-packed hunt and battle scenes, paintings of respected Revolutionary War heroes, and meticulously designed medals. Mr. Bodo has achieved international fame in the art world and has brought added respect in another dimension to Nashville. Along with creating masterpieces, Sandor and his wife, Ilona, are noted painting restorers, having done restoration work for the Hermitage in Nashville and the Polk home in Columbia.

Call for an appointment. Bodo's Art Studio, 6513 Highway 100, Nashville, TN 37205. (615) 352-6050.

Lyzon Pictures and Frames, Inc., Nashville, American art and special frames

Myron King is an artist, featuring American oils and etchings. In his 35 years at Lyzon, he has worked with renowned artists such as Red Grooms and David Burliuk. But Myron has a special talent. Working with Lyzon's over 800 different patterns of moldings from around the world, he can create or copy the frame to complement any artwork. For example, at Travellers' Rest in Nashville, there was a 4-foot-square picture of Judge Overton, and a matching frame was needed for a picture of Mrs. Overton. Myron made one that can't be distinguished from the original. See Myron, too, about your painting or frame restoration work.

Lyzon Pictures and Frames is open 9:00 A.M. to 5:00 P.M. weekdays. 411 Thompson Lane, Nashville, TN. (615) 256-7538.

Susie Justus, Nashville, Interior designer

And finally, Reupen recommends most of all Susie Justus. ([615] 385-9523). She has a degree from the New York School of Design and has an extensive library of authentic materials, papers, and designs to create the proper background for your home and fine furniture. "She's the best interior designer in Nashville, specializing in 'the early look,' but I could be partial. She's my daughter."

English mahogany candlestand, Reproduction by James Horne

Chattanooga's Houston Antique Museum

Anna Safley Houston loved antiques. She especially loved antique glassware, but her passion was for pitchers. When she died in 1951, she left her most prized possessions to her adopted home town of Chattanooga, and her collection of more than 15,000 antique pitchers became the basis for one of Tennessee's truly unique museums.

During the Depression, Mrs. Houston had to choose between saving her home or saving her collections, so she sold her house and moved into an old barn on the outskirts of the city. She lived there until her death in 1951. Her will left her remarkable collection to the people of Chattanooga and named a board of trustees charged with establishing a museum. Since there was no money for that museum, the beautiful pieces stayed in the leaking old barn for almost 10 years until the board and many concerned citizens finally rallied to save the collection with a fund-raising drive. This drive produced enough money to buy the old Victorian house on High Street as a place to display her collection.

Mrs. Houston lived surrounded by her antiques. She had about 50 corner cupboards, all of them jammed with unusual glassware and china. She had sugar chests, blanket chests, highboys, and old tables, all of them laden with her collection too. The rest were fastened to the ceiling on ropes, one reason for the way the museum now displays a part of her collection.

Even though Mrs. Houston was rather eccentric in her later years, she had exquisite taste in antiques. She had the best of Staffordshire, Liverpool, Spatterware, and other varieties in more than 1,000 teapots. There are also priceless Meissen, Dresden, Capo di Monte, Bristol, Chelsea and Staffordshire vases, Betty lamps, Clark's fairy lamps, peg lamps, and other lighting fixtures. But the incredible collection of pitchers makes the Houston internationally known among collectors and dealers in glassware. Many other things are on display too—quilts, furniture, antique music boxes, Toby jugs, and occupational mugs.

The Houston Antique Museum is located at 201 High Street in downtown Chattanooga. It is open Tuesday through Saturday from 10:00 A.M. to 4:30 P.M. and Sunday from 2:00 to 4:30 P.M. Admission is $2 for adults, 75 ¢ for children.

Antique Shops in Tennessee

Sandy Arden Antiques, Knoxville

Here's a shopping trip sure to please the whole family. While Mom is picking out some gorgeous country antiques, Dad and the kids can stroll around a real working farm and visit a lovely log cabin. Sandy has her antique shop right on her property in the "Halls" area. Price range of merchandise is broad, so call for more information or an appointment. 8301 Andersonville Pike, Knoxville, TN 37938. (615) 922-0455.

Kountry Konnection, Ooltewah

Arlene Jenkins paints folk art on wood pieces cut out and prepared by her husband, Bob. She tells us: "It has really been fun working together on these projects and has given both of us a great sense of accomplishment. We have opened the upstairs of our home as a gift shop. This is the best way we knew to avoid 'the empty nest syndrome.' I determined that my shop was going to be unique and would carry some merchandise that other stores in the Chattanooga area didn't have. I also have learned how to refinish antiques and have gotten a lot of satisepction from finding an old painted piece and stripping it to discover the beauty of what's hidden underneath. Bob and I are really kept busy doing special orders for people who want a welcome sign personalized or a shelf made to fit a certain space. My sister is busy doing counted cross-stitch in the country theme for the shop. The prices on our things range from under $1 to over $400 for an old antique kitchen cabinet with stained-glass doors. We feel that our shop has something for everyone—even if you don't like country you're bound to like our gourmet dip mix that comes in four delicious flavors!"

Open Tuesday through Thursday, 10:00 A.M. to 6:00 P.M. or by appointment.

Address: 9300 Janeen Lane, Ooltewah, TN 37363. (615) 892-2816.

The Daffodilly Antiques, Bell Buckle

Lynn Sain and Linda Vannatta look forward to spring when blooming daffodils line the 12-mile stretch of country road leading to their shop. The shop is in a building that opened in 1911 as Clary's Drug Store, and shelves that once held medicine bottles now display antique accessories and memorabilia. Lynn and Linda feature pine and poplar furniture in The Daffodilly, and rope beds and plank tables are their hottest items. However, other special pieces of furniture include cupboards, desks, pie safes, cradles, and chairs. For children or the young at heart, find rope doll beds, ice-cream chairs and tables, and miniature doll furniture. Both women are married to farmers, which makes them well qualified to offer their cookbook, *Potluck Pickin's and Picturesque Places of Bell Buckle.* Be sure to check it out.

Furniture or craft items range in price from 50 ¢ to $1,200. Business hours are 10:00 A.M. to 4:00 P.M., Monday through Saturday.

Directions: Exit I-24 at Shelbyville, Wartrace, Bell Buckle Exit. Go 3 miles on State 64 and take a right on State 82. Go 12 miles (or follow the daffodils in Spring). Railroad Square, Bell Buckle, TN. (615) 389-9663.

Pauline's Antiques and Junk, Collinwood

What began as a hobby will take on added importance for Pauline as a business and country store when she retires in a few years. She specializes in pressed glass, patterned glass, colored glass, and stoneware, priced "from cheap to quite expensive," as her customers say. Hours: after 4:00 P.M. weekdays, most anytime on weekends.

Directions: From Collinwood, turn right on State 13

English mahogany sidechair, Reproduction by James Horne

toward Florence, Alabama. Go 1 mile and see the sign out front. Route 2, Box 19, Collinwood, TN 38450. (615) 724-4370.

Jones Antiques, Murfreesboro

Riverside, the home of Sarah and Claude Jones, was built in the 1830s. It was restored in the 1860s and has been in the Randolph family since 1865; Sarah is the granddaughter of Beverly Randolph, the original owner. There you'll see the tall, white columns glistening in the sun and feel an air of pride and dignity within the walls. The original floral-designed ceiling paper in the parlor blends well with the exquisite antiques.

The original furnishings are now being enjoyed by the third- and fourth-generation descendants of the original owner. But all 13 rooms of Riverside are furnished with other antiques in keeping with the period of the home, and practically everything in the house is for sale. Massive dining room tables, 7-feet-tall pier mirrors, walnut tester and half-tester beds, cherry sideboards, mahogany china cabinets—all make you feel you are shopping in one of the finest historical homes of the South...and you are.

Business hours from 9:00 A.M. to 5:00 P.M. Wide price range. It's best to call first. Route 3, Murfreesboro, TN 37130. (615) 893-8583.

Ellene Sewell, Columbia

Here's a place to drop in and find something different in antiques, paintings, and decorator items. Ellene says, "I've always been interested in anything having to do with the arts and especially in finding beautiful old things of quality and bringing them back to their original state." Most of her interest seems to focus on old paintings and frames. Customers return frequently to observe progress of painting or frame restoration. Prices range from $10 to $2,000. Open 10:00 A.M. to 4:30 P.M. daily, except Sunday.

Directions: In Columbia on US 31N (across from Northway Shopping Center), turn on Riverside Drive. Proceed a few blocks and turn left on Fifth Avenue. House will be on right. 208 Fifth Avenue, Columbia, TN 38401. (615) 388-3973.

Countryside Antiques, Monterey

Get off I-40 East at Exit 300 and see "where the hilltops kiss the sky," as the residents say. If you like scenic drives and antique hunting, take a drive west on US 70 out of Monterey. Nestled back on a hillside sits an old-country-store-looking, barn-wood building with the sign "Countryside Antiques" on it. Stop for a visit with Pat Young, a charming and friendly southern belle, who will be happy to show you antiques, glassware, ironware, graniteware, lamps, and Tennessee split-oak baskets. Another product she is proud to offer is old-fashioned, pure mountain honey, supplied by her beekeeper father, John Lee Tayes. Business hours: Monday through Friday and most Saturdays, 10:00 A.M. to 5:00 P.M.. Other times by chance or appointment. Route 1, Box 108, Monterey, TN 38574. (615) 839-2516.

Anne Johnson, Nashville

Anne sells quality American antiques from the late 1600s to 1850, with a particular emphasis on southern furniture, textiles, pottery, and Tennessee antiques. There is a wide range of products and prices, starting at about $25 for small southern decorative arts on up to $10,000 for some seventeenth-century antiques. Business hours, 11:00 A.M. to 3:00 P.M..

Address: 2204 Crestmoor Road, Nashville, TN 37215. (615) 292-6135.

Joanna's Junque, Tullahoma

You'll find browsing in Joanna's Junque as much fun as prowling around in Grandma's attic. Located in an old converted home, there are 11 big rooms of furniture and primitives, country store items, kitchen gadgets, glassware, plus The Mulberry Bush full of craft items. (Check closets for added surprises!) Although most men enjoy shopping at Joanna's, restless husbands enjoy the pink rockers on the porch. Easy to find and plenty of parking.

Open daily 10:00 A.M. to 4:00 P.M. closed on Monday, Tuesday, and Sunday. 201 South Anderson, Tullahoma, TN 37388. (615) 455-4418.

Dulac Collectibles, Buchanan

This retired couple, Joe and Jessie Scarbrough, enjoys keeping the past alive. Visit their 1871 log house and notice the "shoot out" holes by the door. Inside see quilts, pottery, Depression glass, and furniture for sale, as well as oblong dough trays, stag-handle hunting knives, and even homemade lye soap and Tennessee-grown tobacco, twisted and ready to chew! Open 9:00 A.M. to 5:00 P.M., Monday through Saturday, and 1:00 to 5:00 P.M. on Sunday (if not gone fishing—better call first). Approximate prices: $85 to $100 on trays or knives.

Directions: Approximately 1/2 mile west of Paris Landing State Park on US 79 (on north side of highway). Route 1, Box 88, Buchanan, TN 38222. (901) 642-1520.

Nelsie Anderson Mulkins Antiques, Germantown

Nelsie Anderson Mulkins loves her work. She works every day and shares a partnership in her antique business with her daugher, Lola Mulkins. The only thing unusual about this arrangement is that Nelsie is 92 years old.

Nelsie's father, Herman Anderson, moved to Memphis in 1903 and opened a furniture repair shop in 1906. He started with four employees, eventually expanded to six, and all of these men continued to work for the Andersons until their deaths—the last in 1960. Nelsie married in 1909 and started working in her father's shop in 1928. After Herman's death in 1930, Nelsie and her mother continued to run the business. Eventually they were forced into the antique business because they took old furniture as payment on furniture repair bills.

In 1957, Nelsie and her mother moved to their present location at 9336 Poplar Avenue in Germantown. Nelsie did upholstery work, refinishing, and traveled the country buying antiques. By this time her mother was 87, still acting as hostess and helping customers.

In the last 79 years, the shop has progressed from a small furniture repair shop to one of the finest antique shops in the Mid-South. Nelsie says: "The latchstring is out and there is 'welcome' on the mat. It's been that way for 79 years. I wouldn't trade jobs with anyone."

Go by and see Nelsie and Lola. Open Tuesday through Saturday, 10:00 A.M to 5:00 P.M. and Sunday evenings by appointment. Items priced from $1 to $10,000.

Directions: Exit Interstate 240 at Germantown/Poplar Exit. Go 8 miles from the exit. The shop is on the left. 9336 Poplar, US 72, Germantown, TN 38138. (901) 754-7909.

The Country Collection, Henry

More than 50 years ago, the Routon one-room schoolhouse held a roomful of eager learners. Now it holds avid antique and folk art collectors who pass in and out of its doors 10:00 A.M. to 5:00 P.M., Tuesday through Saturday. Nowadays see a wonderful collection of antiques, crafts, and folk art made and finished in the shop. Pause for a game of checkers at the checkerboard table in the antique section. Prices range from $1 (small items) to $100 or more (antiques).

Directions: Six miles south of Paris on US 79S. Route 1, Box 278, Henry, TN 38231. (901) 644-1550.

Brenda's Antiques, South Fulton

Antique collectors dream of finding that quaint little treasure trove, chock-full of country cupboards, stoneware, and quilts. Here it is! Brenda Jones specializes in country furniture, primitives, and accessories, housing these treasures in a 160-year-old log cabin. Good country antiques and primitives are becoming rare, but if they could talk, what they could tell us! Brenda's century-old sugar chests and pies safes would describe kitchens producing luscious fruit pies with flaky crusts. The hunt table could relate tales of plump, roasted rabbits and geese which fed a hungry Tennessee pioneer family.

Cozy handmade accessories add to the country look, many made by Brenda or local residents, and they are available through mail order too. Prices range from $100 to $1,000 on furniture and from $75 to $250 for quilts.

Find Brenda's hidden away on US 45E, 4 miles from South Fulton. Appointment advised. Route 5, Box 162, South Fulton, TN 38257. (901) 479-3266.

Custom-built Furniture and Reproductions

Nelson and Sons Woodworking Shop, Afton
Custom-made cabinets

The motto "Built to Suit You" lets customers know the Nelsons will build anything in the wood line, given enough time. They specialize in custom-made cabinets and give free estimates on all work.

Directions: From Greenville, take US 11E. Then take the first road to the right past the Greene Valley Developmental Center, and go 1 mile on the blacktopped road. Route 1, Box 13, Afton, TN 37616.

Jack Campbell, Athens, Antique reproduction and folk art
Jack Campbell is the quiet type. He's content sitting in his workshop whittling or sawing boards, pausing now and then to check on another project or have a smoke. "If you find your work to be a chore, you're no good at it," Campbell says. Jack must be good at it then, because he enjoys his work and has a national reputation as an antique expert and craftsman.

Admirers around the country seek the Campbell handmade furniture and folk art. In the furniture line Jack creates made-to-order concept cupboards, Shaker chests, and canopy or pencil post beds—to name only a few items. In the folk line, wooden but luscious-looking fruits and vegetables are big items—carrots, radishes, green peppers, apples, pears, and juicy watermelon slices. Around Christmas time, Jack sells a lot of distinctive, intricately carved wooden Santas and "Merry Christmas" banners.

Visit this family-operated business, or write for a catalogue. Prices range from $2.50 for a carved wooden heart to $1,000.00 for a piece of furniture. Anyone who can use up 7,000 to 8,000 feet of lumber a year must have something you need! Business hours: 9:00 A.M. to 5:00 P.M. Call for an appointment.

Address: 107 South Kilgore Street, Athens, TN 37303. (615) 745-8010.

The Cooke Hill Collection, Athens,
Furniture reproductions

Home owned and operated by Tom and Carmen Wilkins, this unique 1,700-square-feet store features the work of over 80 artisans from all over the country. No imports. The Cooke Hill Collection specializes in fine handmade Early American furniture of pine, oak, cherry, or walnut. Featured is furniture by Thomas E. Wilkins and Sons, also of Athens. Custom orders are welcome, and they ship anywhere in the continental United States. See also hand-loomed rugs, carved decoys, baskets, wheel-thrown and hand-done pottery, and much more.

Located on the courthouse square. Open Monday through Friday 9:30 A.M. to 5:30 P.M.; Saturday 10:00 A.M. to 5:00 P.M. 15 North Jackson Street, Athens, TN 37303. (615) 745-5668.

Thomas E. Wilkins and Sons, Athens, Hand-crafted furniture

Jeff Wilkins, Walter Vincent, and Robert Wilson work with their hands, and their hands turn out fine furniture for home or office, furniture made of white pine, white oak, walnut, or cherry. Jeff Wilkins pretty much taught himself everything from how to get a smooth dovetail edge on a drawer to how to hand-finish wood with linseed oil. He prefers natural joiners such as mortise and tenon or dovetail, the very heart of handmade furniture, rather than nails or screws.

Most Wilkins furniture has very simple lines, and Early American reproductions are specialties. Orders can be delivered anywhere in the United States. Prics depend on the piece of furniture but are always reasonable and competitive. Open 8:00 A.M. to 5:00 P.M., Monday through Saturday.

P.O. Box 509, Athens, TN 37303. (615) 745-6925.

Country Craftsmen, Bristol, Virginia,
Furniture restoration and reproductions

Furniture restoration means more than refinishing the surface of a fine piece of furniture. It may mean completely rebuilding the piece from a heap of wood into something beautiful. Country Craftsmen have refinished, using their unique methods, elaborate Chippendale pieces and simple country pieces dating to the seventeenth century. Their list of pleased customers includes many individuals, businesses, and a local hotel furnished with lovely antiques. Work is priced by the piece. Call for more information, an appointment, or directions. Owners are Charles Cross, Jr., and Phillip Koltunski. 748 Goose Creek Road, Bristol, VA 24201. (703) 669-8754 or (703) 466-6623.

Heartwood, Greenbrier,
Furniture reproductions

Sandra White says: "A few years ago when we were tearing down an 1807 yellow poplar cabin and rebuilding it, we came to cherish the fine wood and wonderful craftmanship in the old house. We tried to make the best possible use of every piece in our new home. It took us four years to build our home ourselves. From that effort came our present business in making things from wood. We specialize in furniture reproduction, custom building in pine, oak, or poplar."

See their rocking horses, storage cabinets with punched-tin paneled fronts, and dry sinks custom-made for a microwave to fit on top. Prices range from $50 to $200. Home furnishings and gifts to warm every heart. Call for an appointment or more information.

Address: Old Distillery Road, Greenbrier, TN 37073. (615) 643-0858.

The Red Fox, Lascassas,
Williamsburg reproductions

See an old sawmill in operation! From the cherry and walnut boards prepared here, John McFarlin and Ransom Jones fashion elegant furniture reproductions. Visit the shop where the furniture is displayed, as well as locally-made quilts, home-grown herbs, antiques, and items of the colonial period. Located on the beautiful Stones River with a great bed and breakfast place, fishing, and swimming nearby. Furniture priced from $85 to $3,000 and up.

Directions: From Murfreesboro, take State 96 East, turn left at Campbell's store, and left again at Jefferson Pike. See The Red Fox on the left, approximately 1 1/2 miles from Lascassas. Old Jefferson Pike, Lascassas, TN. (615) 893-0072 or (615) 896-3525.

James Yannayon, Lawrenceburg,
Furniture, reproductions

Do you know what you want but can't find it in furniture stores? Or if you find it, is it so cheaply made, you don't want it after all? Then James is the person to see. James can build hard-to-find items by looking at a picture or sketch. He uses only solid woods. People around Lawrenceburg say his craftmanship can't be beat, whether he's working on a cherry dining room table, an oak roll-top desk, or a made-to-order outbuilding for a farmer. Prices range from under $20 for a footstool to over $1,500 for a roll-top desk. Business hours: 8:00 A.M. to 6:00 P.M. Closed Sunday and Tuesday.

Directions: From Lawrenceburg, take US 64 about 7 miles. See the shop on left side of the highway. Sign out front. Route 5, Lawrenceburg, TN 38464. (615) 363-7711.

George Ray, Monterey,
Furniture reproductions and clocks

George cuts his own oak, walnut, cedar, or cherry and dry kilns it himself to make sure it's done right. In the small item line, he fashions coal oil lamp holders, reproduction antique mantel clocks, old-fashioned rocking chairs, and porch swings. He custom makes large pieces such as roll-top desks or bedroom furniture; just bring in a picture of what you want and George will fix you up. Call for an appointment.

Prices: Clock—about $80, rocking chair—about $80, and porch swing—about $30.

Directions: Exit I-40 at Monterey. Located about 4 miles north of Monterey on State 84. See sign on left. Route 2, Box 346, Monterey, TN 38574. (615) 839-2328.

Woodcrafts by Overman and Pierce, Pleasantville,
Hickory rocking chairs

Overman chairs and accessories are unique. So are James and Sharon. We'll tell you about the folks first, then the furniture.

James Overman has a master's degree in biological chemistry and a master's of divinity from Grace Theological Seminary, but he earns his living as a master

carpenter. He uses the high degree of carpentry skill he acquired while living with the Amish, and now he makes hickory rocking chairs.

James says: "Our hickory and ironwood are selected in the woods, cut with machetes, trimmed, hauled to the shop, and cut to length. After drying, the limb knots are sawed off, and the sticks are sanded smooth with the bark left on. The main pieces are steamed and bent to shape on forms. Other pieces are bent and nailed directly to the furniture from the steamer. Most of the pieces in our line were designed to complement the Amish-style rocker. Our line adapts itself well to many types of decor, especially the country living emphasis currently in vogue."

Lamp tables, lamps, magazine racks, and footstools are also available, and most recently added to the line are porch swings, end tables, cradles, quilt racks, double rockers, hat racks, and walking canes. Overman products are sold nationally through about 35 top quality craft stores and are shipped anywhere in the United States. Prices range from $3 to $360. Business hours are 8:00 A.M. to 5:00 P.M. Monday through Saturday.

Directions: The Overmans are 75 miles west of Nashville and 30 minutes south of I-40. Take Lobelville Exit from I-40. Call for an appointment. Route 1, Box 61, Pleasantville, TN 37147. (615) 729-5487.

Willows by Phillips, Spring Hill,
Willow furniture, accessories, and workshops

A unique, traditional piece of furniture from a scruffy patch of river willows? Hogwash! But John and Debra Phillips say no—"where there's a willow there's a way."

Willow is a special wood to them. Concoctions from willow bark and leaves have been used since the time of Hippocrates for treating headaches, fevers, rheumatism, eye irritations, and other pain. But Debra and John use "bush" willow to create a "twig" or "rustic" style of furniture which originated in eighteenth-century England. In America, this unusual furniture became most popular in the Adirondack Mountains region of New York during the 1920s and 1930s. All Phillips willow furniture is handmade using an assortment of house and garden tools. They offer items for sale such as baskets, chairs, love seats, or even canopy beds.

Sign up for the one-day workshop and learn the art of willow furniture making yourself. You will be supplied with all you need, except a hammer. Success is guaranteed 100 percent. Participants are amazed at what they learn to do with a pile of sticks. John begins the session with a rousing harmonica song and follows with a lecture on the history and workability of willow. Call for an appointment or more information. Approximate price range of products is $12 to $1,500. Workshops are $65 to $85; they are held May through September, the last Saturday of every month.

Address: P.O. Box 402, Spring Hill, TN 37174. (615) 486-2634.

Charles R. Goolsby, Spring Hill,
Custom cabinets and furniture

Family of Amish rockers by James Overman

Cabinets custom designed to fit your kitchen feature ³/₄-inch wood and wood veneers throughout—even the drawers have ³/₄-inch sides and backs. Furniture items and bookcases are built to fit your location and special purpose in your home. Woods used are poplar, oak, and cherry. Free estimates and kitchen designs available. Business hours: 7:00 A.M. to 5:00 P.M.

Address: Route 2, Sugar Ridge Road, Spring Hill, TN 37174. (615) 486-2800.

Charles Mitchell, Union City,
Furniture designer

Charles is a third-generation bricklayer by trade, specializing in patios, fireplaces, and walks. But on rainy,

cold, or snowy days, and at every other opportunity, he'll be in his workshop—custom building wooden items and furniture. Very seldom does he make any two items alike. Charles is a talented designer and makes his own patterns to achieve what people want in size, color, shape, and so on. His prices range from a few dollars for a simple towel rack to several hundred dollars for a china cabinet. If you like one-of-a-kind, quality hardwood furniture that you can't find in a furniture store, call Charles. You'll be glad you did.

Address: 712 North Third Street, Union City, TN 38261. (901) 885-9063.

Antique Malls

Antiques Unlimited, Bristol, TN

Visitors to Antiques Unlimited say this is one of the largest and most complete malls in the area. Beginning or advanced collectors are sure to find something they need—from lighting fixtures to new furniture and reproductions to country or period antiques. Small items such as quilts, baskets, crocks, china, and miniatures are also available. Wide price range.

Hours: Monday–Saturday, 9:30 A.M. to 5:30 P.M. Sunday, 1:00 to 5:00 P.M.

Directions: On the main street in Bristol, in the restored section near the train station. 628 State Street, Bristol, TN 37620. (615) 764-4211.

The Chattanooga Antique Mall

Susan Dever tells us to invest in the past and shop in Chattanooga's only antique mall, now filled to capacity as it celebrates its first anniversary. The Chattanooga

Willow by Phillips

Antique Mall, located on Broad Street at the foot of Lookout Mountain, in Chattanooga's antique row, offers a variety of antiques and collectibles. Featuring over 50 dealers, the mall is open daily. Free parking.

Business hours: 10:00 A.M. to 5:30 P.M., Monday through Saturday. 1:00 to 5:30 P.M., Sunday.

Address: 1901 Broad Street, Chattanooga, TN 37408. (615) 266-9910.

Clinton Antique Mall

For unusual country primitives, come to Clinton Antique Mall, located in the heart of picturesque Clinton. See quality antiques and collectibles ranging from 10¢ to $500 (dealers' prices are advertised). Browse through their selections of country primitives, folk art, quilts, vintage clothing, baskets, tools and farm implements, glassware, gameboards, toys, and books, among other things.

Open Monday–Saturday, 10:00 A.M. to 5:00 P.M.

Address: 355 Cullom Street, Clinton, TN 37716. (615) 457-9858.

Haggle Shop Antique Mart, Kingsport

Bob and Joyce Grills promise all customers coming to the Haggle Shop that they're always ready "to go one more haggle." Their 85 booths filled with glassware, dolls, quilts, Victorian and country oak furniture, and popular oak furniture reproductions certainly have something for most shoppers. But if you don't want to buy and just want to rest for awhile, sit on an old church pew and play a relaxing game of checkers. You can reach into a nearby candy jar for a tasty treat if you're hungry. The inventory changes almost every day at the Haggle Shop, but it's always bursting at the seams with bargains. Go by and hone your art of haggling.

Open seven days a week: 10:00 A.M. to 5:00 P.M., Monday through Saturday, and 1:00 to 6:00 P.M. on Sunday.

Address: 146 Broad Street, Kingsport, TN (615) 246-8002.

Brentwood Antique Mall

See the finest antiques displayed by 78 dealers in 12,000 square feet of space. Located only 15 minutes south of downtown Nashville, 5 minutes off I-65, Exit 74. Open Monday-Saturday, 10:00 A.M. to 5:00 P.M. Sunday, 1:00 to 5:00 P.M.

Directions: Take I-65 South to the Brentwood Exit. Church Street East, Brentwood, TN 37027. (615) 373-2353.

Eighth Avenue Antique District, Nashville

Visit Nashville's oldest and largest antique district. See fine furniture, primitives, rugs, collectibles, vintage clothes, crafts, and much more in five shops beginning at 2019 Eighth Avenue South and going to 2218 Eighth Avenue South. Be sure to visit with Judi and Ron Lederer at Forrest Valley Galleries. Let the children play with the sturdy handmade wooden toys while you see contemporary artworks complementing Victorian and period furnishings and one of the finest collections of estate linens in the South. Ask about their interior design service.

Hours: Monday–Saturday, 10:00 A.M. to 5:00 P.M. Sunday, 1:00 to 5:00 P.M.

Directions: Exit off I-65S to Wedgewood Avenue. Turn left on Wedgewood Avenue and left again on Eighth Avenue South in Nashville.

Murfreesboro Antique Mall and Antique Village U.S.A., Murfreesboro

Historic Murfreesboro is called the "Antique Center of the South," and the town boasts many dealers and malls. Visitors from around the world come to Murfreesboro seeking hard-to-find collectibles or museum quality antiques. The malls and local shops deal in glassware, china, dolls, rugs, books, paintings, watches, jewelry, clocks, furniture, and other items.

The *Sampler* mentions two large malls that carry many items typical of those found in reputable shops in town. Stop, browse, and ask for brochures and information about your particular antique interests.

Murfreesboro Antique Mall, open Monday–Saturday, 10:00 A.M. to 5:00 P.M.; Sunday, 1:00 to 5:00 P.M. Directions I-24S, Exit 281 on US 231. Call (615) 890-2674.

Antique Village U.S.A., open Monday–Saturday, 8:30 A.M. to 5:00 P.M.; Sunday, 1:00 to 5:00 P.M. Directions: I-24S, Exit 89, Buchanan Road. Call (615) 890-6756.

Goodlettsville Antique Mall

Opened in October 1982 by David and Ellie Meade, Goodlettsville Antique mall provides one of the largest selections of antiques in the area. Housed in a spacious former car dealership building with lots of floor-to-ceiling windows, the mall is called "The Antique Showcase of the South" by its owners. See 123 booths filled with a wide variety of items such as Heisey, Flo Blue, or Nippon glassware; American and Tennessee country furniture; primitives; European antiques, sixteenth-century vases and jewelry; early lighting fixtures; architectural antiques such as mantels, doors, or street lights; dolls; wicker; and vintage clothing. Twenty of the booths offer homemade crafts.

Selections range from hand-dipped candles at 50¢ to an original signed and dated 1742 oil painting for $36,000. Most items range from $5 to $500.

Business Hours: Monday–Saturday, 9:30 A.M. to 5:30 P.M. Sunday, 12:00 noon to 5:30 P.M.

Directions: I-65 North from Nashville. Take Exit 97 and go west to Dickerson Pike, which is also US 31. Turn right and the Antique Mall is two blocks on the right. 213 North Dickerson Road, Goodlettsville, TN 37072. (615) 859-7002.

Antique Reconstruction, Restoration, and Refinishing

Doug Mars Construction, Greeneville

Being a resident of East Tennessee, Doug Myers is used to being called "Dug Mars" by some of the local people, but he doesn't mind. Doug has a very special talent, one that fits well into the warp and woof of our Tennessee heritage. Doug preserves historical structures by repairing and reconstructing buildings native to Tennessee, such as log houses, barns, or mills. He relocates log buildings for those wishing to live in authentic log homes. He uses old bricks and stones to build new chimneys. Doug also does various types of fencing, including the split-rail type. Approximate price range: repair and reconstruction of a log house, $10,000 and up (less for smokehouses and primitive cabins).

Business Hours: 7:00 A.M. to 10:00 P.M.

Directions: Fifteen miles north of Greeneville off Highway 70. Route 11, Box 209, Greeneville, TN 37743. (615) 234-0433.

Bellevue Designs

Michael Wells says your finest antiques will be safe in the hands of a master craftsman. Go see some of his work and find out for yourself, or give him a call to see what he has to say about refinishing your latest antique find. He can also make and repair furniture.

Directions: Located on US 70S, west of Nashville, in the Shacklett community of Cheatham County. 7166 Willow Creek Drive, Bellevue, TN 37221. (615) 646-4231.

Armstrong's Furniture Clinic, Bluff City

Armstrong's Furniture Clinic rebottoms chairs, rebuilds treasures found in Grandma's attic, and refinishes antiques. They are careful to preserve the patina developed over decades of use and have worked on many valuable period pieces, some belonging to Governor Taylor and to Andrew Johnson's family. Randy Armstrong says, "We welcome visitors Monday through Friday, 8:00 A.M. to 5:00 P.M. Visitors may also get to tour Island Mill (an old family-owned three-story grist mill), see a basket being woven, fish for rainbow trout, or just watch the river flow by." Approximate prices: $15 for chair bottoming and other work priced according to what is needed.

Directions: Located on Riverside Road just outside of Bluff City. P.O. Box 85, Bluff City, TN 37618. (615) 538-8877.

Dogwood Hollow Woodworks, Palmersville

Nestled in the gentle hills of northwest Tennessee is Dogwood Hollow Woodworks, a family owned and operated shop offering quality woodenware at affordable prices. Made-to-order bread boxes, spice cabinets, butter molds, churn dashers, boot jacks, and more—all available at finished and unfinished prices. Send a first-class postage stamp for a free catalogue.

Between exhibiting at craft fairs and farming, Jerry Rachels builds oak porch swings and gliders and does custom antique reconstruction. Nelda makes traditional cornhusk dolls like the ones described in the Foxfire books, priced from $3.50 each on up to a delightful fam-

ily grouping at $30.00. If you have any questions, write Jerry and Nelda.

Directions: About 2 miles south of Palmersville off State 89. Go 1 mile on the Old School Road and look for sign. Route 1, Box 171-A, Palmersville, TN 38241.

Antique Specialty Work

The Bell Buckle Bookstore

Intellectuals, pseudointellectuals, or antique buffs, stop here! You can find rare and used books ranging in age from 2 to 200 years and in price from 50¢ to $100. This bookstore features a nationwide out-of-print book search service that has proved successful in helping many people. Another feature, more popular with the under 10 set, is a children's corner with plenty of toys and books.

Store hours: Summer, 10:30 A.M. to 4:30 P.M. Tuesday–Saturday. Rest of year, 10:00 A.M. to 2:00 P.M., Tuesday–Friday; 10:00 A.M. to 4:00 P.M., Saturday.

Directions: 8 miles off I-24E, about an hour south of Nashville. Railroad Square, Bell Buckle, TN 37020. (615) 890-6308.

Reproduction furniture by Alfred Sharp

Reed's Custom Framing, Madison

So often it's hard to find just the right frame for that special memento, whether it's a photograph or a priceless antique violin. Donald and Lou Reed are masters at preserving the things that mean so much to you. Reed's Custom Framing creates one-of-a-kind shadowbox frames for such unusual items as wedding flowers, doctor's tools, dishes, and baby dresses. When they frame needlework, they mount the piece in a unique way to preserve it. The Reeds also have a special service of restoring and gold-leafing picture frames and other antiques. Lou has written a pamphlet, *A Simple Guide to Gold Leafing,* and she does work for the Tennessee State Museum. Even if you're a do-it-yourselfer, Lou will be glad to lend her expert advice and give you step-by-step pointers. Framing prices range from $20 to $300.

Hours: Monday–Saturday, 10:00 A.M. to 9:00 P.M.

Directions: In Nashville on I-65N, exit Old Hickory Boulevard and Madison. Go right on Old Hickory to the second traffic light. Turn right on Douglas. 216 Douglas Street, Madison, TN 37115. (615) 865-2666.

Shacklett's Studio, Murfreesboro

Shacklett's evaluates each picture carefully to determine the best possible procedure for restoring your old family photographs. Box 1333, Murfreesboro, TN 37130. (615) 893-2369.

David Lloyd Swift, Nashville

David owes his knowledge of preserving and restoring documents to his volunteer work at the Tennessee State Library and Archives. If you have letters, newspapers, or other printed memorabilia you'd like restored or preserved for posterity, call or write David. His services start at $15 and go up, depending on the attention required and the condition of the document. Call Tuesday through Friday, 8:30 A.M. to 5:00 P.M.

Address: 6436 Brownlee Drive, Nashville, TN 37205. (615) 352-0308.

Wicker Works, Nashville

Does your wicker look wicked from too much wear? Stana Snodgrass can solve your problem. She has the only shop in Nashville that strips, repairs, and paints old wicker as well as rattan, bamboo, and cane. She sells new and antique wicker and also does chair caning. Stana's furniture repair experiences include doing work for the Chattanooga Hilton and repairing all the wicker furniture in the Hyatt Regency. Other than furniture, Stana also stocks hampers, baskets, shelves, picture frames, and mirror containers. Prices: service—$35 to $200; sales—$95 to $800.

Open: Monday–Friday, 10:00 A.M. to 5:00 P.M.; Saturday, 10:00 A.M. to 1:00 P.M.

Address: 4423 Murphy Road, Nashville, TN 37209. (615) 298-4179.

Carolyn's Corner, Paris

Carolyn Wallis restores antique, china, and modern dolls. Broken heads and limbs are restored or restrung, and dolls are dressed in period costumes. Collectible dolls are also sold, as well as stands, wigs, shoes, and socks. Appraisals and free estimates done. Wide price range. Hours are by appointment or chance.

Directions: Go 6 miles east of Paris courthouse square. Turn right after passing Sally Lane Candy Farm onto Sulfer Well Road. Go 2 miles. Shop in old log house. Route 4, Box 411, Paris, TN 38242. (901) 642-0266.

Tennessee's Special Sittin', Sippin', Spittin', Swappin', and Shoppin' Places

Tennesseans love a get-together, and for generations the general store has been the center of country life, a place to buy staple items, dry goods, farm supplies, and food, and to hear the local news. When it's too wet to plow, the stores fill up with farm folk looking for a game of dominoes, rook, or checkers, or someone to swap knives with.

The stores themselves are a truly unique shopping experience. Many still shelve items from bygone days such as ladies' high-topped shoes and chamber pots.

This is your official *Sampler* invitation to travel Tennessee's back roads and find that country store near you. Here's a baker's dozen of Tennessee's finest to get you started!

Rheatown Food Market

This is a real country store, complete with its complement of "loafers." It has everything from soda pop to stove pipes. Come in and browse a while and talk to Patsy. Prices range from 3¢ on up.

Business hours: Monday through Sunday, 7:00 A.M. to 10:00 P.M.

Directions: East of Greeneville, take US 11E to Afton. Look for sign pointing to Rheatown. Go to the first intersection—there we are, behind the Amoco gas pumps. Route 2, Chuckey, TN 37641. (615) 257-5463.

M. E. Trew

M. E. Trew says his store is the oldest business in McMinn County. Here folks have congregated for four generations to pass the time, solve world problems, and trade for sugar, flour, seeds, and Wolverine boots. Today the store is the daily meeting place of the Used-to Club, composed of retirees who sit around the stove and talk about things they "used to do." Other reminders of yesteryear are a 1914 telephone, a roll-top desk which once served as a post office, some 1890 clothes, and antique farm and home implements.

Open 9:00 A.M. to 5:00 P.M., Monday–Saturday; closed at noon Tuesday.

Directions: Exit I-75 at Calhoun, travel east on State 163 about 10 miles to Dentville. Route 1, Delano, TN 37325. (615) 263-7484.

Crossroads Grocery

This is truly a country store, featuring all types of merchandise and ol' time good service. They've been at the same location and in business since the late 1940s. And no wonder—Crossroads Grocery is the local hangout for community folks, especially when it's too wet to plow. Dominoes are played every day. Stop by for some good visitin'. A garage, a grocery, and a barber shop are all in one building.

Open 6:00 A.M. to 9:00 P.M., Monday–Saturday.

Directions: Located in southeast Greene County at the intersection of State 350 and 357. Camp Creek, Greeneville, TN 37743.

Webb Brothers General Store

Sandra Webb Hyder says: "1986 will be our fiftieth anniversary in business as Webb Brothers. As far as antiquities, we have them beginning with Uncle Oliver who will be 78 in June, to Daddy who was 76 in January, to the old Cherokee Indian bonnets my great-grandparents traded from the Indians for corn, to wooden buttermolds. We cater to the tourist trade and have souvenir items such as bandannas and post cards (pictures taken by my dad with an old camera costing $10 in 1929). Of course Daddy and Uncle Oliver are available for personal pictures and autograph signing. We hand slice cheese and bologna and will sell you a pack of saltines to go along. This makes a nice snack to take trout fishing or just to enjoy our scenery."

Directions: Go 6 miles north of Benton on US 411, then east on State 30, 6 miles. See sign "Reliance" and Webb Brothers General Store on the left. Reliance, TN 38369. (615) 338-2373.

Cumberland General Store

The sweet smell of cinnamon-orange tea and the warmth of a wood stove greet the visitor who walks into the Cumberland General Store. Whiffs of tobacco, cedar churns, leather harnesses, new cloth, and hickory-smoked ham can be detected as the eye takes in an array of merchandise lining the side walls, center aisles, and counters. "Goods in Endless Variety for Man & Beast!" is the official slogan, proclaimed both on billboards in Crossville and on the front of the store's catalog.

Catalogs and merchandise are distributed to every state and to 20 foreign countries each year. The catalog is available for $3 plus 75¢ postage by writing Cumberland General Store, Route 3, Crossville, Tennessee 38555.

Directions: Located in Homestead, about 4 miles south of Crossville on US 127. (615) 484-8481.

Tarkington General Store

R. D. and Edith Tarkington bought this store in 1927. In 1979 R. D. and Edith retired, and now the store is in the hands of their son C. D. The fourth-generation Tarkingtons, one of whom is little Christopher Lee Allen, help in the store.

The Tarkingtons sell most anything you need—groceries, livestock feed, gas, and even brand name jeans. There's a creek beside the store that provides good entertainment for the children.

Open from 8:00 A.M. to 8:00 P.M., Monday–Saturday.

Directions: Take State 100 west of Nashville to Lyles (about 50 miles). Then go about 2 miles on Primm Springs Road. Turn right at sign to get to Tarkington Store. Route 2, Box 168, Lyles, TN 37098. (615) 729-2767.

Miller's Grocery

Mrs. Leo Harrell says: "My son Bill owns and operates a country store which my 84-year-old father has owned since I was about 12 years old. They sell everything from coal oil to sandwiches. Many drop by who work on the railroad, also hunters and people who lived there years ago. Bill collects early American objects and stuffed animals."

Open from 7:00 A.M. to 7:00 P.M.

Directions: Approximately 10 miles south of Murfreesboro on US 231, turn left, and it's about 1 mile to the store. Christiana, TN 37037. (615) 893-1878.

Plummer's Old Store, Museum, and Orchard

For a great taste of southern hospitality, as well as a great taste of a made-to-order 85¢ sandwich, visit H. B. and Mildred Plummer. Old and young alike come to sit, visit, and enjoy the practical jokes of the Plummers. Be sure to visit the mini-museum in back filled with old tools, buggy whips, wood carvings, medicine bottles, and old jail irons. As Mr. H. B. says, "Come grouchy and leave laughing."

Directions: Go I-24 to Clarksville from Nashville. Take Exit 11, State 76, Adams Exit. Go 3 miles. Sign in yard says "As We Like It." Box 60, Clarksville, TN 37043. (615) 358-9679.

Jacksboro General Store

Find regular grocery and hardware items in a 100-year-old building. See antiques on display. Try the delicious hamburgers, hot dogs, and sandwiches and turn your teenagers loose in the game room—two pool tables, pinball, and video games. Open 7:00 A.M.

Jacksboro General Store is on the corner of Jacksboro Road and the old Shelbyville Road. Rt. 3, Morrison, TN. (615) 939-2937.

Anderson's General Store

Clifton and Grace Anderson bought this lovely old store a few years ago from a lady who had owned it 50 years to the day. Located in a picturesque setting, well cared for through the years. Such unusual items as horseshoe nails, mule collars, women's cotton stockings (hard to find for the old-timers and much in demand at Christmas), and last but not least, slop jars are available.

Located between State 71 (Santa Fe Pike) and State 96 out of Franklin, 3 miles north of the Fly community. Leipers Creek Road, Santa Fe, TN 38482. (615) 682-2315.

Championship domino game at Crossroads Grocery
Photo by Lisa Waddell

A. Schwab's General Store

A real shopping adventure is in store for you at Schwab's, the oldest working family-owned general store in the Mid-South. The merchandise has changed little in 109 years. They still sell spats, celluloid collars, 44 kinds of suspenders, an assortment of kerosene lamps, men's pants to size 74, and women's dresses to size 60. Schwab's boasts the most extensive selection of men's hats and caps in Memphis.

For some really captivating items, try these: a Last Supper hand fan, perfect for home or dinner out, 30¢ oils and potions—for casting spells, curses, and maybe even nets—95¢; ugly ties—great gift idea for the dad who never lets you go anywhere or the boss who raises the roof but never your salary, the ultimate bad guy gift at only 24¢.

Free guided tours of the store and museum, plus a free souvenir for every visitor.

What more could you want? For a shopping experience you won't soon forget, visit Schwab's. As their motto says: "If you can't find it at A. Schwab's, you are better off without it."

Open Monday–Saturday from 9:00 A.M. to 5:00 P.M.

Directions: Located on Beale Street between Second and Third Streets. Free parking behind the store. 163 Beale Street, Memphis, TN 38103.

Harbour-Pitts Company

Situated on the banks of the Tennessee River, the Harbour-Pitts Company celebrates 100 years of operation by the same family this year. Joe Pitts can keep you mesmerized for hours telling tales of years gone by—about the Indians who bought the first thing ever sold in the store, why the double-barreled shotgun is hidden under the bolts of gingham, and how and why Harbour-Pitts repossessed a casket. That should take care of the first part of the day.

For the afternoon session, be sure to see the arrowhead collection which numbers in the thousands, one of the largest gun collections in the state, and gorgeous pieces of antique glassware. You might be in the market for a bow and arrow, a fox horn, a black derby hat, ladies high-topped shoes, along with the usual meats, vegetables, or dry goods.

Visitors are welcome any business day—7:00 A.M. until 6:00 P.M., but the store is closed on Sunday, Thanksgiving, and Christmas. On Tuesday nights the store is open until 10:00 or 11:00 P.M. Called "liar's night" by the womenfolk, men gather to swap hunting and fishing stories, buy and trade guns, shells, reloading equipment, and more. Not to be outdone, the ladies play canasta.

Directions: Located 6 miles north of the Savannah city limits. Route 6, Box 120, Savannah, TN 38372. (901) 925-4280.

Duncan's Pharmacy

The sign on the wall says, "Cows may come and cows may go, but the bull in this place goes on forever." That's a strange comment for a drug store, but the customers in Duncan's Pharmacy are a special lot—and they'll be glad to tell you they're not "out to pasture" yet!

Instead of display items in the window at Duncan's, you'll see a window full of people. Yes, a window-seat and various chairs close by are filled with about 15 old-timers of the town who assemble around 8:00 A.M. six days a week to swap stories from each other's never-written autobiography.

Making Gladhill's Healing Oil is a tradition at Duncan's Pharmacy. This marvelous cocoction was invented by E. W. Gladhill, and the formula for making it came with the purchase of the store. Doug Duncan says he makes a gallon a month and sells a six-ounce bottle for $2.75. The label reads: "Gladhill's Healing Oil—Good for Man or Beast—A sure relief for barb wire cuts, scratches, galls, sore shoulders, neck and back, burns, sores, wounds, and all other diseases requiring external application." Drop in and see how folks chuckle, not mope, down memory lane. And while you're there, buy some Gladhill's Healing Oil.

Address: 137 South Main, Dyer, TN 38330. (901) 692-3578.

Outlet Stores

Americans want to be fashionable, but most of us can't afford the high price tags of designer fashions. Even if we could, it just makes sense to shop wisely.

For example, a lady from another state comes every year to Stein Mart in Nashville, Tennessee, gets out of her Rolls Royce, and proceeds to spend several thousand dollars for her family's wardrobe. Stein Mart is an incredible chain of stores (three are in Tennessee—Knoxville, Nashville, and Memphis), which offers designer clothes, shoes, and home accessories for 20 to 60 per cent less than you'd pay elsewhere.

So why pay big prices? You don't have to. While traveling through the Bible Belt, take *The Tennessee Sampler* along as your "Bargain-Hunter's Bible." Save, save, save, and giggle all the way back to your home town bank with that money you *saved*—not spent—on your Tennessee shopping spree.

The *Sampler* has made every effort to select stores that will add the most to your shopping enjoyment as well as keep the most in your bank account. However, we recommend that you call stores before traveling long distances. Due to circumstances beyond our control, a store could have a change of address or management after we researched our information.

Now get your *Sampler* in one hand, your money in the other, and blast off on your Tennessee shopping spree.

Headquarters

This "Headquarters" section precedes the outlet stores' brief listing and is an alphabetical description of chain stores throughout the state. It also lists brand names and other pertinent information.

Acme Boot

Seconds and close-outs in men's, women's, and children's footwear. Great buys. Hours vary; call ahead.

Ashley's Outlet Store

First quality, factory direct merchandise. Close-outs, irregulars, and overruns. Get clothing for the entire family, plus bedspreads, towels, and mattress pads. All famous name brands. Hours vary; call ahead.

Burlington Coat Factory

Coats and sportswear for the entire family at America's number one factory outlet. Featuring famous brands such as White Stag, Jonathan Logan, London Fog, Pauline Trigere, Health-Tex, Pierre Cardin, and more. Hours vary; call ahead.

Cape Craft Pine

Candles, glass, crystal, Early American decorator items, pictures, brass, silk flowers. Brands: Libby, Anchor Hocking, J. G. Durant, Crystal Clear, and Imperial Crystal. Hours vary; call ahead.

Donlevy's Back Room

Very extensive collection of high-fashion clothing and designer labels. All types of women's clothing in junior and misses sizes—dresses, skirts, suits, and coats to sportswear, jeans, and swimsuits. Brands include Gloria Vanderbilt, Bill Blass, Sassoon, Evan Picone, Geoffrey Beene, and Pierre Cardin. Truly a store for the fashion conscious with a small pocketbook. Call ahead for store hours.

Fashion Barn

Current fashions for women of all sizes and age groups. Double your saving pleasure if you hit a sale. For example, a friend bought a fully lined, first quality woman's linen suit here last summer for $25. Open seven days a week.

Harbour Pitts hasn't changed much.

Hit or Miss

Find everything that is "in"—the new look in brand name outerwear—suits, dresses, sportswear, and accessories. This is one of America's finest off-price fashion shops. Hours vary; call ahead.

H. W. Gossard

Jeans, sleepwear, loungewear, support hose, socks, and sweaters for the entire family. Men's and boys' underwear. All types of lingerie (S-XL), overstocks, discontinued, and a few irregulars.

Lichterman Shoe Co.

Find famous brands such as Amalfi, Andrew Geller, British Walker, Florsheim, Nunn Bush, and Van Eli.

Menswear, F. O.

Men's suits, slacks, and shirts, sizes 36 short to 54 X-Long. Brands such as Botany 500, Johnny Carson, Palm Beach, Hubbard, Izod, and Kuppenheimer. Hours: Monday–Friday, 10:00 A.M. to 9:00 P.M.; Sunday, 10:00 A.M. to 6:00 P.M.

Outlets Ltd. Mall

What could be better—a group of outlet stores clumped together for your shopping and saving enjoyment: Choose from 25 stores specializing in lingerie, athletic and camping equipment, books, handbags and luggage, women's and men's fashions, gift items, shoes, children's clothes, linens, and rainwear. Tremendous discounts on brand names you'll recognize. Plan to spend at least an afternoon because there's something for everyone. But better beware, men. Detour to The Outlets Mall on your vacation, and you may not reach your destination!

Simmons Shoe Store

Seconds in top name brands for men and women. Hours vary; call ahead.

Stein Mart

Find famous brand shirts, shorts, shoes, sweaters, and jeans as well as expensive designer labels at drastic reductions. Most merchandise comes direct from the manufacturer with few irregulars, but these are clearly marked. For men, choose from names like Calvin Klein, Izod, Givenchy, or Ralph Lauren. Women find such brands as Gloria Vanderbilt, Pierre Cardin, Jones of New York, and Liz Claiborne—also lots of ultra-suede. Find great selections in linens, kitchen accessories, giftwares, and women's accessories. This is a store the well-dressed person, budget conscious or not, will have to shop.

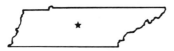

East Tennessee Stores

CHATTANOOGA

American Clothing Company, 180-A East Gate Center. (615) 899-7512. Men's Apparel, 40 to 70 per cent savings. Ties—Pierre Cardin and Halston. Suits—Alfred Downing, Botany 500, Mansfield House. Slacks—Hubbard, Jaymar, Levi's. Sportswear—Tally Ho, Lord Jeff, Wilson, MacGregor.

Buster Brown Outlet, Broad Street. (615) 629-2531. Children's apparel. Manufacturer's outlet for this famous brand.

Carter's Factory Outlet, 6880 Direct Connection Drive. (615) 891-9004. Children's apparel, 20 to 60 per cent savings. All Carter's merchandise—sleepwear, outerwear, and underwear. Girls' sizes, infants—size 14. Boy's sizes, infants—size 20. Women's and men's sportswear, coats, raincoats, socks, sneakers, suits, and dresses. Hours: Monday–Thursday, 9:00 A.M. to 5:00 P.M. Friday–Saturday, until 9:00 P.M.; Sunday, 1:00 to 5:00 P.M.

Factory Footwear Outlet, 4433 Highway 58 North. (615) 894-1089. Family footwear, 10 to 35 per cent savings. Boots—Acme, Dan Post, and Dingo. Shoes—Timberland, Dion-Deb, Wimzees, Arandiamos, Pro-Keds, Grasshoppers, Nunn Bush, Converse. Largest selection in Chattanooga of women's shoes. Hours: Daily, 10:00 A.M. to 8:00 P.M.

Lotties, 5754A Brainerd Road, Brainerd Village. (615) 892-4460. Footwear, 25 to 60 per cent savings. (See "Headquarters" under Lichterman Shoe Co.)

Menswear, F. O., 2133 Rossville Boulevard. (615) 266-6288. Men's apparel, 40 to 60 per cent savings. (See "Headquarters.")

Signal Mill Store, 6503 Slater Road. (615) 894-3753. Lingerie/knits, 30 to 70 per cent savings. (See "Headquarters" under H. W. Gossard.)

Towel and Linen, Inc., 2821 Cummins Highway, US 11 and 41 (West Exit Browns Ferry Road); 6853 Lee Highway (Exit at Shallowford Road). (615) 821-2688. Towels/linens, 25 per cent savings. First quality and some seconds in towels, mats, and accessories. Royal Family sheets. Buy towels by the pound.

GATLINBURG

Cape Craft Pine, Baskin Square. (615) 436-7662. Giftware, 30 to 60 per cent savings. (See "Headquarters.")

Millers Dinnerware, Main Street on the Parkway. (615) 436-5170. Dinnerware, 40 to 60 per cent savings. Seconds of stoneware, Copco, Iroquois, stainless, porcelainized cast iron, hand-blown crystal.

Mountain Camper, 525 Parkway. (615) 436-4453. Camping supplies, 50 to 70 per cent savings. Manufacturer's outlet of supplies for the outdoor person—stoves, sleeping bags, tents, dried foods, goose down and poly-fill outerwear for the entire family. Also jeans, shirts, shorts, jogging shoes, and boots. Open seven days a week.

JOHNSON CITY

Tri-Cities Textile Mill, 3010 Bristol Highway. (615) 282-5531. Bed/bath, 40 per cent savings. Bedding ensembles, towels, curtains, bath items, and kitchen fashions. Call ahead for exact hours.

Vanderbilt Fashions, 1932 Roan Street. (615) 928-2721. Women's apparel, 30 to 75 per cent savings. These stores sell quality merchandise and are also called Captree Factory Outlet, Station Square, Organically Grown, Smart Alec, Pandora, Trolley, Prides Crossing, or Langtry. Call ahead for hours.

KNOXVILLE

Outlets Ltd. Mall, 11221 Outlets Drive, Intersection of 40 West and Lovell Road. (615) 373-5427. (See "Headquarters.")

Second Serve, Bearden Center. (615) 584-1671. Athletic apparel, 30 to 60 per cent savings. Sports clothing for the entire family such as tennis dresses, shorts, skirts, or warm-up suits. Brands: R. R. Sportswear, Quantam, Top Seed, Tail, Paul Sullivan, and John Newcombe.

Textile Wholesale Inc., 8019 Kingston Pike. (615) 693-0241. Bed/bath, 30 per cent savings. First quality linens, kitchen accessories, shower curtains, decorator pillows in brands such as Wamsutta, Fieldcrest, Martex, Dundee, and Springs Mills. Hours: 9:00 A.M. to 5:00 P.M., closed Sunday.

Camel Factory Outlet, Chapman Pike. (615) 577-5070. Camping equipment, 50 per cent savings. Camping equipment, tents, and clothes for the outdoors person—poly and goose down garments, and jeans. Open seven days a week.

Central Shoe Store, 5211 Kingston Pike. (615) 588-7811. Footwear, 30 to 70 per cent savings. Famous brands women's and men's shoes.

Donlevy's Back Room, 1801 Downtown West Boulevard. (615) 690-4261. Women's apparel, 40 to 70 per cent savings. (See "Headquarters.")

Hit or Miss, 4807-B Broadway, Broadway Square Shopping Center. (615) 687-9773. Women's apparel, 20 to 50 per cent savings.

Johnston and Murphy F. O., 5204 Kingston Pike. (615) 584-6688. Footwear, 40 to 60 per cent savings. Manufacturer's outlet for brands like Johnston and Murphy, Bass, Durango, Sebago, Keith Highlander, and British Walker.

Luxury Fabrics, 9715 Kingston Pike. (615) 693-7021. Fabrics, 20 to 50 per cent savings. First quality bedspreads, pillows, upholstery and drapery fabrics, and drapery hardware.

Mill Agent, Inc., 129 South Gay Street. (615) 637-2920. Upholstery fabrics, 40 to 50 per cent savings. Upholstery and drapery fabrics, wallpaper, and carpet. Fabric brand names include Waverly, Burlington, Graber, Gilman, Cabin Craft, and many more. Hours: Monday–Saturday, 9:00 A.M. to 5:30 P.M.

The Mill Outlet, 522 Baxter Avenue. (615) 546-8100. Mens/women's apparel 40 to 60 per cent savings. Men's and women's first quality name brand clothing—Pierre Cardin, Evan Picone, Palm Beach, Country Set, Gant, and more. Hours vary; call ahead.

Normak Factory Outlet, 1507 Ninth Avenue. (615) 525-3081. Men's/women's apparel, 40 per cent savings. Men's and women's wool and wool blend clothing. For men see vests, blazers, corduroy separates, and pants—all in solids, tweeds, and herringbones. Women find skirts, slacks, and outerwear. Hours: Monday–Saturday, 9:00 A.M. to 5:30 P.M.

Stein Mart, Kingston Pike. (615) 691-5111. (See "Headquarters.")

PIGEON FORGE

Cape Craft Pine, Box 1121, Highway 441. (615) 453-8740. Giftware, 30 to 60 per cent savings. (See "Headquarters.")

Clothesworks, 819 North Parkway (inside Brand Name Fashions). (615) 453-1561. Women's apparel, 30 to 60 per cent savings. Manufacturer's outlet for Jack Winter sportswear and other brand names. Sizes 4-18 and petites 6-14. Great prices on pants, skirts, blouses, jackets, and sweaters. Hours vary; call ahead.

Middle Tennessee Stores

CLARKSVILLE
Acme Boot Outlet Store, 100 Providence Boulevard, North. (615) 552-9546. Footwear, up to 50 per cent savings. (See "Headquarters.")

Ashley's Outlet Store, Riverside Drive, Clarksville Square Shopping Center. (615) 552-2523. Family apparel/bed and bath. (See "Headquarters.")

COLUMBIA
Weathertamer Factory Store, Alexander Lane (off US 31S). (615) 388-4522. Family outerwear/fabrics, 20 to 50 per cent savings. Weathertamer produces the only American-made outerwear on the market—other companies have gone to imports. Buy half-price jackets for the entire family or snowsuits for children of the famous Weathertamer name at sale times and get 75 per cent savings. See other brand names such as Izod, Calvin Klein, Gloria Vanderbilt, Wrangler, Sweet and Sassy pageant dresses for little girls, Caron dresses for women, and Terry Sportswear women's blouses all at 20 to 50 per cent savings every day. Save 50 per cent on lovely fabrics sold by the yard and 20 per cent on all notions. Buy polyester batting for quilts and polyester stuffing for crafts at drastic savings. Open 9:00 A.M. to 5:00 P.M., six days a week.

COOKEVILLE
Acme Boot Outlet Store, 803 South Jefferson Street. (615) 528-1110. Footwear, up to 50 per cent savings.

Ashley's Outlet Store, 199 South Jefferson Avenue. (615) 528-2049. Family apparel/bed and bath, 25 to 60 per cent savings. (See "Headquarters.")

GOODLETTSVILLE
Outlets Ltd. Mall, 900 Conference Drive. (615) 373-4527. This mall is well worth the stop, the same great buys and quality shops but about half the size of the big Outlets Ltd. Malls in Knoxville and Murfreesboro. This could be a plus if you have only a few hours to shop and want to make the most of your shopping time. You'll certainly get the most for your $! (See "Headquarters.")

MADISON
Ashley's Outlet Store, 856 Madison Square Shopping Center. (615) 865-5324. Family apparel/bed and bath, 25 to 60 per cent savings. (See "Headquarters.")

Lotties, 838 Madison Square Shopping Center. (615) 868-1978. Footwear, 25 to 60 per cent savings. (See "Headquarters" under Lichterman Shoe Co.)

MOUNT JULIET
The Boot Barn, State 70, next to Lineberry's. (615) 758-9415. Footwear. Aigner women's shoes, Nike tennis shoes, and much more.

MURFREESBORO
Outlets Ltd. Mall, 330 River Rock Boulevard, I-24 at State 96 Exit. (615) 373-5427. (See "Headquarters.")

Rolane Factory Outlet, 911 A & B Samsonite Boulevard. (615) 890-6174. Family apparel, 30 to 50 per cent savings. Great buys in family hosiery and apparel, shoes, handbags, and luggage. Hours: Monday–Saturday, 9:00 A.M. to 6:00 P.M.

Warnaco Outlet Store, 1203 Park Avenue (exit off I-24, follow sign ½ mile to store). (615) 890-6699. Men's/women's apparel, 50 per cent savings. Choose from 300 to 400 women's and men's sweaters, plus brand names including Pringle, White Stag, Puritan, Christian Dior, Spalding, Yves St. Laurent, and more. You won't be disappointed at this place!

NASHVILLE
Ashley's Outlet Store, 6664 Charlotte Pike, Hillwood Plaza. (615) 352-6094. Family apparel/bed and bath, 25 to 60 per cent savings. (See "Headquarters.")

Burlington Coat Factory, 100 Oaks Shopping Center. (615) 385-9455. Family apparel/shoes, 30 to 60 per cent savings. (See "Headquarters.")

Donlevy's Back Room, Bavarian Village, 4004 Hillsboro Road. Women's apparel, 40 to 70 per cent savings. (See "Headquarters.")

H. W. Gossard, 425 Chestnut Street. (615) 242-1611. Lingerie/knits, 30 to 70 per cent savings. (See "Headquarters.")

Handmacher Fashions Outlet, 712 Church Street. (615) 256-2580. Women's apparel, 20 to 60 per cent savings. (See "Headquarters" under Fashion Barn.)

Hit or Miss, 719 Thompson Lane, 100 Oaks Mall. (615) 383-9904. Women's apparel, 20 to 50 per cent savings. (See "Headquarters.")

Lotties, Bell Forge Shopping Center. (615) 834-5616. Footwear, 25 to 60 per cent savings. (See "Headquarters" under Lichterman Shoe Co.)

Martin's Direct Clothing, 1110 Gallatin Road. (615) 226-0066. Men's apparel, 40 to 60 per cent savings. (See "Headquarters" under Menswear, F. O.)

May Hosiery Mills, 425 Chestnut Street. (615) 242-1611. Hosiery, up to 50 per cent savings. Complete line of socks for the family, plus women's lingerie, men's and boys' T-shirts, shirts, and sweaters, toddler's sleepwear, and much more. Hours: Monday–Saturday, 8:30 A.M. to 4:30 P.M.

Mostly Linens, 3900 Hillsboro Road. (615) 297-5722. Bed and bath, 50 per cent savings. All name brand sheets, pillows, bedspreads, towels, and kitchen accessories. Hours: Monday–Saturday, 10:00 A.M. to 5:30 P.M.

Stein Mart, 3760 Nolensville Road, Windlands Shopping Center. (615) 834-6702. Family apparel/footwear/gifts, 20 to 60 per cent savings. (See "Headquarters.")

Tuesday Morning, 5423 Highway 100 (next to Post Office). (615) 353-0141. Tableware, 50 to 80 per cent savings. Really great buys in tableware, giftware, and brass items.

Steiner-Liff Textile, 400 Davidson. (615) 252-2600. Fabrics. For the fabric bargain hunter. Slightly flawed fabrics are sold by the pound. Sift through boxes and boxes in a huge warehouse.

Washington Mfg. Outlet, 224 Second Avenue North. (615) 244-0600. Men's/women's apparel, 50 per cent savings. Women's sportswear in brands like Turtle Bax, Rappers, and Lori Lynn. Men's sportswear and dress slacks. Call ahead for business hours or other branch stores in the Nashville area.

West Tennessee Stores

COVINGTON
Ashley's Outlet Store, US 51, Covington Shopping Center. (901) 476-1216. Family apparel/bed and bath, 25 to 60 per cent savings. (See "Headquarters.")

Another out-of-state shopper speeds to a Tennessee outlet store.

DYERSBURG
Deloach Outlet Store, 104 East Court. (901) 285-0929. Footwear, 30 to 60 per cent savings. (See "Headquarters" under Simmons Shoe Store.)

HUMBOLDT
Ashley's Outlet Store, Bypass 45. (901) 784-7969. Family apparel/bed and bath, 25 to 60 per cent savings. (See "Headquarters.")

Simmons Outlet Shoe Store, 204 South Fourteenth Avenue. (901) 784-4701. Footwear, 30 to 60 per cent savings. (See "Headquarters" under Simmons Shoe Store.)

Wayne Gossard Outlet Store, Route 4, Milan Highway. (901) 784-5341. Lingerie/knits, 30 to 70 per cent savings. (See "Headquarters" under H. W. Gossard.)

JACKSON
Ashley's Outlet Store, 33 Carriage House Drive, North Plaza Shopping Center. (901) 668-7255. Family apparel/bed and bath, 25 to 60 per cent savings. (See "Headquarters.")

Kids Port USA, North Plaza Shopping Center. (901) 668-4434. Children's apparel, 30 to 70 per cent savings. Manufacturer's outlet for quality children's playwear, sizes 3 months—14. Hours vary; call ahead.

Tempos Fashions, Hamilton Hills Shopping Center. (901) 668-4215. Women's apparel, 15 to 60 per cent savings. Designer fashions from Condor, Gloria Vanderbilt, Liz Claiborne, Diane Von Furstenberg, Oscar de la Renta, and more. Call ahead; hours vary.

MEMPHIS
Ashley's Outlet Store, 3732 North Watkins, (901) 357-7105; 5130 Old Summer Road, (901) 683-8151;

4070 Elvis Presley Boulevard, (901) 346-9626. Family apparel/bed and bath, 25 to 60 per cent savings. (See "Headquarters.")

Burlington Coat Factory, 5100 Park Avenue, Suite 7, Eastgate Mall. (901) 682-3650. Family apparel/shoes, 30 to 60 per cent savings. (See "Headquarters.")

Calico Corners, 985 South Yates Road. (901) 767-8780. Decorative fabrics, 30 to 60 per cent savings. Fabrics here meet your every decorating need. Yards and yards of calico, moire, prints, chintz. For draperies—sheers, linings, antique satin, and casements. For upholstery—crewel, tapestry, brocades, velvets, and damasks. How-to books, drapery hardware, notions, and feather and down pillows. Call ahead for business hours.

Lotties, 4670 Knight Arnold Road, (901) 362-9660; 4818 Summer Avenue, (901) 685-8317; 4115 Elvis Presley Boulevard, (901) 398-1546; 4746-48 Yale Road, (901) 388-7537. Footwear, 25 to 60 per cent savings. (See "Headquarters" under Lichterman Shoe Co.)

Famous Footwear, 4657 American Way. (901) 362-8775. Men's and women's footwear, 20 to 50 per cent savings. A real gold mine for shoe fanciers. Choose from such famous names as Florsheim, Robb Lee, Nunn Bush, Aigner, Hush Puppies, Candies, and Mushrooms.

Handmacher Fashion Outlet, 5100 Park Avenue, Suite 11, Eastgate Shopping Center. (901) 767-2019. (See "Headquarters" under Fashion Barn.)

Hit or Miss, 4478 Mall of Memphis, (901) 369-9879; 5052 Park Avenue, Eastgate Shopping Center, (901) 766-9099. Women's apparel, 20 to 50 per cent savings. (See "Headquarters.")

Linens and Things, 5100 Park Avenue, Eastgate Shopping Center. (901) 761-3993. Bed and bath, 20 to 50 per cent savings. First quality and seconds in name brand towels, sheets, comforters, blankets, and other home accessories.

Marshalls, American Way Plaza. (901) 363-7840. Family apparel, footwear, domestics, savings up to 60 per cent. A must for your Memphis shopping spree. Marshalls sells only brand name clothing, footwear, domestics, samples, and designer originals (small percentage of irregulars). Marshalls stands behind everything it sells. Every day is sale day at Marshalls. Don't miss it for savings *and* quality.

Maternity Wearhouse Outlet, Park Place Center. (901) 683-1113. Maternity apparel, 15 to 50 per cent savings. All types of maternity fashions. Call ahead for hours.

Stein Mart, 4310 Summer Avenue. (901) 683-7304. Women's apparel/footwear. (See "Headquarters.")

Tennessee's Unique Shopping Experience— From Art to Burros to Cheese

Whether you're interested in antiques or animals, there are lots of auctions around the state just waiting for you. They're guaranteed to get in your blood. So y'all come and join in the fun. You can bet that Tennesseans are going…going…gone—to the nearest auction!

A SAMPLER FEATURE

Ben Gary's Auction Barn

■ The loud-talking, cigar-smoking, back-slapping comedian surveys the crowd with a sly gleam in his eye. Then he leans toward the microphone, and instead of cracking one more joke, he signals to his assistants, the audience gets quiet, and the comedian changes into a businessman. A rapid-fire, singsong chant begins. It's 5:30 on Friday night, and it's auction time in Tennessee!

Tennesseans love a get-together—any chance to visit with friends, meet new ones, laugh, and eat. If you've never been to an auction, you don't know what you've missed! You need to take part in this sometimes laid-back, sometimes intense entertainment—no admission charged.

Tennessee auctioneers, depending on their qualifications, sell anything from houses, farms, acreage, livestock, and antiques to general merchandise. You can find great one-of-a-kind items and come away with a bargain, or you can be slicked right out of a lot of money and lose your proverbial shirt. Remember cardinal rule number one while in Tennessee—some slow-talkin' folks in overalls can outdo plenty of the fast-talking, tailor-made-suit financiers when it gets down to auction know-how. So don't let those country boys fool you—or you'll be sorry!

Perhaps auctions most fun to observe and participate in are the general merchandise or antique auctions. A typical Tennessee general merchandise auction is held every Friday night, weather permitting, just north of Spring Hill, Tennessee, about 30 miles south of Nashville on US 31. We at the *Sampler* would like to take you there.

Like many auctioneers, Ben Gary comes on with the typical circus air. But watch out. Ben has been auctioneering since 1964 in his Spring Hill Community Auction Barn. People come from all over Middle Tennessee for his Friday night auctions, and most in the crowd know and trust him. He points out all the faults and flaws that are obvious of items he sells and will even re-sell an item if the bidder is unhappy with his buy. One elderly man explains, "If there's a crack, Ben tells you; if it doesn't light properly, he tells you; if Ben Gary tells you something, you can believe it." The trust of the crowd is definitely an asset for an auctioneer's business.

Ben can also call most of the crowd by first or last name, giving the auction a down-home, family flavor when bidding starts. You may hear, "Sold to Mrs. George in the third row," rather than the usual final, cold comment, "Sold to number 71."

Many in the crowd, like farmer and master carpenter Robert George, his wife Evelyn, and their friend Lucille Mathis, are regular Friday night auction-goers. Robert sits in the back with some of his friends watching for old tools at a good price, and Lucille and Evelyn sit up front in seats another friend has saved for them. They love visiting with friends and catching up on community news. As far as they're concerned, an auction is better than the movies.

Think twice about getting into a bidding battle with that woman in the print dress across the barn. She may own the 1,000-acre farm down the road and have more in her bank account than you could count in a month! You never know in Tennessee. Tennesseans must have originated the old saying, "You can't judge a book by its cover."

Everybody's ready to laugh at any of the hilarious things that might happen…like the night Ben tried out a used vacuum cleaner and got too close to a lady's hairdo and sucked the wig right off her head…or the night he sold a dead rattlesnake and a set of false teeth.

But don't think it's all a joke and that all items sold are junk. Besides a good time, the serious auction-goer can also find useful household items (stoves, refrigerators, sinks, kitchen ware) or beautiful handmade linens, glassware, and furniture. Besides the regular Friday night funfests, Ben holds special auctions on July 4 and Labor Day.

Estate Auctions

Check the local paper of any Tennessee town to find advertisements of an auction's location, time held, and items to be sold. For example: "Personal Property: 1973 Ford Fairlane, Norge refrigerator, pie safe, oak bookcase, walnut secretary, antique walnut bed, dresser, and chest, cedar-lined chest, butter churn, wringer washer, 5 h.p. garden tiller, garden tools, other items. The frame home, 1 1/2 acres of land, and personal property will be auctioned on Saturday, April 17, at 2:00 P.M."

Antique Auctions

Another auction in the Middle Tennessee area worth checking out is Adron and Shirley Phifer's Antique Auction, held every two weeks year-round, except in December when they skip the weekend closest to Christmas. Located a couple of miles out State 99 east of Columbia is the Highway 99 Auction Barn. This is a family operation: Adron is the auctioneer, his wife Shirley writes tickets, and Shirley's parents, sister, brother-in-law, and nephews lend helping hands. Be sure to try a peach fried pie made by Shirley and her daughter. That'll make your trip worthwhile even if you're outbid on everything you want!

At Auction 99 see antique glassware, linens, jewelry, coins, decorative items, and furniture, all in varying quality, brought here for auction on designated Saturday afternoons or Saturday nights. (Check the local paper or call to be sure of the time.) Items come from all over—Pennsylvania, Indiana, Ohio, New Hampshire, Massachusetts, or Connecticut—and sell from as low as 50¢ for a fruit jar lid to as much as $4,500 for a fine Victorian bedroom suite. Many fine oak, walnut, cherry, and mahogany pieces may be seen as well as some period pieces. Everyone is welcome; dealers make up about three-fourths of the crowd. Write and ask to be put on their mailing list temporarily if you are planning a vacation to Middle Tennessee.

Tips from the *Sampler* on Attending an Auction

1. Know the auctioneer or talk to someone who does. Find out if he's an honest person. All auctioneers have their techniques of getting the most money out of you. Find out what they are or just observe the first few times.

2. It's very important to arrive early and check out the items you are interested in. Look at the general condition of the item up close. It's risky to bid on anything you haven't examined first.

3. Fix in your mind the price you are willing to pay and don't exceed it…unless you really want it. Sometimes $5 more will buy it. A good rule of thumb is—don't exceed your fixed priced by more than 10 per cent. You will get the feel of bidding as you attend more auctions. Don't let emotions or pride get into your bidding. If you are short on self-discipline, be careful. Some people are hypnotized by the singsong chant of the auctioneer and regretfully spend more money than they should.

4. Don't wave to friends, nod your head, wink, or rub your nose! Such actions may be mistaken for bids, and you may inadvertently buy something you don't want. You see, various methods of bidding range from scratching the nose, touching a fingertip to the mouth, an almost imperceptible nodding of the head, or even jumping up and yelling out a bid. But don't be overly concerned. Auctioneers usually recognize newcomers and overlook such mannerisms, unless there is eye contact too. The experienced buyers never show excitement.

5. Know or find out the local symbol for "halfing" the auctioneer's bid. Sometimes the auctioneer will call out a price you think is too high, and you will want to offer half the amount.

6. Understand the bid system. Usually a clerk will give you a number corresponding to a number as you

Could these men be talking about Ben Gary's Auction?

sign your name on a sheet of paper. Then if you are high bidder on an item, you show your number to the auctioneer, he calls out, "Sold to number (your number)," the clerk records it, and you pay for your item before you leave.

7. Understand the difference between a general auction and an absolute auction. If the words *Absolute Auction* appear at the top of the paper's advertisement, the real estate, acreage, or personal property, whatever is to be sold that day, will be sold no matter what the high bid happens to be. For example, if the high bid is $1,000 on the house and 1½ acres of land, they sell for that low price. If a quilt's high bid is $2, it goes for that low price. If *Absolute Auction* does not appear in the advertisement, the seller and auction company reserve the right to recall items if the high bid is not high enough for them.

8. Keep a list of what you buy and the price paid, or get a copy of items you buy from the clerk as you buy them.

9. After you have bought an item, it's yours, and you are responsible for it. Therefore, it's a good idea to keep your eye on it or even take it to your vehicle if possible, if you are staying till the auction is over.

10. If you are bidding on several items sold at one time, such as a set of antique goblets, be sure you understand if the price the auctioneer sets is for one goblet or the whole group. Better quit talkin', eatin', and visitin' long enough to pay attention!

11. Don't show any excitement or the price may double. On a big dollar item (like land, a house, or a

piece of heavy equipment), don't show interest until toward the end of the bidding.

12. In real estate, if you really want a house or piece of land selling at auction and the auctioneer knows you want it, get someone else to bid for you.

13. When bidding on small valuable items, like antiques, survey your competition. Look for dealers. If a dealer bids on an item you want, hang in there. He knows its value and is going to mark it up for resale. If you don't know the value of an item, pick out the dealers, watch them, and then get in the game at the end when the bidding slows—again, only if you really *want* the item.

Columbia's Mule Auction

Remember the ol' Jimmie Rodgers tune "Muleskinner Blues"? The muleskinners in Columbia don't have anything to be blue about come the first Monday in February each year when the largest horse and mule auction in the world is held.

The sale begins with horse colts, progresses to mule colts and finally to a mixed lot of mules and draft horses auctioned by numbers. This auction itself is one of the most active and fastest you will ever see. Many customers come year after year. The Amish of Pennsylvania come to buy prime draft mules, and others buy animals of higher quality for exhibition at fairs or parades. A pair of first-rate mules may bring as much as $6,000.

George Chamberlain of Los Olivos, California, has been coming for close to 15 years and buys 100 or so mules which he saddle breaks and sells to the United States Forestry Service, dude ranches, or individuals out West. Chamberlain says: "Those who call a mule stubborn just don't know how to train a mule. We're slow and easy with our mules. Mules will do anything you ask, if they understand your wishes. They are very sure-footed on steep, mountainous terrain, and because they are gentle and dependable, mules make especially good mounts for older people."

If you love mules and the things that go with them, you'll feel right at home. On the grounds, trucks and trailers are filled with tack, harnesses, and various leather accessories for sale. If you miss this incredible event and all it offers in February, maybe you will be able to catch two other large sales held by Hub Reese in Lebanon, one on the first Monday in December and the other on the first Monday in March. Hub has mules for sale year-round in Gallatin, where he has sold mules to pull carriages in New Orleans, ride down the Grand Canyon, or to appear in movies. Single mules sell from $500 to $3,500, and a pair sells from $1,000 to $10,000. Call Hub for more information at (615) 452-5554 or (615) 452-5550, or write him at Reese Horses and Mules, c/o Hub Reese, Jr., Route 4, Box 120, Gallatin, TN 37066.

Even if you're not even interested in buying a mule, the *Sampler* recommends a mule auction as an entertaining and educational experience, a chunk of Tennessee heritage.

Livestock Auctions

Now that you know about general auctions, antique auctions, and the big mule auction, have they gotten into your blood? If they haven't, you haven't gone to enough of them. Well, there's one more type you should know about—the livestock auction.

Be ready to experience the sounds of bawling calves separated from mothers, high-pitched squeals of pigs, and bleats of scurrying sheep. (Better wear old clothes and watch out where you step!) Most Tennessee counties have livestock auction barns, and you need only check the Yellow Pages of local phone books.

Area farmers load hogs, cattle, and sheep into trucks and bring them to market. Most of the time the animals are tagged with a number before leaving the truck. They are then graded according to size, age, or weight and put in separate areas. When the auction begins, young animals are generally sold first, then older animals, and old bulls usually take the last spot. Bidding prices are usually by the pound. If you wish to buy, it's best to watch the general procedure awhile before jumping in. Better still, talk to farmers in the crowd. Tennessee farmers are almost always helpful and glad to help newcomers learn country ways. A fascinating experience for someone who's done it all!

A SAMPLER
*****Exclusive*****
An Oak Ridge Boy
Goes Shopping

Many a woman in America loves to go shopping, just about anywhere at anytime. We guarantee any woman would love a shopping trip a lot more if she could go on one with Richard Sterban. He's the hunk with the sly smile who sings those low, low bass parts for the Oak Ridge Boys. You women know the one, but for you men, Richard's the slim guy with the thick brown hair and blue eyes, born in New Jersey, raised a Yankee, but now a Tennessean.

Like all of the other Oaks, Richard's a very busy man. When the *Sampler* talked with him, he told us that one of the most delightful things he ever does is to spend a day shopping in Gatlinburg. We don't know how he keeps from being recognized, but maybe he wears a baseball cap from one of the five minor league baseball teams he's part owner of.

Anyway, Richard will spend the day ducking in and out of the quaint shops, filled with Tennessee crafts and other goodies, which line Main Street in Gatlinburg. Often he's just looking, wondering if so-and-so would like this or that. Richard's the only single Oak so we wonder who so-and-so might be. Sure would make a great contest sometime, Richard, for one of our readers to win an all-day shopping trip with you.

Thirteen Nifty East Tennessee
Shopping Places

In-Town Gallery, Art objects

See a potpourri of paintings, pottery, sculpture, and fibers priced from $5 to $5,000. Open weekdays 10:00 A.M. to 4:00 P.M., and Saturday, 11:00 A.M. to 3:00 P.M. 718 Cherry Street, Chattanooga, TN 37402. (615) 267-9214.

Hotel 1880, Local arts

No more overnight guests for this quaint hotel which opened in 1880. Now the facility showcases local arts, crafts, and antiques. All merchandise is accepted on consignment. Price range: 50¢ to $50. Open 9:00 A.M. to 4:30 P.M., Friday and Saturday, 12:00 noon to 4:30 P.M., Sunday.

Directions: Immediately adjacent to Exit 329 off Interstate 40, east of Nashville. Crab Orchard, TN 37723. (615) 484-2518.

Could Vice-President George Bush be the man behind the ear at Columbia's Mule Auction?

Johnson Hardware

Linda J. Babb says: "We have a family owned and operated hardware. It has been in our family for over 50 years, and we have items for all—the farmer, the professional, and the small business person. When a customer comes in, he not only asks for merchandise, but many times for the "how to use" information as well. We have a furnace that everyone sits around and talks about any and every thing—relevant or not!! We have items priced from a few cents to hundreds of dollars. Open 8:00 A.M. till 5:00 P.M. daily, or until the customers leave."

Address: Route 3, Box 9A, Chuckey, TN 37641. (615) 257-2642.

Tom and Mary Morgan, Stringed instruments

Tom and Mary have 25 years of experience in building and repairing stringed instruments. They make fine banjos, autoharps, mandolins, and guitars, and they are happy to furnish materials, parts, or information that a larger company might be too busy to deal with. The Morgans are also talented musicians. To have the Morgans entertain or provide a display/demonstration/discussion of instrument building, give them a call. Instrument prices: $1,000 to $2,000.

Address: Route 3, Box 204, Dayton, TN 37321. (615) 775-2996.

Alicia Salzman and Pat Grimes, Goat's milk, cheese

Here's your answer to harried shopping ventures that sometimes get your goat. Two former Dominican nuns, Alicia and Pat, make their living by selling goat's milk, cheese, baby goats, and home crafts. They spend fall and winter months making lovely quilts. The sewing room also houses a branch of the Hancock County Public Library, and neighbors drop by frequently to chat and to check out or return books.

Angelica Farm got its name from the angelica plant which grows wild in the southern Appalachians. When Alicia and Pat moved to their 1840 farmhouse a few years back, Alicia planted two angelica plants outside the doorstep. She thought, *As long as the plant survives, so will we.* However, the goats made short work of the angelicas as well as lots of the other flowers and shrubs. Alicia and Pat are surviving nicely—resetting angelicas every spring.

Items for sale which can be ordered by mail include goat milk soap, potholders, place mats, and gift boxes which include a set of potholders, one bar of goat milk soap, 1/2 pound goat cheese, and one jar of homemade jam or relish. Call or write for a price list.

Directions: Take State 33 east from Sneedville to Kyles Ford. At Kyles Ford turn south on State 70, go across river bridge and turn left. Go about 10 miles and turn right before you reach a stone bridge. First white house on the left. Route 1, Box 99B, Eidson, TN 37731. (615) 944-3126.

The Hampton Music Shop, Dulcimers

Jim Miller is a builder and player of hammered dulcimers and has been in business for the past five years. In that short time, Jim has built over 180 dulcimers. He has extensive training in woodworking and has been a self-employed maker of stringed instruments for several years. Jim also does repair work on all stringed instruments. Albums of string music are available as well as instruction on stringed instruments. Prices on instruments range from $225 to $450. Write or call for more information.

Directions: In Upper East Tennessee, from Elizabethton take US 19E south to Hampton. P. O. Box 228, Hampton, TN 37658. (615) 725-3191.

W and LD's Miniature Horse Farm

There are less than 5,000 of these little (34 inches or so) horses in the entire world. That alone makes breeding and raising them very special. Come and see for yourself. They'll win your heart. Approximate price range: $2,500 to $100,000.

Business hours: 8:00 A.M. to 5:00 P.M., Monday through Saturday.

Directions: From Greeneville, go out Erwin Highway (State 107) to Horse Creek Recreation Area. Turn right and drive about 2,000 yards. Box 866, Greeneville, TN 37743. (615) 638-1881.

J. S. Rhea and Sons Tin Shop

Clifford Rhea was a tin man, born with a big heart, a person who became a clever and skillful wizard in his lifetime. He was a colorful Greeneville resident and businessman who died in 1980 at the age of 91. Uncle Cliff and his pet monkey, Chita, saw the business of tin making change through the years from a time of making dish pans and other household items to a time of making gutter and duct work.

Clifford never learned to drive a car or truck, even after winning the first car ever given away at the Greeneville County Fair. He did own 30 or 40 trucks through the years in his business. Many times around town he'd be accompanied by Chita, a circus escapee. They both provided entertainment for two decades to the folks of Greeneville.

Blaine Rhea, Mr. Clifford's nephew, is the last of the Rheas in the tinner field. Blaine's fondest memories are of his Uncle Clifford, the man from whom he learned to make coffee pots and repair antique tin lamps, which he does today. Go by and see him. Business hours vary, so it's best to call first.

Address: 207 College Street, Greeneville, Tn 37743. (615) 638-6262.

Highland Manor Winery, Inc.

A winery in the "hollers" of the Cumberland Mountains? A moonshine still, maybe, but not a winery, you're thinking. But in fact, a world-class winery can be found in these hollers.

Highland Manor is Tennessee's first modern licensed winery and a producer of fine wines and champagnes. Few people realize that making wine in Jamestown was once the dream of Mark Twain. In his autobiography, Mark Twain describes the "fine estate left by his father in the region roundabout Jamestown where wild grapes of a promising sort grew." Almost 100 years passed before Fay and Kathy Wheeler recognized the same grape-growing potential of the area and established their own vineyard just south of town.

Highland Manor became the first American winery, large or small, to be awarded the International Gold Medal for Quality in Madrid, Spain, in 1983. They won again in 1984—another record. Try their famous musca-

Can you guess what Richard Sterban is wearing that he bought in Gatlinburg?

dine wine made from the bronze-colored grape that has been said to be God's gift to the sunny South. Approximate prices: $5 to $7 per bottle.

Tours of the winery are available, and free samples of products are given. Call ahead for large groups. Open daily from 10:00 A.M. to 6:00 P.M., except Sunday.

Directions: Take Exit 317 off I-40 near Crossville. Travel US 127 northward about 29 miles toward Jamestown. The winery is located on the east side of the highway. P. O. Box 203, US 127 South, Jamestown, TN 38556. (615) 879-9519.

Iron Mountain Stoneware

Laurel Bloomery—even the name sounds soothing, warm, and peaceful. Unique? Yes. It's a sleepy little hamlet with a population that tops out at about 70 persons. Yet a product manufactured here can be found in collectors' shops and posh department stores all across the country, from Tiffany's in New York to Gumps of San Francisco.

The product is ceramic dinnerware made by Iron Mountain Stoneware, Inc., one of the few firms in the world producing contemporary stoneware. Much of the process—the molding, trimming, glazing, and painting—is done by hand.

The stoneware is sold in over 600 retail stores from coast to coast, and it is also marketed abroad in Denmark, France, and Belgium. The firm operates an on-site retail store where discount sales are held each year at Thanksgiving and Mother's Day. Sometimes at Thanksgiving close to 10,000 shoppers come from as far away as Atlanta, Memphis, Washington, D.C., and New York.

Address: Located on State 91, about 8 miles north of Mountain City. It is in the very northeastern tip of the state. (615) 727-8888.

Joan H. Thornbury, Needlework and custom designs

Joan's specialty is custom-designed, counted cross-stitch graphs of individual homes. Send Joan a color photograph of the front view of your home, church, or other special building, and she'll chart it on graph paper and provide directions for you to create a family heirloom. Detailed instructions and a color chart will be provided with the graph. The finished size of the design area is approximately 6 by 10 inches.

Send the photograph with your name and address on the reverse side and check or money order for $30. Finished cross-stitch work (unframed) is also available. Other subject matter will be considered upon request.

4604 Wilson Avenue, Signal Mountain, TN 37377. (615) 886-5967.

Mike Vaughn, Woodcarvings

Mike makes one-of-a-kind originals. For his woodcarvings, he uses a chain saw to rough out the larger pieces, then wood carving chisels and a mallet from Germany to achieve finer detail. Nothing replaces the "old eyeball technique" for proportion, says Mike.

In addition to woodcarvings, Mike creates sculptures, illustrations, pipes, and violins.

Directions: State 321 from Pigeon Forge. Left on Valley View Drive. Bear left at fork in road to Little Cove Road, to Vaughn Box 371 on the right on a hill. Route 7, Box 371, Sevierville, TN 37862.

Lee and Dolores Roberson Artwork

The Robersons live what they paint—and it shows. Lee, a descendant of Cades Cove pioneers, is best known for his landscapes—hazy mountain panoramas, mellow old buildings, and sparkling streams. Dolores expresses her love of the delicate members of nature—wildflowers, birds, and animals. Lee's *Wild Heritage* was the official commemorative art print of the fiftieth anniversary of the Great Smoky Mountains National Park. Dolores did the official art poster. Both works are collector's items and are available at many retail establishments or directly from the Robersons. Many Roberson prints hang in more than 300 galleries and frame shops across the nation.

A visit to the Roberson Farmstead and Gallery is unlike a visit to the usual art gallery. In a remote mountain cove at the end of a winding one-lane road is the Robersons' log home and studio. Sundays are special days at the Robersons. Christian church services are held at 10:30, with worshipers gathering on the front porch unless disagreeable weather forces them inside. Everyone is welcome, and it is quite acceptable to come in casual clothes.

Visit the Smokies and take a bit of your vacation home with you…a painting or print by Lee or Dolores. Write for a free brochure, or send $5 (plus postage and handling) for complete color catalog.

Prices range from $10 to $5,000. Open 10:00 A.M. to 5:00 P.M. Monday–Saturday. Closed Thursday. Open by appointment only, Sunday afternoons.

Located about 35 miles from Knoxville, just out of Townsend, on State 321. Wears Valley Road, Townsend, TN 37882. (615) 448-2365.

Mike Vaughn and carvings

A SAMPLER FEATURE
The Amish

■While traveling US 43 north of Lawrenceburg, you might see a horse and buggy carrying dark-clothed, sober-faced folk. No, you are not hallucinating from the last episode of "Little House on the Prairie." Who are these people? Let's get in the time machine and spin backward a couple hundred years.

Located off US 43 between Mount Pleasant and Lawrenceburg is a small community of Amish people. The Amish are hard-working Christians, named for Jacob Amman, a Swiss Mennonite leader of the seventeenth century. The first group of Amish settlers in the New World came to Pennsylvania in 1741. Amish communities were later founded in many other states, Canada, and South America. Often called "Mennonites" by "people of the world," the Amish follow a more straight and narrow path in life, owning no cars, radios, televisions, and turning their backs on many modern-day conveniences and conventions—no make-up for the women, no electricity or inside plumbing, and few store-bought goods.

A small group of Amish people came from Mississippi to settle in Ethridge, Tennessee, in 1944. One long-bearded, white-haired man gleefully recounts the reception they got:

We got off the bus out at the highway and started walking down the dirt road toward our new farm-land. School had just let out and some children were up the road a piece from us. Of course they'd never seen anything like us before, and when they turned around and saw us, they took off running as fast as they could go....I spent my first night sleeping on a pile of corn shucks in a neighbor's barn.

Through the years the Amish appearance and life-style have been accepted in Middle Tennessee, although by choice the Amish remain apart from the rest of the world.

Clothing is handmade for the entire family from brown or black "goods," and everyone wears heavy black, high-topped brogans. Winter and summer, men wear full beards, bobbed hair styles, and loose-fitting shirts and pants. Women wear loose-fitting, long-sleeved blouses without buttons, long skirts, and aprons. Hats for men are of two varieties—a wide stiff-brimmed black

hat for winter and a straw stiff-brimmed summer version, the latter handmade by the women. Women wear neat white bonnets (even indoors) which tie under the chin and a darker sunbonnet for outdoor wear. Children wear miniature versions of their elders' clothes.

A typical home is a family-built, two-story, white, wooden or concrete block structure with a tin roof. Many homes have tall windmills to pump water to the kitchen. A small one-story house will likely be among numerous outbuildings. This is the "Grandpa House" built for aging parents when a son takes over the farming duties and moves into the big house. Inside both homes are bare but clean wooden floors, white walls, and a few pieces of functional, beautifully hand-crafted furniture. Black straight curtains are pulled aside to let in light no coal oil lamp can give. Outsiders and dreamers like us could gaze for hours at these small-paned, spotless windows, looking across the front yard clothesline to see the big Belgian mare slowly pulling the plow. But curtains are not pulled for dreaming. Sewing, weaving, or rug hooking is done by windows.

Metal clothes hooks line one wall, supporting hats or small clothing items. A homemade oak indoor clothesline, several wooden arms fastened to a base, hangs nearby. Amish women are kept busy cooking delicious homegrown food on the wood stove, doing laundry using a wringer washer run by a gas generator, or working on the carefully crafted quilts, rugs, baskets, or hats the family will use or sell.

As in frontier times, Amish families are often large with as many as 8, 10, or even 20 children. Life on a farm is not an easy life in any age, and many busy hands make work easier for all. No modern birth control methods are used, and children are the most prized possession of a home.

Children attend school through the eighth grade. To keep a small class size and enable children to walk to school, five small schoolhouses are spaced throughout the community. The three R's are taught in English and German, and Bible study and hymn singing are done in German, which is the primary language of the Amish. It is spoken exclusively at home, but it also comes in handy for private conversation out in the community. School operating expenses are tallied by a community treasurer who tells each family head the amount due for education. Every family pays, even if there are no children in school.

At the center of Amish life is the worship service, held every other Sunday. Over 20 families gather at different homes for a three-hour period of New Testament Bible study and hymn singing—all done in German. A time of good-eating and visiting follows, making it a day filled with joy for God and His creatures.

Word of fun times spreads fast in the Amish community—"Come and holiday with us" is always a welcome request. Weddings are all-day affairs at the bride's home, food for the invited guests furnished by the bride's family. After the ceremony, many hours of eating, talking, and joking follow. Even hard work is disguised in a "working bee" if a farmer has a barn to be built. Eight or ten men help raise it, each highly paid in strong measures of good food and good cheer.

The *Sampler* Recommends

The *Sampler* has learned from one of the Amish elders that they really do welcome people like you to shop in their community. If you want to take a remembrance of this way of life home with you, here's how. By politely asking buggy travelers, knocking on doors, or watching homemade signs, you'll be able to find outstanding buys in food, crafts, or furniture reproductions.

Please, do be courteous and respectful. *Don't* take photographs. Pictures to them are graven images and are forbidden by the second commandment God gave to Moses. *Don't* try to buy anything or conduct any business on Sunday.

Items available include: sorghum molasses, honey, quilts, buggies, harnesses, dog houses, bird houses, rocking chairs, furniture reproductions, fruit (in season), vegetables (in season), wicker repair, baskets, hats, peanuts, popcorn, and quilt frames. Specific directions: On US 43S, just before getting to Ethridge, look for Phillips Feed Supply on the right. Turn there, to the right on Brewer Road. Turn right again on Brace Road. The Amish community is located between here and Buffalo Road in an angled, rectangular shape. Drive at your leisure, observe, and ask questions if you wish.

Middle Tennessee Hot Spots

Debra Norfleet, Oil painting

Debra's wildlife paintings seem to capture the curiosity and humor of wild animals, just as her portraits of children capture innocence and trust. She also does landscapes of God's outdoor wonders.

Prices: $35 to $200. Contact Debra for an appointment or see her work at the Creative Gallery at Paris Landing State Park or Montgomery Bell State Park. Route 1, Box 117, Adams, TN 37010.

New Hope Studios, Ceramics and metalwork

This husband and wife team form the design firm of New Hope Studios.

Mary Ann Fariello started out as a production potter but has left earthenware to achieve new dimensions in ceramics and porcelain. Her commissioned works include a porcelain mural in the new wing of the Rutherford County Health Department, a series of masks at a performing arts center on the West Coast, and a triptych on the wall of Metro Nashville's Justice Center.

William Rogers is a blacksmith who uses old-fashioned methods to design and create architectural items, crafts and jewelry. Rogers does small items such as kitchen utensils for craft fairs but prefers to do commissioned work or design special items.

Both artists have gained a wide reputation for their one-of-a-kind work. Prices range from $25 to $300. Call for an appointment. Route 1, Box 192, Alexandria, TN 37012. (615) 529-2900.

Ardmore Cheese Company

Ardmore Cheddar is still made by hand according to a centuries-old English cheddaring recipe, and Ardmore cheese lovers insist that their cheddar stands apart from other cheddars. The judges at the Tennessee State Fair have awarded Ardmore Cheese Company the Governor's Trophy for the best cheddar in the state nine times!

Get this award-winning cheddar in mild, mellow, and sharp, and Monterey Jack, colby, caraway, hot pepper, cheddar, flavorful cheese logs, spreads, cheese balls, and even processed and natural cheeses. Priced from $2 to $55 (for the 25-pound hoop).

Open Monday–Friday. 8:00 A.M. till 5:00 P.M.; Saturday, 8:00 A.M. till 4:30 P.M. (615) 427-2191.

Located at 200 West Main Street in Ardmore.

Joe and Shirley Young, Molasses making

Shirley tells us: "Growing cane and making molasses is becoming a thing of the past. It is hard to find pure molasses anymore without syrup added. And nothing beats good molasses and hot biscuits! We do not have a molasses mill to make the molasses. We got Mr. Willie Byford, an old hand at molasses making, to make it on shares for us.

"Going to the mill and making the molasses is the fun part. To get good molasses, the cane must be stripped of the fodder. We hope our three-year-old daughter can have some fond memories, as we do, about molasses making."

Drop in at molasses-making time, mostly in September and October.

Approximate price: $5 per quart.

Location: 7 miles south of Woodbury on State 53. Route 1, Box 227, Bradyville, TN 37026. (615) 765-5337.

Charles Pinckley, Nursery and crafts

Charles and Wanda Pinckley are both retired from Austin Peay State University in Clarksville and spend happy times together working with their combination hobby/business. Stop for a visit at Wandaland Nursery. They do landscaping and also make barnwood frames, miniature doll furniture, and bluebird boxes. Hours: 8:00 A.M. to 4:00 P.M., Monday–Saturday.

Location: US 41A, approximately 5 miles north of Pleasant View or approximately 15 miles south of Clarksville, near Exit 19 (Maxey Exit) off I-24. Route 2, Cedar Hill, TN 37032. (615) 746-5212.

Billy R. McCoy, Dulcimers

Billy tells us, "The word *dulcimer* comes from the Greek word *dulce* meaning 'sweet' and the Latin word *melos* meaning 'song.' It seems most likely that the dulcimer was the outgrowth of a variety of European instruments created from memories of the German, Norwegian, Dutch, and Swedish immigrants who settled in the Appalachians.

"Our dulcimers are constructed from carefully selected woods grown in Hickman County. Several woods are used, but walnut is most often used for the tuning head because of its strength and beauty. Other woods used are wild cherry, oak, pecan, and white walnut (butternut). Sometimes soft woods such as poplar, chestnut, and gum are used for tops to provide a softer tone. We saw our own wood, and we use no kits or plywood."

Dulcimer prices: $125 to $145. Call for an appointment.

Directions: 3½ miles north of Centerville just off State 100. 1704 Bellwood Drive, Centerville, TN 37033. (615) 729-2137.

Thompson Dry Goods

Thompson Dry Goods Company has been in operation since 1837. See priceless antiques and fixtures and new merchandise in an old setting—from sewing notions to clothes for the family. Open Monday–Saturday, 8:00 A.M. to 5:00 P.M.

Directions: Take US 100 southwest of Nashville 50 miles. 307 North Public Square, Centerville, TN 37033. (615) 729-3547.

Three of Billy's dulcimers

Custom Cast, Bronze designs

Cast your eyes on this! Great gift ideas for the men in your life. Bronze creations such as belt buckles, paperweights, and plaques. Available in small and large quantities, reasonable prices, and no minimum order. Send a picture or a rough sketch of what you want and they will do the rest. All work hand done.

Approximate price range for custom designed belt buckle—$50 set-up fee (includes artwork and pattern), plus $12 for the first buckle, unit price decreasing the more you order. Write for a free brochure or call and order as many as you like. Satisfaction guaranteed. Route 1, Panther Creek Road, Christiana, TN 37037. (615) 274-6844.

Dolores Chesser, Artwork

Dolores is an artist whose work in acrylics and pen and ink reflects her love of the Tennessee outdoors. In her peaceful studio located in the woods, she is inspired to create landscapes, flowers, and wild animals. Price range: $20 to $100. Call for an appointment. 2220 Pendleton Drive, Clarksville, TN 37042. (615) 431-3954.

Susan Ross, Watercolors

Susan is a self-taught artist. She does commissioned work from photographs of other regions. Just send photographs, Susan will paint what you want and send you the painting with price tag included. You either pay the price or return the painting. Susan is so good, she's never had one returned. Repeat customers are frequent.

Call for more information. You can see Susan's work at the Creative Gallery at Montgomery Bell State Park or Paris Landing State Park. Route 5, Box 287-B, Clarksville, TN 37042. (615) 645-4166.

Hagatha, Inc., Monogrammed items

Gloria Rasbury says: "I started sewing in my basement for my family. My mother had taught me basic sewing skills, but I soon took a whole new direction in designing. Every dress or suit I made had a purse to match. Purses fascinate me. They can be fun or fancy, practical or pretty. I would appliqué and re-embroider scenes of children, public buildings, homes, or anything to make something personal. Then I would sew it into a tote bag with lots of pockets inside and out for practical purposes. But I soon realized this style would not always appeal to everyone so I started monogramming for local stores. Soon I bought a commercial monogram machine and moved out of my basement. My daughter and I came up with the name of Hagatha, and I opened up for business in 1980. Now customers bring their personal items to be monogrammed, or they order our unique tote bags, cloth bags, aprons, or garment bags. We also do a large mail-order business and send our products nationwide. We are open Wednesday through Saturday from 9:30 to 5:00."

Directions: From the courthouse on the square, go out West Seventh Street three blocks. Turn left at the Episcopal Church. Last house on the right. 812 Walker Street, Columbia, TN 38401. (615) 381-5175.

Tennessee Knife Works, Inc., Knives

Knife traders or collectors know the Colonel Coon Knife to be one of exceptional quality, and it is manufactured right here. Completely hand-crafted, the knife comes in five different patterns: the single blade, the Barlow pattern with two blades, the jackknife with two blades, the three-headed stockman, and the two-headed mini-trapper. Three handle types are available: stag, bone, and the more elegant rosewood. All knives can be custom etched, if desired. Safety awards, commemorative knives, and club knives using logos or commemorative dates are available. All knives come with a written guarantee. Prices range from $20 to $40.

Directions: Located between Columbia and Mount Pleasant on Zion Lane. Columbia, TN 38401. (615) 388-7821.

S & H Honey Farms, Honey, country ham, and sausage

Glenn Stevenson: "You can be dog-tired and eat a spoonful of honey and 15 minutes later, see if you're not a different person. You can use honey to treat burns, fight bacteria, or even combat tuberculosis."

Glenn has been fascinated by bees and the beekeeping process since childhood, and the 12 or 15 hives he got from his father to start his business years ago have multiplied to almost 3,000. His honey is sold all over Middle Tennessee.

If honey doesn't do the trick and your lethargy still needs a boost, start your day with some homemade biscuits, eggs, honey, butter, and some of Glenn's own country ham and sausage. (See "Eatin' Good" for some country ham cooking tips from Glenn's charming wife, Janice.)

Price ranges: honey—8 ounce jar about 75¢ 55 gallon drum about $700; country ham—$2.00 to $2.25 per pound; country sausage (not smoked)—$3.50 per 2 pound bag, (available November 10–February 10)

Hours: Monday–Saturday, 8:30 A.M. to 6:00 P.M. Sunday, 1:00 to 5:00 P.M.

Directions: 4 miles north of Columbia on US 31. White house by the side of the road with sign in front. Come on around to the back. (615) 388-2420.

Lou Jacobs Fruity Patch Farms, Fresh fruit

Large selection of pick-your-own fruits—peaches, apples, pears, cherries, blueberries, plums, blackberries, muscadines, and chestnuts. Prices range from $3 per gallon for some berries to $8 per bushel for apples and peaches.

Come anytime from 8:00 A.M. to 6:00 P.M. when nature produces fruit from June 15–November 15. Best to call first to see what's ready.

Location: 7 miles west of Columbia on State 50, turn right on Brown's Hollow Road, and right at the second driveway on the right. Name on mailbox. Route 4, Box 124, Brown's Hollow Road, Columbia, TN 38401. (615) 583-2494.

The Second Time Around, Clothing

Lucille Courtney says: "I started this business in an attic over a gift shop. Now Lil Moore and I run a consignment shop, and we take mainly women's and children's good clothing, along with a few specialty items like wedding dresses and prom dresses. Some are new, some are not so new but good. We furnished the outfits for most of the women in the movie about Hank Williams, so come by—your dress may be in the movies! We have a wonderful Victorian house with a porch, large windows, high ceilings, and fireplaces. Our many good people tell us to give anything of theirs to anyone who truly needs it. We do. We love to help out the foster mothers. Your clothes are the closest thing to you, and some of them hold such precious memories. From two women who never suffered from the 'empty nest syndrome' but rather enjoyed it—this job is fun!"

Directions: From the courthouse on the square, go out West Seventh Street three blocks. Turn left at the Episcopal church. Last house on the right. 812 Walker Street, Columbia, TN 38401. (615) 381-7222.

Randall and Paula Carr, Wild horse and burro adoption

Cross Plains—the name evokes an image of wide, open plains under western skies, a place where wild horses roam. So it is fitting that the rolling pastures of Cross Plains, Tennessee, serve as home port for thousands of wild horses and burros coming East for adoption. This is the first permanent adoption center in the eastern United States and is a family operation, built and operated for the Federal Bureau of Land Management by Randall and Paula Carr.

Paula tells us that many adopted horses have won endurance races and plowing contests and have made particularly good 4-H projects. Burros make good pets and have been taught to break show calves or break bulls to a lead. Randall and Paula have learned from experience that they are no longer losing calves to wild dogs, thanks to the burros. They chase the dogs and will not let them come into the fields.

The adoption fee is $125 for each horse and $75 for each burro.

For more information, write: Adopt-a-Horse or Burro Program, Bureau of Land Management, Eastern States Office, 350 South Pickett Street, Alexandria, VA 22304; (703) 235-2866 or Southeastern Wild Horse and Burro Adoption Center, Route 2, Carr-Couts Road, Cross Plains, TN 37049; (615) 654-2180.

Directions: Take I-65 north to Exit 112. Turn west and go 4 miles to Cross Plains. Continue 1 mile past town and turn right at Carr-Couts road. Go 1 more mile, taking the right fork of the road. The center is on the left.

Patricia Anderson, Watercolors and quilling

Patricia specializes in watercolors of the iris, Tennessee's state flower. She also does dough art, painted eggs, quilling (a revival of Victorian paper filigree), and stained-glass work. Her watercolors range in price from $5 to $200 and quilling prices range from $5 to $25. Patricia's work is displayed at Creative Gallery at Montgomery Bell State Park Inn, or you may phone her in Dickson for an appointment. (615) 446-9302.

Judy Holman, Square dance attire

Judy makes and sells custom-designed square dance attire. Call her at home or see her work at Five Rivers Arts and Crafts Creative Gallery at Montgomery Bell State Park. Her items range in price form $1.50 to $50.00. To get to the park, take I-40 West from Nashville to State 96, then follow the signs to the park. Contact Judy at 304 Kevin Drive, Dickson, TN 37055. (615) 441-1197.

Marie's Fabrics and Sewing Services, Quilting fabrics

Bill Pearce says: "Our customers come from Alabama, Georgia, Mississippi, and North Carolina, as well as the immediate area. Why? Our large selection of quilting fabrics. We have approximately 200 bolts of 100 per cent cotton prints and solids to choose from. We also have many unique and unusual supplies and notions for the quilter. We have Mountain Mist trademark symbol quilt batting, 100 per cent cotton down-proof floral pillow ticking, and poly/cotton pillow tubing. Buying buttons on cards is frustrating so we stock buttons in drawers just like the good ol' days.

"We serve the fabrics craftsperson with a wide selection of basic and fashion fabrics. We also sell and service Viking sewing machines an⸱ Huskylocks by Husqvarna. Our prices range from 2⸱ ¢ ⸱ $1599."

Directions: From I-65, turn west tṵward Franklin on State 96. Alexander Plaza is the large shopping center on the right. 541 Alexander Plaza, Franklin, TN 37064. (615) 794-6024.

Kari Traditionals, Heirloom sewing

Kari Traditionals is a specialty shop for English smocking and heirloom sewing. The idea for the shop came about when Gayle Gilley's daughter, Kari, outgrew a certain line of children's clothes, and Gayle started looking around for something pretty for Kari to wear. Gayle discovered English smocking and learned how to do it. Then she began to teach others, create designs, and finally make patterns. From her studies, Gayle created a machine-sewing technique which attaches laces and makes tucks by machine rolling, which looks like hand-whipped work. The shop offers imported fabrics, French laces, smocking supplies, DMC thread, copyrighted and other patterns, and handmade gift items. Open Monday–Saturday.

Call Gayle for more information about smocking classes or seminars. 504 West Main Street, Franklin, TN 37064. (615) 794-7922.

Ramcraft, Clocks

Owner J. R. Ramsey tells us that Ramcraft builds all the cases for their grandfather clocks, starting with rough lumber and carrying the process all the way through to the finished product. To these cases are added German movements and dials imported directly from manufacturers. Mr. Ramsey says: "Our product is special because in this fast-paced, high-production world, we cherish the fact that we are a small business of 10 employees, home-owned and family-operated. We sell the finished product to the public at a reasonable price." Approximate price range: $25 to $2500. Open Monday–Friday, 8:00 A.M. to 5:00 P.M.; Saturday, 9:00 A.M. to 2:00 P.M.

Directions: Take I-65 North from Nashville. Exit Two Mile Pike. Bear right to Gallatin Road US 31 and go to Gallatin. Proceed on Gallatin Road to the fourth traffic light in Gallatin. Turn left and go 1 1/2 blocks. Ramcraft is on the left. 331 West Eastland Avenue, Gallatin, TN 37066. (615) 452-7430.

Frank Ellis, Blacksmith

Mr. Frank says: "Blacksmiths' shops aren't on every corner, and there are those like me who don't want the art of the old country blacksmith to fade away. Our young folks need to know that when someone makes an article it's made the best he can, with pride and skill, whether it is a fine fireplace poker or a crocheted shawl. Here at our farm we still kill hogs, make molasses, keep bees, make apple cider, have a huge garden, and work horses and mules. It's hard work, but when some old-timer comes and watches the horses work the sorghum mill and tastes your molasses and says, 'Well, I ain't seen 'em made since I was a boy,' it is all worth the effort and hard work." Price range: From the blacksmith's shop—$1 to $100.

Directions: From Greenbrier on US 41N go to Hinkles Used Cars, turn right, cross the railroad tracks, and turn left on the next road, right at the next, and follow signs to Whippoorwill Forge. Approximately 3 1/2 miles after turning off US 41. Route 1, Box 341, Greenbrier, TN 37073. (615) 643-4842.

Blueberry Ridge Farm, Blueberries

For some gorgeous scenery and scrumptious blueberries, you'll never have a better day than the one you spend at Blueberry Ridge—4 1/2 acres of berries on a high ridgetop surrounded by woods.

Marcelle Ragan says their youngest picker was her 15-month-old grandson (who eats all he picks) and the oldest an 83-year-old lady. Vacationers from Texas, Alabama, California, and New York enjoy the beauty of the area as well as the berries. You'll love meeting and getting to know Miss Marcelle.

Price per gallon depends on the crop for the year but reasonable always. Hours: July 1–September 5, 6:00 A.M. to dusk.

Directions: From Hohenwald 5 1/2 miles south on State 99W (Buffalo Road). Turn right on Dial Holler Road, go 1/4 mile to mailbox with Blueberry Ridge Farm on it. (615) 796-4382.

Helen's Junk Store, Clothing

If you're a bargain hunter, be sure to visit Helen on the square and other "junk stores" in Hohenwald. Many come to Helen's to buy the name brand clothes in perfect condition. Prices from 25 ¢ to $5. Store hours 8:00 A.M. to 5:00 P.M. Get ready to find some unbelievable buys.

Address: 21 South Maple Street, Hohenwald, TN 38462.

Painter's Corner, Oil paintings

See oil paintings on canvas or on such unusual surfaces as saws, milk cans, skillets, coal shovels, buckets, and mailboxes. These paintings have more than the country look. They are re-creations of country life—chickens pecking around a barn, farmhouses with cool, shadowy porches, clothes blowing on a line, woods with darkened log cabins, waterwheels on frozen ponds, or abandoned hayrakes.

Prices: $5 to $300. Open 9:00 A.M. to 5:00 P.M. Closed Sunday and Thursday.

Directions: From State 99, go to the third traffic light, turn left, and go to the end of the block. 26 North Court, Hohenwald, TN 38462. (615) 796-5596.

Fran Salmons, Artwork

Fran enjoys the relaxation of painting on pieces of slate. Old buildings with slate roofs provide her medium, but the slate requires pounding, washing, scrubbing, and drilling before the "artistic" touch is administered. Fran uses acrylics to create her animals and snow scenes. Sizes range from 2 by 2 inches up to about 14 by 24 inches and prices from $5 to $50. Fran also paints pets from their photos for about $30. Call for an appointment. 1708 Deer Hollow Drive, Lawrenceburg, TN 38464. (615) 762-7702.

The Mousetrap Cheese Shop, Cheese and country cured meats

Owner Randle Jones says: "When our family cheese company began back in 1929, we believed that if we took a vat of cheddar cheese and stored it under controlled conditions for just the right amount of time, we could create a cheddar whose taste and texture could not be excelled. Nothing has happened in the last 50 years to change our minds. Also, our Mousetrap brand country cured meats are cured the way our forefathers cured their meat. No additives or artificial flavorings are added. Nothing is injected. You get just the natural flavor of old-fashioned cured meat smoked with real hickory smoke. Each piece is allowed to hang until the smoke has had time to penetrate, cure, and give you the genuine true flavor."

Write for a free catalog or drop by the store in Lewisburg to buy cheese, meats, and candies. Business hours: 8:00 A.M. to 5:00 P.M., six days a week; open Sunday by appointment.

Directions: Come to the square in Lewisburg and take US 31A south after leaving the south side of the square. Go to the first traffic light and turn right. The Mousetrap is 50 yards on the left. P.O. Box 249, Lewisburg, TN 37091. (615) 359-6336.

Fred Warren, Miniature log cabins

Mr. Fred is 71 years young, living all those years in the Rockhouse Creek community, 12 miles south of Linden. In years past he was a carpenter. Now he has scaled down his building trade to turn out authentic copies of rapidly disappearing Tennessee log cabins.

Out in "Pop's Shop" as the grandchildren call it,

Mr. Fred makes the cabins from poplar or red cedar, tiny logs notched and crossed at the corners, chinked with a caulking gun, and topped with an authentic wood shingle roof. Cabins have chimneys, hinged doors, glass windows, and a dogtrot (or breezeway for you city slickers). This tiny treasure is about 36 inches long and 25 inches wide—the perfect size for a pioneer play family. This one-of-a-kind heirloom for tomorrow ranges in price from $200 to $500. (615) 589-2884.

Ellen McGowan, Sculptures

Ellen lives in rural Perry County and sculpts Tennessee people from Tennessee clay. Focusing on the "hidden richness of human relationships," she works from memory, imagination, or short glimpses of everyday people at their everyday activities. Her work is in numerous collections in the United States and abroad.

Approximate price range: $100 to $350 (more for commissioned works, such as portrait busts).

Address: Route 4, Box 197, Linden, TN 37096. (615) 589-5418.

Sculptor Ellen McGowan

Henry and Jewell's Wood and Photo Shop, Custom frames and woodcraft

Henry Beckman is a master craftsman. When he isn't teaching at Loretto High School, he custom-builds fine pieces of furniture. Log benches, cradles, and picture frames show he does "all kinds of whittling and piddling." Every year Henry and Jewell have a big show and sale Thanksgiving weekend. See their wooden items and a collection of antique tools—many still in use. They might even show you their wild mongoose!

Located on Demonbreum Street in Loretto, the shop is right by their house. Referring to store business hours, Henry says, "We're here more'n we ain't." However it might be a good idea to give Henry and Jewell a call before making a trip from a distance. (615) 853-4479.

Doc's Berry Farm, Pick-your-own fruit farm and winery

See a working family farm and pick your own fruit in season—grapes, muscadines, apples, blueberries, and peaches. Then observe, taste, and buy from the winery. Most fruit is sold for 50¢ per pound and wine for $4 per bottle. Open Saturdays regularly, but call at other times, especially when fruits are not in season.

Directions: Go east from Loretto on Lexington Highway, then south on Littrell Lane. Follow signs. P.O. Box 160, Loretto, TN 38469. (615) 853-6911.

Big Creek Knifeworks, Knives

David Rhea began making knives at age 12 when he made a "forge knife" with a trash fire in the front yard. His dad got mad. But if Dad could see the one-of-a-kind treasures David creates now, surely pride would replace that anger. All knives are handmade and all designs original, except for copies of some specific period pieces. David specializes in "art" knives, knives sought for their appeal as collector items. These knives employ exotic blade designs and handle materials, as well as engraving, casting, scrimshaw, and sometimes precious metals and gemstones. However, he produces utility knives priced low enough for field use.

David's work in scrimshaw enhances the beauty of his knives, but now his scrimshaw skills have extended to belt buckles, pendants, jewelry pieces, handgun grips, mounted tusks, and a form he calls "scrimcarve," which is scrimshaw on fully carved pieces.

Price range: Knives—$65 to $150; scrimshaw—$15 to $250. Come by evenings or weekends, or call other times for an appointment.

Address: Route 1, Box 272, Lynnville, TN 38472. (615) 363-5993.

Boyd Brothers Nursery

Shortly after the Civil War, Jonathan H. H. Boyd started a small nursery in Warren County. The business still flourishes after more than 100 years. The fourth and fifth generations of Boyds grow and sell (both wholesale and retail) quality nursery stock from Middle Tennessee. Their seeds and plants grow all over the world, in the gardens of plain folks and in those of presidents. See their own "First Lady Dogwood," the "Pioneer Sweet Cherry," and "The World's Fair White Dogwood." Plants range in price from a few dollars for small items to several hundred dollars for a large shade tree. Open Monday–Saturday, 8:00 A.M. to 5:00 P.M.; Sunday from 1:00 to 4:00 P.M.

Directions: From McMinnville take State 55 toward Manchester for 6 miles. Nursery on right. From I-24, take McMinnville Exit at Manchester and come about 14 miles. Nursery on left. P.O. Box 512, McMinnville, TN 37110. (615) 668-9898.

Le Chevrier Goat Dairy, Goat's milk products

Le Chevrier is one of the few goat dairies in Tennessee and one of the largest goat dairies in the country that milks its own stock and processes the milk into various products. A traditional French raw milk cheese called Montrachet and a goat milk yogurt are produced. At present it is the only goat milk yogurt produced in this country. Folks in the metropolitan New York City area pay premium prices to enjoy these delicacies.

Call for ordering information. Open 10:00 A.M. to 3:00 P.M. Group tours at other times may be arranged in advance.

Directions: Take Livingston Exit from I-40. Take State 111 north, which turns into State 42N through Livingston. Continue 42N 7 miles to Monroe. There is no sign that says Monroe, but look for a gold sign with a goat on the right side of the highway. Turn right and continue 3 miles to front of farm. Route 1, Box 54, Monroe, TN 38573. (615) 823-4604.

Scott Higdon, Artwork

For some rustic scenes of rural Tennessee, you need to see the artwork of a young college student, Scott Higdon. He reflects on camping or hunting trips with his father for his subject matter or on historical images in his mind—brown-toned log cabins, owls, covered wagons, or Walking Horses.

Tennesseans typically have lots of perseverance, but Scott has more than most. Crippled by cerebral palsy since birth, Scott holds a pencil or pen in his mouth to create his detailed drawings. For comfort he

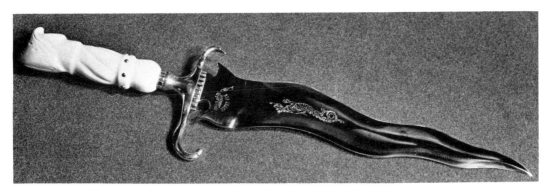

Ivory-handled kriss with dragon by David Rhea

does most of his drawings lying down. Most drawings take 10 to 20 hours of work, but the more detailed ones take 40 hours or more.

Call for an appointment to see these artworks created by a great Tennessean. Average price is $25. Murfreesboro, TN 37130. (615) 890-6245.

Sally Cartwright, Finely detailed pottery and sculpture

Sally says, "My work draws inspiration from the rock and plant forms of this beautiful state. Its lush vegetation provides an endless wealth of ideas."

Some of those ideas include a scuplted, wall-size orchid, a miniature landscape reproduced in clay, and an ornate jar disguised with living woodland flowers, fungi, and lichen. Call Sally for an appointment. Nashville, (615) 385-1100.

Artworks, Etc.

Artworks, Etc. features new, local artists in various fields. Find good buys in fine art and decorative posters, unique gifts, local handmade crafts, and signed and numbered prints of Nashville landmarks. 2817 West End Avenue, Nashville, TN. (615) 327-3153.

Elizabeth B. White, Silhouettes

How much time have you wasted poring over greeting card racks, searching fruitlessly for the card for that special person? Sometimes friends are so special that no commercial card can quite fill the bill.

Rest easy, folks. We've discovered Beth White, a Nashville silhouette artist who creates intricately detailed note cards using an X-acto mat knife on a single piece of folded black paper. Uniquely beautiful cards adorned with finely detailed trees, squirrels, birds, antlered deer, and mythical unicorns may be seen in her exquisite collection. Like her lithe cat on the Queen Anne table, you can almost feel warm sunshine and a gentle breeze blowing patchwork curtains aside. Beth's black-and-white silhouettes are hand cut to her own designs (or your suggestions for designs). Their outstanding artistic quality has earned them a place in the Smithsonian as well as other museums in the Northeast.

What could be better than sending one of these silhouette treasures to a friend? Order a box of 12 cards, each a different design, for $10. You won't be disappointed. In fact, you may even have to come up with a friend-ranking checklist to help you decide who will be lucky enough to receive one of these gems. They're a cut above the rest.

Business hours: 10:00 A.M. to 6:00 P.M. Call to make an appointment or to order.

Address: 1708 Warfield, Nashville, TN 37215. (615) 297-6853.

Michael Amick, Tailor-made clothing

Strange tools of a man's trade—a pencil behind his ear and a tape measure around his neck. Michael Amick clings to an old profession, tailoring.

As a custom tailor for men and women, Michael is

Sally Cartwright's elegant ceramics

proud to show you "quality that doesn't cost but pays." A top quality man's suit can cost about $500 and up, but Michael can make a suit comparable to one by Hart, Schaffner, and Marx for only about 20 per cent more than the rack cost. Michael says, "So many have trouble wearing standard suits because they need a different size pant from the coat size they wear. I make sure everything fits exactly. If my customers can fit through the door, I can fit them." Visit Michael Monday through Friday, 9:00 A.M. to 5:30 P.M.; Saturday, 9:00 A.M. to 4:00 P.M.

Address: 2200 Hillsboro Road, Nashville, TN 37212. (615) 385-0426.

Designer Collections, Pottery, art, and teak furniture

Maki Lin is a production potter and an artist. Designer Collections is a studio where Maki does wheel-thrown pottery, and it's also a gallery where hand-crafted items are displayed. Monthly exhibits feature local, regional, and national artists. Also available is handmade teak furniture imported from Maki's native Taiwan. Stop in and see Maki for some unique gift ideas with an oriental flavor. Prices range from $6 to $3,000. Open from 10:00 A.M. to 5:00 P.M. Monday–Saturday.

Address: 2817 West End Avenue, Nashville, TN 37203. (615) 327-3616.

Nashville Tops, Regional souvenirs

Nashville T-shirts, belt buckles, caps, jewelry, Nashville and Tennessee souvenirs, and western hats and shirts are specialities of Nashville Tops. Satisfied customers come back year after year because of new T-shirt and belt designs and great prices, but we suspect they want to hear another story from owner Bob Foster who played steel guitar on the Grand Ole Opry for 17 years.

Open Monday–Saturday, 9:00 A.M. to 5:00 P.M.; Sunday, 9:00 A.M. to 4:00 P.M.

Located around the corner from the Ryman Auditorium. 424 Broadway, Nashville, TN 37203. (615) 244-1954.

Jane Baxendale, Bronze works

Jane designs solid bronze belt buckles, paperweights, custom plaques, busts, or oval bronze relief portraits relating to heroes of the Confederacy. Jane's bronze works are cast by Morris E. Parker of the New River Foundry in Lavergne, Tennessee. Her heroic size bronze sculpture of Nathan Bedford Forrest, now in the Great Hall of the Tennessee State Capitol, was cast by the famous Karkadoulias Bronze Art Foundry of Cincinnati, Ohio. Prices on custom buckles include a $35 set-up charge and $12 per buckle. Bas-relief portrait buckles of notable Civil War figures are available for under $15. For more detailed information, call or write for a free brochure. 4114 Sneed Road, Nashville, TN 37215. (615) 297-1975.

Sandra Pennington, Nashville goodie baskets

Do you want to send some of our luscious taste treats out of the county, the state, or even the country? Get a woven wooden basket chock full of made-in-Nashville treats: Standard Candy Company's King Leo stick candy and Goo-Goo chocolate clusters, Martha White's Cotton-Pickin' Cornbread Mix, Roy's wild honey, colorful Nashville-imprinted napkins, Jane Marie's pickle relish, and a three-dimensional, hand-painted white chocolate "Dolly-Pop"—our tribute to Dolly Parton. Prices: $5.95 to $25. 205 Jackson Boulevard, Nashville, TN 37205. (615) 356-5155 or (615) 352-4823.

Music City Gemstones, Jewelry

Dan and Judy Lucas are "rockhounds" who search out

Girl with Unicorn, cut paper art by Beth White

rocks and fashion belt buckles, jewelry, bolos, and gem trees from them. Call for an appointment. 919 Timberside Drive, Nolensville, TN 37135. (615) 776-5006.

Wylodean Johnson, Paintings

When Wylodean isn't a Giles County school bus driver, she is an artist. Wylodean paints crosscut saws, hand saws, Skillsaw blades, old disk blades, and "any other old thing." She also paints canvases and woodcrafts cut out by her brother, Bill Eldridge. Take a drive in the country and see Wylodean's art and craft work. Ask her to show you her handmade dolls and pillows—also a picture of her twin grandsons.

Directions: At Campbellsville, turn right at the fork in the road. Go up a long hill to where the road meets another road. Turn left. Go past small store on the right. Wylodean's is the second house on the left. Route 8, Box 261, Pulaski, TN 38478.

Early's Honey Stand, Cured meats and more

About 60 years ago the Early family was in the backyard killing hogs when a motorist stopped and asked to buy 10 pounds of sausage. That motorist liked the sausage so much, he came back for more. That was the beginning of a $1 million a year mail-order enterprise that employs a staff of from 3 to 40, depending on seasonal fluctuation.

The first mail-order facility was 12 feet square and was built because Mother Early told Dad that if he didn't stop wrapping meat and stuff in her kitchen, she was going to quit cooking. In 1979, a 70 by 125 feet, two-story plant and new retail store replaced the old mail-order facility.

Here you will find one of the oldest, largest, and most famous country meat houses in the South. Nearly a half-century of curing and smoking experience goes into each of the products. The old-time methods are still used—curing with sugar, salt, and natural spices. Slowly smoked with green hickory wood to a golden brown, the meats truly have that old-time flavor and taste. There is no needling, pumping, dipping, or doping with newfangled chemicals at Early's. Other typical Tennessee products available are aged cheddar cheese, water-ground cornmeal, cracklin's, smoked seasoning, sassafras, honey, sorghum, hickory chips, and even corn cob jelly. Write for a free catalog or drop by most anytime—open Monday–Saturday, 8:00 A.M. til 5:00 P.M.

Directions: 29 miles south of Nashville on US 31. Box 100, Spring Hill, TN 37174. (615) 486-2230.

Rick Sweeney, Oil paintings

Rick does oil paintings of Tennessee rural landscapes on canvas or metal saws, including crosscuts, hand saws, or circular saws. Sixty per cent of his customers bring a picture of where they grew up and ask Rick to paint it on a saw used by someone in the family. It's a great gift idea.

Rick does most of his painting in the late summer through late December and combines his love for fall, deer hunting, and painting. Wildlife can be seen in almost every painting. Rick says, "Without wildlife, to me the painting is dead." Prices: 8 by 10 oil or small circular saw—$10 (up to $150). Call for an appointment.

Address: Route 2, Kincaid Drive, Spring Hill, TN 37174. (615) 486-2413.

Hainted Hole Dairy Goats, Goat's milk products

Carol and Harold Kiser raise French Alpine and LaMancha (earless) dairy goats. The LaMancha breed is the only American breed of dairy goat. The Kisers give demonstrations at local fairs on milking and cheese making and even visit a local nursing home so the patients can milk or pet the goats: some in wheelchairs even milk! Carol makes several varieties of cheese for sale. Ira Olive, Carol's friend, tells us Carol has one more hidden talent…artwork. Ira says: "Carol is quite an artist. Most of her drawings and paintings are centered on her love for goats, but she has been known to paint landscapes of the surrounding area."

Visitors are welcome to see the goats anytime, and milking hours are 8:00 A.M. and 8:00 P.M. You might call before visiting. Maybe you'll be as lucky as the *Sampler* was. Carol was in the barn bottle-feeding 13 newborn goats!

Directions: From Erin, take State 49 toward Dover. Go left on State 147 through Tennessee Ridge, Stewart, and McKinnon. Go right on highway 232N for 2.6 miles. You'll see the farm on the right. (615) 721-3275.

J & J Molasses Co., Pure sorghum molasses

According to Jack Leath and Jim Howell, the making of pure molasses is fast becoming a lost art. In times past, sugar cane was grown, made into molasses, and used as a dessert or cooking ingredient. The molasses making of today is primarily a Howell and Leath family operation, with both sets of grandparents lending a helping hand. Jack and Jim strive to keep the old-time molasses a thing of the present. They also grow corn and make hominy for their own use, raise geese and pick the feathers for pillows, and make some of their own furniture.

Price is about $12.50 per #10 can. Visitors welcome during months of September and October.

Directions: From Nashville, take 31E North to Westmoreland. Go east on State 52 approximately 2½ miles to the community of Siloam. Stop at Jim Howell's country store. Route 4, Westmoreland, TN 37186. (615) 644-2694.

Linda Pickett, Paintings

As early as six years of age, Linda mixed pokeberry juice and white shoe polish to produce her first creations. Linda still loves her state (although her mediums have changed), and she enjoys expressing that love in her paintings. One of her loveliest recent works is of Ketner's Mill in the Sequatchie Valley near Jasper. Linda says: "I went down there in the late afternoon one fall day when it was quiet and peaceful. There is no detail work in the painting—only feeling and atmosphere— *that* is a painting. It must tell a story; the artist must achieve a mood or it's just another picture."

Linda has a small art and craft shop where her prices range from $50 to $1,000 for paintings and from $5 to $100 on other craft items.

Directions: From Nashville, take I-24S to Jasper, take the South Pittsburg Exit, go north on US 41 to Jasper, turn left on State 27N, and it's about 10 miles from there to Crossroads and Whitwell. Route 3 Box 76, Whitwell, TN 37397. (615) 658-5101 or (615) 658-9636.

Woodward Knives, Knives, swords, and engraving

Harold Woodward says: "I have been making handmade knives and swords for about 12 years now. In August of 1983 I was injured in a motorcycle accident, and after six months in the hospital, I returned to my farm in Woodbury and have been engraving guns and knives. I am getting my machine shop adapted to use from my wheelchair so I can continue with my knife and sword making." Approximate prices: Engraving starts at $10 and custom-made knives begin at $75.

Directions: Take US 70S out of Murfreesboro to Woodbury. Turn right at the Edgefield Branch of the Bank of Commerce (West Adams Street). Proceed ¼ mile to Hollis Creek Road. Turn right and go 1½ miles to the dead end at the Sunny Slope Church of Christ. Turn left and go 1¼ miles to where the pavement runs out. Follow the dirt road ½ mile to the house. There is a stream which comes out of a cave just 750 feet from the house and it is a very nice place to picnic. It's best to call before coming. Route 3, Box 64A, Woodbury, TN 37190. (615) 563-4619.

Tennessee Flea Markets, Big and Small

On a drive around any Tennessee city on any weekend you're likely to see a hand-lettered sign announcing a flea market. Officially defined as "An open-air market for second-hand articles and antiques," Tennessee flea markets range from neighborhood sales to major events which attract hundreds of buyers and dealers and thousands of visitors.

Regularly scheduled flea markets are held in each of Tennessee's four largest cities. The Knoxville flea market is held on the third weekend of each month at Chilhowee Park. In Memphis the flea market is held at the Mid-South Fairgrounds each weekend. The Nashville flea markets take place at the Tennessee State Fairgrounds or Ellington Parkway on the fourth weekend of each month, except for September (when the State Fair is operating) and December. Chattanooga's big flea market is a weekly happening in the 2300 block of Rossville Boulevard.

Who patronizes flea markets? All types of people.

Entertainer Redd Foxx is an ardent collector of flea market furniture. Grand Ole Opry star Roy Acuff is a frequent visitor to the Nashville flea market. In fact, a number of Music City celebrities visit the monthly markets where they are seldom recognized by the crowds.

Flea markets draw buyers and sellers from many states. One woman from New York flies to Nashville every month to comb the booths for a particular kind of jewelry. After spending several hours at the flea market, she takes a taxi back to the airport for a flight home to New York. A buyer from California is another frequent visitor to the Nashville flea market, making at least one stop in Nashville each year.

It is not unusual for an item to exchange hands three or four times at one flea market. Haggling over price is another part of the game and a big part of the fun. Experienced buyers seldom pay the asking price for an item, and experienced sellers rarely expect to get their original price. The art of haggling has become recognized by at least one Tennessee university. Memphis State now offers a course entitled "How to Buy and Sell."

Flea market sellers know that one man's junk is another man's treasure. That is what makes flea markets so much fun to visit.

West Tennessee Shopping

Carrie Haney, Oil paintings

Some folks say she's another Grandma Moses, only better. Carrie Haney has taken up oil painting since her retirement from being a home demonstration agent and home economics teacher. Oil painting is something Carrie always wanted to do. Now the walls are filled with a variety of subjects—flowers, fruit, boats, orientals, birds, and animals. Prices range from $50 to $350. Call for an appointment. Box 33, Decaturville, TN 38329. (901) 852-3382.

Phil Lavely Studio, Paintings

Phil puts on canvas the birds and animals of Tennessee, showing the creatures as they are in their natural habitat. The deer, bald eagles, and racoons practically leap off the painting at you.

Price range: $20 to $2,000.

Directions: Go to Martin and "ask up town for the artist that paints the wildlife of Tennessee." 200 Todd Street, Martin, TN 38237. (901) 587-6107.

Cedar-Oaks, Plantation bells

The plantation bell has always been a symbol of family pride. Like many time-honored traditions, the craft of bronze bell making became virtually extinct in the United States. Small foundries disappeared, and many plantation bells were melted down into cannons during the Civil War. Only a cherished few survived.

Deep in the West Tennessee cotton country, the craft has been reborn. At Cedar-Oaks, the plantation where his family has farmed for more than 100 years, Joe McCraw creates magnificent plantation bells using the same methods developed in colonial times. The bells are each custom designed to bear the name of the family, plantation, or farm commissioning its creation. Each bell is the finest quality bronze and cast as one unit. Cradle mounted, the massive plantation bell with its bronze clapper produces a wonderfully pure sound. One pull of the lanyard conjures up visions of generations past, when the bell would have announced mealtime and brought field hands running.

Whether your "plantation" stretches as far as the eye can see or just reaches the mailbox, a personalized plantation bell will become one of your family's most treasured heirlooms. Cedar-Oaks' custom bells have been shipped all over the United States to individuals, ranches, and churches. Visitors are welcome to watch craftsmen at work. Approximate price range: $225 to $585.

Located 35 miles east of Memphis on US 79. Call for specific directions. Route 2, Box 277, Mason, TN 38049. (901) 594-5300.

Lansky's Department Store, Clothing

One day during the early fifties, owner Bernard Lansky finally invited a young man into his store who was always around with his nose pressed up against the window. Soon Bernard was outfitting America's hottest new singing sensation with everything from stage costumes to street clothes.

Visit Lansky's today and see gobs of Elvis memorabilia. Bernard could write a book of Elvis anecdotes. He says, "Elvis loved pink and black. A few years after he graduated from Humes High, we really fixed him up with an outfit. It was a pink tux, black shirt, black tie, and pink-and-black cummerbund. Elvis was crazy about it." And you'll be crazy not to visit Lansky's while you're in Memphis—Elvis's favorite shopping place. Beale Street, Memphis, TN 38103. (901) 525-1521.

Dan Doty, Dulcimers

Dan and Ethel Doty spend the winter months in their shop preparing for spring craft shows. They work hard to produce a fine musical instrument while holding to traditional styles. Each dulcimer is individually made, numbered, and dated. The Dotys have built over 1,250 dulcimers, and they appear frequently at craft shows throughout Tennessee to perform and to sell their instruments.

Price range: $185 to $450. Album or cassette of dulcimer music containing sixteen songs: *A Show of*

Hands—$7, *Wildwood Flower*—$7. Dulcimer cases—$28 to $55. Call for more information or write for a free catalog/brochure.

Directions: Northeast Memphis in the Raleigh community. 3773 Wychemere, Memphis, TN 38128. (901) 528-4903.

Alice Bingham Gallery, Artwork

The Alice Bingham Gallery specializes in original artwork by Tennessee and regional artists as well as original prints by national and international artists. The gallery is interested in making sure Tennessee art work is seen, appreciated, and purchased not only by Tennesseans but also by people from across the country. Approximate price range: $150 and up. Business hours: Monday–Friday, 10:00 A.M. to 5:00 P.M.; Saturday, 11:00 A.M. to 5:00 P.M.

Directions: Overton Square area in midtown. Overton Square, a tourist attraction in itself, is a group of specialty shops and fine restaurants. Take Broad Street Exit on I-40 West. Turn south on East Parkway; at next light (Poplar Avenue) turn west; at next light (Cooper Street) turn south. Alice Bingham Gallery is near the intersection of Madison Avenue and Cooper. 24 South Cooper, Memphis, TN 38104. (901) 722-8665.

The Woman's Exchange, Hand-crafted items

The Woman's Exchange is an interesting shop where Tennesseans market hand-crafted wares. Senior citizens, handicapped, or the unemployed have items displayed here, including many who might not otherwise have an outlet for their crafts.

They are particularly proud of their quilts, pillows, children's and baby clothes, and heirloom christening dresses.

The motto of The Woman's Exchange is "Helping Others Help Themselves." Do drop by and lend your support. You might even like to have lunch in the tearoom which overlooks an enclosed garden.

Address: 88 Racine Street, Memphis, TN 38111. (901) 327-5681.

Elsie Warmath, Glass painting and woodwork

Elsie is a 65-year-old grandmother who does canvas painting, 3-D art, and glass painting. Her studio is a room in an old house she and her husband lived in when they were first married. Her husband, James, does woodworking and picture framing. Call them for an appointment or more information. Route 4, Box 49A, Milan, TN 38358. (901) 686-8474.

Tanasi Crafts, Tennessee pewter

Tennessee pewter is hand finished in the same manner of America's early pewter craftsmen, so it's easy to care for and safe for everyday use. Specialized gifts, such as a key ring or lapel pin engraved with your company logo, can be tailored to your request.

You are cordially invited to see fine pewter products being made at Tanasi Crafts, the home of Tennessee pewter. If you can't come for a visit, give them a call or write for a free catalogue for more information. Prices range from $3 for a cotton boll key ring to $175 for a pewter coffee service.

Directions: 50 miles east of Memphis on State 57. Located on the square. 35 Charleston Street, Box 37, Moscow, TN 38057. (901) 527-5421.

The Quilt Shoppe, Everything for today's quilter

The only shop of its kind west of the Tennessee River features all supplies needed for quilt making plus the newest quilter's gadgets. Find the area's largest selection of 100 per cent cotton fabrics, quilting notions, books, patterns, and supplies. Beginning to advanced classes are taught on quilting techniques, and the owners will travel anywhere in the state to conduct workshops or judge quilt shows. Tennessee handmade quilts and gift items for sale in the store.

"Quilt-in-a-Day" workshop is for the busy quilter who can't spend months creating a handmade quilt. Vacationers can take home a beautiful Log Cabin Quilt which they complete while visiting Tennessee. Especially for the summer tourist season are one-day or half-day classes in quilting techniques. You "fishing widows" send that husband out on the lake and come on in!

Price range: $25 crib-size quilt, $85 to $650 for large quilts (most quilts in the $200 to $400 range).

Business hours: 10:00 A.M. to 5:00 P.M., Monday–Saturday.

Directions: US 79E (the highway to Paris Landing State Park) directly across from the Avalon Restaurant and one block from the new Best Western Motel. 1316 East Wood Street, Paris, TN 38242. (901) 642-2741.

Anderson Fruit Farms, Fruit and cider

Since 1939 Tennessee's largest orchard and only commercial cider mill in the state has continued to provide high-quality fruits for local residents and tourists from many states. Produce prices range from $1.00 to $14.00. Also known as Cloverport, the farm is approximately 15 miles south of I-40 on highway 138. (901) 658-5524.

Anderson fruit farms also operate roadside markets year round in both Whiteville and Jackson, featuring fresh fruits, homemade apple cider, country ham, all-natural jams, jellies, preserves, and assorted gift items.

The Whiteville Market, nestled in a portion of the orchard, has been in operation for 40 years. Pumpkins, damson plums, pure honey, sorghum molasses, and assorted relishes and butters are market favorites. Citrus fruit from the Rio Grande Valley is usually available in November and December. Take Highway 64 West. (901) 254-9530.

At the Jackson Market, you will find all the same delicious items as at the Whiteville market plus a large assortment of fruit baskets, a full line of produce year round, a commercial pea-sheller, and a remarkable talking pig. Highway 45 South, open 8:00 A.M. till 6:00 P.M., Monday to Saturday. Open Sunday, 1:00 to 6:00 P.M. (901) 422-2388.

Dixie Gun Works, Inc., Muzzleloaders

Sharon Cunningham tells us that Dixie Gun Works, Inc., is the "Muzzleloading Mecca." Haven for thousands of blackpowder shooting enthusiasts throughout the world, Dixie Gun Works was begun as a hobby by owner/founder, Turner E. Kirkland, in 1954. Since that time, the hobby has become a multimillion dollar corporation on the southern edge of Union City, and it provides jobs for 35 full-time employees.

The bulk of Dixie's business is from mail orders of muzzleloading guns, supplies, and related equipment. The in-house publishing division of Dixie, Pioneer Press, issues a 500-plus page catalogue which is sold to blackpowder shooters throughout the world at a modest price of $3 (postpaid). Dixie Wholesale Services supplies small blackpowder dealers with the merchandise made famous by the parent company. There is also an in-house advertising agency and an antique arms division.

Dixie Gun Works welcomes visitors to its large showroom. Business hours are 8:00 A.M. to 5:00 P.M. daily and 8:00 A.M. to 12:00 noon on Saturday. An Old Car Museum (one of Turner's forays into another area of collecting old things) charges a small admission. The collection of Ford automobiles ranges from 1908 to 1942 and also includes a 1912 Cadillac which will knock your eyes out! Just purchased, and now being restored, is a 1924 Marmon once owned by Roger Motlow, son of Lem Motlow of Jack Daniels Distillery fame.

Dixie is located on US 51 South. Go by to see them—they like visitors! P. O. Box 130, Highway 51 South, Union City, TN 38261. (901) 885-0561—information; (800) 238-6785—orders only.

Crafts

We think Tennesseans produce the finest crafts in the world. Of course we're prejudiced—but right, nonetheless. Tennessee artisans use their talents to produce the heirlooms of tomorrow and take great pride in a job well done. Come along with the *Sampler* as you experience our "Insider's Shopping Guide," and be awed, as we have been, by the incredible talents so alive in Tennessee.

A SAMPLER FEATURE

Alex Stewart

Portrait of a Pioneer

■ *John Rice Irwin, founder of the Museum of Appalachia and author of several books on mountain crafts, has conducted interviews over the years with a remarkable man, Alex Stewart. As their friendship grew, so did John Rice's appreciation of Alex not only as a craftsman but also as a man who had totally mastered the way of life the mountains demanded. The Sampler is honored to*

Dixie Gunworks

share some excerpts from John Rice's tribute to those years of friendship, Alex Stewart: Portrait of a Pioneer.

I found Alex Stewart at his sawmill near his home on Panther Creek. Our first meeting a quarter-century ago, could hardly be characterized as dramatic. I remember a little man with overalls too big for him, a well-worn hat, and a pipe full of homemade tobacco that smelled even stronger than it looked. I recall the quick, jovial manner in which he responded to all my questions, but my unrestrained admiration and esteem for him came later—slowly at first, but growing as a thousand remarkable facets of his life unfolded.

After our friendship had grown closer over the years, I thought of that first meeting, and I wondered what had gone through Alex's mind on that occasion. "Well, at first I didn't know what you was up to. But I soon learned what you was interested in. And now I'm awful proud we got acquainted."

What I most remember about that meeting was his response to my question about making a piggin. I remember his amused laugh. "Why, son, I've been out of that business for 40 years. These here store-bought buckets, plastic containers and such, put me out of commission. Anyhow I don't have no timber. It takes good cedar timber to make vessels, and they's not much left. If I had some timber, I'd shore make you anything you wanted."

It wasn't long until I found some large, straight-grained cedars which I cut and took to Alex. He examined them carefully, making some cautiously optimistic comments relative to their quality but pointing out that "a body don't know how timber will work till he splits it open and examines it." Then he threw in a little philosophy, the likes of which I was to hear so often as we spent more time together.

"Timber is just like people. They's all kinds of people in this world, and they's all kinds of timber. They are more alike than anything I've thought about in my life, timber and people. You can go out here in the woods and find you the purtiest-looking tree. You cut it down, and when you get inside, you may find rotten places and dotty places and it's no account. Then you can get an old knotty, scrubby-looking tree, and it'll make the best lumber ever you seen. And that's just the way of people too. I've thought a lot about that. It's a purty good lesson if you just look into it."

After his parable, Alex went on to say that he'd see what he could do with the timber I'd brought. People tend to exaggerate their capabilities and talents, and even if they are capable of performing at the level that they claim, they often just never get around to doing it. I fully expected that the pile of cedar logs would still be lying there undisturbed when I returned three weeks later, but I was mistaken. There wasn't a log in sight.

It was noontime, and Alex was just finishing a sumptuous meal. Both he and Margie, his wife, insisted I eat. This was the first of many great meals I was to enjoy there. Nothing was said about the cedar, and after we had finished eating, we retired to the front porch. Looking back, I now know that Alex was as anxious as a child that I ask him about the cedar. But he talked about the weather, the hateful sweat bees, and the crops that needed rain. His self-imposed protocol forbade him from bringing up the subject of the cedar, and I'm convinced he would have let me leave without mentioning it. I finally did ask about the timber in as casual a manner as I could, for I didn't want to embarrass him in the event he hadn't made anything.

"Well," he said, obviously delighted that the question had finally been raised, "I've done a little something or other." He called for Mutt, his middle-aged son who lived with him. "Here, Mutt, help me set these vessels out." Alex led us back into the house and into a room filled, or so it seemed, with churns, buckets, tubs, and piggins that I had ever seen. Every stave in every item had been split, planed, and precisely beveled. Every white-oak band had been fashioned so that it fitted perfectly the curvature of its container. *A year's work,* I thought, *and yet this fragile little man had done all this in three weeks.*

This was only the first of hundreds of feats that were to impress and amaze me and, as Alex's fame grew, to amaze people throughout the country as well. We carried all these pieces into the front yard and took the photograph of Alex and his work, shown here.

I don't want to portray Alex as merely a remarkable craftsman, for he is much more than that. *National Geographic* featured him on the cover of their book, *Craftsmen of the World,* and he was indeed deserving of that honor, but this and similar publicity have emphasized this one aspect of him while neglecting the other facets of his life. Characterizing Alex Stewart as merely a craftsman is a little like characterizing Thomas Jefferson as merely a farmer.

Alex Stewart
Photo by John Rice Erwin

Alex Stewart, 94, died April 15, 1985. This section on East Tennessee craftsmen is dedicated to this gifted and remarkable Tennessean.

East Tennessee Crafts

Quilts and Wallhangings

Bets Ramsey, Quilt documentation

Bets has a wonderful goal. In her special work with quilts, she strives to give recognition to the anonymous women in history who were artists in their own right but were not recognized in their own time.

In 1971 at the University of Tennessee in Knoxville, Bets did some graduate research in a class, "Crafts in America." As part of this research, she interviewed two of her aunts to find out information about her own family, specifically her great-grandmother, whom she had never known. Through the stories told by the aunts and through examining her great-grandmother's quilts, Bets, in a sense, grew to know and love her great-grandmother who had died in 1907. She was fascinated by the precise workmanship, the eye for design, and the fact that even everyday quilts were not "scrimpy" or dull but exhibited the same lovely workmanship as the "company" quilts. This idea of researching your roots through examining quilts was one Bets knew she wanted others to experience.

Now almost 15 years later, Bets and Merikay Waldvogel document quilts. Certain dates and times are set up across the state at various museums or universities, and quilt owners bring in their quilts made before 1930 for Bets and Merikay to examine. Collected data goes into the quilt survey they are doing, and all records will be available at a later time, if people are interested in genealogical research. Individual quilt owners are able to obtain copies of their documentation and a photograph of their quilt for $5.

Bets offers some valuable tips on the care and preservation of old and new quilts:

Do use quilts. Even old ones used sparingly will resist creases. Air quilts occasionally. Wash, if in good condition, but be careful! When storing, wrap in old sheets or undyed towels. Prewash all material before making a quilt to remove sizing.

Don't put quilts away for a long period of time or fold the same way each time. Don't store quilts in tissue paper (unless it is special acid-free paper) or plastic bags. Plastic locks in moisture, and quilts need to breathe. Don't store quilts in cardboard boxes or in contact with wood.

For more information, send a self-addressed stamped envelope to Bets at 322 Pine Ridge Road, Box 4146, Chattanooga, TN 37405. (615) 265-4300.

Betty Fain, Quilts

Betty made her first quilt 26 years ago when she was expecting her daughter. It was such a long, drawn-out process, she decided she wanted no part of that craft. But 20 years later, that daughter wanted a quilt for a wedding present. So Betty gave it one more try. This time she caught the fever and has been quilting ever since, using both traditional and original designs. Route 5, Cline Road, Dandridge, TN 37725. (615) 397-2833.

Lora M. Creasman, Wallhangings

Lora says: "I have lived on a farm for many years. In this lovely section of East Tennessee every day is a joy. I see the mountains in their shades of blue to purple, and I see the river and the sky in all the azure shades. I cut pieces of fabric and try to match the colors. I use abstract designs and name them. I also write a very short poem about each one and hide a cotton boll somewhere on each wallhanging as my trademark. It is so much fun for me that I laugh and say I would pay people to buy my wallhangings! But, fortunately when I finish one, there is usually someone waiting to buy it."

Address: Route 1, Delano, TN 37325. (615) 338-5282.

Polly Taylor, Statewide quilt reference booklet

Polly has compiled a helpful booklet, *A Directory of Tennessee Quilters,* which lists Tennessee quilt makers and those who teach quilting or hold seminars and workshops on various aspects of quilting. Special sections include addresses of quilt makers listed by Tennessee counties, a chapter on special quilting services and interests, and a section on areas of quilting specialization.

A Directory of Tennessee Quilters is well worth $5 (includes tax and postage) for quilters and quilt lovers alike. Write or call Polly for your copy today or for more information about her quilting seminar held at East Tennessee State University in July.

Address: Route 1, Box 294-A, Watauga, TN 37694. (615) 929-4333 or (615) 542-5907.

Woodcrafts

Sculpture in Wood, Woodcarvings

Of his woodworking cottage and home, Jess Betschart says, "My wife and I built the cottage with no power tools except a chain saw and financed our project by what money we would have used for recreation—I might add it was very little. It was a five-year commitment."

Jess's primitive but elegant woodcarvings inside the cottage attest to the magnitude of his talent. Most of his work has to do with Indian culture or animals, and it is rapidly becoming known in many regions of the South. Prices: Small woodcarvings, $10 or less; finer and more complicated ones, $10 to $300. Commissioned carvings done on request. Hours: Monday–Saturday, 8:00 A.M. to 6:00 P.M. Directions: From I-24 take Exit 134. Located 1 mile down US 41N. P. O. Box 113, Monteagle, TN 37356. (615) 924-2970.

Rick and Reneé Stewart, Coopering and woodcarving

Rick and Reneé are carrying on family traditions. Rick is a fifth-generation cooper, and Reneé is a woodcarver.

They were taught by their famous grandfather, the late Alex Stewart of Sneedville. Rick was apprenticed to Alex for one year to learn the trade of coopering. Reneé was never apprenticed; she just seemed to have an innate ability at woodcarving, and she specializes in the carving of animals.

Rick says: "I have been carrying on the coopering tradition in my family for the last nine years. This craft was brought over to this country by my forefathers from Scotland who settled in the mountains of East Tennessee because of the vast supply of cedar from which they liked to construct their vessels."

Coopering means making wooden vessels capable of holding liquid. These wooden items were the bare essentials of everyday life in the Appalachians many years ago. The cooper was as common and as needed as the shopping malls of today. Some of the items he made were buckets, churns, tubs, and piggins.

Alex once said, "If you haven't got patience and can't control your temper, you don't work with wood. I've only been able to teach four people to do what I do." And surely Rick and Reneé are two of the four. Reneé says: "I have been carving for six years. I enjoy this craft thoroughly, and I am pleased that I was fortunate enough to have a grandfather to pass it down to me as mine did. He was truly an extraordinary person. He told me that when he was a child there were no toys to play with, so people had to carve out their toys. This is why he took up carving. I do carvings of almost any animal on foot or hoof. My favorites are horses, bears, and coon dogs treeing a racoon in a tree. The coon and dogs was one of my grandfather's favorites, and he did these with pride—combining a craft with everyday life. At one time he was a hunter as well as a craftsman. He loved his coon dogs."

Rick and Reneé have sold their crafts to people in every state and to some famous folks like Alex Haley and Brooke Shields. Rick constructs his vessels with care and patience, and Reneé carves her animals with the same Stewart diligence and perfection. The vessels that Rick constructs are made completely of wood; he uses no glue or nails. Recently his churn was selected by the Tennessee Arts Commission and the National Folk Art Committee to represent the state of Tennessee in their national headquarters and leadership center at Reston, Virginia. Rick and Reneé make each item as if it were to be used or admired, much as each generation has in the past. The talent of Alex Stewart lives on in the hands of his grandchildren.

Rick's prices range from $18 to $200 and Reneé's range from $5 to $50. The shop is open Monday through Friday from 8:30 A.M. to 4:00 P.M. and sometimes on Saturday.

Directions: The shop is located 6 miles east of Sneedville on Panther Creek Road, beside a sawmill on the right side of the road. When you get to Sneedville, go past the second traffic light and turn at Tommy's Texaco. Ask the service station attendant if you need further directions. Rick's address is Route 2, Box 328, Sneedville, TN 37869; (615) 733-4214. The shop's address is the same as Reneé's: Route 1, Box 101, Sneedville; (615) 733-2617.

A SAMPLER FEATURE

The Museum of Appalachia

■When Tennessee's early settlers arrived in the coves and hollows of the wilderness on the western side of the Appalachian Mountains, they brought with them an incredible ingenuity, a remarkable resourcefulness, and a rare talent for survival—qualities vividly demonstrated at Norris (16 miles north of Knoxville) in the unique Museum of Appalachia. The museum's 70 acres contain a collection of 30 authentic log cabins and buildings ranging from the Arnwine Cabin, a one-room cabin built around 1800, to the McClung Home, a comparatively elegant dogtrot cabin from the 1850s. The cabins and other buildings form a village representative of the region during the first half of the nineteenth century. But the Museum of Appalachia is far more than just a collection of old log buildings.

John Rice Irwin's fanatical attention to detail and authenticity gives the museum its charm and character. He once refused to open a new cabin for a year and a half because he did not have the right kind of wooden hinges to put on it. Adding to the authenticity is the ax imbedded in a stump surrounded by piles of kindling. A foot-operated lathe using a springy sapling as an ingenious power source holds a nearly completed table leg. A half-finished wagon wheel is in the wheelwright's shop. The church stands ready for a Sunday service. Chickens peck busily around kitchen herb gardens. Roosters crow, turkeys gobble, and peacocks scream for attention. Fields of corn, squash, beans, and tomatoes simmer in the sun behind split-rail fences. It is as if the residents of the village had simply stepped into the woods for a moment.

"People see the plates of dried beans and peppers, the churns and kitchen utensils all ready for use, and they ask, 'Is someone still living here?' It's the best compliment I can receive," says John Rice.

"Around 1962 two events occurred which were responsible for the beginning of the Museum of Appalachia. The first came as a result of my visit to the old home place of my paternal Irwin grandparents, both of whom had passed on by that time. My Uncle Morrel was making plans to tear down the old house, and many of the heirlooms had been stored in a log smokehouse. Someone had rummaged through these old relics and had removed many items from the building into a full exposure to the elements.

"I instantly recognized many items and could even remember their locations in Granny's big house. They had been so important and so aesthetically appropriate when they had been in Granny's kitchen or her parlor or in the upstairs bedroom. But now, they seemed so meaningless and forlorn.

"The second event took place in the fall of 1962. I

Museum of Appalachia

went to an auction of the old Miller estate, which was located on the Clinch River near my home in Norris. I beheld a sight I remember vividly to this day. The treasures from several generations of the Miller family had been carried from the old two-story home, the smokehouse, corn crib, and the barn. Ox yokes were piled next to old spinning wheels and bread trays. An old cedar churn was being sold to a couple from Hammond, Indiana. I overheard the wife say they were going to shellac it, 'electrify' it, and make it into a lamp. An old wagon seat was going to have legs attached and be made into a coffee table. A 200-year-old cupboard was bought by an antique dealer from Knoxville.

"I thought, *How terrible! These items are a part of our heritage and culture, but only if the history and object remain connected. Once an object is separated from its history, its meaning and significance are greatly diminished.* So I started bidding. I bought many of the items and carefully recorded their history. Then I started attending other auctions; but mostly I started making journeys into rural and isolated areas and into the mountains, buying almost anything I could find and afford. I would buy a few items at a time or a truck load.

"My garage was soon filled. Then I bought and rebuilt the General Bunch cabin, furnishing it to the last meticulous detail. Collecting became sort of an obsession, an obsession that eventually evolved into the Museum of Appalachia. But even through establishing the museum, I can never come close to doing for southern Appalachia's charming and unprententious people what they have done for me."

John Rice is too modest, because he has done much for the mountain people around him. The store at the museum houses many craft items made thereabouts which are for sale at reasonable prices. And they are all in one location. The Museum of Appalachia is a great place to discover mountain crafts. John Rice is a recognized authority on these craftsmen, and he's always ready to answer questions.

The Museum of Appalachia, Box 359, Norris, TN. (615) 494-7680.

Baskets

Webb Weavers, Baskets

Roy and Mary Webb gather wild grapevines for basket frames, dye reed from fiber and fabric dyes, and then weave away. Each basket is signed and dated, thus becoming an heirloom to be handed down to a future generation. Special orders are welcome. Prices range from $35 up. Call for more information. 864 Snoderly Court, Alcoa, TN 37701. (615) 982-0836.

Mary Street, Baskets

All kinds of baskets are available, from berry baskets to doll cradles, woven the traditional mountain way. Prices: $5 to $25. Call for an appointment. Route 2, Box 714A, Blountville, TN 37617. (615) 323-4635.

Coker Creek Crafts and Handweavers, Baskets and weaving

"It's not easy making a living on the mountain, but it's worth it," says Kathleen Dalton. The Daltons' materials and methods for making white oak split baskets follow the old traditions. They use only hand tools. They find a suitable white oak tree and cut it into small sections, which they divide with a knife into splints. Then they hand pull, scrape, and cut the splints to proper size for weaving. Their baskets are displayed in places far off the mountain—the White House, Tokyo, and the

Smithsonian. Kathleen also fashions hand-woven place mats, napkins, table runners, and rag rugs made to order. A special service to mail-order customers is gift wrapping and direct mail. Write for a free brochure. Average prices: $10 to $100. Hours: Monday through Friday, 8:00 A.M. to 4:30 P.M.

Directions: State 68S at I-75 in Sweetwater. P. O. Box 95, Coker Creek, TN 37314. (615) 261-2157.

Dorothy L. Basista, Baskets

Dorothy's baskets are *not* just ordinary baskets. They are decorative and useful too. She makes the handle and frames from wild grapevine and then weaves in reeds. She uses natural dyes from blackberries, pokeberries, onion skins, and tomato plants, and she also mixes colors to get a good variety.

Dot travels a lot on the craft fair circuit, and last year her baskets were named Best of the Show at the Appalachian Festival in Cincinnati and Best of Craft in the Jackson Arts Council Spring Fling. Prices are $89 to $445. Write Dorothy about her baskets. 107 Hudson Drive, Maryville, TN 37801.

Earth Sculptures Basketry, Baskets

Nancy Braski is a native Tennessean. Her ancestors came from Switzerland and lived in the small, rural community of Belvidere in Franklin County. Nancy says: "When I was a child, I would play in the fence rows, underneath the honeysuckle undergrowth, and around mossy knolls. When I went to college and majored in fiber design, my thoughts immediately returned to my ancestry and my childhood. My ancestors must have woven baskets to have containers to gather things in. I wanted to weave baskets too! So I began to teach myself, from that moment. I gathered some weeping willow withes and began.

"Since my father claimed to have Indian heritage, I imagined myself a squaw, sitting along the water's edge, weaving a container in which to gather herbs and berries. Now I often sit at the edge of Watts Bar Lake and do just that! There is something magic about soaking the natural material in the lake water. I use kudzu vine, wisteria, wild grapevines, honeysuckle, crossvines, many grasses, and even morning glory vines, iris, and daylily leaves. I achieve texture and color by the adding of wild onions and barks and by leaving the roots and knots on the vines. My sculptural forms begin at $10 and go from there, according to design. Please call for an appointment."

Address: 102 Willow Lane, Oak Ridge, TN 37830. (615) 482-2718.

Beryl Omega Lumpkins, Baskets

Beryl makes baskets from mountain materials and uses only natural mountain dyes. She uses pioneer and Indian designs and weaving methods. Beryl conducts many lectures and workshops on basket making, and she has just published *From Vines to Vessels,* a guide for identifying, gathering, and preparing vines. Price range: $30 to $200. Call for more information. 9820 Bluegrass Road, Knoxville, TN 37922. (615) 690-4461.

A SAMPLER FEATURE

Castle in the Clouds Rug Hooking

■The art of colonial rug hooking is revived each year during the first week in June at the picturesque Castle in the Clouds at Covenant College. Ramona Maddox, president of the local chapter of the National Guild of Pearl K. McGown Rug HooKrafters', Inc., says: "We meet for a week of work and rug hooking—work meaning the joy of working together on the rug of our choice. The method is the same as in the colonial days. We have a workshop on teaching methods of dyeing and hooking, and we teach beginners and those who have enjoyed the craft for years through a one-on-one teaching program.

Many guests stay at the old Castle in the Clouds Inn and enjoy delicious meals from the college cafeteria. Husbands may golf or sightsee while wives are in class.

What is it that draws someone into this relatively unknown art form? For John Young, a 71-year-old stroke victim, it was therapy. Even though his arm and hand movements were impaired, through diligence and the help of Ramona Maddox, his rug was finished and featured in a display at the Chattanooga Choo-Choo in the fall of 1984. He's working on another one now. Others want quality craftsmanship steeped in history and don't mind spending a week learning how to achieve it, even though a finished product may take two, three, or even four years to finish. Sound impossible? Not so, say true hookcraft enthusiasts.

Historians say that rug hooking is the most American form of needlework since most other forms of needlework originated in other countries. But our primitive American craft almost slipped through the pages of history.

It wasn't until the gloom of the Depression years that Pearl K. McGown revived childhood memories of rug hooking. Although her interest began as a hobby, soon her original designs were so popular that a business was started. Many rewarding years followed—years spent designing rug patterns, training teachers, holding seminars, and writing four books. Mrs. McGown died in 1982 at 91 years of age, leaving Jane McGown Flynn, a granddaughter, in charge of the business.

Come and join in a week of fun, work, and relaxation at the Castle in the Clouds. Create a bit of history that will hook the next generation to yours. Castle in the Clouds Rug Hooking Creations, Covenant College, Lookout Mountain, Chattanooga, TN 37421. (615) 892-1858.

Castle in the Clouds rug hooking

Craft Centers, Malls, and Shops

Afton Crafts and Flea Market, Crafts and flea market

At this shopping place yesterday meets today to provide the gift of tomorrow. Find antiques, dolls, stuffed animals, and handmade wooden items. Be sure to visit the outside flea market for real bargains in toys, tools, truck parts, and all size wooden handles. Price range: $50 to $1,000. Open Friday, Saturday, and Sunday, 9:00 A.M. to 6:00 P.M.

Directions: 2½ miles northeast of Greeneville on US 11E By-pass. Box 42, Route 1, Afton, TN 37616. (615) 639-3092.

Laurel Gap Handicrafts, Various crafts

All items handmade by local people, many items unique to East Tennessee. Special orders for quilts, pillows, wallhangings, and more. Prices from $1 to $500. Open 9:00 A.M. to 4:30 P.M., Monday through Friday.

Directions: Take Exit 36 off I-81, then Baileyton Road North. Pass front of Davy Crockett Truckstop and 36 Motel, then look for Village Green sign. Route 11, Village Green in Baileyton, Greeneville, TN 37743. (615) 234-0344.

The Exchange Place, Farm and craft center

The Exchange Place is a restored nineteenth-century farm and craft center, but it once served as a facility for exchanging horses and Virginia currency for Tennessee currency. Buy quality, traditional Tennessee crafts, and enjoy demonstrations, entertainment, and good food. Open weekends, May–October. Free admission. 4812 Orebank Road, Kingsport, TN 37664. (615) 288-6071.

Rose Center, Art and community center

The Rose Center was built in 1892 as Morristown's first public school. In 1910 it was named to honor Civil War hero Judge James G. Rose. Now the Rose center is a community gathering place for exhibits, classes, arts activities, community groups, festivals, and performances. In the front corner room of the main floor, the Rose Garden Gift Shop displays quality arts and crafts. Free admission. Located two blocks north of Morristown. 442 West Second North Street, Box 1976, Morristown, TN 37814. (615) 581-4330.

Barbara J. Briggs, Cornshuck Dolls

Barbara says: "My two daughters and I are carefully handcrafting our 'angel band' dolls. Created in the foothills of the Smoky Mountains, my dolls are lovingly made, using only corn husks and corn silks and accented with dried flowers. No two are alike. Each one, hand-crafted in the tradition of bygone days, bears its own stamp of individuality.

"Some have traveled overseas, and many are in gift shops and galleries. Governor and Mrs. Lamar Alexander have one of our tree-top angels. It is my sincere wish that angel band dolls will put a song in your heart for years to come.

"Our shop is housed in the original smokehouse of the County Line Farm—a very special complex of the Attic Restaurant (see "Eatin' Good") and individual shops at Talbot. Friends of mine have placed some beautiful work here. We have pottery, wooden rocking horses and cradles, dried flower pictures, original art and limited edition prints, baskets, needlecrafts, and, of course, my angel band dolls. Y'all come see us!"

Prices on dolls range from $8 to $25. Open 10:00 A.M. to 5:00 P.M., Monday–Saturday.

Directions: From Knoxville, take I-40E. Exit at Jefferson City and take State 92 to Jefferson City. Turn right at the traffic light. Travel US 11E approximately 4 miles to the Attic and the craft shops. Route 2, Box 420 A, New Market, TN 37820. (615) 475-7187.

Greenwich Village Mall, Craft mall

This mall is a frequent stop for tourists visiting the American Museum of Science and Energy and the Children's Museum (see "Tours and Trails" for more information). This little village is composed of nine craftsmen's studio shops along an angular hallway that pleasantly disguises what was formerly a bowling alley in the 1940s. Tuesday through Saturday afternoons artists are busy working on their crafts but are always happy to stop and chat. Prices range from 60¢ for ceramic napkin holders to $700 or more for commissioned handmade quilts. Crafts include jewelry, weaving, stained glass, and dulcimers. The mall is open Monday–Saturday with individual shop hours varying somewhat. 109 Towne Road, Jackson Square, Oak Ridge, TN 37830. (615) 483-9115.

The Cats' Paw Pottery, Pottery

Amazing to see one-of-a-kind porcelain pots with zinc silicate crystalline glazes. Prices range from $15 to $60, depending on size of pot. See items on display at the Arrowcraft Shop in Gatlinburg or The Tree House (Proffitt's Department Store), downtown shopping center in Oak Ridge, or contact Frances Weeren: 909 West Outer Drive, Oak Ridge, TN 37830; (615) 483-6639.

The Uncommon Market, Craft shop

This shop is dedicated to promoting East Tennessee craftspeople. It features the finest in available crafts and is always searching for more interesting items to offer the public. Owners Leigh Ann Koksal and Sallie Hurt welcome dealer inquiries that would bring these crafts to other locations of the United States. Without a ready market for their crafts, many fine craftspeople would have to turn to other jobs for their livelihood. This shop/showroom caters to both retail and wholesale trade. Price range: $1 to $500. Open 10:00 A.M. to 8:00 P.M., Monday–Saturday; Sunday by appointment.

Directions: On the main highway into Pigeon Forge, next to Holiday Inn. 413 Parkway C-I, Holiday Shopping Plaza, Pigeon Forge, TN 37863. (615) 453-1118.

A SAMPLER FEATURE

Arrowmont School of Arts and Crafts

■ Set apart from the sounds and bustling activity of the thriving tourist community of Gatlinburg, the Arrowmont School of Arts and Crafts is situated on 70 acres of unspoiled hillside land adjacent to the Great Smoky Mountains National Park. The atmosphere of creativity and visual stimulation provides an unending source of energy for those who attend. Men and women of all ability levels, all ages, practical backgrounds, and educational attainment attend this nationally recognized visual arts school for year-round one- and two-week sessions, special conferences, and weekend workshops. People gather from all parts of the United States as well as foreign countries to study with prominent artists and craftspeople, perfect their artistic skills and aesthetic understandings, and exchange ideas and points of view. Students may elect to receive graduate or undergraduate credit, or they may audit courses in clay, enamel, fiber, fabric, metal, photography, stained glass, paper, graphics, painting, drawing, leather, and bookbinding.

The Arrowmont Gallery provides monthly changes of juried, invitational, theme- or media-oriented feature exhibitions. Objects by faculty and students that are part of the permanent collection are displayed in the Atrium Gallery and throughout the Arrowmont buildings. Arrowmont School of Arts and Crafts receives financial support from the Pi Beta Phi Fraternity in addition to private and corporate funding. Accreditation is received through the University of Tennessee-Knoxville, College of Liberal Arts, Department of Art.

Write: Arrowmont School of Arts and Crafts, P. O. Box 567, Gatlinburg, TN 37738. (615) 436-5860.

Craft Potpourri

Ruth Miller, Various Crafts

Ruth is the person you need to call to fix up that one-of-a-kind shower or wedding gifts. For example, a crocheted bedspread is $400; afghan, $50 to $80; tablecloth set, $1 to $20; placemat set, $11 to $20; bun warmer set, $10; candlewick pillow, $25; or three sizes of hand-woven baskets, $15 to $22. Forget the stress of shopping and call Ruth. 2628 Broad Street, Bristol, TN 37620. (615) 764-5272.

Stitch and Frame Place, Counted cross-stitch/candlewicking

Visit the Stitch and Frame Place in the heart of historic downtown Elizabethton, a half-block from the famous Covered Bridge built in 1882. See counted cross-stitch and candlewicking samples of nearly 2,000 books and charts on various subjects. Special favorites are "The Four Seasons of the Covered Bridge" and "Rhododendron Gardens of Roan Mountain." Be sure to ask owners Ruth or Bill Ziletti about other local places to visit. 619 East Elk Avenue, Elizabethton, TN 37643. (615) 543-4115.

Jonesborough Art Glass, Stained glass

Stephen and Tava Cook specialize in the design and construction of custom stained-glass lamps and windows. Their work has been displayed nationally as well as abroad, featured in many East and Middle Tennessee newspapers, and has won several Best of Show awards. Prices: Suncatcher and ornaments—$6 to $50; lamps and window prices vary with the design. Open 10:00 A.M. to 5:00 P.M. daily. Sunday by appointment. 101 East Main Street, Jonesborough, TN 37659. (615) 753-5401.

Bev's Bears, Teddy bears

When the price of antique teddy bears got too high, Beverly Lyons decided to make her own. Through trial and error, Beverly made her own patterns and experimented with ways to articulate the head, arms, and legs. She scoured flea markets and antique shops, searching for old furry coats, antique coverlets, glass beads for eyes, and old lace for collars. The results—lovable, furry little creatures, some with bow ties and jackets, sure to please that special person on your gift list. Price: $20 to $100. Put in your order today. Beverly also sells from The Exchange Place in Kingsport. 1814 Ft. Robinson Drive, Kingsport, TN 37660. (615) 247-8316.

Jessie and Betty Rushing, Farm/crafts

Take the family to visit Jessie and Betty and their two daughters, Amy and Sarah. Their Valleyview Farm is located on a scenic rural valley on State 58 east of the Tennessee River in Roane County. They have sheep, berries, fruits, and vegetables for sale. While you're there, see some of the lovely craft items the family makes—wreaths, hats, and baskets, decorated with dried herbs, plants, and flowers. A great way to spend an afternoon.

Directions: 6½ miles south of Kingston on west side of State 58. Call if you need more information. Route 1, Box 168, Kingston, TN 37763. (615) 376-2923.

Middle Tennessee Crafts

Dolls and Teddy Bears

June and Bob Beckett, The Deer Lodge Doll Makers

In the world of doll making, wooden dolls are a rarity because doll makers have traditionally relied on porcelain, ceramics, and modern plastics. June says, "As wood carvers, we are bringing the elements of nature to doll making. We love the feel of wood—it's the inspiration that causes us to enjoy our art. We also love to study children, who are the basis for our sculpture."

"We carve the hair on some models and also the

toes if we do not carve or dress them in shoes," remarks Bob. The dolls are carved and labeled as 'continuing series,' 'limited series,' or 'one of a kind.' Some have soft bodies with carved heads and limbs, and others are made completely of wood. When wigs are not used, the hairdos are carved in pageboys, ponytails, and other styles typical of small children.

Each Beckett original is copyrighted, signed, and dated. Each doll is dressed, and the outfit is tagged with the Beckett label. Although most are part of a named series, each doll is slightly different since its own distinct personality emerges during carving.

June and Bob Beckett have also developed a line of teddy bears. June's bears look like antiques, thanks to materials salvaged from old coats and blankets. "Teddy bears seemed like the perfect companions for our dolls," June says. "I especially like to use the small ones as toys for our 'Kinnygarten Angel' dolls."

Price range: $100 to $400. Call for an appointment. Closed on Saturdays. Box 127, Deer Lodge, TN 37726. (615) 863-3506.

Just Bearly, Old-fashioned teddies

Karen Hargrove says: "I make antique-style, fully jointed teddy bears, with an old-fashioned hump on their shoulders and locked-in, shoe-button eyes. They are dressed differently, according to what they like to wear or what a customer would like—from a Halloween bear with mask and ruff to a bear with a cross and Roman collar, which I made for a friend who is a priest. My bears range in size from 8 inches to almost 22 inches and in price from $30 to $75. They come in natural bear colors. I work at home in Christiana, a small community which grew up around a railroad depot constructed in 1882."

Call to make an appointment or to order. P.O. Box 840, Murfreesboro, TN 37130. (615) 890-0314.

Pea Ridge Purties, Traditional dolls and quilts

You must meet Belle, Miss Alma, Annie, and Wally Bear. They are all part of a unique collection of traditional fabric dolls, made from fabrics aged with natural dyes to make them appear well used and extra charming. See also the Pea Ridge Quilt, a watermelon basket, and taste-tempting primitive watermelon slices...wooden, of course. Pea Ridge items are sold in craft shops, antique shops, and various stores throughout the country specializing in Americana. Prices range from $21 for the smallest doll to $500 for large quilts. Catalogues available for $1.

Directions: Corner of Cherry and Adams Streets in Fayetteville, TN 37334. (615) 433-6084.

Olivia Derryberry, Dolls/doll quilts

Olivia says: "I think my soft-sculpture baby dolls have a cuter face than some dolls you can buy these days. I may get into trouble with kids for thinking that, but my dolls are very cute, soft, and cuddly. I also design doll quilts which are personalized for a specific child. I made the quilt for my four-year-old niece out of scraps of material that have a special meaning to her—a piece of her baby blanket, pictures of Raggedy Ann, Care Bears, Merry-Go-Round." Prices: Dolls—$25: quilts—$20. Call for an appointment. Route 1, Box 188, Spring Hill, TN 37174. (615) 486-2580.

Martha Hutton, Corn shuck dolls

These dolls are handcrafted from the husks and silks of dried corn and can be seen at the Westbrooks Country Store at Cannonsburgh Pioneer Village in Murfrees-boro. See Martha and her friend Darlene Gray demonstrate how to make the dolls at the village, the last Saturday in April and September. Prices start at $2. Call Martha for more information. Route 1, Box 146, Ready-ville, TN 37149. (615) 563-2772.

Quilts

Joyce Hailey, Quilts

Joyce does quilting in her spare time. She especially enjoys making baby quilts. Give her a call and go see the beauty of her work. Prices: Baby quilts, around $25; queen-size quilts, around $125. 4724 Arapaho Bend, Antioch, TN 37013. (615) 834-2751.

Quilter's Haven, Quilts, quilt supplies, quilting instruction

About a mile from Bell Buckle lies the beautiful farm of Edgar and Mildred Locke. There you'll find Quilter's Haven, your one-stop shopping place for anything having to do with quilts. They carry a large variety of 100 per cent cotton calico and solid color material, hundreds of books, patterns, stencils, hoops, batting, notions, and many handmade gift items. Also, they offer beginner, intermediate, and advanced classes in quilt making. Mildred is widely recognized as a leading quilt authority and travels all over the United States lecturing and conducting workshops.

Quilter's Haven has a beautiful array of quilts for sale. They carry patchwork, applique, and whole cloth quilts, but specialize in the Log Cabin pattern. These quilts are heirlooms that can be handed down from generation to generation and are an investment that will appreciate in value as time goes by.

Address: Wartrace Road, Bell Buckle, TN 37020. (615) 389-9371.

Jean Anglin and Mary Herbison, Quilts and quilted throw pillows

Mary has pieced and quilted her mother's quilt patterns for a long time. They sold for $20 in the 1930s and about $150 now. The pillows are a sideline and make nice gifts. Jean has helped Mary, her mother, since she was six years old. Call for more information. Prices: Quilts from $125 to $250; pillows, $10 up.

Directions: North of the public square in Center-ville. 982 Highway 100, Centerville, TN 37033. (615) 446-7334, (615) 729-4561.

Mary Johns Kelley, Quilts

Mrs. Kelley taught school for 38 years before she retired. Relying on skills learned as a child, she now makes quilts as a hobby. Prices range from $250 to

Detail of Tennessee Quilt
Photo courtesy of State Museum and Archives

$1,000. Call for an appointment. 126 Greenwood Acres, Columbia, TN 38401. (615) 388-1834.

Julia Read Clark, Quilts

Julia Clark has organized a little band of textile artists and set up a miniproduction line. She acts as manager and plans quilt patterns, decides on colors and fabrics, and provides each quilter with materials needed to complete each project. When each quilt comes off Julia's drawing board, it goes to Mrs. Joe Haley of Bone Cave. Mrs. Haley says: "I've pieced quilts all my life. If I work steady, I can cut and piece one in two weeks." Although Mrs. Haley concentrates on piecing now, she has made many quilts through the years from start to finish. "I had 11 at one time, all from one woman, that I had to quilt, and I've made quilts for all five of my grandchildren."

From Mrs. Haley's hands the quilt passes to Euna Bryant of Spencer or Mildred Geer of Yankeetown. Mrs. Bryant, another lifetime quilter says, "I had 25 quilts when I was married," that she and her mother had made, "but now they're either worn out or given to family." Mrs. Bryant is one of the quilters of the group and spends three or four weeks sewing elaborate floral or geometric patterns into each quilt. Mrs. Geer is the other master quilter, having quilted since she was 13.

Julia and the other ladies "quilt to order" and design quilts to fit unusual size beds or particular color schemes. The most popular patterns are the Flower Garden, Log Cabin, Windmill, Double Wedding Ring, Fan, and Trip-Around-the-World.

Watch for the 1985 *Southern Living Christmas Book* to see Julia's pattern for a quilted Christmas tablecloth. A former home economics teacher, Julia also offers for sale handmade quilt racks and copies of her cookbook, *Julia's Favorite Recipes*. A childhood dream was to write a cookbook, and this one has been very successful. Although Julia had pieced a quilt before she was 16, she prefers cooking to quilting and leaves the production to other team members.

Business hours: 7:00 A.M. to 3:00 P.M., winter; 7:00 A.M. to 5:30 P.M., summer.

Prices: Quilts from $150 to $600; quilt racks, $50; wallhangings, $75; Christmas table cloth, $42.50; and cookbooks, $12.95 (plus tax).

Route 1, Camp Clements, Doyle, TN 38559, (615) 657-5390.

Pauline Coffey, Contemporary quilts

Pauline employs precision cutting and accurate stitching, and she uses well-coordinated color schemes. She does most piecing and quilting by machine for durability, and she designs many original patterns herself. Baby quilts are $50 to $75; patchwork place mats, $6 to $8 each; vests, $50. Call Pauline for an appointment or see her work in the Creative Galleries at Montgomery Bell State Park or Paris Landing State Park. Route 1, Box 251-A, Dover, TN 37058. (615) 232-6771.

Strictly Amish, Quilts/wallhangings

Rosie Wade's "quilting roots" go back to her childhood days when she spent a lot of time under a quilt on a quilting frame with women from her mother's quilting circle sitting around it. She recalls: "My brothers and I would get underneath the quilt frame and push the needle back through for the ladies. They would put their thumb on the spot where they wanted the needle to come back through. I think it was their way of keeping us busy and out of trouble. Even when the weather was unbearably hot, it was always cool underneath the quilting frame."

Now Rosie adds a new twist to an old art form. She designs individual quilts to complement wallcoverings and carpet; in essence, she's an interior quilt designer. After designing the quilt, she creates the image in watercolors on the fabric. Then she sends the quilt to an Amish woman for the quilting. Rosie has done various quilt designs based on Williamsburg, states, roses, and even oriental fans. Quilts range from $200 up; custom quilts from $375 up; and wallhangings from $50 up. Call Rosie for an appointment.

Address: Cedarmont Drive, Franklin, TN 37064. (615) 794-7684.

Rosalie Sumper and Myrtle Reed, Quilts

Rosalie and Myrtle are sisters who make lovely pillows and quilts, each made to order as to size and color. Every stitch is hand-sewn, not done on a machine. Call Rosalie and Myrtle today to place your order or make an appointment to see some of their lovely handiwork. Price: $12 to $20 for pillows; up to $300 for quilts. Route

3, Box 305, Hohenwald, TN 38462. (615) 796-2629.

Once Upon a Quilt, Quilt service

Owners Andrew Davis and Peg Marlin love quilts, as do the two dozen craftspeople at Once Upon a Quilt. Here are the services they offer: custom-made quilts for sale, professional cleaning of keepsake quilts, restoring old quilts, quilt binding, quilt piecing, comforter tying, quilt supplies for sale, quilt basting, and professional appraisals. Call for more information. 2108 Crestline Drive, Nashville, TN 37214. (615) 889-6403.

Mrs. George B. Fly, Quilts

Mrs. Fly says: "I am a housewife who likes to quilt. When I retired after 25 years of public work, I started out crocheting afghans and capes in my spare time. Now I mostly quilt the pieced tops that people bring me. Some are over 50 years old and belonged to the customers' grandmothers. Now they're keepsakes. I also do some piecing and quilting myself."

Prices: Quilts, $75 to $300. Call to make an appointment or to order. 84 Lester Avenue, Apartment 727, Nashville, TN 37210. (615) 244-5051.

Harriet B. Hightower, Clothing from quilts

This is certainly one-of-a-kind attire. Simple lines show off designs and patterns of old quilts. Scraps are used to make sashes, heart pillows, and pin cushions. Prices: $2 to $365. Call for an appointment. 958 Graybar Lane, Nashville, TN 37204. (615) 297-0883.

A SAMPLER
***** *Exclusive* *****

Janie Fricke,
Quilt Maker

Janie Fricke's roots are in the heartland of Indiana, where she was born and reared on a 400-acre farm near South Whitley. In 1975, Janie came to Nashville and became a back-up/jingle singer. As a jingle vocalist, her voice was featured on national commercials.

In 1982 and 1983, she won the Country Music Association's Female Vocalist of the Year. In 1984 she accepted her second consecutive *Music City News* Female Vocalist of the Year award and her first Academy of Country Music Female Vocalist of the Year award. Some of her most famous songs include "He's a Heartache," "Tell Me a Lie," "It Ain't Easy (Being Easy)," and "Don't Worry 'Bout Me Baby."

Janie loves to visit Bell Buckle, Tennessee, about an hour's drive from Nashville near State 82 near Shelbyville. Bell Buckle is a picturesque little town that hosts an annual crafts fair each July. Janie's favorite shop in

Janie Fricke, a spare-time quilter

three governors and eight Rhodes scholars. The original building is a museum today.

Over the past decade, artists and craftspeople have set up shop in a two-block business district area. All of them use native materials and try to preserve traditional crafts such as pottery, basketry, quilts, and others. The delightful blend of things for sale includes antique furniture, books, woodcrafts, fiber goods, dolls, stained glass, and hand-forged wrought iron objects. The downtown cafe features home-style cooking. At the old-fashioned diner, baked goods are made on a cast iron stove, and the menu includes natural country foods.

Anne speaks for many of the craftspeople when she tells us, "I'm lucky! I am doing *what* I want to do, *where* I want to do it, with all my favorite people."

See "Fun Times" for information on special events at Bell Buckle.

Hours: Most shops are open 10:00 A.M. to 5:00 P.M., Monday–Saturday.

Directions: 8 miles from I-24, Exit 97, 50 miles southeast of Nashville. Bell Buckle Crafts, Railroad Square, Bell Buckle, TN 37020. (615) 389-9371.

town is Quilter's Haven, owned by Mildred and Edgar Locke. Mildred teaches quilting and Janie has taken her classes. As a result, she has made two quilts of her own (a biscuit quilt and a silk tie quilt). One of them hangs on a wall in her Texas home.

Maybe a visit to Bell Buckle will enable you to make your own quilt and carry a little Tennessee tradition back to wherever you like.

Bell Buckle Craft Center

Bell Buckle boasts a total population of 453 people and looks like a sleepy little town from a Norman Rockwell painting. Anne White-Scruggs, local resident and potter, says, "We have a place that harks back to an earlier age—of Main Streets, large homes, and neighbors who care for each other. Dogs sleep on the maple-tree-lined streets, and the porches have swings. We're only 8 miles from I-24, but it seems like 80 years sometimes."

The town got its unusual name around 1800 when a bell and a buckle were discovered carved on a tree in what is now the town square. Bell Buckle reached its commercial peak around 1900 because of its stockyards and Webb, its college-preparatory boys' school. Webb is now co-educational, and its graduates include

Woodcrafts

Clarence and Mai Graham, Woodcarving/bread cloths

Several years ago Clarence picked up a stick and went to whittling. That was the beginning of a hobby he still enjoys, and he says, "it keeps me out of meanness." Clarence now makes necklaces, picture stands and frames, furniture, canes, fern stands, magazine racks, and lots of wooden pliers of all sizes. He keeps small sets of pliers with him all the time, and if he sees a child somewhere in town, he'll say, "Do you have a bicycle?" If the child says yes, Clarence says, "Well, you might need these to work on it," as he hands a pair of pliers to the child. Clarence likes to personalize items. For example, walking canes have the owner's name and birthdate burned into the wood.

Mai is not idle while Clarence is whittling. She makes tatting of all designs and then attaches it to cloths for bread baskets. These sell for $10. Clarence's items range from 50¢ to $100. Go by and meet Clarence and Mai. You'll be glad you did.

Directions: 6 miles south of College Grove between College Grove and Chapel Hill on US 31A. Rigsby's Garage is at Allisona. Clarence and Mai live in the fifth brick house past there. Route 2, College Grove, TN 37046. (615) 368-7668.

Piney Creek Woodworks, Woodcrafts

Wanda Howell says: "My family is involved in a cottage industry called Piney Creek Woodworks, situated along the creek banks of the West Piney River. Many of the people here live on land that has been in their family for generations. I was born and raised here, as was my father before me. I have in turn raised my sons here. This is very much our home and an inspiring setting in which to create.

"In our spare time we produce specialty wood-crafts. My husband Don is a quality woodcrafter by night, and I am the wood finisher and tole painter. Wood-work is in my blood because my father built the house I was raised in. Sounds of saw and hammer and the scent of fresh-cut lumber are vivid childhood memories.

"Much of our work is personalized in some way. It is made to order. We do, however, keep available items such as a log cabin birdhouse, complete with front porch, miniature rocking chair, and rain barrel, and our own Tennessee Rocking Horse, quilt racks, and bread, recipe, tater, and novelty boxes. Visitors welcome any-time, but please call first! Prices range from $5 to $100."

Address: Route 5, Box 790, Dickson, TN 37055. (615) 441-1451.

Woods and Flowers Gift Shop, Woodcrafts/silk flowers

Unique ideas abound here, making every visit to Woods and Flowers a treat. See handmade Shaker furniture, shelves with Shaker pegs, sconce sets, quilt racks, door stops, pineapple hangers, toy boxes, bread boxes, name signs, drop-leaf tables, and wooden horses. Other wooden items are made to order. Silk flowers are often placed with wooden items, and arrangements can be custom designed.

Prices: $1 and up. Business hours: Thursday and Friday, 4:00 to 8:00 P.M.; Saturday. 8:00 A.M. to 8:00 P.M.

Directions: From Nashville take State 100. Turn left to Fairview, through a four-lane section of highway. From the end of the four lane, the gift shop will be ¼ mile on the left. Route 2, Box 416, Fairview, TN 37062. (615) 799-8223.

Roy K. Pace, Woodcarving

Roy grew up in the woods. His grandfather was a log-ger, his father a cabinet maker, and Roy proudly carries on the tradition—but from a different angle. He creates carvings of historic or working-class people. Called primitive folk art, some of his well-known carvings are of famous Tennesseans Andrew Jackson, Andrew John-son, James K. Polk, Davy Crockett, and John Harding. A delightful grouping is "The Revival," depicting an old-time tent-meeting scene, a part of American heritage Roy feels should not be forgotten.

Visit Roy and Jean at the Rock Castle where they are resident directors. See Roy's work in the shop, open 10:00 A.M. to 5:00 P.M., April–October, or call for an ap-pointment at other times. Prices: $75 to $1,000.

Directions: 2 miles off Gallatin Road (US 31E), turn right at traffic light onto Indian Lake Road, beside Hen-dersonville High School. Drive 2 miles straight to the Rock Castle. 139 Rock Castle Lane, Hendersonville, TN 37075. (615) 824-0502 or (615) 824-6560.

Hobby Horses & All Wooden Things, Hobby horses

Earl Peterson loves children. He also loves to work with wood and says that "the smell of freshly cut sawdust and wood is one of life's joys." Put those together and the result is a sturdy but lovable rocking horse that can withstand lots of tumbles and wet diapers. Earl also cus-tom makes other things—cabinets, furniture, cradles, and other children's toys. But his favorite is the hobby horse. He says, "I start work at 6:00 A.M. and go to mid-night most days. I enjoy what I'm doing. I don't use cheap materials, and I've never had anything brought back for fixing." Reasonable prices. Call for an appoint-ment.

Directions: From Hermitage Boulevard, go south on Central Pike and take the third left on Melvin Road. Go two blocks and turn right. Second house on the right—397 on the mailbox. Tanglewood Trail, Box 397, Hermitage, TN 37076. (615) 758-3281.

Jane P. Kinney, Wood sculpture (birds)

Jane does unbelievably detailed basswood carvings of song birds, game birds, and decorative decoys. She says, "I just keep whittling till the bird starts showing," trying to make the process sound easy. But when you see these designs, you'll agree that they came from the hands of an artist, not a whittler. A moment in the life of a wild creature has been captured. Each is original, hand-painted in oils, feet crafted of copper or brass, and then mounted on driftwood and native walnut. A lot of Jane's work is on display at Five Rivers' Arts and Crafts Association at Montgomery Bell State Park. Prices range from $10 to $500.

Call Jane for an appointment. Route 3, Box 268, Hohenwald, TN 38462. (615) 796-3779.

Jane Kinney's quail takes flight

Sledge-Crafts, Woodcrafts

When Brad and Trevor Sledge were 5 and 9 years old, they would go to the basement and "help" their dad as he worked at making cabinets at night. They'd hammer and saw and play and have a great time, just like lots of "helpers" everywhere. Then the summer when they were 8 and 12, they helped their mom with her crafts when she taught vacation Bible school. Their wooden crafts were so good, the brothers got an offer to display items at a craft booth. Boom! Sledge-Crafts was off to a great start, with the executive officers both under 15 years of age.

Brad and Trevor have been business partners for 8 years now and have developed many other interests along the way. But that special talent for woodworking remains much alive and the boys are still turning out excellent wooden products—rocking horses, children's table-and-chair sets, and personalized desk plaques which grace the desks of some Tennessee legislators.

When Brad was in high school several years back, he made a scale model of Shakespeare's Globe Theater for a junior English project. Later, this outstanding model won first place over 3,000 other entries in a national crafts contest.

Folks, these boys know what they're doing! They can create just about any wood project you can think of. Give them a call and see for yourself.

Address: Route 1, Murfreesboro, TN 37130. (615) 893-4652.

Tom and Linda Morris, Woodwork and counted cross-stitch

The Morris family is very crafty. Linda, her two daughters, and oldest son cross-stitch, and Tom does all the framing and woodworking. Some pieces take over 500 hours of work. Prices are $10 and up. Call for an appointment. 108 Elm Street, Smyrna, TN 37167. (615) 459-4046.

William Glenn West, Chain saw sculptor

Glenn, a barber who owns the City Barber Shop on the square in Waynesboro, has a unusual hobby. He uses his chain saw to carve such things as animals, birds, dough trays, bowls, chairs, tables, Indians, and totem poles. Glenn says, "I don't draw a pattern; I just fire up my saw and begin to carve."

Glenn adds, "I am often inspired to do a carving by what I see in the tree while it is still standing. For instance, on my first carving—an Indian brave—I saw his face on a cedar log. I have one giant eagle with a 6 foot wingspread from one giant tree trunk. I have a totem pole in Wayne County at Natural Bridge, two totem poles at Cherokee Landing, located in Middletown, Tennessee, and two in my own front yard.

"The door is always open to everyone all day from 8:30 A.M. to 5:00 P.M. each day except Wednesday and Sunday. You are all welcome to come in and browse around, view the scenery, and maybe get a haircut or a shave and a piece of bubble gum. We recently went up on haircuts to $3. The barber shop has been in operation approximately 40 years, and in the beginning haircuts were around 15¢ We are still getting complaints today about raising the prices to $3! I promise I won't use the chain saw on your hair."

Address: c/o City Barber Shop, Courthouse Square, Waynesboro, TN 38485. (615) 722-5611.

Knitted, Crocheted, Tatted, and Woven Products

Heike's Sweaters and Things and Jean's Craft Shack, Soft-sculpture dolls/sweaters

See a variety of custom-made soft-sculpture dolls as well as hand-knitted sweaters, afghans, doll clothes, stuffed animals, pillows, and more. Heike and Jean show their crafts by appointment or take orders over the phone and send them COD. Dolls are priced from $30 to $45, and knitted items range from $6.50 for a newborn's sweater to $85 for a king-size afghan. Call for more information.

Directions: I-24, Exit 8, turn west on Rossview, going toward Clarksville. Go 1.9 miles and turn left on Basham Road. They're the first house on the left. 2115 Basham Road, Clarksville, TN 37040. (615) 552-0525 or (615) 645-1200.

Sara Brown, Knitted and crocheted items

Sara says she enjoys knitting and crocheting, and she takes pride in doing them right. She stands behind the workmanship of all her afghans, bedspreads, and smaller articles too, priced from $20 to $60. Call Sara for an appointment or see her work at the Creative Gallery at Montgomery Bell State Park or Paris Landing State Park. 313 Willow Heights, Clarksville, TN 37040. (615) 647-7549.

June McClanahan, Clothespin dolls/hand-knit sweaters

June makes original clothespin dolls and hand-knitted sweaters. Call her for an appointment or see her lovely items on display at the Creative Gallery at Montgomery Bell State Park or Paris Landing State Park. Route 4, Box 476, Dickson, TN 37055. (615) 446-3265.

Gayle Helen Powell, Crocheted items/poetry

Gayle tells us: "I live out in the country. In the winter you can most often find me near the wood stove crocheting one of my treasures for a gift or for sale. I crochet many hours a week, and I would like to share more of my handwork with the public. I crochet everything from bookmarks to afghans, whatever people want. I also write inspirational poetry."

Call Gayle to place your order or to make an appointment. Crocheted items range from $1 to $60 or more. Poetry books are $3. Route 2, Box 198, McEwen, TN 37101. (615) 582-3160.

Mr. and Mrs. Percy Redmon, Knitted items

Mrs. Redmon tells us: "Percy has a lot of hobbies. He knits, crochets, makes baskets, wreaths, ceramics, and does lace weaving. He is 72 years old and a very good husband."

Percy says: "Knitting is relaxing, and it gives me something to do while I'm not busy with something else. I learned how to knit during World War II just watching my mother-in-law. I like complicated designs now, and I think the fun in knitting is mastering a design."

The first article Percy made was a coat for his wife. It was so good, it won a blue ribbon in 1942 at a local trade fair. Percy still likes to make clothing as well as afghans for people. Give him a call for your knitting needs.

Address: 2506 Central Boulevard, Murfreesboro, TN 37130. (615) 896-9210.

Doris Finch Kennedy, Tatting/weaving

Doris has been a quilter since she was 16, and a weaver for the last 13 years. As a child she learned tatting from her grandmother. Doris says: "I was teaching high-school home economics in a small farm community in Kansas. There I was able to spend the time perfecting the skill of tatting and gaining the speed to really call myself a tatter.

"Tatting is a form of knotting that can appear complex but is created by repeating a single knot. Because it is a knotting technique, tatting is more durable than crocheting and knitting. It is familar to most people who are over the age of 30, even if they don't know how to create tatting. Many have watched grandmother's fingers use the tiny shuttle to create lacy trims, doilies, baby booties, or a baby's bonnet.

"I'm basically a traditional artist in weaving, quilting, and tatting. I like to add a today look but use the old patterns. The last five years I've been involved along with my family in a textile documentation project in the state of Tennessee and co-authored with Sadye Tune Wilson *Of Coverlets: The Legacies, the Weavers*."

Approximate price range: Weaving—coverlets and counterpanes, $500 to $1,000. Tatting—edging, $10 to $50/yd.; baby bonnets, $70 to $200. Quilts—crib, $90 to $150; double, queen, or king, $500 to $1,000.

Directions: Take Briley Parkway to Murfreesboro Road and go east on Murfreesboro Road for one block. Turn left on McGavock. School Lane is second left off McGavock. 1263 School Lane, Nashville, TN 37217. (615) 367-0268.

A SAMPLER
FEATURE

Of Coverlets:
The Legacies, the Weavers

■This definitive book culminates a five-year study of early textiles in Tennessee, early Tennessee weaving in particular. It was written by Sadye Tune Wilson and Doris Finch Kennedy, both expert modern-day weavers. Wilson has been a weaver since 1954 and has a Ph.D. in special education and psychology. Kennedy has been a weaver since 1970 and has a Ph.D. in textiles.

This book is no dry account of technical terms. Beautiful color and black-and-white illustrations introduce flower and diamond patterns and geometric motifs and present to the reader delightful country, yet explicit, names for patterns: Cat Tracks and Snail Trail, Sunrise with Cross Center, Braddock's Defeat, or Pine Cone Bloom. The book is warm with humor as it traces weavers and their descendants who inherited priceless coverlets.

The weaving of coverlets is so much a part of Tennessee's heritage—its history, legends, and lore. Looms were built by loving husbands and fathers, and some even dreamed up patterns and learned to weave themselves. There are funny anecdotes about couples "courting" at the loom, and one yarn gives a sure-fire way to get rid of company. A particular coverlet was very heavy and named Company Cover because you couldn't sleep under it comfortably, and it would be sure to shorten a guest's stay.

Of Coverlets: The Legacies, the Weavers was called "an epic" and "a classic" the day of publication. It sells for $70 and can be ordered from Mrs. Wilson at the address below. Following Mrs. Wilson's address is a sample listing of Tennessee weavers today. Contact them to order coverlets, shawls, tapestries, wallhangings, place mats—or whatever you fancy—for the heirlooms of tomorrow.

Tunstede, Sadye Tune Wilson, 212 Vaughn's Gap Road, Nashville, TN 37205. (615) 352-0971.

Weavers : Doris Kennedy, 1263 School Lane, Nashville, TN 37217; (615) 367-0268. Anna Louise Loftus, P. O. Box 120343, Nashville, TN 37212; (615) 383-7190. Beth Smathers, 3002 Simmons Avenue, Nashville, TN

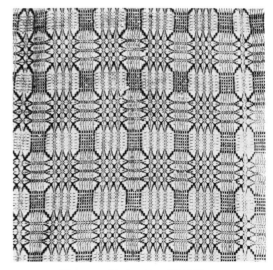

Pine cone bloom coverlet pattern

37211; (615) 331-4619. Mary Ayleen Bryan, Route 1, Moss Bennett Road, Ashland City, TN 37015; (615) 746-8338. Kaaren Reid, 5831 Ridgeval, Memphis, TN 38119; (901) 682-6940. Susan K. Wallace, The Silver Shuttle (weaving supplies and crafts), 1465 Madison Avenue, Memphis, TN 38104; (901) 274-6302. Chloe C. Northington, 1650 Hopkinsville Highway, Clarksville, TN 37042; (615) 645-4447. Betty Emerson, Greenwich Village Mall, Oak Ridge, TN 37830; (615) 482-2173.

Glass and Pottery

Catherine Lowry, Fabric arts/stained glass

Catherine relates to Thomas Edison's observation that "genius is 1 per cent inspiration and 99 per cent perspiration," because her fabric inventions are guaranteed to have a little share of her heart woven into the fabric. Catherine designs fabric murals which are layers of artfully appliqued animals and lovely stained-glass windows, all with the same graceful sense of design. Call for an appointment. Peytonsville Road, Franklin, TN 37064. (615) 790-9543.

Popcorn Studio, Pottery

Ray and Susan Allen are a husband and wife team who produce functional yet aesthetically pleasing stoneware pots. Their pots are extremely durable and safe for oven, microwave, or dishwasher. Some of their unusual items include rolling pins, milk pitchers, colanders, steamers, champagne buckets, wall mirrors, and vases or planters. Prices range from $6 to $300, but most pots are under $30. Call for an appointment. 2031 Nelson Lane, Murfreesboro, TN 37130. (615) 896-9167.

Classic Glass Studio, Glass work

Ask Drew and Jan Trahan about their custom work, which is represented in over 26 states and 3 foreign countries. They've designed pieces for many notable people including Jerry Reed and Huey Lewis.

Drew and Jan use unique textures and subtle hues in their glasswork, creating a work of beauty and a piece of glass that will allow privacy without blocking out light. They do custom beveling, stone-wheel engraving, sandblasting, and etching. Popular items are suncatchers, lovely boudoir lamps, kaleidoscopes, large standing mirrors, and room dividers. Prices from $20 to $2,000. Business hours: 9:00 A.M. to 5:00 P.M. when not at craft fairs. Best to call ahead.

Directions: 65 miles east of Nashville. State 56, 8 miles south of I-40, and 2 miles south of the Appalachian Craft Center. Route 3, Box 348, Smithville, TN 37166. (615) 597-4608.

Baskets

Sherry Brock, Appalachian-style baskets

Appalachian basketry is an age-old craft. Sherry makes egg, hen, and potato baskets the same way they've been made for years, adding her own personal touches of color. A teacher and mother of four, Sherry makes baskets for relaxation. Her seven-year-old daughter and the rest of the family make baskets too. Prices: $5 to $125. Call for an appointment. Route 1, Box 128, Cowan, TN 37318. (615) 967-3838 or (615) 967-7053.

Something Mary's, Baskets

Mary Tedford uses reeds from tropical vines and Rit dye to create her beautiful baskets. She also offers classes in basket making and basket supplies for sale. Baskets and classes range in price from $10 to $40. Open every day except Wednesday and Sunday. Call for an appointment.

Directions: Located 1½ blocks off Madison Street behind Memorial Hospital. 222 Cherokee Trail, Clarksville, TN 37043. (615) 552-0802.

Richard Spicer, White oak baskets

Richard thinks Tennessee is a great state because traditional values learned 100 years ago are still alive today. Richard is trying to keep one of Tennessee's many traditional crafts alive too—weaving white oak baskets. Living in rural Perry County, Richard has a ready source of white oak available to him, and selling his baskets is his only source of income. Richard's baskets grace many homes in Tennessee, including the Executive Residence in Nashville.

The Spicers' home is their business place too, open from 8:00 A.M. to 5:00 P.M. Located in Poplin Hollow in Perry County, just off State 20 on Poplin Hollow Road halfway between Hohenwald and Linden. Route 3, Box 146, Linden, TN 37096.

Estel Youngblood, Baskets

These fine quality split white oak baskets are made by a fellow who's followed the basket trade since boyhood. The *Sampler* highly recommends them. Individual price depends on style and shape, but range is from $35 to $150. Call for appointment, Monday through Friday. Directions: From Murfreesboro, take US 70S to Wood-

bury. Located 8 miles on 70S at State 146 junction (to Smithville). First house on right. Route 2, Box 169, Woodbury, TN 37190. (615) 563-4204.

Willie McLerran, White oak baskets

Willie's baskets will last a lifetime if you take care of them—just like the one his family has used for 43 years. It still looks as good as new.

For 30 years Willie has been weaving baskets, the type his grandmother used to deliver eggs to the store and then fill with coffee, salt, and matches to bring home. Sometimes she brought a piece of candy for a lucky child. Take home a piece of Tennessee heritage, a McLerran basket. Price range: $10 to $35. Visitors and observers welcome, but call ahead.

Directions: 5 miles west of Celina on State 52. Route 2, Celina, TN 38551. (615) 258-3231.

Two exhibition galleries allow visitors to view traditional and contemporary Appalachian crafts, ranging from basketry and quilting to watercolor paintings. Overnight accommodations are available to visitors, and the center also offers facilities for private banquets, meetings, and conventions.

Guided tours of the facility are available if arranged in advance. Self-guided tours are always possible. Hours: Weekdays 9:00 A.M. to 5:00 P.M., all year except between Christmas and New Year's Day.

From I-40 take Exit 273 (about ½ hour east of Nashville) and head south on State 56 for about 6 miles. Follow signs and cross Hurricane Bridge over Center Hill Lake. Then take a sharp left up a winding but well-paved road. For more information, contact: The Joe L. Evins Appalachian Center for Crafts, c/o TTU, Box 5106, Cookeville, TN 38505. (615) 597-6801 or 528-3051.

A SAMPLER FEATURE

The Joe L. Evins Appalachian Center for Crafts

■The Joe L. Evins Appalachian Center for Crafts is a unique, new educational facility located on almost 600 acres overlooking Center Hill Lake in Middle Tennessee. It provides the opportunity for students to explore contemporary art as well as traditional crafts in five basic media: clay, fibers, glass, metals, and wood. Made possible by the largest federal grant ever awarded for crafts, the center is currently funded by a combination of state allocations, federal grants, donations from foundations, and revenues generated by student tuition and workshop fees.

Currently a bachelor of fine arts (BFA) degree is available in conjunction with Tennessee Technological University in Cookeville, which operates the center. Additionally, a unique bachelor of science (BS) degree in crafts marketing has been established. For those who are interested in a learning experience but who do not require college credit, the center provides alternate programs—the apprenticeship, the internship, and the certificate of accomplishment. In addition to these programs, short workshops and evening classes are offered on a year-round basis, with a concentration of one- and two-week workshops during the summer months. These workshops are open to anyone with a desire to learn a craft. Well-equipped facilities are available on the premises and students enrolled in a degree program are eligible for financial aid.

The Sales Gallery has a truly outstanding selection of fine crafts for sale that includes items from all over the Appalachian region as well as those produced at the center. The gallery will gladly ship purchases for you.

Craft Potpourri

Hollis Ramsey

Hollis and his cousin Edgar Ray are carrying on a tradition started in the early 1800s by their rail-splittin' great-grandfather, Larkin Ray. They make white oak split baskets and buckeye dough bowls, reseat chairs with hickory or chestnut, and make maple syrup.

Hollis sells his crafts and the maple syrup at a roadside stand in front of the home he shares with his mother. See Hollis and Ray selling these wares along the road or call them at home. Baskets range in price from $50 for the 9 inch roundbottomed, bulging-sided egg basket to $100 for the 18 inch bushel basket. Hollis said the egg basket is sometimes called a 'gizzard basket' because turned upside down it looks like a chicken's gizzard or a "fanny" basket (you can figure that out for yourself).

Directions: Exit I-40 at Cookeville. Take State 42 to Livingston and 52 to Allons. At Allons turn right at the Willow Grove Resort sign and go 4 miles, until you see Hollis's sign saying "Hand-made Mountain Crafts." Route 1, Box 46, Allons, TN 38541. (615) 823-4467.

Finishing Touch, Gingerbread spice shapes/wreaths/wooden crafts

Gingerbread shapes and wreaths give off a distinct cinnamon aroma and can be used year-round—tied on a grapevine wreath, in a flower arrangement, or as an ornament. They will decorate or spice up your home for months. Wholesale prices available. Prices: Spice shapes—$3 per package (two per package); wreaths—$7 to $20; crafts—$3 to $25. Contact: Judy Smidt, 1410 Devens Drive, Brentwood, TN 37027. (615) 794-6923.

Becky's Originals, Handmade cloth crafts

Becky Anderson makes hand-quilted pillows, sock monkeys, baby dresses, coverlets, wallhangings, and personalized or monogrammed gifts. She also takes special orders and designs many original patterns for customers. Call Becky at home or see her work at the Creative Gallery at Montgomery Bell State Park. Route 4, Box 478, Dickson, TN 37055. (615) 446-6183.

Joe and Arlene Alford, Rockcraft

Joe and Arlene are "rock artists." By using the natural shape of rocks, they form human and animal shapes by expertly adding paint and epoxy glue. See some of the cutest and funniest characters you've ever seen in their slim, fat, wide, short, and tall men, elves, frogs, bears, tigers, rabbits, doctors, preachers, and even a "good ol' boy" with a handmade "kat-hat." Priced from $1 to $15. Call for more information or see their "rock creatures" at the Creative Gallery in Paris Landing or Montgomery Bell State Park. Route 2, Box 383, Dover, TN 37058. (615) 232-6250.

Juanita's Fashions and Crafts, Fashions/crafts

Juanita makes her own patterns on many clothing or craft items and sometimes combines them with store-bought patterns. She hand paints from cards or pictures and designs special things for customer orders, especially for Christmas or other occasions.

Prices 50¢ to $300. Open 10:00 A.M. to 5:00 P.M., Monday, Wednesday, and Thursday, or other times by appointment.

Directions: Take I-40 east of Nashville. Take the Carthage-Gordonsville Exit 258. Go south on State 53 to US 70. Located in Maggart Community, Sullivan's Bend Road. Route 1, Box 215, Elmwood, TN 38560. (615) 897-2721.

Katherine K. Simmons Corn shuck dolls, Baskets, vine wreaths

Unique dolls and corn shuck flowers are made from all-natural material. The honeysuckle baskets are all different and are more like sculptures than baskets. Prices: $1.25 to $15. Open by appointment only. Route 6, Box 43 A, Fayetteville, TN 37334. (615) 433-3229.

The Attic, Custom Christmas ornaments

These ornaments are wooden, hand cut, and hand painted back and front. They are designed to be personalized. Keep them or share them. And remember, ornaments can be given year-round for baby gifts, weddings, anniversaries, or birthdays. Price range: $3 to $10. Write for a free brochure or call for an appointment: Gayle Brinkley or Becky Waldrop, P.O. Box 1122, Franklin, TN 37065-1122. (615) 794-7801 or (615) 794-5646.

Log Cabin Herbs, Herb wreaths, potpourri, herbs, dried flowers

"An herb garden is a thing of beauty in all seasons," says Jean Dixon. Jean makes wreaths from herbs and teaches classes on how to grow and cook with herbs.

Jean and her husband grow and dry all the herbs, herb flowers, and wildflowers used in the wreaths. They make the straw wreath formations, as well as potpourri, herb vinegars, seasonings, and teas. In the spring and fall, herb plants are for sale.

Visit their garden and experience the wonderful fragrances of peppermint, lemon, verbena, nutmeg, and rose. On the picturesque wildflower trail, see wild herbs such as ginseng, bloodroot, and goldenseal. Truly an experience worth remembering.

Prices: $1 to $25. Open Tuesday, Wednesday, and Thursday, 9:00 A.M. to 4:00 P.M. Give them a call first to be sure they're around. Send a self-addressed, stamped envelope for a map and more details.

Directions: From Hohenwald, take State 20 east toward Summertown. Turn right on Grinders Creek Road. Route 3, Box 139, Hohenwald, TN 38462. (615) 796-4780.

Mrs. A. N. Stancie, Rag rugs

Mrs. Stancie says: "I am 75 years old and live on the farm I grew up on. I make rugs for sale. An elderly Pennsylvania Dutch woman taught me how to make these rugs over 50 years ago. I make them with a wooden needle this woman's husband whittled out. Then we called them rag rugs, like rugs made in the colonial days. I suppose they were called rag rugs because they were made from old clothes and blankets.

"I first made a rag rug to donate for a local auction sale by my Sunday school class. After that people wanted me to make them one. I make round or oval sizes, mostly oval, about 48 by 30 inches. But I have made them as large as 4 feet in diameter. I make them because I really like to, and I need something to do."

Call Mrs. Stancie for an appointment. Larger size rugs priced around $50.

Address: 370 Wesley Chapel Road, Lawrenceburg, TN 38464. (615) 762-2813.

Robert and Margaret Steele, Dolls/clothing/pickles/horses

Here's a shopping experience in the country. Margaret offers quilts and larger size clothing for the beautiful but big woman. Be sure to try a pint of her special homemade kosher dill pickles, made from her German grandmother's recipe. Helen Skiles, Margaret's mother, sells clown, hobo, and court jester dolls. See Robert about the B and M Stables, where Tennessee Walking Horses are bred. Prices: Pickles about $2 a pint; clothing starts at $8; quilts at $65; dolls are under $20; and horses $1,000 and up.

Address: Route 2, Box 193-C, Muddy Pond Area, Monterey, TN 38574. (615) 445-7855.

Don Thompson Sign and Craft Shop, Custom sign painting, fiberglass fancies

Don can do anything from painting a sign to creating totem poles. So if you have a fancy for something unusual, Don is the man to see for what you can't go downtown and buy—like a wingspread eagle, a horse, or a lion at your home-site entrance. If you're near Murfreesboro, see Don's original 32-foot, fiberglass totem pole in the Cripple Creek area, Uncle Dave Macon's old stomping ground. Call for more information.

Directions: 7 miles east of Murfreesboro on US 70S (Woodbury Road). Woodbury Road, Route 5, Murfreesboro, TN 37130. (615) 893-5474.

Shirley Douglas, Quilts/dolls

Shirley makes quilts, rag dolls, teddy bears, and a few crocheted items. Prices: Clown doll—27 inches tall, $16; Raggedy Ann and Andy—35 inches tall, $20 each; full-size quilts—$100 to $175; baby quilts—$20 and up.

Directions: About 9 miles from Murfreesboro on State 96W, across from the Bill Rice Ranch. Look for sign in the yard. Route 2, Franklin Road, Murfreesboro, TN 37130. (615) 896-3880.

Mary E. Pryor, Crafts

Mary is a real woman's woman. She raises ducks, chickens, guineas, and mules, and she still milks a cow by hand. Ask her to tell you some funny animal stories or something about the history of Defeated, Difficult, or Pleasant Shade, Tennessee. In her spare time, which must be in the wee hours of the night, she custom makes soft-sculpture dolls, tater bags, broom covers, and stuffed chickens. You can see some of her work at the B and L Grocery at Difficult, Tennessee, or at her home. Call for an appointment.

Directions: From Nashville, take I-40 East. Take Carthage Exit. From Carthage, take State 25 (toward Hartsville) but turn right on State 80 and go to Pleasant Shade. Route 2, Box 12-B, Pleasant Shade, TN 37145. (615) 774-3437.

W. R. Arnold, Decoys, knives, and more

Here's a fellow who's actively enjoying his retirement years. Mr. Arnold makes snipe decoys; custom-etched knives; cherry, walnut or maple writing desks; powder horns of goat or cow horns; and banjo-type barometers and clocks. Call or write for more information. Route 1, Box 43, Readyville, TN 37149. (615) 895-2236.

Jocie Parsley, Purses/curtains

Jocie says: "I make Naugahyde purses, luggage, throw pillows, and many other smaller items. This is a self-taught craft I began over 20 years ago. I also make Priscilla-style curtains, with nostalgic ruffles and bow tiebacks. I make quilt tops, decorative kitchen towels, and various types of cloth and bed pillows."

Call Jocie for more information. Route 3, Smithville, TN 37166. (615) 597-4517.

Donna Davis Carter and Sharon Davis Fowler, Hand-painted crafts

Donna and Sharon make dolls and paint various scenes on saws, coal scuttles, shovels, and plow points. They do pen-and-ink drawings from photographs supplied by customers—a favorite church, an old home place, a barn, or whatever. Prices range from $8 to $100. Route 2, Box 12A, Woodbury, TN 37190.

Craft Facilities

Laura's Loft, Country crafts shop

Laura Beard specializes in high-quality handmade crafts at reasonable prices. About 20 craftspeople display their wares at Laura's Loft and frequently stop and chat with customers. The country-style crafts are perfectly showcased in a lovely two-story, hand-hewn long house. Since Laura caters to neighbors as well as tourists, she tells us her prices are 25 to 30 per cent lower than market price and the range is from $1 to $400. Open Thursday through Saturday, 10:00 A.M. to 6:00 P.M.; Sunday, 1:00 to 6:00 P.M.

Directions: From Nashville take I-40 West and exit at Exit 182, which is State 96. Go 4/10 mile toward Dickson. Route 1, Box 541-A, Burns, TN 37029. (615) 446-2470.

Creative Crafts, Country crafts

Carolyn Sykes's shop specializes in the country look, and her slogan is, "A touch of country, a touch of love." She does all her own painting on canvas, wood, or saw blades, and she enjoys watercolors most. Bring in a picture of what you want painted. Art supplies, silk flowers, and needlework available as well as lots of other crafts. Many items in the $5 to $8 to $10 range, very few over $50.

Directions: Erin is less than 30 minutes west of Clarksville on State 13. In the center of town is Old Town Village, and Creative Crafts is the first shop inside. Route 3, Box 96, Erin, TN 37061. (615) 289-4052.

Log Cabin Crafts, Craft shop

Visit the only craft shop in the resort area of Fairfield Glade, 10 miles from Crossville. See a wide variety of handmade local crafts displayed in a charming log cabin. Prices: $2 to $250. Hours: 9:30 A.M. to 5:00 P.M. daily. Closed Sunday.

Directions: On the edge of Fairfield Glade on Peavine Road. Take I-40 Exit at Peavine Road and come north about 6 miles. Fairfield Glade, TN 38555. (615) 484-2691.

Foothills Crafts, Craft facility

Foothills Crafts is operated by the Coffee County Craft Association, a nonprofit educational organization dedicated to the preservation of quality craft work. Over 200 members exhibit and offer their crafts for sale, including items of wood, clay, metal, glass, and fiber. Find the best quality hand-crafted items in the area. Prices: From $1 souvenir items to collectibles valued at several hundred dollars. Business hours: Monday—Saturday, 9:00 A.M. to 5:00 P.M. Directions: Exit 110 from I-24, 60 miles south of Nashville. Turn south on State 53 and go ½ mile. See store on left. 800 Woodbury Highway, Manchester, TN 37355. (615) 728-9236.

Porterfield Crafts and Trading Post, Crafts

Eloise Rains says, "My father-in-law cuts out things in wood, and my mother-in-law and I tole paint them. My grandmother makes dolls of all sizes, especially black ones. We also do cross-stitching, candlewicking, chicken-scratch, quilted items in hoops, pillows, and ruffled wreaths. Our prices are very reasonable, and we also have some antiques in the store. Business hours: 9:00 A.M. to 5:00 P.M., Monday—Saturday. Visitors are welcome, and we do take orders."

Directions: From Woodbury, take US 70 toward Murfreesboro. Turn right onto Porterfield Road, beside Dick's Chair Shop, approximately 5 miles from Woodbury. Go all the way to the end of the road. The store is on the left. Route 1, Box 156, Milton, TN 37118. (615) 273-2313.

Barnes-Yard Crafts, Country creations craft shop

Janet Barnes makes mostly wooden items—cats, bears, geese, cows, potatoes, apples, watermelon slices, small lapel pins, and wreaths or plaques with various symbols. Many of her creations are custom designed, bought as gifts and sent as far as Texas or Hawaii. Vicki, Janet's sister-in-law, specializes in counted cross-stitch which is made into pillows, placed in frames, hoops, or washboards. They also make aprons and decorate picture-brim hats or grapevine wreaths.

These girls have established a reputation for their uniqueness and quality. Reasonably priced; 'most everything under $25. Open Monday—Saturday, 8:00 A.M. to 5:00 P.M., but it might be best to call before traveling long distances.

Find them out in the country about 11 miles from Woodbury on the Pleasant View Road. You can reach this road by traveling on US 70S or State 53. A farm sign in the barnyard identifies Barnes-Yard. Box 212, Route 3, Morrison, TN 37357. (615) 765-5243.

Yours Truly, Craft shop

Yours Truly is a unique shop that has been in operation eight-and-a-half years. They carry hand-painted and handmade things as well as art, craft, and needlework supplies. Silk and dried floral arrangements can be made on the premises for homes, parties, or other affairs. On the second weekend in October, Yours Truly sponsors an arts and crafts show held in a huge tent in front of their store. Here they teach classes and offer handmade items for sale.

Directions: In Jackson Heights Shopping Plaza on Northwest Broad Street in Murfreesboro. This is also US 41 between Nashville and Chattanooga. Murfreesboro, TN 37130. (615) 893-6744.

Country Cottage Crafts, Handmade small items

Lots of handmade items such as afghans, ceramic dolls with lace dresses, hand-painted wood churns or cross-cut saws, and ceramics. Something new every day and reasonable prices from $1 to $100. Open: Monday—Saturday, 9:00 A.M. to 5:00 P.M. Directions: Take Franklin Road to Murfreesboro. Turn right on Broad Street. Go through two traffic lights. Shop is fourth building on left. 323 Southeast Broad, Murfreesboro, TN 37130. (615) 893-7853.

Centennial Art Activity Center, Art activity center

Tourists visiting Nashville usually have Centennial Park and the Parthenon on their list of things to see. While you're at the park, be sure to visit the Art Activity Center, the one-story block building on the left of the Parthenon, beside the children's playground. Craft classes such as tole painting, basketry, pottery, painting, weaving, spinning, and ceramics are taught here year-round for a very modest fee—no charge for senior citizens or children under 18. Of special interest to visitors is the art and craft display of items hand crafted by Tennessee artists. See items such as porcelain dolls, quilts, paintings, and woodcrafts, all available at modest prices. This display has a featured craft or artwork which changes monthly. In November there is a Student Show in which art/craft students offer their work for sale.

The center is open daily. Call and ask for Darlene Carson. Hours: 9:00 A.M. to 9:00 P.M., Monday—Thursday; 9:00 A.M. to 6:00 P.M., Friday. Centennial Park, Nashville, TN 37209. (615) 259-6446.

A SAMPLER FEATURE

Mrs. Aggie Smith
Tennessee's Quilting Angel

■Aggie Smith has been quilting since she was 12. That's a quilting career of about 75 years. She used to quilt entirely by hand, but now she uses a machine. In the past 8 or 9 years, Aggie has made approximately 1,000 quilts, but then something happened—she lost her eyesight. Thankfully, in May of 1984, an operation

restored this vital sense for Aggie, and last winter she made close to 100 quilts.

In the past 20 years, Aggie has given away more than 120 quilts to friends, family, and the needy. The most quilts Aggie did in one season was 240, and that was in the fall and winter months of 1969.

Aggie could teach us much about love for our fellow human beings as well as about the hard times she's seen. But Aggie's not a braggart nor a complainer. She worked in the steamy cotton fields of West Tennessee until 12 years ago and could pick as much as 300 pounds of cotton in the blistering heat. Now Aggie's sold her 66-acre farm, but she still tends 3 acres and a garden.

Aggie is typical of Tennessee's country and mountain folk. They are unsung heroes…out-of-step pioneers in an age when no one has time to unload the dishwasher. The Aggies of Tennessee know about the virtues of struggle, perseverance, and triumph. We salute you, Aggie Smith of Bradford, Tennessee, and the lessons of love you have taught so many.

West Tennessee Crafts

Craft Shops

Made in Memphis

This shop specializes in fine handicrafts and original art made by Memphis artisans. Find everything from pottery to pillows, wallhangings, woodwork, quilts, and all sorts of unique, often humorous gadgets and goodies. Prices range from $1 to $600. Open 10:30 A.M. to 5:30 P.M., Monday–Saturday. Located in the Poplar Plaza Shopping Center at Poplar and Highland in the Poplar Plaza Gallery. 3460 Poplar Avenue, Memphis, TN 38111. (901) 323-6016.

Norma's

See lots of counted cross-stitch and other crafts. Located in downtown Milan, about ½ block from the post office. 343 South Main, Milan, TN 38358.

The Craft Basket

Kathy Gray, manager of The Craft Basket, tells us: "Our business is truly family operated—my father does much of the wood cutting, my father-in-law and husband make grapevine wreaths and baskets for the shop, an aunt

does our framing, and mother and I teach classes and make many of the craft items.

"Our store began in 1978 with little capital but a big love for crafts. We sell supplies and teach classes weekly for basketry, cross-stitch, quilting, painting, cut and pierced lampshades, metal punch, scherenchitte (paper cutting) stenciling, and more. Handicrafts lovingly made by our customers today will be cherished by future Tennesseans, hence our slogan—'Today's Pleasures, Tomorrow's Treasures.' We carry an assortment of craft supplies comparable to that found in larger city craft shops. In addition, we sell many hand-crafted gift items made right in the shop by area crafts people. Visitors and observers are always welcome. We might even teach them a new 'old' craft."

Located in a renovated building in downtown Union City. 223 South First, Union City, TN 38261. (901) 885-2880.

Fiber Artists

Eugenia G. McPherson, Fiber and clay designs

Eugenia's interest in handiwork began more than 50 years ago when she fashioned an embroidered doily for her baby sister's first birthday. When Eugenia was around nine, her grandmother taught her to crochet and tat and later to sew.

When Eugenia got married she decided to use wallhangings instead of pictures to decorate her walls, so she made floral needlepoint pictures. Today her clay wallhangings are different from her fiber designs but equally appealing. Some of the clay hangings are used as planters. Eugenia does mostly experimental work in different clays and glazes. Call for an appointment or more information. Route 2, Box 303, Big Sandy, TN 38221. (901) 593-3749.

Wanda Clayton James, Fiber artist

Wanda is reviving the traditional craft of weaving rag rugs, mats, and traditional quilts as well as producing contemporary tapestries for corporate and private collections. Her paper work, an emerging craft, incorporates weaving and stitching. Wanda employs good craftsmanship, design, and color in all her work. One of her quilts and some tapestries are displayed in the Tennessee State Permanent Crafts Collection, and she has an ongoing account with shops in South Carolina. See Wanda quilting and selling her wares at the Mid-South Fair in October each year at the Memphis Pink Palace Museum.

Address: 6265 Valleydale, Memphis, TN 38115. (901) 794-5003.

Weaver's Choice, Yarns, looms, accessories

Get congenial service in a congenial atmosphere. Spinning demonstrations upon request—from raw fiber through preparation to final product—whenever there's a project on the loom. Hand-woven items done by special order. Price range: $5 for hand-spun yarn to $350 for tailored hand-woven suit. Call Kaaren Reid for an appointment. 5831 Ridgevale, Memphis, TN 38119. (901) 682-6940.

Knitted, Crocheted, and Cross-stitched Products

Brenda Medlock, Knit and crochet

Brenda thinks "The Tomato Patch" would be a good name for her crafts enterprise because, like her husband's grandmother before her, she always goes to the tomato patch for privacy or to get away from the children.

Brenda's knitting and crocheting act as therapy for arthritis. She does small craft items on up to larger, more detailed pieces. Call Brenda for more information or see her work at the Creative Gallery at Montgomery Bell State Park or Paris Landing State Park. Route 2, Box 402, Paris, TN 38242. (901) 642-4842.

Ruth E. Sipes, Crochet

Ruth creates all sorts of crochet critters of her own designs. There are lovable Smurfs, fat turkeys, alligators, geese, bunnies, dogs, gingerbread men, skunks, and even Mickey Mouse. She also crochets more traditional items such as afghans and bedspreads. An unusual craft is her delicate tin art you must see to believe. It closely resembles the old paper art form, quilling. Prices: $5 to $100. Call Ruth for more information. 726 El Capitan, Bolivar, TN 38008. (901) 658-5820.

Alma Medlock, Crochet

Alma does beautiful crochet work. She has been crocheting about 50 years and works everything from fine cotton yarn to four-ply, depending on the project. Alma can create small items like doilies to large items like beautiful bedspreads. Price range: $2 and up. Call Alma to place your order or see her work at the Creative Gallery at Montgomery Bell State Park or Paris Landing State Park. Route 2, Box 402, Paris,TN 38242. (901) 642-0389.

Brenda Riddick, Cross-stitch pillows

Brenda does cross-stitch, mainly pillows, and sells to the public. She likes to cross-stitch various sayings about friendship or love, so people can better express their feelings to friends or relatives through gift giving. Prices on pillows range from $20 to $30. Call Brenda to place your order, or see her work at the Creative Gallery

at Paris Landing State Park or Montgomery Bell State Park. Route 1, Box 56, Greenfield, TN 38230. (901) 235-2342.

Craft Potpourri

Custom Craft Ceramics

Give yourself or someone you know a gift of ceramics. The wide range of ceramic items includes pitchers and bowls, Christmas trees, fruit, crocks, lamps, and other lovely items. Classes taught on Tuesday and Thursday nights. Call Mildred Burke after 4:15 any weekday or all day on weekends. 183 Broad Street, Dyer, TN 38330. (901) 692-2825.

Charles G. Wilson, Woodburnings

Charles does original woodburnings of most wildlife and custom work of people's pets. He does these on wood from freehand drawings and then burns them on wooden plates or frames them as pictures. Small likenesses are reproduced on boxes or spoons. Prices range from $2 for spoon etchings to $35 for pictures and plates. Call for an appointment. Route 2, Box 39C, Lexington, TN 38351. (901) 968-5420.

Peggy Hutchison, Various crafts

Peggy has compiled a cookbook of over 250 delicious recipes, and she makes baby quilts, delightful "Mouse" or "Mammy" broom or toaster covers, and lovely honeysuckle wreaths, which she decorates with ribbons and dried or silk flowers to suit your color scheme. Call Peggy to place your order or see her work at Creative Gallery at Paris Landing State Park or Montgomery Bell State Park.

Prices: Cookbook—$5; quilts $40; covers and wreaths—$20; and as a special souvenir from Tennessee, a beautiful 16 by 20 color photograph of a purple iris, the state flower—$6 plus $1.50 for postage and handling. (Send a self-addressed stamped envelope for price list.) Route 2, Box 44, McKenzie, TN 38201. (901) 352-3783.

Agnes Stark Pottery

Veteran potter Agnes Stark makes a statement for all craftspeople when she says: "I suppose I want what every craftsman wants for his or her work. I want my pots to have a 'presence,' a vitality and strength that includes joy." Agnes creates functional stoneware and decorative porcelain. Her strong design and glaze technique combine to produce work that is widely recognized for its originality. The stoneware has all of the safeguards necessary for kitchen use.

She sells her work to shops and galleries all over the country. Agnes creates an interesting variety of pieces which have been exhibited at Brooks Memorial Art Gallery in Memphis, American Crafts Council Show in Dallas, the Old State Capitol in Baton Rouge, and the governor's mansion in Nashville. Prices range from $4.50 to $300.00.

Directions: Her studio is near Memphis State University. Take Highland Street and turn on Cowden between Poplar and Central. Call for an appointment. 3598 Cowden Avenue, Memphis, TN 38111. (901) 458-2354.

The Butterfly Duo, Accent wreaths

Frances Crenshaw and Denise Russell tell us, "Tennessee's unique arts and crafts are not found only in East Tennessee's mountains. One of the newest cottage industries calls a small farm on the bluffs of the mighty Mississippi home. Christmas wreaths and original custom decorator accent wreaths that grace some of the state's best home interior showrooms and gift shops are hand-crafted in a large rambling farmhouse by The Butterfly Duo. Yes, sometimes in the summer we even work on the screened-in front porch where the scent of honeysuckle and magnolia blossoms fills the air. If you're looking for a weatherproof, indoor-outdoor creation, 12 inches to 20 inches, you've found it! Say you're 'crafty'? Call us for an appointment—give us two to three hours and we *guarantee* you'll love it or we don't take you money. (Even men do a great job!) Now you call us before you come! Some days we just play hooky and fish in our lake."

Prices: Group class prices available. Wholesale prices available to retailers (minimum three). Retail prices range from $45 to $75. Hurri-candle rings available to mix or match.

Address: 6603 Millington Road, Millington, TN 38053. (901) 872-1414.

Debbie Britton, Tole painting/waterfowl

Debbie works with driftwood and carved wood for her welcome signs and shore bird decoys and with grapevines to make her wreaths. Call her for an appointment. Prices range from $5 to $50. 404 Blanton Street, Paris, TN 38242. (901) 642-7484.

Patty's Ponys, Stick horses

Although Patty's Ponys are primarily for children, some folks buy them to give as a token of love or as a decorator item. Pat Epperson calls them Tennessee Walking Horses or heirloom horses because their quality workmanship will allow them to be handed down as heirlooms.

Pat says, "To date we've made 420. We add velvet noses, make the bridle from leather shoestrings or macrame, and have a secret way of putting on the head so it won't come off. Each pony has its own gift card. Our ponies have won the first place ribbon in the handmade toy category of the Henry County Fair for the last three years."

Price range: $15 to 35. Call Pat to place your pony order or see her ponies at the gift shop in the Nashville Airport. Pat also sells her ponies the third weekend of each month at the Memphis Flea Market at Mid-South Fairgrounds and the fourth weekend of each month at the Nashville Flea Market. Route 1, Box 236 A, Paris, TN 38242. (901) 782-3396.

Mary Sue Nelson, Suncatchers

Mary Sue creates original suncatchers finished with a very hard coat of a polyester-epoxy mixture. She re-creates nature items in plaques and paperweights, all priced from $3 to $75. Call Mary Sue to place your order or see her work at Creative Gallery at Paris Landing State Park. Route 4, Box 62, Paris, TN 38242. (901) 642-8617.

Kit's Country Baskets

Kit Benson is a self-taught basket weaver. Now she teaches clases in basketry, hoping to preserve a part of our southern mountain folk art and heritage. Each of Kit's baskets is signed, numbered, and dated on the bottom, priced from $2 to $60. Call Kit for more information about her baskets and/or classes. 509 North Poplar Street, Paris, TN 38242. (901) 642-5297.

Polly's Page's Mountain Crafts, Carved dolls

Polly carves dolls from red cedar, dolls designed from pioneers that we don't know about, but we read about. Polly feels she is a part of her dolls; after all, she's known them for 40 years! Polly's dolls are in permanent collections at the Tennessee State Museum and the Smithsonian Institution, and they are owned by Dinah Shore and Betty and Winfield Dunn. In 1976, Polly was featured in a chapter from noted doll maker Helen Bullard's book, *Crafts and Craftsmen in Tennessee.* You'll fall in love with 9 inch Uncle Pink and Aunt Jenny, 6 inch Hitty, and 5 inch Mack and Rafin. Priced from $35 a pair to $100. Call for more information or drop by during regular working hours. Polly loves visitors. P.O. Box 174, Pleasant Hill, TN 38578. (615) 277-3402.

Joyce White, Quilts/dolls

Joyce's quilts have received both local and national recognition. She also makes her Coleslaw Cuties, a doll similar to the Cabbage Patch doll. Her Mr. T doll and Mr. T bear are best-sellers. Prices: Quilts—$1,000 and up; pillows—$35 and up. Call for an appointment or see a sample of Joyce's work at the Creative Gallery at Paris Landing State Park. Route 1, Box 560-A, Springville, TN 38256. (901) 642-5724.

A SAMPLER

SPECIAL

Homer Hardison

The *Sampler* feels fortunate indeed to have Homer Hardison in our craft section. It was quite by accident that we discovered him. The other day while going through the mail, we opened a letter from Homer's neighbor, Osroe Hilham. Osroe wrote: "Y'all's book won't tell nothin' about Tennessee crafts if you'uns leave out Homer. He's just like that boy from Memphis wuz a few years back—what them city folks call 'undiskevered talent.' " (We think he was referring to Elvis Presley.)

We contacted Osroe to find out more about his amazing neighbor. The information we received was so wonderfully intriguing that the *Sampler* staff got in our corporate vehicle, Peter's pickup with the camper shell, and set off to Woodburg, located in West Tennessee near the banks of the Mississippi.

We met Osroe just east of Memphis since he had agreed to be our guide into the swampy woodland where Homer lives. We followed Osroe until the highways became byways, and soon we were forced to say good-by to civilization—and the pickup. Next we strapped on our backpacks and hiking boots and started overland, following Osroe down the Old Salt Lick Trail that looked like it had been traveled often by cottonmouths. When all of us (except Peter) thought we couldn't crawl another step over the murky, humid terrain, Osroe said, "Here we are"—and we thankfully collapsed into a dugout canoe.

After what seemed like miles of swatting giant mosquitoes and dodging muskrats, we spotted the top of a magnificently carved totem pole. Osroe told us that this was an example of Homer's extraordinary woodworking skill.

We disembarked from the dugout and got further directions. Osroe wanted to stay, but he had a pressing appointment at the Antenna Club in Memphis (see "Music"), so he gave us hurried directions and left, promising to return by sundown. So we pressed on to Homer's workshop.

What the *Sampler* found at Homer's, the world would find hard to believe. In fact, we held a meeting of the entire staff before we left Woodburg in order to decide if we should include Homer's talent in the *Sampler* or keep it secret. It was decided, by one vote, that the rest of Tennessee and the world must know of Homer Hardison, truly a "woodman of the world."

Typical of many Tennesseans, Homer is quiet and mild-mannered. His speech is still flavored with many Indian words and grunts. We were forced to use primitive forms of sign language when our conversation with him came to a standstill. There in his shop were incredibly beautiful hand-carved songbirds, quaint martin houses, sturdy bows and arrows, stocks for Daniel Boone-type long-barreled muskets, and even wooden safety tips for bulls' horns. Most unusual were Homer's custom-designed outhouses. These had seats formed in the shape of various animals such as the ground hog, the skunk, or the opossum. Homer's love for animal life was

Early Tennessee crafts family

further evident in his delicate woodcarvings depicting mules winning in various feats of strength, opposing mountain lions, bears, bobcats, foxes, or snakes.

Perhaps the most impressive item was Homer's lovely custom-carved musical instrument, the "guitoe," which closely resembled a guitar, but was made to be played with the toes. For the leisure minded (which definitely includes the *Sampler*), there were luxurious hammocks fashioned of panther skin.

Needless to say, the *Sampler* wanted one of every unique item Homer had on display, but we had to think of the trip home. So we said our good-bys to Homer and promised him fame and fortune by including him in our book. As we strapped on our backpacks, we noticed wooden barrels brimming with small wooden disks. When we asked Homer about these, using his broken English, sign language, and various gestures, Homer explained his latest invention—wooden computer disks. Then we all understood what Osroe meant when he referred to Homer's "*undisk*evered" talent!

Craft Catalogs

Catalogs featuring work of Tennessee craftspeople:

Collectibles—Tennessee Craftsmen, 1102 Hunters Court, Franklin, TN 37064. $1.00.

The Uncommon Market, Route 13, Box 396, Maryville, TN 37801. $2.50.

Pea Ridge Purties, 311 East Washington Street, Fayetteville, TN 37334.

Country Collectibles, P. O. Box 81, Springfield, TN 37172-0081. $1.00.

THE GREATEST OUTDOORS

GREATEST OUTDOORS HIGHLIGHTS

✳Explore Tennessee's Mountains✳

The Sampler's special tour of the Smokies by Peter Jenkins and Smoky Mountain Ranger Dwight McCarter

✳Take an I-40 Tour of Tennessee Terrain✳

The mountains, the plateaus, the valleys

✳Watch Tennessee's Best✳

Walking horses, bird dogs, cars, miniature trains, eagles, and coon dogs

✳Take a Tennessee Adventure✳

Caves and caverns, 4 of Tennessee's best hang-gliding sites, cross-country and resort skiing, and Tennessee's greatest canoeing rivers
A Sampler Special: The Cyclone Silo Cycle Club

✳Fish the Greatest Outdoors✳

A Sampler Feature: Charlie Ingram, World Champion
Tennessee Record Catches
When and where they're biting
TVA lakes, Army Corps of Engineers lakes
A Sampler Exclusive: An Oak Ridge Boy Hits the Lake
Chattanooga's hot spots and houseboating in Tennessee

✳Hunt the Greatest Outdoors✳

Ducks, deer, wild turkey, wild boar, and more

✳Tennessee's Best Bargains✳

Tennessee's State Natural Areas
6 resort parks where you'll be pampered
The Sampler's 12 "Picks of the Parks"

Introducing the Greatest Outdoors

Tennessee has it all. Undiscovered caves. Unspoiled coves. Streams and springs in abundance. Virgin forests. Hiking trails you'll have all to yourself. Cold-water trout streams. Warm-water lakes that lure bald eagles from Canada each year. Boar hunting. Bear hunting. Deer hunting. Duck hunting. Turkey hunting. Coon hunting. World-record fishing. Natural bridges. Underground lakes, rivers, waterfalls. Championship golf courses and skeet shooting. Cross-country skiing at Roan Mountain. Ice climbing at Foster Falls. Hang gliding off Lookout Mountain. White-water careening down the Nolichucky. Placid floating on the Hatchie. All of this and much more!

Tennessee has always taxed human powers of description. The Indians worshipped the Greatest Outdoors, for it was life and death to them. It was greater than anything they could imagine. The white settlers, when they came, often stated that the hand of God had been at work in Tennessee. They liked to compare it to the biblical Garden of Eden, as if the Lord might have spent His day of rest here in creative relaxation! Geologists have spoken of long-ago forces and movements in the earth that produced Tennessee. However it is explained, everyone who really experiences Tennessee's mountains, valleys, forests and hills, lush farmlands and beautiful waterways agrees that here is an unequalled variety of nature's splendor.

Tennessee! For thousands of years it waited for habitation, a paradise of game and fertile soil. It was covered with climax forests where giant oaks, hickories, beeches, chestnuts, poplars, fiery-sweet maples, and cedars had won the battle for sunlight centuries before. Unless nature itself uprooted them, they soared majestically over lesser species of bush, flower and fern capable of living in their dark shadows. Exceptions to the great forests were the mysterious bloom-covered balds in the mountains and a small midwestern prairie trapped in the south-central part of the state. Flowing everywhere were the pure streams and salt licks where the eastern buffalo congregated by the thousands.

To the Indian, this land was abundant with spiritual as well as physical life; with spirits of animals, plants, and birds. He studied them all, and found clues to human character in the actions of nature's creatures. He harvested and used everything the Greatest Outdoors had to offer. He girdled the trees and tilled corn in the rich river bottoms. He farmed, hunted, fished, fought. He survived. When survival became marginal, he moved. But *always* he fought, and never achieved the kind of cooperation with other tribes which might have kept the whites from taking his land.

But one thing the Shawnee from the North, the Cherokee from the East, the Chickasaw from the West, and the Creek from the South agreed upon—Tennessee was *worth fighting for!* It became a hunting ground for many tribes, a place all desired, for it was incredibly rich

in the game, herbs, and trees they depended upon for meat and medicine.

Tennessee was crisscrossed by trails made by the buffalo, the greatest natural engineer of prehistoric times. Over millenia, these had become warrior paths and permitted rapid movement of bands of Indians. Indians would often raid, retreat, and lie in wait to ambush those in pursuit. White settlers quickly learned of the dangers of the open trails. The trails are still here. Some, like Franklin Road out of Nashville, are paved over, but others still wind through virgin timber and look as they must have when the first Indian strode down them.

In The Greatest Outdoors, *The Tennessee Sampler* will give you glimpses of Tennessee through the eyes of some of its premier hunters, hikers, canoers, fishermen, and cavers. Whether you've scarcely broken in your hiking boots, or whether your pack is worn from years of outdoor adventure, you'll find the experiences of a lifetime in The Greatest Outdoors!

Tennessee's Majestic Mountains

Whole books have been written about the Great Smoky Mountains, its history, and the history of the Indians and the settlers, the two peoples who gave up their homes in the Smokies so there could be a park. We at the *Sampler* would like to dedicate this section on these mountains to Lem Ownby, the last resident in the Smokies, who died in 1984 after spending 95 years at his homeplace. Lem lived the kind of independent life that the mountains demand. We're glad we got to know him for a little while.

Peter Jenkins Revisits the Smokies

It was 1973 and a mean wind gushed from the west, picking up speed as it blew down Grandfather Mountain. I was walking across America and had only been on the road for two months. The frigid air carried a lot of snow and seemed to be trying to cut me in half. A lot of the time I was blinded, and now the snow was freezing to my beard and icing my eyes shut. These winds wouldn't stop me because I was headed for the Smoky Mountains. I'd wanted to see them all my life, but growing up in Connecticut had kept me from them till then.

Somewhere out there were Clingmans Dome and Hooper Bald. There were countless lesser-known peaks and spring-fed creeks with names like Whistling Branch and Abram's Creek. It was great to be seeing these Smokies from the top of a mountain, but I wanted to be in the middle of them.

I walked for about a week and got in the middle of these Smokies. It was winter, so I decided to stop and spend some time with them. I got a job in a sawmill and experienced their many moods and complexities as gray winter turned to the pale greens of spring and spring exploded into my first Smoky Mountains summer. Everything was so green, and the swimming holes were so pure and cool. But my time came, and the rest of America called. I had to walk on.

I saw them again at the end of November 1983.

Ten years later, "Hello poplar trees," I said, "you've grown bigger. It's nice to see you, mountains. You look about the same. Ten years has changed me a lot more than it's changed you. Since I left your hollows and peaks, I've crossed the Rockies and lived amongst them. I've strolled across New Mexico's prairies that seemed as endless as oceans. I've hiked through knee-deep snow trying to get over the jagged peaks of Oregon's Cascade Mountains. I've seen a lot since I left you, Great Smoky Mountains, but as one of my neighbors would say, 'I ain't seen nothin', nowhere, like you.' "

As I walked through the Smokies that Thanksgiving weekend of 1983, I refreshed my memory of them and became even better acquainted. Not only did I get to make new friends with different hollows, trails, and creeks, but I was walking along with other people.

My wife Barbara was with me. One of our friends, Lamar Alexander, was walking with us too, and I heard tell that he was born near these mountains. He comes from the tribe of people they call East Tennesseans. His wife (everyone calls her Honey) comes from Texas. Someone told me that the difference between a Texan and an East Tennessean is that if you want to know what a Texan thinks, just hold your breath for a split second, and he'll tell you. If you want to know what an East Tennessean thinks, live around him all your life, and you might find out a thing or two.

Lamar and I were talking about the fact that the summer of 1984 would be the fiftieth Anniversary of the Great Smoky Mountains National Park, and wouldn't it be great to get together and celebrate that. I suggested that it would be fun to find out how the original pioneers made their way through these narrow passes and dense forests, and retrace some of their routes.

Dwight McCarter would be our guide. He's a back-country park ranger. I guess you could say that Dwight's best friend is the Smokies. There is probably no man or woman alive who knows them better and enjoys sharing them more.

On this walk we met an extraordinary man who has since died. Lem Ownby was almost 95 when we met him. When the government was buying up land for the park, many people didn't mind selling. Much of the land was in large tracts owned by lumber companies. But some settlers who lived on this land didn't want to leave and wouldn't sell. Lem Ownby was the only one left. Although he was blind, he lived alone in a weathered cabin, surrounded by many beehives.

Lem was sitting in a chair by his Warm Morning stove when we arrived. I imagined ol' Lem spent much of the wintertime in that chair. His DeeCee overalls were faded.

"Why didn't you sell your place and leave when everyone else did?" I asked him. The cabin smelled strongly of wood smoke and chewing tobacco.

Lem Ownby and Governor Lamar Alexander, Honey and Drew Alexander, and Peter and Barbara Jenkins

"Because I was born here." He spat into a can. (Lem said he'd been chewin' since he was 15. He chewed "Blood.") "You see that corner?" He pointed to a corner of the house by the old fireplace. "My mother was kneeling in that corner praying one day for her seven brothers to come home from the Civil War. They were in the Union. They all walked into the yard together while she was on her knees." A single light bulb hung from the ceiling above Lem's head. "My mother, there never was a better woman who tramped dirt."

Lamar was sitting on the old man's bed, and he decided to enter the conversation.

"We haven't had many governors from East Tennessee before," Lamar said.

"Yeah. And we ain't had many that didn't steal, either," Lem said. Lem couldn't see, but surely he sensed what everyone was thinking. He paused and then said, "I ain't never heard nothing on you yet." Everyone laughed. That was classic East Tennessean.

"Did you know that a lot of them people that sold their places here in the mountains for this here park died of homesickness?" Lem asked. He never did answer me directly about why he didn't leave, but then again he did. He'd lived almost a century, and when he died, it wasn't of homesickness. These mountains and hollows and woods and creeks grab hold of a person and sometimes won't let go. You've got to fight hard to make them feel like home, but maybe that fighting makes them hard to give up.

I was so glad that we met this blind man who was the last person who could really call the Great Smoky Mountains National Park home. The beginning of our trail went by his house and up into the woods.

As we continued our hike, Dwight immediately pointed out things I would never have noticed. "See there—that's an old chestnut stump. The settlers cut it down to make a chestnut rail fence. Down there you can see where they piled rocks so that they could farm these hillsides." These hillsides were steep. By now, the trees had taken back the land.

We hiked on. "There, those are wild boar tracks. …Those hemlock trees weren't much good for lumber, but the old-timers could boil that hemlock and commit suicide if they had a mind to….This is a wild cherry tree," Dwight stopped us all. "See the claw marks, that's where a young bear's done climbed up to get the cherries this summer."

Dwight, the back-country ranger with the wild laugh, whose best friend is the Great Smoky Mountains, made all of us feel like we knew his best friend much better.

Honey and Lamar and Barbara and I felt much closer to the adventuresome, resilient, tough pioneers who made their way here and stayed. Yet, even more than that, we had to thank all the pioneer families who gave up their homes and their roots so that there could be a place like the Great Smoky Mountains National Park.

I expect that my grandchildren's children will come back and make friends with its crystal pure creeks, its Cades Cove, and its mountain tops covered with hoar frost. And I plan to come back and see the mountain laurel brighten the spring woods and take my son, Jed, who is now two years old, to see poplar trees that he and I can't stretch our arms around. The Smokies are already the most visited park in the USA. It's our responsibility not to love the Smokies so much that we hurt them and yet encourage those who need these woods and creeks and hollows to not be so busy they miss getting to know them. Life's too short to miss this place. "Them Smoky Mountains. There ain't nothin' like them, nowhere!"

The *Sampler* Guide to the Smokies

When it came time to capture the mystery and adventure of the Great Smoky Mountains for our readers, the Sampler knew exactly the man to see, our friend Dwight McCarter, Smoky Mountain Ranger. Could he take us and our readers on a special guided tour of some of his favorite places in the Smokies? "Shucks, just let me know when we're going!" was his response. So here we are, ready to have the experience of a lifetime.

If you're reading this at home in your easy chair, it should make you eager to join the millions of visitors annually who see the wonders of the Smokies. If you're at the park while reading this, just grab a map in one hand, your Sampler in the other, and prepare to follow these directions for a unique insider's driving and hiking tour of the Smokies.

Dwight's Driving Tour of Cades Cove

We met Dwight early in the morning at the Elkmont Campground near Gatlinburg. The April weather and wildflowers in abundance made this a perfect time to be in the mountains. The campground is on Little River Road in the Great Smoky Mountains National Park, the most-visited national park in America. We'd spent most of the last two days exploring all the shops and fun things to do in Gatlinburg (see "Tours and Trails") and were all ready to hit the woods.

After introductions all around, we all piled into the van and headed along the Little River Road west toward Cades Cove. Dwight sat up in the front to navigate. The kids wanted to know, "What does a ranger do?"

"Well, now," Dwight said. "I'm a back-country policeman. I'm a firefighter. I'm a naturalist. I'm a wildlife officer. I'm a trails maintenance man. I'm a tree cutter. I'm a forest researcher. I'm a tracker of man and nature. All this and a lot more, because these mountains demand so much more sometimes."

Captivated, we drove slowly, not wanting to miss a single detail of the brilliant colors around us.

We hadn't gone very far when Dwight said, "We've got to stop at Metcalf Bottoms first." So we detoured on the unpaved road at the Bottoms, named for a settler family. About 2 miles north of the Bottoms, we came to Greenbrier School, a one-room schoolhouse. Dwight took us to the cemetery in front of the school. "You notice these headstones are all facing east. That's because the mountain people believed in the Resurrection, and the second coming of Christ from the east. Look at these headstones here made out of mountain slate. It was good for this purpose because it was easy to chisel out. But the nearest slate quarry I know of is on Panther Creek, 40 miles from here. So it would take a good journey to get a homemade headstone." Dwight also pointed out the huge timbers, mostly tulip poplar, used to construct the school.

We returned to Little River Road and drove about 2 more miles to the Sinks, on the left by the Meigs Creek trailhead sign. After looking briefly at the deep pool of water at the base of the Sinks, Dwight led us up an old dry riverbed starting from the left of the parking area. The river had flowed here perhaps many thousands of years until it cut a new course. Following the old riverbed, we came to a swampy area with cattails growing up, a sight you wouldn't expect in the mountains!

Farther on, we came to an old farmstead. "These piles of rock," Dwight said, "were cleared out of the fields." The old cabin chimney was still standing. "If you'll notice, this hearth opening is square, which is common west of Gatlinburg. East of Gatlinburg, the top opening of the chimney will be arched, just like most of the bridges around there. The arch lasts longer than the square, because it handles the load better. This metal piece is a wagon rim, pounded flat. The settlers would usually dismantle the wagon and use the rim for chimneys. They would build a homemade sled to haul off all the rock out of the field."

Then for a special treat we went farther down the old riverbed and found the settler's spring, which had ice-cold water. Pretty soon we crossed the Meigs Creek Trail that comes up from the parking area where we left the van. It goes on to Meigs Mountain, about 6 more miles. We kept on down the dry riverbed and came to the present Little River. We turned upstream and headed back to the parking area.

As we walked, Dwight meditated. "You know, this Little River starts as a spring 2 miles west of Clingmans Dome, on the Appalachian Trail. We call that Double Springs. Part of that water goes into North Carolina as Forney Creek and part into this Little River. That water flows both ways about 100 miles and comes back together again at Tellico Reservoir. That's remarkable."

We got back onto Little River Road and stopped after about 2/10 mile to look at Meigs Falls on our left. Dwight explained that waterfalls, like the one at the Sinks and here, usually occur at fault lines, where harder rock wears away slower than softer rock. After about 2 more miles, we drove under a rock jutting over the road. Dwight told us it was Indian Face Rock.

At the Townsend Y we turned right and drove 2 miles into Townsend for some soda pop. Townsend is in beautiful Tuckaleechee Cove. A few days before, we had visited the cave there and had thoroughly enjoyed ourselves. The Indians called this cove "Tikwalitsi," which means "peaceful valley."

We went back to the park and up Laurel Creek Road toward Cades Cove. About 3 miles up the road we stopped at the Schoolhouse Gap trailhead on the right. About 1/4 mile up the trail, Dwight pointed out old wagon ruts in the creek bed. "These were made by settlers in the 1830s," he said. "This old road was called Anderson's Turnpike. He's the same fellow that founded Maryville College. He had this dream to build a road to connect with one from the North Carolina side. He figured there would be a lot of trade as a result and a lot of money to be made. But the North Carolina road never happened. Anyway, these wagon ruts can be found in Laurel Creek between here and Cades Cove. The settlers used Anderson's road mainly to take cattle up to Spence Field, a grassy area, to graze."

Then we continued to Cades Cove. Just before we descended into the Cove, our windshield fogged up. Dwight said there was a cave about 100 feet to our right that released warmer air at that point and caused the fogging.

At the Cades Cove Loop Road entrance, we picked up a tour booklet. "How did this place get its name?" Brenda asked. "Well, most believe that it was named after Kate, the wife of Chief Abram of the Chilhowee Indian village that was 10 miles downstream on Abram's Creek. The spelling got changed somehow."

As we drove along the Loop Road, we saw many deer, which got Dwight talking about animals. "I've been told any deer you see will be within 2 miles of his or her birthplace. Now, look at those deer feeding. See, the tails are down, like the head. But just before he raises his head, that tail will flick back and forth and then go up. When he looks around and is satisfied there is no enemy, then head and tail both go back down. And look over yonder at them turkeys scratchin' around! That reminds me of a time I was camped under a group of turkeys roosting in pine trees above me. They kept losing their grip on the limbs when they fell asleep, so that's all I heard all night—turkeys falling out of the trees and trying to get back up in them!"

Soon we were at Stop 8, Rich Mountain Road. "This was the original settlers' road into the Cove, a traders' route prior to that, and an Indian and buffalo route prior to that. One of the first traders to enter Cades Cove was named Vaughn, from Virginia, in 1740. He used this trail until 1754. He said these trails were old when he first saw them. His route of trade started at the

French Broad River near the present I-40 Dandridge Exit, went up the Little Pigeon River to the village of Sevierville, through the present Wear Valley to Tuckaleechee (or Townsend), through Rich Gap to Cades Cove and across the Appalachian Trail at Ekaneetlee Gap, down to Fontana and to the upper Indian towns at Deep Creek." Dwight got more and more excited just talking about this man who traveled the wilderness 240 years ago.

At Stop 9, Dwight pointed out the location of an ancient Indian village called the Otter Place, down the valley to our left. We went into the Cable Mill complex and marveled at this early engineering feat. We also saw the unusual cantilevered barn.

Right behind it was Mill Creek on our extreme left, joining Forge Creek to its right. "Hold on, now, I'm going to show you something," said Dwight. He stepped out into the water and picked up a small piece of metal. "This is a piece of slag from the iron forge that operated about 1 mile up Forge Creek in the 1830s. D. D. Foute ran the forge and sold iron ingots in Chattanooga. He sent them by wagons. Anyway, this slag was useless and was discarded into the creek. It washes further downstream with each high water."

We kept on around the Loop Road to Bicycle Hill, known to the settlers as Orebank Hill. It was about 1/4 mile past Stop 14. "Here was one of the three locations iron ore was quarried for the forge," Dwight said as he pointed to a big pit in the earth.

At the mention of supper, we drove back to Elkmont.

Dwight's "Haint" Tales

After eating around the campfire, Rebekah asked Dwight if there were any haunted places in the Smokies. The fire crackled and flared up as Dwight poked at it while he thought. "Well, I'm going to tell you honestly about some of my own experiences. There's two places in the Smokies that are bothersome to me. Both are at old home sites where people died mysteriously. One is at Ace Gap on Hurricane Mountain. An old widder woman died there. This place only bothers me if it's after dark and I'm alone. A breeze hardly ever stirs in Ace

Packhorse crossing icy creek in the Smokies

Gap. The quietness of the place is disturbing. Every time I am there alone I sense someone or something watching me and circling around me. If I am not alone, I never have this feeling.

"The same thing happens at Knewt Prong, about a mile upstream from the junction of Knewt Prong and Jakes Creek, in the Elkmont area. A few years back police were looking for a murderer. He disappeared, but his bloody car was found at Jakes Creek. The last time I was there, I was eating lunch near the creek, when something started watching me and circling me. I was so disturbed I had to leave. I couldn't tell you if the watcher is human, animal, or apparition, but I know it's there."

This wasn't enough for 12-year-old Andrea. "But how do you know it's there if you can't see it?" she wanted to know. "It's my life to know if I'm being watched," said Dwight. "I've spent my life in the forest, and I know when I'm being watched just like the animals. The Indians knew not to lock their stare onto a deer they were stalking, because if they did, the deer would get nervous or spooky."

Julia, the youngest, had heard enough. "I'm putting my sleeping bag next to Daddy!" she announced.

Dwight's Hiking Tour to Mt. LeConte

The next morning we had the full *Sampler* country breakfast right around the campfire, with biscuits, eggs, sausage, pancakes, and country ham we brought with us from Middle Tennessee. Dwight encouraged everyone to fill up. "Eat plenty, folks, 'cause today we're going to do some walking." (As if we hadn't yesterday!)

By 8:00 A.M. we were headed through Fighting Creek Gap on the Little River Road. When we got to the Sugarlands Visitor Center, we turned right and drove up the Newfound Gap road. Right above the Chimneys picnic area we stopped at the overlook. "The Chimneys are named for a hole in the center that draws air up like a chimney does," said Dwight. "The Indians called the Chimneys the forked antlers."

About a mile farther we came to an overlook, called Fort Harry. "Here are earthworks and gun emplacements built by Confederate Colonel Thomas in 1862 to guard Alum Cave. Let's go see where the guns were." So we parked at the overlook and went down the bank to the earthworks.

Our next stop was the parking area at the Alum Cave trailhead, which was full of day hikers like us. As we started up the trail at the first footlog, we saw a sign that said bears were very active on this trail.

Soon we came to Alum Cave Creek. Dwight explained that this creek is devoid of any aquatic life. No trout, no larva, no nymphs live in the water. He picked a rock out of the creek just as slick as it could be. "Now there ought to be nymphs of the may fly sticking to this rock. The reason there aren't any is upstream. There are landslides on the mountain. They release iron pyrite, or iron ore water, into the stream. This water comes from the Anakeesta formation, the oldest rock in the Smokies. Maybe 400 to 600 million years old. Fish nor nothing else can live in this water!"

Heading on up the trail we started looking at all the trees and flowers in April bloom. Just before Arch Rock, we had the kids get into a giant hollow beech tree for a picture. They were reluctant to oblige and happy to get out. Dwight said, "I love beech trees. You know the Indians revered them. Said lightning wouldn't hurt them if they got under their friend the beech tree. Come to think of it, I've never seen one hit by lightning, but I can't guarantee that it might not happen." Soon after that we saw Arch Rock, a hole cut through the rock outcrop by water. Then the trail crossed the creek, and we started climbing the mountain. As we crossed a small dry branch we smelled a strong odor, and Dwight pointed out the reddish color of the rocks. "Now, that's the Anakeesta formation I told you about," he said.

About ¼ mile farther we stopped at a large red spruce tree. "Look here," said Dwight. "See this scarred area about 6 feet up? A mama bear's been marking her territory. She bites and claws this tree and others around the corners of her home. She'll have about 2 square miles marked off. Somewhere in there is her den tree. She had her babies in there in January. It'll have an opening about 40 feet up the tree where she dens or sleeps. They don't all den in the top of a tree, but most do. Every now and then they'll find rock outcroppings to den in or turned-over logs. They mark like this every spring—see the hair stuck in the sap?—and right here at this same place her great-great-great-grandmother did the same thing. We're apt to see a bear anytime now!"

Farther up we came to Inspiration Point, with a view of Alum Cave to our right. Dwight pointed out Peregrine Ridge straight ahead and Anakeesta Ridge to our extreme left. The peregrine falcon used to be seen in the Smokies until the late 1940s. "I'm right proud of helping bring the peregrines back to the Park," said Dwight. "We placed some over at Greenbrier Pinnacle near Campsite 31, and we hope they'll come back from South America this year. We'll hack eight more soon." Julia was afraid *hack* meant chopping up the birds.

"No, *hack* means putting the birds out in the park so they can live here," Dwight reassured her.

We went on up the trail and stopped at an overlook. We realized we still had a way to go to get to Clifftop on Mt. LeConte. We were humbled by the majestic forest of red spruce and balsam fir. Ravens flew overhead, their "Awk! Awk! Awk!" answered by the "Chickadee-dee-dee!" of the chickadee. Everywhere was evidence of landslides, some of them healed over with mountain grasses and flowers.

Farther on, we saw cables bolted to the mountain, and Dwight showed us why. A vast rock slide extended hundreds of feet below. Finally we had finished our 2600-foot climb. Dwight introduced us to Tim and Lisa, who manage LeConte Lodge, and we decided to eat our dinner on the clifftop in the bright spring sunshine.

The world was spread out before us. The same ravens that had been lording it over us awhile before now flew below us. At this altitude, and on these currents, they could bob up and down as if on ocean water, but not move forward or backward. Andrea wanted to know about the name, *Smokies*. "The Indians called these mountains 'Sha-cona-ge,'" said Dwight, "which meant 'blue like smoke.' They always have a smoky blue haze. They are very old. At one time they were 18,000 feet high, but they have been wearing down ever since by wind, rain, freezing, and thawing. Sometimes I'll find a round, river-worn rock on top of a lowland ridge, and I'll know a river flowed there once. The bear, buffalo, Indians, and settlers all saw the mountains change, and they're changing while we're sitting here talking."

About 1:30 we started back down the way we came. There was still so much to see that it felt like the first time we'd been over the trail. But Rebekah hadn't seen a bear yet, and that was bothering her. Then Dwight pointed out some rocks that had been turned over since we had come through. "This time of year, the bears are eating a lot of ant eggs, squaw root, and stinging nettles, but mostly ant eggs. She's turned these over just a little while ago. She's real close by." Sure enough, down the trail she had marked as her own, we saw a mama bear and two cubs! She popped her jaws shut a few times and huffed! "She's telling us to stay back," said Dwight. So we did as she asked, and she and the cubs moved on. "Always make a lot of racket, whistling, shaking bushes, and such when you think there's a bear around," Dwight advised.

We saw a lot of other hikers when we got down to Alum Cave again, and the kids had to tell them all about the mother bear and cubs. Dwight just said, "That's the Smokies for you. Once you're here, you'll never be the same. These mountains will change you."

Sampler's Guide to the Smokies' Biggest Trees

Exactly where you are in the Smokies determines the type of forests you will find. The spruce-fir forest, on the high peaks, is made up of beautiful evergreens. The Spruce-Fir Nature Trail off the Clingmans Dome Road is the best place to see these forest kings. The hemlock forest is on slopes up to 4,000 feet or so and along streams. These may be seen near Grotto Falls or Alum Cave Bluffs. Drier slopes and ridges are covered with forests of pine and oak which may be seen at Cades Cove on the Pine-Oak Nature Trail. At Newfound Gap and Clingmans Dome Road, intermingled in spruce-fir forests, are some stands of northern hardwood, usually beech and yellow birch. But the most valuable to loggers, both for variety of trees and ease of logging, was the cove hardwood forest. For this reason, virgin timber of this type is harder to find.

Three places with exceptionally large trees:

Albright Grove

Located in the Cosby (northeast) section of the park. The hike up to the grove is a 7-mile round trip but worth it for the sight of huge tulip poplars, hemlocks, and silver bell trees. The trail is moderately difficult,

with a climb of about 1500 feet. The trail begins at the park boundary adjacent to the privately owned Safari Campground on US 321 about 15 miles east of Gatlinburg. It follows an old road through 3 miles of second-growth forest to a walk (1½ miles) through a virgin cove hardwood forest. (See Smokies map, number 41) There is another way in from the Indian Camp trailhead, about 3½ miles up to Albright Grove. You'll need to stop at the Cosby Ranger Station for specific directions.

Laurel Falls

Another great tree adventure begins after you have made it up to the falls. At Fighting Creek Gap just east of the Elkmont campground on the Little River Road, the blacktop trail up to the falls begins. By all means, stop and enjoy the falls. That's all most people do. But, if you'll notice, a dirt trail continues past the falls. Take this trail about ¼ mile, and you'll be dwarfed by some astounding forest giants. A farmer owned 600 acres of timber here that he jealously guarded from loggers. The trees are truly awesome, mostly tulip poplar and hemlock.

Ekaneetlee Trail

This trail is abandoned now, but it runs through a mighty mountain forest. (You'd better not try it if you don't feel comfortable in the woods or have someone with you who does.) This adventure starts from the Cades Cove Visitor Center. From there, drive south on the Forge Creek Road (two-way), and park where it changes to the one-way Parson Branch Road. Then start up the Gregory Ridge Trail toward Campsite 12, the Forge Creek campsite. About 1½ miles up the trail, you'll cross a footlog. Hike for ½ mile or so on the right side of the stream. You'll come to a huge poplar stump. Turn left directly behind the stump. In 30 or 40 yards, you'll hit a creek. Head upstream. The Ekaneetlee Trail crisscrosses the stream numerous times, and about a mile up the trail there are huge poplars, big buckeyes, and hemlocks that are seldom seen by people. On the way you'll encounter plenty of rhododendron bushes and, the scourge of Tennessee hikers, sawbriers. So it won't be a fast hike. Be sure you're wearing boots and jeans for protection. In season, though, you'll be rewarded by some of the Smokies' best blackberries!

Basic Smokies Information

The park superintendent's address is Gatlinburg, TN 37738. Brochures on the park are available from the Superintendent of Documents, U. S. Government Printing Office, Washington, D.C. 20402. The *Sampler* recommends Handbook 112, *Great Smoky Mountains,* and Handbook 125, *At Home in the Smokies,* both available from that office for a modest fee. Also very helpful is Randolph Shields's *Cades Cove Story* published by the Great Smoky Mountains Natural History Association (1977).

No hunting is allowed in the park. Overnight backcountry camping requires a permit (for your protection). Food cannot be left unattended (for the bears' protection). Don't drink any back-country water without boiling it! Come prepared for all kinds of weather, and know the symptoms of hypothermia. Hikers have died from hypothermia in midsummer at high altitudes, usually because they didn't have rain gear and got soaked to the skin.

A word about bears. They are not in the Smokies for the enjoyment of man. They just happen to live there, perhaps as many as 600 of them. They don't all behave the same way, and generalizations about what to do around them are dangerous. Feeding the bears is prohibited, and by all means stay away from mothers with cubs.

There are seven developed campgrounds and three primitive camping areas in the park. Camping is limited to seven days, and reservations are taken for two camping areas in Tennessee—Elkmont and Cades Cove. For these, call the park and find out the current fees, and then send the appropriate amount in a money order to Ticketron, P.O. Box 2715, San Francisco, CA 94126. Over 100 commercial campgrounds are located nearby. The Tennessee list can be obtained by writing to Knox-visit Welcome Center, 901 East Summit Drive, Knoxville, TN 37915. (615) 523-2316. Ask for *Fishing and Camping in East Tennessee.*

The Smokies has hiking trails for the handicapped as well as for all levels of hiking abilities. Of course, the Appalachian Trail winds through the Smokies too. Some waterfalls are only visible on back-country trails. Be sure to get the *Great Smoky Mountains Trail Map Folder* from the superintendent's office, or the Sierra Club's *Hiker's Guide to the Smokies* at a visitor center. *Walks and Hikes,* a leaflet available from the park office, in-cludes 50 popular day hikes. So whether you hiked in on the Appalachian Trail and plan to spend months hiking every place in the park, or whether you drive up for one of the day hikes, you'll have a great time walking in the Smokies.

Horseback riding, bicycling, fishing, and birding. The Smokies offer miles of horseback trails. You can ride your own steed or rent one from a park concessionaire by the hour or the day. Write the superintendent for the do's and don'ts of horsebacking the Smokies.

No question about it, the best bicycling in the Smokies is the Cades Cove Loop Road. The 11-mile ride is breathtaking anytime, and we're talking about the scenery. The ride itself is a paved, level-to-rolling country road. Saturdays in the summer after 6:00 P.M. you and the other bikers will have it to yourselves—no cars allowed.

Fishing enthusiasts in the Smokies go after smallmouth bass, rock bass, rainbow trout, and brown trout. No bait fishing. Only single-hook artificial lures. The native brook trout are being protected to allow them to build back up in number, so their waters are closed to fishing.

The Other Mountains—The Cherokee National Forest

The Greatest Outdoors has more mountain experiences for you than just those in the magnificent Smo-

There's some great trout fishing in the Smokies.

kies. The Cherokee National Forest presents tremendous opportunities for hiking, camping, off-road-vehicle riding, hunting, and fishing in its 624,000 acres. We can't do much more than introduce you to the riches of the Cherokee in this *Sampler,* but we encourage you to take advantage of all it has to offer.

Rock Creek Gorge Scenic Area, the Watauga Scenic Area, the towns of Elizabethton, known for its covered bridge, and Reliance and the Ocoee Flume are to be found in and near the Cherokee. The forest is a great place to discover on trip after trip to East Tennessee.

There are 29 developed camping areas in the Cherokee, with almost 700 units. There is no reservation system for the campgrounds, so you'll just have to show up and see what's available. Of course, you can primitive-camp almost anywhere, but be sure to haul out everything you haul in.

Various Cherokee trails are great for horseback riding, bicycling, riding motorcycles, driving off-road vehicles, or hiking. Some have been described in self-guiding brochures which may be obtained from the Forest Service. By all means, if you're hiking in the back country, keep the rangers advised of your plans. The John Muir and Warriors' Passage Trails, the Appalachian Trail, and the Citico Creek and Big Frog Mountain trails systems are some of the more notable trails. The Citico Creek Wilderness is right on the state's boundary line just south of the Smokies. The wilderness is easily reached from Knoxville, Oak Ridge, Cleveland, and Chattanooga. The Citico is widely known for outstanding fall colors. Although the timber is mostly second-growth, due to overzealous logging and a terrible fire in 1925, the forest is abundant and full of black bear, wild boar, deer, and wild turkey.

The Harvey Broome Group of the Tennessee Sierra Club has put together an excellent and most accurate guide to the hiking trails of the Citico Creek Wilderness. You need to get a copy of it if you plan to hike any of these trails, but here are some of the sights you can see.

The Crowder Branch Trail follows the creekbed of its namesake for about 2½ miles, climbing 1,440 feet in the process. The trail crosses the creek numerous times, so be prepared to get your feet wet. The trail passes a waterslide, pool, and waterfall, goes through rhododendron patches and up to an old homesite with an orchard, meadow, and delicious, cool spring. Here it joins with the Fodderstack Trail, if you're interested in pressing on.

The Falls Branch Trail goes for only one third of a mile from the trailhead next to a bridge on the Tellico Plains-Robbinsville Road. You'll need to turn beside the bridge northeast along an old roadbed for about 400 yards and watch for the hikers' sign on the left. On this short trail, you'll pass through great hemlock trees, cross a creek, and go through a deep fracture in a large boulder to a gorgeous waterfall. Be careful of slippery rocks when approaching the falls. The trail and the falls are majestically beautiful.

Five of Tennessee's premier white-water rivers flow through the Cherokee—Ocoee, Hiwassee, French Broad, Tellico, and Nolichucky. Areas for swimming, boating, and skiing are available within forest boundaries.

Hunting and fishing regulations in the park are set by the Tennessee Wildlife Resources Agency. They may be contacted toll-free at (800) 262-6704. Fishing enthusiasts are usually after the rainbow, brown, or brook trout, while hunters seek black bear, wild boar, deer, squirrel, grouse, and turkey.

For more information, write: Supervisor's Office, U.S. Forest Service, 2800 North Ocoee Street, Cleveland, TN 37311, or call (615) 476-9700. Free maps and brochures are available for the park as a whole, and wilderness area maps may be purchased for $1.

Yep, They're All in Tennessee!

1. Spectacular **Ruby Falls**—1120 feet beneath Lookout Mountain. The tallest underground waterfall, and the deepest commercial cavern in the United States.

2. World's largest natural **rhododendron field**—600 plus acres at Roan Mountain.

3. **Virgin Falls,** which emerges from one cave only to disappear into another, after a fall of over 100 feet.

4. **Fall Creek Falls,** the highest waterfall in the eastern United States.

5. **Reelfoot Lake,** formed by earthquakes in 1811–12, which caused the Mississippi River to flow backward and may have been the most severe quakes in North American history.

6. The largest remaining **natural prairie** in the eastern United States, near Manchester.

7. What may be the **largest pecan tree** in the world at Natchez Trace Park.

8. More species of **salamanders** than anywhere else in the world.

9. The **largest virgin forest** of its kind in North America, near Savage Gulf.

10. The **Great Smoky Mountains National Park,** America's most visited national park. The Smokies have more varieties of plant life than the continent of Europe!

11. The **oldest manmade tunnel** in the United States. You'll have to float the Harpeth River in Middle Tennessee to see it.

12. The **largest red cedar forest** in the United States—at Cedars of Lebanon State Park.

13. The **largest cave room** in eastern America, Cumberland Caverns.

14. The **largest wall of onyx** in the world—Forbidden Caverns.

15. The best **hang gliding** in the eastern United States, off Lookout Mountain, Raccoon Mountain, and in Sequatchie Valley.

16. The **world's largest underground lake,** The Lost Sea, near Sweetwater, Tennessee.

An I-40 Tour of Tennessee Terrain

When you look at a map of our state, you notice a couple of things right off: Tennessee's horizontal boundaries were set by people; Tennessee's vertical boundaries, her "living lines," were set by nature.

In fact, if you go through West Tennessee from north to south or East Tennessee from northeast to southwest, you'll experience a Tennessee that looks, except for city and country differences, pretty much the same. People will be growing the same crops on land that looks just like the acreage you drove past a few miles back.

Actually, Tennessee has eight strikingly different land types, but the only way you'll be conscious of them is to travel from east to west, as the first settlers did.

In this way you will experience terrain, forest types, and climatic changes equivalent to a drive from Canada to the Louisiana Delta, all in one state—Tennessee.

Now, the reason this is so important for you, the *Sampler* reader, is that these land types determine how you experience the Greatest Outdoors—where you white-water canoe or where you float, where you explore caves, stand under waterfalls, or ride updrafts on a hang-glider. So keep your thumb on the *Sampler's* map section, because we're going to drive across one of Tennessee's newest highways, Interstate 40, which bisects the entire state, to talk about Tennessee's oldest geographical features, the contours of land and water that make the Greatest Outdoors.

The Unaka Mountains

We'll assume you're coming in on I-40 from Asheville, North Carolina, deep in the Blue Ridge Mountains. When you hit the Tennessee line, you'll be in the Unaka Mountains, as they're called in Tennessee. (The Great Smoky Mountains are that part of the Unakas inside the Great Smoky Mountains National Park.) The Unakas run diagonally from northeast to southwest, and make up the eastern boundary of Tennessee.

The Unakas are old. Unlike many of the world's younger barren and rocky mountain ranges, they are teeming with animal and plant life. The terrain is rough and rugged, with deep impenetrable forests, high-velocity streams, and many splendid waterfalls.

Mountain coves like Cades, Wear, and Tuckaleechee, are renowned for their beauty and fertility. Here also are puzzling, naturally cleared areas known as balds. Scientists are still arguing about how these came to be. Here are colorful fields of natural wildflowers, such as the rhododendrons on Roan Mountain. The val-

leys are from 1,000 to 1,500 feet above sea level. Among the peaks, the highest point in the state is Clingmans Dome, which is 6,642 feet. Several other mountains are over 6,000 feet in elevation.

If you were actually in the car driving, you'd want to stop and spend some time in the mountains. They are breathtakingly beautiful, and much of Tennessee's mountainous land is publicly accessible in either the Great Smoky Mountains National Park or the Cherokee National Forest.

Tennessee's mountains are there waiting for you to visit. But before you make your reservations, let's continue this tour of Tennessee terrain.

The Valley and Ridge

If you stay on I-40 you'll travel only a very few miles before you begin to notice that the land is changing. Near Hartford, the descent from the mountains has brought you into the next geological division, which is known as Valley and Ridge, or sometimes the Valley of East Tennessee. The ridges alternate with broad, fertile valleys, all running on the same diagonal as the mountains. Some of these are Clinch Ridge, Powell Ridge, and Bays Mountains (3,097 feet) in the north, and Whiteoak Mountain (1,495 feet) in the south.

The ridges were folded up at the same time the mountains were pushed up. Then erosion made this area of Tennessee what it is today. The ridges were harder rock and the valleys softer. Most of the valleys have streams in them, but some waterways, including the Tennessee River itself, that run across the grain of the diagonal and must have started from fractures that ran across both the ridges and valleys.

East Tennessee's major towns—Chattanooga, Oak Ridge, Knoxville, Johnson City, Kingsport, and Bristol—and largest lakes are all in this Valley and Ridge section. The alternation between valley and ridge made this the premier area of Tennessee for hydroelectric power and lake building. It is both Tennessee's prime industrial corridor and one of its most beautiful areas at the same time.

If you were actually driving I-40, you'd really be tired right now. After all, you've driven many miles into the Greatest Outdoors. So just 20 miles west of Knoxville, take exit 364, turn toward Oak Ridge, and eat wonderful fried fish at the Crosseyed Cricket Restaurant. If you have time, they'll let you catch your own supper. (See "Eatin' Good" for directions). There, boy, that was dee-licious! Now, back to the map.

The Cumberland Plateau

After you've traveled on I-40 through Knoxville, past Oak Ridge, and just beyond Kingston, Tennessee, you'll begin ascending again.

On the map, you can virtually define the limits of the Cumberland Plateau by taking the distance between Kingston and Monterey and running it on the same East Tennessee diagonal we've already pointed out to you. This is part of the Appalachian Plateau that reaches up into New York. From the east, the plateau is defined by cliffs averaging 900 feet in height. On the west, it gradually dissolves into foothills and rolling terrain.

Farmer plowing a Tennessee ridgetop
Photo by Joe Clark

There's no doubt when you reach the plateau on I-40. The highway begins ascending at the Rockwood-Harriman exit, takes a turn to the southwest, and goes right up the face of the plateau. Once you're up on the Cumberland, then the highway turns northwest toward Monterey. This should help you realize that long ago the plateau was a real barrier. Then, travelers had to pass through the Cumberland Gap to cross the plateau. Now, you can make it up and over in your Winnebago!

Deep gorges cut into the sandstone plateau, and there are two beautiful valleys, the Elk Valley to the north and the Sequatchie Valley to the south. I-75 north out of Knoxville takes a turn up by Buckeye and runs right along the crest of Pine Mountain. You can look to your left and see Elk Valley the whole time you're on the crest. In Tennessee the Sequatchie Valley is over 60 miles long, 5 miles wide, and has cliffs 1,000 feet high on each side. (See "Tours and Trails" for drives in the Sequatchie.)

Fall Creek Falls and Burgess Falls are two of the Cumberland's many beautiful waterfalls. Just north of

Oak ridge is the highest point on the plateau, 3,534-feet Cross Mountain.

The Highland Rim

When you get to Monterey on I-40, you'll be making the descent into the Highland Rim. You'll keep descending all the way through Smith County. The rim surrounds the Central Basin (the fifth area we'll talk about). So as you head westward, you'll drive through the Eastern Highland Rim, then through the Central Basin, and then the Western Highland Rim.

The Rim includes all kinds of terrain, rolling hills and deep-cut narrow valleys, streams and waterfalls. Parts of the rim are very flat, such as an area in Coffee, Cannon, and Warren counties known as the barrens. This includes the May Prairie near Manchester, southeast of Nashville, where unique native grasses have survived for tens of thousands of years. There are plenty of caves and sinkholes, and a lot of rainfall off the Highland Rim drains underground. All of this makes for unusual rock formations and a cavers dreamscape.

The average elevation of the rim is 1000 feet, but 2,074-feet-high Short Mountain, visible from US 70 S, is a remnant of the Cumberland Plateau. The western half of the rim has the highest elevations, especially in Lawrence County around Summertown.

The Central Basin
Between the two halves of the rim lies the elliptical Central Basin. On I-40, you'll be descending into the basin in Smith County at about the 255 mile mark. You'll stay in the basin until just past Nashville.

The Central Basin includes what some Middle Tennesseans like to call the "Dimple of the Universe" south of Nashville toward Columbia down US 31. The first settlers found the Basin thick with native bluegrass.

The basin features lush rolling farmland. Steep Highland Rim hills, some up to 1,300 feet in elevation, thrust up here and there above the basin floor. The basin is crisscrossed with countless meandering, slow-moving streams, and thousands of springs. Here too are many caves and sinkholes.

The middle part of the basin has an average elevation of 600 feet, sloping up to 750 feet at the edges. This accounts for the beautiful rolling hills that visitors to Nashville have long admired. The city is on the edge of the basin and the Western Highland Rim. Parts of the basin are rocky and covered with cedar glades. These glades, due to the limestone so close to the surface, harbor their own distinctive species of wildflowers and other plants.

Few people can drive through Nashville without stopping to hear some great music. After all, this is Music City. But after you've sampled its country, jazz, and bluegrass (with the aid of *The Tennessee Sampler's* music section, of course) you'll feel ready for Memphis and the blues. So bundle up the kids, gas up the van, hit the restrooms, and head west on I-40 again.

The Tennessee River Valley
After you pass through the Western Highland Rim, some 75-odd miles from Nashville near the Cuba Landing Exit, you'll be in the Tennessee River Valley. If you keep driving, you'll be across the valley in jig time, since it spans only 15 or 20 miles at its widest. The Birdsong Road exit marks the other end of the valley.

The Tennessee River flows north across the state for more than 100 miles. Its valley is crossed by many smaller streams all flowing into the Tennessee. The flood plain of the river itself is about 1½ miles wide at the Kentucky line and about 3½ miles wide at the southern border. But soil deposited by the river is to be found well up the sides of the surrounding hills, indicating that the water level was pretty high at one time. This was possibly due to the advance and retreat of the polar ice caps.

The area of the Tennessee River Valley has its own rich culture based on the River itself as a source of food and commerce. Not only fishing, but digging for clams and mussels, and harvesting shells and pearls are a way of life for most dwellers in the valley.

The Coastal Plain
Well, as they say, it's all downhill from here! Soon after you come out of the Tennessee River Valley, the Interstate enters Natchez Trace State Park. Here begins the West Tennessee Uplands, and then, about a third of the way to Memphis, the West Tennessee Plain.

From the Tennessee River westward, the underlying rock begins to slope down toward the Mississippi, and the ground on top of it does the same. West Tennessee topsoil has a sandy base underlying it. It is in most respects a coastal plain, just like Southern Louisiana or Mississippi or the coast of the Carolinas. In the uplands, such as in the Natchez Trace State Park, there are hills, but gone are the limestone caves and waterfalls of the eastern two-thirds of the state. West Tennessee waters are just as beautiful—the Hatchie, Big Sandy, and Beech Rivers—but more subdued. The farmland here looks the way you would expect that of the Plantation South to look. When you arrive at the very edge of the Coastal Plain, just before you drive into the Mighty Mississip', you'll see the last prominent geological feature of West Tennessee, low bluffs along the Mississippi usually about 100 feet high.

The Mississippi River Valley
Now, hold on. Just because you've made it to Memphis, don't shut your *Sampler* and rush off to Graceland, because we've got one more area to talk about. Ol' Man River gives Tennessee her last geological region. He actually gives it and takes it away with great fickleness.

At times 14 miles wide in Tennessee, the Mississippi River Valley is as changeable as it is fertile. It includes swamps, lakes, and islands all created by the restless river.

At its northern end is remarkable Reelfoot Lake, up in Lake County. Reelfoot was formed by the Great New Madrid Earthquakes of 1811 and 1812, when eyewitnesses saw the river run backward for a time! The land sank, and creeks, springs, and maybe the river itself formed this warm-water lake in a matter of weeks. The middle Mississippi Valley has seen its share of earthquakes, and some believe those bluffs we were just talking about are fault-line markers in the Greatest Outdoors.

Something to Think About
We're through with this little geological tour of Tennessee, but we want to leave you something to think about, or "study on" as a wise Tennessee friend of ours would say. Think about the ways that land shapes people. It determines the animals and birds they can hunt and the fish they can catch. It determines their building materials. The land determines the things they have to do to make a living and how hard that living is apt to be.

If they are farming, it determines whether they can afford hired help and whether or not they can plant cotton, tobacco, or soybeans.

On the banks of abundant rivers such as the Tennessee, people fish or dig mussels and find pearls for a living. They mend their nets and build their boats just like Louisiana Cajuns.

Where eons-old trails converge, and the Cumberland River flows, they set up government and commerce, as at Nashville.

Where the Mississippi narrows and concentrates the wealth of a continent, they build a port city, Memphis, as busy and wealthy as if it were on the seacoast.

Where East Tennessee ridges separate wide valleys, they dam up rivers, creating lakes for flood control and power generation, and industries that forever alter our relationship to our environment.

And back in the mountains where the White Man first entered and the Red Man last clung, they stay fiercely independent. There the mountain people still take what they can from the land and make much of what they need for the taking.

So today, Tennesseans are still living according to generations-old accommodations to their land. Some of us work with computer chips, and some with cow chips, but all of us are shaped by the Greatest Outdoors. And the variety of our land is reflected in the variety of us who *are* Tennessee.

If you want to read more about Tennessee's geology, the best source, written for the layman, is Ned Luther's *Our Restless Earth* (UT Press, 1977), available from the State Conservation Department.

Evan Means' Guide to Tennessee Trails

Evan Means and his sturdy walking stick have hiked more miles of Tennessee's wooded trails than anyone else the *Sampler* knows. He has given us, in *Tennessee Trails,* one of the best trail guides any state possesses. We asked Evan to share his favorite trails with you, and he has done just that, with clear directions and a few stories that will make you want to hike them all.

A good way to get acquainted with Tennessee's geography and history is to hike on her many trails, from the Mississippi River to the high mountains along the North Carolina border. There isn't a continuous footpath from the "Father of Waters" to the mountains, nor do any of the trails run directly from north to south or from east to west. Tennessee's geography is somewhat "on the bias."

In the book, *Tennessee Trails,* we covered the trails from east to west because that was the way the pioneers moved across the state in settling the land. However, to make it easy for the twentieth-century traveler to follow the map, we'll take them from left to right—from west to east.

The traveler driving south from St. Louis on I-55, or from Chicago on I-57, should switch over to US 51 at Cairo (pronounced "Kay-ro"), Illinois. After crossing Kentucky into Tennessee, stay on 51 until you're near Alex Haley's native town of Henning, then turn west on State 87 to visit Fort Pillow State Historical Area. This was the site of some heavy fighting during the Civil War,

on the first Chickasaw Bluff, site of Fort Prudhomme, built by French explorers in 1682.

The Fort Pillow Historical Trail is listed in *Hiking Trails of America,* published by Historical Hiking Trails, Inc., in Memphis, and we used Ken Humphreys' description in *Tennessee Trails.* It provides striking views of barge tows on the Mississippi and of Fulton, Arkansas, across the river.

There are few trails in West Tennessee, but some have been added and others are in the planning stage since we did the research for the book. Meeman-Shelby Forest State Park, just north of Memphis, has an elaborate trail system which is popular with school groups and Scout troops. Mosquitoes are a problem there in spring and early summer, but the birds and plant life are interesting. Tall poplars (tulip trees) and beeches with initials carved on them populate the deep woods.

Leaving Memphis from Union Avenue on US 72 and State 57, veer left at Collierville and follow 57 east through Grand Junction. Watch for the sign pointing to Big Hill Pond State Environmental Education Area, a short distance east of Pocahontas. This area lies along the Mississippi border, and its 19 miles of trails follow creeks, go across a swamp on a board walk, and include a long wooden footbridge over an arm of the lake. I ate my fill of muscadine grapes there in September.

Leaving Big Hill Pond, it's a short trip to the east to Pickwick Landing State Resort Park, which has plush accommodations, a campground, and a marina, plus some well-marked trails for walking in the woods. From Pickwick, you have the option of doubling back to visit Shiloh National Military Park or going north after crossing Pickwick Dam to connect with US 64 at Savannah.

On US 64 you cross the Natchez Trace Parkway east of Waynesboro and arrive at David Crockett State Park at the edge of Lawrenceburg. There's a nice trail system here that you can walk out in less than a day. I followed signs pointing to Crockett Falls on the Shoal Creek Trail and arrived at a pretty little waterfall only about 3 feet high. This was the site of a grist mill operated by Davy Crockett before he moved on to the cane brakes of West Tennessee.

If you have time for a side trip, take State 50 from Fayetteville to Lynchburg for a tour of the famous Jack Daniel Distillery, then continue eastward on State 55 through Tullahoma to Manchester to visit the Old Stone Fort Archaeological Area. An excellent trail leads past waterfalls on the Duck and Little Duck Rivers and traverses the "fort," an apparent prehistoric fortification that has puzzled archaeologists.

From Manchester, take I-24 from US 41 at Mile 114 and ascend to the top of the Cumberland Plateau at Monteagle, 20 miles to the southeast. Go left on State 56 and stop at the South Cumberland Recreation Complex Visitor Center for maps and orientation. There are some 100 miles of trails in the South Cumberland Complex. The Fiery Gizzard Trail begins in Grundy Forest Natural Area at the edge of Tracy City and runs to Foster Falls Public Use Area (TVA). The Great Stone Door at Beersheba Springs, 19 miles north of Tracy City on State 56, is the start of a system of day-use trails and a backpack trail connecting with Savage Gulf State Natural Area.

At the Stone Door a trail leads down through a giant fissure in the sheer bluff, into the Big Creek Gulf near its junction with the Collins River gorge. I was walking on a level section of the Cumberland Plateau when I found myself at the edge of a yawning gorge some 500 feet deep. A red-tailed hawk soared high above the canyon floor but still 200 feet or more below me. I took the Big Creek Gulf Day Loop to the right and soon flushed a flock of grouse.

A connecting trail drops to the floor of the gorge and takes you to Savage Gulf. By highway, take State 108 east from State 56 and follow the signs. Mack Prichard's account of the history of Savage Gulf in *Tennessee Trails* is well worth reading. The Savage Gulf trails were described by Robert D. Brown, cofounder with Prichard and this writer of the Tennessee Trails Association (TTA).

Bob was leading a winter backpack trip on the North Rim Trail, and they spent the night in the hunters' cabin at Hobbs Camp. A member of the party woke up in the night to discover a skunk enjoying the warmth under the wood-burning stove. Luckily, they were able to usher the visitor out without getting sprayed.

Leaving Savage Gulf at the North Rim trailhead, continue north to the junction of State 8. Here you have the option of going north on State Routes 8 and 111 to the south entrance to Fall Creek Falls State Park or turning south to US 127 to go to Signal Mountain and the southern terminus of the Cumberland Trail. Fall Creek Falls has a great backpack loop and shorter day hikes.

Governor Lamar Alexander has set a goal for completion of the Cumberland Trail in 1985. The original section of this trail, from Cumberland Gap to Oliver Springs, was proposed by this writer in 1965. It was included in the State Scenic Trails System when the act was passed in 1971 and extends from Tristates Peak in Cumberland Gap National Historical Park to Signal Mountain, a distance of more than 180 miles. It is complete from Cumberland County to Tristates Peak.

The southern terminus of the Cumberland Trail is near the Alexian Brothers Home in Signal Mountain. The first leg goes past Edwards Point where there is a magnificent view of the "Grand Canyon of Tennessee," and on to a parking area in Prentice Cooper State Forest. A flood wiped out a section of the trail in 1982, and it has been relocated to the top of the plateau. Purple rhododendron (*Rhodendron Catawbiense*) blooms here in May, a month to six weeks earlier than in the famous gardens on Roan Mountain. Lush patches of Jack-in-the-pulpit grow in moist spots below the rim of the canyon.

Coming out of Memphis toward Nashville, you have the option of US 64 and State 100 to Chickasaw State Park, which has camping and trails, or I-40 past Jackson to Natchez Trace State Park and Forest. The 40-mile Red Leaves Backpack Trail in Natchez Trace is the longest state park trail in Tennessee. This is an easy trail in gently rolling woodland. Continuing east on I-40, take State 48 to Dickson and US 70 to Montgomery Bell

State Park, where there is a 12-mile overnight trail which winds around lakes and streams and passes an old iron furnace.

Several good trails are easily accessible as you travel east from Nashville. First is a new system in Long Hunter State Park, south from the Mt. Juliet Exit, Mile 226. Volunteers from the Tennessee Trails Association helped build this system. Hidden Springs Trail in Cedars of Lebanon State Park, on US 231 south of I-40, is a day-use loop trail that gives the hiker a rare opportunity to view topography known in only one other place in the world, in the Karst Mountains in Yugoslavia. The trail area is home to 19 rare species of plants that grow nowhere else.

Continuing south on 231, the eastern trailhead of the Twin Forks Trail, 22 miles of parallel hiking and horseback paths, is located at Walter Hill Dam, 26 miles from I-40. This trail on Corps of Engineers land around J. Percy Priest Reservoir was built and is maintained by TTA and volunteers from Murfreesboro and Rutherford County.

Returning to Lebanon, go east on US 70N to Carthage, turn left on State 25 and right on State 85 to the Defeated Creek Recreation Area on Cordell Hull Reservoir. The 6-mile Bear Waller Gap Trail provides beautiful views and a variety of plant life. Continue eastward on State 85 through the Cumberland foothills, and you come to the south access to Standing Stone State Park and Forest at Hilham. The main entrance is on State 52 at Timothy, 11 miles north of Livingston.

I like the 5-mile loop on the Overlook, Bryan's Fork, and Lake trails. This loop provides variety: cedar glades, deep woods, and lakeshore scenery, plus abundant bird life. Standing Stone is only a little more than 30 miles from I-40 at either Cookeville or Monterey, but if you have time, continue eastward on State 52 to Jamestown, turn left on US 127, and right on State 154 to Pickett State Park and Forest.

Pickett is classed as a rustic state park, situated in a remote area on the Kentucky line. There are campsites and cabins and more than 30 miles of trails. You can see grouse, deer, rare plants, natural bridges, and much more. It is worth a day of your time to hike the Hidden Passage and Rock Creek trails. Pickett is also the starting point for the John Muir State Scenic Trail. Not many people know that the great naturalist walked across Tennessee in 1867, long before he founded the Sierra Club in California.

John Muir walked from Louisville to Florida, passing through Burkesville and Albany, Kentucky, and Jamestown, Tennessee. He angled across the Cumberlands to the Emory River and downstream to Kingston. This walk is described in *The Thousand-Mile Walk to the Gulf*, which can still be found in some libraries. Muir went across country from Kingston to Philadelphia, visited a gold mine at Coker Creek, then went up the Hiwassee River to Murphy, North Carolina. The United States Forest Service has built a section of the John Muir Trail along the Hiwassee in Cherokee National Forest.

You are now getting into hiking country. From Pickett, take the Leatherwood Ford Road across the Big

Spectacular wilderness scenery at the Big South Fork

South Fork National River and Recreation Area to Oneida. Much of the extensive trail system in the Big South Fork area is complete, and you can get information at the Park Service Visitor Center on Leatherwood Ford Road. Going south on US 27 from Oneida, the traveler may take State 63 eastward through the highest range of the Cumberland Mountains to Cove Lake State Park, headquarters for the north end of the Cumberland Trail, or go on south to Wartburg and east on State 62 to Frozen Head State Natural Area.

You should not leave the Big South Fork area without a hike on the Honey Creek Trail, developed by Hiwassee Land Company (Bowater). Turn west on State 52 toward Rugby and watch for the Pocket Wilderness sign. This is the most interesting, most rugged trail I hiked while doing research for *Tennessee Trails*. There are "rock houses," sheer bluffs, and a breathtaking view of the gorge of the Big South Fork of the Cumberland River. There are ladders to get over impassable bluffs.

If you choose Frozen Head as your next stop, you won't regret it. This wild area is a favorite with backpackers, naturalists, and wildflower lovers. I caught up with four male school teachers from Florida on top of Frozen Head Mountain on a Thanksgiving weekend. They had been making too much noise and hadn't seen any wildlife. I passed them and flushed a grouse 300 yards on down the trail.

Park headquarters at Frozen Head is only 25 miles from Oak Ridge's North Ridge Trail, the first National Recreation Trail designated within a city's limits. If you don't have a copy of *Tennessee Trails* with you, maps may be obtained at the Oak Ridge Public Library. From Oak Ridge, you have the option of taking State 61 through Clinton and Norris to Big Ridge State Rustic Park, which has my favorite state trails. The Big Valley Trail follows Big Ridge to the rock outcropping where Indians ambushed the pioneer Peter Graves in 1790, then drops off to the site of Sharp's Station on Norris Lake, the first settlement west of the Blue Ridge. Or you can take State 95, I-75, and State 68 to Tellico Plains, gateway to the south end of Cherokee National Forest. There are around 100 trails in Cherokee National Forest, and the best of them are in the Tellico Ranger District. A deer trotted down the trail ahead of me on the Fodderstack Trail, along the border of the Joyce Kilmer Wilderness Area. A grouse flushed and landed quickly. I paused a moment, then walked forward quietly. It was standing beside the trail, head held high, waiting to see if I was chasing it.

Before we skip over the Great Valley of the Tennessee from the Cumberlands to the high mountains of the Blue Ridge range, we should visit Bowater's Piney River Trail near Spring City and the Laurel-Snow Wilderness at Dayton, where the famous Monkey Trial was held in 1925. The former follows the Piney River, Duskin Creek, and Newby Branch 10 miles over easy grades, with steel bridges across the streams. Laurel-Snow provides spectacular views of the TVA lakes and the Cumberland Mountains.

As we mentioned in the opening paragraph, Tennessee geography is somewhat on the bias. The Great Valley of the Tennessee angles from northeast to southwest, from Bristol to Chattanooga. Indian war paths followed the valley, and there was a trade route from Ohio to Florida through Cumberland Gap, long before it was discovered by Dr. Walker in 1750. These are all highway routes today.

Taking State 68 from Tellico Plains, you come to the old town of Coker Creek. An unimproved road leads from there to Unicoi Gap on the first toll road from North Carolina into Tennessee in pioneer days. The Unicoi Trail drops down the mountain to State 68, and the Unicoi Mountain Trail continues to the mouth of Coker Creek. I am told it is still possible to pan gold there.

On the Unicoi Trail, a grouse stepped into the path ahead of me. I froze before he got a good look at me, and he wasn't sure what I was. He fluffed his ruff and bobbed his tail, trying to get me to move, but he held his ground until I started forward, and then he flew away. I camped one night in the Ocoee Ranger District near the Cohutta Wilderness on the Georgia line, where I enjoyed an owl serenade. Screech owls made forays through the camp a couple of times, then a tenor "hoot owl," obviously immature, sounded off just before I fell asleep. Just before dawn, a barred owl sounded its deep-chested hoots nearby.

There are six ranger districts in the Cherokee National Forest, and maps are available in each office. On the north end, north of Great Smoky Mountains National

Park, are the Watauga District at Elizabethton, Unaka at Erwin, and Nolichucky at Greeneville. The Appalachian Trail crosses these, and there are many shorter trails. Roan Mountain State Park, Horse Creek Recreation Area, and Houston Valley Recreation Area are good jumping-off places for exploring them.

On the south end, the Tellico District Ranger Office is located in the forest off Tellico River Road, upriver from Tellico Plains. The Hiwassee District Office is on US 411 at Etowah, and the Ocoee District Office is on US 64 at Parksville, east of 411. Maps of the entire Cherokee National Forest and the wilderness areas may be purchased from the Forest Supervisor's Office, 2800 North Ocoee Street, P. O. Box 2010, Cleveland, TN 37311.

I have not included Great Smoky Mountains National Park here, since so much has been written about trails in the Smokies. There are more than 300 trails in Tennessee, from short nature walks to overnight backpack trails, so we can mention only a few. Maps of the state park trails are available at park offices and from the Tennessee Department of Conservation, Division of State Parks, 701 Broadway, Nashville, TN 37203.

There are also some excellent trails in TVA's Small Wild Areas. The River Bluff Trail at Norris Dam is the best wildflower walk I know of in the spring. Lady Finger Bluff, on the east bank of Kentucky Lake near Perryville and Linden, has views of the lake and some rare gnarled cedars on top of the bluff. Information about TVA recreation may be obtained from their Information Office, 400 West Summit Hill Drive, Knoxville, TN 37902.

Spectator Sports in the Greatest Outdoors

The Iroquois Memorial Steeplechase

On the second Saturday in May one of the nation's rarest horse racing events takes place in Nashville, Tennessee, at Percy Warner Park. On a Tennessee spring afternoon, the Iroquois Memorial Steeplechase and other races will unfold across waves of shimmering spring grass. Before the blue haze of distant hills, eight exciting races will entertain a crowd of over 40,000.

There is no admission charge for hillside viewing, and spectators are encouraged to bring blankets and lawn chairs and spend a delightful afternoon enjoying this great rite of spring.

Between the races, members of the crowd will dip into their food baskets. The music of portable radios will float on gusty breezes that dance with Frisbees and an occasional kite. Suddenly across the clovered hills, the famous Iroquois bell sounds, alerting riders and their mounts of the next race. The crowd will stir, the starter will drop the flag, horses will break, and the roar of the crowd will sound like any other horse race. But this race

is like no other. It is strictly for amateurs and strictly noncommercial. In 40 years of running the race, there has never been a scandal. The losers and winners trot off side-by-side, still friends. The people attending the steeplechase come for the pleasure of being in the countryside, watching horses and riders race their best.

Besides the grand exhibition of fine horse flesh, the Iroquois makes enough profit—from the sale of box seats, program ads, concessions, and private donations—to donate substantially to the Vanderbilt Children's Hospital. In 1983, contributions totaled over $137,000. As one ad man put it, "The horses run now so that children will later."

The Iroquois Memorial Steeplechase honors the only American-bred horse to win the English Derby. Iroquois, stabled and raised at historic Belle Meade in Nashville, won in 1881. His victory signaled the racing world that the American challenge had begun. Iroquois retired to the fields of Belle Meade and died in 1899, but his memory lived on.

Regardless of the records and winners, the Iroquois serves as an enjoyable springtime event that brings the Nashville community and friends together. Percy Warner Park, site of the races, is located southwest of Nashville on Old Hickory Boulevard between Hillsboro Road and State 100.

The National Field Trials

It has been called "the Super Bowl of bird dogs, the World Series of the hunting fraternity, the Olympics of the canine world." *It* is officially known as The National Field Trial Championships. Beginning on the third Monday of each February, bird dog enthusiasts from all over the United States converge on the Ames Plantation in Grand Junction, Tennessee, some 50 miles east of Memphis for 8 to 10 days of intense competition to decide the National Champion Bird Dog.

Ames Plantation has been synonymous with the quest for the best bird dog since the turn of the century when Hobart C. Ames brought the competition to Grand Junction and established the guidelines used in selecting a champion.

"It is an honor just to be allowed into the national competition," explains Ames Plantation superintendent Jim Anderson. "There are strict qualifications each dog must meet, so that by the time the competition actually gets underway eliminations have already reduced the

field to the top 30 or 40 dogs."

For those top dogs, the National Field Trials represent one of the most grueling tests of endurance in the sports world.

"February can bring almost any kind of weather to Grand Junction," Anderson says. "Sometimes it is sunny and mild, but we are just as likely to have rain, snow, or sleet. A dog must be able to compete properly in whatever conditions exist. He must hunt through thickets, sand, ditches, creeks, and all type of terrain.

"The dogs at Grand Junction are primarily hunting for quail, although there are usually some woodcock on the plantation grounds during February. During the three-hour hunt, each dog will cover a linear distance of 11 to 12 miles, but he will actually run much farther than that, which means a dog must be in absolutely perfect physical condition to have any chance at all in this caliber of competition."

For the large gallery of spectators following the hunt on horseback, there is the chance to assess the competition or just to enjoy the spectacle of a bird dog doing what he does best. For the judges and dogs, however, it is a test of style as well as talent and stamina, and the Amesian standards are high.

"The dog must have great bird sense," Hobart Ames declared in setting those standards. "He must show perfect work on both coveys and singles. He must possess speed, range, style, character, courage, stamina, and good manners always. He must hunt the birds, and not the handler hunt the dog. He must be bold, snappy, and spirited."

Although the dogs are the main attraction during the field trials, Ames Plantation itself is one of Tennessee's most interesting places. Built in 1847, the plantation was purchased by Hobart Ames in 1901 and quickly developed an outstanding reputation for its livestock and agricultural programs. Angus cattle bred on the plantation since 1913 have won scores of blue ribbons all across the United States. Today, the 18,600-acre Ames Plantation is a part of the University of Tennessee system.

Bristol's Blistering Speedway

Tucked away in the Blue Ridge Mountains just south of Bristol, Tennessee, is a motorsport complex that attracts racing fans like a magnet. Spaciously laid out across hundreds of acres, the complex consists of two separate racing facilities: Bristol International Raceway and Thunder Valley Dragway.

The Raceway is a mecca for NASCAR Winston Cup racing fans. Unlike many tracks, the Raceway offers a totally unobstructed view where fans can take in all the exciting, split-second action. From watching pit crews change two tires and pump 20 gallons of gasoline in 13 seconds to gasping as their favorite driver swaps paint and races door handle to door handle at 100 MPH, everything can be seen out in the open.

The track is a .533 mile oval. Straightaways are short, but the turns are banked high and steep—the steepest of any in motorsport (36 degrees). Consequently, high speed is especially the name of the game on this compact raceway. In fact, it holds the record as the world's fastest 1/2-mile track at 112.5 MPH

Because of its high-banked construction, drivers have to overcome extraordinary circumstances. The "G" force is so powerful, drivers must don a special helmet harness that combats the relentless centrifugal force pulling against their heads and necks. In addition, during each grueling three-hour race, drivers really cannot relax, for they are constantly turning.

The Raceway annually hosts 2 of the 30 NASCAR races in America. The Valleydale 500 is a daytime event

Flatwood Hank, 1985 Champion
Photo by Henry Reynolds

in early spring, and the Busch 500 takes place at night in late summer. Both attract top drivers like Bobby Allison and Darrell Waltrip.

Within walking distance of the Raceway is the headquarters for the International Hot Rod Association (IHRA), a drag-racing sanctioning body, as well as the drag-race strip itself.

Thunder Valley is an apt name, for the strip is laid out in the center of a narrow valley with tree covered hills on either side. As vehicles blaze down the strip, engines roar and echo, filling the air with high-powered intensity. Engines are revved so high that fans sitting next to each other must shout to be heard, and the vibrations cause fans to actually *feel* the power.

The strip is made of asphalt and is three quarters of a mile in length. Two vehicles at a time blast off from a standing start at one end, and streak down the strip for a timed quarter-mile race. The extra half-mile is needed for these super-quick vehicles to stop.

Pure acceleration is the essence of this sport. Therefore before the races start, officials spread a substance akin to industrial-strength superglue on the track in order to create maximum friction between tire and surface. Heating up the tires also increases velocity.

Of the eight IHRA events held across the country, two occur here: the Winston Springs Nationals and Fall Nationals. Each event includes two professional categories and six sportsmen (amateur) divisions. Anywhere from 500 to 700 cars participate in each three-day event.

Many fans feel the pro funny car category is the

most exciting. Powered by nitro methane—which some say "is like putting dynamite on the pistons"—cars can disappear down the strip in 5.7 seconds at 250 MPH, less time than it takes to read this sentence.

So grab your earplugs and head for Bristol. You might turn into a real racing fan yourself!

Columbia's Miniature Steamers

In fall and spring the Mid-South Live Steamers Club meets in Maury County Park outside Columbia, Tennessee, to run their 1½ inch-scale steam locomotives, re-creating an era when steam was king in America. The locomotives run over 4,450 feet of 7½ inch-gauge track, providing club members and park visitors with a miniature, imaginary journey into railroading of the 1800s.

Locomotive hobbyists dwarf their small engines as they ride down the rails, but the difference in size seems unimportant as spectators note that the engineers are busily stoking the engines with coal, checking boiler pressure, and working as hard as linemen of by-gone days to ensure a safe and smooth ride. Simple scale-model cars carry the children of club members and visitors around the track.

The September meet is one of two official meets held every year in the park. The spring meet brought club members together from as far away as Arizona with scores of locomotives.

The locomotives that run on the tracks range from Roy Stewart's elaborate brass, bronze, and steel model to Marshall Dugger's endearing wood cab engine.

"Marshall is a railroad man with the Norfolk Southern Railroad," remarked Dave Halloway, club president and locomotive engineer for the Seaboard Systems. "He and I are unique as club members because we work for the railroads. Most of the club members work at other jobs and have always dreamed of being engineers. All of us are in love with steam engines and the romantic history of the locomotive."

The craftsmanship of the model engines is remarkable when you remember that the machines are built from scratch. "By metal bar, sheet, and piece; from the ground up" is the way one Steamer describes his labors in creating an engine. Club members work from old drawings or old photographs. This, too, is remarkable since technical drawings before 1870 are extremely rare.

The pioneer period of the American locomotive ended in about 1855. The machine developed from a squat little boiler on wheels in 1830 to an elegant, well-proportioned mechanism in 1900. Both types are represented at the meet in the Maury County Park. The locomotive was regarded with great pride in the nineteenth century as the carrier of civilization and a product of man's genius. That same pride and genius are evident to anyone who visits the park and encounters the Steamers and their engines.

Reelfoot's Bald Eagles

The annual return of the eagles has become a major event in northwestern Tennessee. The opportunity to view a live American bald eagle brings scores of visitors each winter to Reelfoot Lake State Resort Park, located in the extreme northwestern corner of the state.

For the eagles, the attraction is fish. Flying south from the Great Lakes states and Canada, the majestic birds come to where their food source is readily available in the ice-free waters of Reelfoot Lake. During the winter months, Reelfoot has perhaps the highest concentration of bald eagles east of the Mississippi River. The shallow lake, with its partially submerged forest, is one of the world's largest natural fish hatcheries and home to some 58 species of fish.

Park-sponsored eagle tours are conducted seven days a week from December 1 through mid-March, when the eagles usually begin the long journey back to their homes in the north. Tours originate at the park's Airpark Inn at 10:00 A.M. daily. Visitors are encouraged to make advance reservations by contacting the inn at (901) 253-7756. There is a charge of 50 per person for the tour. Visitors should dress warmly and bring their cameras and fieldglasses. Park rangers provide a spotting scope.

The swamp forests and marshes surrounding the lake provide home and sanctuary for a variety of plant and animal species. The northern portion of the lake is included in the Reelfoot National Wildlife Refuge, a 10,000-acre area managed by the United States Fish and Wildlife Service.

Reelfoot is a major stopover point for waterfowl along the Mississippi Flyway, and ducks and Canadian geese are found in abundance during the fall and winter months. Peak populations reach or exceed 250,000 ducks and 40,000 geese, according to Refuge Manager Wendell Crews.

"The refuge is visited by 235 different species of birds during the year," Crews said. "Reelfoot is listed in all the field guides as one of the best songbird areas in the country. We've had birdwatchers come here from as far away as New York, New Mexico, and California."

The refuge headquarters, located off State 22 on the eastern side of the lake, has recently opened a small museum with excellent exhibits of wildlife that inhabit the area. Refuge officials will conduct tours for groups with advance notice (901) 538-2481.

World's Biggest Coon Hunt

The raccoon is a tricky, hard-to-catch animal that has fooled and frustrated many a hunter. It also happens to be the state animal in Tennessee. Therefore, it seems only fitting the Volunteer State play host to the World's Biggest Coon Hunt at Parsons, Tennessee, every April.

"Excitin', danged excitin' is what it is," drawls Benny Jordan, originator of the event and chairman of this year's hunt. "We'll have a total of about 600 hunters from 30 or 40 states participating in the hunts. It's a million dollar's worth of fun."

It's also worth a great deal of money in a literal sense. You see, the hunt is also the biggest independent fund-raising event for St. Jude Children's Research Hospital in Memphis. St. Jude's is the largest child cancer treatment and research center in the world and is supported entirely by grants and donations. This year they expect to raise $100,000.

The unusual weekend event includes a number of activities centered on the hunt which takes place Friday and Saturday. These strictly competitive hunts only judge a coon dog's ability to track and "tree" (identify the tree where the coon is hiding). Guns are forbidden, so no raccoon is ever shot or killed.

Since a raccoon is a nocturnal creature and searches for food at night, the hunts always occur after dark. Hunters are chosen at random and divided into casts or groups of four with their favorite dog, and a judge. Judges are supplied by the various county coon hunting associations involved with the hunt.

Territory of where to hunt is also chosen by lot. Some casts hunt in locations as far as 150 miles from Parsons, and convoys are escorted by local sheriff departments and the Tennessee State Highway Patrol.

Once out along the river bottoms and the brush, points are tabulated on a scoreboard when a hound makes a "strike" (barking when he has picked up the raccoon scent) and when he trees a coon. The quicker a dog strikes or trees, the more points he is given. Pursuing and catching two of the unpredictable and elusive raccoons during the three-hour hunt each night is considered good.

One of their deceptive tricks is to jump out of a tree, hit the ground with a soft thud which is covered by the noise of hounds, and scamper off again—triggering a whole new chase. Other clever stunts include swimming in water, running the same track, and even hiding up in a tree for long periods of time.

The most popular breed of coon dog is a Treeing Walker, although some champion coon hounds have been mixed breeds. It takes about six years for a hound to reach prime, and they are trained solely for raccoon hunting. Once trained, they are worth up to $25,000.

Since hunters come back to town at all hours of the night, a concession stand sponsored by the Jaycees and Jaycettes will remain open around the clock for 54 continuous hours during the weekend. It features a full menu, and most of the food, including the hundreds of pounds of delicious barbecued pork and chicken, has been donated. More good times are guaranteed each evening thanks to a live country band which plays until 3:00 A.M. each morning. Other events include an auction and radiothon Saturday afternoon.

Good coon hounds have been prized for decades.
Photo courtesy of State Museum and Archives

Adventure in the Greatest Outdoors

Tennessee Underground

Tennessee is a cave lover's paradise because so much of Middle Tennessee and East Tennessee rests on limestone. The damp nooks and tight crannies in the vast majority of these caves are seen only by hard-hatted, mud-splattered spelunkers, but several particularly grand and unusually beautiful caves have been developed commercially. Visitors may savor these subterranean wonders in safe and well-lighted surroundings in the care of competent guides.

Cumberland Caverns, near McMinnville, was opened for tourists in 1956. The second largest cavern system in the United States, Cumberland Caverns was discovered in 1810 by Aaron Higgenbotham. Venturing into the cave alone, he was trapped for three days on a high ledge when his torch went out. According to legend, when a rescue party reached him, his hair had turned white. Years later, this same cave was mined extensively for saltpeter during the Civil War.

Raccoon Mountain Caverns, named for the mountain near Chattanooga which contains them, are still growing. They are said to contain more formations in a natural state than any caverns in the region.

Deep inside nearby Lookout Mountain lies **Ruby Falls,** containing the highest underground waterfall open to the public. Since the cave has no natural opening, visitors reach it by means of an elevator shaft drilled through solid rock. A short walk leads to the room where the spectacular waterfall tumbles from the ceiling in a sheer drop of 145 feet. At 1,120 feet below the surface of Lookout Mountain, Ruby Falls is also the deepest commercial cavern in the United States.

The Cherokee Indians played an interesting part in the history of **Bristol Caverns,** in Upper East Tennessee. The caverns' many passageways offered a hideaway for the Indians who would attack settlers on what was then the western frontier, race back into the cave, then emerge from a back entrance to stage still another raid on the nearby villages and farmsteads.

Near Sevierville, moonshiners, rather than Indians, played an active role in the history of **Forbidden Caverns.** In fact, the original 'shine still found in the caverns can be seen during a one-hour tour. Among the other attractions are natural chimneys, a waterfall and the largest wall of onyx known to exist in the world.

According to the *Guinness Book of World Records,* The **Lost Sea** near Sweetwater is the home of the world's largest underground lake. Just 1,000 feet from its entrance, visitors can glide in glass-bottom boats on the surface of this 4.5-acre lake stocked with huge rainbow trout. Almost half the world's known supply of rare anthodites, or "cave flower" formations, line the walls, leading the United States Department of the Interior to designate the cave as a Registered Landmark.

What is billed as "The Greatest Sight Under the Smokies" can be enjoyed in **Tuckaleechee Caverns,** located near Townsend. Tuckaleechee's rooms are vast in size with high ceilings and deep gorges. An underground stream flows through the main corridor, and natural wonders include lofty "totem pole" stalagmites and "Flowstone Falls", a curtain of beautiful flowing onyx.

One of the more unusual methods of exploration is offered by **Wonder Cave,** the oldest commercial cave in the South, near Monteagle. The winding, one-hour tour is enhanced by the use of lanterns rather than electric lights.

A SAMPLER FEATURE

Doug Plemons
Tennessee Speleologist

■ *Doug Plemons is a speleologist. That means he explores caves. In fact, Doug has been underground in Tennessee more than some groundhogs we know. We at The Tennessee Sampler wanted to talk to an expert about caving in Tennessee, and we think you'll find Doug the perfect guide to introduce you to caving in our state. Doug and his friends in Tennessee's "Grotto Club" chapters of the National Speleological Society stand ready to help you discover the thrill of Tennessee underground. We like their motto: "Take nothing but photographs, leave nothing but footprints."*

Tennessee is *the* cave state, no matter what Missourians or Kentuckians would have you believe. There are a *reported* 4,000 caves or pits of various lengths and depths, ranging from your basic backyard crawlway to vast subterranean systems boasting ten or fifteen entrances. More new caves are being found almost *every* day.

I am a caver associated with the Nashville Grotto, Tennessee's oldest established chapter of the National Speleological Society. There are seven such chapters in Tennessee; our Grotto has over 100 members, and the list is growing each month as curious cave-loving individuals find out what professional caving is all about. The society as a whole contains over 7,000 members from the United States and abroad. Anyone who is interested in caving with an organization dedicated to the exploration and conservation of caves is encouraged to join! Grottoes are friendly, generally boisterous and life-loving clubs in which a caver will make lifelong friends as well as take up the challenge of a lifetime. Caving can be an endurance sport, a part time hobby, or for some a way of life. I must stress that people should not go caving unless they have had some supervision by more experienced cavers. There have been many accidents and even some fatalities associated with caving.

To date, no NSS member has been killed in a Tennessee cave.

Since space is limited here, I will tell about only some specific kinds of caves: historic/prehistoric caves (with artifacts related to Tennessee history), the highly prized and jealously guarded formation caves, some of the more popular "tourist" caves (not the widely advertised commercial caverns), and vertical shafts, or pits. I will not give away the locations of the more sensitive caves for safety or conservation reasons. If after you read this you become interested, you are invited to come to a Grotto meeting or write the NSS. We know about some pretty impressive caves! Tennessee boasts the largest single cave room *and* the deepest open air freefall drop in the Eastern United States!

First the historic caves. Tennessee was one of the first areas to be settled during the 1700's, and of course one of the major battlegrounds of the Civil War. Caves have always been an integral part of that history. Saltpeter for gunpowder used to fight several wars came from deep inside some of the state's more well-known caverns. Many saltpeter caves are scattered throughout the hills and valleys of Tennessee. Most are easy caves to traverse, with their smooth, flat floors and dry passages. These are my favorite caves since they involve little more than lighting up the passage as you stroll down it, seeing the relics such as leaching vats, stirring paddles, and water troughs that were placed in the cave up to 200 years before.

Other historic caves predate the wars of the 1800s; a humble little 200-feet long cave near Donelson was the birthplace of the first white child born in the Middle Tennessee area. And long, long before the coming of the white man to this continent, a man estimated by caving scientists to be around 10,000 years old left his footprints in the soft clay mud of a cave in Middle Tennessee. Next to these prints were those of a jaguar! Perhaps the cat was the prey; perhaps the man. We may never know.

Next in line are the formation caves. These highly prized works of nature are rarely found but when they are, grotto photographers win national awards for their photos of them. Formations such as dripstone or flowstone can take on every color of the rainbow! These formations are often seen in commercial caves, but in wild caves the colors seem much more intense, more vivid. These caves are very jealously guarded against vandals, but trips are available through the state's grottos.

Then come the so-called sacrifice caves, caves which are so well known that even your granddaddy has been there. Caves such as *Snail Shell Cave, Lost Creek Cave*, and *Indian Grave Point Cave* see heavy traffic every weekend. Snail Shell, near Rockvale in Rutherford County, is a 13-mile-long stream cave system actually composed of two separate caves, and the dry sections of the cave are well traveled. But the upstream, deep-water section is reserved for wetsuit cavers with inner tubes and electric lights. Recently two inexperienced teenagers met a watery death in that part of the cave.

Lost Creek Cave is located ten miles south of Sparta in White County. Its entrance is an immense sinkhole with a mini-Niagara waterfall, a very popular place for campers and cavers from all parts of the state. The cave is over 3 miles long, and composed mostly of extremely large-sized walking passages up to 90 feet tall and wide! It is truly a grand sanctuary, one of the most scenic places in Tennessee. Indian Grave Point Cave is also well-known, located one mile south of Dowelltown, Tennessee in Dekalb County. It seems as though every caver worth his salt has been all through this 3-mile-long cave.

All three caves are located in the bottoms of giant sinkholes. Of the three, Lost Creek has by far the most scenic, gaping sink. It is about 100 feet deep, and 200 or 300 feet long, and a 60-feet-high waterfall forms one end of the sink. Easy foot trails lead down into the sink, and there are many other caves nearby, although none has the size of passage of Lost Creek. It is by far one of my favorite places in Tennessee!

Last but certainly not least come the vertical shafts. Much vertical experience and training by professional vertical cavers is a prerequisite for the bottoming of these shafts. Several innocent bystanders have fallen into some of these vertical fissures, some of which are well over 200 feet deep. Some of the more well-known are *Thunderhole* (144 feet deep), *Conley Hole* (163 feet), and the unbelievably huge *Cagle Chasm* (183 feet). There are dozens of others much, much deeper. One near Chattanooga is an astonishing 281 feet deep, so large that you cannot see the walls when you are on descent. Again, let me stress that vertical caving is for the experienced, confident, well-trained spelunker only. It's a long way down to the bottom if you fall!

I know of many hair-raising incidents associated with caving. A friend of mine was climbing a 115-feet freefall drop outside Monterey when part of his equipment failed and he nearly turned upside down on the rope, hanging 100 feet off the floor! It scared him so bad he didn't go vertical caving for a week. Some other friends of mine once found a human skeleton in the bottom of a very remote cave. That led to the eventual arrest and conviction of a murderer.

Good times just happen, like when the bat in a Davidson County cave decided he liked the back of my shirt better than the cold, clammy cave ledges for a place to snooze. It didn't bother me, I just gently brushed him back into his regular hiding place. He didn't like that at all, hissing at me like a kitten before settling back into his nap. People think bats are scary, but actually they are some of our best friends. So, don't ever kill a bat! There are several endangered species in Tennessee caves.

The cavers of the Tennessee Grottoes and the members of the National Speleological Society invite *you*, the outdoors enthusiast or conservation-minded individual, to join a Tennessee Grotto, learn how to cave safely, and see some of Tennessee's most valuable and hidden treasures. The Nashville Grotto meets the first Thursday of each month at 7:30 PM in the Cumberland Museum. Come see us!

Tennessee—there's no place under the world like it!

For more information, write:
Nashville Grotto, PO Box 23114, Nashville, TN 37202

Chattanooga Grotto, 6647 Botsford Drive, Chattanooga, TN 37421

East Tennessee Grotto, 924 Corning Road, Knoxville, TN 37923

Holston Valley Grotto, Box 3585 CRS, Johnson City, TN 37601

Mountain Empire Grotto, PO Box 842, Blountville, TN 37617

Smoky Mountain Grotto, Box 8297, U. T. Station, Knoxville, TN 37916

West TN Chapter of the NSS, 4518 Lawrence Road, Memphis, TN 38122

The National Speleological Society, Cave Avenue, Huntsville, AL 35810.

Soaring Above the Greatest Outdoors

Tennessee Gliderports

Perhaps you've heard of the Soaring Society of America out of Los Angeles. Well, each state has an SSA governor, and Speedy Bond is Tennessee's governor. In fact, Speedy is the first woman governor they ever, ever had in the United States. She says, "It really boils down to a glorified unpaid PR job." She is also manager of Eagleville Soaring School.

For any who may not know, gliders are aircraft without motors which are pulled aloft by powered aircraft, then released to glide on wind currents.

There are two great commercial gliderports in Tennessee. One is Chilhowee Gliderport, 5 miles north of Benton (between Cleveland and Etowah) on US 411. The owner is Mike Reisman, and you can contact him at 15 Fairhills Drive, Chattanooga, TN 37405, (615) 338-2000 or 266-1767. Lessons and rides are available on a daily basis. The fee is approximately $30 per half-hour.

The Eagleville Soaring School is in Eagleville, 35 miles south of Nashville on US 41A. Bill McFarlane is the owner, and Speedy Bond is the manager. Open yearly on weekends. Phone for appointment or just come and watch! (615) 893-2727 or 274-6341.

We think you would really enjoy doing this. Speedy is only about a 30-minute drive from Nashville, and Mike is only about a 30-minute drive from Chattanooga and an hour from Knoxville.

Hang Gliding in Tennessee

Most of us are fascinated with the flight of hawks and eagles as they drift and soar high above us. From Icarus to the Wright brothers, man has tried to experience flight himself. Now, through engineering miracles and space-age materials and the natural thermal updrafts of the Greatest Outdoors, you can make this "flight of fantasy" come true.

It's called hang gliding and for years Tennessee has been recognized as the hang-gliding capital of eastern America. In fact, Tennessee has four prime locations for the practice of this sport: Raccoon Mountain and Lookout Mountain, both outside Chattanooga, and Hinson's Gap and Whitwell, both in the Sequatchie Valley. Here, in the geographic center of the Tenneseee River Valley where the Appalachian and Cumberland Mountains come together, geological forces have built up a series of ridges. These towering bluffs, coupled with gentle breezes and steady thermals, insure a long, warm season for this increasingly popular sport.

The pilot of a hang glider is suspended below the wing and by shifting his weight, causes a change in either direction or speed. In order to maintain flight the glider must always move forward through the air currents.

The average student takes about seven days to learn these techniques. Lessons begin with ground handling demonstrations and progress to mini-launches on the hillside, eventually culminating in a launch from the top of Raccoon Mountain 835 vertical feet above the landing field. An ingenious device, the world's only hang gliding simulator, is used for practicing maneuvers.

The simulator consists of a real hang glider attached by pulleys to a 700-foot steel cable. The cable is stretched from a launching ramp 110 feet up the side of the mountain to a sawdust-filled landing zone on the ground.

After the pilot is secured in the harness, the glider is launched from the ramp and glides for an exhilarating 25-second flight which soars as much as 100 feet above the ground. A rubber tire mounted on the cable near the bottom terminal causes the glider to flare to a soft landing. In addition, a safety brake on the launch site is controlled by one of the five instructors to insure a risk-free ride.

There have been no mishaps in the thousands of simulator flights. Pilots have ranged in age from 5 to 80 years old. The cost is $5.00 for two rides for those who just want to try it out.

The simulator is not the only advantage for enjoying this close-to-nature kind of excitement on Raccoon Mountain.

Unlike most hang-gliding areas where a flight is followed by a long, tedious climb back up the mountain, the Sky Ride, a half-mile tram, carries riders and gliders up to the top launching site in only a few minutes. Special racks, to hold the folded gliders, have been installed for easy transportation.

For information call: High Adventure Sports (615) 825-0444. If you are an experienced hang-glider pilot, be sure to bring proof of your rating and logbooks with you. For lodging, contact Chuck Toth at the Crystal Air Sport Motel (615) 821-2546. For information on hang gliding in Tennessee you might also want to contact the Tennessee Treetoppers, P.O. Box 136, Lookout Mountain, TN 37350.

The FlyAway at Pigeon Forge

"Did you ever have a dream about flying? It's just like that!"

"Loved it! To me it compares to a helicopter ride without the helicopter, looking out at 45 degrees."

What in the world are these folks ardently proclaiming, you ask? They are searching for words to adequately describe their own bobbing, floating, soaring, dipping experience in FlyAway, a brand-new $1 million attraction in Pigeon Forge. In essence, FlyAway is a vertical wind tunnel where customers actually soar through the air. Like a bird. With no strings attached.

"I got the idea for building it in the fall of 1981 by watching a TV show about the FlyAway in Canada," explains general manager and ex-hang-glider, Les Thompson. "I've always had a desire to fly and make money, and this way I can realize both goals. Of the three FlyAways in the world today, mine is the only one east of the Mississippi River."

The focal point of the solidly made, red brick structure is a wide silo, 57 feet high. It contains the chamber for the fliers as well as the spectators' viewing area which spirals around the chamber. The 50 windows built into the chamber permit gazing inside at fliers from any angle.

Beneath the silo is a 600-horsepower diesel engine and a DC-3 aircraft propeller. Winds up to 110 MPH are generated in the 20-feet-wide chamber, and fliers float up to 21 feet above the floor.

For safety precautions, the chamber floor is a bouncy steel cable netting strong enough to support a truck and trailer. A similar netting is fastened at the top. Special padding 6 inches thick lines the interior, while cushions around the bottom are a full 18 inches thick.

To further prevent injuries, all participants are required to wear knee and elbow pads, goggles (which even fit over eyeglasses), tennis shoes, a helmet, ear plugs, and flight overalls. The baggy flight suit is made of light canvas with custom-made vents in the armpits and ankles, which allows more surface area for extra lift.

Before entering the chamber, all fliers must attend a brief but thorough preparation session. Here they are taught how to correctly jump into the main jet stream of air and to maintain a stable position once aloft. Additional teaching covers forward tracking and backward movements.

Once inside the chamber, most groups consist of two instructors and three fliers. All stand just to the side of the main wind thrust. Then, one by one, the fliers dive directly into the air stream and take flight.

For skydivers, FlyAway's advantages are obvious. At 10,500 feet of elevation, a skydiver has only 45 seconds to practice relative work (movements). Here, customers are always given a generous five minutes to practice whatever aerobatics—even flips—they long to perfect. It's quality preparation time for novices or experts.

The FlyAway costs $1.00 to watch, and $9.57 to fly, which includes flight time, equipment rental, and necessary instruction.

Ski Tennessee!

Ober Gatlinburg's Downhill Slopes

The challenge. The thrill. The unquestionable magic of snow skiing is now yours for the asking in Tennessee. Southeastern skiers who have previously looked to the Rockies or New England can now take the plunge at Ober Gatlinburg, located just a blink away from the Great Smoky Mountains National Park.

Although this southern ski resort overlooking the resort city of Gatlinburg has been around since the 1960s, it has just recently given birth to serious skiing. Thanks to an ambitious $4.5 million expansion campaign, Ober Gatlinburg now boasts 10 slopes for all levels of skiers.

Swiss-born ski director Rolf Lantz designed the new slopes, and he feels that the current facilities are on par with any major ski resort. At 5,200 feet long, "Ober Chute" is the resort's longest slope. Its vertical drop is 600 feet. "Grizzly" also descends 600 feet but is only 3,800 feet long—which translates into a steep, ego-testing run that lights up the eyes of expert skiers. Just a slope away is a new, specially designed beginner's run, complete with a private service lift. This protected area separates advanced skiers from the uninitiated and prevents veterans from having to dodge novice skiers on the slopes.

Another obvious and most welcome addition for impatient skiers is a quad ski-lift system capable of carrying four people at a time up the mountainside.

"These two are the only quad chairlifts in the South," stresses Lynn Janutolo, Ober Gatlinburg's director of marketing. "It gives us an incredible uphill capacity of 6,000 people per hour, which virtually eliminates standing around, waiting in lift lines."

To offset the unpredictability of Tennessee snowfalls, the resort has installed snow-making machines on every slope. They have both the compressed air and airless models. Under ideal conditions, slopes can be blanketed in 18 inches of snow in eight hours.

The ski school is staffed with certified instructors, and its huge stock of rental equipment can fully outfit 2,000 skiers. In addition, every slope is furnished with powerful lights to illuminate the runs for night skiing.

The slopes are open seven days a week with two sessions daily Monday through Saturday (9:00 A.M. to 4:30 P.M. and 3:00 P.M. to 10:00 P.M.) and one on Sunday (9:00 A.M. to 4:30 P.M.). Snow-making weather usually prevails through February.

However, even when it gets too warm to make snow, visitors can ski year-round on the world's largest artificial ski surface. Five full acres of Astro Turf are covered with millions of tiny, polyurethane beads, then sprayed with water and a silicone solution.

For ski rates and snow reports at Ober Gatlinburg, call (615) 436-5423 in Tennessee or toll-free (800) 251-9202 (out of state). Snow-skiing packages are offered by several Gatlinburg hotels.

Cross-country Skiing in Tennessee

"Every year millions of people visit the Great Smoky Mountains National Park, but only a few ever see it like this!" Jim Jenkins, a cross-country skiing outfitter based in Gatlinburg, paused for a breather on a snow-covered road leading to Clingmans Dome, the highest point in the park.

"If you came here in midsummer, there would be bumper-to-bumper traffic on this road. But during the winter months, cross-country skiers have it all to themselves. It's a totally different world from what exists the rest of the year."

Winter transforms the majestic Smokies into a cloudland of snow-capped peaks and crystalline forests. Far removed from the crowds of summer, it is a world of silence and solitude— a world best explored on a pair of cross-country skis.

"Most people can pick up on the basic techniques with an hour of instruction," Jenkins said. "As the saying goes, 'If you can walk, you can ski cross-country.' "

The skis are attached at the toe only, so that the heel can lift off the ski during the kick-and-glide movement. The rest of the foot is free to move in any direction, which removes the danger of sprains or broken ankles during a fall.

"There is the danger of exposure or hypothermia, so proper clothing is very important," Jenkins added. "It's best to wear several layers of light clothing, so that you can adjust as you go along. A warm cap, gloves, and sunglasses are essential. If you plan to ski a long distance, bring a light-weight pack with drinking water and some high-energy snacks."

Another advantage of Nordic skiing is that you don't have to spend a fortune on a chic wardrobe. Old clothes from the back of the closet will do fine in the wilderness.

Only three ingredients are needed for Nordic skiing: the basic equipment, land open for public use and, of course, a good supply of the white stuff. Another excellent place in Tennessee to find all three is at **Roan Mountain State Resort Park,** located about 30 miles southeast of Johnson City.

Roan Mountain is the South's only cross-country ski resort state park. The park has developed three winter experience trails, which range in difficulty from gently rolling terrain to very steep grades that should be attempted by experienced skiers only. The resort park now has its own ski center, operated by High South Nordic Guides, so you can rent your equipment right in the park. The center also offers skiing instruction and guided tours on the park's trails and to the heights of Roan Mountain.

Two-day ski packages at Roan Mountain include two nights' lodging at one of the 20 fully furnished modern cabins; on Day One, an all-day cross-country tour, including free equipment rental, instruction, and a hot lunch on the trail; on Day Two, a half-day of equipment rental free.

Prices depend on the number of people in the party. For example, for a party of two, the price per person in 1985 was $75.97. For a party of six, the price per person was $45.44. Ski packages are available on Sunday through Thursday nights.

For information, call or write Smoky Mountain Outdoor Center, P.O. Box 670, Gatlinburg, TN 37738, (615) 436-5052 and Roan Mountain State Park, Route 1, Roan Mountain, TN 37687, (615) 772-3303.

Canoeing the Greatest Outdoors

Bob Lantz's Favorite Streams

Bob Lantz has been one of Tennessee's premier canoeists for years. Meanwhile he co-authored, with Bob Sehlinger, A Canoeing and Kayaking Guide to the Streams of Tennessee, the most complete guide in print to Tennessee's floating and paddling experiences. If you're going to canoe Tennessee, you need this book with detailed maps, crammed with useful information. It is available from Menasha Ridge Press, Route 3, Box 58-G, Hillsborough, NC 27278.

An avid conservationist, Bob is a past director of the Tennessee Scenic Rivers Association, a group that has done more than any other to promote and protect our state's waterways. The TSRA's organized statewide activities are the best way for beginners and new residents of Tennessee to be introduced to the finest river and stream adventures to be had in any of the 50 states.

When Bob, an aerospace engineer, and some friends decided to build canoes made just for Tennessee's boulder-infested white-waterways, the Blue Hole

Whitewater canoers alert for danger downstream

Canoe Company of Sunbright, Tennessee was born. Blue Hole Canoes are made for those licks that canoes have to take in Tennessee waters. If you have the misfortune to wrap one around a rock, just pound it back straight and keep on going.

Now settle down in your easy chair, adjust your reading lamp, and get set for Bob's descriptions of some of Tennessee's finest canoeing adventures.

Tennessee is as long, narrow, and stretched out as its name. It offers a varied array of land forms and waterways, which in turn provide a wide variety of paddling experiences for canoeists. From the small-watershed, cascading mountain white water in the east to the meanderings of bottomland swamp water in the west, literally hundreds of canoeable streams flow across the diverse Tennessee lands. As a well-watered southeastern state, Tennessee has at least 106 floatable stream segments greater than 25 miles in length, according to state and national inventory results. Only California exceeded Tennessee in quantity of streamways in those government listings, and undoubtably, Tennessee surpasses California in quality of those flowing waters.

There are favored floats all across Tennessee. The six described below are only examples of the type of floats found in four divisions of Tennessee: the hardrock Smoky Mountains in East Tennessee; the Allegheny sandstone uplands of the Cumberland Plateau; the bluegrass limestone basin lands in Middle Tennessee; and the flat, deep-soil bottomlands of West Tennessee.

East Tennessee. Streaming off the slopes of Big Frog Mountain from deep in the Cohutta Wilderness, a little crystal-clear gem of the woodlands, the **Conasauga River,** flows into southeastern Tennessee as a State Scenic River. A native trout stream, the water is clean enough for a paddler to drink, a rarity among eastern rivers. In the springtime (only) when there is water sufficient for floating, the small-watershed Conasauga River plays host to paddlers from all over Tennessee as a moderately technical float stream. With cold water, swift flow, and many rocks to maneuver around, the stream is not too pushy and is simply beautiful. A trail (using a long-abandoned, narrow-gauge railbed) follows the stream for low-water enjoyment of the area. (But be forewarned that the trail crosses the river more than once.)

Further north, but also flowing westward off those high mountain flanks, the **Tellico River** is the favored all-around, free-flowing, white-water float river in Tennessee—beautiful mountainous setting, clean water, and a watershed big enough to supply an extended paddling season. The Tellico requires technical whitewater paddling skills with proper equipment and precautions. (If you've never had to wear a helmet while paddling an open canoe on a river, you probably do not have the skills to paddle the Tellico.) The Tellico is known and favored by active white-water paddlers throughout the eastern United States, especially those in Tennessee who have ready access to those mountain waters.

Cumberland Plateau. Extending southward from the Alleghenys of Pennsylvania, Tennessee's Cumberland Plateau is an uplifted sandstone range to the west of those hard-rock Smoky Mountains. Buried in the middle of those sandstone uplands lies the only National Wild and Scenic River in Tennessee, the **Obed River.** There's good reason for the national designation: the Obed is indeed a wild and scenic river. Sandstone erodes very slowly. After eons of time, water flow only cuts the hard material in one direction—down. The riverway is embedded deep in the rock and steep-sided gorges, and high-guarding bluffs on both sides are common along the Obed.

The paddler feels remote while floating through those Obed gorges because the paddler *is* remote. Rescue is difficult, if possible at all. Undercut boulders, which can trap paddlers and boats underwater, are common hazards in the stream. With practically no flood plain in the gorges between the bluffs, heavy rainfall can cause river flow levels to increase dramatically in hours.

Some sections along the Obed are only moderate in technical difficulty, and some sections are almost too difficult to survive in an open canoe. Sometimes one section leads into the other without opportunity to leave the riverway. But for those who have the skill, have done their homework, and paddle with competent companions who know the area, the experience in the fresh, green, laurel-bound, boulder-filled riverway can be breathtaking.

Middle Tennessee. The limestone-based Central Basin of Middle Tennessee provides lush, pastoral bluegrass fields. A float down the central drainageway, the **Harpeth River,** is an enjoyable pastoral float backward into history. There are no difficult rapids on the Harpeth, and the upper stretches mostly have pleasant rock-bottom riverbeds.

The early route of the Natchez Trace coincides with some of the upper runs. Early remnants of the settlement of Nashville can be found along the way, and the part of the Harpeth that runs through Nashville is designated for protection as a State Scenic River. Farther downstream pre-Civil War industrial uses of the river can be noted at the cannonball foundry sites. Then pre-Indian mounds and bluff markings can be found as you paddle on into the prehistory era.

The Harpeth is a valuable respite hard against a major metro area in Tennessee. Precautions concerning weather, swimming ability, and snakebites (in season) are all that is required for adventurous members of the family. Serenity, scenery, and perhaps a sense of history will be the rewards for sampling the pleasures of the Harpeth.

Along the western edge of the great Central Basin, the **Buffalo River** flows freely for more than 100 miles through rural woodlands and along cave-dotted hillsides. This river has introduced more people to the joys of river floating and canoeing than any other river in Tennessee. The Buffalo is renowned for its fishery. And floating the river is the best way to sample those waters. Boy Scouts annually hold a 50-mile canoe race down the river. Overnight canoe camping is a common family venture on the Buffalo. Tree snags are the primary hazard, and many unwary canoeists have learned that water flows through those snags but not canoes. Almost always the canoe capsizes during such lessons. There are both swift-current shoals and deep-water pools along the river. The scenery is pastoral. The Indians used the lands along the Buffalo as a hunting ground, and many Indian artifacts still crop up in the nearby plowed fields. Springs and sinks occur along the way. A float on the Buffalo is a genuinely mellow experience.

West Tennessee. The deep wind-driven soils of West Tennessee cause strange water-flow erosion patterns on the flat, cotton-field-type landscape. Oxbows and meanders keep the flow slow; swampwater paddling opportunities appear. The prime river experience in West Tennessee can be found along the 100 miles of the quiet-water **Hatchie State Scenic River**. Large cypress trees with exposed "knees" provide havens for beaver. Deep-rooted, gigantic hardwoods form the cover forest for the swamp-water streamway, and birdlife abounds. Every species of woodpecker common to Tennessee maintains winter quarters along the waterway. Warblers sound out from streamside foliage.

The meanders to the river can stretch out a trip surprisingly, so skills in map reading are helpful for safety's sake. Be self-contained (carry water and stoves), for dry campsites are hard to locate. A rare and relatively unknown experience for Tennessee floaters is available in the cypress swamp atmosphere of the Hatchie River. It is well worth the effort.

Other well-known floats are the Little River and the Nolichucky near the Smokies, the Big South Fork in the Cumberlands, the Stones and Duck rivers in Middle Tennessee, and Reelfoot Lake in West Tennessee. Any of these would serve as a good example of Tennessee canoeing, and there are many more throughout the state. There's one near you.

Other Tennessee Streams

The Ocoee
"One thing to remember. If you go out of the raft, keep your feet pointed downstream so you can bounce off the rocks without getting hurt. Don't worry about going under. Your life jacket will keep you high in the water."

The speaker is Marc Hunt, one of the founders of an Ocoee River rafting service. His audience is a tense-faced bunch of novice white-water rafters about to challenge one of the most exciting rivers in the eastern United States.

The Ocoee is a new river for white-water enthusiasts. Located in the Cherokee National Forest about 65 miles east of Chattanooga, the waters of the Ocoee were diverted for more than a half-century by a wooden flume line which carried most of the river's flow to a downstream power plant. When the flume line was removed from service in late 1976 and the river returned to its natural bed, local canoeists and rafters were quick to discover that the 250-feet drop in the 5-mile stretch of river had created a new playground. Seven full-time

Obed National Wild and Scenic River
Photo by Jim Robertson

rafting companies now operate on the Ocoee along with several part-time ones.

The Big South Fork
A vast, new back-country area is opening to the public in a plateau and gorge region of northern Tennessee and southern Kentucky. The Big South Fork National River and Recreation Area will eventually encompass over 100,000 acres atop the Cumberland Plateau on the Tennessee/Kentucky border due north of Crossville, Tennessee. Area boundaries are less than 50 miles from two interstates, I-40 to the south and I-75 to the east.

The Big South Fork is one of the first attempts to combine the concept of a National River with that of a National Recreation Area, and the project represents a significant shift in focus for Corps of Engineers planners. The idea is to develop the Big South Fork's potential for outdoor recreation, while carefully preserving one of the last great undeveloped back-country areas in the eastern United States. The river and gorge area will remain virtually untouched, except for developed trails, overlooks, and river access sites. All other development will be in the adjacent plateau area.

The rivers and forests are open for fishing and hunting, subject to state regulations. Many of the old forest roads are open for four-wheel-drive vehicles. Back-country hikers can camp anywhere on public domain, provided the site is over 300 feet from the trail. While land acquisition is incomplete, there are over 70,000 wild and scenic areas to explore.

The dominant feature of the Big South Fork is the river gorge, and a float trip takes you to beautiful, remote sections of the area that are otherwise inaccessible. The sheer cliffs of the gorge rise to 1,700 feet above sea level in places. Rock gardens in the riverbed are strewn with boulders the size of houses.

There are over 80 miles of prime canoeing waters in the area, ranging from easy floats for novices to violent white-water runs for experts. Rafting trips are a great way for beginners to challenge such rapids as the Washing Machine and Devil's Jump.

River guidebooks are available for 35 from the National Park Service Headquarters in Oneida, Tennessee (615) 569-6963. The guidebooks show access points, distance in miles between points, difficulty of the various streams, and the best time of year to float each stream. The Park Service also has information on rafting outfitters.

Another great way to see the sites is aboard the Big South Fork Scenic Railway. Weekend excursions originate in Stearns, Kentucky, and travel 5.5 miles down into the gorge, passing through a 200-feet-long tunnel along the way. For ticket information, contact the BSF Scenic Railway, (606) 376-5330.

For more information on the Big South Fork, contact the Corps of Engineers, P.O. Box 1070, Nashville, TN 37202; (615) 251-7161.

The Nolichucky River

The Nolichucky River gets its name from an old Cherokee word meaning "rushing waters." Anyone who has challenged the raging rapids of this upper East Tennessee river will tell you that it is well named. It is one of the most rugged and isolated rivers in the South.

"The Nolichucky is really an undiscovered jewel," said Bill Kohler of Nolichucky Expeditions, an outfitting company headquartered near Erwin in Unicoi County. "It is a premier white-water stream, and yet you can go 100 miles in any direction and most people have never even heard of it."

White-water experts claim that there are few raftable rivers in the eastern United States that can match the Nolichucky for scenic beauty, water clarity, and sheer excitement. Its waters originate high atop Mt. Mitchell in North Carolina, and the river thunders into Tennessee through a spectacular canyon carved out of the Unaka Mountains. It is the deepest river gorge in the Southeast, with peaks towering over 2,000 feet above the riverbed.

"The 9 mile section of the river that we run has an average drop of 36 feet per mile," Kohler said. "In the springtime, the rapids have an overall rating of Class IV."

Class IV rapids are described by the American Whitewater Association as "Very difficult: long powerful rapids with irregular waves, dangerous rocks, and boiling eddies." The Nolichucky is all that and more.

Each rafting trip begins with a brief training session to explain paddling strokes and safety techniques. It's best to pay close attention because there is little time for practice after putting in. The river almost immediately plunges into the first set of rapids, known as "Last Chance" (as in last chance to chicken out). The shouts of the guides can barely be heard above the roar of the rapids. The raft, half-submerged in the white foaming

waters, is swept between two huge boulders. Screams of fear become shouts of triumph as the raft emerges, its occupants wide-eyed and soaking wet.

Last Chance is only a warm-up for such rapids as Jaws, Rooster Tail, and On the Rocks (which is where some rafts end up). There are over 20 Class II, III, and IV rapids in the 9-mile run.

Even on a rambunctious river like the Nolichucky, white-water rafting is less hazardous than most adventure sports. Helmets and life jackets are provided, and with the stability of the rafts and the expertise of the guides, the chances of injury are slim. The trick is to stay *inside* the raft.

More adventurous souls can try their luck going "solo" in a Funyak, an inflatable craft shaped like a canoe. Complex white-water skills are not needed to shoot the rapids in these one-man crafts, which combine the stability of a raft with the agility of a kayak.

The river mellows out toward the end, so that rafters can unwind and soak up the magnificent scenery. The canyon is surrounded by the Cherokee National Forest, and there are few intrusions on the serenity of the wilderness. About the only sign of civilization on the entire trip is the old Clinchfield Railroad, which runs parallel to the river.

Rafting trips on the Nolichucky are available daily from March through November, although currents are swiftest in spring and early summer. Costs for the six-hour trip range from $30 to $35 per person, which includes all equipment, a guide in each raft, and lunch served during the trip. White-water beginners are more than welcome, but there is a minimum age limit of 12. For information, write: Nolichucky Expeditions, Box 484, Erwin, TN 37650.

The Clinch River

Winding past wooded hills and limestone bluffs less than 25 miles from downtown Knoxville is one of the most scenic and cleanest float streams in East Tennessee, the Clinch River. The Clinch provides a safe float trip, since there are no rapids or major hazards along the 14-mile stretch between Norris Dam and Clinton, although at lower water levels, rock shoals add a little excitement to a canoe trip without presenting anything more dangerous than a scratch to the bottom of a misguided canoe.

The Clinch offers the perfect opportunity to beat the summer heat with a leisurely float, a chance to observe the varied wildlife, birdlife, and wildflowers along the river. The river also offers the prospect of fresh rainbow trout sizzling in the pan. Flowing clear and cool from Norris Dam, the river's rate of flow requires little paddling. The trip will take from four to seven hours, depending on water levels, how lazy your crew wants to be, and how often you stop or explore side streams.

The Clinch is fast becoming one of East Tennessee's premier tailwater trout fisheries, with an active stocking program and TVA's strong commitment to develop the river into a first-class trout stream. In addition to pan-sized rainbows, the Clinch is beginning to yield some in the 3 to 5 pound category. Brown trout of 2 to 4 pounds are commonly caught and some of up to 9 pounds have been netted from the river. The upper 3 miles below Norris Dam are easily accessible to waders and bank fishermen, while access to the middle and lower reaches of the river is mainly limited to a few isolated trails or those choosing to float-fish from canoes, rafts, or john boats.

Clinch River Outdoors, located on the banks of the river at Massengill Bridge, provides full float service, including canoe or raft, life jackets, paddles, dry bags, and shuttle service back to your vehicles, which may be left in their parking lot where security in provided. Each canoe or raft is also provided with a detailed floater's guide and map to help you make the most of your trip.

Floaters have a choice between paddling a canoe for added maneuverability and easier access to creeks and side streams or going Huck Finn style in comfortable and sturdy inflatable rafts. Either way, the Clinch offers a perfect afternoon's recreation for the entire family. For more information, contact Clinch River Outdoors, River Road at Massengill Bridge, P.O. Box 220, Lake City, TN 37769; call (615) 494-9207.

The Hiwassee River

The Hiwassee River originates on the northwest slopes of the Blue Ridge Mountains along the Appalachian Trail in northern Georgia and flows into North Carolina before turning west through Polk County in Tennessee. It drains over 750,000 acres of mountain land, most of which lies within the confines of Chattahoochee, Natahala, and Cherokee National Forests. This area is over 90 per cent forested, a condition which is reflected in the purity and crystalline clarity of the Hiwassee's waters.

The Hiwassee River provides an exceptional setting for white-water canoeing and rafting. Fishing opportunities are great with an abundance of largemouth bass, yellow perch, catfish, and brown and rainbow trout. The river valley affords beautiful mountainous vistas.

The Hiwassee River is cooperatively managed by

Made in Tennessee—A Blue Hole canoe

the Tennessee Department of Conservation, the Tennessee Wildlife Resources Agency, the United States Forest Service, and the Tennessee Valley Authority. For more information, write the Hiwassee River Office, Box 255, Delano, TN 37325.

A SAMPLER
SPECIAL

The Cyclone Silo Cycle Club

You'd expect the Greatest Outdoors to produce some equally great outdoor adventurers. Sure enough, in preparing the *Sampler,* we've come upon any number of outdoor activities that are tremendously thrilling and/or dangerous and many fearless people who are expert at them.

So we were unimpressed when one of our friends told us to get in touch with the secretive and exclusive Cyclone Silo Cycle Club from Belle Meade. What could be more boring than a bunch of corporate executives on their expensive motorcycles cruising the countryside, right?

Were we ever wrong! We rode with the Cyclone Silos for a whole weekend and were amazed by their unique high-tech approach to Tennessee outdoors adventure. You see, a silo standing majestically alone in a field is not just a thing of beauty to these guys. It is a challenge. A Mount Everest!

We all met in a parking garage in Belle Meade where their Honda Gold Wing motorcycles were kept. These cycles had radar, TV's, radio communication, synchronized stereos (so they could all listen to National Public Radio at the same time), fish finders, and fuzz busters.

The Cyclones were really pumped up. It was Friday afternoon on their cycling weekend. Forgotten were their stocks and bonds. It was time for the Cyclone Silos to hit the road!

They were already "high fiving" each other as they shed their three-piece suits and put on their special black leather jackets. Each jacket had a huge studded silo on the back with a sequined cyclone dancing about on top of it. Each group member wore an aviator scarf in magenta, mauve, or chartreuse. "Magenta for officers, mauve for senior members, and chartreuse for junior members," said Jeff, the leader of the Cyclones, when we asked about the significance of the colors. "The difference is in the number of silos you have conquered. Right now, I have 22."

We were feeling out of place on our big Harleys and in our traditional Dirty Dogs leather jackets, but Jeff said it was OK. "We'll just tell everyone we hired bodyguards," he said.

"Why is the group such a secret?" we asked.

"Well," said Jeff, "it's strictly an insurance thing. People think we ride around on our Hondas, and it's easy for us to get life insurance. If they knew what we really do, no insurance company would touch us!"

"So what you do is dangerous?"

"Well, now, silos are nothing to trifle with," interjected Rocky, the group's tactician. "We had a member die in one last year."

"What happened to him?" we wanted to know.

"He ran himself to death looking for a corner to…"

"Shut up, Rocky!" interrupted Jeff. "I don't approve of making jokes about sacred subjects, and silos are definitely sacred."

Rocky was laughing so hard he almost dropped his polishing cloth.

After checking out our radio communications system, we hit the road, heading into the rich farming area south of Nashville. "That's real silo country down there!" said Jeff, as we cruised past two awestruck state troopers at a sedate 50 MPH.

"What makes a good silo?" we asked.

"We don't look for just any silos," said Rocky, "only the old empty stone ones."

Well, the mystery was solved soon enough. On a scouting trip, Rocky had discovered a promising silo on a farm outside Spring Hill. Soon we were pulling off on a private driveway up a hollow almost a mile long which opened out on a gorgeous Victorian home and barns, hills punctuated by Jersey dairy cattle, and a truly magnificent silo. All the Cyclones jumped off their bikes and started high fiving again. "It's never been tried before. I guarantee it!" Rocky gushed.

Meanwhile Jeff was talking to Mr. Campbell, the landowner, about what they proposed to do.

What happened next was the most amazing outdoor sport the *Sampler* has ever witnessed. First, the Cyclones set about removing the interior ladders in the empty silo (with the owner's permisson, of course). Then they built a small embankment just inside the door. Meanwhile, another group of Cyclones was busily working around some trailers they had pulled behind them. We went over to see, and they were checking out three tiny bikes with big puffy tires like you see on those little three-wheelers. They were propelled by nitro methane, the same fuel used in drag racers, sometimes called "liquid dynamite."

All the time our photographer was busily clicking away, since the Cyclones had promised to go public in the *Sampler.*

When the jet bikes were ready, Jeff made the long climb up the outside ladder to the top door of the silo, opened it and left something on the sill, then climbed down, leaving the door open.

Rocky was the first one to attempt this silo. The noise when he fired up the small jet bike was so intense that the audience of cud-chewing Jerseys fled in disarray. Rocky darted down the dirt path, disappeared into the silo, and all we heard for about seven seconds was that tremendous engine noise as he spiraled his way up the silo's interior.

"Watch the doorway!" shouted Jeff as he pointed to the top. A black-clad arm plucked the object that Jeff had left out of the doorway, and about 10 nail-biting seconds later Rocky emerged from the lower door to the cheers of the group.

"No doubt about it, it's the best ever!" he shouted as he pulled off his helmet and popped the top off the object he had grabbed at the top of the silo. It was a bottle of lime-flavored Perrier.

By the end of the weekend, three chartreuse Cyclones had moved up to mauve, and Rocky and Jeff had accomplished the rare, almost impossible, simultaneous silo ascension, although Rocky had grabbed both bottles of Perrier, much to Jeff's annoyance.

Only one jet bike had been totaled. Rodney, one of the new members, had gotten his scarf caught on some metal projection about halfway up the silo. The bike was a mess, but Rodney survived, although he had turned purple by the time he was rescued.

The *Sampler* was disappointed that none of the pictures turned out, but we do have an address for the Cyclone Silo Cycle Club to give our intrepid readers. If you are at least a vice president in a Fortune 500 corporation in Tennessee, then you may qualify to ride with the Cyclone Silo Cycle Club. If you are interested, write to the *Sampler* at Box 20, Franklin, TN 37064, and we

A solitary silo offers its challenge

will put you in touch with Jeff and Rocky, if they are still alive.

Don't laugh the next time you see a group of cyclists with bright scarves gliding down I-65 on flashy Hondas with silos on the backs of their black leather jackets. The pride of Belle Meade, the fearless Cyclone Silo Cycle Club, is riding again!

Fishing the Greatest Outdoors

A SAMPLER FEATURE

Charlie Ingram
World Champion

■When Charlie Ingram was a boy, his mama would give him a quarter for lunch money, but Charlie had wading creeks and fishing on his mind. So he would get a nickel candy bar and buy fishing lures with the rest at Dalton's Grocery. He'd start up by G. T. Curry's farm and work his way south with the gentle curves of Carters Creek. In a pool by the bank, behind a chunk of exposed root, might be a 3½ pound smallmouth bass. Sometimes young Charlie would catch so many fish that he couldn't carry them all home.

That young Tennessee country boy gave away a bunch of fish before he got out of high school. Then he went to college at MTSU in Murfreesboro. He arranged his schedule so that he had to go to class only on Monday, Wednesday, and Friday. He fished the other days. You might say he majored in bass fishing and minored in college.

Now Charlie Ingram is the world's champion bass fisherman. Fact is, Charlie won $89,000 in 1984 just fishing for largemouth bass! It's been about 30 years since Charlie first waded Carters Creek. These days the bass man lives in the fast lane of fishing. He's graduated to the pro circuit of bass fishing, in which there are six major tournaments a year in huge lakes from upper New York State to Florida, from Wisconsin to all over the USA. In 1984 the Tennessee fishin' man won three of these tournaments, an amazing feat!

Charlie lives in Maury County, so we had to ask him about the places in our state he would take friends and neighbors fishing. We wondered aloud where Charlie would take someone who had won him for a dream bass fishing trip.

Charlie liked that idea.

First, he said, the trip would not begin until the moon was three-quarters full. Then you'd head out of Nashville on I-40, turn north and drive through Charlotte, Erin, and Dover to Lake Barkley around Bumpus Mills.

After that you and Charlie would head for Kentucky Lake in West Tennessee for two days. Then you'd cruise south to Pickwick Lake for some night fishing.

By then you'd be ready to cast into some Middle Tennessee lakes. First, you'd head to Tims Ford Lake near Fayetteville for some more night fishing. Charlie likes to fish these beautiful lakes at night because they're so clear. The bass are sensitive to light so they come up to feed at night.

Next you'd head north to Normandy Lake on the upper Duck River near Manchester on I-24.

By now you'd be getting a deep tan, and if some of Charlie's skills were rubbing off on you, you'd have sore arms.

Don't give up now, though, because you're fishing with the world's champion. Just think. Maybe you could catch more fish than he did on one of these lakes!

Next you head northeast for some more night fishing on Center Hill Lake. After fishing all night you'd stop for coffee, biscuits and country ham.

Then you'd have to head east on I-40 to Fort Loudon and Tellico Lake just southwest of Knoxville. They're two lakes with a canal connecting them, but they're totally different lakes, according to Charlie. In fact, at the upper end of Tellico you can even catch trout. To end your dream fishing trip on the great waters of Tennessee, you'd head back west and splash into Watts Bar Lake. Charlie would drop you off at your car, probably sleep some, and then get back after those bass, the ones he's been wading after since he was seven.

Charlie Ingram, world bass fishing champion

Charlie's Angles. Charlie fishes Pickwick more than any other place in Tennessee, but he's fished every lake in the state. These are the lures he uses to bring home the big bass.

If the water temperature is above 60 degrees, Charlie goes with the L. C. Plastic Worm, 6-inch or 8-inch.

If the water is below 60 degrees, he uses the L. C. Bass Bug, with Razorback Bo-Frog trailers.

In the spring and fall when the fish are in shallower, darker-colored waters, Charlie uses the L. C. Single-blade Spinner in white and chartreuse colors. He uses the same-color L. C. Buzz-bait if the water temperature gets above 65 degrees. "Bass will come up as much as 20 feet to take this one," Charlie says.

For all-around year-round casting, Charlie recommends Bagley's Diving Bee II, a crank-type bait, silver-foil color in the fall and Tennessee shad color in the spring.

Tennessee Record Catches

Crappie State Records:
    Black Crappie—3 lbs. 6 oz.—Pond in Cumberland County
    White Crappie—5 lbs. 1 oz.—Pond in Dickson County

Trout State Records:
    Rainbow—14 lbs. 8 oz.—Obed River below Dale Hollow Dam
    Brown—26 lbs. 2 oz.—Dale Hollow Tailwaters
    Brook—3 lbs. 14 oz.—Hiwassee River

White Bass State Record:
    4 lbs. 10 oz.—Pickwick Tailwaters

Bluegill State Record:
    3 lbs.—Fall Creek Falls

Walleye State and World Records:
    25 lbs.—Old Hickory Lake

Muskellunge State Record:
    42 lbs. 8 oz.—Norris Reservoir

Striped Bass or Rockfish State Record:
    49 lbs. 8 oz.—Lake Norris

Spotted or Kentucky Bass State Record:
    5 lbs. 4 oz.—Chickamauga Lake

Largemouth Bass State Record:
    14 lbs. 8 oz.—Sugar Creek

Sauger State Record:
    7 lbs. 6 oz.—Below Pickwick Dam

Smallmouth Bass State and World Records:
    11 lbs. 15 oz.—Dale Hollow Reservoir

Catfish State Records:
    Channel Catfish—41 lbs.—Fall Creek Falls
    Blue Cat (Class B)—130 lbs.—Fort Loudon Reservoir

Flathead Cat (Class B)—82 lbs.—Big Sandy River Brown Bullhead—2 lbs. 14 oz.—Chickamauga Reservoir

When and Where They're Biting

WEST TENNESSEE
Reelfoot Lake
    Bluegill: Daytime, May–June. Crappie: Daytime, April–June, Sept.–Oct. Yellow Bass: Daytime, May–June, Sept.–Oct. Bullhead Catfish: Night in summer.

Kentucky Lake
    White Bass: Daytime below Pickwick Dam, March 1–May 1. Sauger: Daytime below Pickwick Dam and Sycamore Landing area, Dec. 15–March 15; can be trolled for on gravel bars during May and June. Catfish: Night or day, Pickwick trailrace sector and all main-stream areas, May–Oct.; best months for whopper cats are July, Aug., and Sept. Largemouth Bass: Daytime, best months are May while they're spawning and June during mayfly hatches; nighttime in July and Aug. with top water. Smallmouth Bass: Daytime, restricted to area above and below Pickwick Dam, Sept., Oct., Nov. Stripers: Restricted to area below Pickwick Dam during April–May, Aug.–Oct. Crappie: Year-round; TWRA fish attractors.

Pickwick Reservior
    Smallmouth Bass: Nighttime, June–Sept.; anytime balance of year along bluffs and old river channel. Largemouth and Spotted Bass: Peak for large fish March–April, Oct.–Nov.; easy school fish up to 3 lbs. late May and first two weeks of June; around dam (upper side) and along main channel, Feb.–Sept. Bluegill: On crickets during spawning period shallow in late May; on crickets, worms, and ultralite in 10 to 20 feet depths June–Sept.

MIDDLE TENNESSEE
Cheatham
    Largemouth Bass: Fair April–June during day; summer at night. Bluegill (Bream): Good May–June, primarily in embayments and sloughs. Crappie: Fair March–May, primarily in embayments. Catfish: Fair May–June, Sept.–Oct. Stripers: Fair in tailwater Jan.–March. Sauger: Fair in mouths of creeks and tailwaters in winter and early spring.

Percy Priest
    Largemouth Bass: Fair in April–June during day; summer at night. Smallmouth Bass: Fair March–May, Oct.–Nov. Bluegill (Bream): Fair May–June, Sept.–Oct.

Crappie: Good to excellent April–May and Sept.–Dec. Catfish: Good May–June and Sept.–Oct. White Bass: Good to excellent March–April in headwaters; May–June in lake. Stripers: Fair shallow early spring and fall; deep summer and winter; early spring runs up creeks and rivers.

Tims Ford

Largemouth Bass: Excellent March–June, Sept.–Dec. Smallmouth Bass: Good to excellent March–April, Oct.–Nov. Bluegill (Bream): Good May–Aug. Crappie: Good to excellent spring and fall; early spring run up Elk River; deep in summer and winter. Walleye: Excellent, June–Aug. in reservoir; Feb.–March up Elk River. Trout: Tailwaters year-round, good to excellent.

CUMBERLAND PLATEAU AREA

Dale Hollow

Largemouth Bass: Daytime, April–June 15; night in summer. Smallmouth Bass: Daytime, March 15–May 30; night during June with full moon. White Bass: March–April in the headwaters; night during summer. Walleye: Headwaters in March–April; lake in June and early July. Crappie: March–April and Nov.–Dec. Catfish: June–Aug. Bluegill: June–Sept. Muskie: Dec.–Jan. trolling. Trout: May 30–Sept. in lake; tailwater trout depends on stocking.

Watts Bar

Largemouth Bass: April–June daytime; July–Aug. at night. Smallmouth Bass: Oct.–Dec. Bluegill: Summer, willowfly in July. Crappie: Spring and fall. Catfish: June–Aug.; June when spawning. White Bass: Aug.–Sept. Rockfish: Oct.–Nov. at Moon Island; spring and fall at Thief Neck Island and below dam. Sauger: Below dam Nov.–Feb.

EAST TENNESSEE

Tellico-Chilhowee

Largemouth and Smallmouth Bass: Best in April–May. Crappie: Late April–May, Oct. Bluegill: June–Sept. Trout: April–May; good at night in summer.

Fort Loudon

Largemouth Bass: April–June; night in the summer. Smallmouth Bass: March–May, Oct.–Nov.; night in the summer. Crappie: Mid-April–May, Oct. White Bass: March–April; occasionally in the summer when they're feeding on the surface. Catfish: Best in the summer at night; lake holds state record blue cat (130 lbs). Bream: April–Oct. Sauger: Below dam in Feb.

Norris

Largemouth Bass: May–June; use light tackle and fish deep. Smallmouth Bass: April–May, Jan.–Feb.; fishing live bait off points. Crappie: Late April–May near fish attractors. Walleye: Feb.–March in the headwaters,

sometimes at night in the summer trolling in the lake. Catfish: Spring and summer. Striped Bass: April–May; can be caught through the summer fishing live bait in open water; state record at 49½ lbs. from Norris in 1978. Bream: Spring through fall.

Douglas

Sauger: Feb.–March in the river from US 25 bridge upstream. Largemouth Bass: April–May. Crappie: Usually March–May, occasionally earlier; excellent fishing. White Bass: Feb.–March, sometimes to mid-April in the headwaters. Bream: April–Oct.

TVA Lakes

Dotted across the landscape of Tennessee are some 20 lakes operated by the Tennessee Valley Authority (TVA) as part of its broad-based program to develop the natural resources of an entire river valley. The lakes and dams help to control floods, provide transportation, generate low-cost electricity, and are major outdoor recreation resources. Local and state parks and commercial resorts and marinas located along more than 7,000 miles of shoreline offer opportunities for boating, fishing, camping, swimming, picnicking, and many other outdoor activities.

Fort Patrick Henry, Boone, South Holston, and Watauga

This series of mountain lakes in upper East Tennessee ranges in size from 872 to 7,580 acres. Built mostly in the early 1950s, plenty of secluded, deep-water coves make these lakes particularly suited for smaller boating activity. Watauga Lake boasts 13 species of game fish. Easily accessible from I-81, the area is a rugged one where recorded history dates from the Revolutionary War era.

Cherokee, Douglas, and Davy Crockett Lakes

Located about 30 miles east of Knoxville and surrounded by rolling pastures and farmlands, these 30,000-acre lakes have been providing fishing enthusiasts with hefty catches of bass and crappie. Cherokee and Douglas lakes will accommodate nearly any boat class. As on many TVA reservoirs, considerable private, second-home acreage surrounds Douglas Lake although public access is frequent. TVA's Nolichucky Environmental Education Center and Waterfowl Sanctuary is located on Davy Crockett Lake, a few miles south of Greeneville. Historic Greeneville was the capital of the Lost State of Franklin and the home of President Andrew Johnson.

Kentucky Lake

Stretching 180 miles, Kentucky is the last of nine mainstream lakes on the Tennessee River. It is by far the largest, most developed, and most popular in the TVA lake system. Scattered along its shoreline are five state parks, the Shiloh National Military Park, over 80 resorts and boat docks, and TVA's Land Between the Lakes.

Annually, midwesterners are enticed to Kentucky Lake for the spring crappie runs. Sauger, a cousin to the walleye, is also a popular catch. More than 1,000 tons of fish are caught in this lake each year. If your preference is boating, you will find 160,000 acres to explore and hundreds of secluded coves with sand beaches.

Chickamauga, Fort Loudon, Watts Bar, and Nickajack Lakes

These spacious lakes are the first on the mainstream of the Tennessee River as it begins its 650-mile journey to the Ohio River. Suited to any type of boating from sailboats to large cruisers, these lakes have attracted vacationers for over 35 years. Chickamauga and Watts Bar are great for family vacations with their more than 40 commercial resorts and boat docks. Chickamauga Dam, which backs up a 35,000-acre lake, is adjacent to Chattanooga.

Norris, Melton Hill, and Tellico Lakes

Norris, the first dam built by TVA after the agency was created, is located 20 miles northwest of Knoxville. Along the lake's 800 miles of shoreline are three state parks, two state wildlife management areas, boat docks, county parks, and public access areas. Clear, deep water produces excellent catches of rockfish, walleye, and smallmouth bass, as well as the usual species found in other area lakes.

Melton Hill Lake is downstream from Norris on the Clinch River. Its wide expanses of water are suitable for most boating, and a lock at the dam provides boaters with access to the main Tennessee River channel.

Tellico, about 30 miles southwest of Knoxville, is one of TVA's newest lakes. Connected to Fort Loudon Lake and the mainstream of the Tennessee River by a canal, the potential for long-distance cruising is unlimited.

Normandy and Tims Ford Lakes

Both lakes are located near Tullahoma in Middle Tennessee. The 3,100-acre Normandy Lake is good for fishing and small boating, while the larger Tims Ford, at 10,600 acres, accommodates most types of boating. A state park is located on the Tims Ford shoreline.

For more information, write the Information Office, Tennessee Valley Authority, 400 West Summit Hill Drive, Knoxville, TN 37902. Tennessee residents can call TVA's toll-free Citizen Action Lines at (800) 322-9250. Residents in the other Tennessee Valley states can call (800) 251-9242.

Army Corps of Engineers Lakes

Dale Hollow Lake

Lying in the Highland Rim section of northern Tennessee and southern Kentucky, the area surrounding the lake is a forested plateau with scattered farming and low population density. The water quality of Dale Hollow is superb, and the crystalline waters are conducive to virtually all water sports, including scuba diving and spearfishing. Dale Hollow also boasts the world record smallmouth bass, an 11 pound, 15 ounce beauty. Several modern campgrounds meet the needs of camping vacationers. Immediately below the dam is a National Fish Hatchery open to the public. For more information, contact the Resource Manager, Dale Hollow Lake, Celina, TN 38551; (615) 243-3136.

Cordell Hull Lake

This lake, located at the base of the Highland Rim of Middle Tennessee, has ample acreage for numerous recreational pursuits. Modern campgrounds and day use areas, excellent hunting and fishing, hiking, and horseback riding trails are just some of what you'll find here. The two loops of the horseback riding trail cover 22 miles and vary from easy, flat riding to rugged, steep terrain along precipitous bluffs overlooking the lake. The Bearwaller Gap hiking trail (6 miles) has received highly favorable comments from Scout groups. Canoeing is excellent in the Roaring River section of the lake. An extensive wildlife management program is administered by the Corps, and hunting is a popular sport. For more information, contact the Resource Manager, Cordell Hull Lake, Route 1 Box 62, Carthage, TN 37030; (615) 735-2244.

Old Hickory Lake

Just northeast of Nashville, Old Hickory Lake has undergone extensive private development next to the narrow fringe of public property surrounding it. The Old Hickory Nature Trail, designated in the National Trails System, is a must for trail buffs but is appealing to most everyone. Good fishing and duck hunting make the lake popular year-round. The world record walleye (25 pounds) was caught in the upper section of the lake in 1961. Two off-road vehicle trails at Rockland Recreation Area allow drivers to test their skills. Sailing and yachting are popular, and regattas are held frequently. Its central location and accessibility to interstate highway systems make Old Hickory Lake a popular choice for traveling campers. Contact Resource Manager, Old Hickory Lake, P. O. Box 511, Old Hickory, TN 37138; (615) 847-2395.

Lake Barkley

Lying in the gently rolling hills of southwestern Kentucky and north central Tennessee, this huge lake is known nationally for exceptional fishing and duck hunting. The numerous Corps recreation areas and TVA's Land Between the Lakes recreation area (located on the western shore) offer visitors almost unlimited recreational opportunities. Minibike, horseback riding, and nature trails comprise a well-rounded trail system. Special points of interest include Cross Creek National Wildlife Refuge. Contact Resource Manager, Lake Barkley, P. O. Box 218, Grand Rivers, KY 42045.

Fishing on a foggy morning

Center Hill Lake

Nestled in the Cumberland Mountains of Middle Tennessee, Center Hill is noted for its smallmouth bass, walleye, and white bass fishing. Fancher and Furgess Falls are on the Falling Water River arm of the lake. Bluffs and steep, forested hills enrich the natural beauty of this lake. For more information, contact Resource Manager, Center Hill Lake, Lancaster, TN 38569; (615) 858-3125.

Cheatham Lake

Passing through an area of rolling hills and moderately steep terrain typical of scenic Middle Tennessee, the impoundment of the Cumberland River forms Cheatham Lake which meanders through the heart of Nashville and past the famous Opryland complex. History comes alive in a visit to Cheatham Lake and the surrounding area. The remnants of Lock A, Harpeth Shoals, and Indian Town bluff are exciting reminders of the area's colorful past. Reconstructed Fort Nashborough overlooks the lake in downtown Nashville. Excellent duck hunting and lunker bass are just waiting for you. Rockfish in the tailwaters reach weights of over 30 pounds. Contact Resource Manager, Cheatham Lake, Route 5, Ashland City, TN 37015; (615) 792-5697.

J. Percy Priest Lake

Located near metropolitan Nashville, J. Percy Priest is a relatively small but popular lake. The rockfish stocked in the lake by the TWRA have been a big hit, and fishing for other game and panfish species is good despite heavy fishing pressure from nearby Nashville. Multipurpose recreation areas dot the lake, providing good access and recreation opportunities throughout. Many campers use the lake as a base while visiting Nashville's many attractions. A cooperative effort between the Corps and TWRA plays a major role in managing the wildlife here. For a panoramic view of the lake, go to the award-winning Visitors Center near the dam. For more information, contact Resource Manager, J. Percy Priest Lake, P. O. Box 2377, Nashville, TN 37214; (615) 889-1975.

A SAMPLER
★★★★★Exclusive★★★★★

An Oak Ridge Boy Hits the Lake

When we hear the high lead vocals of one of the many Oak Ridge Boys' hits, we immediately picture a slim, curly-haired guy with big, round eyes. Joe Bonsall, like the other three Oaks, wasn't born in Tennessee, but he lives here now and loves it!

The Oak Ridge Boys are so popular that they aren't

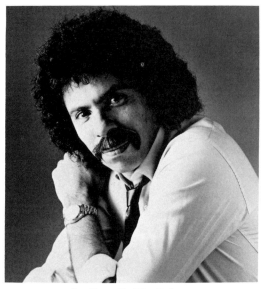

Joe Bonsall of the Oaks

home a lot, since they play about 200 dates a year, from the main rooms in Las Vegas hotels to a sold-out Carnegie Hall. You've surely seen them on "The Johnny Carson Show" or in countless other TV appearances.

When Joe is home in the great state of Tennessee and the weather's right, he heads for the his favorite place, Old Hickory Lake. There he fires up his high-powered boat and points it toward some hidden cove or inlet. On the often glassy waters he can ski for hours with friends, then lounge in the rays, being soothed by the gentle waves that rock his boat.

Joe told the *Sampler* that he also loves to crank up his boat in the fall and go out on Old Hickory to get a very special view of the colors that are so vivid and inspiring there. The blues of the lake reflect the reds and yellows and oranges and make Joe thankful to be alive.

Next time you're skiing or fishing or relaxing on Old Hickory Lake, you may see Joe. He's not only one of "The Boys," he's one of us.

A SAMPLER FEATURE

Chattanooga's Hot Spots

by Dan Cook

■ *Chattanooga may be closer to more great fishing areas than any other city in Tennessee. We've asked our friend Dan Cook, Outdoor Editor of the* Chattanooga News/Free Press *to give you all the specifics on hot spots around his town. So get your gear together and try these for yourself!*

Lake Chickamauga

Convenient to Chattanooga, this TVA reservoir offers some superb bass and crappie fishing as well as top angling for bluegill and rockfish. The Chattanooga Bass Association is an organization formed by local bass clubs in which prize money is offered for top catches. The association sponsors a series of tournaments which are held on Chickamauga and the adjoining Nickajack and Watts Bar lakes. Although this series of tournaments attracts many local anglers, it is open to tourists and others as well.

Entry fee for 1985 was $30 per person, with the amount including breakfast in the restaurant at Bass Bay Marina. Bass Bay is where the weigh-ins are held for the monthly series scheduled from March through October. Fishermen who stay with the series have a shot at the season-ending "classic" in which a boat and trailer rig are usually awarded to the winner of competition between top point producers (points awarded on the basis of ounces caught in the tourneys). Interested fishermen should write Bass Bay Marina at 9718 Hixson Pike, Soddy-Daisy, TN 37379, for more information or call (615) 842-5391.

Two beautiful camping areas are located on the lake. One is the city-owned Chester Frost County Park reached by taking State 153 off I-75 in Chattanooga north to Northgate Shopping Center and turning right onto Hixson Pike. The park offers a lovely view of Lake Chickamauga. Rates are reasonable for camping spaces. There's a two-week limit on lakeside locations, but visitors may stay elsewhere in the park as long as they wish. Sites rent for about $6 per night, hookups and bathhouses with running water included. Senior citizens can rent sites for half-price. That address is Park Headquarters, Chester Frost Park, 2318 Gold Point Circle, Hixson, TN 37343. It's located close to several shopping malls.

The other major camping location is Harrison Bay State Park on the opposite end of the lake from Chester Frost Park. Harrison Bay is a Tennessee state park offering a marina and picnic areas with camping sites near the lake. To reach the park, drive north from Chattanooga on State 58. The address is 8411 Harrison Bay Road in Harrison, TN 37341. Or call (615) 344-6214. Top fishing spots in Lake Chickamauga include Wolftever Creek, which enters the lake near Loret Marina just off State 58 north, and the area upriver where the Hiwassee River flows into the lake. At Loret Marina, sailboats and motorboats are available. Call (615) 344-8331 or write Loret Marina, 6701 Highway 58, Harrison, TN 37341. Big Ridge, (615) 842-5828; Chickamauga, (615) 622-0821; Gold Point, (615) 877-2501; Lakeshore, (615) 877-6468; Lakesite, (615) 842-0431; Sale Creek, (615) 332-6312; and Shady Grove Harbor, (615) 332-5613— all are facilities available on Lake Chickamauga.

Nickajack Lake

This is the first lake you'll cross when approaching Chattanooga from Nashville. An old railroad bed located near I-24 has provided some top crappie and bass fishing. Nearby Nickajack Dam offers fishing from

You can do more than fish on Lake Chickamauga

the wingwalls jutting out into the water on the south side of the dam. In that area Benny Hull of nearby Rossville, Georgia, who holds several line-class, fresh-water, world-fishing marks, caught the world record fresh-water drum weighing slightly more than 50 pounds. Ross's Landing Marina is located in downtown Chattanooga just a few miles below Chickamauga Dam on Nickajack Lake. It offers overnighting for sailboats traveling the Tennessee River. It is located within walking distance of downtown motels and stores.

Watts Bar Lake

Located north of Chattanooga near Dayton and Rockwood, this lake offers more of the same top crappie and bass fishing. New Port Resort in Rockwood has boat slips. Several other marinas are located in the area.

Hiwassee River

This may be reached by driving east on I-75 from Chattanooga, taking the first Cleveland Exit, and following US 64 east until it intersects with Highway 411 (the old Atlanta-to-Knoxville main route). This is one of Tennessee's top trout fisheries, with some whopper brown trout taken from it. It is regularly stocked by the Tennessee Wildlife Resources Agency in prime trouting season. About an hour-and-a-half drive east of Chattanooga, Webb's Store at Reliance offers bait and other supplies. Two primitive camping areas are located close by.

Tellico Section of Cherokee National Forest

Located just east of Tellico Plains, it offers the beauti-ful Bald River Falls and the breathtaking streams that are regularly stocked. This is about a two-hour drive east of Chattanooga. Contact the United States Forest Service's Cherokee National Forest Office in Cleveland for maps and other details.

Chickamauga Creek

This stream flows through the heart of Chattanooga and offers trout and other types of fishing. The trouting is best on the north end where it is stocked by TWRA. Craft's Chickamauga Sport Shop on State 58 in Chattanooga is located near the creek. Baits and other supplies may be purchased there.

Fall Creek Falls Lake

This small lake in Fall Creek Falls State Park has produced one line-class world record catfish and the state bluegill standard. Boats with electric motors and canoes may be rented at the park marina in season. The lake is a part of the view from the park's golf course, which has received acclaim as one of the nation's top 50 golf spots by one publication. The park is located near Pikeville and offers some cabins extending over the lake, making it possible to fish from the porch. Waterfalls, trails, crafts, and swimming in pools are other features.

Sequatchie River

The Sequatchie Float Service at Dunlap offers rental canoes for this peaceful stream which offers trouting.

Battle Creek

This trout-stocked stream is located just to the right of I-24 as the visitor descends massive Monteagle Mountain when approaching Chattanooga from Nashville. It's regularly stocked with trout.

Conasauga River

For the canoeist, this is a lovely, peaceful trip as the river juts from its point of origin in Georgia across the line into Tennessee and back into the adjacent Peach State again. Visitors should arrange for a shuttle system since few businesses offer that in the area. To reach it, travel east on I-75, taking the directions for the Hiwassee River, except that the visitor should turn right (south) when reaching Highway 411. The river is located near the Tennessee-Georgia border. A dirt road leads to the left along the north side of the stream, and there are various access points in the trees to the right. Redeye bass are a favorite catch. Don Hixson at Canoeist Headquarters, 4825 Hixson Pike, Hixson, is a top canoe source who can provide more information on the canoeing phase of the Conasauga. His shop also has a wide variety of supplies, publications, and other items pertaining to the sport. The phone number is (615) 877-6256.

Houseboating In Tennessee

One of Tennessee's best-kept vacation secrets is houseboating on the state's many scenic waterways.

Renting a houseboat can provide you with a fine vacation, and it often costs less than renting a cabin for the same amount of time.

From the Father of Waters in the west to Watauga Lake high in the eastern mountains, Tennessee has one of the most diverse water systems in the whole nation. The state contains 29 major lakes and reservoirs and thousands of miles of beautiful shoreline. Through the engineering marvel of locks and channels, the recreational boater can travel from one end of the state to the other without ever setting foot on land!

This natural blessing has helped make Tennessee a leader in the manufacture and registration of houseboats. The making of these boats has come a long way from Noah's 300-cubit gopherwood model. Today's most expensive houseboats are really luxurious and speedy enough to pull waterskiers. These boats can be rented at almost 40 marinas across the state. As a rule, two people can capably handle these houseboats, and marina staff will be glad to give you all the training you need for safe operation of the craft.

Perhaps the most pleasant aspect of a houseboat trip is that you may travel at your own leisurely pace. You can spend your days sightseeing, swimming, sunning, and fishing, and your evenings cooking fresh fish and enjoying the gorgeous sunsets. Many people bring along a small boat for exploring the inland streams. Shallow lake points and submerged islands are a treasure trove of arrowheads and other Indian artifacts. Dale Hollow Lake in upper Central Tennessee has clear water, a bright shale bottom, and all kinds of fish to make it a favorite for underwater photography. If you want to engage a rare fresh-water jellyfish in a meaningful conversation, Dale Hollow is the place for you.

Plenty of quiet, sheltered coves allow families to get away by themselves. The solitude and tranquillity are so rejuvenating that many boaters come back summer after summer. Some even houseboat in cold weather, when they can really have the lakes to themselves. The *Sampler* recommends houseboating as one of the gentlest and most rewarding ways of getting acquainted with Tennessee and seeing areas that are inaccessible from the land.

Hunting the Greatest Outdoors

Tennessee hunters are smart! They must be among the smartest in the world. They have to be. For one thing, the animals they hunt and trap are smart. Not only smart, but dangerous, some of them. For another thing, they have to be smart just to figure out when, where, and what they can hunt and trap. Because although the Tennessee Wildlife Resources Agency does a great job with its pamphlets and brochures, hunting regulations are still complicated.

So the first thing for you to do if you're interested in Tennessee hunting and trapping is to write the TWRA at its central office, Ellington Agricultural Center, P. O. Box 40747, Nashville, TN 37204. (Or call 360-0500.) They'll send you brochures and tell you how to get in touch with people who can help you have a successful hunt.

The *Sampler* is just going to hit the highlights of game and duck hunting in Tennessee. But first, we need to say that we realize hunting's not for everyone. Many people would rather hunt wildlife with binoculars and camera than with a gun. But you'll find that most serious hunters are dedicated conservationists who help manage wildlife populations. They are interested in keeping Tennessee's animals very much a part of the Greatest Outdoors. Many groups of hunters, like the Coon Hunting Associations, never take the animals; they just hunt, confirm a treeing and leash up the dogs and go again. Tennessee hunters are an asset to our state.

Duck Hunting

Duck hunting in Tennessee can be simple or complicated. The *Sampler* has met hunters who get in a small boat on Duck River (naturally) and just paddle down the river, surprising the ducks as they float around curves in the stream. (Incidentally, that's a good way to squirrel hunt too.) The surprise could also be a cold dip in the Duck, if sudden movements are made!

Other Tennessee duck hunters own scores of decoys and duck calls, build blinds, and devote hundreds of hours to preparing for the season. Although wild ducks are in every Tennessee county, the largest population is in the western portion of the state, the big wetland areas such as Reelfoot and Kentucky lakes that are in the Mississippi Flyway. Duck hunting takes great patience and a total disregard for weather conditions. True-blue hunters will go out in any weather.

Tennessee's duck hunting is set up on a points basis. The hunter who bags a canvasback or black duck is through for the day because all 100 points are used up with one bird. Male mallards and ringnecks, for example, are 25 points each. So if you've got the stuff in you of which great duckhunters are made, go with some experienced hunters or guides (some Tennesseans guide fishers and hunters for a living all year long) until you learn the ducks. The *Sampler* knows hunters who can tell the types apart just by flight patterns or calls while they are still several hundred yards away.

Deer Hunting

Deer hunting is perhaps the most widely practiced hunting in Tennessee, except maybe for rabbits. Middle and West Tennessee are the best places to hunt, just because of the large deer populations in some of the heavily farmed and wooded counties that provide abundant food and cover. Hickman, Perry, Giles, Fenton, and Hardeman counties are among the best deer hunting areas. Deer hunters do extensive scouting before the start of the season to search out the trails. Once the season starts, though, the deer get much more cautious and will usually change their routes.

Hunters under 16 need to take a Hunter's Safety

Course offered by the TWRA. We've heard this course highly recommended by several parents who took it with their children. Don't forget to obtain permission from the landowner if you're going to hunt on private property. State, federal, and industrially owned lands offer fine hunting, though, and you can get a complete listing of these just by writing the TWRA office.

Mountain Hunts

"Mountain hunting offers the most risk of any hunting in Tennessee." So said Charles Kirkland, a friend of the *Sampler* and an experienced East Tennessee hunter. In mountain areas open to hunting are not only deer but wild turkeys, black bears, and wild boars, the latter being descendants of some escapees from a hunting preserve decades ago. The terrain is almost as dangerous as the prey. In combination, the bears, boars, and boulders have done some hunters bodily harm.

But the hazards of falling out of trees, getting hung in briars with a boar's "tushes" right on your tail, or sliding down cliffsides on your backside are nothing to the aggravation of chasing hunting dogs through mountain laurel.

"The laurel grows as tall as a man, thick and interlaced, like hackberry limbs," Charles said. "Now, the bear, he's got a wedge shape to him. He cuts right through the stuff. So does the wild boar. But a man, it'll fight him every step!" So a hunter can get really angry at a dog who chases rabbits through a big laurel patch when wild boar is what the hunter wants to see.

Charles and some friends and 10 hunting dogs participated in a three-day wilderness hunt in Cherokee National Forest just about Christmas a few years back. Use of hunting dogs is limited to these three-day hunts. They were hunting on the North River off Tellico Plains, in the Cherokee wilds. On these hunts, you can get a bear and a boar apiece. That's the limit. On this hunt, only three of the dogs would even track a bear. The rest of them had never smelled one and wanted nothing to do with the critter.

They had somewhat better luck with the wild boars, but they got off to a slow start. Most of the hunting dogs they brought were large-breed hounds. But two old boys in overalls with one single-barrel shotgun between them had brought two small, brown, nondescript-looking dogs with them. The big hunting dogs were too slow to catch the boars and turn them and keep them at bay. Those boars would just keep running, the dogs chasing after them, and the hunters had to wade through laurel

A Sampler *safety tip: Always check you aim*
Photo courtesy of State Museum and Archives

and rhododendron after all of them. So Charles and the biggest bunch of the hunters got nothing but sore feet that first day. Meanwhile, the two old boys with their little feisty dogs had gotten a boar every two hours, just like clockwork. Those dogs would catch the boar and hold it till the men got there with their antique shotgun. After that, most of the hunters were following those two, and they wound up with 14 wild boars, some wonderful barbecue, and a lot of great sausage.

Another favorite among Tennessee hunters is wild turkey. We asked Charles about the turkey, and he said, "That's the sharpest, quickest-reacting animal in the woods! You'd better do a lot of good scouting before the hunt, wear all the camouflage you can, and know how to call him up. Then, don't move anything but your eyeballs, or he's gone. He's faster than a white-tailed deer. There's an old saying among turkey hunters. 'Always shoot high at a turkey! Those feathers will turn shot like a flak jacket.' "

The *Sampler* wanted to know if there was any other way to catch the skittish birds. "Well, the old timers used to take a box without a bottom, and dig a hole under it with a trench big enough for the turkey to come through. Then they'd trail corn to lead that gobbler into the box. Once he straightened up, he was caught. He'd just walk around in that box and never look down and go back out! They called one old boy around here 'Turkey Jack' because he built a big trap like that and caught six or eight turkeys. He took the lid off and jumped in there to get one, and they like to have beat him to death, and all got away!"

As we mentioned above, the best way to begin hunting in Tennessee is to get in touch with hunting groups, experienced guides, and thoroughly understand the laws and regulations governing hunting. So write for pamphlets, be cautious, and good hunting to you!

Our Greatest Outdoors

Our Greatest Outdoors are all those special places in Tennessee that belong to each of us. Of course we're talking about our 51 state parks and other state-owned recreation areas. Tennessee's park system is one of the finest in the nation and the *Sampler* would love to tell you about each and every one. Since space won't permit that, we've decided to describe some of the scenery and special features of a few of our favorite parks. We hope you'll go to see each of these and be inspired to discover the rest of our Greatest Outdoors.

Unless we note otherwise, all of these parks offer a variety of camping experiences, special programs such as hikes and hayrides, and complete facilities for day uses such as picnicking. Campsites with tables, grills, and electricity are $7.75 per day at all of Tennessee's state parks. More primitive sites are less expensive. These prices plus Tennessee's scenic beauty make for an unbeatable combination.

For information and reservations on *all* state recreational areas in Tennessee, write or call: Tennessee Department of Conservation, 701 Broadway, Nashville, TN 37203; Phone (615) 742-6667, Toll Free Number for Reservations: (800) 421-6683

Tennessee's State Natural Areas

Scattered across Tennessee are certain special places which show no evidence of the hand of man. Tennessee has identified and designated 29 of these as State Natural Areas. They are rare gems set in the crowning glory of the Greatest Outdoors. They include virgin forests, splendid waterfalls, cave systems, unique rock formations, deep river gorges, bottom lands, and the largest remnant prairie in the Southeastern United States, ranging in size from the 18,000 acres at Reelfoot Lake to a two-acre Natural Bridge site near Sewanee.

Most of these are open to the public, but don't expect to find tennis courts or cabins around. By law these sites must be conserved and protected, and this results in access which is much more restrictive than state parks. The idea is to allow as little impact by man as possible. The foot trails you will use are virtually the only evidence of man's activity.

Here are the *Sampler's* picks of Tennessee's State Natural Areas:

Virgin Falls

Virgin Falls is unique in that there is no visible stream leading up to or away from it. Eons ago, a sinkhole collapsed, laying open a section of underground river. The year-round stream emerges from a sinkhole, runs over a flat rock surface for 70 feet, falls 110 feet, and then disappears into another cave in one of nature's miracles of design.

Virgin Falls is one of the most beautiful spots in Tennessee, but be ready to expend some energy to get to it! It is one of 11 natural areas owned privately. The Bowater Southern Paper Company, which owns over 180,000 acres of Tennessee timber, opened Virgin Falls in 1970. Bowater developed the trail system, which demands a vigorous 4-mile hike to reach the falls. Primitive camping is allowed in a designated area near the falls, but keep in mind that you have to carry out everything you carry in, so pack sparingly. Allow 6 to 8 hours for the full round trip.

Virgin Falls access is in White County, 8 miles south of US 70 near De Rossett. Take Mourberry Road south out of De Rossett about 5.9 miles. Turn right on the access road at the "Chestnut Mountain Wilderness" sign.

Radnor Lake

Only a 15-minute drive from downtown Nashville, the 957-acre Radnor Lake Natural Area contains an abundance of plant and animal life. The 61-acre lake attracts geese, heron, and other birds as well as many species of salamanders, turtles, and many of Tennessee's most beguiling mammals. Radnor also has some

Fall Creek Falls in wintertime

of the highest hills in the Nashville Basin. Wildflowers, ferns, and mosses in abundance are a feast for the soul. The area is laced with trails for strolling through gorgeous woods which make it a welcome and relaxing getaway from pressure-cooker living. Guided nature walks can be arranged by contacting the Radnor Lake staff at (615) 373-3467.

Radnor is located on Otter Creek Road one half mile east of Granny White Pike and 1½ miles west of Franklin Road (US 31). Parking is available at east and west ends of the lake.

For information, write: Radnor Lake State Natural Area, 1050 Otter Creek Road, Nashville, TN 37220.

Frozen Head State Natural Area

About 10 miles east of Wartburg and 40-odd miles west of Knoxville is a 12,000-acre natural area named for one of the highest peaks in the Cumberland Mountains. Frozen Head's name comes from the fact that the peak is often shrouded in ice and snow during winter months. The Frozen Head observation tower provides an incredible vista of the Cumberland Plateau. Over 55 miles of foot trails meander through the majestic hardwoods in the area. Primitive campsites, picnic areas, and an amphitheater are also available. Above all, don't miss Frozen Head in the springtime. It is one of the richest wildflower areas outside of the Smoky Mountains. Every spring the Frozen Head Wildflower Pilgrimage is one of the most popular events on the Cumberland Plateau.

From I-40, take State 61 Exit north, go north on US 27 to Wartburg, turn right on State 62, and follow the signs.

Big Bone Cave

For those of you who like to avoid the sunshine, the *Sampler* recommends Big Bone Cave, located on a 334-acre site in northwest Van Buren County. Big Bone Cave was named after the discovery of fossil remains of prehistoric mammals, including a Pleistocene jaguar and a giant ground sloth.

Situated on Bone Cave Mountain on the Eastern Highland Rim, the historic cavern was a center for extensive saltpeter mining during the War of 1812. The cave was mined by hundreds of men at a time who dragged sacks of nitrous earth out to leaching vats near the entrance. These activities were duplicated during the Civil War.

The vats, tramways, and ladders are still inside the cave in an excellent state of preservation. For this reason Big Bone Cave is on the National Register of Historic Places. As a significant Pleistocene vertebrate fossil site it has been designated as a national landmark by the United States Department of the Interior.

Visitors may tour the cave with a state park ranger.

From US 70S between McMinnville and Sparta, turn on Bone Cave Road just a couple of miles south of Camp Parish (Boy Scout camp). Bone Cave Road will go due east for a few miles, then head to the southeast. About a mile past the intersection with Laurel Creek Road, turn left on Bone Cave Mountain Road. Follow it just over 2 miles to McCoy Road, which accesses the natural area.

A SAMPLER FEATURE

The South Cumberland Has It All!

■The Tennessee *Sampler* urges you to discover the South Cumberland Recreation Area. Not only does it offer an almost unparalleled variety of outdoor experiences, but nearby is a host of fascinating historical and tour sites, including Sewanee, Fall Creek Falls, Monteagle, and the Sequatchie Valley. (See "Tours".)

S.C.R.A. Visitors Center

Whatever you plan to do at the South Cumberland, start off at the Visitors Center located between Tracy City and Monteagle on State 56. Maps, trail information, and directions to park areas are available here seven days a week. The Visitors Center also has a narrated music and slide show which provides an armchair tour of everything the South Cumberland offers. Brochures describe in detail what you will need for any park activities.

Savage Gulf State Natural Area

The Savage Gulf Natural Area contains 11,400 acres with approximately 85 miles of back-country trails and nine primitive campsites. A ranger station is located at each access point for visitor registration and assistance. A permit must be obtained for hiking through the virgin timber sections of Savage Gulf. Be prepared for some rugged hiking, and make plans to carry out everything you carry in.

Savage Gulf was obtained by the State of Tennessee in 1973 in order to protect one of the last-known "mixed Mesophytic" stands of virgin timber in the United States. This type of hardwood forest, once disturbed by logging, never comes back in the same mixture of trees.

The Savage Gulf entrance is also the eastern access point to the Savage Gulf-Stone Door trail complex that winds through some of the most rugged and scenic sections of the park. At this entrance is a 2-mile loop trail to Savage Falls that the *Sampler* highly recommends.

Named for the Great Stone Door, a 150-feet-high crevice at the crest of the plateau, the Stone Door entrance is the western access of the Savage Gulf-Stone Door trail complex. Steep bluffs that offer excellent rapelling are to be found at the Stone Door. About 6 miles out is a section of trail that passes among the fringes of the virgin timber. The trails are well maintained, but rugged.

Grundy Lakes State Recreation Area

Grundy Lakes offers swimming and picnicking facilities in one of Grundy County's most historic areas. It is the site of the Lone Rock Coke Ovens where locally mined coal was converted to coke using convict labor until 1892. The coke ovens remain as eloquent monu-

ments to the desperation of life and labor during those times.

Grundy Forest State Natural Area

Grundy Forest covers approximately 212 acres and is the northern entry point for the Fiery Gizzard Trail. The trail is accessed just behind Tracy City Elementary School. This trail winds past numerous waterfalls and spectacular sandstone formations and eventually leads to Foster Falls. About halfway down the trail is the "blue hole" swimming hole—just right for a cool plunge during summer hiking. There are two primitive campsites along the Fiery Gizzard Trail. We recommend that hikers leave a car at each end of the trail, if possible. The trail is about 13 miles one way and with a stop or two along the way, will take most of the day to walk.

Foster Falls TVA Small Wild Area

Foster Falls provides picnicking and primitive camping close to the 60-feet-high falls for which it is named. In winter it offers excellent ice climbing for a small group of Tennesseans and visitors who practice this difficult sport. From the parking and camping area, it is just a short walk to two waterfalls.

Sewanee Natural Bridge State Natural Area

From the South Cumberland Visitors Center, take US 64 into Sewanee, turning left at State 56 to Sherwood. Then look for the park signs. Located a short walk from the parking area, the Natural Bridge stands 27 feet high, a marvel of nature's engineering, weathered from solid sandstone.

Carter State Natural Area

Hikers can enter the Carter State Natural Area along the Buggy Top Trail. This trail is 2 miles long and leads to the main entrance of Buggy Top Cave. The entrance is one of the most impressive cave mouths in the state. It is 100 feet wide and 30 feet high and opens up at the base of an overhanging bluff 150 feet high. The creek that formed the cave disappears into the ground at the big sink more than a mile north of the cave mouth. Be sure to bring flashlights if you expect to go very far into the cave. Also, plan to get your feet wet and see a lot of bats.

The area around the cave is full of wildflowers in the spring and has a forest of oaks, hickories, and maples as well as many shrubs. Wildlife is abundant with deer, grouse, and numerous squirrels coming near the trail. Some of the flora and fauna in this area are very rare, so don't pick up specimens or leave graffiti. Just find a rock to sit quietly beside the trail, and we guarantee you'll have a real wildlife adventure.

For more information and reservations contact: South Cumberland State Recreation Area, Route 1 Box 144-H, Tracy City, TN 37387. (615) 924-2980.

If you want to camp near the South Cumberland but need hookups and electricity, the *Sampler* recommends Jim Oliver's Smokehouse Campground in Monteagle, TN, 37356, at the intersection of I-24 and US 64. It offers a swimming pool and playground, and all the amenities of a campground at reasonable prices. Call Jim at (615) 924-2268.

Tennessee's Resort Parks

Imagine stepping out on your balcony to a view of a crystal-clear Tennessee lake or wooded hillside instead of just another concrete convention hotel across a crowded city street! Tennessee's Resort Parks offer you attractive, comfortable sleeping rooms with all the amenities, such as air conditioning, color television, in-room coffee, and room telephones. For a different type of meeting experience, you may want to consider sleeping accommodations in one of Tennessee's fully appointed cabins, which range in style from ultra-contemporary to rustic.

Although our Resort Parks give you the advantage of escaping the hustle and bustle of the city, you'll still have plenty to do in your leisure time. Championship golf courses, tennis, fishing, swimming, boating, biking, and hiking are just a few of the activities available. Or maybe you'd like to try your hand at skeet shooting or archery. The Resort Parks have something to appeal to all ages and interests.

Paris Landing State Resort Park

Paris Landing State Resort Park, on the western shore of Kentucky Lake, is named for a steamboat and freight landing on the Tennessee River dating back to the mid-1800s. From here and other landings on the Tennessee and Big Sandy rivers, supplies were transported to surrounding towns and communities by ox cart.

Nearby attractions include TVA's Land Between the Lakes outdoor recreation area, a 170,000 acre, 40-mile-long peninsula between Kentucky Lake and Lake Barkley. Thirteen miles east of Paris Landing is Fort Donelson National Military Park, which contains a museum and numerous authentic replicas of the Civil War. During the last week in April, in nearby Paris, the World's Biggest Fish Fry takes place. Fresh Kentucky Lake catfish is the star attraction along with all sorts of exciting activities. (See "Fun Times.")

Reelfoot Lake State Resort Park

Reelfoot Lake State Resort Park lies in the northwest corner of Tennessee in Lake and Obion counties. It covers about 18,725 acres, 18,000 of which are water. The area is said to be the greatest hunting and fishing preserve in the nation. It harbors almost every kind of shore and wading bird, as well as the golden and the American bald eagles. Other animals are also diverse and abundant here. Its many species of flowering and nonflowering plants attract botanists from all over the country. Cypress dominates the margins of the lake, but many other trees and shrubs are also present. In 1973, Reelfoot was reclassified as a resort park, and many new facilities were developed including a resort inn and restaurant, picnic area, playgrounds, an air strip, and a camping area. Tennis courts and a pool were completed near the inn in 1977.

Henry Horton State Park

Located on the former estate of Tennessee's forty-first governor, Henry Horton State Park was one of the first resort parks in the Tennessee Outdoor Recreation Area System. Its 1,135 acres border the historic Duck River and boast a resort inn, scenic golf course, and one of the finest skeet and trap ranges in the nation.

Montgomery Bell State Resort Park

The iron industry has long been extinct in Tennessee, but traces of it may still be found within the 3,782-acre Montgomery Bell State Resort Park. The remains of the old Laurel Furnace and the ore pits, where men once scratched iron ore from the earth, lie quiet and abandoned. The hardwood forest, heavily cut to clear farmland and to produce charcoal for the iron furnaces, has slowly healed its wounds.

The park has a beautiful 40-room inn and restaurant open year-round except during the Christmas season. Blending contemporary architecture with the colorful warmth of Tennessee Crab Orchard stone, this structure is located in a peaceful setting among the trees overlooking scenic 35-acre Acorn Lake.

Family camping, swimming, boating, fishing, and hiking are favorite activities. The Frank G. Clement Golf Course is the newest recreation facility at Montgomery Bell. The course furnishes a challenging 18 holes and a modern pro shop.

While at the park, get directions to the Harpeth River for a wonderful float trip. After canoeing several miles on the meandering Harpeth, you finish within a few hundred yards of your original departure point. While you're paddling, you'll see the famous "Narrows of the Harpeth" tunnel built by Montgomery Bell.

Fall Creek Falls State Resort Park

Fall Creek Falls State Resort Park is one of the most spectacular outdoor recreation areas in America. Its waterfalls, cascades, sparkling streams, gorges, timberland, and an unmatched variety of recreation facilities and activities have made it one of the most popular parks in the Southeast. Fall Creek has the highest waterfall east of the Rocky Mountains. It plunges 256 feet into a shaded pool at the base of its gorge. The park's other falls (Piney, Cane Creek, and Cane Creek Cascades), though smaller, are just as impressive.

The oak and hickory forest that covers most of the park gives way to tulip poplar and hemlock forest in the gorges. The plants and animals of the moist, protected gorges are somewhat like the species found in southern Canada. Mountain laurel and rhododendron are abundant throughout the park, as are other plants and animals.

Natchez Trace State Resort Park

Natchez Trace State Resort Park straddles I-40 in the West Tennessee uplands. The park came into being

World's largest pecan tree at Natchez Trace State Park

in 1939 when the state leased 42,000 acres from the United States Forest Service. Many of the existing buildings and improvements were also taken over by the state. Additional developments, including the Pin Oak Lodge and day-use complex, were completed and dedicated in 1975.

The area provides not only recreation and managed hunting, but also the largest and most successful continuous pine tree planting and cutting operations in the state. Here, too, is one of the largest pecan trees in North America. With its roots buried deep in Tennessee soil, its trunk soars 118 feet into the sky, stretches its limbs 136 feet, and has a circumference of 18 feet 2 inches. The legend is that one of General Andrew Jackson's men returning home from the Battle of New Orleans gave a pecan to Sukey Morris who planted it.

The *Sampler* Picks of the Parks

EAST TENNESSEE
Warriors Path State Recreational Area
Warriors Path State Recreational Area is named for the park's proximity to the ancient war trail or "warriors path" used by the Cherokees when they went raiding or hunting in Virginia. It is situated on the shores of TVA's Fort Patrick Henry Reservoir on the Holston River. Warriors Path has eight wonderful hiking trails, including ridgetop trails which offer views of Bays and Roan Mountains and much of the geology of the Valley-and-Ridge province of Tennessee.

Warriors Path has one of the finest Par 72, championship, 18-hole golf courses in the state. A driving green and a practice green are next to a fully-stocked pro shop. Warriors Path is located in the Tri-Cities area of upper East Tennessee. It is 2 miles southeast of Kingsport and accessible via US 23. From I-81, exit on US 23 and go north for 2 miles to the park entrance.

For further information contact: Superintendent's Office, Warriors Path State Recreational Area, Kingsport, TN 37663 (615) 239-8531.

Red Clay State Historical Area
Red Clay State Historical Area is located in the extreme southeast corner of Bradley County, just above the Tennessee-Georgia state line. The park encompasses 275 acres of narrow valleys formerly used as cotton and pasture land. Forested ridges average 200 feet or more above the valley floor.

The site contains a natural landmark, the great council spring or blue hole, which rises from beneath a limestone ledge to form a deep pool that flows into Mill Creek. The spring was used by the Cherokees for their water supply during council meetings.

Red Clay served as the seat of Cherokee government from 1832 until the forced removal of the Cherokees in 1838. It was the site of 11 general councils, national affairs attended by up to 5,000 people. Those years were filled with frustrating efforts to ensure the future of the Cherokees. Principal Chief John Ross led the fight to keep their eastern lands, refusing the government's efforts to move his people to Oklahoma. Controversial treaties, however, resulted in the surrendering of land and the end of the Cherokees' future in the east. At Red Clay, the Trail of Tears really began, for here the Cherokees learned that they had lost their mountains, streams, and valleys forever.

Today an automobile route takes you along the approximate route of the Trail of Tears. Tour maps are available at the park office.

The James F. Corn Interpretive Center, located near the park entrance, houses a theater, a resource reading room, and exhibits. A Cherokee farm and council house of the period have been reconstructed to show how the area might have looked 140 years ago.

The great council spring is located near the council house and is accessible by a paved trail designed to accommodate the handicapped. The council spring is presently 11 feet deep and produces over 400,000 gallons of water a day.

Recreation facilities include a 500-seat amphitheater, a picnic pavilion with tables, an outdoor picnic area with tables and grills, and a 3-mile loop trail with a limestone overlook tower. Red Clay is designed for day use and has no facilities for camping.

For information write or call Red Clay Historical Area, Route 6, Box 734, Cleveland, TN. (615) 472-2627.

Pickett State Rustic Park

12,000-acre Pickett State Rustic Park and Forest is situated in a remote section of the upper Cumberland Mountains, and it possesses a combination of scenic, botanical, and geological wonders found nowhere else in the state. Of particular interest in this wilderness country are the uncommon rock formations, natural bridges, numerous caves, and the remains of ancient Indian occupation.

Some say Pickett is second only to the Great Smoky Mountains in botanical diversity. World War I hero Sergeant Alvin C. York was raised in these mountains as was Cordell Hull. In fact, you may visit Hazard Cave, where York and his brother kept their cows penned in years past.

Pickett adjoins the Big South Fork of the Cumberland River National Recreational Area, which is now under development. This area consists of 150,000 acres of prime eastern wilderness country.

Pickett State Park is located 45 miles north of the Crossville-Jamestown exit on I-40. This exit is about 114 miles from Nashville and 70 miles from Knoxville. From the exit, take US 127 north through Jamestown. Turn right on State 154 and go 13 miles to the park.

For further information: Superintendent's Office, Pickett State Rustic Park, Polk Creek Route, Box 174, Jamestown, TN 38556. (615) 879-5821.

Roan Mountain State Park

This beautiful park is nestled beneath the 6,285-foot peak for which it is named. From the park it is only 10 miles along US 143 to the highlands of Roan Mountain itself. Roan Mountain is rich in beauty and unusual plant and animal life. Here you may find a northern flying squirrel or the tiny white flowers of Michaux's saxifrage. During the middle of June, above 5,000 feet the Catawba rhododendron bursts into bloom, forming the largest natural rhododendron garden in the world.

One of the most beautiful sections of The Appalachian Trail crosses the highlands of the Roan. It runs west from Carvers Gap to US 19E, and takes you across the largest expanse of grassy balds in the southern Appalachians. Impressive views, thick carpets of moss, and many wildflowers are waiting for you along these high mountain ridges.

Roan Mountain State Park is located in Carter County about 20 miles southeast of Elizabethton. To reach the park, turn south from US 19E onto US 143 at the town of Roan Mountain. The park, entirely within the boundaries of Cherokee National Forest, is only two miles from the town of Roan Mountain.

For further information contact: Roan Mountain State Park, Route 1 Box 50, Roan Mountain, TN 37687.

MIDDLE TENNESSEE
Long Hunter State Recreation Area

Long Hunter State Recreation Area is situated along the shore of J. Percy Priest Lake, a lake that was formed by the impoundment of Stones River by the U.S. Corps of Engineers.

Pleasure boating and water-skiing, as well as year-round fishing, are very popular on the 14,000-acre J. Percy Priest Lake. Catches include large and small-mouth bass, rockfish, crappie, bream and catfish. Long Hunter offers two launch ramps on J. Percy Priest Lake, one at Bryant Grove and one at Couchville Lake.

Prior to the 1700s this territory was in the possession of the Choctaw, Cherokee, and Chickasaw Indians. The territory was a favored hunting ground since buffalo, elk, deer, and small game were plentiful here.

Many of the early explorers were known as *long hunters,* so named for the duration of their excursions and the long rifles they carried.

Couchville Lake is totally barrier free. In fact, that's the main reason the *Sampler* wanted to tell you about Long Hunter Park. It is completely accessible to the handicapped, and programs involving the handicapped and elderly are regularly offered. Facilities include a fishing pier and boat dock and a 2-mile, hard-surfaced nature trail.

For Further Information Contact: Area Manager's Office, Long Hunter State Recreation Area, Route 1, Hobson Pike, Hermitage, TN 37076. Phone (615) 885-2422.

Standing Stone State Rustic Park

The almost 11,000 acres of Standing Stone State Rustic Park and Forest are situated on the Cumberland Plateau of north-central Tennessee. This quaint and rustic park is noted for its outstanding scenery, spring wildflowers, fossils, beautiful hardwood forest, fall colors, and other natural diversity.

Standing Stone is located in Overton County within a triangle formed by highways connecting Livingston, Gainesboro, and Celina.

The park takes its name from the "standing stone," which was supposedly used as a boundary line between two separate Indian tribes. The stone was sandstone and about eight feet tall. It sat upright on a sandstone ledge. After it fell, the Indians placed it on an improvised monument to preserve it. The stone may still be seen at Monterey, Tennessee.

Year-round fishing is excellent in 69-acre Standing Stone Lake. Dale Hollow Lake is only five miles from the park and offers some of the finest fishing, boating and skiing in the state. Eagles have been sighted at Dale Hollow in winter.

The best season to go to Standing Stone, though, is the fall. Standing Stone's incredible hardwood forest puts on an October and November spectacular! And, by all means, rent one of the chestnut log cabins during the cold weather, build a fire in the fireplace, gather some friends around, and really enjoy yourself. Ten miles of trails through the wilds of Standing Stone State Rustic Park and Forest offer everything from today's wildlife to fossils millions of years old.

For Further Information and Reservations Contact:

Superintendent's Office, Standing Stone State Rustic Park, Livingston, TN 38570. (615) 823-6347.

Cedars of Lebanon State Day-Use Park

Cedars of Lebanon State Day-Use Park is named for the dense cedar forest that existed in the biblical lands of Lebanon. However, our own "cedar" is not a true cedar, but a close cousin, the juniper.

Of the park's 8,887 acres, 901 acres are used for intensive recreation. The remainder of the area is operated by the Parks Division as a natural area and by the Forestry Division as a State Forest. This is the largest red cedar forest remaining in the United States. Its open limestone glades, peculiar to the cedar forest area, host an array of rare wildflowers and other native plants and animals.

Eight miles of hiking trails twist through the cedar forests and glades. One of these is keyed to a self-guided trail brochure available at the Nature Center. Trails take visitors past wildflowers, sinkholes, caves, and numerous other natural and cultural features. Twelve miles of horseback riding trails with rental horses are available at the park stables.

Don't miss the Spring Wildflower festival at the park. Also, Cedars of Lebanon hosts a great square-dance every Saturday night. (See "Music.")

For Further Information and Reservations Contact: Superintendent's Office, Cedars of Lebanon State Day-Use Park, Lebanon, TN 37087. (615) 444-9394.

Old Stone Fort

Two hundred years ago, when white settlers first came to what is now Middle Tennessee, they found a system of manmade walls on the banks of Duck River, near the present city of Manchester in Coffee County. This mysterious structure, commonly referred to as "the Old Stone Fort," became the object of romantic legends which purported to explain its origin.

Actually this isn't a fort, but a church! Based on evidence unearthed on the premises, archaeologists have announced the following conclusions about the ancient structure:

—The ancient walls were built by prehistoric Indians;

—The walls were raised in the first four centuries that followed the birth of Christ;

—It was a ceremonial site, holy ground to the Woodland Indians.

Today the Old Stone Fort lies in ruins on the bluffs high above the Duck River, where it cascades down the Highland Rim near Manchester. Its builders located the enclosure between the forks of a river, a few hundred yards from the point at which the two tributaries—Little Duck and Big Duck—come together to form the main stream which flows westward to the Tennessee. Bluffs from 60 to 100 feet high form natural barriers on two sides of the enclosure. The manmade walls, on the north and south sides, cross the neck of land between the forks and terminate where the bluffs afford natural barriers. The south wall alone stretches 2,111 feet from one stream to the other, attesting to the size of the project. The total area enclosed by the walls and bluffs is about 54 acres.

Perhaps the most distinctive feature is the entrance to the enclosure. The single opening, located on the north wall, consists of two parallel walls that extend into the enclosure to form a narrow passageway some 120 feet long.

Several miles of foot trails are developed within Old Stone Fort State Archaeological Area. These trails parallel the fort walls, the Big Duck and Little Duck Rivers and wind through the park. River trails provide unmatched views of picturesque waterfalls, shimmering white water, and placid pools.

A naturalist is available in the park throughout the summer months to conduct tours of the fort and demonstrate the American Indian way of life during the Archaic and Woodland periods.

The state maintains a 9-hole golf course adjacent to the main park. This scenic course is located within the Duck River floodplain. There is a small pro shop and rental carts are available.

Old Stone Fort is located just off US 41, about 1½ miles west of Manchester just east of Big Duck River Bridge. From I-24, turn south at either the first or fourth Manchester exit and follow the signs to the park.

WEST TENNESSEE

Meeman-Shelby State Park

The mighty Mississippi River forms the western boundary of Meeman-Shelby State Park. The developed sections of the park sit atop the Chickasaw Bluffs. These bluffs and the river bottoms below are rich in Indian lore, and they host one of the finest arrays of plant and animal life in the state. Wild turkey and deer abound in the 9,000-acre bottomland hardwood forest, along with other animals from bobcats to bobolinks. Miles of scenic trails put you within reach of all these animals and trees, and take you right to the banks of the Mississippi. Amazingly, all this is less than 15 miles north of metropolitan Memphis!

The park is located in West Tennessee within Shelby County. It is 13 miles north of Memphis near Millington and is accessible via US 51.

For information call or write: Meeman-Shelby State Park, Millington, TN 38053. (901) 876-5201.

Nathan Bedford Forrest State Historic Area

This park was named for General Nathan Bedford Forrest, the intrepid Confederate cavalry leader, who on November 4, 1864, attacked and destroyed $1,500,000 worth of federal supplies and munitions at (Old) Johnsonville at the mouth of Trace Creek. His operations were concentrated along the river in the vicinity of the park and the town of Eva. The fall of Union-controlled Johnsonville represented not only a Confederate victory but the first defeat of a naval force by a cavalry force in military history.

Today you may visit the scene of Forrest's operations, see impressive views of the Tennessee River, and

Eagle at Reelfoot State Park

study the park's rich fossil deposits at many points along a beautiful trail system.

The park's proximity to Kentucky Lake, one of the great fishing and hunting lakes in the South, makes it even more attractive to Tennessee outdoorsmen and visitors.

Pilot Knob, the highest elevation in West Tennessee, houses the Tennessee River Folklife Interpretive Center featuring the life, folkways, and customs of river people along the Tennessee.

For Information Write: Superintendent's Office, Nathan Bedford Forrest State Historic Area, Eva, TN 38333. (901) 584-6356.

Fort Pillow State Historic Area

Fort Pillow was occupied throughout most of the War Between the States by Union or Confederate forces. The fortification was named after General Gideon J. Pillow, a Mexican War hero.

Early in the war the Confederacy saw the necessity for defending against a Union invasion of the South by way of the Mississippi River. Fort Pillow was one of several fortifications constructed as a part of a river defense system. The fort was built on the first Chickasaw Bluff overlooking the river. Batteries of cannon were constructed facing the river. An extensive system of breastworks was dug for the protection of the river batteries in case of land attack. During the war, the fort's river batteries were close to the river, but since the war the river has moved a mile west.

The 1,650-acre park provides sanctuary for deer, turkey and many other animals. The Mississippi kite can often be viewed from the bluffs during the summer. Many species of small birds can be observed as they follow their spring and fall migration routes.

Today the original breastworks remain in good condition. The park's extensive trail system follows the breastworks in many places. The fortification defended by Union forces in the controversial 1864 battle has been restored after an extensive archaeological study. If you're a Civil War buff, this is a must!

Fort Pillow State Historic Area is located in Lauderdale County on the first Chickasaw Bluff overlooking the Mississippi River. The park may be reached by turning west off US 51 on to State 87. Proceed 17 miles and turn north on State 207, which leads to the park entrance.

For Further Information contact: Fort Pillow State Historic Area, Route 2 Box 108 B-1, Henning, TN 38041. (901) 738-5581.

Pinson Mounds State Archaeological Area

Pinson Mounds is set aside by the state to protect one of the greatest mound complexes of the Woodland

Indians known to exist. It has a dozen Indian mounds, related earthworks, and crematory areas.

Archaeological work has been recently undertaken at Pinson Mounds, but many questions still remain unanswered. The Indians who built the mounds lived in the area long before historically known Indian tribes. Most of the site is believed to date from the Middle Woodland Period, about A.D. 1–500. The site was used for ceremonial purposes. Indians did not live there. Pottery from areas as far away as Georgia and Louisiana has been found. The largest mounds were used for ceremonies, while a few of the smaller ones held burials. A number of cremation areas have been found nearby.

In the summertime, Pinson Mounds offers you the chance to view archaeological field work in progress, with an archaeologist in residence and a $1.5 million museum full of fascinating artifacts and exhibits. Mounds include:

Sauls Mound, at 72 feet, the second tallest in the United States;

Ozier Mound, 32 feet high, second tallest at site, ramped. It has been Carbon-14 dated to A.D. 190; the oldest known mound of its type;

Geometric Earthworks—a 1200 feet remnant of the earthworks believed to have encircled this area. Similar structures have been found in the Ohio Valley;

Duck's Nest—a rimmed circular depression atop a rise, with a large firepit in the center. It was used for a single ceremony. Two nearly complete pots have been found here.

Pinson Mounds State Archaeological Area is located on US 45, just south of Jackson, TN.

Get Involved in the Greatest Outdoors!

Today, the buffalo are gone as are the chestnut trees; a few things have been added, such as interstate highways and wild boar in the Smokies and manmade lakes. But halfway through the 1980s Tennessee has achieved a unique and enviable balance between conservation and utilization. Whole areas where fragile ecosystems survive are protected by law from the intrusion of humans. Tennessee's sports enthusiasts, resident and visitor alike, find an abundance of fish and game and clean water. Alert citizens groups work hand in hand with state government and industry to ensure this will always be so.

Place Names in Tennessee

Arp	Free Communion	Ninth Model
Bitter End	Gilt Edge	Nough
Boring	Hanging Limb	Peeled Chestnut
Calfkiller	Hardscrabble	Rascal Town
Cornpone	Hoodo	Scaife
Crackers Neck	Lick Skillet	Skullbone
Crucifer	Marrowbone	Tranquility
Defeated	Motch	Yell
Difficult	Nameless	Yum Yum
Dismal	Nankipoo	Whodathotit

If you're interested in hiking and backpacking, there's an organization you should know about. The Tennessee Trails Association was founded in 1968 to promote proper use of trails and to develop new trails. Members are directly involved in constructing the Cumberland Trail, which will skirt the eastern rim of the Cumberland Plateau for 200 miles. The association has an adopt-a-trail program which allows you to select a state, federal, local, or private trail, inspect it twice yearly with an evaluation form, and remove brush and litter. Supporting membership is $15. Write to Tennessee Trails Association, Inc., P. O. Box 4913, Chattanooga, TN 37405.

Another active organization is the Tennessee Scenic Rivers Association. It is dedicated to the protection, restoration, and enjoyment of Tennessee's free-flowing rivers. It offers a full schedule of float trips and hiking trips all over Tennessee, all geared to enjoying the rivers. The association also sponsors a school for canoeists and kayakers with instruction for all levels of experience. Basic membership is $10. For more information, write the Tennessee Scenic Rivers Association, P. O. Box 3104, Nashville, TN 37219.

Other Volunteer Environmental Groups:

Tennessee Environmental Council, 1720 West End Avenue, Suite 300, Nashville, TN 37203.

Tennessee Native Plants Society, c/o Department of Botany, University of Tennessee, Knoxville, TN 37916.

South Eastern Regional Representative, Sierra Club, S.E. Office, P.O. Box 11248, Knoxville, TN 37939-1248. Sierra Club trails brochures are available for $3.80.

FUN TIMES

FUN TIMES HIGHLIGHTS

20 feature articles on Tennessee Festivals

East Tennessee Ramp Festivals
Knoxville's Dogwood Arts Festival
Gatlinburg's Highland Games
Chattanooga's June Jaunt
Jonesborough's National Storytelling Festival
Nashville's Italian Street Fair
Columbia's Mule Day
Smyrna's Air Show
A Sampler Exclusive: Hank Williams, Jr., and the World's Largest Fish Fry
South Fulton's Banana Festival
Memphis' Pink Palace Crafts Fair

January-December listings

Dozens of festivals for East, Middle, and West Tennessee
Note: Music Festivals can be found in the Sampler's Music Section

The Celebration of a Heritage

Autumn in the Smoky Mountains is breathtaking. Leaves of red and gold shimmer in the afternoon sun while clear streams thread quietly down the mountain.

A warm summer's evening on the Mississippi is just as soothing. The quiet of the deep waters is interrupted only by the sounds of musicians making their jazz stretch into the night.

Five hundred miles separate the mountains from the river. What lies in between is a land and a people as diverse as the natural boundaries that border them.

Being so spread out, it's not surprising Tennesseans are as different as they are. Consider that Bristol, Tennessee, is closer to Canada than it is to Memphis. And Memphis is closer to Houston, Texas, than it is to Mountain City, Tennessee. No wonder the bluegrass music they play in Erwin doesn't sound a bit like the bluesy tunes that rise from Beale Street in Memphis.

Yet out of this diversity have arisen many outstanding people: astronaut Rhea Seddon, country music greats Dolly Parton and Roy Acuff, Olympic gold-medal swimmer Tracey Caulkins, and countless others.

We Tennesseans respect the state's diversity as part of what makes us special. It has not prevented us from celebrating those things we have in common, such as spirit, determination, and a love for the simple things in life. Tennesseans believe in these things. We boast of plain, straight-forward values that are timeless and strong.

Because of our pride and this love for our heritage, Tennesseans have joined hands to celebrate who we are and how we got to be that way—Tennesseans celebrating being Tennesseans. And that's what Tennessee Homecoming '86 is all about.

It's the largest statewide celebration in Tennessee's history. Homecoming '86, simply, is part reunion, part history lesson, and part good old-fashioned hoedown. It's a time to look at the past and plan for the future.

The core of the celebration lies in communities across the state that are researching their roots, discovering what is special about *their* part of Tennessee, and planning a project based on that heritage. Everyone who has ever lived in Tennessee—and anyone who hasn't—is invited to come home and see Tennessee's three thousand special homeplaces.

The Start of Something Big

Tennessee's Governor Lamar Alexander is the author of the idea for Tennessee Homecoming '86.

During 1978, while he was campaigning for his first term in office, the young candidate walked 1,022 miles across the state to meet the people of Tennessee. In 1982, Governor Alexander returned to these communities and rolled up his sleeves to join work days in which citizens were restoring and beautifying their towns.

The pride and spirit that evolved from the walk and the community work days sparked the idea for a similar statewide program that would span an entire year and

reap results that would last a lifetime. Such a program, the governor thought, would give Tennesseans an opportunity to celebrate and display their best to the rest of the world.

It was an idea he couldn't resist. So Tennessee Homecoming '86 was launched during Governor Alexander's second inaugural speech in January 1983.

"Let's have our own kind of homecoming," he said, speaking from the steps of the capitol. "Let's all come home ourselves to the values which make our Tennessee so very special."

Sitting with him on the reviewing stand that day were ten special guests—Tennesseans who had once lived elsewhere but had "come home" to live in the state. Three well-known Tennesseans were among them: Grand Ole Opry star Minnie Pearl (Sarah Cannon); Pulitzer Prize winner Alex Haley, author of *Roots;* and Peter Jenkins, the man who walked across America and wrote two best-selling books about his trip.

"They all could live anywhere they wanted to," said Alexander of his special guests, "but they all came home to Tennessee."

Bringing Folks Together

Tennessee's diversity makes for an interesting array of Homecoming projects and celebrations. The showcase extends from Mountain City to Memphis, with almost every kind of spruce-up activity in between.

Each community is following a four-step plan to prepare for the 1986 celebration:

—research the community's roots;
—plan for the community's future;
—select a specific Homecoming project; and
—plan a community-wide celebration sometime in 1986.

When the planning, nail-pounding and finishing touches are completed, sounds of celebration will rise as each community becomes absorbed in the Homecoming spirit.

Jonesborough is celebrating Homecoming '86 with Jonesborough Days, July 4–6. The annual festival attracts thousands who are interested in local crafts, food, and music. The city's Heritage Project is a new library that will house old documents signed by Andrew Jackson.

Just twenty-five miles away in Greeneville, Andrew Johnson's home, residents are planning one activity for every month in 1986. The Youth Builders Club will have their fortieth reunion on Memorial Day, and September 20–22 will be the weekend for the Fall Festival, which will re-create the lifestyle of early tobacco farmers in all kinds of music, crafts, exhibits, and festivities.

Carter County has set aside March 30 for its Homecoming '86 Celebration: the annual Peter's Hollow Egg Fight. And it's just that—a battle with eggs! Everybody who enters starts with several dozen eggs. The winner—after all the dodging and throwing—is the one with the most unbroken eggs left.

In Chattanooga, Vision 2000 is the talk of the town. The city's plan for the future fits right into Homecoming '86 as a Vision Project. Their celebration, the Riverbend Festival, is scheduled for June 17–22 on the banks of the Tennessee River. The annual event features a world-class circuit boat race, plenty of concerts, dancing in the streets, food, and crafts.

For those who are nuts about peanuts, Waverly's got the perfect Homecoming celebration: the Peanut Jubilee, featuring the Peanut Butter Jam sock hop on Friday, July 25. Down the road in McEwen on Saturday, fourteen thousand pounds of mouth-watering barbecue will be served up to anyone who's got a hankerin'.

The Donelson/Hermitage Chamber of Commerce will travel 160 years back in time during their Homecoming '86 celebration, Andrew Jackson Day. The home-place of the legendary, fiery president will come alive on May 18 with dueling exhibitions, military drills, horse races, nineteenth-century marketplaces, and crafts.

Agriculture buffs can stop in Milan for the July 24 No-Till Field Day. The annual workshop/exhibition attracts nearly five thousand folks interested in the latest farming techniques and equipment. Milan residents will unveil their Heritage Project, the West Tennessee Agriculture Museum, on that day as well.

Union City will be teaching black history on July 3. Black History Recognition Day will feature a luncheon and speakers versed on the events of black America's past.

And down in Pulaski/Giles County, residents are preparing their own study of black education. Despite prevailing attitudes in the South, Giles County was the first in Tennessee to integrate its school system. Oral interviews with former teachers and students, as well as artifacts from the early schooling days in the county, will be on display in the county museum. Their celebration is set for June 29–July 6.

Tennessee even has its own ghost town, and McNairy County plans to bring it back to life on July 4–5. Purdy was the original county seat—a boom town in the 1800s, full of Civil War history. The living history days will re-create the town with signs, maps, clothes from that period, tours, and Civil War activities. The fun doesn't end there—on the 6th, everyone will pick up and head fifteen miles down the road to Selmer, the present county seat, for a parade, square dance, and gospel singing.

At least three Tennessee homeplaces will be honoring the legend of Davy Crockett in '86. Crockett County celebrates its namesake in good ol' country fair style during Davy Crockett Days, July 4–6. Rutherford residents are preserving one of Crockett's original cabin homes for their Homecoming Project. Furniture, crafts, and artifacts from the period will be used to restore the interior to look exactly as it did when Crockett lived there. Lawrenceburg is dressing up for its own Davy Crockett Days August 15–17.

In Fayette County, a town full of antebellum mansions will open its doors for visitors. La Grange will host a Tour of Homes October 10–12.

Just outside Memphis, the town of Bartlett plans to celebrate Homecoming '86 during the entire month of September. Each weekend will feature different kinds of activities such as sports, reunions, and heritage and Homecoming festivities.

Hundreds of celebrations are scheduled through-out 1986, and Tennessee is inviting her neighbors to come join in the fun. We're taking time out to celebrate our heritage—the many different lifestyles and beliefs we've handed down for generations. And with the variety of tastes and talents to be found across the state, Tennessee is bound to have something to please everyone.

Tennessee Homecoming '86 means different things to different people, but just about everything we're doing has to do with feeling at home, feeling good about ourselves and where we are—not just for today, but for a lifetime.

We think that's worth celebrating.

—by Elise Smith

East Tennessee Area

Ramp Festivals

Once you've tasted this onionlike mountain plant, you're not likely to forget it anytime soon. It's been described as the "sweetest-tasting, vilest-smelling vegetable that grows." Generations of mountain folk have considered the ramp a delicacy having wonderful medicinal properties. Eaten raw, parboiled, or fried, the ramp was regarded as a necessary spring tonic to overcome the sluggishness of a long winter.

Back in the 1950s, the small town of Cosby introduced the ramp to an unsuspecting world by establishing an annual festival in its honor. Over the years the Cosby Ramp Festival has grown into a major spring event, attracting thousands of visitors and celebrities ranging from Harry S. Truman to Tennessee Ernie Ford.

In contrast to Cosby where ramps are brought down to the festival site, participants in the Polk County Ramp Tramp must go up to where the ramps grow on the slopes of Big Frog Mountain. A craft show, blue-grass music, and welcoming ceremonies at the People's Bank in Benton, Tennessee, are parts of the festivities too.

On Saturday morning, the Ramp Trampers gather at Cherokee Corner on US 64 about halfway between Ocoee and Parksville and begin the 2½-mile hike to the ramp feast site. Big Frog Mountain lies within the Cohutta Wilderness Area where motorized traffic is not permitted, so the only way to lunch is to hike or to ride horseback.

Lunch consists of fried ramps in eggs, fried potatoes, streaked meat, corn bread, and soft drinks. The lunch costs $2 for adults, $1 for children under 12. At the Cosby Ramp Festival you may purchase a lunch that does not include ramps. At the Ramp Tramp, however, participants are clearly warned, "If you don't like ramps, bring your own lunch."

For the undecided and those unfamiliar with the properties of the ramp, the following conversation be-

Some people just love their ramps
Photo Courtesy of State Museum and Archives

tween two youngsters on Kineavista Hill one sunny Ramp Festival Sunday might be enlightening:

"Did you eat a ramp yet?"

"I ate 10. They won't let me in school tomorrow."

Dogwood Arts Festival

About 30 years ago, widely traveled author John Gunther made the mistake of calling Knoxville, Tennessee, "the ugliest city in the world." But maybe that wasn't a mistake after all. His comment spurred Knoxvillians into action to prove him wrong. Thus, they began a beautification battle which they have most certainly won.

The native dogwood trees were already one source of beauty in East Tennessee, so the concerned coalition decided to emphasize and expand that aspect of the surrounding area. Now, Knoxville's April Dogwood Arts Festival has grown into one of the nation's largest and most successful seasonal celebrations. In addition to the opportunity to see some of the nearly one million dogwood trees, events including major art exhibits, parades, craft shows, home tours, flower shows, sporting events, and a variety of entertainment draw visitors from all over the world.

The first day of the 17-day spring spectacular begins with an inspirational message at the annual Prayer Breakfast. Market Square Mall, a year-round, open-air shopping plaza in downtown Knoxville, serves as a focal point for activities with daily arts and craft shows, catered lunches, and live entertainment of all kinds.

But the awesome beauty of Knoxville in the spring is what draws most visitors to the festival. Each year the festival selects a number of neighborhoods as "dogwood trails," and motorists can drive through more than 50 miles of them in all parts of the city. Free bus tours of the dogwood trails are offered.

Would Gunther change his mind if he could see the Knoxville of today? He would likely agree with countless others that Knoxville in April is perhaps the most beautiful city on earth, a fantasy land of pink and white.

Highland Games

What does a Scotsman wear under his kilt? You might just find the answer to that age-old question at the Great Smoky Mountains-Gatlinburg Highland Games every May when more than 35 different clans from all across America bring authentic Scottish customs, music, dances, and athletic contests to the mountains for a long weekend of rip-roarin' fun.

Kilts will be provided for anyone wishing to take part in the activities and sporting events held at Mills Park, 2 miles north of downtown Gatlinburg. The misty outdoor setting here bears a strong resemblance to Scotland.

The carnival-like sights and sounds of the Highland weekend actually begin Friday night with a parade through downtown Gatlinburg, followed by a banquet and a Scottish country dancing exhibition. On Saturday, men, women, and children dress in eye-catching tartans and take part in individual Highland dance contests. But the exciting athletic contests grab center stage for attention. Whether participants heave a caber (a 20-foot wooden pole weighing 120 pounds) end over end or toss a 16-pound hay sheaf with a pitchfork over a bar, all seven events require skill as well as a great deal of strength. Other events are unusual weight throws, wrestling, and a 1-mile race in kilts. Classes are broken down into amateur and professional divisions, and first-timers are encouraged to compete with seasoned athletes.

Just for fun, any man may enter the "bonniest knees" competition—guaranteed to be a laugh-producing event where seven blindfolded females use their tactile ability to judge the masculine legs.

Imported foods such as meat pies and shortbread abound, and quality Scottish merchandise as well as clan ancestral information may be obtained.

Fascinating demonstrations show the uncanny ability of border collies to guide and control sheep in an open field.

A Sunday morning worship service is held on the grounds of Mills Park, followed by a moving ceremonial blessing of the tartans and the clans they represent. Sunday afternoon is the women's haggis-hurling event. (Haggis is a tasty spiced pudding cooked in the sheep's stomach.) A spirited tug of war among the clans occurs before the closing ceremony.

Even the night crawlers drive fast in Tennessee

Worm Race

In June, the Johnson City Public Library sponsors an annual worm race as a kickoff for the summer reading club. The racing worms symbolize the "bookworm," and the event is designed to attract more children to the library. This sporting event pits worm against worm in three categories: slimies (night crawlers), fuzzies (woolly worms), and 'pedes (centipedes). After a tragic first year when most of the vermicular contenders died of sunstroke, the heats are now held in the shade on mud-covered cardboard. For more information, contact Jo Puckett, Children's Librarian.

June Jaunt

Memorial Day and Independence Day celebrations are old southern traditions. Chattanooga has a unique way of celebrating both. The June Jaunt, a month-long event, begins on Memorial Day weekend with a Pops in the Park concert by the Chattanooga Symphony at the huge Chickamauga-Chattanooga National Military Park. An Independence Day Downtown Block Party featuring live entertainment, food, and a spectacular fireworks show is the finale of the Jaunt.

There's everything from a major juried arts show in Miller Park to the Pat Boone–Bethel Celebrity Sports Spectacular in which many celebrities, including Pat and Debby Boone, compete. One of the highlights is the annual Riverbend Festival, six days of activity and entertainment at Ross's Landing Park on the banks of the Tennessee River in the downtown area. A live concert is given by big name artists, and there are performances by local bands and entertainers too. The Outboard Marine Corporation's Formula One boat races, offering $50,000 in prize money, always draw a top field of boat drivers and pit crews.

As if a major national powerboat race were not enough, the June Jaunt also includes the Great Tennessee River Raft Race, where hundreds of rafts attempt a 6-mile race from Chickamauga Dam to Ross's Landing Park.

During the month of June, many Chattanooga hotels, attractions, and restaurants offer discount coupons available through the Chattanooga Area Convention and Visitors Bureau. To get more information about the June Jaunt, Tennessee residents may call toll-free (800) 338-3999, and out-of-state residents, (800) 322-3344.

The Overmountain Victory Trail

In 1780, the war had been raging for four years, and British commander Lord Cornwallis had a near stranglehold on the South. His only disturbing problem was the remote "overmountain" settlements in what is now the western Carolinas and eastern Tennessee. In an attempt to solve this problem, Major Patrick Ferguson threatened, "Desist opposition to British arms...or I will march my army across the mountains, hang your leaders and lay your country to waste with fire and sword."

On September 18, 1780, colonels Issac Shelby and John Sevier met at Sevier's home on the Nolichucky River to plan a course of action. They decided to answer Ferguson's message in person—and in force.

The word spread like wildfire through the settlements along the Watauga, Holston, and Nolichucky rivers. More than 1,000 men answered the call to arms, including militiamen from Virginia and North Carolina. The mustering at Sycamore Shoals (now Elizabethton) on September 25, 1780, was a dramatic event on the frontier and one of the great moments in Tennessee history.

The Overmountain Men caught up with Ferguson's retreating forces at King's Mountain in South Carolina. The battle was brief but furious. In one hour and five minutes all of Ferguson's Loyalist Militia were either killed or captured.

Two centuries later, the Overmountain Men are preparing to march again. The first Overmountain Victory Trail March re-enactment was made in 1975, according to Elma Gray, whose late husband, Thomas, was instrumental in establishing the event.

"Tom had been interested in that trail ever since he was a child. He and a lot of other people around Carter County believed that the Overmountain Men never got the recognition they deserved. The March was established as a way of honoring them. Along the way, people from the small towns and communities will come out and meet us. Lots of times they share stories that have been passed down in their community about when the original Overmountain Men passed through."

The September festivities at Sycamore Shoals include traditional music, a muzzleloading rifle shoot, and demonstrations of pioneer crafts such as basket weaving and bullet making.

National Storytelling Festival

When Donald Davis talks, even E. F. Hutton listens. Donald Davis is a storyteller whose tales about his family and friends in the North Carolina mountains have earned him national recognition as a master wordsmith. Who could resist a story that begins: "Aunt Laura was a floater. She floated from one relative to another, and she could hear the crack of dawn"?

Swapping ground at the National Storytelling Festival

Donald Davis loves to tell tales about the wonderfully wacky Jolly family who never bothered to name their children. "They figured a person had to earn his name....They'd wait until something important happened. One of the Jolly boys stepped on a rake one day. It flew up and hit him in the face, so they named him Rake."

Donald is just one of the dozens of master storytellers who will gather in October in the quaint little town of Jonesborough to spin their yarns for enthusiastic audiences at the annual National Storytelling Festival. Other storytellers are Ron Evans, a Chippewa-Cree Indian from Saskatchewan, Canada; Maggie Peirce from Belfast who tells Irish stories; Ephat Mujuru from Zimbabwe who relates African stories; and Moses Aaron from Australia. The impressive line-up of American storytellers includes Anne Izard from New York, Spoons Williams of Philadelphia, Kathryn Windham of Alabama, and Ray Hicks of North Carolina. They weave their own versions of ghost stories, slave stories, and Appalachian stories and Jack Tales.

The three-day event takes place in three separate tent sites where the storytellers will be working constantly. In addition to the tent locations, the popular "Swappin' Ground" is a place where anyone with a story to tell may do so and where many of the master storytellers not engaged in the formal program gather to share some of their stories.

Tickets for the three days of storytelling cost around $30. One-day tickets are available for $15 on Friday and $20 on Saturday. Half-price tickets are available for children, 7 to 12. Family rates are also available, and there is no charge for children under 6. There is no admission charge for the Swappin' Ground, for the Sunday afternoon session in the park, or for the popular Saturday night session of ghost stories and tales of the supernatural told around a roaring bonfire in the 200-year-old Jonesborough cemetery.

More East Tennessee Fun Times

JANUARY

Knoxville Flea Market. Held the third weekend each month at Chilhowee Park.

Chattanooga Flea Market. Held weekly at the 2300 block of Rossville Boulevard.

FEBRUARY

Black History Month Celebration, East Tennessee State University, Johnson City, TN 37614. Sponsor: Carroll Reece Museum. Contact: Helen Roseberry, (615) 929-4392. Crafts and music.

MARCH

Cumberland Mountain Craft Show, Cumberland Mountain State Park, Crossville, TN 38555. Sponsor: Tennessee Division of Parks and Recreation. Contact: Andy Lyon, (615) 484-6138. Fine arts and crafts, about 1400 attend.

Knoxville Boat Show, Convention Center. Contact: Ralph Green, (615) 588-1233.

APRIL

Homefolks Festival, East Tennessee State University, Johnson City, TN 37614. Sponsor: Carroll Reece Museum. Contact: Helen Roseberry, (615) 929-4392. Folk music, original work with attendance about 500. No admission.

Dogwood Arts Festival, 203 Fort Hill Building, Knoxville, TN 37915. (See feature article.)

Spring Wildflower Pilgrimage, Gatlinburg, TN. Chamber of Commerce, (615) 436-4178. Nature studies, guided photo trips, motor and hiking tours to explore the spring flora of the Great Smoky Mountains National Park. For professionals and amateurs.

Springfest Celebration, Johnson City, TN 37614. Two-week festival includes sports competition, games, family fun.

Polk County Ramp Tramp, Benton, TN. Don Ledford, County Agent, (615) 338-2841. (See feature article.)

Foothills Folk Festival, Foothills Mall, Maryville, TN 37801. Sponsor: Maryville-Alcoa-Blount County Recreation and Parks Commission. Contact: Rebecca Hahn, (615) 983-9244. Fine arts and crafts. Attended by approximately 10,000.

First New Moon Arts and Crafts Show, Old Signal Mountain Hotel, Signal Mountain, TN 37377. Sponsor: Signal Mountain Lions Club. Contact: Sam Powell, 506 Brady Point, Signal Mountain, TN 37377. Fine arts and crafts displayed. Attended by 5,000. Admission: $1.

Spring Festival, Warriors' Path State Park, Kingsport, TN. Contact: Marty Silver, park naturalist, (615) 239-8531. Participate in nature seminars taught by professionals and walks guided by trained naturalists, each highlighting a different area of natural history.

MAY

Mountain Music Homecomin', Gatlinburg, TN. Chamber of Commerce, (615) 436-4178. Celebrates the return of spring to the Smokies with bluegrass and fiddle contests, crafts, demonstrations.

The Cosby Ramp Festival, Cosby, TN. Dr. Jack Clark, (615) 623-5410. Huge dinner on the ground, featuring the ramp, the "sweetest-tasting, vilest-smelling plant that grows." Gospel and country music. Bring plenty of mouthwash!

Highland Games, Gatlinburg, TN. Chamber of Commerce, (615) 436-4178. (See feature article.)

Spring Music and Crafts Festival, Historic Rugby Inc., Rugby, TN. (615) 628-2441. British Isles and Appalachian music and dancing, craft demonstrations and sales, walking tours of remaining buildings of this unique colony, settled in the 1880s by British author Thomas Hughes. A two-day festival.

Sevier County Music and Arts Festival, Sevierville, TN 37862. Contact: Mary Sue Poe, executive director, (615) 453-1515. Attendance 5,000. Bluegrass bands, old-time gospel groups, cloggers, arts, and crafts.

Carter Mansion Ball, Sycamore Shoals Historic Area, Elizabethton, TN. Contact: Herb Roberts, Sycamore Shoals Historic Area, Elizabethton, TN 37643; (615) 543-5808. Eighteenth-century dance demonstrations. Music by 20 to 75 artists. Attendance: 500 to 600.

Spring Festival, Museum of Appalachia, Norris, TN. (615) 494-7680. Musicians, craftsmen, and celebrities gather each May to sample authentic mountain recipes, homemade apple cider, mountain music, and see demonstrations of early Appalachian mountain lifestyle.

Ole Time Radio Reunion, Jonesboro, TN. Celebrates the region's importance to the growth of country music radio. Stage performances and pickin'.

Appalachian Music Days, Bristol, TN. Celebrates the roots of country music with live performances.

Lake Chickamauga Spring Festival, Chattanooga, TN. Bluegrass music, arts and crafts.

Appalachian Music and Craft Festival, Children's Museum, Oak Ridge, TN. (615) 482-1074.

Azalea Festival, Oak Ridge, TN. (615) 482-7821.

Strawberry Festival, Dayton, TN. Beauty pageants and various activities honor Dayton's famous fruit.

JUNE
(See "Music" for information concerning East Tennessee music festivals.)

June Jaunt, Chattanooga, TN. Contact: Visitors Bureau, (615) 756-2121. Powerboat racing and other sporting events, street fairs, art exhibits, and music ranging from jazz and bluegrass to gospel and chamber concerts. Celebrity spectacular, circus, and raft race. (See feature article.)

Covered Bridge Celebration, Elizabethton, TN. Contact: Chamber of Commerce, (615) 543-2122. Festival centers around a picturesque, century-old covered bridge. Arts and crafts, entertainment—three-day celebration.

Rhododendron Festival, Roan Mountain State Park, Roan Mountain, TN (615) 772-3303. Festival focuses on the 600-acre garden of rhododendrons in full bloom atop Roan Mountain, one of the highest peaks east of the Mississippi River. Arts and crafts, guest speakers, gospel singing. Three-day event. (See "Tours and Trails" for more information.)

Norris Dam State Park Arts and Crafts Fair, Lenoir Museum, US 441, Lake City, TN. Sponsor: Norris Dam State Park. Contact: Angie Crowell, ranger, (615) 426-7461.

Chattanooga Riverbend Festival, Ross's Landing Park, Chattanooga, TN. Sponsor: Friends of the Festival, Inc. Contact: Bruce Storey, P. O. Box 886, 518 Lookout Street, Chattanooga, TN 37401. Dance, literary, music, and theater. Six-day celebration. Admission $3 to $5 for six days.

Annual Blue Ridge Quilting Exhibition, East Tennessee State University, Johnson City, TN. Sponsor: Carroll Reece Museum. Contact: Helen Roseberry, P. O. Box 22300 A, ETSU, Johnson City, TN 37614. Crafts only—quilted items.

JULY

Historic Jonesborough Days. Contact: Jonesborough information, (615) 753-2888. Three days of fun which include a muzzleloading rifle shoot, live music, arts and crafts, southern-style cooking, and old-fashioned fun in Tennessee's oldest town.

Gatlinburg Craftsmen's Fair. Contact: Everett Brock, (615) 436-7479. A five-day event featuring the nation's finest craftsmen.

Kingsport Fun Fest. Contact: Chamber of Commerce, (615) 246-2010. A week of more than 150 fun events for the entire family including celebrity entertainment, sports clinics and tournaments, taste of Tri-Cities, hot air balloon rides, fun shop, lectures, and hoe-down.

Warriors' Path Folklife Festival, Warriors' Path State Park, Kingsport, TN 37663. Contact: Marty Silver, (615) 239-8531. Celebrate the good old days with old-time music, basketry, weaving, whittling, apple butter making, games, clogging, and contests. All events free!

"The Wataugans," Sycamore Shoals Historic Area, Elizabethton, TN 37643. Contact: Herb Roberts, (615) 543-5808. Theater production. Fifty performers. Attendance: 2,500. $3 admission.

AUGUST

Historic Rugby Pilgrimage of Homes, Rugby, TN. Contact: Historic Rugby, Inc., (615) 628-2441. Over a dozen of the historic British colony's public and private buildings will be open for tours. Enjoy a period concert, slide programs, and British Isles refreshments. (See "Tours and Trails" for more information about Rugby.)

Tipton-Haynes Historic Farm Festival, Johnson City, TN. Tipton-Haynes Farm, (615) 926-3631. Craft festival including tours of farm and cave. Let the children enjoy pony rides at this living history farm. A re-enactment of the Battle of the Lost State of Franklin, children's dramas, contests, and music are some of the festival's events.

Sportsfest, Morristown, TN. Contact: Mark Sudheimer, (615) 586-6382. More than 30 sports events are planned for participants and spectators. Major softball tournament, karate tournament, plus fishing, archery, soccer, and more.

Frozen Head Folklife Festival, Frozen Head National Area, Wartburg, TN 37887. Contact: Duane Wyrick, (615) 346-3318. Dance and folk music. Attendance: 3,000.

SEPTEMBER

Mountaineers Folk Festival, Fall Creek Falls State Park, Pikeville, TN 37367. Contact: Stuart Carroll, (615) 881-2197. Bluegrass and traditional gospel music, crafts, and lifestyles featured. There will be ballad singing, 1700 Tennessee life re-enactments, and contests such as log splitting, animal calling, crosscut saw competitions, and cake walks. "Come and enjoy a slice of life on the mountain." Attendance: 2,000.

Roan Mountain Folklife Festival, Roan Mountain State Park, Roan Mountain, TN 37687. Contact: Jennifer Wilson, (615) 772-3303. Fine arts, crafts, folk music. Attendance: 2,000.

National crafts Festival, Pigeon Forge, TN. (615) 453-4616. Over 100 craftsmen gather for an outstanding outdoor festival at Silver Dollar City, a theme park dedicated to traditional crafts Closed Wednesdays and Thursdays.

Apple Festival, Sevierville, TN. Contact: Sevierville Chamber of Commerce, (615) 453-6411. September 12 to 21. There are dances, golf tournaments, a beauty pageant, road race, dance and ball, and kids' day. Street dancing, entertainment, and large parade through downtown Sevierville on Saturday, September 21. Demonstrations and craftsmen from many states are there with "cracklin' bread," corn pone (made while you wait), and all varieties of apple products. Being a general kind of celebration, it gives tourists the opportunity to see and talk with the local people in the area without the atmosphere of a tourist town. This is the fastest growing festival in the state! Sponsor: Sevierville Chamber of Commerce and the City of Sevierville, (615) 453-6411.

Overmountain Victory Trail Celebration, Elzabethton, TN. (See feature article.)

Oktoberfest, Jamestown, TN. Contact: Beggar's Castle. (See "Eatin' and Sleepin' Good" for more information on Beggar's Castle.)

Fall homecoming, Museum of Appalachia

OCTOBER

Hawkins County Heritage Days, Downtown, Rogersville, TN 37857. Contact: Mrs. Buford Street, (615) 272-3143. Over 100 booths of arts and crafts.

Coker Creek Autumn Gold Festival, Coker Creek, TN 37134. Contact: Frank Murphy, Jr. Visit what was once the gold panning and gold mining center of Tennessee. See the long toms, sluice troughs, and gold pans in full operation. Buy handmade or hand-crafted items displayed by 90 artists. Board splitting and syrup making from years ago featured, also a beauty contest with girls dressed in pioneer costumes. Delicious mountain food is available.

Mountain Makin's Festival, Rose Center, Morristown, TN 37814. Contact: Bill Kornrich. Crafts only—8,000 to 10,000 in attendance.

Gatlinburg Craftsmen's Fair. Contact: Everett Brock, (615) 436-7479. A gathering during the month of October of the nation's finest craftsmen.

National Storytelling Festival, Jonesborough, TN. Contact: Jimmy Neil Smith, (615) 753-2171. (See feature article.)

Tennessee Fall Homecoming and Fiddle Contest, Norris, TN. Contact: Museum of Appalachia, (615) 494-7680. Huge festival with music competition, crafts demonstrations, foods, and exhibits. Held outdoors at the 70-acre Museum of Appalachia.

The Autumn Leaf Special, Chattanooga, TN. Railroad Museum, (615) 894-8028. Round-trip steam train rides from Chattanooga to Crossville travel across the beautiful Cumberland Plateau when fall colors are at their peak. Reservations needed.

Fall Color Cruise and Folk Festival, Chattanooga, TN. Visitors Bureau, (615) 756-2121. Two weekends of music, dance, crafts, and a wide variety of entertainment, plus cruises through the "Grand Canyon of the Tennessee River" in its autumn splendor.

Bethel Country Fair and Festival, Hixson, TN. Bethel Bible College, (615) 842-5757. Arts and crafts, hay rides, foods, auction, games, flea market, all benefit Bethel Bible Village in Chattanooga.

NOVEMBER

Christmas Crafts Show, Sycamore Shoals Historic Area, Elizabethton, TN. Contact: Herb Roberts, (615) 543-5805. Fine arts and crafts, original work only. Attendance: 1,000 to 1,500.

Foothills Craft Show, Oak Ridge Civic Center, Oak Ridge, TN. Contact: Judy Housteau, (615) 689-6360. A two-day event, with about 90 members of the Foothills Craft Guild exhibiting woodworks, pottery, jewelry, weaving, and scrimshaw.

DECEMBER

Twelve Days of Christmas, Gatlinburg, TN. Contact: Chamber of Commerce, (615) 436-4178. The four weekends prior to Christmas are filled with special holiday events such as yule log burnings, Festival of Christmas Past, choral celebrations, madrigal feast, Christmas Craft Fair, Candlelight Ball, and Living Christmas Tree.

Winterfest, Elizabethton, TN. Contact: Anthony Lyons, (615) 542-2462. Christmas tree exhibit, snow queen pageant, parade, special tours, and musical presentations.

Christmas in the City, Knoxville, TN. (615) 523-2300. Annual celebration offers a wide variety of yuletide festivities to delight young and old.

Madrigal Dinners, Milligan College, TN. (615) 929-0116. Representation of English sixteenth-century Christmas feast, period costumes, entertainment, songs, and music.

Middle Tennessee Area

The Americana Sampler Crafts, Art, and Food Fair

The Americana Sampler, held at the Tennessee State Fairgrounds in Nashville, presents crafts from across Tennessee as well as from many other states. Held indoors, this delightful three-day event provides welcome relief from the dreariness of Tennessee's February weather. Nearly 200 craft and folk art professionals come from all over the country to give demonstrations or to display their wares, products of Appalachian basket making, doll making, quilting, weaving, wood carving, broom making, or other skills.

Antique dealers offer antique linens, clothing, and textiles as well as period furniture and primitives. A preview party with entertainment the first night is a good opportunity to do some shopping ahead of the crowds.

Cultural Heritage Festival

For a great April day of family fun and a truly educational experience, try this unusual festival. A cultural exchange effort, the festival provides an opportunity for people from other countries now living in Nashville to show their host city and area something of their native culture through dance, music, and colorful costumes. Individual booths raise funds for such projects as building temples or churches or supporting student exchange programs. Many participants stroll from tent to tent, sampling foods from other lands, admiring displays, and asking questions about other cultures.

Egyptian native Zainab El-Berry says of Nashville International Cultural Heritage, Inc.: "We are sort of an international Welcome Wagon. We help newcomers become adjusted to the community. If you came to Nashville, and you wanted to contact someone from your home country, we would help. If someone needed a translator, we could help."

Come and have a family reunion on a global scale!

Mule Day

Mules as far as the eye can see. That's the impression a bystander has when attending Columbia's Mule Day Parade, always held the first weekend in April (unless there is an Easter weekend conflict). More typical parade entries certainly contribute to the colorful festivities, but the reason-for-being for the celebration is mules, the hybrid offspring of a jack and a mare.

Columbia, about 50 miles south of Nashville, has long boasted the proud title of "Mule Capital of the World." In the 1840s mule dealing began in Columbia. The area quickly developed into a crossroads for mule dealing in the United States. Young mules were shipped in from Missouri and then traded off or sold to the sugar and cotton plantations of the South. The street sales became nationally known, and in 1934, Columbia's "Market Day" on the first Monday of April expanded to a bona fide celebration complete with a parade and special activities. Mule Day took an intermission during the war years and for a time thereafter. Its revival in 1974 is credited to the Maury County Bridle and Saddle Club.

One obvious distinction between a horse and a mule is a mule's long ears. This distinction is the point of a story about Kit Carson—for whom Fort Carson is named. According to the story, Carson, at 16, shot his own mule while on guard in a wagon train camp when he mistook the mule's long ears one dark night for an Indian's two-feather headress.

The Mule Day celebration begins on Friday night with the Liars' Contest at the Central High School Auditorium. Anyone with a far-fetched true story or just an outright good lie is welcome to enter. Others can just listen and get their ears stretched.

The Mule Sale Saturday morning is a reminder of the days when Columbia was a mule-dealing crossroads. Southern Livestock conducts the sale on the east side of the Courthouse Square. The parade begins Saturday and follows a route through downtown Columbia. A Mule Day queen and her court and the "King Mule" are chosen in similar contests but with slightly different standards of beauty. Prior to the parade, the Culleoka Lion's Club offers an all-you-can-eat pancake breakfast for $2.50 at the Memorial Building, right on the parade route. Other events are staged at the Maury County Park: mule pulling contests, a mule show, a log skidding show, a tobacco spitting contest, a checkers contest, a square dance, and a crafts festival and knife show.

Mule Day royalty

Annual Old-Timers Day

This special May weekend was designed to honor Dickson County's older citizens for their accomplishments and contributions to our way of life. It's a homecoming, a time for visiting old friends, making new ones, or recalling old traditions.

The highlight and most unusual event of the fun-filled weekend is "The Miss Old-timers Day Beauty Contest," featuring beauties of the senior-citizen set. Miss Ora Rushton, Miss Old-timer of 1982, said: "They kept asking me to be in it and I told them I didn't want them to make a crazy out of me. I finally said I'd do it...if I didn't have to wear a swimsuit." On relinquishing her crown to Ethel Baxter, the 1983 winner at 87 years young, Miss Ora said, "Clay [her husband] really got carried away when I won last year. He didn't know I was pretty till then."

Old Timers Day is also one of the greatest festivals for Tennessee traditional dancing (see "Music").

Tennessee Crafts Fair

One of the largest statewide craft fairs is held the first weekend in May each year in Nashville. Almost 150 selected Tennessee craftspeople offer their wares on the green in front of the Parthenon in Centennial Park. Over 50,000 eager fair goers come, rain or shine, with children and dogs, Frisbees and footballs and, of course, their abiding love for quality Tennessee crafts.

Enjoy the sights and sounds in the many booths and tents, especially in the large tent in the center. See continuous demonstrations of more than a dozen different crafts. Try your hand at quilting, watch a raku pot being pulled from the kiln and plunged into sawdust for smoking, marvel at how felt is made, and ask questions of the spinners and weavers. Listen to the melodic sounds of a handmade bamboo flute or a mountain dulcimer. A supervised area provides children opportunities to try their hands at a number of crafts.

Try the tempting dishes from several local restaurants and eat at the picnic tables set out under the trees. You'll find something for everyone, whether it's eating, watching, buying, or just restin' in the shade.

Threshermen's Show

Blue July skies of Adams, Tennessee, fill with clouds of black smoke and the shrill whistle of escaping steam when the Tennessee-Kentucky Threshermen's Association presents its annual wheat-threshing and steam engine show to the public. Some 400 members join with over 20,000 people in a three-day country fair extravaganza of crafts, antiques, music, and machinery.

The Threshermen's Show is held on the grounds of the former Bell Elementary School located on US 41, 13 miles north of Springfield, Tennessee, and 7 miles south of Guthrie, Kentucky, and US 9. The school grounds at Adams are home of the Bell Witch Opry and an antique mall, both open to visitors free of charge.

Craftsmen display their wares and demonstrate country arts such as quilt making, toy making, blacksmithing, and flour grinding. Several concession stands offer a variety of soft drinks and food, especially white beans, cornbread, and barbecue. Under giant shade trees the miniature and small steam engine buffs gather to show off their machines. Across the shaded grove of trees is a steam-powered sawmill, sawing giant logs of walnut, cherry, and whatever is brought in from the community.

Some other special features are exhibits of antique cars and early gas tractors and mule demonstrations. There are performances of bluegrass and country music, gospel singing, a square dance, and an antique tractor pull.

Ernest Williams, one of the association's founders, says: "The threshing of wheat was always a community affair. Several men would arrive with a thresher and would spend days going from farm to farm or setting up in a field where farmers could bring their wheat in on wagons. The women gathered with food and water and spread blankets under the trees. Today, we are celebrating that tradition at our show."

National Rolley Holes Marbles Championships

In Clay County, the game of marbles is a blood sport, particularly when over $500 in prize money is at stake, as there will be in August at Standing Stone State Park in neighboring Overton County during the National Rolley Hole Marbles Championships.

Dumas Walker of Moss, Tennessee, was the Minnesota Fats of the marbles world until he broke his arm a few years ago and retired from active competition. He says: "I just couldn't get the proper English anymore. When you've been the best, it's aggravating when you can't play as good as you used to."

The team game called "Rolley Hole" is played on a rectangular court 40 feet long by 25 feet wide which has three small holes evenly spaced down the middle. The object of the game is for both partners to get their marbles into each hole, down the court, back, and down again—three times. It's not as easy as it sounds.

Watching a shooter like Russell Collins knuckle down to a 10-foot shot which sends an opponent's marble spinning for a dozen feet, and leaves his own within inches of the hole, is a lesson in marble artistry and a warning not to bet the mortgage payment in this kind of competition.

Nobody knows exactly why Clay County and environs became such a hot spot for champion marble shooters, but the whole area is full of marbleyards. And more than one corn crop has fallen victim to a heated game of marbles. The sport is sort of a family tradition, and no self-respecting marble shooter would be caught dead with a store-bought marble in his pocket.

Bud Garrett declares: "The marbles I make are tougher than agate." Garrett's highly regarded handmade marbles are generally made of flint, and they are works of art. At this year's festival, Bud will be making his marbles, and there will be craft demonstrations, bluegrass music, and a Saturday night square dance.

Standing Stone State Park is located on State 52 about 20 miles north of Cookeville, Tennessee, between Livingston and Celina. The state park offers overnight accommodations in 20 cabins, each sleeping up to 10 people. A recently renovated 35-space campground, a swimming pool, bath house, tennis and volleyball courts, fishing, boating, and other forms of recreation can be found there too.

The Italian Street Fair

Thirty years ago the Nashville Symphony needed $5,000. So they tried having an Italian Street Fair. The Fair was so successful, it single-handedly kept the city from losing its symphony in 1954 and has lived on to be one of Nashville's longest-running festivals.

The first fair was quite different from the fair of to-day. It lasted from 10:00 A.M. to dusk one October day, spaghetti and spumoni were served, there were a few rides for children and an organ grinder with a monkey, and four members of the orchestra strolled around playing Italian music. Sweet and simple, but successful.

But watch out, Nashville! Now the fair lasts four days over the Labor Day weekend and nets close to $200,000 for the symphony and hours of pleasure for Middle Tennessee residents. Music may be jazz, rock, bluegrass, or classical played by small groups or the whole symphony.

You won't be able to resist trying the mouth-watering, waist-bulging Italian specialties like meatball sandwiches, pizza, spaghetti, and delicate pizelles for dessert. Children enjoy rides, art activities, puppet shows, fun photos, and "bocce." Adults love all the bargains—bargains made possible because everything is donated to the fair. At the auction, bid on things like a sailboat ride or an Italian dinner for 20. Real bargains come on the last day when all booths are emptied and the contents auctioned off. Anybody need 30 dozen hamburger buns for $5? On the other hand, be sure and buy a raffle ticket and win a trip to Naples, a Fiat, or Ferrari...maybe.

Tennessee Aviation Days

Fighter jets swooping and thundering overhead. Ribbons of puffy white smoke from vintage aircraft spiraling across the sky. Skilled parachutists forming stars a mile in the air, then gently floating to earth. These are just some of the amazing sights and sounds to be enjoyed at one of the largest air shows in America, Tennessee Aviation Days, in September 1986. This event is always held on even numbered years in Smyrna, just 15 miles south of Nashville.

The exhibit on the field is one of the most varied anywhere and is virtually a museum of aviation history. Everything from nostalgic wood and fabric biplanes to contemporary aircraft—including the C-5A, one of the world's biggest airplanes—to futuristic jets lined with ultrasophisticated equipment will be shown.

Overhead, aviation superstars perform all afternoon. Heading the list are the United States Navy Flight Demonstration Squadron, the Blue Angels, distinguished for their flawless maneuvers. The Blue Angels' diamond formation epitomizes the beauty and grace that can be achieved through exact timing and precision in formation flying. In this routine, all six jets blaze across the sky at approximately 500 MPH—yet remain only an arm's length from one another. The Golden Knights, the official United States Army parachute team, will put on a show equal to their world-famous reputation. All 12 jumpers in the show will demonstrate the high-altitude aerobatic expertise that has set more records than any other parachute team in history. All these events keep audiences spellbound.

Gates open at 10:00 A.M., and main flying acts begin about noon and last until 5:00 P.M. Cost is $5 for adults.

More Middle Tennessee Fun Times

JANUARY
Nashville Flea Market. Fourth weekend every month except September and December. Tennessee State Fairgrounds.

FEBRUARY
Middle Tennessee Boat Show, Opryland Hotel, Nashville, TN. Call Opryland information, (615) 889-6611.

Charlie Daniels' Volunteer Jam, Municipal Auditorium, Nashville, TN. Contact: Municipal Auditorium (615) 259-6271. (See "Music.")

Heart of Country Antique Show, Opryland Hotel, Nashville, TN. Contact: Debbie Dale Mason or Elizabeth Durham, (615) 242-1210. Three-day show having booths of over 100 exhibitors from all over the country plus exhibitions, specialty booths, and lectures.

Grand-Ol'-Goodies Craft Show, Tennessee State Fairgrounds, Nashville, TN. Contact: Tennessee State Fairgrounds, (615) 255-6441.

Americana Sampler Crafts, Art, and Food Faire, Tennessee State Fairgrounds, Nashville, TN. Contact: Tennessee State Fairgrounds, (615) 255-6441; or Mary Ingram, Tennessee Craft Sampler, P. O. Box 8222, Nashville, Tn 37207, (615) 228-5370. (See feature article.)

Great Lakes of the South Outdoor Show, Municipal Auditorium, Nashville, TN. Contact: Vernon Williams, (615) 245-1111.

MARCH
Annual Lawn and Garden Fair, Tennessee State Fairgrounds, Nashville, TN. Contact: Exchange Club of Nashville, Civic Hall, 321 Charlotte Avenue, Nashville, TN 37201; (615) 256-4724. Leave the dull landscape outdoors and come inside to view gardens, borders, trees, lush flowers, waterfalls, and colorful displays. Sights and lectures appealing to both backyard and "big time" gardeners. See the latest in home, lawn, and garden products. Two-day event. Admission charge.

The Southern National Antiques Show and Sale, Tennessee State Fairgrounds, Nashville, TN. Contact: Tennessee State Fairgrounds, (615) 255-6441. Over 100 exhibits of eighteenth- and nineteenth-century furniture and accessories, porcelain and pottery, jewelry and silver, paintings and folk art, rugs and crafts. Lots of southern hospitality for all, plus lectures and a gala preview party.

Opryland Opens for the Season, Nashville, TN. Last weekend. Contact: Opryland information, (615) 889-6611.

APRIL

Old Time Fiddler's Championship, Clarksville, TN. Chamber of Commerce, (615) 647-2331. Musicians from across the United States will be competing in various bluegrass singing, dancing, and music categories.

Mule Day, Columbia, TN 38401. Chamber of Commerce, (615) 388-2155. (See feature article.)

Riders in the Sky, Annual Music Round-up, Nashville, TN. Contact: Hospital Hospitality House, 214 Reidhurst Avenue 3, Nashville, TN 37203. (615) 329-0477.

Annual Opryland American Music Festival, Grand Ole Opry House, Nashville, TN. Contact: American Music Festival, Opryland Sales Department, 2802 Opryland Drive, Nashville, TN 37214.

Al Menah Temple's Shrine Circus Municipal Auditorium, Nashville, TN. (615) 259-6217.

Franklin's Main Street Festival, Franklin, TN. Contact: Barbara Kurland, (615) 790-7477. Food booths, live entertainment, crafts.

Cultural Heritage Fair, Nashville, TN. (See feature article.)

MAY

Franklin Rodeo, Franklin, TN. Contact: Ed Moody, Box 609, Franklin, TN 37064. (615) 794-1504. One of the biggest rodeos in the South.

Annual Tennessee Crafts Fair, Parthenon, Centennial Park, Nashville, TN. Contact: Tennessee Crafts Fair, (615) 383-2502. One of the largest in the state. (See feature article.)

Opryland Gospel Jubilee, Nashville, TN. Contact: Opryland information, (615) 889-6611.

Nashville Summer Lights Festival, Legislative Plaza. Contact: Nashville Symphony, 1805 West End Avenue, Nashville, TN. (615) 329-3033. Sculpture, painting, theater, dancing, music, plus marketplace for gifts and foods.

International Folkfest. A festival of folkloric talent with dancers and musicians in traditional costumes from different nations.

East Main Street Festival, East Main, Murfreesboro, TN 37130. Sponsor: Arts and Humanities Council of Murfreesboro and Rutherford County. Contact: Marlane Sewell, (615) 896-0201. On the last day of the International Folkfest, a parade and abbreviated dance exhibitions are held and all area crafts people and artists are encouraged to participate. 150 artists attend.

David Crockett State Park Arts and Crafts Show, US 64 West, Lawrenceburg, TN. Sponsor: David Crockett State Park. Contact: Kevin Tipps, Lawrenceburg, TN 38464. Fine arts and crafts. Attendance: 25,000.

Annual Cannon County Good Ole Days, Public Square, Woodbury, TN. Sponsor: Bank of Commerce. Plays, square dances, break dances, bluegrass, various contests (bubble gum blowing, best dressed pig, toilet paper dressing), outhouse race, arts and crafts show.

Portland Strawberry Festival, Portland, TN. Contact: Chamber of Commerce for information. Buy plump, delicious strawberries and take in the festivities too, such as the parade and square dance.

Annual Old-timers Day, Dickson, TN. (See feature article.)

JUNE

Oaklands Association Antique Show and Sale, Murphy Center, MTSU, Murfreesboro, TN. Contact: Oaklands Mansion, Maney Avenue, Murfreesboro, TN 37130. (615) 893-0022.

International Country Music Fan Fair, Nashville, TN. Contact: Fan Fair, 2804 Opryland Drive, Nashville, TN 37214. (615) 889-6611. Country music stars mix and mingle with thousands of fans. (See "Music.")

Annual Pioneer Heritage Show, Municipal Auditorium, Nashville, TN. Sponsor: Tennessee Arts and Crafts Guild. Contact: Mary Baker, (615) 868-0891. Fine arts and crafts.

Horse and rider show the intensity of the Tennessee Walking Horse National Celebration in Shelbyville

Grinder's Switch Arts and Crafts Show, Centerville, TN. Sponsor: Hickman County Arts Guild. Contact: Pat Floied, (615) 729-3930. Crafts only. Attendance: 10,000.

JULY

Fiddler's Jamboree and Crafts Festival, Smithville, TN. Contact: Lavelle D. Smith, (615) 597-4971 or 597-4571. Gigantic music competition with 21 categories for musicians, singers, and dancers. Continuous jam sessions under the trees around the courthouse. 200 or more arts and crafts exhibitors. (See "Music.")

Uncle Dave Macon Days, Murfreesboro, TN. Contact: Jesse Messick, (615) 893-9326. A rollicking three-day festival that honors "Uncle Dave," one of the first stars of the Grand Ole Opry. Enjoy the music competition, crafts, and food. 15,000 attend.

Nashville 420 Stockcar Race, Nashville Raceway. (615) 242-4343. The Winston Cup Grand National event provides night stockcar racing at its finest.

Tennessee-Kentucky Threshermen's Show, Adams, TN. Contact: Emerson Meggs, (615) 696-2883. (See feature article.)

Frontier Days, Lynchburg, TN. Contact: Lynchburg (Moore County) Chamber of Commerce. For three days and nights Moore County, the home of the famous Jack Daniels Distillery, celebrates the Fourth of July with square dancing, bingo, livestock show, country cooking, tobacco spitting, and a giant flea market. It's small-town fun at its best.

Country Fair, Bell Buckle, TN. Contact: Bell Buckle Merchants Association, (615) 389-6908. This popular event features arts and crafts, antiques, plants, fresh vegetables, jams, jellies, freshly baked treats, and good food in general.

AUGUST

Tennessee Walking Horse National Celebration, Shelbyville, TN. "The Celebration," (615) 684-5915. Shelbyville is known as the "Walking Horse Capital of the World," and this show determines which of the thousand or more entries is crowned World Champion. Ten days and nights of pageantry and excitement.

Italian Street Fair, Nashville, TN. Contact: Dolores Sorey, (615) 865-2926. (See feature article.)

International Grand Championship Walking Horse Show, Murfreesboro, TN. (615) 890-9120. More than 800 horses parade in this show featuring the Tennessee Walking Horse, bred in Middle Tennessee and renowned for its smooth gait.

Summer Sampler Annual Craft, Art, and Food Faire, Nashville, TN. Contact: Mary V. Ingram, director, (615)

228-5370. Outdoor craft and art fair for traditional, folk, and contemporary work. Food and entertainment. More than 130 exhibitors from 14 states.

National Rolley Holes Marbles Championship, Standing Stone State Park, Livingston, TN 38570. Contact: Billy Markin, (615) 823-6347. (See feature article.)

Antiques Show and Sale, Murphy Center, Murfreesboro, TN. Contact: Murfreesboro Antique Association, Rt. 6, Elam Road, Box 342, Murfreesboro, TN 37130.

Annual Hee-Haw International Clogging Championship, Nashville, TN. Contact: Opryland Sales Department, (615) 889-6600.

Davy Crockett Days, Lawrenceburg, TN. Contact: Lawrenceburg Chamber of Commerce, (615) 762-4911. Laugh at the rolling-pin throwing contest, tobacco spitting and liars' contests, and enjoy the beauty contest and giant sidewalk sales offered by local merchants.

SEPTEMBER

Tennessee Aviation Days, Smyrna, TN. Contact: Smyrna Chamber of Commerce. (See feature article.)

Buck Dancing Contest and Old Time Music Day, Drakes Creek Park North, Hendersonville, TN. Contact: Juliette Armer, Box 64, Hendersonville, TN 37075. Dance. May register the day of the event. Cash awards. Entry fee $3. Attendance: 1,000. No admission for dancing. Crafts fair and music—attendance: 3,000; admission $1.

Pickett State Park Old Timers Day, Pickett State Park, Jamestown, TN. Contact: Bobby Fulcher, (615) 726-7463. Music and crafts. Attendance: 3,000.

Annual Tennessee Grassroots Days, Centennial Park, Nashville, TN. Contact: Anne Romaine, (615) 331-0602. Fine arts and crafts. Dance. Music. Attendance: 15,000. No admission. This celebration brings together the music, folklife, and old-time survival ways to Tennessee working people.

OCTOBER

Octoberfest, Fairgrounds Park, Clarksville, TN. Contact: Karina Long, (615) 647-1007. Sponsored by the Edelweiss Club, whose purpose is to uphold and promote German heritage. Enjoy two German bands, lots of dancing, authentic German food, costumes, and beer. Everyone invited to join the fun.

Ketner's Mill Country Fair, East Valley Rd., between Whitwell and Jasper, TN. Contact: Clyde Ketner. Work of more than 80 regional craftsmen, country food, entertainment, and demonstrations against the backdrop of beautiful Sequatchie Valley in autumn.

Sand Bar Arts and Crafts Show, Rock Island, TN. Contact: H. G. Deaton, (901) 686-2429. Arts and crafts. Attendance: 8,000 to 9,000.

Meriwether Lewis Craft Fair, Meriwether Lewis Park, Hohenwald, TN. Sponsor: Maury County Arts Guild with the National Park Service. Contact: Mary Ann Blalock, (615) 381-2428. Held the second weekend in October, this fair has delighted Tennesseans for almost 20 years. See 65 to 70 booths of pioneer crafts, demostrations of a grist mill, beekeeping, and weaving, all against the backdrop of the beautiful fall foliage off the Natchez Trace. Try the craft food booths which offer foods peculiar to pioneer days—apple fritters, fried pies, or white beans and corn bread. Free wagon rides for children. Attendance: 40,000. No admission.

Webb School Arts and Crafts Festival, Bell Buckle, TN. Contact: Bell Buckle Merchants Association, (615) 389-6908. This annual festival is held on the Webb School campus during the third weekend in October. 100 artists and craftspersons display and sell contemporary work as well as traditional folk art and crafts. Watch demonstrations, make purchases, and enjoy glimpses of the past—whittling, cider making, dancing, and fiddling.

NOVEMBER

Tennessee Fall Crafts Fair, Tennessee State Fairgrounds, Nashville, TN. Contact: Alice Merritt, (615) 383-2502. Original craft work only. 100 to 120 artists. Attendance: 10,000.

Opryland Closes for the season, Nashville, TN. Opryland information, (615) 889-6611.

Christmas Village, State Fairgrounds, Nashville, TN. Contact: Barbie Bachman, 1807 Harpeth Drive, Brentwood, TN 37027. Beautiful Christmas crafts provide an early shopping spree.

Harvest Craft Festival, Volunteer State Community College, Gallatin, TN. Contact: Page Jackson, (615) 452-4500. Crafts only by about 75 artists. Attendance: 5,000.

Yuletide Seasons Show, Municipal Auditorium, Nashville, TN. Contact: Mary Baker, (615) 898-0891. Attendance: 50,000.

The Christmas Sampler, Recreation Center, Springfield, TN. Contact: Maxine Elliott, Route 1, Adams, TN 37010. Sponsored by the local Women's Club. Crafts of all kinds available and delicious food too. Robertson County is noted for growing dark-fired tobacco. At this time of year notice the "smoking barns" along the roadside. The tobacco must be smoked to achieve proper color.

Arts, Crafts, and Quilt Show, 510 Woodland Street, Nashville, TN. Sponsored by Christian Counseling

Services Lady Auxiliary. Call (615) 254-8341 for more information.

Arts and Crafts Fall Festival, New Prospect Community, Lawrenceburg, TN. Contact: Mrs. A. N. Stancie, (615) 762-2813. (See feature artice.)

DECEMBER

Christmas at Twitty City, Hendersonville, TN. Contact: Dan Stupka, (615) 822-6650. Conway Twitty's showplace displays holiday spirit with more than a quarter million lights, performances by local chorus, live nativity scene, and Christmas crafts. Nightly 6:00 to 9:00.

Trees of Christmas, Nashville, TN. Cheekwood, (615) 356-3308. Exquisitely decorated trees are enhanced with other Yuletide exhibits. Plant shop and holiday bazaar.

Tennessee Crafts Sampler and Friends, Julia Green School, Nashville, TN. Contact: Mary Ingram, (615) 228-5370 or 226-3168. Original arts and crafts. Attendance: 6,000.

Country Christmas Craft, Art, and Antique Fair, Opryland Hotel, Nashville, TN. Contact: Mary Ingram, (615) 228-5370 or 226-3168. Fine arts and crafts. 125 artists. Attendance: 50,000.

Annual Christmas Boutique, Tullahoma, TN. Contact: Lucy Hollis, (615) 455-1234. Crafts only by 30 artists.

An Old-fashioned Christmas, Bell Buckle, TN. Contact: Bell Buckle Merchants Association, (615) 389-6908. THe town celebrates Christmas as it was in the 1890s. The first Saturday in December is set aside for Christmas shopping, singing carols, renewing ties with friends and neighbors, and delighting in the old-fashioned decorations which evoke memories of yesteryear. Those of you who remember Christmas as it was, and those of you who want to discover Christmas as it was, will want to be there.

West Tennessee Area

The World's Largest Fish Fry

Hungry for food and fun? Try this to whet your appetite. Start with 1,500 pounds of cornmeal, 250 pounds of salt, and 9,000 pounds of fresh Kentucky Lake catfish. Set up old-time black kettle pots over gas burners and heat 240 gallons of vegetable oil. While waiting for the oil to heat to the proper temperature, mix your cornmeal and salt together, roll each piece of catfish in the cornmeal-salt mixture, and drop into the heated oil until each

Everyone loves Catfish at Paris, Tennessee

A SAMPLER
*****Exclusive*****

Hank Williams, Jr., and
The World's Largest Fish Fry

We heard a true story about Hank Williams, Jr., the other day. It seems like last summer Hank was out on his tractor bushhogging one of the pastures on his farm. (For those of you that ain't country, that means he was cutting the grass.) It was a hot southern afternoon, and Hank was covered with sweat and dirt and grass clippings. Anyway, one of the local folks motioned for Hank to drive over and said, "Listen, boy, when you get finished with that field I got some fields for you to cut." The man barking out the orders didn't recognize Hank and thought he was some hired man. Hank didn't say anything except "Yes, sir," and after finishing his pasture, he cut that man's fields too. Hank never did get paid for his work.

That's just the kind of person, Hank Williams, Jr., is. He's country, not because he has to be but because he wants to be. Listen sometime to the powerful, cutting, fun-and-emotion-packed lyrics of his songs to find out for yourself. Listen to one of his greatest songs, "A Country Boy Can Survive." Anyway, one of Hank's favorite things to do in the world is go to the World's Largest Fish Fry every April in Paris, Tennessee. While Hank's in Paris he loves to eat at the Oak Tree Restaurant, especially for breakfast. The place is built around several large oak trees.

piece is deep fried to a crispy golden brown. Add mountains of cole slaw, buckets of white beans, and wagon loads of hushpuppies, and you have a recipe guaranteed to draw huge crowds to Paris, Tennessee, for the World's Largest Fish Fry.

For the past 30 years, Paris has hosted the annual Fish Fry at the Paris Fairgrounds near the banks of the huge Kentucky Lake. Paris has developed a well-deserved reputation for the quality of its catfish and the traditional Tennessee method of preparing them. Although catfish are pretty much the same everywhere, it ain't the fish that matters, it's the preparation. And the people of West Tennessee know how to fry a catfish. Notice that the man wearing the apron behind that big black kettle is no teen-ager. It takes a lot more skill to fry a catfish than it does to grill a Big Mac.

The four-day celebration in April includes a lot more than just the fish feast. The schedule is jammed with parades, street dances, square dances, sporting events, a carnival, and a full-scale rodeo. There are arts and crafts shows, a high-school baseball tournament, and a junior fishing rodeo. Still, the star of the event is unquestionably that big old, hairy-faced creature called the catfish. Serving begins in the fish tent at the Paris Fairgrounds, and for $5 you can eat as much as you want.

If you want to make a weekend of it, the Kentucky Lake area is filled with all sorts of resorts, motels, and marinas, including Paris Landing State Resort Park with its new 100-room inn, large campgrounds, championship golf course, and other attractions on the banks of Kentucky Lake. The resort park inn also has an excellent restaurant; just guess what their specialty is!

Hank Williams, Jr., and fish-eatin' grin

Most of all Hank, Jr., loves to fish on Kentucky Lake for largemouth bass and crappie. This man carries on the family tradition by not only loving the outdoors but by introducing his son to it too. The *Sampler*'s just heard that Hank has taken his young son up in the wilderness of Alaska hunting grizzly.

Although most of Hank's rowdy friends have semi-settled down, if you're in Paris fishing or enjoying the fish fry and you're having trouble settling down to a night of reading a book on real estate, head over to Hank's Club, owned by Hank Williams, Jr., and Partner. They book some mighty hot, hard-core country bands to play here, including Hank's band, Bama. You may look up some night and see Hank, Jr., his-own-self, standing there sippin' and enjoying the place as much as you.

By the way, if you're a stranger to these parts and want somebody to talk to at Hank's Club, especially if you want to talk about huntin', fishin', guns, and survivin' southern-style, ask for Hank's good friend, Jerry Richardson. We'll see you either fishin' or at "The Fry!"

Strawberry Festival

Humboldt proudly claims that there's no place on earth where a sweeter, juicier, or more colorful strawberry can be grown. You will certainly find no argument with that around these parts of West Tennessee.

The annual Strawberry Festival Horse Show begins the May celebration. Other activities include dancing in the streets, which features country and rock music, and a Junior Parade. An unusual aspect of this parade is that all floats are hand-drawn, and vehicles are pulled by youngsters or ponies, dogs, or goats. No motorized vehicles are allowed. That evening the stage band festival provides a real showdown for stage bands and great entertainment for everyone.

During the week the Strawberry Show and Strawberry Products Show give farmers the opportunity to show off their pick of the crop and the preserves, jams, and vinegars produced from the fruit. For athletes of the area, there are softball, baseball, and golf tournaments, a bike ride, and a 10K run. Funseekers of all ages enjoy the Barbecue Cook-off and carnival. A Grand Float Parade and a selection of Strawberry Festival Queen are part of the doings too. A country western concert brings the festivities to a close.

Banana Festival

The most unusual of Tennessee's fun-time events is a four-day September celebration in honor of a product not grown in Tennessee or even in the United States, the banana. South Fulton's unique devotion to the banana did not come about by accident. It all started over 80 years ago when the twin cities of Fulton and South Fulton were key railroad towns on the New Orleans to Canada route. At this time the Illinois Central Railroad (now Illinois Central Gulf) had developed the refrigerated rail car, and Fulton had the largest one-story ice plant in Mid-America. Since bananas must be kept at a constant, cool temperature on their way to market, it was only logical that Fulton became an important checkpoint along the route. For nearly six decades it was the redistribution center for 70 per cent of all the bananas brought into America, and the title "Banana Capital of the World" was a fitting one.

By the mid-1960s efficient trucking lines and modern methods of refrigeration had replaced Fulton's facilities in the distribution system. But in honor of its proud history, a banana festival was begun. Nearly 40,000 banana-curious visitors are expected to turn out for this year's festival to see a children's banana-split-eating contest; a Kiddie Parade; a sidewalk bazaar; arts and crafts show and flea market; a fashion show; and a banan-a-rama. A 10K race, a "fun run," and a parade featuring the world's largest banana pudding also take place.

When the parade finally concludes in the city park, this incredible 2,000-pound banana pudding is scooped into cups and served as 10,000 free desserts. Unusual events held in the park are a banana eating contest and ribbons awarded for the prettiest, ugliest, and fastest turtle and for smallest, fastest-jumping, and farthest-jumping frog. A parachute team will perform mile-high tricks, and a swinging fiesta ball will round out the evening entertainment.

Pink Palace Crafts Fair

Formerly known as the Mid-State Crafts Fair, the Pink Palace Crafts Fair has been called "the ultra-suede crafts fair of Memphis." Over 100 select craftspeople demonstrate and offer for sale both pioneer and contemporary handmade objects. Jewelers, basket weavers, stained-glass artists, toy makers, and sculptors are only a few of those featured.

The October fair presents the perfect pastime for families looking for fun. For less than $10, a family of four can enjoy the country music and dancing on the fair's stage and visit the craftsmen in the educational tent.

A number of artisans demonstrate dying crafts such as spinning, weaving, chair caning, or blacksmithing. The ring of the blacksmith's hammer blends with the happy sound of down-home bluegrass music or the stomp of the cloggers' feet. Civil War buffs can join for a few hours an authentic wartime encampment, complete with tents, campfires, drills, and all the other necessities of army life. Visitors may smell and taste the past as they inhale the sweet aroma of the sorghum mill on their way to sample freshly pressed apple cider. For many who attend the fair, these demonstrations are the only glimpse they'll have of this way of life from the past.

The event is sponsored by the Friends of the Pink Palace, the volunteer group which supports the museum. Live demonstrations with animals and artifacts are provided by museum staff, special shows at the museum's planetarium are featured, and all craft fair ticket holders can tour the museum free.

Lain Whittaker of the Pink Palace publicity committee tells us: "One reason the fair has survived for 13 years is due to the attachment Friends of the Pink Palace and craftspeople have developed for the event. Some of the same people have been working at the fair since its inception.

"Dee Moss, woodcarver from Jackson, has an eagle he's been working on for the last five fairs. Having invested over 2,000 hours in it already, he declares it has crossed over into the domain of 'priceless' pieces. Another veteran of the fair is Babe Howard of Millington whose mule-powered sorghum mill has been a featured attraction for a number of years. In 1982 he began a tradition of donating a barbecued pig and hosting a dinner for craftspeople and Friends. After the torrential rains of that year, workers gathered in the lobby of the old museum for a bit of food and fun before going their separate ways.

"Clarence Saunders, a millionaire whose palatical 'pink palace' was the first home of the museum, would not have imagined a more unlikely crew than the middle class Memphis matrons and blue-jeaned craftsmen who lounged on the marble steps munching barbecue and becoming better acquainted. Occasions such as these make the fair something to anticipate each year."

The creations for sale are all handmade. Unusual items are much less expensive here than in the specialty stores where they usually appear. One-of-a-kind silk batik fashions, pipes made from antlers, or carefully crafted metal fountains are only a few of the items that vie for the attention of the discriminating eye. Original stone carvings or dramatic raku pottery may delight the art lover, while puppets, puzzles, and dolls attract a younger audience.

The usual array of culinary delights will be on hand for the country crafts gourmet—from pronto pups and the best homemade doughnuts ever created to quiche and bean sprouts for the health conscious.

More West Tennessee Fun Times

JANUARY
Memphis Flea Market. Third weekend each month at the Mid-South Fairgrounds.

Eagle Tours, Tiptonville, TN. Reelfoot Lake is one of the prime wintering areas for the American bald eagle. Guided tours daily at Reelfoot Lake State Park from December 1 to March 15.

FEBRUARY
National Field Trial Championships, Grand Junction, TN. Ames Plantation, (901) 764-2167. Bird dog owners from across the country converge on Ames Plantation for 10-day competition to determine the National Championship bird dog. Visitors may join mounted galleries to view the action.

MARCH
Memphis Artist Craftsmen's Association/Theater Memphis Show, 630 Perkins, Memphis, TN. Sponsor: Memphis Artist Craftsmen's Association. Contact: Charlie Gardner, 3462 Hallshire, Memphis, TN 38112. 20 to 30 artists.

APRIL
World's Largest Fish Fry, Paris, TN. Contact: Bill Wensler, (901) 644-1155. (See feature article.)

Soybean Festival, Dyersburg, TN. Contact: Dyersburg Chamber of Commerce, 121 Masonic Street, Dyersburg, TN 38024. (901) 285-3433. Dyersburg honors this major cash crop with a full week of activities such as a parade, softball tournament, street dance, and a beauty contest in which the contestants have suspiciously hairy legs. The gastronomical highlight is the great Bean Cook Off, and for sheer excitement there's the Riding Lawnmower Race, proving again that people will race anything that has wheels attached to it.

MAY
Strawberry Festival, Humboldt, TN. Week-long celebration. (See feature article.)

Memphis in May International Festival. Month of art, music, and special events honoring the history and culture of a selected country. Annual events are the Beale Street Music Festival, Sunset Symphony, and International Barbecue cooking contest. (See "Music" for more information.)

Cotton Carnival Musicfest, Memphis, TN. 10-day music festival at the fairgrounds with every type of popular music represented. Contact: Memphis Area Chamber of Commerce for more information, (901) 523-2322.

Blues in the Park, Handy Park, Beale Street, Memphis, TN. Sponsor: The Blues Foundation. Contact: Joe Savaring, The Blues Foundation, P. O. Box 161272, Memphis, TN 38186-1272. (901) 332-6459. Music. All blues performers. Daily in September. 100 artists. No admission.

JUNE
Moscow Summer Games, Moscow, TN. Games for all ages include adult tricycle race, 10K race, marble

shoot, horseshoes, arm wrestling, and more. Medallions for winners.

JULY

Doodle Soup Festival, Bradford, TN. Contact: Bradford Chamber of Commerce. The Doodle Soup Festival, held at Bradford, the Doodle Soup Capital of the World, includes beauty reviews, softball tournaments, country western music, a three-wheeler rodeo and suicide race, quilt show, senior citizen cake walk, a carnival, horse show, parade and, or course, plenty of Doodle Soup. (See "Eatin' and Sleepin' Good" for the recipe for this delectable delight.)

Okra Festival, Bells, TN. Contact: Chamber of Commerce (Haywood County), (901) 772-2193. A street carnival, softball tournament, flower show, rodeo, beauty contest, tractor pull, and craft show honor the town's favorite vegetable—okra.

AUGUST

Elvis International Tribute Week, Graceland Mansion, Memphis, TN. (901) 332-3322. Memphis's favorite son is honored in a city-wide event featuring talk sessions with Presley's friends and associates, performances by his back-up musicians, memorabilia exhibits, and more. (See "Music" for more information.)

SEPTEMBER

International Banana Festival, South Fulton, TN. (See feature article.)

Forest Festival, Bolivar, TN. Contact: Chamber of Commerce, (901) 658-6554. Held each year to promote forestry throughout Tennessee and awaken the public to the dangers of the fall fire season. See educational displays. Enjoy the logger's breakfast, arts and crafts fair, antique car and street rod show, Paul Bunyan Run, and beauty contest. "Smokey the Bear" is on hand as an ever-present warning about forest fires.

Carroll County's Pork Festival, Huntington, TN. Contact: Huntington (Carroll County) Chamber of Commerce, (901) 986-4664. A week-long salute to the pork industry and "Miss Piggy" specifically. There are a sausage breakfast, white bean and ham hock dinners, and barbecue suppers. The beauty revue and octoberfest are enjoyed by all. Hog-calling and tobacco-spitting contests are always fun, plus flea markets. Downtown merchants provide lots of bargains. In Carroll County, everyone goes hog wild and pig crazy this week!

Annual Casey Jones Village Labor Day Arts and Crafts Festival, I-40 and the 45 By-Pass, Exit 80-A, Jackson, TN. Contact: Norwood Jones, (901) 668-1223. Arts, crafts, music. Attendance: 5,000.

Festival, Paris Landing State Park, Paris, TN. Contact: Shirley Casey, (901) 642-5577. Arts and crafts. Attendance: 18,000.

Mid-South Fair, Memphis, TN. Contact: Shelley Robbins, (901) 274-8800. Arts, crafts, music, dance. Attendance: 400.000.

OCTOBER

Octoberfest, Memphis, TN. Contact: Wanda Carruthers, (901) 526-6840. Arts, crafts, music. 16 to 25 craft booths and 22 to 25 bands. Attendance: 40,000. No admission.

Pink Palace Crafts Fair, Pink Palace Museum, Memphis, TN. Contact: Lain Whittaker, (901) 454-5600. Original crafts only. Attendance: 2,000 to 3,000. (See feature article.)

Reelfoot Lake Arts and Crafts Festival, Tiptonville, TN. Contact: Kathleen Downs, (901) 253-6204. Original crafts only. Over 300 artists. Attendance: 10,000 to 15,000.

Fayette County Egg Festival, Somerville, TN. Contact: Gayle Bowling, (901) 465-8690. Fayette County's salute to the people and the product, the egg industry. Barbecue-chicken-cooking contest, meringue-throwing contest, decorated egg trees, the Egg Scramble 5K run, ice-cream-eating contest, an omelet brunch and, last but not least, the Chicken Beauty Contest.

Davy Crockett Days, Rutherford, TN. Contact: Joe Bone, (901) 665-7771. A craft fair, flea market, parade, and pet shows all honor the pioneers who settled in Rutherford, foremost of whom was Davy Crockett.

NOVEMBER

"Christmas by the Lake" Arts and Crafts Festival. Creative Gallery, Paris Landing State Park Inn, Buchanan, TN. (901) 642-4311. This festival features approximately 50 exhibitors from Tennessee and surrounding states.

Mid-South Arts and Crafts Show and Sale, Memphis, TN. Contact: Bill Miller, (901) 363-4178. Nearly 400 artists and craftsmen from 24 states take part in this large indoor show.

DECEMBER

The Liberty Bowl Football Classic, Memphis, TN. Liberty Bowl, (901) 278-4747 or 458-2674. Annual holiday classic features two top NCAA teams.

For additional information about fun times in Tennessee, contact the following offices:

Tennessee Department of Tourist Development, Room T, Box 23170, Nashville, TN 37202. (615) 741-1904.

Tennessee Arts Commission, 505 Deadrick Street, Suite 1700, Nashville, TN 37219. (615) 741-1701.

A TREASURY
OF TENNESSEE
WIT &

Wisdom

A Treasury of
Tennessee Wit and Wisdom

A Year or so ago, we asked people to tell us what they thought about Tennessee. We heard from thousands of Tennesseans—professors, realtors, students, housewives, and farmers. They all had something important to say about The Volunteer Sate, and one of the reasons we did *The Tennessee Sampler* was to give them a place to say it. Here is that place.

We are especially honored to present to you some of the wonderful photographs of Tennessee in decades past made by Joe Clark HBSS (HillBilly SnapShooter) and published in his books *I Remember, Back Home,* and *Back Home Again.* Joe and his son Junebug have for years taken "pictures that tell a story." *The Tennessee Sampler* dedicates this Treasury of Tennessee Wit and Wisdom to Joe Clark.

So get ready for a heartfelt tribute to Tennessee. Here are fresh interviews with Cousin Minnie Pearl, Amy Grant, and Michael W. Smith, comments from Larry Gatlin, and insights into Tennessee character from Wlma Dykeman. Enjoy!

A Tennessean's special place

A Sense of Place

Home at Last

I was not born among these green and rolling hills,
The graves of my ancestors lie in a windy, far more rugged place.
But I have become a daughter of this state
In my heart, where it counts most.

It was all foreign at first—the summer's heat, the
Speech, the slower way of doing things,
But one day, returning from my native land,
I crossed this state's green borders,
And felt, at last, at home.

Ruth Garren, McDonald, Tennessee

Cumberlands Prayer

Grant that, when I am old and my eyes are dim,
I need only wander the halls of memory to once again know
This evening's masterpiece of mist and mountain:
Eastern valleys veiled in shrouds of rain;
Ridges dark with dripping maple, oak, and hickory,
Pleated foothills shimmering wet in the rising fog,
The storm's thundering down long valleys and breaking with
The late evening sun over the Cumberlands.

Charlotte A. Shea, Huntsville, Alabama

Racoon Mountain

Today
for the first time
in my life
I saw an eagle
flying free.

The symbol
of my country
proud
majestic
strong.

Wings beating
in measured strokes.
A swift descent

to the surface
of the water.
Talons snaring a fish
I could not see.
Victor again
in the age old
struggle.

I did nothing
to change
that eagle's life.

But he
changed mine.

Hugh Clements, Hixson, Tennessee

Small Creek

Small creek, run dry, who stole your vital flow?
Has rain not come and washed you clean again?
Time's made you hold the things you wish would go.
Could you have been like this when I was ten?

Each day new treasures there in you I found:
A rusty key, rare rocks, or clay of gold,
A fort with roof of leaves and floor of ground,
Or arrowheads, quite old, as I was told.

I made a path which led down through your bank,
But now it's gone, my wonder with it too,
Though everyday this journey I did take.
Your mark on me is gone, as mine on you.

Your fertile banks still hide what children seek,
Have you run dry or is it I, small creek?

Lee Ann Hearn, Nashville, Tennessee

The Come-Back Rock

To most it's an ordinary rock. Not to us. It's our come-back rock. It came from a mountain stream near Townsend.

What's it doing in Texas? It's our pledge that we'll come back home to the mountains.

On special days we dip it in water (icy cold, of course). Soon we're looking for deer in Cades Cove, riding the sky-lift above Gatlinburg, sitting about my parents' fireplace.

When we get home, we'll return our rock to its stream. Then we'll all be where we belong.

Steve Bobitt, Orange, Texas

Chattanooga Lights

A Chattanooga man huddled against an icy rail on the crest of the Ridge and shook the snow from his curly hair. Behind him, his huge truck idled and blew a steamy invitation for his quick return.

He hesitated, shrinking from the bitter wind, then blew steaming coffee clutched with trembling fingers.

One more glance…

The moon, floating peacefully above, smiled down upon a hundred thousand Chattanooga lights beckoning, twinkling… winking boldly at the cold.

One more glance, and then he turned to go…

Rita L. Hubbard, Chattanooga, Tennessee

The magic of a Tennessee childhood

A SAMPLER
·····*Exclusive*·····
Michael W. Smith

Nashvillian Michael W. Smith is one of Christian Contemporary music's most gifted composers and most exciting performers. In 1985 he won a Grammy with his album *Michael W. Smith 2.* Out of the two hundred or so songs Michael has written, 175 of them have been recorded, an amazing percentage. Songs like "How Majestic is Your Name," "Great is the Lord," and "Friends" are already classics.

The *Sampler* asked Michael what it was that made Tennessee special for him. "It's Tennesseans who have made Tennessee home for me," he answered. "Friends. I moved to Nashville seven years ago from West Virginia, so I guess I represent people who live in Tennessee with roots in other states. But Nashville is home now. I met my wife Debbie here, and we've started a family."

"One afternoon we were getting ready for a farewell party for a friend, Bill Jackson, who was moving to Mississippi. Debbie writes most of my lyrics, and two hours before the party she told me we ought to write a song for Bill for that night. I told her we couldn't possibly write a song in two hours, and went outside to feed the dog. I came back in and she had these wonderful lyrics all written out.

> Friends are friends forever,
> If the Lord's the Lord of them.
> And a friend will not say never
> 'Cause their welcome will not end.
> Though it's hard to let you go
> In the Father's hands we know
> That a lifetime's not too long to live as Friends.*

So I sat down at the piano and wrote the music and we sang Bill his song that night, and all cried together. I guess I'll always think of friends when I think of Tennessee."

To that, we at the *Sampler*, some of us transplanted Tennesseans, say a hearty "Amen!"

riverrhythm

wrinkled old men, shriveled and brown.
withered hands transporting cumbersome cotton
bales on barges with inert familiarity.

little children basking in the fierce summer sun.
small fists tightly wound around drippy ice cream cones.
tiny toes squishing themselves into my rich, muddy mire,
penetrated with the essence of my existence.

sparsely scattered sunlight filtering through watery grey-brown fluid,
touching my deepest abysses.
sky and water and land pulsating together,
each a part of a throbbing, rhythmic sensation.

i am the River.

Jennifer Less, Memphis, Tennessee

Cousins in Detroit

We've all got cousins in Detroit. People who left because there wasn't any work and took a little bit of Tennessee with them to the mills and factories in the North. But the jobs are here now, and their children are coming home.

Peggy O'Neal Peden, Nashville, Tennessee

God's Country

Joe Clark, HBSS states in his book, I Remember:

Many of us spent the days of our youth in a different place from where we live now. Time and distance have softened that childhood place, and it has mellowed in our memories and dreams. It became, through the years, God's country. The only difference between your home community and my home community is that Tennessee really is God's country.

Rainbarrels and Swimmytails

Rainbarrels and swimmytails
And happiness in an hour.
Woodsmoke and laundry soap
Mingled in my hair.

Pine groves and honeysuckle coves,
The woods were our domain.
Crowfoot and Indian Corn,
We knew them all by name.

Grapevines and swimmin' holes
On lazy summer days.
Whoopee-hide and lightnin' bugs
All in the twilight haze.

It was a time out of childhood then,
A time out of endless time.
A time that my heart never knew was joy
'Til I was far from my Tennessee home.

Evelyn M. Bales, Kingsport, Tennessee

Grandfather's Mountain

Every person has a peaceful place. A place where things are simple and pure. A place one runs to when everything is falling apart.

My grandfather's mountain has always been my peaceful place. Nature almost untouched by human hands.

My grandfather is a small man, but never disobeyed by anyone in our family. Papaw is a quiet man; studious, hardworking and religious. When I was small I used to ask him about the Garden of Eden and Adam and Eve...and if it was all right for me to eat apples. He always had an answer and he always spoke "my language," the simple, honest language of a child.

I can still remember sitting on his front porch on summer nights. In the darkness one could see the fireflies among the branches of the mountain. The frogs and the crickets that were always so much louder at night echoed down the "holler." In the kitchen my grandmother would be working; singing hymns. At times Papaw would talk about our family. People I knew only from pictures in an album. Sometimes he would talk about right and wrong, truth and love, honor and honesty.

I've never decided if my grandfather made the mountain, or if the mountain made my grandfather. Both still stand strong and tall.

Susan Cook, Knoxville, Tennessee

The land is a treasure

Land or Money

An early summer morning in McPheeters Bend brought sounds of dove and bob white. Sunshine made sparkles on the dewy garden. Off behind the garden was the blue hazed mountain. On the porch, Grandfather and I rocked. "My father divided the land between Ida and Guy and me—so much river bottom so much upland. Clyde got money," he said. "Would you rather have land or money, Granddaddy?" I asked. He hesitated only a moment. "I'd rather have land."

Helen Gilbert, Jonesboro, Tennessee

Ain't God Good To Tennessee?

Supper's done, the dishes all are washed and put away,
My Little Leaguer's had his bath, he's tired from his play.
From the porch we hear the squeak of Daddy's rockin' chair.
We know that he is waitin' for us, to be with him there.
"Mamma, what are fireflies signalin' with them little lights?
And what are the owls gigglin' at, long into the night?
And what do the cicadas say, talkin' in the tree?"
"My Son, they're all just sayin', Aint God good to Tennessee!"

Mrs. Jayne L. Kelly, Norris, Tennessee

Grandpa and Grandma

A Sense of Humor

Politikin

He came to kiss the baby fair,
Or so at least he claims;
What really brings him out this way
Is my 'X' beside his name.

Says he, "This road could use some oil.
Would take away the sludge,

I might could get it done for you
If I were County Judge."

Says I, "This road don't need no oil,
'Cause it don't go nowhere;
The one that leaves this road alone,
Deserves the Judge's chair."

Frank Andrews, Franklin, Tennessee

Grandfather's Mule

My grandfather lived his life on a farm in Overton County, Tennessee. Returning from a late summer walk, we stopped to drink from the spring. His mule was eating apples from the tree behind the barn. "I'd better go chase him away," he said, walking off to fetch his herding pole. "Red's as old and worn out as me, and the apples ain't much good, but I've always chased him away from that tree, and he wouldn't know what to think if I stopped now."

Kenneth Roberts, Antioch, Tennessee

One of the Sampler's favorite funny people is WSM radio 650 personality Al Wyntor. Every morning on WSM's Waking Crew he honors us with "That's Not All the News." Here's a real gem!

Six Warning Signs of Stupidity

There is a silent, sneaky-pete disease that every year inflicts itself on thousands of unsuspecting Americans. Yet, because of the stigma attached to it, we seldom hear about it, let alone admit we may have it ourselves. The malady of which I speak is, of course, stupidity. The American Stupidity Association is seeking to find the root causes of the condition, to find a cure and to warn the public of the dangers of acting dumb. Therefore, in the interests of us all, we present, "Six Warning Signs of Stupidity."

1. Are you convinced "duh" is the 4th letter of the alphabet?
2. Have you ever been given a refund for an I.Q. test?
3. Does your bathroom have a sand floor?
4. Can you carry on a meaningful dialogue with a Cabbage Patch doll?
5. When tying your shoes, must you consult the owner's manual?
6. Are you the only person at the office who fastens his shirt with twist ties?

To learn more about stupidity, the U.S. Library of Congress has prepared several manuals on the subject and has available a number of books. We suggest, *My Life as a Plant Hangman, You Can't Be a Blood-brother to a Fire Hydrant,* and *Lost in the Lobby.*

Al Wyntor

There's truth in Tennessee

Tree-climbin', creek-wadin', vine-swingin',
Cow-chasin', horse-stompin', deer-runnin',
Canoe-rowin', tobacco-hoein', corn-pullin',
Cotton-pickin', strawberry-snitchin', watermelon-crunchin',
Bar-b-que munchin', tractor-pullin', pick-up haulin',
Folk-singin', square-dancin', banjo-plunkin',
Fiddle-bowin', Bible-thumpin', church-prayin',
Chalk dustin', book-learnin', college-goin',
Confederate-troopin', Dan'l Boon-carvin',
Tornado-turnin', thunder-rollin', snow-fallin',
Sun-shinin', moon-shinin', mountain-smokin',
City-slickin', sky-scrapin', money-makin',
Hand-shakin', friendly smilin', home-comin'
Truth in Tennessee.
Honest!

K. Campbell Norskov, Fayetteville, Tennessee

Watermelon crunchin'

A SAMPLER
·····*Exclusive*·····
Cousin Minnie Pearl,
The Soul of Tennessee
Wit and Wisdom

"I'll never forget the first time I took Brother to town. We both had on our best clothes. I knew I looked nice—several men smiled at me, one of them laughed right out loud! Anyhow, we got a ticket and climbed aboard the train. We hadn't been there for long, settin' there big as life and twice as natural, when a feller came by with a basket full of apples and 'nanners. Brother never had had a 'nanner before, so he borrowed a nickel from me and got one. This other feller across the aisle got one too, and when Brother asked me, 'Minnie, how do I eat this thing?' I said, 'Just watch that feller there and do whatever he does.'

"Well, this feller peeled down the 'nanner in his hand and Brother peeled down the 'nanner in his hand.

"The feller took a bite of the 'nanner in his hand. Then Brother took a bite of the 'nanner in his hand, and just then we went into a long dark tunnel. When we came out, Brother was jest settin' there, not sayin' a word—jest lookin' at the 'nanner. 'Ain't you gonna eat the rest of your 'nanner?' I asked him. And he said, 'I ain't gonna eat no more! I took one bite and went stone blind!' "

Fans of the Grand Ole Opry will have already recognized one of Minnie Pearl's most famous stories about Grinder's Switch. Grinder's Switch is a delightful storehouse of country characters like Brother that Sarah Ophelia Colley Cannon, alias Minnie Pearl, created in fifty years of making audiences laugh.

Uncle Dave Macon, Homer and Jethro, Grandpa Jones, and many others have told country stories or sung humorous songs, but only Minnie, Jerry Clower, and the late Grady Nutt in recent years have kept country comedy alive as a pure form. Today, Minnie is as funny as ever, twice as natural, and three times a lady.

The *Sampler* interviewed Cousin Minnie Pearl at her beautiful new museum near Music Row. "Welcome to my yellow gingerbread house!" Minnie said. Inside we found her collection of rare memorabilia—photographs of her life and fifty years of entertaining. There was a complete model of Grinder's Switch and what had to be the world's biggest Minnie Pearl hat on the ceiling. We saw Minnie's rare film footage collection of Grand Ole Opry stars including Roy Acuff, Tennessee Ernie Ford, and of her first network TV appearance in 1957 on "This is Your Life." After this special tour conducted by Minnie herself, we headed over to Tavern in the Row for lunch and a long conversation with this fascinating lady.

Minnie Pearl's motto she got from her dad, "If you can't beat em, confuse em!" Thomas Kelly Colley, her father, kept popping into the conversation. He was obviously a fundamental shaper of her values and perceptions. "People down in Centerville used to say they'd rather have Tom Colley's word than the signature of the president of the Chase Manhattan Bank." But her mother's family thought their 18-year-old daughter was going into the wilderness when Tom Colley married her and took her to Centerville, in Hickman county. He was a tall, spare, 36 year old in the lumber business, and most of the county was virgin timber back then.

"People used to say you couldn't raise an umbrella on that land!" Well, maybe not umbrellas, but kids were a different matter. Minnie was the last of five daughters raised in a household full of love and excitement.

She had plenty of spunk by the time she showed up at Ward-Belmont College in 1930 in Nashville, one of the few girls there who had not been brought up with a houseful of servants. She had already started to listen and learn from all types of people, and her father's importance in their small town had gotten her used to meeting the demands of most social situations.

But, as Ophelia Colley from Centerville, she was a little out of place in a status-conscious place like Ward-Belmont. She says the buildings at Belmont even *smelled* different from her big old house back home.

"They smelled like European antiques and furniture polish; our house smelled like wood smoke from the fireplace!" With the help of three unconventional college friends who called themselves Hot, Dot, and Annie she quickly found her niche as an entertainer, and got her first practice at being funny for groups.

After graduation, she traveled around rural areas of the south for a while putting on dramas and song and dance programs at schools. There she first learned to put her observations of country life to use. Her father deplored the fact that she had gone into "show business" which he considered too dangerous for a young single woman.

While she was doing this traveling she began to shape her country characters. "In 1936 they sent me to Baleyton, Alabama, in the north Alabama highlands. On Brinlee Mountain I stayed with an elderly man and his wife in a mountain cabin for 10 days. They were kind and hospitable. But she was funny. Everything she said was just naturally funny! I came away from there telling her stories. Then I kept my ears open for other country stories and the expressions people used in telling them."

Then her father died, and she returned to be near her mother, working for the WPA for $50.00 a month keeping a recreation room open in Centerville upstairs over the school. Those were hard times, and she still remembers how they had to sew up their silk stockings when they snagged because they could not afford new ones. By this time, Minnie Pearl was a well-established part of Sarah's repertoire. "I dressed Minnie like I thought a country girl would dress trying to get a fella at a square dance—a clean cotton dress, low heel Mary Jane shoes, and a hat. The price tag came after I went on the Opry. It was an accident, but people liked it, so I kept it."

Minnie's debut on the Opry came in 1940 at the War Memorial Auditorium. "I was deathly afraid," she says, "because although I had been working on Minnie, I'd never done her on radio." She got $10 per appearance for the Opry, and the fact that she and her mother needed the money so much undoubtedly added to her fear that night. She was a great hit to Opry fans from the beginning, and her career began a growth which has never slowed down to this day. Now she has added many years of TV appearances, including regular stints on "Hee Haw," to her experience.

The *Sampler* asked Minnie what her hopes were for country humor. She said, "I'm disappointed that more people aren't getting into country comedy. You know, the real country people are just as funny as ever, and the great stories are still out there waiting to be found by someone who can do something with them. We need some creative new blood to get some of the spontaneity back into our humor on radio and TV. Some of the funniest stories in country are being done by songwriters instead of comedians."

How about practical advice for young storytellers?

"You have to take a gag on the road," says Minnie, "and try it out on people before you use it on the Opry. It's the same for anybody. Most of humor is listening to people and putting ideas together. But you still have to work, work, work." Sounds just like the sort of thing Tom Colley from Centerville might have said, doesn't it?

The Queen of Country Humor and the King of Country Music—Minnie Pearl and Roy Acuff.
Photo courtesy of Henry Cannon.

Explanation of Tennessee Words and Terms:

Possum: a critter not worth much till you get him in the sack
Sassafras tea: a brew for eliminating the weak
Mountain dew (could say white lightnin'): a brew for eliminating the strong
Holler: a small valley
Valley: a big holler
Mountain: a big hill haired over with trees.
Sorghum molasses: soppins for your winter biscuits
Sparkin': starting an uncontrollable fire by looking into a girl's eyes
Bean shellin': an excuse for kids to do a little work and a lot of sparkin'
Corn huskin': same as bean shellin' except it's played in the barn by seein' how close you can get to the fire without gettin' burnt

From I Remember *by Joe Clark, HBSS.*

Outdoor baptizin'

Reminiscences of Aunt Sadie Belfield

When I was a young'un churches weren't air conditioned. We used to fight to sit next to an open window, especially the one that had a big ole sugar tree just outside. It had the coolest breeze. Anywhere else we'd nearly smother.

The preacher would take off his coat and loosen his tie. The sweat poured as he paced back and forth, gesturing wildly, his voice like thunder.

Hell has never seemed more real, nor heaven more desirable than they did then.

Carrie Leech, Columbia, Tennessee

The Way Back Home

If you get lost in Tennessee, you won't stay lost for long.

One scorching summer day, I stopped at a roadside general store for directions back to Nashville. The two elderly men inside immediately engaged in an amiable argument over the best route to I-40. Many minutes later, I left the store with *two* maps, *two* sets of directions, and *two* frosty soft drinks "for the road."

As I reached my car, their conversation continued in full swing, "If she turns left past the bridge…"

L.D. Montgomery, Nashville, Tennessee

Nashvillese

The Sampler *agrees with Jesse Hill Ford that "Nigh-ish-vul" has a special language. Thanks to* Nashville Magazine *we're glad to reproduce this brief survival guide to help you "get on" in our fair city:*

Nashvillese	Translation
wekum waggin	welcome wagon
moe tail	motel
hee-yull	hill
rat fur piece	far
far	fire
tail	tell
plum tard	fatigued
coldern hail	chilly
hottern hail	warmish
crazern hail	insane
barnt up	angry
tear out	run
toe out	ran
prar meeten	church service

Christy Butler of Nashville adds a few other rib-ticklers:

dawg	man's best friend
backer feel	tobacco field
hail far	discontentment
Ov-air	(use when pointing to nearby area)
up-air	high
back-air	behind You
mucha bliged	thank You
painin	hurt or Ache
naw	disagree
a mess	a lot of something

Christmas and the Blue Tick Hound

Christmas was approaching, and it was during some bad financial years that old Rambler went away. Pa sold Rambler that December, and it almost broke Pa's heart. Old Rambler fetched in $300.00, an outrageous price in bad times for a coon dog. Santa came Christmas night, and Pa looked real proud. Pert near every Christmas since then that old Blue Tick Hound is remembered and an humble prayer is said. Perhaps Rambler didn't mind too much because after all he was a sporting dog.

Mary Bratton, Williamsport, Tennessee

Recess from joke telling, 1943

A Sense of Family

Tennessee Woman

She saw the stars
Sunrises
Sunsets
Autumn leaves
Falling snow
A rushing stream
Flowers in spring
And sewed them all
Into her patchwork quilts.

She baked biscuits soft and light.
Her garden thrived.
She learned the healing power
Of mountain plants
And nursed her neighbors back to life.
She delivered babies in their cabin homes.
She played her fiddle at hoedowns.

Now she lies in the churchyard
But in the mountains
And the cities
There are granddaughters,
Great-granddaughters,
Survivors,
Whose middle name
Is Tennessee.

Malra Treece, Memphis, Tennessee

Homestead

The house no longer stands—the chimney's toppled.
All that remains are huge foundation fieldstones set
By man and time and log-of-poplar pressure.
And now spring comes as usual, no regret
Evident at her tender, pulsing temples,
The smoothness of her forehead, her warm mouth;
Forsythia's flower-falls are bright as ever
Thorn, touched to bloom by soft winds from the south.
But where the lilac bends its plumes of purple
There seems the gentle swish of phantom skirts,

And by the leaning fence late jonquils whisper
Of other springs, until earth's great heart hurts.
The yard, once nurtured with a loving care,
Breathes lonely, sweet remembrance everywhere.

Webb Dycus, Duck River, Tennessee

Feeding Grandma's chickens

Auctioneer's Song

The man trailed along behind the auctioneer,
Every line on his face showing the
Nervousness he felt.
Now that his tobacco was on the floor
Excitement overtook fear as the auctioneer
Sang a final call of $2.00 per pound.
Surely the price was a New Year's blessing.
Every bill he owed could be paid in full, with
Enough extra money left to buy tires—and a baby bed.

Sharon B. Welch, Nolensville, Tennessee

Grandma's Clothesline

Hanging sheets in the
  cool morning air.
The smell of bleach and sunshine
  in Grandma's sheets
  lines that ran forever
  became my maze.
Down the sheet-draped rows
  I would run
  laughing with Grandma
  as she "tried" to catch me.
I would spin in circles
My arms wrapped in
  clinging wetness
Falling to the ground.
Dragging cool, damp sheets
  with me—
And Grandma,
Laughing as she fussed.
Then falling asleep at night
  under the scent of
  bleach
  and sunshine.
And laughter with Grandma.

Rebecca Britt, Knoxville, Tennessee

Neighbors

It was a cool October day in Tennessee, when our house burned. I watched the flames lick at the sky and thought I would surely die from the pain in my heart.

We had started with nothing. Now we had nothing again. I didn't see how we would survive.

Then they came. Our neighbors. People we knew and those we didn't. They brought clothes, furniture, food and money, but most of all they brought hope and love. We survived together.

Mildred Aday, Adamsville, Tennessee

Our father's hands

Our Father's Hands

Our Father's hands were calloused and his skin was tough and tanned. We know now that he toiled very hard on the old Tennessee Central Railroad, driving spikes, tamping ties, and shoveling rocks in the blazing suns of summer and the icy blizzards of winter.

But we didn't know then and he never once told us. Our only thought was of running to meet him on payday when he brought home the penny candy the groceryman gave him when he paid his grocery bill.

Mrs. Minnie B. Winfree, Watertown, Tennessee

Tennessee Summer Song

Afternoon,
July breeze flows on bird song through kitchen windows.
It comes lately from among
Stalks of growing green corn,
And tomato laden vines,

Blessing a bowl of sugar soaking berries,
Set to bake your supper pie,
That fat cabbage we cut last night
To chop for slaw, and
Two daughters we made, napping in the lazy afternoon.

Afternoon,
A moment, my senses slice a treasure,
Fling it prayerward to our God,
In celebration
Of His Good Pleasure
In making me your Tennessee wife,
Their Tennessee mother.

Betty Jones, Bon Aqua, Tennessee

Decoration Day

The women folk were busy
A-spreadin' out the food
On new board tables
Below the dove that cooed.

Men folk were a-jawin'
And fannin' with their hats.
The children were a-rompin'
Around like dogs and cats.

Brother Fate said the blessin'.
We gobbled down our meals,
Walked round the graveyard,
And talked of family deals.

We looked at the flowers
In jars and coffee cans,
Touched weathered headstones,
And dreamed of Glory Land.

Robert Michie, Sparta, Tennessee

October Winds

The October winds whisper, softly calling out to me,
This was mama's favorite time of year in Tennessee.

The grass is now fading, flowers gently bow their heads,
As the greenery of summer past transforms to gold and red.

The rolling country displays its beauty, God is everywhere you gaze,
From the frost out on the hayfields, to the forest thru the haze.

Woodland creatures busily preparing for they know what lies ahead,
Firewood being gathered, ranked neatly in the shed.

Mama, it's your favorite time of year in Tennessee
And knowing how you loved it so, makes it even more special to me.

And now when I think of you in the fall of the year,
I smile, swallow hard, and brush away a tear.

Connie Littleton Conner, Bon Aqua, Tennessee

A Civil War Story

When I was a little girl, there were many stories told about the Civil War, but this one I will never forget.

When my Uncle Joe was six years old, his father and my grandfather took him to Franklin after the battle of Franklin was over. There was a wounded soldier sitting in a chair, and he called to Uncle Joe to come there. He told him he had a little boy at home about his age. Uncle Joe went to sit in his lap and the man died.

James Emma Knapton, Columbia, Tennessee

I'm Home Grandma!

The doors are nailed shut.
The roof is leaking, and the porch needs repair;
But there hangs the old porch swing, and there are sprouts from the walnut tree
    that grew outside Grandma's bedroom window.
The old well needs a new cover.
It's spring, been a long long time since I lived with Grandma in this house.
The dogwood is blooming on the mountain, old rosebushes and violets are
    blooming in the yard.
And I've come home Grandma!

Mildred Copeland Fielding, Whitwell, Tennessee

Recollections of Gibson County, 1914

The gypsy walked from the dirt road to our porch. She was young (about my age), with distinctive Indian features and coloring. She asked to tell my fortune. "Not for money," she added, "for a bed quilt." With mutual respect, we bartered.

As she left, my little boy and I walked out to see the waiting covered wagon. We watched the gypsy climb into the seat and unfold the patchwork quilt. Someone handed her a baby; she bundled it up.

Story told by Mrs. Ida Harrison
Written by her granddaughter, Pat Harrison Martin
Memphis, Tennessee

A SAMPLER
·····*Exclusive*·····

Amy Grant

" **A** nother tender Tennessee Christmas,
The only Christmas for me.
With the love gathered around us
Like gifts around our tree.
Though I know there's more snow
Up in Colorado
Than my roof will ever see
A tender Tennessee Christmas
Is the only Christmas for me."*

A few Decembers ago, just after moving to Tennessee, the *Sampler* heard a song so beautiful we just had to pull off the road and listen. We had no idea who was singing or who had written the song, but it captured the love we already had for our adopted state after only a few months as official Tennesseans. Since then, we've heard a lot about Amy Grant and Gary Chapman, the singer and writer of the song that stopped us in our tracks that cold day.

In recent years, Amy Grant has reached more people with her music than any other contemporary Christian artist. Amy was brought up in Nashville, and started writing songs about her faith in God when she was 13. A few years later she made a tape for some friends which was played over the telephone to a record company executive in Texas, and Amy had a recording contract. Now there have been nine albums, including *Age to Age,* the first album of its type to go platinum. Her new album, *Unguarded,* includes the single "Find a Way," which has moved fast on pop as well as Christian radio stations.

Amy and Gary, her husband, make their home on a farm close to Nashville, and the *Sampler* asked Amy

about the love for their state which is so obvious in the song "Tender Tennessee Christmas."

"It's really a song about family," Amy said. "There are years of memories written into those lyrics. Christmas in Tennessee is always a time when families and friends gather and show their love in special ways. My sisters and I are very close, and over the years our parents and grandparents and the Good Lord have given us some really wonderful tender Tennessee Christmases. Gary and I are looking forward to building those memories for our own family."

We Tennesseans know that we're not the only people with a profound sense of family roots. So we send this out to all of our readers enjoying Wonderful Washington Christmases, Lovely Louisiana Christmases, and Heartfelt Hawaiian Christmases. May you always be able to gather the love of your family around you.

A SAMPLER FEATURE
Wilma Dykeman

■ *When we invited Tenneseans to send poems and stories about their state, we heard from more than a thousand people. They wrote from the heart. They wrote pieces that would make you laugh, or cry, or swell with pride. But the amazing thing was that all of these people wrote about Tennessee in terms of two realities: their home place and their family.*

Homestead

We at the Sampler *weren't sure why this was so, but we knew who to ask—our friend Wilma Dykeman.*

Wilma is one of Tennessee's unique voices. Through years of study she has gotten to know our state better than perhaps anyone else. Books like the The French Broad, The Tall Woman, Highland Homeland, *and* Tennessee: A Bicentennial History *have won her an enduring place among Tennessee writers.*

Tennesseans might be described as the ultimate American frontier people. When the colonists along the Atlantic Coast began to cross the formidable Appalachian barrier, they faced the treasures and terrors of a wilderness they would claim from the green pinnacles of the Unaka Mountains to the rolling waters of the mighty Mississippi. In a later century their state would become one of the birthplaces of the Atomic Age. Frontiers.

And from yesterday to today Tennesseans have revealed certain characteristics in responding to the challenges of each frontier. Described most simply, two of the more dominant characteristics might be: a strong sense of place and a continuing sense of family.

This sense of place has informed the work of writers as different as critically acclaimed short story craftsman Peter Taylor and poet Nikki Giovanni, music as different as mountain ballads and cottonfield blues.

The winning and losing of this place called Tennessee involved a tragic confrontation of contrasts: between Europeans disinherited or dispossessed of a homeland who yearned for land of their own, and those native tribes already here for whom the earth and its forests and creatures were part of a complex mythology and religion.

Memory of those Cherokees, Chickasaws, Creeks and other Indians once here still defines mountains, rivers, towns, the very state itself, in proud, exotic names: Tennessee and Chickamauga, Tullahoma, the Chilhowees and the Mississippi. Unfamiliar with the concept of "owning" land, the Indians made European settlers pay dearly for winning of that land for settlement of each place. From this struggle legendary heroes and heroines emerged.

One of these was Sally Ridley Buchanan. She weighed more than 200 pounds and she was strong: she could heave a 150-pound sack of corn to her shoulder and carry it, if the need arose. She was stout of heart, courageous and kind, winning the respect of all those who lived in the fort known as Buchanan's Station, on Mill Creek in Middle Tennessee, during early frontier days.

An Indian attack was mounted against the fort in the autumn of 1792 and during the desperate fighting Sally Buchanan took the place of several men. There were only 17 men to defend the station against some "four hundred of the flower of the Creek and the Chickamauga." One historian has said, "There never was such a battle in all the bloody annals of Tennessee.

There never was such a defender as Sally Buchanan, either. As the men began to run low on ammunition she "came amidst the raking fire of bullets" with a bottle of whiskey in one hand and an apron filled with bullets. Again and again she went the rounds. When a young mother in the fort, half crazed with fear, tried to open the fort gate and run out, Sally Buchanan brought her back. No wonder that one of the bronze highway markers across the state commemorates "Mrs. Buchanan." Her allegiance to place was hard won.

Closely allied with a sense of place is the Tennessean's sense of family.

Sometimes the families have been large. John Sevier, often called the father of Tennessee, had two wives and 18 children. Super-star Dolly Parton was the fourth of 12 children and Olympic champion Wilma Rudolph was the twentieth of 22 children. But it is not the size of the immediate family that is as noteworthy as the strength of bonds linking the extended family. These are the relationships that are described in many ways, from precise genealogical terms to the informal vocabulary of "second-cousins-once-removed" and "kissing-kin."

It is the extended family that gathers during those summer and autumn celebrations known as "homecomings." Then the descendants of some particular family gather from places far and near and reminisce, sing songs, listen to an informal program arranged by some of the "homefolks," feast on food spread on groaning boards beneath the leafy trees or inside some pleasant shelter—and reminisce some more. Tears and laughter intermingle.

Two distinctive American novels grew out of this Tennessee sense of family. James Agee's *A Death In the Family* captured the subtle complexities of family relationships and a young boy's coming of age in the town of Knoxville. The novel won its author a posthumous Pulitzer Prize. *Roots* won Alex Haley a worldwide audience. From family memories gathered on the

Freedom

vine-shaded porch of a home in the West Tennessee town of Henning, the author pursued his extended family back to an African village. The true story of that search, which became an all-consuming adventure, inspired a renewed sense of family around the world on a scale that could only be described as awesome.

Nowadays, Tennesseans are still frontier people.

Choices posed by today's frontiers reflects a delicate balance between yesterday's values and tomorrow's prosperity.

"How far is it from Oak Ridge to the Great Smokies?" a visitor once asked.

And the answer came back: "About a hundred years."

The answer was accurate. The distances separating people and places of Tennessee are often distances of time as much as space. Yesterday has not been completely relinquished; tomorrow has not been fully embraced, and today is taut with the pull between the two. Poised between tradition and change, there are those who hope to have the best of each.

Working toward that ideal, Tennesseans will find strength in their cherished sense of place and deeply rooted sense of family.

Father of Waters

My head is cold;
My feet are warm;
My neck stretches through the Mid-west.
My arms reach out to all parts of the nation.
But my heart is in Memphis.

Jann Tarnowski, Memphis, Tennessee

Germs

We didn't fight germs
When I was a kid.
We ettem.
Alive.

by Joe Clark, HBSS

Germs

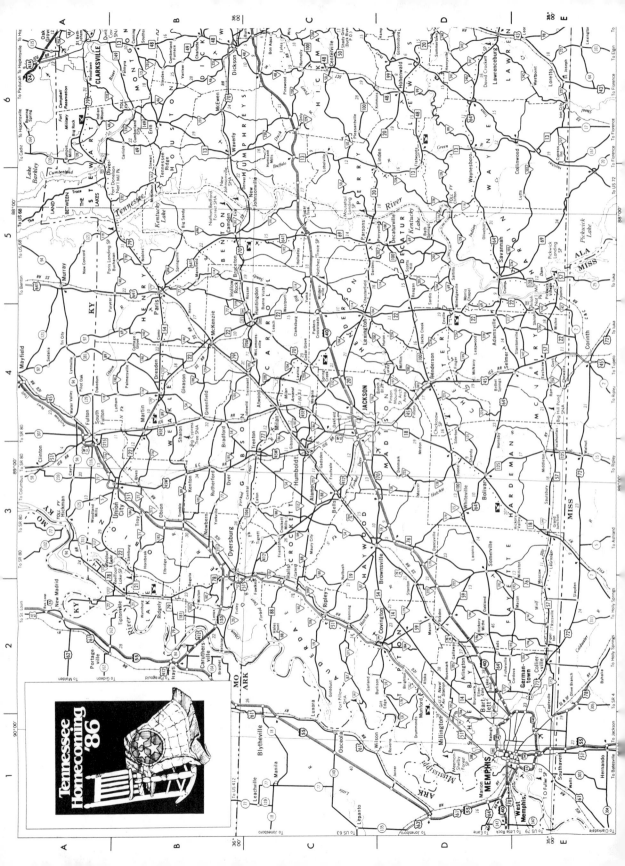

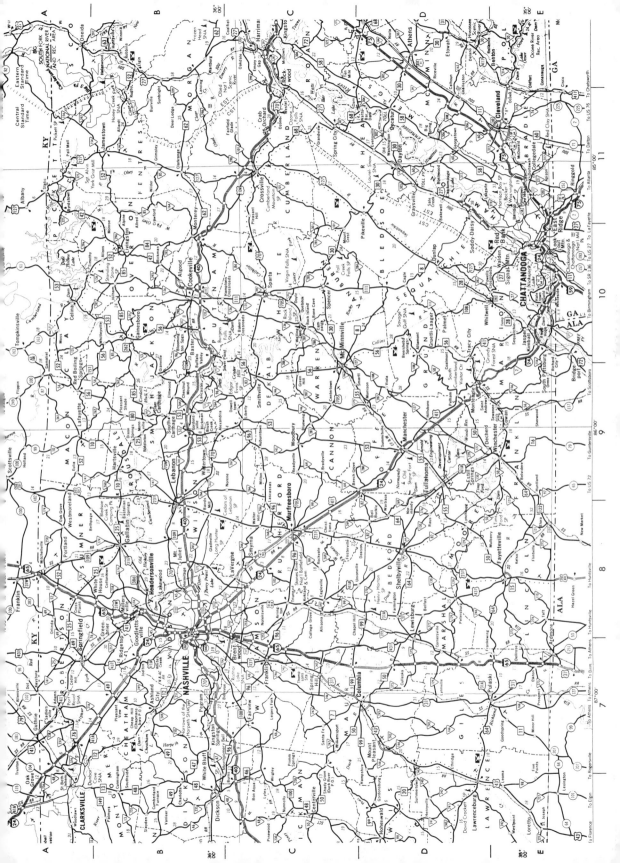

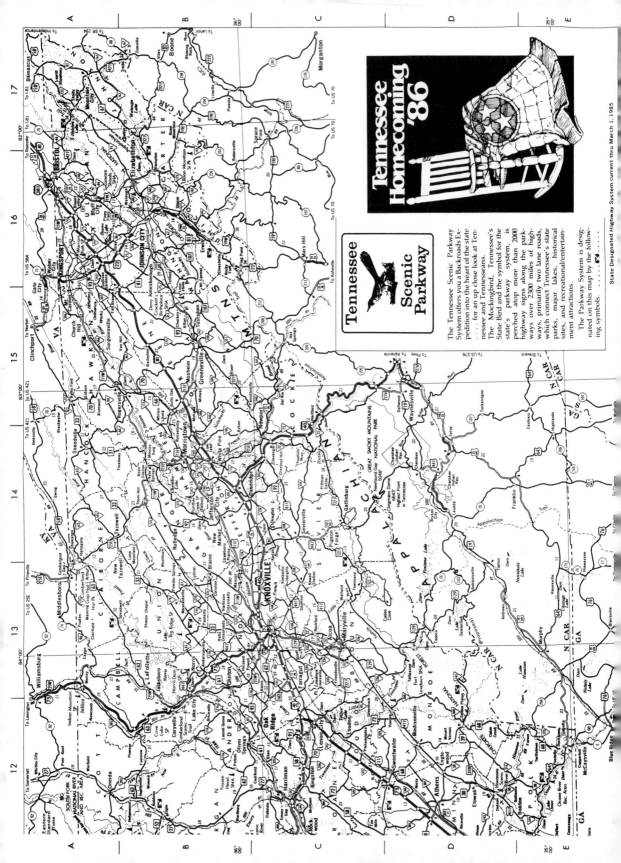

Tennessee Homecoming '86

Tennessee Scenic Parkway

The Tennessee Scenic Parkway System offers you a Backroads Expedition into the heart of the state . . . for an up close look at Tennessee and Tennesseans.

The Mockingbird, Tennessee's State Bird and the symbol for the state's parkway system, is perched atop more than 2000 highway signs along the parkways over 2300 miles of highways, primarily two lane roads, which connect Tennessee's state parks, major lakes, historical sites, and recreational/entertainment attractions.

The Parkway System is designated on this map by the following symbols.

State Designated Highway System current thru March 1, 1985

How to get in the Next Tennessee Sampler

Already we're hearing from many of you across the state who didn't make it into the *Sampler* this time. We'd like to tell you how to submit information for possible use in the next edition of *The Tennessee Sampler.*

If you want the world to know about your excellent restaurant, the craft you have for sale, your inn, bed and breakfast establishment, or the quaint gift shop you run, drop us a line along with the following information:

Your name, complete mailing address, and phone number.
The name and nature of your business.
Newspaper or magazine clippings about your business, if available.
5 x 7 black-and-white glossy of the restaurant, craft, gift shop, product, etc.
Samples of your work, if possible.

Please tell us as many interesting things about your business as you can. The more you tell us, the easier it will be to feature your product or convince people to stop by your gift shop or eat at your restaurant.

Send a $5 processing and storing fee and make the check payable to Sweet Springs Press. (Note: This is not an advertising or entry fee, nor does it guarantee inclusion in the next *Tennessee Sampler*.)

Mail to: TENNESSEE SAMPLER
             P.O. BOX 20
             FRANKLIN, TN 37174

If you, a friend, or a member of your family would like a complimentary copy of our newsletter, "Our America," send your request to the same address.

We look forward to hearing from you!

INDEX TO TENNESSEE COUNTIES, CITIES AND TOWNS